SECOND LANGUAGE ACQUISITION

A Book of Readings

D0111033

Evelyn Marcussen Hatch
English Department
University of California at Los Angeles

NEWBURY HOUSE PUBLISHERS / ROWLEY / MASSACHUSETTS

Library of Congress Cataloging in Publication Data

Main entry under title:

Second language acquisition.

   Bibliography: p.
   Includes index.
   1. Languages, Modern—Study and teaching—Addresses,
essays, lectures. 2. Children—Language—Addresses,
essays, lectures. 3. Bilingualism—Addresses, essays,
lectures. I. Hatch, Evelyn Marcussen.
PB36.S37   401   77-9335
ISBN 0-88377-086-5

Cover design by Wendy Doherty.

NEWBURY HOUSE PUBLISHERS, INC.

 Language Science
Language Teaching
Language Learning

ROWLEY, MASSACHUSETTS 01969

Printed in the U.S.A.   First printing: April 1978
                           5   4   3   2

for

Professor Werner F. Leopold

with respect and admiration

MANGE TAK

I would like to thank the contributors for allowing me to include their studies in this volume. Special thanks to my colleagues and friends—especially Judy Wagner-Gough, Brina Peck, Russ Campbell, John Schumann, Diane Larsen-Freeman, Brad Arthur, and Steve Krashen—for sharing their ideas with me and listening to mine too. I appreciate all the people who have kept me on their mailing list even when I never answer them. They have done their best to keep me up to date on second language research.

And with special love and thanks to Sue and Geoff, Dion, Edgardo and all the others at home.

Contents

Figures (continued)

TABLES

Tables (continued)

SECOND LANGUAGE ACQUISITION

A Book of Readings

SECOND LANGUAGE ACQUISITION

A Book of Readings

Introduction

In 1945, Professor Werner Leopold published a call to linguists for serious study of child language and infant bilingualism:

> We have studied language and languages of every conceivable type, standard languages, dialects, languages not written, languages of special groups with ever varying methods throwing light into every nook and cranny of the speaking activity. Why then should just child language, which is uncontestably a province of language, be outside the pale of linguistic inquiry? (1945, p. 9)

While linguists heard his plea they responded slowly. Nevertheless, the field of child language has grown year by year to become one of the most important areas of linguistic research. The child language bibliography includes hundreds of studies not only from linguistics but also from cognitive and developmental psychology, from the areas of semantics and logic in philosophy, from verbal and cognitive development in education, and from conversational analysis in sociology.

While the interest in child language has grown slowly over the years, the rediscovery of second-language acquisition as an important area of research has been overwhelmingly sudden. Susan Ervin-Tripp, addressing a national conference more than twenty-five years after Professor Leopold made his plea, noted that:

> It has taken surprisingly long for scholars of language learning to envisage the relation between first and second language learning, and to view theories of the human language acquisition system as having a bearing on what they study. (1974, 1)

1

But once that relationship was made clear, new studies, theses and dissertations appeared. Second-language acquisition became a central area of research in applied linguistics. Tables Intro-1 and Intro-2 give a notion of how important this area of research has become since 1970. The climate had changed.

From Dr. Leopold's call of 1945 until the early 1970s, no one in this country seemed to consider second language acquisition (either simultaneous acquisition of two languages or sequential acquisition) of importance to our understanding of either verbal learning or verbal behavior. Aside from Dr. Leopold's classic in the field, Ronjat's less explicit thesis on his child's bilingual development, Kenyeres' study of sequential acquisition of a second language, and a few papers of lesser interest, little work was done. One reason for the lack of research was that linguists were more interested in language description and in language change than in the nature of language acquisition. Another was that researchers interested in child bilingualism frequently lacked linguistic training; many reports were comprised of vocabulary lists rather than data relating to acquisition of the phonological, semantic, syntactic, or discourse systems of either language. When both linguistic training and a bilingual subject were available, the time and patience needed to carry out the detailed work required for such projects, may have been too demanding. Acquisition case studies are extremely time consuming and frequently frustrating. But as our methodology for data collection and analysis evolved, some of these problems have been overcome.

A great deal, of course, had been written about bilingualism during this period. The ERIC (Educational Resources Information Center) file alone contains hundreds of evaluation studies of bilingual education projects. These evaluations, however, were not addressed to the issues of language acquisition. They were not concerned with how the child learns a second language and what this can tell us about the language acquisition process. Rather they were directed towards questions of how to evaluate bilingual education.

A great deal of speculative thinking about second language acquisition has also been published. And much of this literature is both important and interesting. Based on classroom observation, on listening to accents and noting syntactic "errors" of foreign immigrant populations, teachers and researchers have formed a whole body of literature on what needs to be taught in second language classes, what probable errors students will make, and the source of these errors.

Speculation on the source of errors has been the most important theoretical issue in this literature. With intensive study of the two languages—the learner's first language and the second language to be learned—linguists have provided teachers with contrastive analysis studies. In the strongest claims made for the contrastive analysis hypothesis, it was assumed that wherever the two languages differed, interference would occur. That is, the second language was learned through the screen of the first language. One could then predict errors and explain learning problems by looking at the areas of difference between the two languages. The strong claims for the contrastive analysis hypothesis have long

Table Intro-1   Observational studies of second language acquisition   (Arranged by age of subject)

Subject Name(s)	Age	Languages	Investigator(s)	Year
Hildegard	Complete record emphasis on first three years	English & German	Leopold	1939-1949
Douchan	First 2 years	Serbian & French	Pavlovitch	1920
Eta, Ester	First 3 years	Serbo-Croatian & Hungarian	Mikeš	1970
Girl child	1st year	Russian & Georgian	Imedadze	1960
Carlito	1st 3 years	Spanish & English	Mazeika	1972
Mario	1st 5 years	Spanish & English	Fantini	1974
Sandra	1st 3 years	Swedish/Finnish & English	Murrell	1966
Louis	1st 3 years	German & French	Ronjat	1913
Stephen	1st 3 years	Garo & English	Burling	1959
Caroline	2; 4	English & French	Celce-Murcia	1975
Michael	3	French & English	Swain & Wesche	1973
Sven	2 - 4	Swedish & Estonian	Oksaar	1973
Takahiro	2:6 - 3:1	Japanese & English	Itoh	1973
Rebecca	3	English & Urdu	Hansen-Bede	1975
Miki	3	Japanese & English	Yoshida	1976
6 unnamed subjects	range 2½ to 8 years	Chinese & English	LaMarche	1972
4 unnamed Ss;	range 3:7 - 7:6	English & German	Wode	1974
Lars, Inga, Heiko, Brigit	range 3:4 - 9:6	German & English		

Table Intro-1 (continued)

Subject Name(s)	Age	Languages	Investigator(s)	Year
Uguisu	5	Japanese & English	Hakuta	1974
Paul	5	Taiwanese & English	Huang	1970
Marta	5	Spanish & English	Cancino	in progress
Rune, Reidun	6 and 3:9	Norwegian & English	Ravem	1968
Toko, Maija & 2 other Ss	range 4½ - 8	Several languages & English	Keller-Cohen	in progress
Julie, Guy	5 and 7	English & German	Felix	1974
Homer	5:11	Assiryian, Persian & English	Wagner-Gough	1974
10 unnamed Ss	range 4:11 - 5:9	Spanish & English	Adams	1974
8 unnamed Ss	mean age 5:7	English & French	Swain	1972
12 unnamed Ss	5 - 7	English & Spanish	Flores	1973
			Boyd	1974
6 unnamed Ss	range 5½ - 6½	English & Spanish	Dato	1972
Girl child	6:4	Spanish & French	Tits	1948
Alma, Juan & Enrique	range 5½ - 6½	Spanish & English	Young	1974
Lydia	6	Arabic (Egyptian) & English	Rizsk	in progress
Eva	6:10	Hungarian & French	Kenyeres & Kenyeres	1923
Akio, Haruo	6:11 and 7:6	Japanese & English	Gillis & Weber	1975
Daniel	7	English & French	Savignon	1974
Ken	7	Japanese & English	Milon	1972
Angel	8	Spanish & English	Peck	1976

Table Intro-1 (continued)

Subject Name(s)	Age	Languages	Investigator(s)	Year
31 unnamed Ss	range 4 - 9	English & French	Ervin-Tripp	1973
3 unnamed Ss	range 7 - 10	Indonesian & English	Isman	1973
3 unnamed Ss	unknown	Zaire, Spanish, Arabic (Saudi) & English	Nielsen	1974
5 unnamed Ss	range 8 - 15	Spanish & English	Warshawsky	1975
Male child	10	French, Spanish & English	Chamot	1972
Male child	12	Arabic (Egyptian) & English	Rouchdy	1970
Jorge	13	Spanish & English	Rosansky	1976
Ricardo	13	Spanish & English	Butterworth	1972
Marta, Cheo,	2 children	Spanish & English	Cazden, Cancino,	1975
Juan, Jorge,	2 adolescents		Rosansky & Schumann	
Alberto, Dolores	2 adults			
Ginger	adult	English & French	Johnston	1972
Female S	19	Arabic (Saudi) & English	Hanania	1974
Rafaela	adult	Spanish & English	Brunak, Fain & Villoria	1976
2 unnamed Ss	adult	Spanish & English	Schwartz & Fain	in progress
		Vietnamese & English		
Zoila	adult	Spanish & English	Shapira	1975
Wimmi	adult	Punjabi/Hindi/English and English	Gasser	1975
Alberto	adult	Spanish & English	Schumann	1975

Table Intro-2 Experimental studies of second language acquisition

N	Age/Grade	Languages	Investigator(s)	Year
			(St. Lambert Project)	
X	1st grade	English and French	Lambert and MacNamara	1969
38	1st grade	English and French	Lambert, Just and Segalowitz	1970
26	2nd grade	English and French		
39	1st grade	English and French	Tucker, Lambert and d'Anglejan	1972
19	6th grade	English and French	Bruck, Lambert and Tucker	1973
30	3rd and 5th grades	English and French	Markham, Spilka and Tucker	1975
X	Kindergarten, 1st, 2nd grades	English and French	Genessee, Tucker and Lambert	1975
30	4th and 6th grades	English and French	Hamayan, Markman, Pelletier and Tucker	1975
			(Culver City Project)	
19	kindergarten	English and Spanish	Cathcart	1972
15	1st grade	English and Spanish	Broadbent	1973
19	1st grade	English and Spanish	Lebach	1974
12	2nd grade	English and Spanish		
14	2nd grade	English and Spanish	Cohen	1974
3	2nd grade	English and Spanish	Cohen	1975
X	2nd grade	English and Spanish	Waldman	1975
24	Kindergarten to 3rd	English and Spanish	Plann	1976
X	Kindergarten to 3rd	English and Spanish	Jashni	1976
40	Kindergarten to 4th	English and Spanish	Ramírez	1976

Table Intro-2 (continued)

N	Age/Grade	Languages	Investigator(s)	Year
			(OISE Project)	
24	Kindergarten	English and French	Barik, Swain and McTavish	1974
30	1st grade	English and French	Barik and Swain	1974
20	2nd grade	English and French		
112	1st and 2nd grade	English and French	Naiman	1974
40	3rd grade	English and French	Swain	1974
15	2nd grade	French and English	Hébrard and Mougeon	1975
12	range: 6:1 - 8:3	Italian and English	Kessler	1971
55	range 6-8 years	Chinese and English	Dulay and Burt	1974
60		Spanish and English		
50	range 5-8 years	English and Spanish	Olmstead-Gary	1974
115	Kindergarten - 3rd grade	Spanish and English	Ramírez	1974
18	3rd - 5th grades	Spanish and English	Cohen, Fathman and Merino	1976
32	elementary school	Spanish and English	VanMettre	1972
115	Grades 3, 6, 8, 10	Spanish and English	Johnson	1973
12	3rd grade	Hebrew and English	Bassan	1973
8	adults			
98	5½ - 8½	Hebrew and English	Ben-Zeev	1976
188		Spanish and English		

Table Intro-2 (continued)

N	Age/Grade	Languages	Investigator(s)	Year
120	6 to 14 years	Korean, Spanish and English	Fathmann	1975a
200	6 to 15 years	Mixed and English	Fathmann	1975b
144	1, 2, 3, and 10th grades	English and Spanish (native vs. non-native)	Natalicio and Natalicio	1971
46	Elementary grades	Spanish and English	Ramírez and Politzer	1975
21	adults			
30	9 to 11th grades	Spanish and English	Hartford	1975
69	3 years to adult	English and Dutch	Snow	1975
60	8, 11 years and adults	Arabic and English	Hamayan, Saigert, and Larudee	1975
149	high school	English and Spanish	Tran	1972
124	16 - 20 years	English and French	Buteau	1970
50	adult	Czech and English	Dušková	1969
160	adult	English and French	Sodhi	1969
36	adult	Japanese, Spanish, Arabic and English	Heckler	1970
5	adult	Japanese and English	Linde	1971
16	adult	English and Persian	Henning	1973
356	adult	Mixed and English	Oller and Ziadhosseiny	1970
20	adult	Mixed and English	Cook	1973
73	adult	Mixed and English	Bailey, Madden and Krashen	1974

Table Intro-2 (continued)

N	Age/Grade	Languages	Investigator(s)	Year
X	adult	Japanese, Spanish and English	Bertkau	1974
24	adult	Arabic, Japanese, Persian, Spanish & English	Larsen-Freeman	1975
X	adult	Mixed & English	Bailey, Madden & Eisenstein	1976
44	adult	English and German	LoCoco	1975
48	adult	English and Spanish		
50	adult	Arabic, Persian, Japanese, Spanish and English	Schachter	1975
25	adult	Russian and English	Tanka	1975
40	adult	English and French	d'Anglejan and Tucker	1975
20	adult	Spanish and English	Taylor	1975
423	adult	Mixed and English	Kempf	1975
18	adult	Spanish and English	Perkins and Larsen-Freeman	1975
28	adult	English and Spanish	LoCoco	1976
10	adult	Japanese and English	Dickerson	1976
6	adult	Cantonese, Portuguese, Korean & English	Tarone	1976
8	adult	Mixed and English	Robbins	1976
3	adult	Persian, Korean, Spanish and English	Schlue	1976

since been rejected (Wardhaugh, 1970; Riebel, 1971; Dulay and Burt, 1973) on a number of grounds. First among these is the empirical evidence. Errors which are predicted on the basis of contrastive analysis frequently do not occur and unpredicted errors do.

Stockwell, Bowen and Martin, in the best of the contrastive analysis publications (1965), proposed a hierarchy of difficulty as a theoretical basis for error prediction dependent on a much more sophisticated analysis of types of differences between the two languages. However, this hierarchy, much more complex than a simple interference model, has never been rigorously tested against case study data or in experimental research.

A number of other writers claimed that the "errors" one hears in the speech of the second language learner are reflections of a provisional grammar that the learner is creating. That is, the learner is constructing his new language in much the same way that the child learns his first language. Corder (1967) has, in fact, asked for any evidence, strong or weak, to show that second language learning is substantially different from first language acquisition. Richards (1970) suggested that students learning English as a second language share a wide set of "errors" which in many cases cannot be accounted for as language transfers. Rather, he claims, these errors are proof of a common learning system. While granting differences in success and in motivation, he assumes that the same process takes place in acquisition despite age range, first language of the learner, or the number of languages learned. All these factors may make the learner more sophisticated in the range of possible predictions made in learning a new language, but the process remains the same for all language learning.

Selinker (1972) proposed five different sources for the provisional grammar, the language form produced by the second language learner. He uses the term "interlanguage" to refer to this system. Interlanguage, according to Selinker, can be traced to interference from the first language, instruction, second language learning strategies, second language communication strategies, and overgeneralization of the target language rules and semantic features. These categories are obviously not mutually exclusive, but they do give factors other than interference alone as a way of accounting for the "errors" heard in second language learners' speech.

Schumann (1975) has suggested that the pidginization process should also be considered in any discussion of second language learning. While many linguists have refused to include "imperfect" second language learning in their research data, others have included it since the provisional grammar of the learner, while not a pidgin, is an example of the pidginization process. That is, it shows "consistent reduction of the function of language both in its grammar and its use" (Hymes, 1971).

Interesting as all these theoretical papers are, without studies of language acquisition, they can only be speculative. Nothing certain can be said until second language acquisition has been studied in tangible case histories or until empirical evidence has been obtained.

It has taken us the thirty years since Professor Leopold made his plea to begin to realize the importance of second language acquisition studies, the importance of reliable, empirical data. Now the revitalization has taken place. Students of language acquisition are collecting case data and capable researchers have been found to answer Professor Leopold's call:

> America offers countless opportunity for observing infant bilingualism in the making. Children in immigrant families and in the Spanish-speaking Southwest often grow up with two languages. . . . I appeal to the few who are capable of carrying out such an investigation to add sorely needed case histories of infant bilingualism and infant language to the available material, as indispensable spade work for the higher purposes of linguistics. (1945, 11)

The papers presented in this volume are a first answer to that plea. They are the first papers in which empirical, data-based claims about the second language acquisition process appear.

Many of these early studies of second language acquisition are derivative of first-language research. This is not surprising since many of the people involved have studied or worked on first language acquisition projects. It is also not surprising since we want to investigate the similarities and differences between first and second language learning. If one wants to compare data, then the methodology and analysis must be similar. On the other hand, many of the most important papers in first-language acquisition are based on the early second-language work of Leopold, and on the work of Mikeš and Murrell. So the sharing works in both directions. Other studies in this volume are less comparative in nature, either rejecting first language methodologies or looking instead at specific strategies for second language learning.

The studies included in the volume cover five major areas of research: 1) studies of infant bilingualism (the simultaneous acquisition of two or more languages by very young children); 2) studies of young children adding a second language; 3) studies of adolescents and adults learning a second language; 4) a sample from the experimental literature; and 5) discourse analysis papers. Obviously no book could publish all the important studies in our rapidly-expanding field of inquiry. An abstract section has been added to make the picture more complete. Many of the most important studies have had to be presented in abstracted form since they were either too lengthy to include, not published in English, or were widely available in child language collections.

The studies in the first section focus primarily on phonological and semantic areas along with general acquisition strategies. The studies in sections two and three focus on the development of the auxiliary system, negation, and question formation. The experimental studies reflect the area of most interest in the early 1970s—the order of acquisition of morphemes. The final papers present summary information and a look at discourse analysis as a new direction in second language acquisition research.

The age range represented in the studies allows us to look at many of our assumptions about the success of children compared to the frequent failure of adults in the second language learning task. Surely, the difference in success across the age range is not open to question. There are a number of generalizations about this difference, however, that I hope these papers will dispel. First among these is our notion that the child acquires a second language without any effort on his part. The corollary of this notion is that the child has no meta-awareness of language (that is, that language is part of the child and not a separate entity for him). What we seem to mean by this is that the child has some sort of mysterious language acquisition device which does everything for him while he expends little—if any—effort on learning. Such a claim simply means that we have nothing interesting to say about the process by which he learns; but, indeed, there is *much* to be said about this process. Recent work in first-language acquisition (on preverbal behavior by Bulowa, Sinclair and others; on vocabulary development by Nelson, Clark, Reich, and others; in acquisition of phonology by Moskowitz, the Stanford child phonology project team, and others; on presyntactic language by Bloom, Scollon, and others; and on pragmatics by many researchers but especially by Keenan and Atkinson) shows that the process is a very long, very demanding, and frequently frustrating one for the child. I believe the same can be said about second language acquisition.

Not only is second-language learning a long and difficult process for the child, but there are children who do not learn the second language as "automatically" as others. The studies presented in this volume concern learners, in some cases spectacularly successful learners. In contrast, the reader might want to review the case study conducted by Denise Young which speaks to the issue of the non-learner. Her third subject, Alma, did not acquire English as a second language although she attended an American school for the eight months of observation. Initially, Young was tempted to drop her six-year-old "non-learner" from the study. Then she decided that Alma might be a "late bloomer" who was using extended listening as a strategy for learning (the strategy is explained in detail in Olmstead-Gary, 1974). Her hypothesis was that once Alma began speaking English, her production would be quite advanced or that she would move much more rapidly through syntactic development stages. This did not happen. When Alma did begin speaking English after eight months, it was the same kind of data that we find in sessions with most learners during the first month of observation. While no I.Q. testing was permitted at the school, Alma was not "retarded" in any other way. She was able to respond appropriately to all kinds of language stimuli and language tasks in Spanish. She was extremely well coordinated. However, she was in almost all circumstances an extremely passive, quiet, and withdrawn child in the classroom. This was in sharp contrast to her bubbly, out-going, aggressive nature at home where, of course, everyone spoke Spanish.

Though we have little data on non-learners, the studies presented in this volume show that some children learn a second language much more rapidly than others. For example, Harumi Itoh's two-and-a-half year old child, Takahiro, developed strong language interaction patterns with adults and children after an initial stage of complete rejection of English speakers (this included hiding and crying). He acquired vocabulary and syntactic structures (within limits) at a rapid rate. In contrast, Midori Yoshida's three-year-old Japanese subject, Miki, took a much longer period of time to begin producing English. His utterances, after a school-year period of observation, were one or two words in length in most cases, and his interaction patterns were not as strong as Takahiro's. There are also differences in kinds of structures and interaction patterns for two five-year-olds, Paul and Homer, both presented in this volume.

Not only do some children not learn much, and some children learn a great deal, but in almost every diary study presented here, there is mention of experiences in which the child shows the same frustration, withdrawal, and "paranoia" as adult language learners. The Kenyeres and Kenyeres study of their 7-year-old daughter, Eva, is a classic case of language/culture shock. When they knew that they were moving to Geneva, they tried to interest Eva in learning French. She absolutely refused, saying that she would see the mountains and wildflowers and then come back home. In the first week in Geneva, she went with her family to visit friends who had young children. She came away determined to learn French so that she could play with them the next week. Unfortunately, when enrolled in a French school, she was acutely unhappy and had nasty things to say about French speakers and about the country. She was sure none of the children liked her, and she was angry that her father had not taught her French. However, she *was* motivated; she worked hard at learning the language in a very conscious way, reciting gymnastics commands to herself, working on vocabulary in picture books, practicing small dialogues with her dolls. After months in Geneva and spectacular progress in French, she loved her school, her teacher, and all things French. She then began to complain about having to speak Hungarian because she was obliged "to find the words."

When displeased, Eva would shout "disgusting!" in Hungarian, marking one of the few instances in which she still used her native language in Geneva. Gough's five-year-old subject, Homer, used his first language to verbalize threats when his playmates provoked him. Rarely were these threats acted upon, but they allowed him a way to release some of his frustration in the second-language environment:

Mark: Stupid, now quit messing up my things.
Homer: (in Assiryian) Now, I'm going to swear at you and now I'm going to throw this.
Mark: I'll get you.
Homer: (in Assiryian) This is a real gun. I'm going to hit him with it.

Like Eva, he too complained (after three months) about having to use one of his first languages (Farsi), claiming that he no longer understood the questions occasionally asked of him in Farsi.

In Leopold's study, we see the same kind of rejection of alternatively English and German. When asked to speak English by her mother in Germany, she would feign crying, and finally would burst into tears when her mother spoke English. At first they assumed this was temper, but:

... yesterday we were able to ascertain that the reason was not merely a lack of inclination to do so under the influence of her environment. . . . Playing store with her, the mother pretended to be a new storekeeper from America who did not know German. Hildegard entered into the idea, but the only thing which she could still do smoothly in English was counting money. She had to ask for the English names of goods for sale, sometimes repeatedly, and even then she came out with combinations like *die book*. Loath as she was to interrupt a game, at one point she said sadly: "Mutti, ich kann gar nicht mehr englisch sprechen."

There are other examples of children who can understand but cannot/will not produce the language. (Cf., Ronjat's description of Humboldt's 1791 study of Adel and Gabrielle. Adel would answer questions asked in German with Italian. She would not speak German while Gabrielle spoke both languages fluently.)

Such case records lead us to believe that the task of learning a second language is not as easy and effortless either psychologically or linguistically for some children as folklore would have us believe. Nevertheless, the skill that many children display as second language learners is truly dazzling.

The children described in these studies also offer comments which show an amazing meta-awareness of language. At the very earliest age, children acquiring two languages simultaneously seem to realize that there are two ways of talking. Ronjat's child Louie (French-German) at 1:8 called this "comme papa" and "comme mama" and, at this early age, actively solicited vocabulary equivalents in the two languages. At 2:0 Burling's child Stephen (English-Garo) talked about word equivalents in the two languages—pointing to his nose, he would say "English nose" and "Gawo giŋ -tiŋ." At 4:5, Louie asked if there were people who spoke other than French and German. Imedadze (Russian-Georgian) claims that during the first year, his subject did not separate the two languages and would frequently use translation equivalents together in sentences. During the second year, the child separated the two languages for communication with different people. At the beginning of the third year, she began to use the expressions for "in Russian/in Georgian" and would ask for translation equivalents in learning new words. She also referred to whole communication situations, "Don't talk Georgian; Irakli doesn't know Georgian" (said in Russian). Imedadze interprets "the subsequent development of metalinguistic interest at this early age . . . in terms of the special linguistic demands placed upon a bilingual child."

Bilingual children show this metalinguistic interest in a variety of ways. For example, Louie "reacted with defiance" when guests mixed two languages in speaking. When his mother used French words in her German utterances, he told her not to. He recognized and was critical of pronunciation errors of others. He also gave explanations about how to produce French phonemes. At 58 months, he said, "Je plie ma langue pour *a*, on ouvre tout; pour *m*, tout est ferme, et pour *p* d'abord ferme, puis ouvert." He also talked about morphological endings, which words took -ier endings. As mentioned earlier, he continually elicited translation equivalents in a manner reflective of many field linguists. At 36 months: "Mama, purée de pommes de terre, wie heisst?" After the mother named a dish "Gefüllte Tomaten" he asked his father, "Comment tu dis, toi?" to get "tomates farcies."

Hildegard was also conscious of errors in the speech of others. She felt superior to her mother in handling German, tried to help her or "took a hand in search of German articles." Hildegard also recognized her own German was not always right. When she mixed in English words, she would say that she was speaking her "funny German" (4:6).

Eva, the six-year-old, commented a great deal on the language she was learning. She wanted to know if *jeudi* came from *jour de jeu* (since there was no class that day). She was astonished that *7* and *week* were not the same word as they are in Hungarian. She asked (making a joke) whether *langue française* was because it pulled the tongue when one spoke it. She asked why *ouest* and *est* were similar in French but not in Hungarian. She immediately noticed and disliked nasalized vowels. But she loved the *ui* sound and practiced it continually (Suisse, huit, etc.). The French *r* was especially hard for her and she would lie in bed at night practicing it ("bonjou*r*, papa che*r*i"). She wanted to know which language has more sounds and how they were represented in letters. She asked if there were a *tz* sound in French. She was aware not only of segmental differences but also of intonation differences between the two languages. In May, she was shocked by the French errors a Hungarian visitor made and said, "you don't speak French well, you let your voice fall."

These child language learners also gave rules, sometimes correct and sometimes incorrect for the languages they were learning. At 3:4, Louie gave the following rule for plurals (which happens to be wrong): "On dit chevaux quand il y en a un, cheval quand il y en a beacoup." At 4:2, Hildegard gave a similar rule, "If there is one, you have to say Schuh; if there are two, you have to say Schuhe."

Gender fascinated Eva, the six-year-old French learner. She wanted very much to have a semantic rule to determine gender. She began by using her own logical classes: *la* fleur, le jardin, not *la* jardin because the garden was the mother of the flower; la chaise, la table, not *le* table because the table had to be the papa. She then decided that everything that was good and beautiful would be feminine. At a later stage, she gave a phonological rule for gender, refusing to say *la dame* because she didn't like the vowel euphony and then refusing to say *le monsieur* because of the three oe's. She also became angry when she learned that *oiseau* had only one gender and she wanted *le* and *la* for dolls. In January, she decided to carry gender over to verb conjugations. She said "je fera" and, when corrected, she objected that it had to be *je fera* because she was a *la*.

Sandra Plann (1976) investigated the metalinguistic awareness of English-speaking children enrolled in the Culver City Spanish school. The children are, of course, quite aware of the fact that they are learning a new language (though they receive no overt language "instruction"), and have many interesting comments to make about this (see Lebach, 1974). Using the Bilingual Syntax

Measure (Dulay, Burt and Hernández) to elicit both oral and written data, Plann then questioned the children about the errors they made. Here are a few samples of their responses:

1. Gender

Adult: Ah, y aquí, ah . . . tú me dijiste que 'éstas son las ventanas de *los dos casas.' ¿Está bien decir '*los dos casas'?

Child: No.

Adult: ¿Qué es de decir?

Child: Estos son los, es . . . estos, oh ¿éstas son las ventanas de los-las dos casas?

Adult: Uh-huh, muy bien. Y ¿por qué tenemos que decir 'las'?

Child: Porque 'casa' termina con 'a' y, mmm, tiene, es 'la casa.'

Adult: Uh-huh.

Child: And (heh-heh) y casas, luego 'las' con 's,' es 'las.'

2. Gender and number

Adult: Y tú dijiste 'ella va a llevar comida a sus bebitos, a sus *pajaritas' y lo cambiaste a 'pajaritos.' ¿Por qué dices 'pajaritos' y no '*pajaritas'?

Child: Por el mismo . . . ahh . . . es, cuando dices 'niño' es un niño, 'niña' es una niña, pero todos es 'niños.'

Adult: ¿Todos que?

Child: Todos los niños. Y si hay muchos niñas y niños se llaman niños, y hay muchos pajaritos aquí.

3. *De la* vs. *Del*

Adult: Dijiste que 'esta puerta es *del casa azul.' ¿Está bien? Es '*del casa azul'?

Child: Sí.

Adult: ¿Por qué dices '*del casa?

Child: De la, de la casa. 'Del' es como . . . es corta para 'de la.' Ah . . . ah . . . sí . . . de . . . la, en unas veces. El otro es, debes usar 'del.'

Adult: ¿Cuándo usas 'del' y cuando usas 'de la'?

Child: Marina del Rey. (!)

4. Subject-verb agreement

Adult: Okay, y aquí dijiste 'él *viven en este casa.'

Child: Sí, él . . . él vive . . . en este, este, este casa?

Adult: ¿Está bien eso, 'él *viven, o el vive? ' ¿Cuál?

Child: Vive.

Adult: Uh -huh, y ¿por qué tienes que decir eso?

* = error discussed.

Child: Porque 'viven' es como, umm, tres personas, o um, dos o tres
         personas.
Adult: Uh-huh, ¿verdad? Y ¿decir '*este casa'?
Child: Esta casa.

5. Ser/Estar

Adult: Y dijiste que él está limpiando el barco 'porque *es muy sucio.'
         ¿Eso está bien? 'El barco *es sucio'?
Child: No, pero yo no sé que es mal.

6. "In a hurry"

Adult: . . . aquí dices por ejemplo, aquí (points to number 7 on the page)
         la manzana cayó pero aquí dices '*los manzanas'. ¿Cuál es correcto?
Child: 'Las.'
Adult: Uh-huh. Y ¿por qué 'las'?
Child: Porque manzanas termina en 'a.' Yo, yo hizo este porque estaba
         escribiendo rapido porque Joana no lla- lla- lla- me llamo una uh
         'slow poke.'

7. "Testing"

Adult: Y el hombre, ¿dónde?
Child: (whispers to herself) Está en el . . . (normal voice) El hombre . . .
         *estás . . . oh . . . no.
Adult: Uh-huh?
Child: *Están . . . no, porque ese es muchos.
Adult: Sí, son muchos, están, si es uno . . . ?
Child: *Estamos . . . oh . . . ay! Está en el barco.
Adult: Okay. Y ¿por qué 'está'? El hombre—
Child: Porque solamente hay una persona.

In all of these examples we see parallels to those judgments given by adults (cf.,
Schlue, 1976; Robbins, 1976; or Stafford and Covitt, 1976). They say "I know
the rule, I don't know the rule, it sounds right, it sounds better, I made a mistake
because I was in a hurry," or show no awareness of error. The children whisper
to themselves to try out what "sounds best," they self-correct as they speak, and
they can do this kind of linguistic analysis about their written errors as well.

The data in these studies, and in other studies in this volume as well, show
overall similarities in acquisition strategies whether the learner is child or adult.
Conversely, the studies show considerable variation among learners at one age
group and also across the age range. One of the most important questions in our
research is how to account for these apparent similarities and differences.

The purpose of this volume, then, is to acquaint the reader with the
empirical studies of second language acquisition in natural environments—that is,
language acquisition outside the classroom. An attempt has been made to give
the novice researcher examples of the wide variety of methodologies used in
longitudinal and cross-sectional studies. While the selections are admittedly
biased towards work done in this country since 1970, an attempt has been made

to include representative work from Europe and Canada, and to use case studies which involve as many different languages as possible.

The questions asked in this research are many: What are the differences, if any, between first and second language acquisition? How does simultaneous acquisition of two languages by the young child differ from the addition of a second language for the older child or for the adult? How does the learner, whatever his age, after a period of inarticulateness, manage basic communication, no matter how ungrammatical that communication may be? Is there a sequence in order of acquisition of particular language structures? Why do certain language forms emerge later than others? How does the learner eventually attain native or near-native use of the second language? It is toward these questions that the following studies of second language acquisition are directed.

Part I
Case Studies

Simultaneous Acquisition
of Two Languages

1 A Child's Learning of Two Languages

W. F. Leopold, *Northwestern University*

INTRODUCTION

At the 5th Annual Round Table at Georgetown University, Professor Werner F. Leopold presented a summary of his famous study on infant bilingualism. That study stands as the most complete record of a child's acquisition of two languages; it is the classic of our field.

The Georgetown summary, reprinted here, gives the reader a brief look at the bilingual process, a notion of what Leopold's careful, day-to-day study revealed. Any attempt to summarize this monumental four-volume work can only give a few highlights. Hopefully, the serious student of language acquisition will turn to the complete study for a full account of Hildegard's acquisition of English and German.

The diaries themselves reveal the development of the child, Hildegard, through her language record. The charm of her speech and the interaction of child and father are a delight for the reader. Everyone who studies the diaries comes away not only with a wealth of ideas for research but also with his or her own collection of favorite anecdotes. My favorite for the student of child development is Hildegard's fascination with numbers, weights, and measures:

> She has a desire to learn German, because she would like to be taken along to Germany some time. Once she offered me her entire wealth of ten cents to enable

> me to pay for the journey... Favorite prices for her are $3.00 and 10 cents; they have no particular individual value. The other day she measured herself with a ruler and declared that she weighed sixty pounds. (Vol 4, p. 43)

The last sentence is then footnoted:

> This item drives home to me the value of the daily diary. In my memory the incident had become transformed thus: she looked at a thermometer and said she weighed $60.00. This version improves the story, which I have told many times when I did not feel the weight of scientific responsibility.

And, for those interested in language switching and mixing, perhaps one of the most moving exchanges is an entry when Hildegard was ill with chicken pox and didn't want her father to leave the room. In a final plea she says, "Papa, wenn du das licht ausmachst, then I'll be so lonesome." (5:4) This is a beautiful example of heightening emotional content of a message by language switching.

To the linguist and to those interested in child development, this record of one child's development of the phonology, semantics, and syntax of two languages is without parallel. Each of the four volumes has served as a resource for some of the finest work in first language acquisition—e.g., the work of Breyna Moskowitz in phonology, Eve Clark's work in semantics, and Patricia Greenfield's research into the child's early syntactic development. While other records tell us much about beginning stages of bilingual development, only Leopold, with his careful notation in a day-to-day record form gives every student of second language acquisition a complete, detailed source to turn to for comparison data.

Reprinted with the permission of the author and Georgetown University Press from *Georgetown University Round Table on Languages and Linguistics,* 1954, 7, 19-30.

* * *

In the area of bilingual learning of small children, the problems of description are complicated by the fact that infants exposed to two languages from the beginning do not learn bilingually at first, but weld the double presentation into one unified speech system. A further complication in the case studied by me, the language learning of my daughter, is the fact that English and German are so closely related that the structural differences cannot be reflected in the primitive early speech of a child. I am going to separate the initial formative stage of the first two years from the later phases of learning.

The small child first learning the language of the environment faces an enormous task. Subconsciously he must make a complete structural analysis of the language and slowly, step by step, learn to imitate the system in active speaking. In the field of sounds and words, the process goes hand in hand with the gradual development of perceptive and articulatory faculties. In the higher reaches of the syntax, which cannot be learned by imitation of relatively tangible material (sounds), but requires the grasp of abstract patterns, growth of intellectual maturity is a prerequisite for successful learning.

No wonder then that in the learning of language patterns the child appreciates and reproduces at first only the coarsest contrasts. It takes time and much effort to learn ever finer subcontrasts, until eventually the whole complex structural mechanism of the developed language is assimilated. This process of learning first rough contrasts and then finer and finer ones can be demonstrated in the learning of phonemic patterns: in vowels and consonants, in syllable and word structures. It operates also in syntax. After a long stage of speaking in single words, the art of putting two, three and more words together in a sentence is slowly learned. The relationship between the words in the sentences is not always the same. Such standard patterns as subject—verb—object are gradually learned as vehicles of communication, long before any formal indication of the relation is attempted, with the exception of word order. As the last step the morphological devices which serve as the formal signs of syntactic relations are also learned, often in the third year of life. All this refers to the learning of the patterns of one language. Bilingualism, the separate learning of two sets of patterns, amounts to a further refinement of contrasts, which is naturally learned late.

During the first two years of life, on which I have concentrated my attention in my study, no clash of phonemes due to the presentation of two languages can be said to have occurred. The phonemic structures of German and English are roughly the same, and "roughly" is the only measure that can be applied to a small child's language learning as long as only the coarser contrasts of the model are appreciated and imitated. Of course there are certain phonemes in the use of which the two languages do not agree, like the English dental fricatives and the vowels [æ] of hat and [ʌ] of but or butter, and the German rounded front vowels and voiceless domal fricatives (the ich and ach sounds). But these are all sounds which are late in the learning of monolingual children. They are normally not acquired before the third year.

In examining the sound learning of my daughter during the first two years, I paid special attention to possible bilingual effects, and found very little. Practically the only feature worth noting was the treatment of the consonant [l]. It is one of the more difficult sounds; it was not learned well during this early stage. In initial and medial position it was usually replaced by the easier glide [j]. In terminal position it was represented by vowels, and here a difference between the two languages showed up. In German words the flat [l] was rendered by the front vowel [ɪ], whereas the English [l] with its raised back tongue was rendered by the vowel [u]—most strikingly in the word Ball, which was [baɪ] for the first ten months of the second year, but then became [bau] because the child had switched from the German model to the English ball. Since the diphthongs [aɪ] and [au] were otherwise not confined to one of the two languages, no phonemic separation resulted. At the end of the second year the [l] was sometimes reproduced correctly in initial and medial position. The child then heard terminal syllabic and consonantal [l] and sometimes reproduced it as [l], but it could not yet stand in terminal position. She added the vowel substitute to the [l], *bottle* becoming [balʊ], *oil* [ʔɔɪlo]. The German word in which medial [l] was frequently rendered as [l] was *alle*. The consonant was however at first the velarized English [l]; via the palatal substitute [j] it developed into the correct flat German [l] in the last two months. There was only one English word in which medial [l] was not omitted or rendered by the normal substitute [j], namely *hello*; its [l] was the correct English variety. Thus the child used the two kinds of [l] at first as allophones of one phoneme, without separation by languages. At the end of the second year the models began to be followed more accurately, but the dearth of examples and the subsequent history make it hazardous to speak of two phonemes. Normally [j] was the substitute for [l] in both languages, and the substitutes for terminal [l] tended eventually to settle into [ə] in both.

Another phenomenon worth a glance is the habit which this child developed of using a glottal stop as the introduction of any German or English word beginning with a vowel. Since this is the rule in standard German, the thought arose that it might be an influence of German on her English. That may be the correct explanation. But on the other hand this child's syllable pattern was consonant—vowel for many months. Practically no words began with a vowel, and terminal consonants were not added until the latter months of the second year, and then by no means always. This syllable pattern favored the use of the introductory glottal stop, which is of course quite common in English in isolated words emphatically pronounced. When the child's speaking became rather suddenly more fluent, at the age of 2 years and 4 months, and the syllable patterns became more varied, the use of the glottal stop receded markedly. Again we cannot speak with assurance of bilingual interference in the child's phonemic system.

A further rule of the child's speech as late as the third year was that consonants at the end of words, after they began to be added to the syllable pattern, could only be voiceless; voiced consonants of the English model were either omitted or lost their voice. This is again a rule of German, not of English. But I find terminal devoicing in the literature of child language for monolingual children speaking English and French. It is a special category of assimilation which cannot be attributed to the bilingualism.

Two German words beginning with the cluster [ts], *zu* and *Zunge,* were attempted. The affricate was not handled successfully, which might be thought to be due to the fact that English does not use it initially. But consonant clusters were not mastered at this stage anyway; the same affricate medially and terminally, positions in which it is common in English, was handled just as unsuccessfully.

English long vowels, especially [e], lost their diphthongal off-glide, except in terminal position, becoming pure vowels as in German. But again, this simplification has been observed with monolingual English-speaking children.

Of the two typically German fricatives [ç] and [x], the child did not learn the former in the first two years and seemed to avoid words containing this common German sound. That might be due to the lack of support from English.

Yet, the other fricative, [x], was learned in two words. More frequently, to be sure, it was omitted or replaced by the stop [k], and in many other instances when the sound occurred, it was merely a non-standard off-glide of terminal high vowels, English as well as German.

Thus the child had, by the end of the second year, a slightly wider experience with sounds than monolingual children; but they still belonged to a unified set of phonemes not differentiated by languages.

In the syntax the situation is similar. The free mixing of English and German vocabulary in many of her sentences was a conspicuous feature of her speech. But the very fact that she mixed lexical items proves that there was no real bilingualism yet. Words from the two languages did not belong to two different speech systems but to one, which was bilingual only in the sense that its morphemes came objectively from two languages. Correspondingly, the vocabulary choice was not yet determined by the person addressed; she used German words for English speakers and vice versa.

As far as syntactic structure is concerned, there was no structure during the stage of one-word utterances. The one-word stage is a long one with many children. In my case it lasted from seven to twelve months, depending on what you count as a word, and on what you count as a structured combination of two words. As soon as two words were put together in a non-enumerative fashion, the learning of syntactic patterns began. Combining a subject with a predicate (which was not necessarily based on a standard verb) was learned at the age of 1 year and 8 months. The learning of the pattern verb—object began one month later and took several months. The sophisticated combination subject—verb—object was acquired, with a heroic effort, during the last month of the second year. These patterns, along with simpler ones like adjective—noun, are however, the same in the two languages. Their learning did not require the acquisition of two separate sets of syntactic combinations.

There was one construction in which a bilingual clash could have occurred, namely the English pattern, *Watch this roll, Watch me string beads, Watch me open the sandbox.* This simplest form of a complex sentence, in which the subordination of the second clause has almost no formal expression in the standard language, is common in English, but has only a very restricted use in German. The child began to learn this pattern during the last month of the second year, and two months later (2;1) it was used freely (the examples are from 2;1)—regularly with English words, however. That does not mean that she reserved this pattern for use in English sentences; there was actually one example (1;11) in which a German adverb acted as the second predicate: *Ask Mama this aus,* "I am going to ask Mama to take this off." By that time her speech had become so predominantly English for a time that German words were not too likely to intrude. Thus a bilingual clash was avoided.

In the morphology there was also little occasion for bilingual interference. The child was still operating with syntactic patterns devoid of formal expression beyond word order. Nouns and verbs were used in single base forms, without distinctions as to number, person, tense, etc. The only bound morpheme which began to appear occasionally at the end of the second year was the ending [ʃ] for possessives and plurals of nouns. For possessives the German and the English endings resulted by phonetic rules in the same substitute; it cannot be decided whether her form [mamaʃ] was based on English *Mama's* or German *Mamas*. For the plural the ending is definitely based on English; but it was not transferred to German nouns, and no German pattern for contrasting singular and plural was attempted. The plural category was barely beginning to be appreciated.

Summarizing this first part of the scrutiny, we find that the child was not really bilingual during the first two years. She combined two models into one speech form. No clash between two sets of patterns occurred in sounds, syntax, or morphology. Compound nouns and verbs were sometimes hybrid; but that, too, does not mean a clash of patterns; the two languages use the same patterns.

The situation changed in later years, when the child became conscious of the bilingualism which faced her, and learned to keep the two languages apart. The first signs of this consciousness came soon after her second birthday. This seems to be the normal time; it is reported by other observers, too. She commented on the language difference, the first time even with the use of the language name, German, which we had not introduced to her. Usually she would contrast "I say" with "you say," speaking to me. Sometimes she asked me, "How does Mama say it?"—a sly contrivance to get me to say an English word, without success. Thus, with the consciousness of bilingualism had come the principle of associating a language with a person—in her case associating German with me, the lone German speaker in her world. When she was a little over four years old, she asked, "Mother, do all fathers speak German?" This question confirms the operation of the person-language principle, together with a generalization which shows that the bilingual status of our family had previously not revealed itself to her as exceptional, and with the first doubt about the correctness of the generalization. At the same time she commented once on the fact that a radio speaker was "talking German," with pleased surprise: only fathers were expected to speak German, not radios. Just once, four weeks later, she asked me, "Papa, why is it that you speak German?" The question was not a criticism, although her own language was by that time definitely English; but it was a sign that bilingualism was now a conscious problem. At the age of six and seven she showed by occasional utterances that she was proud of her own bilingualism.

After this excursion I turn to some observations from the later stage, after the second birthday but before the interlude in Germany at age five, the stage when bilingualism had begun to be conscious, but when the child had turned rather resolutely to English. During the third year most of the remaining phonetic imperfections were ironed out and most of the missing sounds were added. For instance, the English vowel [æ] of *hat* began to replace the substitute [a] at 2;3; [ʌ] of *hut* began to be correct at 2;4, so that two new vowel phonemes were added to her stock. She was less successful in imitating German rounded front vowels; her developing English sound system overshadowed the German one. [y] was sometimes rendered by [u], frequently by [i], once decomposed into the diphthong [uɪ], and only occasionally imitated correctly. [ø] was correct in the last month of the third year, [y] by 3;3; but she still slipped sometimes into unrounded forms of the vowels in the fourth and fifth years. These German phonemes were not very stable because the support from English was lacking.

There is evidence that the child was beginning to separate the phonemes of German from the phonemes of English. At 3;6 she thought that she could make the word *candle* German by pronouncing it [kandl]. At 3;8 she used the English verb *to hand* in a German sentence, but transposed it into the form [hant]; she realized that [æ] was not a German vowel. She added immediately the question, "Is [hant] right?" It was not; the question shows that her German speech feeling was ahead of her speaking practice. She also tried pseudo-German [blak] for English *black*; there were many other instances at the same time. Once she used the German word *stimmen*, "to tune instruments," in English: "They are stimming," but with adapted sounds, [st] instead of [ʃt]. She had developed "conversion patterns" (Weinreich) which proves the existence of two sets of patterns.

For consonants also the English system was perfected in the third and fourth years. [v] and [f] were learned at 2;4. Terminal voiced consonants, previously omitted or devoiced, began to be learned in the middle of the fourth year. The learning of the *th*-sounds took until the fourth year. Consonant clusters were gradually acquired. In short, English consonants progressed slowly but steadily to adequate imitation of the standard. German consonants however were wavering. At 2;4 she achieved correct *ich* and *ach* sounds, but replaced them just as often by [k], in the same month. Later, as the English consonant system became stronger, the two German sounds became even more uncertain. They were often articulated correctly, but substitutes, which were normal English consonants, intruded again and again. There was no steady progress toward correctness as in her English. Initial [ts] as in *zu* was still simplified to [s] in the fourth year. This may not be due to English influence; English *furniture* was pronounced without [t] at the same time. But after she had learned the correct articulation at the beginning of the fifth year, throwbacks to the simplified [s] pronunciation continued to occur because of the stronger English speech habits.

In the syntax and morphology, the learning of English patterns progressed with astonishing rapidity early in the third year. Prepositions, articles, auxiliary verbs, all previously omitted consistently, were learned, beginning at 2;3 and 2;4. The verb acquired the ending of the third person singular and past tense forms, both weak and strong. The plurals of nouns had endings more frequently. With the increasing fluency at 2;4, clauses were combined into coherent utterances. The first co-ordinating conjunctions appeared, and practically at the same time she began to use a variety of complex sentences introduced by subordinating conjunctions. The English syntactic and morphological patterns, which had been very primitive at the end of the second year, were perfected rapidly.

At the same time the German syntax was stagnant. She said only the simplest sentences, usually stereotype repetitions of a few requests. German had become decidedly recessive and needed bolstering to preserve it from extinction. Since her active German concerned mostly vocabulary items inserted into English sentences, it was not surprising that German nouns occasionally received English plural endings in the fourth year, or that she used a German plural as a singular. The principles of the several German classes of plural formation were not yet recognized. Rather is it surprising that the simple English plural form did not influence German nouns more often. The child realized that the two languages have different patterns, and while she did not master those of German, she chose to abstain from German utterances in preference to casting them into English patterns—without consistency, to be sure. There were such examples as *"Kann ich haben das?"*—a purely German sentence in purely English word order; or *"Ich will dich zu komm rauf mit mir"*—an English construction impossible in German, and with an imperative instead of an infinitive. On the other hand she did not allow German patterns to intrude into the English system. My remark, *"Ich hab dich lieb,"* was immediately answered, "I like you too." She appreciated that the German idiomatic pattern, which she understood, had to be changed completely in English.

From the end of the fifth year the child spent half a year in Germany with us. She was left alone with German speakers for four weeks, and that time sufficed to give her complete fluency in German while English receded; she was unable to say more than a few very simple English sentences after these four weeks. However the German, while fluent, was by no means correct. Idioms and word order remained strongly influenced by English. She said *"alle von diesen,"* which is English "all of these," not German. A "butterfly" became a *"Butterfliege"* instead of *"Schmetterling."* Instead of *"nicht wahr?"* she used the English idiom, *"Können wir nicht?"* etc. But the most conspicuous influence was in the word order, in which English and German differ greatly. At first infinitives and participles were placed too early in the clause, as in English; but that was corrected almost at once. She had a little more difficulty with the inversion of subject and verb after an introductory word or clause; but the wavering was overcome within a month, and inversion was mastered. The greatest difficulty was the verb-last position in subordinate clauses. It took her three months to learn, and then it became correct quite suddenly. The German pattern, unimportant to her because it was not essential for communication, had suddenly dawned on her.

Pronunciation of the few English words which she still occasionally used was quickly affected by German. After a few weeks in Germany she said "I [kant]," although she corrected it into "I [kænt]." This was of course not a slip into a different type of English pronunciation, but an intrusion of a German vowel. At first she retained the American [r] in German words, but after about four months the German uvular [ʀ] came in with a rush, and after six months it was used even in English words, along with American [r]. Obviously the two forms, different as their articulation is, were merely phonetic variants of the same phoneme. Her [l] was the flat German variety even in English words, and in general she pronounced English words with a decided German "accent" a month after the arrival in Germany.

Half a year's sojourn in Germany was sufficient to straighten out most of the deficiencies of her German in pronunciation and sentence structure—not quite all of them; a few English peculiarities survived the whole period, although her English was then quite inactive.

After the return to America the process of adaptation was reversed. The first day she was unable to say much in English. After a few days she could converse with her English-speaking friends. Half a month after the return she spoke English fluently again, with some German interference. After one month German and English were in balance. After four months she had some difficulty in speaking German; but after six months the reaction was overcome. Both languages were fluent; only the vocabulary was more ready at hand in English. From that time on she was really bilingual—not in the ideal sense of the word: English was much stronger; but she continued to speak both languages separately—German mostly to me, English to others.

It seems that the features of German which she had learned last were the first to be forgotten. In the beginning German [l] and uvular [ʀ] were still used in English and German words. But after one month the latter was receding even in German words; later she learned it again. A year later the rounded vowels were again often unrounded; it took years before they became stable. Immediately after the return she used German pure long vowels in English words like *play*. Nine months later she introduced the English diphthong into German words. At the age of seven she occasionally used [su] for *zu* again, although by then the adaptation was exceptional. Her German sounds were less firmly anchored in her speech habits than were her English ones—except for the limited period in which German was dominant.

There were instances to show that in her bilingual state she had a good feeling for regular sound correspondences. At 6;2 she used German *steif,* which means "stiff," wrongly in the sense of "steep." She had transposed the [p] of the English word correctly into its normal German correspondent [f] ; unfortunately, German does not have such a cognate of *steep.* Before and after the time in Germany she often used the English word *number* in German adaptation, *Numbern,* with a German stressed vowel and plural ending; the real German word lacks the [b]. At 6;6 she called a window *screen* in German a [ʃkrin] —sound adaptation for a practically untranslatable word. A year later she used in a German sentence the mysterious word *Stümpfe,* which turned out to be a conversion of English *stamps* into German, with a most surprising use of zero grade for normal grade in the vowel.

In the word order, too, the German patterns asserted themselves in English for a while after the return from Germany. After one month she said "Then is here your school" and "When one nine years old is," although the transfer of subordinate word order into English was rare. Two months after the return: "I

was earlier there" for "I was there first," German in word order and idiom.
After four months in America: "Where my tooth out is, that's where I bite,"
again marked as very rare in my diary. On the other hand, the verb-last position
of German subordinate clauses was not always correct any more after less than
a month in America, under English influence, and idioms were already affected.
There was clearly a struggle of patterns. However, at other times the child
showed that she had a feeling for the separation of pattern sets. During the first
month in German she had tried to translate *"Ich kann dich nicht verstehen"* into
her atrophied English. She started: "I can't you . . . " and then gave up—not
because of a lexical deficiency, but because she felt the pattern discrepancy,
which she was unable to cope with. Now, a month after the return, she said,
"She wanted me to come over" and immediately translated, *"Sie wollte mich
zu . . . "*; that was a false start; she checked herself and finished correctly,
". . . dass ich rüberkommen soll." With reference to her doll she said, *"Die ist
ja auch nicht–schlafen,"* but then rejected the English pattern, "is not sleeping,"
and corrected herself, *"Die schläft auch noch nicht."* During her seventh year
her bilingualism became more complete. She used correct word order both in
English and in German. She had learned to keep the two sets of patterns apart.

In the morphology there were a few instances in which English verbs were
used with German infinitive and past participle markers, and rare examples of
English nouns with German plural endings, in German contexts, which means no
more than English fill-ins for lexical deficiencies, within German patterns. On
the whole it is remarkable that there were so few such instances, although lexicon
and idioms were the one area in which the child did not mind crossing the two
languages, because no comprehensive patterns were involved. The more real
bilingualism developed, the less interference of patterns was observable. Since
her bilingualism was not ideal, German being decidedly the weaker half, there
remained an influence of English on vocabulary, idioms, and, to a limited
extent, syntax, but practically none on sounds, morphology, and word formation.

Looking back, I think I have given a picture of a mixed language, particularly
during the preliminary stage when the child was still trying to build up a unified
language system out of the double model. I have also outlined the struggle which
led to the separation of two systems, to bilingualism. I do not know whether I
have contributed much to the solution of the problems of bilingual description.
It seems to me that there is a parallelism between the bilingual learning of a small
child and adult bilingualism. In both cases two separate patterns must be mastered,
and to keep them separate means a struggle. The natural thing for both children
and adults seems to be to operate with one language system, and the walls between
the two systems are brittle, unless bilingualism is cultivated with effort. Then
however it is possible to achieve separation; I think the resultant broadening of
the linguistic base leads to an enrichment of the personality.

On the Psychological Nature

2

of Child Speech Formation

under Condition of Exposure

to Two Languages

Natela V. Imedaze, D. Uznadze, *Institute of Psychology, Tbilisi, USSR*

INTRODUCTION

Languages which have a variety of case markers and grammatical gender pose somewhat different problems for the learner than does English. Imedadze, in this study, presents data from a child acquiring Russian and Georgian. The study parallels nicely that of Mikeš who studied two infant girls acquiring Hungarian and Serbo-Croatian, language systems which also require a variety of case markers. The simultaneous acquisition of two languages with important syntactic differences has allowed these two researchers to ask such questions as 1) are forms acquired in one language simultaneously acquired in the other; or 2) is there a separate order of acquisition within each language; 3) which categories or groups of grammatical categories are acquired late in each language and why. Unfortunately, this brief report of Imedadze's work does not give us great detail on the research. The reader may also wish to look at the Mikeš study for an examination of the acquisition of case, gender, person, number, tense and mode.

    The Imedadze paper is best known, however, for the suggestion that the child's alternative autonomous functioning in two languages might be explained on the basis of Uznadze's set theory. The notion of set, an important research area in psychology, has been further explored by Sodhi and by Cummins and Gulutson for second language learning.

Oksaar, in her study of Sven (Estonian-Swedish), presents an alternative model to explain the data which Imedadze classifies as a stage of "mixed speech." The Oksaar model posits an L_3 to account for the child's speech production. A "mixed stage" label, she claims, does not allow us to account for the fact that children learning more than one language create rules and elements that cannot be found in either of the languages he hears.

The need for further information on Soviet research is obvious. While we believe we are breaking new ground in the field of second language acquisition, we may be quite mistaken. The amount of research that has been going on in the area of bilingual education and language instruction in the USSR since the early 1920s is monumental. It is likely that if an information exchange could be worked out, we would find more studies like those of Imedadze to add to our knowledge.

Reprinted with the permission of the International Union of Psychological Science and Dunov, Publisher, Paris from *International Journal of Psychology*, 1967, *2*, 2, 129-132.

* * *

The object of the present study was: a) the possibility of the autonomous functioning of two languages in the speech of a child simultaneously mastering these languages; b) the character of their interaction.

Systematic observations were made of the language of a child from the start of his active speech up to the age of 4, in accordance with the principle of "one person—one language" *i.e.*, one part of those surrounding him invariably spoke with him one language while others used another language: in the present case, the mother and the father spoke Georgian, while the grandmother and nurse spoke Russian.

The first words of the child were partly of Russian and partly of Georgian origin: *tsiti* ("flowers" in Russian), *buti* ("a ball" in Georgian). Not withstanding their objectively distinctive linguistic source and the fact of their acquisition through intercourse with persons speaking different languages, subjectively these were elements of the child's single vocabulary, so that he addressed the adults around him indiscriminately, employing all available linguistic means.

At the very beginning, words of the two different languages did not coincide in meaning. But from the age of 1;2, the child mastered the first pairs of equivalents in the two languages. However, this mastering occurred without signs of their inhibition (as may have been expected on the evidence of Epstein (1918), for example). The child used Russian and Georgian equivalents side-by-side, the two coinciding in a single speech act like synonyms of one language. This was first observed at the age of 1;3: *modi ak* ("come here" in Georgian), *idi, idi* ("come here" in Russian), *ai* ("that is") *sakhli* ("house" in Georgian), *domik* ("house" in Russian) and so forth. The child's ordinary speech began to contain sentences that partly consisted of Russian and partly of Georgian words of different meaning, e.g. *puri* ("bread" in Georgian) *khochish* ("want" in Russian) *chama* ("eat" in

Georgian), *Vidish* ("see" in Russian) *Dali* (girl's name) *buti* ("ball" in Georgian) *nalisu* ("draw" in Russian). Sentences constructed at this stage are completely devoid of grammatical structure.

Beginning with the 20th month, the situation changed: phrases of mixed composition and simultaneous use of equivalents occurred less and less often; the child now begins to address the adults consistently speaking with each one language and only in that language. Thus, the child is sharing his impressions of a walk with his mother (1.8.25) in Georgian: *Patabla bichi chamovalda, satskali bichi* ("the little boy fell down, poor boy"). The child's grandmother says in Russian: "What are you telling about?" The child at once repeats the same in Russian: *Adin mal'chik upal, ba-dina* ("a boy fell down, Granny").

On the basis of the foregoing evidence, two stages are identifiable in the development of the child of the present study: (a) the stage of mixed speech (up to 1;8) and (b) the stage of discriminated language systems (from 1;8).

How common these stages are in bilingualism developing under analogous conditions may be judged by the observation materials of Ronjat (1913), Pavlovich, Leopold (1939). Ronjat, for example, notes the existence of "a common vocabulary composed of word pairs, identical in meaning." The speech of Leopold's child up to two years was "a hybrid system," a blend of English and German and it is only from 1;10 that there appears "a first flicker of the later unfolding of two separate language systems."

The formation, by the end of the second year, of two independent vocabularies coincides with the start of an intensive grammaticizing of the child's speech. Its analysis has shown that the sequence and periods of mastering grammatical forms by the bilingual child under discussion only partially coincide with the corresponding development of monolinguals (Gvosdev, 1949; Avalishvili, 1961); delay and difficulty were observable in mastering those grammatical forms in either language that basically differ as to their means of denoting one and same relation. Thus, the relation between the subject and the object in Russian requires nominative-accusative control and in Georgian—the dative-nominative. During the first half of the second year, it was expressed in preinflectional form. Beginning with the age of 1;8, the ending of the accusative case appears in the child's Russian speech. Some time later inflectional changes also occur in equivalent Georgian expressions; however, they are mostly erroneous, for they are built on the Russian pattern where it is the object that undergoes inflectional changes and not the subject as required by the rules of the Georgian language. For example: *Dali unda tsignis,* instead of: *Dalis unda tsigni* ("Dali wants the book"). The forms that are analogously constructed in both languages, *e.g.,* the instrumental case, were mastered simultaneously and without difficulty. Thus, forms of the genitive case of possession (1;9): *Natelina plati* ("Natela's dress" in Russian) and *Babuas satvalebi* ("Grandfather's spectacles" in Georgian) and those of the instrumental genitive: (2;7–2;10), *Jokhit vtsem* ("I shall beat him with a stick" in Georgian); (2;0), *ukoy adeyaltsem* ("Cover with a blanket" in Russian) appeared in both languages at the same time.

The cause of these phenomena is apparently to be sought in the mechanism of mastering grammatical forms that presupposes not only the acquisition of a formal grammatical symbol but also the isolation of the relation expressed by the given form from the overall concatenation of phenomena. In mastering a corresponding grammatical form in another language, this process is facilitated by the already isolated relation. If the means of designating the same actual relation in the two languages differ sharply, difficulties arise in the course of mastering the respective grammatical forms: the individual has to regroup phenomena by submitting them to new grammatical generalization, without awareness, of course.

These facts show that parallel mastering of two languages is not a mechanical juxtaposition of two processes of mastering the language, but the formation of language systems under conditions of complex interaction. The character of the above second stage in the speech development of a bilingual child shows that, at a definite point in the development of language systems, the child's speech intercourse with those around him becomes differentiated: in each concrete speech act it is the words and the grammatical structure of only one language that become actualized. The ever increasing autonomy of the two languages is graphically illustrated by the following fact: in the presence of the person who consistently speaks to the child in Georgian, the child either gives no answer to questions put to him in Russian or answers in Georgian, and vice versa. Thus at the age of 2;3, the child while traveling with his mother in a funicular carriage kept silent when asked by a Russian tourist where he was going. He answered a repeated question: *puniculeze* ("ze" in Georgian corresponds to the preposition "to"); the question in Russian: "Where do you live?" is replied: *Chonkadzis kucha* ("Chonkadze street" in Georgian).

Such autonomy in the functioning of two languages is inexplicable from the position held by most investigators of bilingualism known to the present writer. W. Stern (1928) and Ronjat (1913) speak of the independent spheres of application for either language, of the child being aware that one collection of words is used with one parent, and the other with the other parent, so that he must, for example, address his mother *Brot* and his father *pain*. It is difficult to agree with this explanation which attempts to transfer the basis of the speech activity of a 2-3 year old child to the level of conscious activity. Theodore Elvert (1959) points to habit (*Gewohnheit*) as the mechanism responsible for the differentiation in the use of the language involved. Again, this offers only a partial explanation of the facts. Traditional associationism (Epstein, 1918) reduces the facts of confusion of languages to the mechanism of associative inhibition, and this will be stronger, proportionately to the strength of the connection between the word and the idea. The existence of stages in the speech of the child of the present study is not only felt without explanation, but is in conflict with this proposition.

In the present writer's view, the mechanism of the alternative autonomous functioning of two languages in the child's speech is explicable on the basis of D. Uznadze's concept of set, according to which the occurrence of a speech activity requires a need for communication and the situation in which it may be gratified as well as the availability of means or instruments of communication (vocabulary, speech habits and skills).

Selective speech behavior is preceded by the determination of the type of speech situation. Speech situation in the present writer's use involves both speech and non-speech components, the former implying some sequence of stimuli set up in accordance with the structure norms of a concrete language (determinative of the type of situation), the latter implying the persons, the places and the field of activity constantly connected with one language.

According to Osgood (1957) a definite integration evolves as a consequence of co-occurrence of stimuli. I suppose that on the basis of an integration of speech and non-speech components, there occurs a kind of completion or reconstruction of non-speech situation to a speech situation. Determination of the type of situation by the individual makes the need for concrete communication, which results in the emergence in him of a state predetermining the structure of purposeful speech behavior, i.e. a set for speaking a concrete language. Consequently, the presence of a non-speech situation component proves sufficient for the actualization of the words and habits of the respective language.

Thus the functional autonomy of the two language systems emerging at a definite stage in the speech development of a bilingual child is determined by the evolving of two distinctive sets, alternately actualized.

The Simultaneous Acquisition

3 of English and French

in a Two-year-old Child

Marianne Celce-Murcia, *University of California, Los Angeles*

INTRODUCTION

The following paper, presented by Dr. Marianne Celce-Murcia at the 1975 TESOL conference, is a description of her daughter's language production at age 2:4. While Caroline's stronger language is English, she has much more than just a passive understanding of French. She uses many French lexical items, but she has not yet attained a balanced system with matched fluency in each as claimed by Ronjat for his child, Louie. Yet Caroline's production is far in advance of the French-English bilingual child studied by Swain and Wesche. Their subject, Michael, appeared to understand a great deal of English but, at the beginning of their study when he was three years old, his responses to English were frequently nonverbal or in French:

Michael: (M picks up microphone and holds it to doll's ear)
Adult: No, he doesn't speak out of his ear. He speaks out of his mouth.
Michael: (M moves microphone to doll's mouth)
Adult: That's right. (long pause) Can you hear anything?
Michael: (M puts microphone to his own ear and listens) *Non.*

Uneven development of the two languages is common in all studies of infant bilingualism. The child develops faster in the language which is used most in his environment.

38

In giving us a description of Caroline's development at one stage, Celce-Murcia is able to focus particularly on phonology and the role that it plays in the child's choice of lexical items from each language. Her discovery of Caroline's avoidance of phonologically difficult words in each language (even when she knew the corresponding word in each language) gives us a new way of understanding the bilingual child's mixing of the two languages in the early stages of bilingual development. In addition, the discovery of avoidance phenomena in young children gives us a nice parallel to the avoidance strategies of adults described in detail by Schachter in her experimental research (1974, 1975).

While the focus of this paper is on Caroline's lexical choices and the relationship to her phonological development, there are many other interesting observations made on Caroline's syntax as well.

The reader who is particularly interested in French bilingualism will no doubt also enjoy reading the fine research work of Swain, Savignon, and Ronjat, and the reports of the OISE and St. Lambert's projects. In addition to Leopold's work, the reader might also wish to investigate other research on the child's lexical development in such studies as Yoshida (in this volume) and Ben-Ziev (1976).

What follows is a description of the English and French that my daughter Caroline had acquired when she was two years and four months of age (date of birth: Oct. 27, 1972).

Caroline's father, who is a native speaker of French and who spends several hours a day with her, speaks to her primarily—though not exclusively—in French, whereas I, a native speaker of English, use predominantly English with her and spend somewhat more time with her than her father. Caroline hears us speak to each other in both languages. (It would have been artificial to keep the two languages apart as has been the case in some other studies, e.g. Leopold (1939-1949), since we both speak the other's language fluently. Moreover, having been married for seven years prior to Caroline's birth, we had become accustomed to using either English or French with each other.) Therefore, Caroline is growing up in an environment where it seems natural for adults to speak both English and French.

Outside the home, Caroline spends three full days per week with a babysitter (a monolingual speaker of English) who has two children—a five-year-old boy and a six-year-old girl. English, therefore, has the edge over French in vocabulary and syntax. However, French is well-understood by Caroline and many vocabulary items and some syntactic patterns and sounds are distinctively French.

Caroline is physically large for her age (2; 4). She is 38½" tall, weighs 34-35 lbs., wears a dress size of 4 or 5, and her shoe size is 9. Her features are also mature in appearance with the result that people often guess her to be 3; 6 or even 4 years of age. She started to walk between 10 and 11 months of age and is very active: runs, jumps, climbs and does not sleep much. She was saying the words "Mama" and "Baba" to me and her father at 10 months of age and she used these two words in her first major piece of communication at the age of 12 months. I came home from UCLA about 5:30 p.m. Caroline heard my key in the door and came running. She said, "Mama, Mama." Then she pointed toward the kitchen where her father was cooking some vegetables and said, "Baba." Then she ran to the kitchen and addressed her father, saying, "Baba, Mama!" while she pointed toward the front door.

Caroline has a personality to match. She is aggressive to the point of being a bully; she is uninhibited, she sings, dances, or screams whenever and wherever it suits her; she is sociable (i.e. likes people), outgoing, demonstrative, and very jealous of her father's attention.

The data reported below were collected during the two-month period when Caroline's age ranged from 2; 2 to 2; 4. They were collected from memory rather than through tape recordings. Every evening, after putting her to bed, I would spend at least 10 to 15 minutes transcribing on 3x5 cards all the new words and "sentences" I had heard her produce that day. Care was taken to capture her deviant and often varying pronunciations.

SYNTAX

In this brief discussion of Caroline's syntax, the deviations and variations in her pronunciation are minimized to facilitate better understanding of her grammar.

Caroline's syntax is very limited at this point. Two-word pivot/open utterances of the following type predominate.

A. *Social*

  1. Come, $\begin{Bmatrix} \text{mama} \\ \text{papa} \end{Bmatrix}$.

  2. $\begin{Bmatrix} \text{Hi} \\ \text{Bye-bye} \end{Bmatrix}$, $\begin{Bmatrix} \text{mama} \\ \text{boy} \end{Bmatrix}$.

  3. $\begin{Bmatrix} \text{Milk} \\ \text{Cookie} \end{Bmatrix}$, please.

  4. $\begin{Bmatrix} \text{Oui (Fr. "yes")} \\ \text{No} \end{Bmatrix}$, papa.

B. *Possession*

  1. car $\begin{Bmatrix} \text{mama} \\ \text{papa} \end{Bmatrix}$ (i.e. Mama's car, Papa's car)

2. my $\left\{\begin{array}{l}\text{bike}\\\text{book}\\\text{milk}\end{array}\right\}$

At this stage, Caroline appears to use pattern (B1) for a noun possessor but (B2) for a pronominal possessor. It is possible that (B1) is due to French influence.

C. *Negation*

no + $\left\{\begin{array}{l}\text{bed}\\\text{change}\\\text{milk}\\\cdot\\\cdot\\\cdot\end{array}\right\}$

D. *Subjectless (1st person sing. understood) "want"-constructions*

1. want $\left\{\begin{array}{l}\text{book}\\\text{that}\end{array}\right\}$

2. want $\left\{\begin{array}{l}\text{talk}\\\text{dance}\end{array}\right\}$ (i.e. one of us is on the phone and she wants to talk on the phone, too)
(i.e. an order to play the phonograph so she can dance)

E. *Subjectless (1st person sing. understood) "want go"-constructions*

1. *direction*: want go $\left\{\begin{array}{l}\text{up}\\\text{down}\\\text{out}\end{array}\right\}$

2. *activity*: want go $\left\{\begin{array}{l}\text{dodo "sleep" (Fr. baby talk)}\\\text{peepee (Fr. }pipi\text{)}\\\cdot\\\cdot\\\cdot\end{array}\right\}$

3. *location*: want go $\left\{\begin{array}{l}\text{park}\\\text{beach}\\\cdot\\\cdot\\\cdot\end{array}\right\}$

F. *Constructions with Adjectives*

1. *attributive*: big $\left\{ \begin{array}{l} \text{dog} \\ \text{lion} \\ . \\ . \\ . \end{array} \right\}$

2. *predicative*: (without copula) $\left\{ \begin{array}{l} \text{mama} \\ \text{my (= I)} \\ \text{papa} \end{array} \right\} \left\{ \begin{array}{l} \text{happy} \\ \text{mad} \end{array} \right\}$

G. *Noun plus Verb Constructions*

1. *statements*: $\left\{ \begin{array}{l} \text{my (= I)} \\ \text{papa} \end{array} \right\} \left\{ \begin{array}{l} \text{tombé (Fr. "fell down")} \\ \text{jump} \\ . \\ . \\ . \end{array} \right\}$

2. *imperatives*: $\left\{ \begin{array}{l} \text{mama} \\ \text{papa} \end{array} \right\} \left\{ \begin{array}{l} \text{dance} \\ \text{come} \\ . \\ . \\ . \end{array} \right\}$

H. *Present Progressive (without copula)*

baby crying
man working

I. *Indefinite Article plus Noun*

(this) an $\left\{ \begin{array}{l} \text{book} \\ \text{boy} \\ \text{park} \\ . \\ . \\ . \end{array} \right\}$ i.e. "a $\left\{ \begin{array}{l} \text{book} \\ \text{boy} \\ \text{park} \\ . \\ . \\ . \end{array} \right\}$ "

For a while I was puzzled by the appearance of a fairly strongly stressed indefinite article (i.e. [æn]) in Caroline's speech. At first, I thought it was the numeral "one," but this did not make sense semantically. Then I realized that what she had acquired was the phonologically more prominent French indefinite article (i.e., an approximation to the masculine form) and that she was using it in combination with her largely English vocabulary. This seems to be a nice example of Slobin's "perceptual saliency" principle (Slobin, 1973), which posits that what is more prominent acoustically tends to be learned first.

J.   *Conjunction*

    1. *phrasal*:
      a. Georgy, Bu, Brian
         (Occasionally varying with)
      b. an(d) Georgy, an(d) Bu, an(d) Brian

    2. *clausal*:

$$\text{my } (= I) \begin{cases} \text{go beach} \\ \text{go potty} \\ \text{dance} \\ \text{talk} \\ \cdot \\ \cdot \\ \cdot \end{cases} \text{too.}$$

K.   *Yes-No Questions*—are signaled by rising intonation.

    mama happy?
    my (= I) go park?

    The above is both a common developmental pattern and the most commonly used yes-no question pattern in informal, colloquial French.

L.   *Wh-Questions*—are very rare, but not a productive pattern yet.

    1. the only common one: what that? (a fixed form perhaps)
    2. playful imitation/repetition of an older child or adult: why not!

    Caroline has also developed some expansions of the two-word (M) and three-word (N) constructions she regularly uses.

M.   *Expansions of Two-Word Constructions*

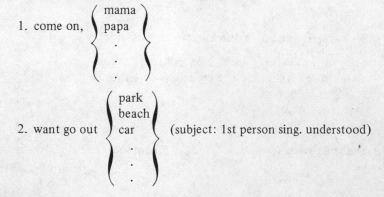

$$\text{1. come on, } \begin{cases} \text{mama} \\ \text{papa} \\ \cdot \\ \cdot \\ \cdot \end{cases}$$

$$\text{2. want go out } \begin{cases} \text{park} \\ \text{beach} \\ \text{car} \\ \cdot \\ \cdot \\ \cdot \end{cases} \text{(subject: 1st person sing. understood)}$$

N.   *Expansions of Three-Word Constructions*
     (All seems to involve *go* as a special activity-type auxiliary verb.)

1. $\begin{Bmatrix} \text{mama} \\ \text{papa} \end{Bmatrix}$ go work

2. $\begin{Bmatrix} \text{my (= I)} \\ \text{baby} \end{Bmatrix}$ go dodo (Fr. baby talk "sleep")

A final syntactic-semantic development of some amusement has been Caroline's three successively different answers to the question "What's your name?" Her first response was "baby," then for a while she said "my," and lately she has produced an approximation of her name, /kalayn/. This follows one of Brown's patterns for child vocabulary acquisition, i.e., the pattern he favors where vocabulary acquisition mirrors cognitive development in children by going from general to specific (Brown, 1958).

PHONOLOGY

In terms of phonological development, which I will go into in some detail, Caroline displays most of the simplification patterns discussed in some detail in Oller (1974).

1. Her vowel system was more fully developed in the early stages than the consonant system.

Early vowels were the front vowels and the low central vowel:

```
    /a/—mama
/e/, /i/—baby
    /E/—bed
   /ay/—hi!
```

Back vowels were more difficult and came later:

```
 /o/—dodo (Fr. "sleep" baby talk)
 /u/—pupi (Fr. "doll" baby talk for poupée)
 /ɔ/—ball
/ɔy/—boy
/aw/—c(l)own
```

The tense vowels /i/, /e/, /o/, and /u/ do not seem to have strong *y* and *w* glides yet.

She sometimes has problems (not always) with:

/ʌ/—/a/, e.g., *bus* /bas/
/ɪ/—/i/, e.g., *big* /big/
/æ/—/a/, e.g., *happy* /(h)api/

The biggest problem is /ʊ/—/u/, e.g., *book* (i.e., /bʊk/) probably pronounced as /buk/.

She can produce the two rounded French vowels nicely:

[y] *bus* (Fr. "bus"), *barbu* (Fr. "the bearded one")
[œ] *oeufs* (Fr. "eggs"), *E* (French pronunciation for the letter "E")

She does not produce most nasalized French vowels consistently—the only two words that she nasalizes with consistent accuracy are:

[p̃ɛ̃] *pain* "bread" and *bain* [b̃ɛ̃] "bath."

Other French words she uses like *papillon* "butterfly," *poisson* "fish," *maman* "mother," typically occur without nasalization.

2. Her consonant system is much more difficult to describe.

Stops

Initial voiceless stops are usually not aspirated and in fact are often voiced:

papa—[baba]
pain—[b̃ɛ̃] (Fr. "bread")

Her final stops are heavily articulated and voiced stops are typically devoiced:

bed [bɛt]
mad [mat]
big [bik]
dog [dɔk]
egg [ɛk]
etc.

Her medial "t" is strongly articulated, e.g., *potty* /pati/ perhaps in imitation of her father.

The three English nasals all occur.

initial and final:
m—/mama, dumdum/ (= (chewing) "gum")
n—/nunu/ (Fr. *nounourse* "Teddy Bear")
    /Endien/ (i.e., Indian)
final:
ŋ—/wiŋ/ (= swing)
    /wɔkiŋ/ (= working)

Fricatives

This is a real problem area for Caroline.

Initial /h/ is usually deleted—except for a few words like "hi!"

/θ/ —→ /s, š/   *teeth* /tis—tiš/

/θ/ —→ /d/   *thank you* /dankyu/

/ð/ ——→ /d/   *that* /dat/

/f/ —→ /k/   *off* /ɔk/

/f/ —→ /w/   *fifi* /wiwi/, *coffee* /kɔwɛk/, *phone* /won/

/f/ —→ /s/   *F* /[ES]

/v/ ——→ /w/   /wal/ (= *cheval* Fr. "horse")

                  /wæ̃n/ (= *vin* Fr. "wine")

/s/ —→ /z/   *Susan* /zuzan/, *sorcière* (Fr. "witch") /zɔzio/

/s/ —→ /θ/   *bus* /baθ/, *kiss* /kɪθ/

The fricative /s/ is also deleted in many environments. For example:

juice—/du/
mouse—/mau/

/š/ is often omitted initially:

shampoo /æmpu/
chapeau (Fr. "hat") /apo/

/ž/ —→ /š/ in *rouge* (Fr. "red") /us/

/ž/ —→ /y/ in *jaune* (Fr. "yellow") /yon/

/z/ is relatively easy:

Leslie /zezi/
bisou (Fr. "kiss") /bizu/
zoo /zu/
zebra /ziba/
zip /zɪp/

Affricates

These complex consonants are often simplified to stops initially:

ǰ—*juice* /du/
č—*chair* /tiya/
        /tæ/
   cheerios /tiyo/

Caroline has better success with affricates medially and finally:

> ǰ—*Georgie* /dɔdǰi/
> č—*witch* /wɪtš/, *bewitched* /biwɪtš/ (learned from watching the TV
> program with Elizabeth Montgomery)

Liquids

The sounds /r/ and /l/ are very difficult for Caroline.
/r/ is often deleted pre-vocalically:

> *rouge* /uš/
> *raincoat* /eynko/

/r/ is always deleted post-vocalically:

> ca(r), chai(r), ca(r)po(r)t

r → n *Morrie* /moni/
l → y (initially): *light* /yayt/
lion /yayon/
lunch /yantš/
l → ∅ (finally): *ball* /bɔ/
owl /aw/
etc.
syllabic [l] → o/u: *apple* /apu/ or /apo/

Semi-Consonants

The semi-consonants /w/ and /y/ are produced with ease in initial position:

> w—*one* /wɔn/
> *water* /walo/
>
> y—*yes* /ya/
> *yuck!* /yak/

Consonant Clusters

As would be expected, there is a great deal of simplification in this area:

/s/ dropped: *(s)wing* /wɪŋ/

(s) $\left\{ \begin{matrix} b \\ p \end{matrix} \right\}$ *oon* / $\left\{ \begin{matrix} b \\ p \end{matrix} \right\}$ un/

ba(s)ketball /bækɛtbɔ/

/r/ dropped: *wo(r)k* /wɔk/
cit(r)on (Fr. "lemon") /sito/

/l/ dropped: *c(l)own* /kawn/

There's also a simplification of:

/kr/ → /w/: *cry* /way/

In other medial positions we see medial /rd/ or /rt/ before /i/ go to /l/, e.g.,

birdie /bɛli/
party /pali/.

Also, medial /n/ before /i/ goes to /nd/, e.g.,

bunny /bandi/
Dany /dandi/
tennis /tɛndi/
Stanley /tandi/

The sequence of medial /t/ followed by a liquid in the next syllable seems to be reinterpreted as /lo/ or /lu/, e.g.,

water /walo/
bottle /balo/ or /balu/

Reduplication

While Ferguson and Farwell (1975) point out reduplication is one of several general strategies in child phonological development, Caroline's is perhaps also reinforced by French.

French:

Reduplicated forms used by adults:

maman	*pipi*
papa	*caca*
tata	*tchintchin*
tonton	

Reduplicated forms in French baby talk:

dodo	*nounou*
bobo	*coucou*

Reduplicated forms in nicknames:

Fifi	*Kiki*
Mimi	*Jean-Jean*

English is much more limited with forms such as:

mama
papa
bye-bye

Caroline's extensions:

/kokakoka/ "coca cola"
/pantapanta/ (Fr. *pantalon,* "pants")
/lili/ (Fr. *lit,* "bed")
/dumdum/ "gum"
/pelolo/ (Fr. *Père Noël,* "Santa Claus")

Other Phonological Phenomena

There are certain words or phrases (mainly French) that Caroline uses for *play* or *enjoyment*:

/kalawet/ (Fr. "peanuts" *cacahuète*)
/woila/ (Fr. *voilà* "Here/there it is; that's it; (then) it happened, etc.")
mama mi! (French version of the Italian exclamation, Mama mia!)

Caroline also appears to have an idiosyncratic form—something so difficult to articulate that she formed an easy though far-fetched approximation:

/andy/ "ice cream"

VOCABULARY—ENGLISH AND FRENCH

There are four categories of vocabulary in Caroline's speech with respect to English and French:

1. Caroline knows both the English and French expression and uses both:

/wal ~ hɔrΘi/ "cheval"/"horse"
/butey ~ balo/ "bouteille"/"bottle"
/pupi ~ dali/ "poupée"/"doll"
/wazo ~ bɛli/ "oiseau"/"bird"
/gato ~ keyk/ "gâteau"/"cake"
/œ ~ ɛk/ "oeufs"/"eggs"
etc.

2. Caroline is confused when the words are similar. She would hesitate or would use both (i.e., she does not know which to use).

/kun/, /kawn/ "clown"
/bys/, /bas/ "bus"
/ybɛ/, /yuba/ "Hubert" (name of her stuffed toy lion)
/kol/, /kul/ "école"/"school"

3. Sometimes Caroline is exposed exclusively or mainly to one form (i.e., the English or the French) and therefore knows only one:

English	French
milk	pipi "peepee"
dog	caca "BM"
car	coq "rooster"
money "coins"	dodo "sleep"
book	nounou "Teddy Bear"
raincoat	barbu "bearded man"
potty	babaou "boggy man"
cookie	

4. By far the most interesting category are those cases where Caroline has been exposed to both the English and French equivalent for an object—but where she avoids or refuses to say the one that is phonologically more difficult in terms of her system—e.g.:

   couteau/*knife /kuto/
  * cuiller/(s)poon /pun/
   papillon/'butterfly /papiyo/
  (*)maison/(home) (*house) /om/
   camio(n)/*truck /kamio/
   poisson/*fish /paso/
   citron/*lemon /sito/
  (*)garçon/boy /bɔy/
   dame/*lady, woman /dam/

This last strategy has been extended to more complex vocabulary items and, in one instance, resulted in mixing within a compound. As far as Caroline was concerned, all team sports on TV were basketball. After repeated correction (re: *football* by her father and me—recall Caroline's problem with /f/ and that the French word for *foot* is *pied*), she finally understood the distinction and settled on *piedball* /peybɔ/ to avoid the /f/ and persisted in using this form for a long period of time.

DISCUSSION

The above data contain some interesting theoretical and pedagogical implications that I would like to explore at this point.

First of all, we will briefly consider Caroline's second category of words (i.e., French/English cognates with minor variations in pronunciation). It has often been noted that adults who are learning a second language that has many cognate words sometimes studiously avoid these cognates in speech (though perhaps not in writing) because of phonological difficulties. Heller (1976), for example, cites cases of Spanish-speaking adults in evening ESL classes who avoid using cognates because they think such words are Spanish and not English.

Caroline has demonstrated a certain hesitation and vacillation in the use of such words—often switching back and forth several times, wondering which pronunciation to use:

   e.g., /bas/ . . . /bys/ . . . /bas/ for *bus*

Evidently, it is hard for her to keep the two languages apart where she has learned cognates with similar sounds. She is not avoiding the cognates but is quite confused.

Could her parents' performance with respect to the use of cognates be partly responsible for the confusion? Her father tends to retain French pronunciation of cognates when speaking English. There is no apparent avoidance—just a tendency to retain as French everything first learned in French even when speaking English. I have always been conscious of the differences in pronunciation between French-English cognates and try to make appropriate adjustments when speaking French. Likewise, there is no avoidance of cognates on my part.

This certainly is an area of language acquisition that deserves further study since so many different strategies are possible concerning a second language learner's use or nonuse of cognates and performance with respect to using cognate words when speaking and/or writing in the second language.

Secondly, let us focus on Caroline's fourth category of words (i.e., phonological avoidance). The strategy of "avoidance" has recently been spotlighted by Jackie Schachter, who suggests that the adult second-language learner will "avoid"—either consciously or unconsciously—structures and words that he is unsure of and make use of synonymous forms or circumlocutions. She further suggests that phonological avoidance or paraphrase is not as likely to occur since the speaker would have to learn to cope with difficult sounds whether he wanted to or not. This is why, speculates Schachter, contrastive analysis has greater predictive value in the area of phonology than in the areas of syntax and lexicon, i.e., one cannot paraphrase or avoid certain sounds (Schachter, 1974).

These conclusions may be valid so long as one refers to adult acquisition of a second or foreign language after the native language has been established (i.e., Schachter's frame of reference). However, if one looks at monolingual children acquiring their native language, a number of studies refer to avoidance of difficult sounds or "persistent avoidance of particular sounds" (Ferguson and Farwell, 1975, p. 436).

Moreover, the above data from Caroline indicate that Schachter's hypothesis regarding the relative nonexistence of phonological avoidance should be modified particularly in those cases where children are acquiring two or more languages simultaneously. In the data reported above, phonological avoidance was observed as a general and pervasive strategy.

An important question to be asked, of course, is whether other children acquiring two or more languages simultaneously also exhibit the same phonological avoidance strategy that Caroline did—i.e., is the strategy general or idiosyncratic? Rina Shapira (personal communication) provides some affirmative evidence from her own experience of being raised in a family environment where all the children acquired Hungarian and Hebrew simultaneously, and she recalls that phonological avoidance was a strategy frequently used by all the children. Also, Leopold in his study of his daughter Hildegard, who was simultaneously acquiring English and German, comments, " . . . she generally avoided altogether any words the meanings and form of which she could not successfully cope with." (Leopold, 1939-1949, Vol. I, p. 172). It should be pointed out that the word "form" as used in this quote refers specifically to phonological form and not syntactic form.

More examples of phonological avoidance from case studies of child language acquisition and also cases of adult phonological avoidance are needed before one can generalize definitively; however, it seems reasonable to assume that the avoidance strategy can manifest itself in any language area or language learning situation where choices are open to the speaker/learner. In other words, the fact that a monolingual adult learning English as a foreign/second language usually has no phonological choices (i.e., is neither learning two words for the same referent as Caroline does nor simplifying to the extent that monolingual children do) is due to his age, learning environment, limited vocabulary and teacher expectations, etc. It is *not* due to the fact that phonological avoidance or paraphrase *per se* is less likely to occur than syntactic or lexical avoidance or paraphrase. In fact it seems that lexical and phonological avoidance would be hard to separate completely since difficult pronunciation may be one of several reasons why a lexical item might be avoided—other possible reasons being the user's certainty as to the word's meaning, spelling, syntactic restrictions, etc.

If phonological avoidance is indeed a natural and generalized strategy that may naturally occur whenever circumstances permit, there is an important lesson in all of this for the language teacher or the writer of language textbooks. A brief anecdote will demonstrate what I mean. One of my former students, who happens to be a junior high school English teacher in Japan, complained to me about the first-year English textbook he has to use in his classes. In the first lesson the students are introduced to the main character of the text, "Roy," an American their age, and they are expected to learn to understand and say sentences like "This is Roy." "Roy is an American." etc. The problem with this, according to my former student, is that the "r" sound is so hard for the students to articulate, that they feel frustrated and defeated before they ever start to learn English. Often insurmountable attitude problems develop during the very first lesson (Mamoru Nishimura, personal communication).

It appears that unnecessary phonological barriers cause psychological problems, stunt fluency, and inhibit ease of learning a foreign language—especially in the initial stage. The writers of the above textbook could easily have used an American proper name like "Eddie," which would have been less excruciating for Japanese-speaking students to produce than "Roy." What the preceding data and the above anecdote suggest is that, as far as possible, initial vocabulary items should be selected with reference to the phonological structure of the learner's native language and on the basis of ease of articulation from the learner's point of view. Although common function words with difficult sounds cannot be avoided, proper names and other content words are often arbitrarily selected, and it is these items that should be more carefully chosen so that they pass easily through the beginning learner's phonological filter and facilitate (or at least do not impede) the initial language learning process. Phonologically problematic words and sounds should be dealt with at a later stage and perfect pronunciation should *not* be insisted upon initially, despite the many audiolingual/behaviorist prescriptions to the contrary.

There is additional support for this position from special instances of language use sometimes exhibited by adult English-speaking monolinguals. Ferguson and Farwell (1975), for example, observe that an adult may systematically—even consciously—avoid in his speech words that are difficult to pronounce, and they recommend that studies be carried out to document and further explore this phenomenon (p. 434). Surely language teachers and textbook writers should not deliberately go against such a natural tendency when preparing materials or lessons for the beginning-level student of English as a foreign/second language!

Language Development

4 of a Garo and English-speaking Child

Robbins Burling

INTRODUCTION

In 1955, Burling conducted this study of the simultaneous acquisition of English and Garo, a language of India, by his son Stephen. Stephen's language development in Garo was much stronger than in English during the period of this study. Many concepts were developed with full linguistic form in Garo but not in English. This makes an interesting contrast to the Mikeš and Imedadze studies and relates to Kessler's basic research assumption as well.

Imedadze, for example, studying the simultaneous acquisition of Russian and Georgian, noted that concepts were learned almost simultaneously in the two languages when the linguistic forms were similar. For example, instrumental case markers were learned first in Georgian and three days later appeared in the Russian data. In certain instances where one pattern appeared to be easier than its corresponding pattern in the other language, her subject would use the easier system for both languages.

The unevenness of development in Stephen's two languages, however, is not exceptional (cf., Leopold, Fantini, Celce-Murcia). Perhaps more unusual is Stephen's early acquisition of morphology. In fact, this study has often been cited as evidence against the principle that syntax is acquired by the learner before morphology is learned. Most children acquire at least basic word order in the new language before attending to morphological details; the same is true of most first language learning. In most languages, one can communicate quite adequately without using morphological markers—as Leopold says "without the frosting on the cake." Perhaps Stephen's early development of morphology in Garo is, as Burling points out, due to the importance of morphology in that language. It would be worthwhile to look for comparable data in other second language acquisition studies.

Reprinted with the permission of the author and the Linguistic Circle of New York from *Word*, 1959, *15*, 45-68.

* * *

Toward the end of October, 1954, I arrived with my wife and small son Stephen in the Garo Hills district of Assam, India, where we were to spend most of the next two years making a social anthropological study of the Garo.[1] These people number a quarter of a million and speak a language belonging to the Bodo group of Tibeto-Burman.[2] When we arrived, Stephen (who was born on the last day of May, 1953), was one year and four months old and was just beginning to attach meanings consistently to some of the vocal activity that he had been emitting in profusion for many months. His first few words were English, but he immediately came into regular contact with Garo speakers and soon added Garo words to his vocabulary; in fact, for the greater part of the time we were there, his Garo was significantly more fluent than his English. Since there have been few studies of child language in non-Indo-European languages, I kept a record of my son's linguistic development and have assembled the results here.

The study of a child's speech is a delightful one, not the least satisfying aspect being the frequent enjoyment that one's informant shows in having so much attention paid to him by his father. Nevertheless, it is beset with difficulties that never arise in the study of adult language. Children won't repeat themselves the way good adult informants can be persuaded to do. It is next to impossible to try to compare minimal pairs directly, both because of the poverty of the children's vocabulary and because of the difficulty in getting them to repeat forms. Moreover children speak with less precision and much less consistency than adults. With wide variation within the limits of a phoneme and with the difficulty of comparing minimal pairs it is frequently impossible to specify precisely the time when the child first makes a new contrast within the range of speech sounds that had formerly been a single phoneme. Nevertheless the ideal for which I have striven is an analysis of the successive additions of the distinctive features rather than a detailed description of the ever changing phonetic minutiae of his speech.

Stephen began to use Garo words within a few weeks of our arrival, but his English vocabulary grew steadily and it was several months before Garo became clearly predominant. The eventual triumph of Garo was aided by a protracted hospitalization of his mother which, except for short visits, removed him from close contact with his most important single English model. She was hospitalized through most of March and April, 1955, when he was one year and nine and ten months old. At this time, I spoke to him frequently in Garo, which diluted the effectiveness of the second major English source. Even after this the continued illness of his mother forced him into greater contact with Garos than might otherwise have been the case. The result was steady progress in the Garo language, which I believe he learned in much the same way as any Garo child.

PHONEMES AT ONE YEAR AND FOUR MONTHS

When we arrived in the Garo Hills, Stephen was one year and four months old and had a total vocabulary of a mere dozen words, but even those required a considerable phonemic inventory. He seemed to distinguish three vowel positions; a low unrounded vowel, generally central, though sometimes varying toward the front, as in *papa* "papa"; a high front unrounded vowel as in *kiki* "kitty"; and a mid or high mid back and strongly rounded vowel, as in *tu* "door."

As these examples also show, he clearly distinguished three stops in roughly the positions of *p, t* and *k.* Usually the stops were unaspirated and somewhat varyingly or mildly voiced, and in this case they were used with voiced vowels. Occasionally, however, the stops were strongly aspirated and without voicing, and in such cases they were invariably accompanied by unvoiced vowels, resulting in an explosive whisper: [k'a ‸k'a ‸] "custard," [p'a ‸] "up." He interpreted all English voiced stops as unaspirated, but voiceless stops were sometimes interpreted in one way and sometimes in another, although he was generally consistent for any one word. For instance, "papa" and "kitty" never had aspiration, while "custard" and "up" always did. He also confidently used two nasals, *m* and *n,* as in *ma* "more" and *nana* "banana." I never heard the nasals used except with fully voiced words. He had then three vowels, five consonants, and a distinction of voice and aspiration that cut across both the vowels and stops.

At this time all of his words were of the form CV or CVCV; if the latter, the two syllables were always identical. The first progress after our arrival came at one year and five months when he learned suddenly and decisively to use two different syllables in the same word, including either different vowels or different consonants. "Kitty" was then pronounced as *kiti* rather than as the earlier *kiki* and one of his first Garo words was *babi* (standard Garo *ba-bir-si*) "cook," his name for our cook.

If this appears to be an extensive phonemic repertory, it should be emphasized that it was available to Stephen at the very threshold of his use of meaningful speech. Though I did not keep careful records of the preceding period, my impression is strong that most if not all of the distinctions which I have described were present in the babbling which preceded his real speech.

Though these phonemes were first used for English words, he soon began using them in Garo words as well. For a considerable time he formed words from both languages with what amounted to a single phonemic system, and so for the first part of the record it is largely possible to ignore the existence of two languages. For the remainder of the paper, rather than adhering to strictly chronological account, I will discuss in turn the development of various aspects of his speech, and in the final section I will make a few general observations and some comparisons with other children whose speech development has been described.

CONSONANTS

About a month after our arrival, at one year and five months, he began to use a lateral in *lala* "Emula," the name of his Garo "ayah" (nurse). Soon afterward he began experimenting with affricates and aspirants. The affricate was established first in *ci* "cheese," but by the age of one year and seven months, he had both this affricate and a spirant in *sosa* (Garo *so-si-a*) "wet." Both š and č were pronounced intermediate to the position of the nearest English sounds (s and š; ts and č) and from the beginning were very similar to the Garo phonemes.

At about the same time he began to use a labiodental approximating English *f*, and with refinement in the voiced/voiceless opposition that was achieved just shortly afterwards, he briefly used *v* as well. Garo does not have phonemes near to this position, and presumably as a result, *f* and *v* failed to become established. In fact they disappeared completely for a period and were replaced in English words by the bilabial stops.

The disappearance of *f* and *v* can be taken as marking his real transition to the Garo language. Everything earlier might be considered to be just as much English as Garo, but only Garo influence can explain the loss of these phonemes. He began to use *f* and *v* once more at two years and four months, but even at 2;7 (years and months), a full year after they first appeared, these consonants were inconsistently articulated.

By 1;7, the rather ephemeral distinction between voiced and unvoiced vowels, and the associated distinction between unaspirated and aspirated consonants, had disappeared, being replaced by a consistent distinction between voiced and unvoiced stops. At that time *p t k* and *b d g* became consistently distinct in the prevocalic position, and the associated vowels were invariably voiced. Stephen's pattern then came considerably closer to both that of Garo and of English, since the languages share the voiced/voiceless contrast. In Garo the contrast is made only for syllable initials, and this is the only position in which Stephen made it for most of our stay.

At just about the same age (1;7), he began to use *w* amd *h* both for the English phonemes, and for the Garo phonemes, which are phonetically similar to those in English, as in *hai* which in Garo means "let's go" and the English word *wet*.

At 1;9, he added *n* to his roster of phonemes. This does not occur initially in either Garo or English and so its appearance had to await the development of more complex syllables than he had had when the other nasals were first used. An example is *do?oŋ* (Garo *jo?-oŋ*) "bug." This example also shows that at this same age the intervocalic glottal stop appeared. It was several months before he could use the glottal stop in the other positions in which it occurs in Garo.

With the addition of these phonemes, there was only one other Garo consonant outstanding: *j*, a voiced affricate which is intermediate as to position between English *dz* and *ǰ* and is thus the voiced counterpart of the Garo *c*. A *j* first appeared at one year and ten months, but for several months thereafter, Stephen used it only irregularly, frequently substituting *d* both for the *j* phoneme of Garo and for its nearest equivalents in English. As soon as *j* was well established (by two years and three months), Stephen had all of the basic phonemic distinctions of the Garo consonants.

Correct pronunciation involves more than simply keeping the phonemes distinct from each other, however, and further refinement in his consonants consisted of increased precision and vigor in articulation, wider distribution of some consonants, growing sensitivity to allophonic distinctions, and better mastery of clusters.

An example of the way in which he gradually gained precision in his articulation is provided by his velar stops. He had had these since we arrived in the Garo Hills, but at first it was impossible to describe them more precisely than simply velar stops. Possibly because of the sheer small size of the mouth, but also because of imprecision and variation, one could not hope to specify the exact point of articulation. By one year and three months, however, his *k* and *g* had settled into the far back postvelar position which is characteristic of Garo, and he interpreted English *k* and *g* the same way, giving a distinctively foreign quality to English words with these phonemes.

At 1;6 his syllable pattern was expanded to include the CVC pattern when he was able to use a final *t* in *dut* "milk."[3] Final *n* followed at 1;7 in *mun* "moon," ŋ appeared finally (its only position) only at 1;9 and final *m* and *l* appear in my records at 1;10. The *k* sound was used finally by 2;0 but *p* was not regularly used in that position until 2;4. Until then, he substituted either *k* or *t* in place of final *p*, as in *jit* "jeep," and *cik-a* (Garo *cip-a*) "shut." The *s* sound was used finally as early as it was used in any other position and in this Stephen surpassed the Garo pattern, which has final *s* only in a small number of imperfectly assimilated loanwords.

From the beginning his word-final stops were unreleased and therefore corresponded to the Garo allophonic pattern. This was carried over into English so that the final consonants of such words as *bed* were consistently unreleased. Medially he was at first inconsistent. Stops might be aspirated once and unaspirated the next time, so that at 1;10 he pronounced "papa" either as [pʻapʻa] or as [pʻapa]. At 2;0 he learned to make the consistent distinction between syllable initial and syllable final allophones of the stops which contrast with each other medially, syllable initials being aspirated like word initials, and syllable finals being unaspirated. Garo has no true medial consonants since every one must be

Table 4-1   Development of language skills by Stephen Burling

Age (years and months)	Consonants	Vowels	Other linguistic progress	Important nonlinguistic events
1;4	p t k m n	i u a		Arrival in Garo Hills
1;5	l			
1;6	c	Vowels rapidly shifting		
1;7	s w h (f) (v) voiced/voiceless contrast	i u (e) o a		
1;9	ŋ			Mother in hospital
1;10	intervocalic?			Mother in hospital
1;11	(j)	ʌ	First unambiguous morpheme substitution	
2;0		e	Syllable and word juncture in Garo	
2;1		æ	Recognizes the existence of two languages	Living away from Garo, but contact with Garo continues
2;2				Return to Garo Hills
2;3	j	I		
2;5	[r] allophone of l		English developing rapidly	
2;6	Clusters with glottal stops			
2;8		Systematic differentiation of Garo and English vowel systems		

associated with either the preceding or following vowel, and the difference can be summarized by specifying the position of syllable juncture. At two years, then, with the establishment of some of the consonantal allophones, syllable juncture was also becoming established.

There is a single phoneme in Garo which if syllable initial is a flap, but if syllable final varies from a lateral much like the English *l* to a sound intermediate between a lateral and a flap, with considerable free variation. At first, Stephen pronounced every instance of this phoneme as [l], which amounted in some cases to the use of the wrong allophone of the correct phoneme. Thus in place of Garo *ra-ma* "road," he would say [lama]. This is a substitution which I heard small Garo children make, and in fact Garos recognize it as typical childish speech. At two years and three months, Stephen began to shift his initial examples of this phoneme in the direction of a flap and by 2;5 he could execute an expert flap. However, even at 2;7 he occasionally continued to replace the flap with [l] in words that he had known for a long time. New words were pronounced correctly, but some that had become firmly fixed before he was able to articulate correctly were slow to shift.

At two years and five months, also, he was suddenly able to use the glottal stop in clusters (phonetically these are glottalized consonants, though I find it easier to analyze them as clusters), and also in the phonetically distinct situation of preceding a consonant in the following syllable. He was then able to produce beautifully such Garo words as *na?ŋ -ni* "your"; *ma?n-a* "to be able"; and *a?-kor* "hole," and also said /jʌ?m-bo/ with a glottalized *m* substituting for the *mp* cluster of the English "jump," together with the Garo imperative suffix *-bo*, so this word expressed the command "jump!", an example of the phonetic and morphological assimilation of English words into Garo that was typical of his speech.

Garo is not rich in consonant clusters, but my data are not complete even for those which it has. An isolated initial *st* cluster appeared as early as 1;10 in *stas* (English "stars") but these were not regularly used for many months. Initial combinations of a stop with *r*, which are the commonest Garo clusters, apparently first began about 2;5. At 2;8 he could make the initial *hw* in English, and could consistently add English plural *s* after other consonants, but other English clusters were still regularly simplified.

The result of this progressive development was a steady approach to the Garo consonantal pattern. He used more consonants prevocalically than postvocalically, which is in accordance with the Garo pattern, and his allophones were settling down to the Garo pattern.

At 2;8 Stephen's English consonantal system still had several lacunae. The single Garo *s* was used in place of the four English phonemes /z, ž, s, š/. Though he eventually learned to make a voiced spirant in imitation, he never did so spontaneously. English *r* was replaced by *w*; postvocalically it was sometimes omitted all together. He never substituted the phonetically very different Garo *r*. The spirants Ө and ð were replaced by various other phones: *den* "then," *ti*

"three," *ala* "other," *samsiŋ* "something," *bæfwum* "bathroom." The labio-
dentals *f* and *v* were fairly distinct by 2;8. Occasionally they were pronounced as
good labiodental fricatives, but more often were bilabial fricatives. Even this latter
position kept them distinct from any other phoneme. He did not keep voiced and
voiceless consonants distinct in the final position.

VOWELS

I have pointed out that at the time of our arrival Stephen had three distinct
vowels. At 1;6 several new vowels appeared with great rapidity, and for some
time his vowels were in such a state of flux that it was difficult to analyze them
systematically. His vowels were always much less well defined than the consonants, and more variable in successive utterances. He sometimes experimented with
various vowels, used one briefly and then abandoned it. I once heard him
pronounce the word "moon" with high front rounded and unrounded vowels, a
mid central vowel, and a high back rounded vowel in rapid succession, giving
every appearance of groping for a sound that suited him. At 1;6 vowel clusters
first appeared with *ai* in *kai* "Karen." The two vowels were quite distinct and
most easily considered as separate syllables. Other vowel sequences soon appeared:
i following a front rounded vowel toward the end of the month, and *oi, au, ui,* and
ia occurred occasionally at 1;7, all of them being bisyllabic. Most of these were
relatively rare at this time, but by then *ai* was well established and frequently
used. It is the commonest vowel sequence in Garo. By the end of 1;7 I felt that
mid front and back vowels were fairly well established, as in *we* "wet" and *po*
"Paul," though "teddy" was still pronounced occasionally as *tidi* rather than as
tedi.

Various other vowels were heard occasionally. He used a mid central
unrounded vowel in [vʌvʌvʌ] for a noise that a dog makes, with the vowel more
emphasized than most examples of the mid central English vowel. A mid front
rounded vowel was recorded first in conjunction with a following *i,* but later also
alone in [tö] "toy," which was also sometimes [töi]. This even appeared briefly
in an unvoiced form in [kʻö ʌ kʻi ʌ] "cookie." This and a higher front rounded
vowel occurred occasionally through 1;7, but by the end of that month, I was
inclined to feel that they were nondistinctive variants of the back rounded vowels.
The use of [ʌ] was occasional, but not consistent until later. By the end of 1;7,
then, he seemed to be settling into a five-vowel system much like the Garo one.

For some time after this, however, *e* gave him trouble and it was only six
months later, when he was just two years old, that it was unambiguously distinct
from both *a* and *i.* In fact, for a while the *e* disappeared, and once when he was
one year and ten months old, I was unable even to get him to imitate it successfully, though he would imitate many other vowels easily. When trying to imitate
e he would substitute either [i] or [ai]. The failure of the *e* to become well
established until later seems surprising both since *o,* which first appeared at about

the same time, was by 1;10 thoroughly established, and because both Garo and English have unrounded vowels in the mid front position, so there would seem to have been ample chance for him to hear these vowels, and model his own speech upon them.

At 1;10 the mid central [ʌ] was reasonably well established in English words, and by his second birthday, the mid front e was again secure. At two years and one month, he seemed to be differentiating a separate and lower vowel from e toward the æ position of English, although Garo has no comparable vowel. The addition of [ʌ] and æ represented his first enduring progress beyond Garo.

By 2;1 Stephen's vowel system was well enough defined and his articulation precise enough to make possible a more conventional synchronic description:

/e/ was a front mid, unrounded vowel. It was close to the correct position of Garo but was used also for the English /e/ of "bed," which is similar.

/æ/ had become distinct from /e/ and was used in English words only, even though these were generally incorporated into Garo sentences.

/a/ remained a low central vowel, used for both the Garo and the English vowels which are similar to each other.

/o/ was a back rounded vowel, intermediate to the cardinal positions of [o] and [ɔ], and therefore close to the proper position for the Garo vowel. It was also used for English words with similar vowels.

/u/ was settling down to the position of conventional Garo: high, usually central and not quite so sharply rounded as the early high back vowel from which it has been derived. This vowel appeared also in such English words as "turn."

/ʌ/ remained rarer than the other vowels. It was phonetically not too different from the nonfinal allophone of the Garo /i/ (for a discussion of which see just below), but as his speech developed /ʌ/, which was used only in English words, seemed clearly to become separated from /a/ while the nonfinal allophone of Garo /i/ was derived from the more extreme high front [i]. That is, if there was uncertainty about an English word containing /ʌ/, the uncertainty always was whether or not it was distinct from /a/.

/i/ was a high front and unrounded vowel, something like the English vowel in "beat" but with no glide. The Garo /i/ has several striking allophones, but for the most part at this time, Stephen used a high front unrounded vowel in all positions.

He used vowel sequences of all sorts easily. He did not tend to diphthongize them, but maintained the syllabic division between them which is appropriate to Garo.

The most serious imperfection in his Garo vowel system at 2;1 was the absence of some of the allophones of /i/. Improvement came at 2;3 when he began to make a consistent allophonic distinction between the /i/ of open and closed syllables. Nonfinal Garo /i/ was then pronounced somewhat lower than final /i/ in just about the position of English vowel [ɪ] in "hit." This was not yet exactly the proper position of the Garo allophone, which in adult speech is pronounced considerably to the rear of the English [ɪ], but at least some allophonic distinction was being made. The same phone [ɪ] was used in English words such as "hit" while [i] was used for the English nucleus [iy]. In his speech the contrast between the high [i] and the slightly lower [ɪ] was actually phonemic, since the higher one could be used in English words where it appeared nonfinally (such as "feet"), though this is an impossible position for the similar allophone of the Garo vowel. What in Garo were allophones were actually separate phonemes in Stephen's speech of the time, since he used them in English words, in positions not found in Garo. The next step in the development of his high front vowels was not clearly established until 2;8, when the non-final allophone of the Garo vowel shifted securely to the rear to its proper position [i]. This meant that [ɪ] was used only in English words and [i] only in Garo words. But by this time, as is described below, several other developments had brought about a systematic separation of the vowel systems of English and Garo.

At 2;7 Stephen had still not acquired any further distinctively English vowels. For the complex vowel nuclei of English he either used nonfused sequences of Garo-like vowels, or simple Garo vowels. Thus for /ey/ of "make" he generally substituted the Garo sequence /e-i/ without the fusing of the English nucleus. Similarly for /ay/ of "pie" and /aw/ of "out" he substituted /a-i/ and /a-u/ respectively. For /iy/ of "heat" he substituted the simple high Garo /i/, for /ow/ of "boat" the Garo /o/, and for /uw/ of "food" the Garo /u/.

I have described Stephen as having phonemes that are distinctively Garo ([ʔ]) and others that are distinctively English ([ʌ, æ]), as well as many that were used in words of both languages. At least until early in his third year, however, his speech was most efficiently described as a single phonemic system. It was an approximation to Garo, with the addition of a few phonemic distinctions which are not found in that language. Even at the age of 2;7 his Garo was clearly better than his English, and he could still be described as speaking a variety of Garo that happened to have a great many English loanwords. Some of the phonemes of his speech were found only in these loanwords, but there was no indication that he recognized these words, or these phonemes, as having any special status. Other English phonemes were interpreted by him according to Garo speech patterns.

By 2;8 and 2;9 I felt that Garo and English were becoming differentiated as phonemic systems. Many English vowels now seemed to be becoming fixed in positions slightly different from the nearest Garo vowels, although since the differences were often small and since there was so much free variation in his speech, it was not easy to specify exactly the moment of separation.

At this time [ɪ] was used exclusively for the English phoneme and the nonfinal allophone of the Garo high front vowel had moved away to the rear. English /e/ also seemed to be consistently pronounced slightly lower than the Garo /e/ and English /ɔ/ of "dog" was now lower than Garo /o/. The high back vowels seemed less stable but again English /u/ of "put" was at least sometimes pronounced further to the rear than the high mid Garo /u/. I could detect no distinction between Garo and English /a/, which are virtually identical in adult speech.

Most of the complex nuclei were becoming more thoroughly untied as diphthongs in the manner appropriate to English rather than to Garo. This was true of /ey, aw, ay, ɔy, ɔw/ and /uw/. For /iy/ he continued to use the high front Garo /i/ which lacked any glide.

In other words, in the two months from 2;7 to 2;9 a systematic separation of the two vowel systems took place, and it was impossible to continue to describe them as one system. This is in contrast to the consonants, where—except for the addition of *f* and *v*—Stephen never went beyond the Garo system, and for as long as we were in India, he simply used the closest available Garo phones as replacements for the English phonemes.

SUPRASEGMENTALS

Garo, although a Tibeto-Burman language, does not have phonemic tone, and so the history of Stephen's speech cannot include the development of recognized tones. However, he fleetingly used a distinction which, even if idiosyncratic, was based partly upon tone. At the age of 1;6, I noticed that he made a fairly clear and consistent distinction between the words "papa" and "bye-bye" on the basis of length and tone. Both had unaspirated consonants and voiced vowels, but the word "papa" was pronounced with a higher tone and very rapidly, while the word "bye-bye" was pronounced with a lower tone and more slowly. Some other words seemed to have similar characteristics, though none were as clear as this pair, and the distinction did not last for long.

A month later at 1;7, length was clearly used as a distinctive feature of certain words which represented noises, such as [di:di::] to represent the noise of an automobile horn, and [ʔoʔoʔo::] for the sound of a crowing rooster. This rather marginal use of the glottal stop actually preceded its use in nononomato-poetic words by at least a month.)

At 1;7 he used the exaggeratedly high and then falling intonation which is used by Garos to emphasize great distance. Even by two years, however, his speech was not connected enough to do more than begin to catch incipient intonational patterns. At two years he sometimes used the slightly rising intonation which terminates Garo words, and I heard the typical low and falling English intonation with the word "there" to convey the sense of "there, that's done." Stress does not have an important role in Garo, and I heard no significant stress variations, except for the emphasis of shouting.

MORPHOLOGY AND SYNTAX

At one year and seven months, I began to notice a few utterances which, from an adult point of view consisted of more than one morpheme. He would say *cabo* (< Garo, *caʔ*—"eat" and *-bo*, the imperative suffix); *galaha* (< Garo *gar-* "fall" and

-a-ha "past"); *kukigisa* (Garo *cookie ge-sa*) "one cookie"; *giboi* "good boy." At 1;10 he was occasionally attaching the form *-gipa* to strings of speech or to nonsense, but only occasionally in positions where this suffix (which makes modifiers out of verbs) could have made any sense. I also recorded different inflectional forms of the Garo first person singular pronoun, *aŋa aŋasa*, and *aŋnisa*, which have somewhat diverse meanings, though presumably he learned these individually and did not construct them himself. His closest approach to substitutability was in phrases with the word *ba-o* "where" as in *po bao* "where's Paul?" I heard this word used once or twice with nouns other than "Paul," but was still doubtful that these were formed by him. It seemed more likely that all were learned as entire phrases. His speech could thus not be described as having utterances of more than one morpheme, since the constituents were not substitutable. Gradually he acquired more such forms, particularly combinations of verb bases with one or another of the principal verb suffixes which indicate such things as tense. He regularly used the suffix which he heard most often with the verb, as the imperative forms of "eat" and "get dressed" and the past of "fall," since "falling" was most often discussed after it happened.

Then on the first day of May, at one year and 11 months, I was sure for the first time that he could use suffixes freely and add any one of several suffixes to any verb. This was a decisive step and after that, he constantly produced new forms. On virtually the same day, he also was able to form syntactical constructions with a noun subject and a verb. Both morphological and syntactical constructions came at the same time and once the initial ability to make substitutions was gained, he went forward rapidly with more and more complex constructions.

From his first use of the constructions of verb with a principal suffix, he used the suffixes *-gen* "future," *-bo* "imperative," *-a-ha* "past," and *-a* "present or habitual," which are probably the ones most commonly used by adults. Shortly there followed *-gi-nok* "immediate" or "intentional future" and *-jok* "recent past," but even a month later at two years these were not used so readily as the others.

Soon after his second birthday he was beginning to use some of the adverbial affixes, which form a characteristic feature of Garo. These affixes are placed directly after the verb base but before the principal verb suffix, and modify the meaning of the verb base in various ways. Early in his third year it was difficult to know how freely he was using these, but the ability to form new constructions with them seemed to be beginning. By then I had recorded the following: *-ja-* "negative," *-eŋ-* "continuous," *-at-* "causative," *-ba-* "progression toward the speaker," *-aŋ-* "progression away from the speaker," and *-be-* "very."

Shortly after his second birthday I had also recorded a few constructions with another class of verb suffixes, a class which follows the principal verb suffixes and which can be called terminators. He did not use these frequently but I recorded *-ma* "neutral interrogative," *-mo* "interrogative anticipating agreement," and *-de* "emphatic."

He also used a few noun suffixes, though none of them as freely as the principal verb suffixes. The most frequently used was *-ci* "in the direction of," while its more emphatic and precise near synonym -*ci-na* was somewhat less frequent. At various times -*ba* "also," -*ni* "possessive," and -*na* "dative" were used, most commonly with the pronoun for "I."

The third and last inflected class of Garo is that of numerals, which are formed from numeral classifiers and the quantifiers. Just before his second birthday Stephen began to experiment with combinations of classifiers and quantifiers, putting them together in the correct way, but with no apparent understanding of their meaning. A few days after his birthday, however, he saw a small bug, and said *jo?oŋmaŋsa* "one bug," including quite correctly the classifier used for all animals, *maŋ*-. A few days later I recorded him saying *gegini* in referring to two pieces of a cookie, correctly joining the classifier *ge*- to the word for "two," -*gin-i*.

The only English morphological construction which he had even incipiently used was the plural, which I recorded in isolated instances such as *ais* "eyes" and *stas* "stars." But the plural marker was not used freely and could not be substituted. Although this English plural marker appeared substitutable, it was elaborated as were the Garo affixes. At the same time he gradually acquired a few English phrases such as "get down," "come in," and "good night," all of which were of course learned as units, and their parts were not substitutable in any way.

Stephen's first freely formed constructions involving more than one word were those which combined a noun as a subject and a verb as a predicate. The construction in Garo is much like that in English, but his first sentences were clearly Garo. For one thing, they almost at once included a Garo principal suffix on the verb, so the sentences included three morphemes. Examples are: *ba-bi on-a-ha* "Babi (the cook) gave (it to me)" and *do?o bilaŋaha* "bird flew away." He continued often to use verbs alone without a subject, but since this conforms to adult Garo, where the subject need not be expressed if no ambiguity arises, this was not a babyish trait on his part.

Soon after his use of subject-verb sentences, he started to use verbs with nouns in other cases. My first recorded example is on May 17, two and one half weeks after his first construction: *papaci reaŋna* "go to Papa." On June 4 I recorded two three-word sentences (four and five morphemes respectively): *aŋa tolet naŋa*, "I need toilet," and *lala bi taleŋa* "Emula is preparing the bed." In both these examples one word was derived from English, though the word order, morphology and phonology were all completely Garo. This assimilation of English words into Garo was characteristic of his speech for as long as we were in the Garo Hills.

By 2;0 he was also using possessives correctly, attaching the possessive suffix to one noun, most frequently *aŋa* "I," and then following it by a name of the thing possessed. At that time also there were the first constructions of a noun with a numeral, examples of which have already been given. By early June, then, just after his second birthday and a bit over a month after he first clearly used morpheme substitution, he had used the following constructions (those marked with * were used most freely and frequently, while those in parentheses were only incipient, and those left unmarked were well established, though not among the commonest):

Morphological constructions
    verb base plus adverbial affix
    *verb base (with or without an adverbial affix) plus principal verb
        suffix
    complete verb plus terminator
    noun plus principal noun (case) suffix
    (numeral classifier plus quantifier to form a numeral)
Syntactical constructions
    *noun (in various cases) plus verb to form sentence
    *possessive noun plus noun
    (noun plus numeral)

Even at this early stage I had never noticed him using obviously incorrect morpheme order. He spoke in a simplified way, of course, and sometimes left things out, but he did not reverse the proper position of morphemes or words. This is perhaps not remarkable since given the freedom of word order (not morpheme order within the words), incorrect word order is not easy to achieve in Garo. In learning these constructions, he apparently always used the construction first in certain specific examples which he learned as a whole and by rote. After using several of these for a while, he would learn to generalize on the construction, and to substitute different morphemes or words in the same construction.

For the next few months, until 2;3, his grammatical development was largely a matter of consolidating and improving the steps that had already been begun in May at 1;11. By September he was freely and correctly using many adverbial affixes and principal verb suffixes. Both these classes had been considerably expanded. At 2;1 I recorded his use of the general suffix *-kon* "probably," and by 2;2 he was using it in such a way as to show that he understood its meaning. At 2;2, I recorded the suffix *-ode* "if," but could not tell whether he understood its meaning or could use it freely. These innovations are significant in that they involve members of still another class of suffixes that had not been represented earlier and which are inserted after the principal suffix but before the terminator if there is one. He also used several of the principal noun suffixes (case markers) correctly and readily. Of the noun suffixes, the possessive marker continued to be used most regularly. His syntax included the simple form of the Garo sentence with nouns in various cases, followed by the verb. However, he sometimes put one noun, often a pronoun, after the verb, which is a correct Garo way of giving emphasis to the noun. More elaborate constructions, with phrases, clauses, conjunctions, and the like, were still absent from his speech.

The only English construction which he could freely use at 2;3 was that with "more," such as *mo ci* "more water." Here *ci* is the Garo for water, but the construction is quite foreign to Garo, and is clearly English. The few other English phrases which he used, including even such complex ones as "what are you doing," had been memorized as units and the parts were not separable.

By the age of two and a half, he had the system of verb inflection essentially complete, including the use of at least some of the members of every class of verb suffix, and all of the common ones. He used many adverbial affixes easily. I heard examples of as many as three adverbial affixes in one word, which is as many as adults commonly use, though it is not a formal limit. He had also begun to use members of a group of verb suffixes which can convert verbs to a substantive function. At 2;6 he was able to use the important verb suffix *-gi-pa*, by which Garo verbs are put into a form which can be used to modify nouns. He had used *-gi-pa* much earlier, appending it to strings of nonsense, but such "babbling" had stopped by 2;1, and now the suffix was used correctly and with understanding. A few weeks after this appeared, he added the somewhat similar suffix *-a-ni*, which is used to make abstracts from verbs, such as "heat" from "hot" or "walking" from "walk."

He also used members of every class of noun suffix, though he did not use every single suffix. He used most of the principal noun suffixes and a good many of the secondary noun suffixes which follow the principal suffixes, and he frequently and easily used the terminating noun suffixes *-san* "only," *-dake* "like, in the manner of," *-ba* "also," and *-de* "indeed." Personal pronouns, which in Garo act grammatically like nouns, were added slowly. He had used *aŋa* "I" since 1;11, but *naʔa* "you sg." was recorded only at 2;4, *ciŋa* "we exclusive" at 2;5, and *bi-a* "he, she" at 2;6. Others were even later.

At 2;6 he could use numbers incompletely and tried to count, but frequently got the order reversed. Two months later he was able to count to ten with occasional mistakes in Garo, and more consistently correctly in English, and he understood the numbers at least to three. He used several numeral classifiers in Garo quite readily, though except for *-sak* (for people) and *-maŋ* (for animals) it was doubtful whether he really understood their meaning.

He was weaker in the use of particles. He used few adverbial particles except *bak-bak* "quickly," and only a few of the conjunctions. Lacking most of the conjunctions, he was able to form few complex sentences, though by 2;6 he was making the balanced type of Garo sentence in which two similar verbs, one generally positive and the other negative, are paired together with their associated nouns, without an intervening conjunction.

Reduplication is used grammatically in a number of ways in Garo, but by this time I had not yet detected Stephen using any reduplicated forms. The slow acquisition would seem to indicate that the grammatical reduplication of adult speech has little to do with the reduplicated forms of infantile speech which occur so ubiquitously and which Stephen had used from the beginning of his speech.

SEMANTICS

Besides making steady progress in phonology and grammar, Stephen spoke about a continually widening range of subjects. In some cases he learned a new word in either Garo or English, and for some time used that word in all circumstances, without ever using an equivalent in the other language. In other cases, however, he simultaneously learned English and Garo words with approximately the same meanings, as though once his understanding reached the point of being able to grasp a concept he was able to use the appropriate words in both languages. I first recorded the English word *swallow* and the Garo *min-ok-a* "swallow" on the same day. He learned to count in the two languages in parallel fashion, and could recite numbers in either one and keep the two sets generally distinct even before he became confident and consistent in reciting them in the right order. It was clear that in both languages he could recite numbers before he had any real ability to count or to understand the meaning.

By one year and ten months he was beginning to use color terms in both English and Garo, with great interest, but with little understanding. He would point to something and mention a color term in either language that had no relationship to the color of the object. When later at 2;9 he suddenly grasped the meaning of color terms, and was able to consistently call a red thing red, he was able to do so in both English and in Garo simultaneously. At about the same time he started to use various indicators of time, such as *last night, yesterday morning*, and corresponding Garo terms, again with little understanding except that he kept terms for past time separated from those for the future. This imprecise use of time markers was in striking contrast to his correct use of spatial terms such as *here, there,* and various Garo equivalents, which he had started to use correctly much earlier.

At 2;9 Stephen began for the first time to ask explicitly about words. He would occasionally start to speak, pause, point to something, and ask *wats dis*; receiving an answer, he would proceed to use the word in his sentence. He asked such questions equally well in both English and Garo. He also talked about words, though it was difficult to know how well he grasped the sense of the sentences he used. For instance, he would point to his nose and say *in English it is nose,* or *in Gawo it is giŋ-tiŋ*, but he would sometimes get these reversed and call a Garo word English or vice versa. When he was two years and ten months old, I was able to interest him in playing a game with me. I would ask him a question such as "What does hand mean?" and he would promptly supply the Garo equivalent; or, if I supplied him with a Garo word, he would return the English. He gave no indication that he noticed which language I presented him with, but consistently gave the opposite one. When I asked for the meaning of the word "table" however, for which the Garos use a word borrowed from English which is phonetically similar to the original, Stephen paused only briefly and then supplied the translation "dining room table." At 2;9 also, he started using the word *said* and its Garo equivalent *a-gan-a* correctly and with understanding in direct speech—another indication of his growing awareness of speech as a phenomenon that can be talked about. In either Garo or English he was able to say such things as *I said "sit down!"*

BILINGUALISM

As early as the age of 1;6, not quite two months after our arrival, I recorded what then seemed to me like translation. If we asked him if he wanted milk, he would unhesitatingly indicate the affirmative with the Garo equivalent *dut* "milk." However, six months later I could still find no evidence that he was really aware of the existence of two different languages in his environment. As in the case of *milk* and *dut* he did recognize that there were two words for certain things and sometimes he would say them together, one after the other, clearly recognizing that they were equivalents. But all his constructions at that time were completely Garo, the only significant English influence being lexical.

We spent about two months from the middle of July to the middle of September (2;1 to 2;3) in Gauhati, Assam, away from the Garo Hills, where Stephen came into contact with several English speakers, as well as numerous Assamese speakers. He continued to be cared for to a great extent by his Garo "ayah," who even sought out the compansionship of other Garos, so his contact with that language was never broken. But while we were in Gauhati, I began to feel that he really recognized the existence of the separate languages. He quickly learned who did not speak Garo and rarely attempted to speak to them. He was always more shy with them than with Garo speakers. By 2;3 he could understand a considerable amount of English, but spoke little. He then showed a facility for translating exactly what was said in English into idiomatic Garo. If I asked him a question in English, he was likely to give an immediate and unhesitating reply in Garo.

After returning to the Garo Hills, life was somewhat more normal. He had more continuous and intimate contact with his mother than he had had for some months. This finally resulted at the end of 1955, when he was two and one half years old, in an explosive expansion of his ability in English. Though his English never caught up with his Garo as long as we stayed in the Garo Hills, he developed a taste for speaking English with native English speakers and to my chagrin he came to prefer to speak English with me. Occasionally, when I failed to understand his still very foreign English, he would with obvious condescension translate into Garo, which, being said more correctly, was easier to understand. He translated without hesitation and with no apparent difficulty in switching from one language to the other. He frequently spoke to me in idiomatic English and immediately repeated it in just as idiomatic Garo for someone else's benefit.

We remained in the Garo Hills until October, 1956, but the pressure of other work prevented me from keeping detailed records of Stephen's speech after April (2;10), while his increasing tendency to speak English with me and the increasing skill with which he spoke in both languages made it both more difficult and less rewarding to do so. When we left the district, there was still no doubt that Garo was his first language (when he spoke in his sleep, it was in Garo) but English had become a flexible means of expression as well. We spent about a month traveling across India. At first he attempted to speak Garo with every Indian he met, but by the end of the month was learning that this was futile. I tried to speak Garo with him from time to time, but he rarely used full Garo sentences even then.

The last time he ever used an extensive amount of Garo was on the plane leaving Bombay. He sat next to a Malayan youth who was racially of a generalized southern mongoloid type, so similar to many Garos that he could easily have passed for one. Stephen apparently took him for a Garo, recognizing the difference between him and the Indians that had failed to understand his language in the past weeks. A torrent of Garo tumbled forth as if all the pent-up speech of those weeks had been suddenly let loose. I was never again able to persuade him to use more than a sentence or two at a time. For a couple of months he would respond to Garo when I spoke to him, but he refused to use more than an occasional word. After this, he began failing even to understand my speech, though it was frequently difficult to know just how much was really lack of understanding and how much was deliberate refusal to cooperate. Certainly at times he would inadvertently give some sign that he understood more than he meant to, but increasingly he seemed genuinely not to understand, and within six months of our departure, he was even having trouble with the simplest Garo words, such as those for the body parts, which he had known so intimately.

CONCLUSIONS

In the preceding sections I have described the manner in which one child acquired speech. A few general observations about his linguistic development and a comparison of it with that of some of the other children whose language-learning has been previously described remain to be made.

The earliest stage recorded here, with three stop positions, three widely spaced vowels, and two nasals, corresponds closely to the pattern which Jakobson (1956, 37-42) suggests to be characteristic of an early stage of speech, except that to these Stephen added temporarily the cross-cutting distinction of aspiration in the consonants and unvoicing of the vowels. Stephen was not slower to articulate velar stops than the others, unlike some children that have been studied (Leopold, 1939-1949, 417). Some advances, notably the acquisition of the voiced/voiceless contrast, were systematic and added several new phonemes together, though even this was not carried so far as to add a voiced spirant, which Garo lacks, or (until later) a voiced affricate, which Garo does have. Other phonemes seemed to be added individually and it is difficult to see any consistent pattern in their order of appearance.

Viewing his speech as developing by the successive addition of distinctions, or minimal contrasts, provides for the most part an efficient means for analyzing his progress. However, progress was not without its interruptions. Some new steps, such as the acquisition of the contrast between voiced and unvoiced stops or the ability to make glottalized consonants, appeared so rapidly as to be almost datable to the day. In most other cases, however, months elapsed between his first tentative efforts to use a new sound, and its final unambiguous incorporation into his phonemic system. This meant that his language was progressing on several fronts simultaneously and later developments were often beginning before earlier ones were completed.

Apparently Stephen developed phonemic contrasts more rapidly than some children in comparison with the speed of expansion of his vocabulary. Velten (1943, 287), for instance, notes the large number of homonyms in his daughter's speech which appeared as her vocabulary outstripped her ability to produce phonemic contrasts adequate to keep all the items distinct from one another. This was never the case with Stephen, and from a linguist's point of view the problem was more often finding minimal pairs for comparison. Homonyms arising from failure to make the proper contrasts were not common.

It was notable that in the earliest stages of his speech, he briefly used several distinctions (voiceless vs. voiced vowels, tone, length) that are found in neither of the languages that he was learning. One presumes that if these features had been present in his environment he would have started learning them from that time. It might be suggested then that learning a language is not only a matter of learning not to make certain phones, but also of learning not to make certain contrasts which arise apparently spontaneously as a child first tries to speak.

Two and a half years seems remarkably early to have acquired all of the phonemes and all of the important allophones of the language. However, the fact that at the age of four years and four months, almost a year after returning to the United States, he had not yet completed his English phonemic inventory (/Θ/ and /ð/ were inconsistently articulated) would seem to deny any extraordinary precociousness, although in general he did seem to be an early talker. Perhaps this provides some objective measure of one's intuitive feeling that Garo does have a simpler phonemic system than English.

Most studies of child language have put heavy stress on the number of words used in a sentence. This is true of much of the psychological literature, but it is also true of Leopold's work. My feeling as I observed Stephen's language, and my conclusion now, is that the number of words or morphemes is perhaps the least important criterion of grammatical progress. What from an adult point of view are multimorphemic words, or multiword sentences, were used before their complex nature was recognized by Stephen. The most significant single advance in his ability came when he learned to make substitutions, and once this was achieved, he was soon able to make sentences with not just two morphemes but with three and more. One simply cannot reasonably speak of a two-morpheme stage of his speech development. (Since Garo has such complex word formation, it is more significant to consider the number of morphemes in a sentence than the number of words.)

It has generally been assumed that syntactical constructions precede morphological ones. Leopold (1953-1954, 10) states baldly, "In the field of grammar, syntax comes before morphology. The student of child language becomes very conscious of the fact that the morphological devices are a luxury of fully developed languages. The small child gets along quite well without them, for a short or long time." It is difficult and perhaps arbitrary in many languages to draw the line between morphology and syntax, but it is extremely convenient to make such a distinction for Garo, since there are stretches of several syllables set off by characteristic junctures which can be called words, and the grammatical devices used to form these words are very different from those used to join words together. If the distinction is made, Stephen defied the generalization that syntax comes first by learning to make both types of constructions simultaneously. Some reasons for this are obvious: What I am calling morphology in Garo is much more essential than the morphological processes of English, or even of the other European languages. Morphology is not a "luxury" of the fully developed language. Moreover, it is far more regular, and therefore no doubt easier to learn than the morphology of European languages. What I am calling Garo morphology, then, has somewhat the character of syntax in the European languages, but Stephen's method of learning this morphology was not comparable to that by which other children have been observed to learn English syntax. Most histories of child speech have reported a period in which many words are used together with minimal regard for the standard order. Children have been described as using ill-connected sequences of words, and only gradually learning to join them closely together with proper order, juncture and intonational pattern.

One of the striking features of Stephen's speech was the rarity with which he reversed the order of morphemes or words. This was true of his earliest Garo sentences and also was true of his English when it finally began. This was in marked contrast to my own daughter who learned English as her first language two years later, and to other children such as Velten's daughter (Velten, 1943, 290). My daughter regularly produced such garbled masterpieces as *reading a mommy a book Nono* "Mommy is reading a book to Nono" (her nickname) or *Nono falling Nono jammies pant* "Nono's pajama pants are falling down." Stephen never distorted normal order in this way. I do not know whether this is due to peculiarities of the Garo language or to Stephen. It is true that word order is freer in Garo than in English, but he was consistent in phrases where word order is not optional (such as that formed from a possessor and possessed noun) and he was entirely consistent from the very beginning in the order of morphemes within words, which is as rigid in Garo as word order in English, even though these morphological constructions were as early as syntactical constructions. I could readily observe the gradual acquisition of new grammatical constructions and repeatedly the same pattern was followed. He would first learn a number of examples of the construction by rote and at this stage it was generally difficult to tell whether he understood the meaning of the construction or not, though for the most part this seemed unlikely. He would then generalize the construction and learn to substitute other appropriate forms in the same construction. Even after this, one could not always be sure whether the meaning was grasped or whether he was simply generating sentences mechanically and for the pleasure of it. Whatever the case, however, these constructions were rarely grammatically incorrect, and sooner or later it would become clear that he was using them under semantically appropriate conditions. Considering the progressive acquisition of new constructions brought the same clarification to his grammatical development as considering the successive acquisition of phonemes brought to the analysis of the phonetic record.

As soon as Stephen began to form constructions of his own, he incorporated English morphemes and words into Garo sentences. He appended Garo suffixes to English words without the least hesitation, but there was never any doubt that his early sentences were Garo, since the morphology and syntax were Garo even if the lexical items came from English. I once heard the sentence *mami laitko tunonaha* "mommy turned on the light" where the roots of every word were English, but the suffixes (*-ko* "direct object marker" and *-aha* "Past tense"), word order, and phonology were Garo and there was no doubt that the sentence should be considered a Garo one. When he finally began to form English sentences, he just as readily adopted Garo words into English. This mutual borrowing was made early partly because his models did the same. All the English speaking adults around him constantly used Garo words in their speech, and Garos borrow readily from English. However many morphemes might be borrowed, there was seldom any question as to which language he was using since affix morphology and syntax were either all Garo or all English. After his vowel systems became differentiated at 2;8, the phonology was also appropriate to the choice of grammatical system. It was only shortly before the systematic separation of the vowels that he used many English sentences. Before that, he spoke with a single linguistic instrument, forged largely from Garo, but with the addition of English vocabulary and a few extra English phones. Later, when he did have two linguistic systems, the two never appeared to interfere with each other. He spoke one language or the other, never a mixture of the two.

One final comparison with Leopold's daughter is worth making. Leopold (1953-1954, 13) insists that a striking effect of bilingualism was the looseness of the link between the phonetic word and its meaning. His daughter never insisted on stereotyped wording of stories. Leopold believed that this was due to the fact that she heard the same thing constantly designated by two different phonetic forms, so that form and meaning were not rigidly identified with each other. There can never have been a child more obsessional in this respect than Stephen. When we read to him, he instantly protested the slightest alteration in any familiar text. This was true even though we read to him in his second language, English, where one would suppose the form and meaning to be least rigidly identified. It must have been an idiosyncratic trait rather than bilingualism that freed Leopold's daughter from insistence upon stereotyped wording.

In the fall of 1958, at the age of five and a half, Stephen is attending kindergarten in the United States. He speaks English perhaps a bit more fluently and certainly more continuously than most of his contemporaries. The only Garo words he now uses are the few that have become family property, but I hope that some day it will be possible to take him back to the Garo Hills and to discover whether hidden deep in his unconscious he may not still retain a remnant of his former fluency in Garo that might be reawakened if he again came in contact with the language.

Notes

1. This paper is an expanded and revised version of one read at the 1958 summer meeting of the Linguistic Society of America. The opportunity to work in the Garo Hills was provided by a fellowship from the Board of Overseas Training and Research of the Ford Foundation.

2. I have assembled a descriptive grammar of the Garo language which is to be published shortly.

3. Those acquainted with the Indic languages may recognize some familiar items in my examples. Garo has borrowed heavily from Bengali, including the word for "cow's milk" as opposed to "mother's milk." Stephen learned these as Garo words, which indeed they are, and I do not distinguish between them and older Garo words.

Second Language Acquisition:

5 *A Case Study*

Harumi Itoh and Evelyn Hatch, *University of California, Los Angeles*

INTRODUCTION

Sequential acquisition of a second language is different in many ways from simultaneous acquisition of two languages. Itoh's study is a mixture of both simultaneous and sequential acquisition. Her subject, a two-and-a-half year old child, had not yet fully acquired his first language, Japanese. His attempts at stabilizing fricative contrasts for the two languages is a case in point. As in Leopold's study there is evidence of confusion of similar sounds, substitutions from the first language. This contrasts with Ronjat's claims that there was little evidence of phonological interference during the simultaneous acquisition of French and German for his child, Louis:

> Le prononciation de Louie est dans les deux langues celle d'un enfant indigène, et je n'ai jamais relevé un échange de phonèmes de langue à langue qui soit authentique et durable . . . On ne peut reveler aucun fait authentique et durable d'influence phonetique d'un langue sur l'autre. (Ronjat, 1913, p. 16)

In some ways Takahiro, the subject of this study, had to deal with acquisition of both language systems at the same time. In other ways, the study is definitely sequential. Central concepts, e.g., negation and question formation, were already present in his first language development.

Takahiro's responses to the second language were, in some instances, quite similar to those of Hildegard. Just as Hildegard at times rejected one or the other

76

of her two languages, Takahiro attempted to reject the second language situation. Takahiro's attempt to avoid English speakers and his obvious preference for his first language have given us evidence that simultaneous and sequential acquisition of two languages is not as easy for the child as we might want to believe. However, after a few months, Takahiro did give up his avoidance posture and began to actively solicit English-speaking sessions with those around him.

Similarly, Kenyeres had noted that Eva, a 6;10 year old, avoided learning the second language until she discovered she would need it in order to play with other children:

> Ce qui lui était indifférent jusqu'ici prend subitement une grande valeur à ses yeux, grâce à son désir de jouer avec les enfants. L'instinct social et le besoin de jouer sont donc des stimulants bien puissants dans le cas d'Eva. (Kenyeres, 1938, p. 323)

This was not the case with Takahiro. Since he did not yet truly play with other children, the nursery school experience did not show him the value of learning the new language. Rather, it was the affectionate interaction with an adult, his aunt, which produced the change in attitude toward learning the second language.

The reader might want to compare this study with other studies of Japanese-English bilingual children by Yoshida (Miki), Hakuta (Uguisu) and Gillis (Akio and Haruo).

Takahiro, an only child, was born on April 14, 1970 in Japan. He came to Los Angeles with his parents in September, 1971. In November, 1972 he was enrolled in a nursery school serving a lower-middle-class neighborhood in West Los Angeles. He attended school two mornings a week from 9:00 to 12:00. This report, then, is a case study of Takahiro, a Japanese 2½ year old, as he learned English as a second language and perfected his first language, Japanese.

Our observations began on November 6, 1972, when Takahiro was 2;6, 22 and ended May 13, 1973 when, at the age of 3;1, he returned to Japan with his parents. During that time we had a chance to see the very beginning stages of second language acquisition and a chance to consider many questions that have been posed about differences between first and second language acquisition.

The data consisted, first, of a journal of observations from each session at the school, 38 three-hour sessions over the 6 month period. During the early data collection, attempts were made to use a wireless microphone to record the data. The microphone was sewn into a small bib on Takahiro's playclothes. All that resulted was a dismal record of thumps, scrapes, squeals, and bangs; no useful speech data was obtained. The observational log included as detailed a record of speech and setting as possible. The context and setting of all speech acts were noted.

Since it was impossible to obtain taped data at school, during the last four months of the study the observer (hereafter HI) visited the home, recording Takahiro's speech data in a variety of play situations. The tapes were transcribed immediately following each session so that they could be accurately supplemented by notes on context. Transcriptions were made in regular orthography except in those cases where a finer phonological record seemed necessary. The tapes and the observational log comprise the data for this report.

In order to describe Takahiro's acquisition of his second language, it was necessary to categorize the data in a summary form. None of the current methods of describing data (rule writing, MLU, T-unit counts, or morpheme counts) seemed to fit the data. Each method seemed to lose the process that the journal revealed. In the end, the most sensible way to talk about the data seemed to be in three general stages which we have called 1) a rejection stage, 2) a repetition stage, and 3) a spontaneous speech stage.

REJECTION STAGE (NOVEMBER-JANUARY)

The first three months at the nursery school have been labeled as the rejection stage. One might think it less subjective to call it an extended listening period. However, the evidence that he was listening to anyone but his mother or HI is slight. His early days at nursery school were spent mostly on a tricycle and not with the other children, especially not the English-speaking children. Takahiro was not the only non-English-speaking child at the nursery school. There were five such children: two other Japanese children, a girl and a boy; a Dutch boy; a German boy; and a Chinese girl. They had acquired various levels of English proficiency. Even when he played in proximity to these children, it could scarcely be said that they played together. His play and that of most of the younger children was isolated; each child absorbed in his own toys and games. Except for laughs, shouts, squeals and cries, there was little verbal interchange among the younger children. When speech was directed at anyone it was to their teacher, or, in Takahiro's case, to his mother or HI, both of whom spoke Japanese.

Takahiro did not respond to his English-speaking teacher. The teacher had to rely on HI or his mother to bring him in for juice and crackers, to persuade him to join the group to listen to stories or to participate in other group activities. He would move away from the group to another part of the room to play with toys if it were at all possible. Takahiro gave the appearance of being a docile, quiet child. He even watched his sandcastles being destroyed without verbal objection. He did, however, like to race the other boys on the tricycle; and he did enjoy being pushed and pulled in the wagon with the other children.

During the first two months (November and December) Takahiro's mother stayed with him at school. Recognizing that this special treatment might be one of the causes of his non-interaction with the teacher and other children, she decided at the beginning of the third month to leave him at school. After her departure, he continued to turn to HI for help and comfort, avoiding interaction with the other children and with the teacher whenever possible.

It was not clear whether Takahiro's seeming avoidance of anyone who spoke English was, in reality, avoidance of English or of the entire nursery school situation. It seemed possible that he might respond positively to English outside the school environment. And, of course, it would be easier to tape record his speech data in other situations. Arrangements were therefore made to visit Takahiro at his home as frequently as possible, usually once or twice a week.

At home, Takahiro was affectionate, outgoing and noisy in contrast to his reserved, shy behavior at school. However, his reaction to HI when she spoke English was exactly the same. At each visit, we tried to get Takahiro to attend to English but with little or no success. For example, spinning the wheels on his toy truck, he was encouraged to stay "stop" to make the wheels stop spinning. Though he finally managed a whispered "stop," he preferred stopping the wheels with his hands. Each time HI spoke English to him, he ignored her, turned away, or ran out of the room.

Two explanations seemed plausible for this rejection. First, the nursery school experience was difficult for him and he turned to those he knew (his mother and HI) for comfort. He avoided everyone else; these people happened to speak English. His avoidance of HI when she spoke English was because this was unexpected behavior from her. Although we tried in the beginning to speak only English in his presence, he knew that HI was Japanese. If this explanation is correct, he did not reject English but rather the situation which he was in.

A second explanation was that he was attempting to avoid dealing with the second language much as adults do, hoping it would not be necessary to cope with this new learning task.

Takahiro's rejection stage certainly must have been caused by a combination of many factors including those mentioned above. Though it did not seem likely, the rejection stage may also have included extensive listening as preparation for learning English. Certainly he had to make a judgment as to the *non*-Japanese nature of what was said to him before he turned away in his avoidance posture. He had to attend to English at least long enough and in enough detail to realize it was not Japanese.

Whatever the cause, his strategy was successful. HI spoke more and more Japanese in his presence and began to record his Japanese utterances. The Japanese data, particularly the phonological aspects, were very interesting. According to a previous study of the articulation of Japanese children (Yasuda, 1970), Takahiro's pronunciation was quite advanced for his age even though his articulation, as with many children his age, showed a good deal of variation. He had particular difficulty with syllables containing fricatives and especially with sibilants. This problem was also evident in his English once he began imitating English utterances. He especially found *su, fu, shu,* and *gu* difficult to articulate correctly.

Metathesis occurred frequently in his speech, particularly in syllables containing /r/. He said *ebereetaa* for *erebeetaa* (elevator), *borotto* for *robotto* (robot), *tebire* for *terebi* (TV), *kutsuru* for *tsukuru* (to make), *hemeretto* for *heremetto* (helmet), and *kopetto* for *poketto* (pocket). The later diary entries show no incidence of metathesis for English words, though many of the Japanese words in which he switched syllables were English loanwords as can be seen from the above examples.

In terms of syntax, his utterances were still short. His MLU for Japanese was 2.36 (Dec. 15). He frequently used "baby talk" expressions, particularly for animal names. He used what has been termed "female style," and he omitted many particles as do all children in learning their first language (e.g., *reeru kokomade* for *reeru wa kokomade*; *koko*? for *koko-ka*?).

However, our aim was not to study his first but his second language acquisition. Our recording of his Japanese was good evidence that his avoidance strategy, whatever its causes, worked.

Since Kenneth, the other male Japanese child at the nursery school, did speak English, HI visited his home, hoping to find some procedure that would work with Takahiro. While Kenneth had acquired a good deal of English, he constantly mixed the two languages. Since Takahiro did not attend to English, HI decided to try to use English as Kenneth did. She began mixing English words into her Japanese utterances to see what Takahiro's reaction would be to a relexification process.

When HI said, "Kore *push* shite goran" (push this), Takahiro repeated doubtfully, "push?" Since he could guess the meaning from gestures, he pushed the toy train. Next time, saying "push," he pushed the train again. With this initial success, we decided to introduce English in this manner. However, and probably fortunately for everyone involved, before we had a chance to experiment further with this method, Takahiro began his repetition stage.

REPETITION STAGE (FEBRUARY 2-FEBRUARY 14)

The beginning of the repetition stage was clearly February 2, the third month, when Takahiro was 2; 9, 18. On this day Takahiro's aunt (hereafter Y) came to visit. She began to play a "repeat after me" game with Takahiro. Drawing figures on a tablet, Y named each one and Takahiro spontaneously repeated the words after her. He repeated whatever English she said for almost three minutes that day. It was so successful that five days later, he played the game for over an hour. Three days later he wanted to play the game again. Transcribing these tapes, one was immediately aware of the phonological variation in his approximations to the model and the influence of Japanese syllable structure on his English pronunciation attempts:

> *eraser*; ireys, reysə, reəs, ireyǰər, reys, ireysə, ireyčə /
> *pencil*; / penšəl, penšɔl, penšɔpu, penšelp, penšawl, penšl/
> *six*; /sič, sik, sekis, siks, seks/
> *square*; /skueəl, skuəl, škuwee, fukueer, šukuwel, skweyl, skwea, šuwel, kuweəl/

Unstressed syllables and final consonants were frequently dropped in this repetition game. Final /r/ was almost always dropped as were plural inflections. Consonant clusters were either simplified or a vowel was added to break up the cluster, as in /æpulu/ (apple), /egu/ (egg). This might be considered as interference from the syllable pattern of his first language where such clusters would not occur.

As mentioned earlier, the fricatives were a problem for him in Japanese and they were in English too. This problem continued throughout the observation period. Fricatives are, of course, difficult for most very young children to control. Interestingly, Takahiro would articulate a sound correctly one day and then differently a few days later. For example, he articulated /Ɵ/ correctly in *three* on February 14 but on April 6 he consistently substituted an /s/ for the /Ɵ/. Furthermore, he articulated difficult sounds correctly in some words without exception (e.g., he always pronounced the /Ɵ/ correctly in *Kenneth*).

Some fricatives were more difficult than others. He had little difficulty with the labiodental pair /f, v/ and great difficulty with the interdental /Ɵ, ð/ and with sibilants. He substituted /š/ for /s/ in most Japanese words (okaashan for okaasan [mother] and otooshan for otoosan [father]). In February he made the same substitution, /š/ for /s/, in English words but on April 6 he used an /s/ for *spoon* and /š/ for all other words. By May 13, he correctly articulated /s/ in all English words, though he still persisted in substituting /š/ for /s/ in some Japanese words. There were a few examples of /t/ substitution for /č/ in English words (wa*t*ch out).

The choice of substitutes for fricatives is interesting because they do not totally agree with the substitutes common for American children learning English. Moskowitz, in her study of such substitutes (1970), displays data that can be compared with Takahiro's:

American Ss (after Moskowitz)					Takahiro's substitutions			
/f/	[p]	[w]			[h]			
/v/	[b-]	[-f]	[-b-]		[b]			
/s/	[d]	[š]			[š]	[č]	[f]	[ĵ]
/z/	[d]	[š]			[č]	[s]		
/s/	[b]							
/z/	[š]							
/Ɵ/	[p]	[š]	[t]	[f] [s]	[s]	[š]	[t]	[p] [f]
/ð/	[d]				[d]	[z]	[ĵ]	

It is not entirely clear what the differences in substitutions should be attributed to. The /h/ substitution for /f/ can be traced to Japanese; in most analyses (e.g., Block, 1950), they are treated as allophones (/h/ is pronounced as [f:] before /t, k, c, č, h/, as [f] before /u/, and as [h] before other vowels). [f, v] are described as both labiodental and bilabial spirants in Japanese so the /b/ substitution for /v/ is not surprising. /Ɵ, ð/, which do not occur in Japanese were very difficult for Takahiro but certainly no more so than the sibilants which occur in both languages. No strong claim is being made for first language interference in this discussion since fricatives are difficult for all young children to articulate. Nevertheless, it would be valuable to have data on substitutions made by other Japanese children learning English so that one could establish whether or not Takahiro's substitutions are typical of Japanese children learning English or simply idiosyncratic. It would also be valuable to look at age range differences since there was little or no evidence of first language interference in Huang's study of a five-year-old child.

Intonation and stress were also important in discovering what parts of an utterance Takahiro would choose to imitate. He began by selecting one word from an utterance, usually the final stressed noun and, as he repeated it, he changed the sentence intonation of the model. If the model were a rising yes/no question intonation, he answered by repeating a noun with falling intonation. If the model was a statement, his one-word response was with rising intonation:

Y: This is a triangle↘   Y: What's that? Snowman↗
T: triangle↗   T: snowman↘

He soon began to repeat more and more words from the model, usually the final part of the utterance: Y: Make it one at a time. T: One at a time↗ While the final segment of the utterance was repeated, he frequently omitted articles, prepositions, selecting only stressed words. He also omitted most morphological endings, particularly the plural and possessive endings. This, of course, could have been because of his problem with sibilants; however, it is characteristic of repetition data of very young children.

How much of the repeated utterances did he really understand? Was this practice in echolalia? Obviously not. He acquired vocabulary rapidly during the first three sessions and began to respond to questions not by echoing them but by giving the appropriate answer:

Y: Draw? What do you want to draw?
T: Draw, draw, draw.
Y: You can draw snow.
T: Snow, draw.
Y: What's this?
T: Choo-choo train.

During these days of repetition, we felt that we were not "teaching" him English; that like other studies in a natural situation, he was simply acquiring without being taught. It was interesting, then, to look at the tapes during his repetition stage for evidence of teaching. There was a good deal of evidence. Vocabulary items were taught by picture reference, by giving answer prompts, and by translation:

Y: What's this? Tiger? (answer prompt)
T: Taigə.
Y: What's this? What's this? Is it a baby lion? (answer prompt)
T: Baby lion.
Y: See, this is mother lion.
T: Okaasan raion? (mother lion)
Y: Yes. This is giraffe.
T: Kirinsan.
Y: Ummm, kirinsan wa ne eigo de giraffe. (kirinsan is giraffe in English) (translation)

In fact, the first few sessions were exactly like a beginning ESL lesson built around the patterns, "This is a NOUN" and "What's this?" In the first two sessions,

Takahiro heard 251 English utterances. Of these, 139 were the following: What's this? What's that? Is this a NOUN? This is a NOUN. That's a NOUN. This is what? How about this? Do you have a NOUN? Can you say NOUN? The other utterances were single nouns and expressions of praise in English. A few other utterances were made by Y as comments to herself more than to Takahiro. Fourteen nouns were translated into Japanese. The English input in the sessions was carefully, though unintentionally limited; the emphasis, again unintentionally, was on teaching nouns.

After the first day of repetition, Takahiro began to show an active interest in all English spoken to him. He soon responded to "What's this?" questions with the new vocabulary he had learned from our sessions, from Y, or at school. During the repetition game, he frequently responded to Y's English questions with Japanese answers as well as English. This evidence led us to believe that he comprehended at least the global meaning of much of what was said to him. As he became proficient in repetition, he was no longer satisfied with repeating just what was said to him. He began to expand on his own spontaneous repetitions by recalling other possible similar patterns:

This is my fork. Fork. This is my fork.
The sun. Sun. This. This sun. This is a sun.
Don't know. I don't know. I don't know, dummy.

At the same time, his behavior at the school began to change. He no longer placidly accepted the destruction of his sandcastles or of his elaborately constructed block houses. He pushed and shoved, and yelled "no" and "don't" just like the older children. He moved from solitary play to parallel play and then began to engage in cooperative play, especially with Kenneth, the other Japanese boy. He ignored HI unless other children tried to engage her in play. Then he reasserted his "right of ownership."

SPONTANEOUS SPEECH STAGE
(FEBRUARY 14-MAY 13)

When Takahiro began responding to questions with answers rather than simply repeating the question, it appeared that he had reached another stage in second language development. This stage began during the fourth month. His repetition stage continued along with his spontaneous speech but his repetitions were usually either to ask the meaning of something he did not understand or to mimic other children by copying both their behavior and what they said.

On February 14 his MLU for English was 2.6. It is, however, difficult to justify morphology counts for the MLU as a valid measure in second language learning. For example, if he said, "This is a blue," it was counted as four morphemes; yet we were fairly sure that "this is a" was not three morphemes for him, but one. If he said, "blue shoes" we counted it as three morphemes though we knew he did not distinguish singular/plural morphemes. The morpheme counts are of interest but are perhaps less than legitimate for this data.

From this point on, Takahiro seldom spoke Japanese to HI, a great change from the early observation period. Since so much of the language input had been "What's this?" questions, it is not unexpected that the frequency of "This is a NOUN" sentences was very high in the data. "This is a" seemed to be an unanalyzed unit; the article always appeared whether appropriate or not:

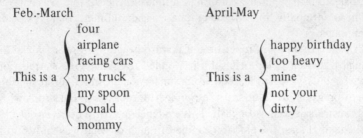

Feb.-March

This is a
- four
- airplane
- racing cars
- my truck
- my spoon
- Donald
- mommy

April-May

This is a
- happy birthday
- too heavy
- mine
- not your
- dirty

By May, however, he began to analyze the "This is a" formula; article and *be*-deletion were frequent:

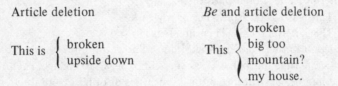

Article deletion

This is
- broken
- upside down

Be and article deletion

This
- broken
- big too
- mountain?
- my house.

While Takahiro's noun phrases developed rapidly, he paid little attention to verbs. He acquired *do* as an imperative perhaps from our urging: "You do it" This became "You do" in Takahiro's imperatives. *Do* indicated whatever action was desired:

You do
- eye! (wink)
- this racer! (race this car)
- broken one! (use the broken one)
- garage here! (come in the garage)

After a few sessions, the *do* disappeared in imperatives: "You bicycle over there!" (ride that bicycle), "You car" (drive the car). As he learned a few new verbs, he dropped the *you*: "Fix engine!" "Sit here!" "Open it!"

Do also appeared as a dummy verb in statements. One of the games he liked to play was "Night and Morning." This consisted of opening and closing the Venetian blinds and pretending to go to sleep or to wake up. Takahiro had learned "good morning" very early in the data collection at school. When he wanted to get up he said, "I'll good morning" ("I'll" appeared to be an alternate form of "I" at this period rather than the modal *will*.) He then extended this with *do*: "I'll do morning" when he wanted to open the blinds to make the room light.

As more verbs were acquired, the *do* in statements was gradually dropped following an intermediate stage when he used both: "You do come on this." "You do you go." But *do* remained the most used dummy verb to the end of the study:

H: Someone is at the door.

T: I do door.

H: Come down.

T: I wanna down. I do down.

Takahiro used very few verbs; his early data shows that almost all of his sentences requiring a verb other than *be* contained the verb *get* (see Table 5-1). *Get* gradually faded out in favor of *wanna* (see Table 5-2).

The modal *can* also occurred during his spontaneous speech stage, again used for many different meanings:

You can car. (You can have/use/take/play with the car.)

I can this. (I'll take/use this.)

I can train. (I'll take/play with the train.)

You'll can. (You can come in.)

I can backward. (I will go in backward.)

Table 5-1   The "I get . . . " pattern

Date	Utterance	Gloss (approximate)
April 6	I get more.	I want more.
	I'll get more.	I want more.
	I'll get this one.	I want this one.
	I'll get strawberry.	I want strawberry.
	I get racing car.	use/want to play with/take?
	I get tire.	I want a tire.
April 9	I get a shovel car.	I can see a dump truck from here.
	I get high.	I am up high.
April 16	I get no garage.	I don't have a garage.
	I get try.	I will try.
	I get high house.	I'm building a tall house.
	I get big.	I'm big.
	I get a house.	I'll make a house.
	I get a tree.	I'll draw a tree.
	I got this.	I have this.
	I get sun.	I'll draw the sun.
	I get big nose.	I'll draw a big nose.
April 19	I got this.	I want to wear this.
	I get Japan.	I'll go to Japan.
	I get shopping.	I'll go shopping.
	I get a shopping.	I'll go shopping.
	I get Santa Monica.	I'll go to Santa Monica.
April 25	I got a pistol.	I have a pistol.
	I got a orange juice.	I want orange juice.
May 2	I get a high.	I want to climb high.

Table 5-2   The "I wanna . . ." pattern

Date	Utterance	Gloss (approximate)
April 25	I wanna orange juice . . . more.	I want more orange juice.
April 28	I wanna driver.	I want to be the driver.
April 29	I wanna ride 'n go.	I want to "ride and go."
May 2	I wanna fire.	I want to be the fireman.
	I wanna get there.	
	I wanna cake.	I'm making a cake.
	I wanna milk.	I want milk.
	I wanna high.	I'm climbing high.
	I wanna two more.	I want two more.
	I wanna down.	I want down.
	I wanna down here.	I want down.
	I wanna jump.	I want to jump.
	I wanna /jakeytow/.	I want to be (superman).
	I wanna tire.	I want to see the tire.
May 5	I wanna more clean.	I want to clean (the room) more.
	I wanna more.	I want to move the chairs some more.
	I wanna down.	I want down.
	I wanna guest.	I want (imaginary playmate)
	I wanna door.	I want you to leave the door open.
	I wanna open it.	I want the door open.
	I wanna school.	I went to school.
	I wanna school today.	I went to school today.
May 13	I wanna mask.	I want to wear the mask.
	I wanna like this.	I want it like this.
	I wanna green same.	I want to use green (crayon) again.
	I wanna helicopter.	I want the helicopter.
	I wanna airplane here.	I want the airplane to fly here.
	I wanna no chair.	I don't want the chair there.
	I wanna play.	I want to play.

Gradually a few other verbs were added but verb acquisition was quite limited in comparison to nouns. He did not mark sentences for tense. There is no data on third-person singular present tense since he did not talk about other people. There are a few examples of verbs in the past tense but they were used in situations calling for present tense. He did use the present progressive (be+ing) usually without the be, but occasionally with the be and no -ing. *Will* appeared as the contraction I'*ll* and you'*ll* but it did not seem to refer to intent or future time. There is little evidence, if any, that Takahiro had begun to develop the AUX system (that is, tense, modal, be+ing) of English at the end of the study. There was some data that suggested he might be on the verge of working out usage for the modal *can* through various trials in the following section near the end of the study:

T: You do garage here. (Put the toy car in the garage.)
H: No. The garage is too small.
T: Small garage?
H: Ummm. I can't come in.
T: Okay. You'll can.
H: You can't come in.
T: I can this. I can. I can backward.

There is no obvious answer to the lack of development in the verb phrase and the limited number of verbs acquired. Our questions directed toward Takahiro almost always asked about things rather than about actions. Secondly, while many nouns were translated into Japanese for Takahiro, there is no evidence of translation of verbs. And, finally, the AUX system of English is extremely complex. To expect that he would concentrate on this area rather than acquire vocabulary for toys, food, and other important objects is perhaps unreasonable.

CONCLUSION

It might seem from the data presented that Takahiro acquired little English during the 6-month observation period but that is not the case. He understood a good deal of what was said to him. True, his utterances were not highly developed but they were developed enough that he could carry on conversations quite easily with others. He even acquired an invisible friend to whom he spoke English:

T: Somebody door.
H: Really?
T: Yeah.
H: I don't think so.
T: Somebody door here.
H: Okay. (Nobody was there so HI began to close the door.)
T: No. Don't do this.
H: Do you . . . keep the door open?
T: Open. Yeah. I wanna boy the girl.
H: You'll have a guest?
T: Boy. This boy. (To an invisible person) Come in.
H: Did he come in?
T: Yeah. My friend. My friend. My friend here. Go . . . go to . . .
H: Japan?
T: Yeah.

It is true that with a more experimental basis, it would have been possible to find out more accurately just which structures Takahiro could comprehend and produce. Diaries and observational studies do have serious drawbacks in the study of second language acquisition just as they have for first language studies. But, nevertheless, this type of observation let us look at day-to-day changes in Taka - hiro's pronunciation, vocabulary acquisition, and structure development in his second language.

Takahiro's pronunciation improved rapidly over the six months. While /š/ vs /s/ was still something of a problem in Japanese, few errors were made in English pronunciation at the conclusion of the study. His vocabulary acquisition reflected his interests. He quickly acquired vocabulary related to cars and car racing. Vocabulary that did not appeal to his interests decayed very quickly even though they were part of the repetition game that Y played with him very frequently. His vocabulary consisted primarily of nouns; verb differentiation was not developed. He used three or four verb forms to cover almost all actions that he wanted to express. In structure, he had learned simple sentence word order; he had not mastered morphological endings such as plurals, possessives, etc. although they were used in some utterances. The AUX system was not developed. Verbs were not marked for tense, contracted modals appeared to be alternative pronoun forms, and the progressive when used was not used appropriately.

The data also showed that, despite our intention that English not be taught to Takahiro, we had taught the language. We had coached him to repeat words after us, we had asked questions and unconsciously prompted the answers, we had frequently resorted to translation. This experience leads one to question how "natural" natural acquisition studies really are, especially when adult observers are the primary contact with the new language for the child.

Adding a Second Language: Young Children

6

The Acquisition
of English Vocabulary
by a Japanese-speaking Child

Midori Yoshida, *University of California, Los Angeles*

INTRODUCTION

Vocabulary acquisition is surely an important part of second language learning, yet few of us have looked at this area other than as a sidelight in analyzing our data. Interestingly, then, one of the most important hypotheses about semantic development is based, at least partially, on second language diary studies. In 1973, Eve Clark presented a collection of examples from many diary studies in support of her Semantic Feature Hypothesis; among them, the second-language studies of Leopold, Imedadze, Pavlovitch, and Kenyeres. Her hypothesis is used to explain the presence of overextensions in the child's learning of the semantic system.

Clark divides the overextensions into several subcategories: related to movement (Pavlovitch: *dzin, dzin,* used for a moving train, then a train itself, and finally for a journey by train), related to shape (Imedadze: *buti,* used for ball, and then extended to toy, radish, stone sphere at a park entrance; Leopold: *tick-tock,* used for a watch, then generalized to clocks, all clocks and watches, gas-meters, a fire hose wound on a spool, a bath scale with round dial), related to size (Kenyeres: *baba,* for baby, then for adults in pictures), related to sound (Leopold: *sch,* noise of a train, to music, noise of any movement, wheels, balls), related to taste (Leopold: *candy* to cherries to anything sweet), related to texture (Leopold: *wau-wau,* for dog to toy dog, to soft slippers, and to a picture of an old man dressed in furs).

Overextension is only one area that Yoshida discusses in the following paper on the lexical development of a 3; 5-year-old child, Mikihide. Since her findings contrast in important ways with those of Clark, Felix, and Nelson, yet agree with those of Celce-Murcia and Fantini, we can now begin to consider factors which might explain variation across learners in the rate and type of lexical development. Certainly, this is an area which needs a great deal of further research.

In studies of second language acquisition by children, contemporary researchers have focused primarily on the acquisition of syntax and have excluded the acquisition of vocabulary. The aim of my research was, therefore, to investigate the vocabulary acquisition of a Japanese-speaking child as he acquired English as a second language in a natural setting. My research questions were as follows:

1) What vocabulary is acquired by this child?
2) What is the process of this child's vocabulary acquisition?
3) Is there any influence of Japanese loanwords from English on this child's vocabulary acquisition?

In the following sections, the observational and experimental data will be presented and discussed briefly.

SUBJECT

The subject MIKIHIDE was three years and five months when the observation started in November, 1975. He had no previous exposure to English in Japan. He came to the United States in September and entered nursery school in the following month. The school was the only place where the subject was totally immersed in English. For the first 5 months, he spent two hours a day, Monday through Friday, and beginning in March, he stayed for three hours a day. At home, his parents do not speak English, but they have given him English-language picture books. In April, the subject became interested in one cartoon program called "Speed Racer." MIKIHIDE is an active and inquisitive child.

PROCEDURES

The data were collected using the following methods and procedures.

A longitudinal observational study of the subject's exposure to English was carried out for seven months, November through May. Both input data and subject's utterances were tape-recorded, and the contexts where the subject's verbal and nonverbal behaviors occurred were described. Observations were scheduled once a week.

In March, April, and May an experimental study was carried out. This study consisted of two tasks: a comprehension test and a production test. Both tests were administered twice (in March and May) using the PPVT (Peabody Picture Vocabulary Test). In addition, two kinds of picture word books were adapted for a production test because the PPVT, which has only noun and verb categories, did not cover the subject's other word categories. Altogether, the subject was tested five times according to the following schedule:

(date)	(test)	(skill)	(material)	(Ss)	(place)	(examiner)
2/5	Pre-test	Production	35 cards	Subject	School	[O]
3/4-11	PPVT Test I	Comprehension Production	PPVT	Subject	School	[T]
4/15	Word Book T.	Production	*W.B.-a	Group	School	[T]
5/8	Word Book T.	Production	*W.B.-b	Subject	Home	[B]
5/10-13	PPVT Test II	Comprehension Production	PPVT	Subject	School	[T]

*W.B.-a = the *Golden Happy Word Book,* *W.B.-b = the *Best Word Book Ever.*

In comprehension tests, the examiner asked the subject, "Put your finger on _____ .," "Tell me where _____ is.," or "Can you tell me where _____ is?," showing the PPVT Book. In production tests, the examiner asked him, "What is this?," "Tell me what this is.," or "Can you tell me what this is?," pointing to a picture. The tests were also tape-recorded.

The criteria for what should be counted as English words were based largely on Nelson's study of first language acquisition (1973, p. 13).

1. Words produced spontaneously by the child were tallied. Direct imitation of a word was not counted.

Example	acceptable		not acceptable	
	[E]	What is this?	*[E]	What is this?
	[S]	Cow.	[Ch.]	A cow.
			[S]	Cow. [imitation]

*[E] = examiner, [S] = subject, [Ch.] = other children

2. All words produced spontaneously by the child were tabulated no matter what their duration in the vocabulary: some were used ephemerally and some were permanent acquisitions.

3. Intonation helps to distinguish spontaneous speech from imitation.

Example	[E]	Do you want some paint?
	[S]	Paint? (↗) [imitation]
		Paint. (↘) [spontaneous]

The following criteria supplemented those suggestion by Nelson.

4. Loanwords from English were considered as English words when they were used in English sentences: the context where a word is uttered may help to

distinguish a loanword from an English word although pronunciation is a key for the distinction.

>   Example   [S]   KORE *ORENJI*. /orēndzi/   [a loanword]
>   [S]   This (∅) orange. /orēndzi/   [an English word]

5. English words were not considered as Japanese words when they were used in Japanese sentences (Mixing): they were counted as English words although a few of them may be loanwords.

>   Example   [S]   KORE small car. (= this is a small car)
>   [S]   O-SAKANA NE, PAPA GA catch SHITA NO.
>   (= my daddy caught a fish)

6. Words which the child volunteered relatively quickly during testing were considered familiar words.

RESULTS

Subject's acquisition of syntax

During the first three months of the observation, the subject produced one-word utterances and at the same time began to use memorized forms which were frequently heard at school. According to the teacher and the subject's mother, he spoke memorized forms more often than I observed at school.

In February, when I gave him a pre-test, I found a filler /z/ and /iz/ in his utterance as in "Mommy /z/, /iz/ . . . ." Then he switched into Japanese as in "Mommy KORE HAITETA NO." (= Mommy wore jeans like this.) This seemed to be his first attempt at English syntax.

In March, the filler /iz/ occurred more often and became productive in his utterances as in "MIKI /iz/ lunch today." (= I am going to stay for lunch today) or "/iz/ moon." (= That is the moon.) Other grammatical features such as possessives, This+Noun, and No+Noun or Verb also appeared in his utterances as in "MIKI's daddy, MIKI's house, my shoes," "This orange juice, This my cooky," and "No airplane, No touch" respectively.

In April, a conjunction "and" appeared as in "owl and cow," and present progressives also appeared as in "Wagon is coming." or "MIKI is coming." A "This+(my)+Noun" form became stable. At the end of April, "I'm/I am" appeared instead of "MIKI is" in subject position as in "I'm MIKI." (= I will be 4 years old soon.) A form "Please+Noun or Verb" was frequent as in "Please more juice." or "Please open."

In May, a "This is (my)+Noun" form turned out to be a productive and stable one. Present progressives often appeared. And "You are +Noun?" with rising intonation was used for a question as in "You are submarine?" (= Have you ever seen a submarine?) or "You are chocolate?" (= Do you have chocolate?). The subject began to express the concept of plurals using "all" and "and" instead of the plural morpheme as follows:

Example   Ship is all.
          All boat.
          One boat . . . one submarine and all, all, all, all boat!
          All house.
          This is house and house and . . . (repeated 11 times)
          Yes, train and train and train.

In summary, the subject's syntactic development was not as fast as had been expected for the first three months. After the filler /z, iz/ appeared in February, his utterances increased, and his attitude and behavior became active and assertive. He seemed confident that he could communicate with others using these few simple syntactic structures.

Subject's acquisition of vocabulary

The data was gathered from three sources: 1) the subject's daily utterances, 2) PPVT Tests, and 3) Word Book Tests. They were analyzed in terms of (A) rate of acquisition, (B) grammatical categories, and (C) semantic categories. The methods of analysis were, again, taken from Nelson's study (ibid. p. 16-17, 32-33), with modifications for second language acquisition. A separate category (D), influence of Japanese loanwords, was added to those used by Nelson, and various modifications were made within each of her categories to account for the data.

(A) Rate of acquisition (data = PPVT only)

The results of PPVT Test I and II showed that the subject's comprehension was far superior to his production: in Test I, the correct responses in comprehension were 72.1%, whereas the correct responses in production attained only 33.9%. In Test II, the former was 72.3%, whereas the latter was 32.0%. In comparing Test I and II, no difference in comprehension was found, but in production the result of Test II slightly declined. This was due to the fact that his wrong answers in Test II increased as he went much further on the questions than in Test I.

The PPVT Tests showed that the subject had a high passive vocabulary. Nelson reported that children who had very high comprehension scores also had high active vocabulary scores. However, this does not seem to be true in this subject's case. He showed high comprehension, but his production was much lower.

Looking at the subject's production, he acquired about 260 words (if his mother's data is included, almost 300 words) after seven months of exposure to English. This is in sharp contrast to Felix's subjects (1975) who were found to produce no more than 40 different nouns and 20 different adjectives after five months of acquiring German. In Felix's study, unknown nouns were usually replaced by demonstrative pronouns such as "dies" (this) and "das" (that). Since

MIKI, the subject in this study, did not acquire English demonstrative pronouns, he did not use them for unknown words. This may be due to the similarity of these forms in English and German and the dissimilar nature of the forms in English and Japanese.

(B) Grammatical categories (data = PPVT, W.B., utterances)

Among the words acquired by the subject, general nominals (concrete objects) indicated the highest score: 60.6%. Action words (verbs) showed the second highest: 13.0%. And the third was modifiers (adjectives, etc.): 10.0%. The remainder were split among many categories.

Most of the verbs were acquired in memorized forms such as "sit down, come on, please push me, take one," which are frequently used at school. After seven months of learning English, the subject did not break up these expressions; that is, he did not use verbs as *a separate grammatical category*. Consequently, when speaking sentences using his own grammatical system, the subject used copula verbs for any main verb, including tense and inflections, as follows.

> Example
> —is— 3 forms: 1) /iz/+NP, 2) NP+/iz/+NP, 3) /iz/, NP+/iz/+NP
> /iz/ Ryan. [complaining to teacher about Ryan]
> /iz/ Claire. [saying "That's Claire's card" in the game]
> MIKI /iz/ lunch today. [I'm going to stay for lunch today]
> MIKI is submarine! [I saw a submarine in Disneyland]
> MIKI is long fish. [I caught a long fish, or "saw"?]
> Is, MIKI is nice. [I look nice in an Indian hat.]
> Is, MIKI's daddy is UCLA. [My daddy went to UCLA
> today] or [My daddy is at UCLA now]
> —am— I am blue. [I have blue color]
> I am! I am! [I do, I do] or [I did, I did]
> I am jacket. [I brought a jacket today, or "have"?]]
> I am parade. [I saw a parade in Disneyland]
> —are— You are submarine? (↗) [Have you ever seen a sub-
> marine?]
> You are teacher? (↗) [Are you a teacher?]
> You are chocolate? (↗) [Do you have chocolate at
> home?]

Even though the subject did not use main verbs properly in English sentences, there are two kinds of evidence that he understood the meaning of verbs which he heard: one is mixing, and the other is his response on PPVT Tests. Regarding language mixing, Uyekubo (1972) reported that her subjects, bilingual children, replaced Japanese verbs with "English verbs + SURU (to do)" in Japanese sentences. MIKI also mixed English verbs in Japanese sentences in the same way as the bilingual children, as in the following examples.

*MIKI drive SURU. (= I'm going to drive, or I want to drive)
MIKI eat SHINAI. (= I won't eat clay dough)
"go" DATTE. (= Brina said "go")
O-SAKANA NE, PAPA GA catch SHITA NO. (= Daddy caught a fish)

*possible use of a loanword

According to the results of PPVT Tests, his comprehension of *verbs* has improved, though there has been no change in production of verbs:

		Test I	Test II
Comprehension:	correct answers	9	14
	incorrect answers	6	2
Production:	correct answers	2	1
	incorrect answers	10	11

Felix (p. 12) found that verbs became productive only very late in his subjects' case. Hakuta (1974) also reported that his subject, a five-year-old Japanese girl, acquired verb inflections late; e.g., she acquired past regular and past irregular much later than did the first language learners studied by Brown or deVilliers and deVilliers. Thus, it should not be surprising that Miki acquired verb vocabulary items rather slowly.

(C) Semantic categories (data = PPVT, W.B., spontaneous utterances)

With regard to the learning of "meaning classes," "food and drink" attained the highest score: 20.9%. The second highest was "vehicles including ships and airplanes": 10.8%. And the third was "wild animals" and "outdoor objects": 8.2% respectively. The rest of the vocabulary items were split among many categories.

As Nelson points out, if a child is really interested in, for example, animals, he will learn an elaborate taxonomy of the family of wild animals. Except for "food and animals" (which Ferguson, 1974, suggests should be taken out and treated separately because of their universal frequency in child language samples), MIKIHIDE revealed his interests in vehicles such as "a hover craft, a submarine, an ambulance" and so forth. He also paid attention to outdoor objects such as "a fence, a bridge, a ladder, a parachute, a cliff." On the other hand, he did not know girls' or women's clothes such as "a dress, a skirt, a ring." It appears that the contents of his vocabulary showed his world—his interests and preference, and his more advanced recognition and perception of objects.

Felix (1975) mentions that the second language learner is both cognitively and intellectually more advanced than the first language learner in the early stages. The subject in this study seems to have been learning words more specifically than the first language learner in the one- or two-word stage. For example, he has never called a cow "a dog," or anything else. Such phenomena as overextension were much less frequent than had been expected. Though the syntactic development of the American children in the nursery school was far superior to that of MIKIHIDE, they sometimes gave inaccurate responses to vocabulary questions. MIKI's responses, in contrast, were either precise or "I /dn/ know." For example, when the teacher asked the children about "the sun," Ryan answered as follows:

	[T]	Can anybody tell me what's shining up in the sky?
	[Ry]	That's xxx morning.
	[T]	What do you think it is?
	[Ry]	It's morning.
	[T]	Somebody colored it all over. What is it?
S–	[M]	Sun.
	[T]	The sun? (⟋) The sun.

In the analysis, several conceivable reasons for the subject's wrong answers in the PPVT Tests are possible. Most of all, association with his previous experiences and knowledge does seem to have affected word learning. Here are some examples of the subject's incorrect answers.

1. Association with previous knowledge

	Q	S's Answer
a-14	skirt—light [the skirt looks like a lamp shade]
a-18	tying—open [probably S has never tied a gift]
a-28	arrow—Indian [American Indians in old days?]
a-35	badge—star [the sheriff badge looks like a star]
b-6	fingers—five [Probably S uses his fingers for indicating his age or numbers] ·
b-14	jacket—Benjie's . . . [Benjie loves to wear a jacket]
b-26	engineer—train man [S might have created it from "milk man" and "mail man"]

2. Specific item in picture for whole (or possible avoidance of "I /dn/ know")

a-9	can—pumpkin [the can has a label on which there are two tomatoes]
a-31	nest—egg [there are 3 eggs in the nest]
b-8	children—boy [2 boys and a girl are in the picture]
b-22	river—boat [there is a boat on the river]

3. No distinction

b-29	rat—mouse
b-12	lamp—light

4. Incorrect answers for verb (action)

b-31	sail—boat, yacht
b-23	ringing—bell
b-24	baking—oven
a-23	pouring—milk, milk is down
b-11	climbing—jump

5. Onomatopoetic expression from Japanese
  b-16   ring—KIRA KIRA ["twinkle, twinkle"]
  b-23   ringing—CHINKARA KOKARA [= "jingle, jingle" as in the sounds of a bell]
  b-30   time—CHINKARA KON [the picture is an alarm clock, which probably associated with the sounds of a bell]

6. Words which *S* never said in English
  a-16   drum—TAIKO
  a-10   chicken—NIWATORI [*S* called broiled chicken "chicken"]
  a-16   blocks—TSUMIKI, OMOCHA
  a-7   clown—PIERO
  *   meat—O-NIKU [from *S*'s utterances]

There seem to be two reasons for Category 6: Hatch and Gough (1974) mention that children use a particular word in one language when it appeals to them more than its equivalent in another language. For example, one child who would never say *blömster* but always said *flower* because she felt the English equivalent sounded better. Celce-Murcia (1975) has pointed out that children avoid words containing difficult phonological elements. It seems likely that MIKIHIDE is avoiding difficult consonant clusters in his refusal to say such words as *drum, blocks,* and *clown.*

(D) Influence of Japanese loanwords

In Japanese, there is a large collection of loanwords from English, and generally these foreign words are adapted to the Japanese sound system (Uyekubo, 1972). Some of the loanwords which the subject said were changed to the English sound system, and some were still pronounced using the Japanese sound system. As far as this subject is concerned, there are two things to be mentioned about loanwords: one is that English stress is important if the subject is to be understood by native speakers of English, and the other is that loanwords seem to help the subject to learn English words more quickly because of their similarity as cognates. There are quite a few loanwords in the subject's vocabulary. The PPVT Tests also show that loanwords seemed to help the subject to comprehend English words: he comprehended 19 words out of 22 loanwords in both tests.

Example

		Japanese	English
Phonological change:	table	/teeburu/	/téybl/
	lion	/raion/	/láyən/
	ice cream	/aisukuriimu/	/áyskriym/
No change:	orange	/ɔrēndzi/	
	drive	/dɔraibu/	
	light	/laito/	
	banana	/bānana/	
	kangaroo	/kangāruu/	

There is one example that shows English stress is important. When the subject talked about a submarine to the teacher, she did not understand him as in the following dialog.

Example	S–[M]	SABŪMARIN, SABŪMARIN, SABŪMARIN, SABŪMARIN
	[T]	What is this? (↗)
	S–[M]	SABŪMARINE
	[T]	. . . . ? [listening to M]
	S–[M]	SABŪMARINE
	[T]	Oh, this sūbma´rine

After this, the subject learned to pronounce "a submarine" with proper stress.

SUMMARY

To sum up the subject's vocabulary acquisition, general nominals had the highest score of all the words acquired for the seven months. "Food" was most productive, "animals," which are universally acquired early in first language acquisition, were also learned by this subject, a second language learner, and "vehicles" and "outdoor objects" revealed the subject's interests toward the world. The subject's motivation and intelligence seemed to be important factors for vocabulary building in terms of precise recognition, perception, and retention. Finally, Japanese loan-words affected the subject's acquisition of English vocabulary. Since there are many such loanwords from English in Japanese, the cognates were very helpful in enlarging Miki's receptive vocabulary. In production, however, his pronunciation of the English source word was not always recognized by English speakers.

In comparison to the second language learners studied by Felix, Miki appears to have learned a very large number of vocabulary items. His strategies also seem to differ from those discussed by Felix. Rather than using demonstratives for nouns, he was extremely explicit in his choice of nouns that he knew. This was not the case, however, for verbs. While he did learn a number of English verbs and used them in Japanese sentences, his early utterances show an /iz/ form in the verb "slot." The /iz/ may have been the English copula or it may merely have been a filler sound which appeared in verb position. Studies of vocabulary acquisition by first language learners reveal a great deal of variation in the learning process. A comparison of this study with that of Felix also shows much variation for second language learners. As our methodology for the study of vocabulary acquisition evolves, hopefully we will find interesting ways to explain the variation that has been found in the data.

Developmental Sequences

7 *in Naturalistic L2 Acquisition*

Henning Wode, *Englisches Seminar der Universität Kiel*

INTRODUCTION

One widely held belief about the differences between child and adult second language learners is that interference is an important factor for adult language learners but not for children. This notion has generated a good deal of discussion (cf., Tarone, Swain and Fathman, 1976) because data from most children does show interference as well as positive transfer from the previously learned language.

Perhaps the strongest position on the negligible importance of first language influence on second language learning is that of Dulay and Burt (1975). They claim, on the basis of their findings in experimental studies involving large groups of children, that "syntactic interference from the first language was almost non-existent for Spanish children learning English in the United States. . . . Interference . . . is virtually nonexistent in child second language acquisition." Kennedy and Holmes, commenting on the Dulay and Burt paper, remind us that all previous learning influences subsequent learning and behavior and that "this phenomenon can be observed in first language acquisition . . . and is often called overgeneralization. It is perhaps a pity that a special term 'interference' was used by habit theorists to describe in second language learning behavior that arises from a similar overgeneralization process." (1975, p. 82)

In the following paper, Wode brings both phonological and syntactic data—data from German and English second language learners—to bear on this issue. As both he and his colleague Felix (see abstract section) note, the problem is not so much in saying whether or not the child relies on his first language strategies but rather whether we can define precisely when interference will occur. One might want to consider Wode's notion of a "crucial similarity measure," Stockwell, Bowen and Martin's theoretical construct of a "hierarchy of difficulty," or a wide variety of other factors such as those proposed by Tarone, Frauenfelder and Selinker (1975), Schumann (1975), Hatch and Wagner-Gough (1975), and LoCoco (1976, 1976) in predicting and explaining transfer (whether negative or positive) and the duration of interference patterns in the learner's speech production.

Reprinted with the permission of the author and the editors of *Working Papers on Bilingualism,* 1976.

* * *

PURPOSE

When in the late 60s and early 70s I was drafting the outlines of my—now—Kiel project on language acquisition, it became obvious that there was a big gap in the activities of the field. Past and ongoing research was concentrated on L1 acquisition and foreign language teaching. Apart from Ravem (1968, 1969, 1970), and oldtimers like, for instance, Kenyeres (1938), there were no modern studies on naturalistic L2 acquisition, i.e., L2 acquisition without the benefit or obstruction from schoolroom instruction. It seemed to me then that if we were ever to get at the mysteries of foreign language teaching, we would have to, at least heuristically, single out different types of language acquisition, such as L1 acquisition, naturalistic L2 acquisition, L2 teaching, etc. This, it was hoped, would lay bare the child's own contribution to classroom language teaching. Moreover, I thought this was one way to find out to which extent language acquisition of whatever type did, in fact, proceed according to universal principles common to all acquisitional types (Wode 1974c). One simply cannot tell, if, for instance, naturalistic L2 acquisition and foreign language teaching are lumped together as in so many studies, recent and less recent (ranging from Valette 1964 to Selinker 1972, and Dulay and Burt 1974). Any claim about the identity of any acquisitional types should be the outcome, if any, of such studies, and not their premise.

    In 1972 I learned that Evelyn Hatch and Roar Ravem had for some time been very active in research on naturalistic L2 acquisition. Since then interest has spread. And it seems to me that now we can notice a sobering swing away from theoretical speculations toward data-oriented empirical research based on—fairly—sophisticated—linguistic assumptions.

    The major issues relating to naturalistic L2 acquisition, as I see the field today, still are:

a) is L2 acquired in a developmental sequence?
b) is there an ordered sequence of stages?
c) are the developmental sequences the same for L1 and L2?
d) what are the variables governing this sequence?
  1. to which extent does the child rely on prior L1 knowledge?
  2. to which extent does his developmental sequence reflect the structure of the L2 target language?
  3. what are the processes and strategies that the child uses to acquire L2?
  4. to which extent are the processes applied in the acquisition of L2 identical with those used to master L1?
  5. do all children apply the same universal set of processes and strategies?

It seems to me that the available evidence, in particular the data to be presented below, will allow us to adopt an affirmative view toward points (a-b). As for point (c), there are those like Hatch and Wagner-Gough (1975), Dulay and Burt (1974), who lean toward expecting the same developmental sequence for a language like English irrespective of whether it is acquired as L1 or L2. I shall disagree. My data force me to conclude that the L1 and L2 sequences for a given language may differ. Furthermore, I am sure that L2 children do rely on prior L1 knowledge (d1). However, it seems to me that the crucial issue is not whether children fall back on L1 knowledge; rather, the issue is to which extent and under which conditions this is done. In the paragraphs to follow it will become apparent that L1 knowledge/structures will lead to interferences only under specific structural conditions. Points (d 3-5) have, more than any other of the points above, captured the interest of researchers. I think that as yet, we do not have either the type, or the variety, of data to go beyond highly tentative global guesses.

DATA AND DATA COLLECTING: THE KIEL PROJECT ON LANGUAGE ACQUISITION

The data that I shall chiefly rely on come from my Kiel University, Germany, project on language acquisition. It is a long-range endeavor aiming, ultimately, at an integrated theory of language acquisition. This theory is to describe, and to interrelate, the various acquisitional types, such as L1 monolingualism; L1 bilingualism; naturalistic L2 acquisition; L2 acquisition under formal teaching conditions; and others. (For details cf. Wode 1974c.) For a year or two our focus has been on naturalistic L2 acquisition. We attempt to contrast systematically the acquisition of two different languages acquired as L2. The languages chosen are German and English. We have, at present, data both from children with English as L1 acquiring German as L2; and from children with German as L1 acquiring English as L2. The age range is, roughly, from 3;4-9;6.

The combinations yield two L2 acquisitional types: L2 German/L1 English, and L2 English/L1 German. In either case we try to look at the data from several points of view. The L2 data for each language are compared with the respective L1 data. This provides hints as to differences or similarities for the L1 vs. L2 acquisition of a given language. Then we compare the L2 data for both languages as to differences and parallels. This, we hope, will provide clues as to the general principles that may govern naturalistic L2 acquisition. Eventually we should be able to use these insights to decide whether and to which extent L1 and L2 acquisition follow the same general principles. (For a more detailed discussion of the issues involved cf. Wode 1974c.)

Throughout the project we have found it useful not to rely on a rigid preplanned data collecting procedure. Instead, it has been our experience that in order to get rich and insightful data, the methodology and the procedure have to be flexible enough to be adaptable to the type of child under observation. Some develop faster, others more slowly; some produce lots of data spontaneously, others need prompting.

For each L2 acquisitional subtype we have two sorts of data: handwritten notes taken spontaneously at the scene of action and including phonetic transcriptions, most likely child intentions, and other information; as well as many hours of tape recordings of spontaneous speech and of experimental sessions.

As for the informants, the data for L1 German come from my two children, Lars, né 1969, and Inga, né 1971. These two together with their older brother Heiko, né 1966, and their sister Brigit, né 1967, are the subjects that have provided the data for L2 English. To get these data, the entire family of six moved to Trinity Center, Cal., for half a year in 1975.[1] It seems to me that this informant situation is as close as one can possibly hope to get for solving the problem as to which extent prior linguistic knowledge is exploited to acquire a second language.

For L1 English we rely on the literature. For L2 German/L1 English we have studied children whose parents have moved to the Kiel area for various reasons. We have extensive records on 4 children aged 3;4 - 7;6. (For further details on the design of the project, the data, the children, and some results cf. Wode 1974a-d, 1976a-c, Wode and Schmitz 1974, Wode and Ruke-Dravina 1976, Felix 1975a-d, Lange 1975.)

SOME ILLUSTRATIVE DEVELOPMENTAL SEQUENCES

I shall outline three developmental sequences relating to different structural areas: phonetics-phonology for the acquisitional type L2 English/L1 German; plural inflection for L2 English/L1 German; and negation L2 English/L1 German as well as L2 German/L1 English. I shall single out the acquisition of negation to discuss in more detail some differences between the L1 vs. the L2 developmental sequences. These comparisons, I think, will at least suggest in outline which kind of evidence a theory of naturalistic L2 acquisition will have to handle.[2]

L2 phonology: L2 English/L1 German

The four children mentioned above did not acquire the local variety of Trinity Center English in a Jakobsonian type of developmental sequence (Jakobson 1941), nor in an approach reminiscent of the feature/process hypothesis implicit in Ingram (1974a-b). Instead, some segments/features were approached through the children's L1 phonological capacity, i.e., the state of development that their L1 German phonological system had reached at the time of their arrival in L2 territory. The second type of segment/feature was acquired in a way that is difficult, if not impossible to relate in any direct way to the children's respective L1 phonological capacity. The first type of phonological elements comprises the stressed and unstressed vowels/vocoids, the syllabic and nonsyllabic consonants/ contoids except /r/ and, possibly, /w/. The acquisition of the latter two, especially /r/, was parallel to the developmental sequence when English is aquired as L1. I shall first illustrate the first type, and then deal with the second.

For the first type of phonological elements the children seemed to proceed along what in Wode (1976b-c) I have termed equivalence relationships, and as set out in Table 7-1. The chart is to imply that the L2 target, as given in the left-hand column of Table 7-1, was regularly substituted by the children by a specific L1 element, i.e., the L1 equivalent to the L2 target. Such substitutions as in Table 7-1 are, at least in part, familiar from foreign language teaching as well as from the numerous studies on languages in contact.

That, in fact, the children were relying on their prior L1 capacity in cases as summarized in Table 7-1, can be illustrated most vividly via the substitutions for the L2 targets /Θ, ð/. [Θ, ð] do not exist as distinctive phonological elements in adult German. However, three of our children, Heiko, Lars, and Inga, had a lisp in the course of their L1 phonological development. By the time the family moved to Trinity Center, Heiko had overcome his without therapeutic treatment. With Lars and Inga the lisp was still strong. Lars used [Θ, ð] as a substitute for German /s, z/, Inga for /ʃ, ʒ, s, z/. Inga employed the same substitutions for her L2 English. Lars' lisp was less consistent. There are many instances from him, where he was lisping in attempting the L2 targets /Θ, ð/ as well as /s, z/. More telling, however, is this: When he talked German in Trinity Center, his lisp was as strong as ever. Among his early attempts at the L2 targets, /Θ, ð/, however, there are many instances where he did not lisp or where he struggled hard to avoid it, thus producing [s, z] or something very close to [s, z]. (For details cf. Wode 1976b.)

The L2 target /r/ does not fit the above generalization. In Wode (1976c) I have argued that the first regular non-∅-substitute for the L2 /r/ in /r-V/ and /Cr-V/ environments is [w]. The next stage is marked by the use of a central frictionless continuant [ɹ]. Retroflex [ɻ]'s were noted only later. Cf. Table 7-2.

I am still undecided on how to interpret the L2 sequencing of [ɹ] vs. [ɻ]. Many local speakers including many local children had [ɹ], others had [ɻ], and many had both. In numerous instances it was impossible to tell

Table 7-1   Some substitutions of L2 segments by L1 equivalents (based on Wode 1976b)[3]

Target L2	Child L2	Target L2-form	Child L2-form	Date	Child
/ ɪ /	[ɪ]	pitcher	pʰɪtʰja	0;6/23	Heiko
/ ʊ /	[ʊ]	pushing	pʰʊʃɪŋ	0;5/22	
/ i /	[i]	please	pʰliz	1;11/59	
/ ɛ /	[ɛ]	ready	ɹɛdi	1;11/58	
/ æ /	[ɛ]	bat	p̥ɛt	0;12/79	
		thank you	θɛŋkʰ ju	0;9/47	Inga
		catch	kʰɛtʰʃ	1;16/519	Birgit
		catch	kʰɛtʰʃ	1;16/519	Lars
/ ʌ /	[a]	some one	sam wan	0;12/77	Heiko
		come on	kʰam ɔn	0;13/86	Inga
		this one	tɪθ wan	0;19/136	Lars
		shut up	ʃalap	0;26/201	Birgit
/ w /	[v]	sandwich	sɛ·ntvɪtʰʃ	0;7/27	Heiko
		Weaverville	vivavɪl	1;8/337	Inga
		wet	vɛt	1;8/353	Birgit
/ θ /	[s]	thank you	sɛŋkʰ ju	0;15	
		three	swɹi	0;23	Lars
/ ɬ /	[l]	Bill Hill	p̥ɪl hɪl	0;12/74	Heiko
		please milk	p̥liθ mɔlk	0;14/98	Inga
		little	lɪtl	0;26/202	Lars
		cold	kʰɔɔl	0;28/236	Birgit
/ əʳ /	[a]	river	ɹɪva	0;13/88	Heiko
		(Trinity) Center	θɛnta	0;5/17	Inga
		(Trinity) Center	θɛnta	0;5/16	Lars
		Carpenter	kʰɔəpʰɛnta	0;14/93	
		Weaverville	vivavɪl	1;9/369	Birgit

whether the children first had [ɹ] as an intermediate developmental stage toward [ɻ]; or whether [ɹ] and [ɻ] are developmentally unrelated. This latter alternative would imply that our L2 children's [ɹ] and [ɻ] are reflexes of different L2 targets.

There is one exception to the acquisition of /r/, and, I think, it is especially telling. Birgit at first had the occasional [w] in her L2. But her favorite was uvular [ʀ], like she uses for L1. Though no foreign language teaching was involved in the whole experiment, Birgit was allowed to take part in the reading and writing activities of the first graders, because she wanted to. However, once school had

Table 7-2   Developmental types in the acquisition of L2-target
[ɻ]/[ɹ]

I:	Substitution by uvular [R]		
L2-form	Child L2	date	Child
Redding	ʀɛdɪŋ	0;12/61	Heiko
right here	ʀaɪtʰia	0;24/176	Lars
Trinity Center	tʰʀɪnɪtʰi θɛnta	0;5/17	Inga
drink	dʀɪŋk	0;28/244	Birgit

II:	Substitution by [w]		
———	———	———	Heiko
Craig	kʰwɛ·k	0;5/15	Lars
Craig	kʰwɛɪk	0;5/18	Inga
Craig	kʰwɛk	1;8/357	Birgit

III:	Substitution by a central frictionless continuant [ɹ]		
(home) run	ɹan	0;6/23	Heiko
Grief	kɹif	0;18/124	Lars
friend	fɹɛ·nt	1;28/793	Inga
crickets	kʰɹɪkʰɪtʰs	2;8	Birgit

IV:	L2-target-like retroflex [ɻ] proper		
Swift Creek Trail	swɪft kʰ ɻ ik tʰ ɻ ɛɪl	1;7/326	Heiko
strike	st ɻ aɪk	1;25/758	Lars
Craig	kʰ ɻ ɛɪk	3;0/1618	Inga
Redding	ɻɛdɪŋ	3;8	Birgit

recessed after we had been there for two months, Birgit gave up her preference for uvular [R], and reverted to the [w] substitutions. Then she continued through the same developmental sequence as the three other children had done or were doing. (For details on the acquisition of /r/ cf. Wode 1976c.)

L2 inflection: L2 English/L1 German plural inflection

The irregular plurals of English were the last to arise with our children. In fact, only Heiko got to the stage where, toward the end of our stay, he had two or three nouns for which he did not form the plural by adding [-s, -z, -əz, -əs]. As for the developmental sequence of the regular plural, it will not do to simply list the allomorphs in the order in which they appeared with the children. There are more regularities to it than that. They will become apparent if the children's intentions are looked at separately from the developmental sequence governing the acquisition of the allomorphs.

Stage I: One form for both plural or singular intention

In the beginning most nouns showed no reflex of target plural inflection. A few others like, for instance, *guys*, did. With these, however, there was no form reflecting the noninflected target. Whether the forms occurred with or without overt plural reflex, these nouns were monomorphemic to the children. They had but one form.

Stage II: Two forms reflecting target singular and plural; singular reflexes used with both singular or plural intention; but with plural reflexes restricted to plural intention.

Stage III: Plural-reflexes restricted to plural intention; singular-reflexes to singular intention.

Nouns now had two forms, like, for instance, *hook* and *hooks*, i.e., reflecting plural and singular target inflection. Forms with singular target reflexes are used with singular intention; forms with plural target reflexes are restricted to plural intention.

The allomorph sequence

Stages I-III mark the acquisition of the principle of plural formation. Tied into these stages is the sequence in which the plural allomorphs /-s, -z, -əz/ are acquired. The first to be used productively starting, roughly, at stage II above, is [-s], next is [-əs]. [-z] and [-əz] are the last to arise.

The reason for the late appearance of [-z, -əz] is very likely not an inflectional one, but rather a more general phonological one, namely the final devoicing rule of German. In German final fricatives and plosives are voiceless. In English they may be voiced or voiceless. It takes all four children a long time to acquire this L2 phonological rule. The plural allomorphs begin to be voiced at approximately the time that voiced fricatives and plosives appear finally elsewhere, too.

The blunders committed by the children are uniform. They never made any mistakes as regards the distribution of [-s, -z] vs. [-əs, -əz]. [-s, -z] were never attached to nouns ending in /-ʃ, -ʒ, -s, -z/; and, likewise, if such nouns were inflected they always had [-əs ~ əz]. This is not to say that blunders did not occur. There were plenty of them. But all are due to inappropriate identification of final target inflectional /-s, -z/'s as part of the stem or by adding [-əs ~ əz] to nouns that should have ∅-inflection. Some instances are (1).

(1)	guyses	[gaɪsəs]	"guys"
	fishes	[fɪʃəs]	"fish"
	basses	[bæesəs]	"bass"
	nutses	[natʰsəs]	"nuts"
	gooses	[gusəs]	"geese"

Likewise, the only type of blunder that I have noted with the children's handling of [-s, -z] is due to the fact that they failed to single out those target nouns that do not take the [-s, -z] plural but, for instance, ∅. Note (2).

(2) trouts   [tʰ˞aɒtʰs]   "trout"
    foots   [fɒtʰs]   "feet"
    feets   [fitʰs]   "feet"
    sheeps   [ʃipʰs]   "sheep"
    cattles   [kʰætls]   "cattle"

The L2 developmental sequence for the regular plural is not totally unlike that known for L1 (Berko 1958, Cazden 1968, Brown 1973). In the Berko study /-əz/ is the last to arise. /-z/ and /-s/ are differentiated from the outset. This is probably due to the fact that the L1 children, at the time Berko did her experiments, had already acquired the phonological rule relating to the voiced vs. voiceless final fricatives. Also the developmental stages I-III are closely paralleled by L1 (cf. Cazden 1968).

Scholars who prefer to explain L2 acquisition in terms of interference will be disappointed. Apart from the general phonological rule, relating to final voiced vs. voiceless fricatives, there is no evidence for interference at all. This is even more striking if one recalls the tempting interference possibilities that a child with German as L1 might have at his disposal. Standard German has a variety of plural formation rules. There is, for instance, the (e)n-plural (*Frau: Frauen*); Umlaut (*Kuh: Kühe*); ∅-plural (*Mädchen: Mädchen*); s-plural (*Auto: Autos*); and others. But, in fact, there is not a single instance in the whole data where a child produced a plural like, for instance [fyt] as the plural for *foot* in analogy to German *Fuß: Füße*.

However, one should not jump to the general conclusion that there will be no interference in the L2 acquisition of any type of inflection. I have noted consistent blunders, for instance, with the possessive inflection. Cf. (3).

(3) Butch's car   [bɒtʰjs] . . .
    Jinx' car   [dʒɪnkʰs] . . .
    Des' car   [dɛs] . . .

It took our children quite a while before they used the appropriate [-əz ~ -əs] in cases like (3). In German, in contrast to English, inflected forms like (3) would be correct. But why is it that at the same time, the same morphological L2 rule should be followed appropriately for the plural inflection but not for the possessive inflection?

Negation

This paragraph will be more detailed, because I want to use the acquisition of negation to illustrate some of the difficulties that have to be overcome in determining the regularities that seem to govern L2 developmental sequences. The data for L1 English and L1 German as well as the two L2 acquisitional types are set out in Tables 7-3 and 7-4. I have listed only the major early stages. For the L1 data cf. Wode (1976a), Wode and Schmitz (1974), Klima and Bellugi-Klima

Table 7-3   Developmental sequences for L1 German vs. L2 German/L1 English

L1 German		L2 German/L1 English (Lange 1976)	
I	nein 'no'	I-IIa	nein 'no'
II	nein, Milch 'no, milk'		nein, da 'no, there'
IIb	nein hauen 'no bang (= don't bang on the table)'	IIb	nein helfen 'don't help me'
III	Honig gibt nicht 'there is no honey' Heiko nicht essen 'Heiko is not to eat anything' die nicht kaputt 'they are not broken' nicht Rasen 'don't sleep on the lawn' Britta nicht 'Britta is not to do it'	III	das ist nicht schöner mit das 'this is not nicer with (= than) that' Milch nicht da 'milk not there' nicht deine 'not yours' nicht fahren there 'not (= don't) drive there' nein, das nicht 'no, that not' Katze nein schlafen 'the cat no (= doesn't) sleep'
IV	Holger kriegt nicht ein Lutscher 'Holger is not to get a lollipop'	IV	das nicht eine Schaf 'that not a sheep'

(1966), Bloom (1970); for the L2 data on German cf. Lange (1975). The data on L2 English stem from my field trip to Trinity Center (paragraph 1).

Even cursory inspection of both the data for L1 and L2 of Tables 7-3 and 7-4 will reveal that there are, or may be, ordered developmental sequences for both acquisitional types. For L1 it was obvious to me from the start of our project that the developmental sequences will differ according to the structure of the target language. For instance, utterances like L1 English *Kathryn no like celery* (Table 7-4, III) have no direct parallel in L1 German. (For details cf. Wode 1976a, Wode and Ruke-Dravina 1976).

When in 1974 our data on L2 German were coming in, I was struck by two observations. These L2 German developmental sequences were ordered; and the developmental stages and the various utterance types were very similar to L1 German. In fact, the few differences that did show up made me suspect that we might have missed something for L1 rather than L2. The differences are: *nein* in medial position as in L2 German *Katze nein sahlafen* (III of Table 7-3). But so far we have had only one L2 child who had—a few—examples of this type. The other children used *nie* /ni/ for "nicht"; a third had both *nicht* and *nie* for "nicht." *Nie* in adult German is "never." To my knowledge no L1 child with *nie* for "nicht" is on record yet.

However, when the data for L2 English/L1 German were in, the situation began to look different. These data support the view that L2 acquisition follows

Table 7-4   Developmental sequences for L1 English vs. L2 English/L1 German

L1 English		L2 English/L1 German	
I	no	I-IIa	no
			no, you
IIa	no, Mom		
IIb	no close	IIb	no play baseball
	'don't close the door'		'let's not play baseball'
III	Katheryn no like celery	IIIa	1) that's no good
	Katheryn not quite through		2) lunch is no ready
	I can't open it		3) I got nothing shoe
			4) John go not to the school
			5) I can no play with Kenny
			6) I cannot hit the ball
		b	I didn't see
		c	I didn't can close it
IVa	you don't want some supper	IVa	don't say something
b	I am not scared of nothing	b	don't tell nobody

developmental sequences, and that these sequences are ordered. They disconfirm
the idea that L2 and L1 acquisition are wholly parallel. Apparently, there may be
parallels, like, for instance, I-IIb and IV of Table 7-4; but there may also be
differences, as in III of Table 7-4. Differences of this sort, I think, are due to the
structure of L1, i.e., the child's prior linguistic knowledge. What is fascinating
about this insight is not that L2 children should rely on prior L1 knowledge, but
that, apparently, they do so in highly restricted ways, i.e., only at specific points
in their development are they liable to fall back on L1. Apparently, specific
conditions relating to the structure of the languages involved have to be met for
interference from L1 to take place at all. I shall explore this lead in a preliminary
fashion in the following paragraph.

THE GENESIS OF A L2 DEVELOPMENTAL SEQUENCE: L2 ENGLISH/L1 GERMAN NEGATION

Data as in Tables 7-3 and 7-4, it seems to me, are, above all, a challenge to devise
an appropriate theory of L2 acquisition. The kind of theory that I have in mind
should not be one that specualtes post hoc whether a given "error" is due to
"interference" or not. A theory of L2 acquisition should aim at predictive power.
That is it should be formulated in such a way that it will be possible to predict
the developmental sequences for, for instance, L2 English/L1 German, L2 English/
L1 Japanese, L2 English/L1 Norwegian, etc. (For some L1 attempts to devise

such theories for specific structural areas cf. Wode 1974b and 1974d, for interrogration; Wode and Schmitz 1974, Wode 1976a, for negation.) Amongst other things such a L2 theory would have to handle the differences between L1 and L2 acquisition. The job essentially amounts to answering points (a-c) in the first section of this paper.

Obviously, it is no help at all if these points are answered in a grand way by claiming that, for instance, L1 and L2 acquisition are not the same; that the child does exploit L1 knowledge; and that processes like overgeneralization are involved. In all cases, we have to be, and we can be, much more specific as to what type of, and under which conditions, prior linguistic knowledge is made use of. Likewise, it is not enough to claim that overgeneralization occurs in L2 acquisition. We cannot make any predictions about developmental sequences unless we know under which circumstances, i.e., at which point in a developmental sequence overgeneralizations are likely to occur. It seems to me, that what we need above all is detailed information on how the many variables interact. I shall briefly go through the developmental sequence for L2 English/L1 German negation to illustrate the complexity of these interactions.

The point of this paragraph is not to arrive at a, perhaps, tentative theory for the L2 acquisition of negation. This cannot be done at present, because of lack of appropriate contrastive data. I shall content myself with two things: to show how complex the interaction of the various processes and strategies is; and to illustrate that L1 knowledge is apparently drawn on only at specific points in the developmental sequence(s).

For many stages there will be several explanatory alternatives. In most cases no attempt can be made to single out one alternative as definitely correct. To do this would require, again, appropriate contrastive data from L2/L1 types structurally different from those which we have to date. The aim of this paragraph, therefore, is to illustrate the variety of alternatives that, apparently, have to be reckoned with, and to show how the various regularities may interlock for a given developmental stage. The procedure, therefore, will be to compare, stage by stage, L2 English/L1 German with L1 English as set out in Table 7-4. Across the four children there will be commonalities as well as individual variations. They are discussed in separate paragraphs.

Developmental commonalities

In contrast to L1 English, we do not have any convincing evidence to suggest that the structural types I and II of Table 7-4 are developmentally ordered for L2. Morphophonologically both types must relate to English. However, whether the word order of IIa is a reflex of English or of German, cannot be decided since, intonation aside, the structure is the same for both languages.

IIb is without parallel in target English or German. Nonetheless the developmental type IIb is superficially the same for L1 and L2. Both seem to be overgeneralizations from IIa; but it cannot be decided whether the overgeneralization in L2 English IIb is due to target English or whether it relates in some way to German.

The commonality of L2 IIIa is that the negative element is placed after the verb. Adult German has such a general rule; adult English does not. In English, the negative element is placed after the auxiliaries. If there are none, *do*-support is required with negative positioned in front of the full verb. It is hard to say just what the children did with respect to the placement of the negatives in L2 IIIa. If we want to give credit to prior L1 knowledge, we would have to claim that the children applied their German rule. This would lead to correct placement of the negatives in L2 utterances containing an auxiliary (IIIa 1-2, 5-6); it would lead to blunders in utterances lacking an auxiliary (IIIa 4).

Alternatively, we might argue that the L2 types IIIa were acquired by relying directly on English. The first utterances of this type, i.e., IIIa 1 have negatives after reflexes of the copular *be*, i.e., *'s* (IIIa 1). Next, the usage is extended to utterances like IIIa 2. Utterances of this type cannot be based on English in the same way as IIIa 1, since the negative element is *no* instead of *not ~ -n't* as required by the target. There would have been some generalizations involved from stage IIIa 1 to IIIa 2. Type IIIa 3 is difficult to explain by relying exclusively on English. It turned up only with our two girls. IIIa will be discussed below, individual variations.

Still clinging to the alternative, that type IIIa goes back directly to English, we would have to claim with respect to IIIa 4 that utterances of this sort must be overgeneralizations of the types IIIa 1-2. This is awkward. No L1 children are known to have done this. Milon (1972) did not find this type for L2 English/L1 Japanese; but Ravem (1969) found it for two children with L2 English/L1 Norwegian. And, sure enough, Norwegian has much the same positioning rule as German.

Type L2 IIIb marks a real advance in that now negative appears in front of the full verb. At first, forms like *didn't, don't* are monomorphemic. This is closely parallel to L1 both positionwise and regarding the morphemic status of these negative forms. But note what happens next. In L2 IIIc the use of *didn't, don't* is generalized in such a way that these negatives appear also in front of the auxiliaries. This type of structure has not yet been reported for L1 English. It seems to me that the children were generalizing both on L2 IIIa and L2 IIIb, thus still clinging to some properties of the German, i.e., L1, negative placement rule. German does not differentiate between auxiliaries and full verbs as regards the placing of *nicht*. In IIIc the children treat full verbs and auxiliaries alike, which is one basic aspect of the German rule. However, the advance as against IIIa 4 is that now negative appears in front of the verb, no matter whether auxiliary or full verb, which is not in accord with the German rule.

The L2 stages I-III as listed in Table 7-4 do not exhaust every detail relevant to the developmental sequence that I have observed with the four children. Nor does type IIIc mark the end of their achievements. These developments will not be discussed here, for reasons of space. However, I have added two stages for the acquisition of the negative indefinites, like *some: any: nothing; somebody: anybody: nobody;* and the like. Here again, there is a close parallel with L1. At first, our children had structures like IVa. Note that the negative *don't* is at first combined with the positive *something,* just as in *L1.* Next is double negation. And only then did our children consistently use the forms with *any-.* Neither German nor English can have provided the direct model for IVa-b. The children must have relied on some prior structure of their own. But which one? I shall deal with this problem in another paper.

Individual variation within developmental sequences

The preceding section was focused on the commonalities among the four children. This should not blind one to the fact that not all children proceed in exactly the same way. That is to say that though there are developmental sequences which seem to set the major stages of development, these developmental sequences do also allow for some degree of individual variation. And, consequently, any theory of L2 acquisition will not only have to handle the commonalities, but also the individual differences. To give some illustrations, I shall first go briefly through the L2 German developmental sequence of Table 7-3. The examples come from four children aged 3;4 - 7;6.

For type III, David, aged 5;3, had some utterances with *nein* in medial position (*ich nein essen, Katze nein schlafen, das nein Bauer*). But he quickly turned to *nicht* in that position. Geoffry, aged 3;4, used *nicht* the moment he got to stage III. Julie, aged 5;4, and Guy, aged 7;6, preferred *nie* [ni] in the sense of "nicht." David had both *nie* and *nicht* for "nicht." The form *nie* was not intended in the sense of "never," though if there is to be a German model, then it most likely should be *nie* "never."

Recall also, that only two of our four children with L2 English had type IIIa 3 of Table 7-4. This type is hard to explain by relying exclusively on English. What comes to mind more immediately, is to relate this type to German *kein.* That is, in German we can say *ich habe nichts* "I have nothing," which can be paraphrased under certain conditions as *ich habe kein(e)* "I have none." In English this is communicatively equivalent to utterances like *I have nothing.* This, in turn, may have led the children to equate *nothing* with L1 *kein* and to use it in contexts where German *kein* would be appropriate but where the analogy with English *nothing* breaks down—for English. In fact, only two of our four children had the structural type IIIa 3 of Table 7-4.

CONCLUSIONS

I think the above data do suggest more than merely highly tentative hints in answer to at least some of the points (a-d) in the first section of this paper.

L2 developmental sequences (points (a-b))

I have no doubts that naturalistic L2 acquisition follows ordered developmental sequences. This insight is not at variance with other investigators' findings. In fact, the orderliness is such that, in the long run we should be able to devise a theory for L2 acquisition that will predict the course a L2 child will take, including the range of child idiosyncratic variations.

L1 = L2: The identity hypothesis (point (c))

I find my own results and views in conflict with quite a bit of recent research. There are researchers like Corder (1967), Hatch and Wagner-Gough (1975), Dulay and Burt (1974), who hold, or lean toward, the view that L2 is acquired like L1. In Wode (1974c) I have called this position the identity hypothesis. In particular Hatch and Wagner-Gough (1975) seem to have in mind that the L1 and L2 sequences should be the same in terms of the surface structure of the utterances that can be observed: The L1 sequence matches the L2 sequences; and the latter are the same irrespective of which language the child has picked up as L1 before. I think that this superficial version of the identity hypothesis must be rejected, but that the hypothesis itself might be maintained in a deeper sense.

L2 developmental sequences are not, on the surface of them, exactly like the respective L1 sequences. For example, L2 English IIIa 4 of Table 7-4 with the negative element *not* following the full verb does not have any parallel in L1 English at all. However, type IIb does. The identity or non-identity between L1 and L2 can, therefore, not be found in the surface forms. Consequently, if the claim that L2 and L1 acquisition are the same is to be upheld, as I think it should for the time being, it can only be that L2 and L1 acquisition are governed by the same set of principles. These principles will lead to different surface forms depending on the total information the L2 child has at his proposal, i.e., depending, mainly, on the structure of the respective L1. Beyond this, I do not think that the question whether and in which way L2 acquisition is the same as L1 acquisition can, at the present state of our knowledge, be decided in any profound way. We do not yet have the proper data to decide the issue.

Prior L1 knowledge (points (d1-2))

A comparison between L2 German and L2 English suggests to me that L2 children, indeed, may, or always do, make use of prior L1 knowledge. Furthermore, I think we have all reason to believe that this is done in systematic ways. The real challenge seems to be to discover what the systematicity is. I think the major variable is the formal type of linguistic structures involved, both from L1 and L2.

The types of evidence to come to grips with include studies like Milon (1973) and the material reviewed in Hatch and Wagner-Gough (1975). Both studies report no (noticeable?) reliance on L1. But the data of this paper do suggest just that. For instance, the L2 negation type IIIa 4 of Table 7-4 is not attested in Milon (1972). I suspect that this is due to the structure of the languages involved. Only if L1 and L2 have structures meeting a crucial similarity measure, will there be interference, i.e., reliance on prior L1 knowledge. For instance, Norwegian and German have much the same positioning rule for negation. As already pointed out in the section on developmental commonalities, Ravem (1969) did find the L2 type IIIa 4. More than that, he also has an instance of type L2IIIc of Table 7-3. This type, too, didn't turn up in Milon (1972).

Unfortunately, we do not yet have the appropriate data to warrant speculations as to what constitutes the essentials of this crucial similarity measure in terms of the—formal—types of linguistic devices used in natural languages. (For a first attempt relating to the acquisition of the various "r"'s cf. Wode 1976c.)

Processes involved in L2 acquisition (points (d3-5))

I have been unable, so far, to identify any language acquisition process for which I cannot think of some parallel phenomenon from L2 acquisition, at least with a little bit of imagination. Overgeneralization, for example, which hardly any discussion on L2 acquisition, whether schoolroom or naturalistic, fails to mention, can be documented both in L1 and L2 developmental sequences.

What is needed is much more detailed precision. Above all, the psychological correlates of such processes/strategies have to be investigated on the basis of close inspection of language data. It will not do to come up with principles such as, for example, Slobin (1973) has suggested for L1 acquisition. What use is there to tell the child to "pay attention to the end of words"? Such principles/advice will have to be ordered developmentally if they are to allow both child and investigator to use them as guidelines for progress. Not until we have this type of information will we be equipped to take a stand on point (d5) in the first section, i.e., whether all children are universally endowed with, or have at their disposal, the same set of principles, processes, and strategies.

SUMMARY AND OUTLOOK

To sum up: I have no doubt that L2 acquisition in a natural setting proceeds according to specific principles. These principles account for the high amount of uniformity across children with the same language background acquiring the same L2. These probably universal principles must be such that apart from the commonalities reflected in developmental sequences, there must be room enough to allow children to proceed according to certain individual idiosyncrasies. It seems premature to me to speculate on the precise nature of these principles. And also on the precise way in which these principles interact to produce such ordered developmental sequences as illustrated here. However, I have no doubt that it will not simply do to list the set of principles. The main task is, if a theory of second language acquisition is to have any predictive capacity at all, to state the conditions which have to be met for a given principle to be applicable by the child. Furthermore, we have to state the conditions that obviously have to be placed on the information available to the child if it is to make use of this information at all. Recall, for example, that the devices used for plural formation in both English and German are—formally—inflectional in type. But the specific plural formation rules of German were not carried over to English. However, quite a few of the German regularities relating to the positioning of the negatives were apparently carried over to English. This seems to imply, that certain conditions have to be met for what is commonly called interference to take place at all. Therefore the notion of interference has to be developmentalized if it is to provide any fruitful insights.

Notes

1. I gratefully acknowledge a grant by the Landesregierung, Kiel, toward meeting part of the expenses for this trip.

Special thanks are due to Trinity Center's two local teachers, Mrs. Cleo Carpenter and Mr. John Cain. They have cooperated admirably with the design of the project. They have gone to great troubles to make our children feel at home and to integrate them into the school activities. Above all, they have taken great care not to subject our children to any type of formal foreign language teaching.

2. Various people on our research group have helped me with sorting out the data and investigating the details of the developmental sequences to be discussed below. Thanks are due, notably, to Werner Praus for L2 /r/, Jens Bahns for L2 English plural inflection, and Jörg Kruse together with Wolfgang Schaar for L2 English negation.

3. The transcription is basically IPA: [R] uvular /r/; [⤙] retroflex /r/; [ɹ] central frictionless continuant; [ɵ] tense rounded back vowel slightly more open than [o]; the lax, front, rounded vowel as in German *Köcher* "quiver," *Knöchel* "ankle," *Wörter* "words" is transcribed as [Ø]; the vowel [ɔ] as in German *Loch* "hole," *komm* "come" is slightly closer than the British English vowel in *not, pot, slot*; raised ⁻ above consonants indicates flapped articulations, as, for instance, with [t̄] in *Betty*.

As regards items with /ð, ɵ/ it should be noted that Lars and Inga had a lisp in their L1.

The time of exposure is given in months and days. Figures following / are project internal file numbers.

8

A Chinese Child's

Acquisition of English

Joseph Huang and Evelyn Hatch, *University of California, Los Angeles*

INTRODUCTION

After Leopold's study, there was a considerable gap in time before the appearance of another study of second language acquisition in this country. During that time interval, however, important work was going on in the field of first language acquisition. The case reports on three children by the Harvard group (the famous Adam, Eve, and Sarah); and on three other children by Braine (Gregory, Andrew, and Steven) set a model at that time which influenced other first language studies and our plan for the study reported here as well.

The methodology current at that time in first language acquisition suggested that data be collected from child subjects on a weekly basis. Data analysis was directed toward Noun Phrase elaboration, and the development of question and negation structures. Another area of interest was identified, following Jean Berko's experiment, to test the acquisition of English morphemes. Another popular activity was the attempt to write rules to describe the evolution of, for example, questions or negatives in the child's speech over a series of stages.

Huang's thesis then is a report of the first attempt to apply this model from first language acquisition to second language acquisition data. One problem was immediately evident. The child, Paul, had to be observed more frequently than once a week. The speed with which the new language is learned can be so fast that daily observations are necessary if anything is to be said about the sequence of acquisition of features of the new language. So daily observation of the child at nursery school was done. A second problem was transcription style, the number of hours that had to be spent transcribing data and adding notes that were made of context was almost prohibitory. At that point, one could appreciate Leopold's plea that linguists be found who had the time and patience to carry out such work. That Huang was able to do all this was unbelievable in itself. However, even more decisions had to be made about analysis. How much of the data could be analyzed and how should it be analyzed. Was rule writing an important procedure or not, could it be done or not—there was no way to find out unless it was tried. And Huang wrote rules. (For a notion of what this entailed, please see Huang's full report and/or the work of Dato on American children learning Spanish in Spain which appeared two years later.)

The report given here has as its focus many questions which seem perhaps overworked now, but questions which had never been talked about before. For example, could one legitimately separate out part of the data and say that these parts were unanalyzed chunks that the learner had acquired? If not, then no clear acquisition process could be seen. When could one talk about these same units as part of the child's rule-governed language system? How could one discuss the role of imitation in the child's language learning process at a time when linguistic theory said imitation was of negligible importance. If one found structures similar to that in first-language data, could this be called developmental? If first language acquisition papers claimed that many structures were learned late because the child had not yet developed the cognitive basis for such syntactic relationships, then what was the explanation for a second-language learner who already had the cognitive foundations? Why should he acquire structures in a similar order? All of these questions were first tackled by Huang in his research on the child, Paul. I have added a number of sections to this study at various times—for example, sections on input and the notion of frequency as an important factor. The study has also served as a resource for comments on language play, discourse analysis, and a wide variety of other areas.

Again, the reader is asked to consult the complete study for a picture of the contribution that Huang has made to the field of second language acquisition research.

Much has been written about how children acquire language. But so far the literature refers either to first language acquisition or to the simultaneous acquisition of two languages. Since circumstances surrounding a child's acquisition of a second language are clearly different from those of his first language, we felt that much could be learned by observing Paul Chen, a Chinese child who arrived in Los Angeles on December 13, 1969, as he acquired English as a second language.

Before Paul left Taiwan with his grandmother, he spoke only Taiwanese; he watched only Taiwanese TV programs; he had no exposure to English. It is likely that he first heard English during his air trip to Los Angeles. In Los Angeles, Paul lived with his grandmother, his parents (both of whom worked during the day), and his three-year-old brother. The two boys spent the day in the care of their maternal grandmother who did not speak English. They played at home; they were not encouraged to play with other children in the neighborhood. While there was a television set in the home, neither the grandmother nor the children watched it. Taiwanese was the language spoken in the home.

One month later, when Paul was 5 years, 1 month old, he was enrolled in a play-school with American children. For a four and a half month period (the 19-week period from January 22 to June 6) observational data was collected at the school, 5 mornings a week from 9:00 to 11:30. In addition, there were 13 recorded sessions on weekends which totalled an additional 14 hours of data. Notes were also taken on utterances the informant made in the car on the way to and from school.

It seems important to emphasize the close observation throughout the study. Since the investigator (hereafer JH) was with Paul at all times when he could be exposed to English, exact information on time and order of acquisition of utterances could easily be established. The only other possible exposure to English would be with the parents during the evening. While they customarily spoke no English at home, it seems unlikely that they never spoke to Paul in English once he began to acquire the language.

The playschool schedule involved 1½ hours of classroom activities, the rest of the morning being spent on the playground. Paul could easily participate during the classroom period (dancing, playing games, playing with toys, "singing," art work and listening to stories) by observing and copying the activities of the other children. Language was not necessary. Indeed, the teacher did most of the talking. Therefore, he neither had the need nor the opportunity to speak. On the playground, the opportunity to talk was unlimited. The investigator was always within hearing distance both on the playground and during the classroom period, taking careful notes on Paul's utterances and his nonverbal responses to remarks of those around him. All events were noted as completely as time permitted in order to clarify the situational context. All notes and tapes were transcribed in regular orthography.

A number of questions had to be taken into consideration almost immediately in summarizing and analyzing the data if a true picture of language acquisition was to be obtained. For example, if during the first few days, Paul said, "Mary had a little lamb," did he know the structure or how much did he know about it? Did he know the words or morphemes in the sentence or how many of them did he know? Did he know the meaning of the sentence, or how much did he know about it? It should be no surprise if he knew nothing about the structure and possibly nothing about the meaning for he might happen to repeat it in an echolalic fashion after the teacher without knowing anything about it at all. But it might also be possible that he had happened to meet a girl named Mary and thus knew what "Mary" was; that his mother happened to have shown him a picture of lambs and had taught him the word "lamb" without our knowing it. And, finally, someone might have paraphrased the sentence for him in his first language. All of these are highly unlikely but had to be taken into consideration in examining the data. Another question which had to be posed was: could he use or understand other sentences of similar structure? For example, was he responsive to, or could he say "I have a little lamb" or "Mary had a little dog." In other words, what evidence was there to indicate any knowledge of English in either the comprehension or production data? In the first month of the study, the analysis focused on these questions.

Paul's prompt non-verbal responses to verbal commands were frequently misleading. For example, on his second day at school, when his teacher (hereafter E) said, "Paul, would you like to sit there?" he smiled and sat down immediately. If he responded to any verbal cue at all it would be to "Paul." More likely he saw the other children seating themselves and E pointing to a chair as she spoke to him. His response was the expected one and could not be taken as evidence of sentence comprehension. He might also have been responding to intonation, though it seems unlikely in this case. During the first day at school, Paul nodded when E said, "Are you through now?" with an exaggerated rising intonation. Exaggeration was necessary to get this response at the beginning of the study. For example, after Paul returned from toilet, he was asked, "Have you washed your hands?" He gave no response. Yet, when the question was repeated later with exaggerated rising intonation, he responded immediately with a nod. Sometimes what might be considered a response to verbal command was, in fact, just something he happened to be in the act of doing. For instance, having parked the car, JH said "Open the door" and Paul moved to the door, opened it, and got out. But, rather than Paul understanding the utterance and acting on it, JH himself, was actually labelling an act Paul would have performed anyway.

Global comprehension, however, was almost always quite clear. In the third day of the observation, Paul began muttering, "Get out of here" to himself. On the way home, he asked what it meant. When JH, instead of telling him, asked what had happened, Paul replied that a boy had said "ma-ai-den-me chia la" (don't be/stay here) to him. A day later Paul was on a tricycle. Another child, M., holding onto the handle bars, kept bothering him. In exasperation Paul shouted, "Get out of here!" Paul had learned the utterance as an unanalyzed unit. He knew the meaning of none of the words separately. When asked about the words, his response each time was "m-chai" (I don't know). Yet he understood its meaning in a global sense, stored it in memory, and recalled it for use in the appropriate situation.

There is no doubt that Paul learned words, phrases, and greetings by imitation (Table 8-1). In the first three weeks, most of these were imperatives, perhaps because they were used with great frequency in both teacher and peer language: "Get out of here! Let's go! Don't do that! Don't touch!" Statements said frequently, such as "It's time to eat and drink" (said every day before snack time) were also imitated. Frequency seems to be one clue as to which utterances would be imitated.

Table 8-1   Imitation and rule formation examples

Week	Imitation	Rule Formed Utterances
2	Get out of here.*	
4	It's time to eat and drink.*	
	Let's go. Don't do that. Don't touch.	
6	Are you ready? See you tomorrow.	This+++kite.
	Excuse me. Hold my hand.*	Yeah, that+++bus.
	Kenny, sit down.	Ball+++no.
7	Are you going too?*	This+++money?
	It's time to go home.*	Paper+++this. Cow+++this.
	Here we go.* Scoot over.*	Mother+++no. Tree+++no. No+++ball.
		Wash hand? Two cat.
8	I'll see you. You shut up.	Kenny car.
	What do you like?	This good. This ball?
	Hi, how are you?*	This+++boat. This+++paper.
	We are going home.	No ice cream. No candy.
		Ball doggy?
9	How are you doing?*	No money. No turtle.
	This is mine.	No more truck. Paul+++baby.
		This+++freeway.
		This not box.
10	Get out of here. Scoot over.	
	All the birds up in the tree now that	
	spring is coming . . . (singing)	

* = immediate repetition of another's speech, but later used in appropriate situations

It was almost always true that once he had "memorized" such utterances, Paul used them either in identical situations or closely similar ones. Occasionally, Paul misinterpreted utterances. For example, after learning "good-bye" he heard and repeated "Good-bye, see you tomorrow" which he then produced, regardless of situation, as an extended form of good-bye.

Another example of wrong meaning assignment was "I'm finished" which Paul interpreted as "ngwa me lei-ke ah" (I want to go). One day, Paul and M. were doing easel painting. M. finished first, turned to E. and said, "I'm finished." When E. said, "Okay, you can go," M. took off her smock, put it away and went to play. After that, when he finished too, Paul said, "I'm finished," and was treated in the same way. His misunderstanding was not corrected but it is interesting that Paul used this structure only in the context of painting. Perhaps this is because the language cue was not recognized well enough to be separated from the specific situation. That is, in the first stage of learning, utterances were usually learned in conjunction with a repeated situation. It is possible that he felt that this "go" utterance applied only in this particular situation. Of course, it wasn't long before he corrected his interpretation. By the end of the study he used "I'm finished" appropriately in many different circumstances.

This discussion of the problems of analysis may give an inaccurate picture of Paul's ability to imitate utterances of considerable length, to store and recall them for use in appropriate situations. In fact, he was so talented at mimicry, both verbal and non-verbal, that without careful checking in a variety of ways, it appeared that he understood almost everything that was said to him (see Table 8-1).

For the first month of observation, imitation appeared to be the sole method of language learning. If it were the only way, Paul would not have gotten very far. While he was very talented, it's unlikely that he could have memorized all the sentences he needed for communication, let alone associate them with the right contexts in which to use them.

It was no real surprise then, in the second month of observation, to find a second kind of utterance which clearly was not based on imitation. On March 3, Paul produced the utterance: "This+++kite," the first indication of development of his own syntactic system for English. More examples of two-word utterances followed during the next few days. These data brought with them a new set of questions to be answered: 1. What is the difference between a sentence learned by imitation and an utterance formed through Paul's own syntactic system? What are the criteria for judging whether an utterance is the former or the latter? 2. Was imitation always the strategy applied first to produce new sentence types? 3. Did imitation continue to apply after he started his own syntactic system? 4. Did Paul's developing syntactic system reflect Taiwanese interference?

As mentioned earlier, Paul's imitated sentences were grammatical (he sounded like a native-speaker of English), and he was not aware of the smaller units within such utterances. He made no attempt to break up these sentences and recombine words into new sentences during the first month. While he said, "It's time to eat and drink" along with other children as juice and crackers were put on the table, he didn't say "It's time to" anything else. Conversely, it could be said that the criteria for judging utterances as of his own rule-formation, were familiarity with the smaller units and ill-formedness.

The first utterances of his own syntactic system (see Table 8-1) were: "This+++kite." "Yeah, that+++bus." "This+++car." There is a pause between the two words and each is equally stressed so that it sounds neither like "this kite" in the sentence "This kite is bigger than that one" nor "I bought this kite yesterday." There is a distinct juncture between the two words with falling intonation on each word.

The first problem is to prove that the omission in these utterances is not simply due to faulty imitation. The most striking evidence is that Paul had already shown himself to be a flawless imitator. He did not omit the copula or article in such imitations as "If you have *a* nickel" or "All *the* birds sing up in *the* tree" or "Tha*t's* all right." He was clearly capable of hearing and reproducing word final consonant clusters and unstressed words. The fact that he paused between the two words "That+++bus" indicates it is not an imitation of some utterance like "That's a bus." Moreover, none of the children in the playschool used the sort of two-word utterances with internal pause that Paul was producing. There is no possibility that Paul was imitating anyone else. He had no contact with children learning English as a first language who might be at the "two-word utterance" stage described by Bellugi, Braine, Bloom and others, where sentences identical to Paul's would be typical.

Another problem was the possibility that these utterances were evidence that he was simply plugging English words into his first language system, a sort of relexification process. The fact was that in Paul's Taiwanese dialect, the omission of the copula in the sentence $NP_1 + cop + NPx_2$ where NP_1 is a demonstrative pronoun is acceptable. However, in his dialect (that spoken in Southern Taiwan) the omission of the copula is optional in such sentences. Furthermore, the copula (*shi*) can only be deleted in affirmative sentences. And, it cannot be deleted where NP_1 is a proper N or a personal pronoun: Table 8-2 shows examples from Taiwanese, the predicted form if Paul were using Taiwanese syntax, and Paul's utterances. Paul did not follow the predicted forms. Two further points made us sure that these were not examples of Taiwanese interference. First, Paul's parents did not omit the copula in any of these forms, and felt there was something unacceptable about copula deletion *chen dzu* even where it was a grammatical optional form; secondly, the one time Paul was observed deleting the copula in Taiwanese, there was no pause between the two NP's.

We felt justified, then, in claiming that Paul, like American children learning English as a first language, was beginning to develop his own English syntactic system. In the literature on first language acquisition, the two-word utterance has been explained in a number of ways. One explanation is that memory span and physical ability are not developed enough for the child to produce more than two words in a string. However, in this study, we have similar data even though Paul obviously had the physiological ability and the memory necessary to repeat much longer utterances. For example, at the same time he said "This+++kite" he could also say such things as "Okay, this is your turn" or "I want to open the window." And of course, he spoke much longer sentences in Taiwanese.

As in the literature on first language acquisition, it was frequently difficult to establish the exact meaning of Paul's rule-formation utterances. For example "ball+++doggy?" might mean the ball belonged to the doggy or it might be a question as to whether or not Paul could give the ball to the doggy. The tapes, even with context given, do not always help in clarifying meaning:

JH: Throw the ball to me. (P does.) Good. Now give it to Joe.

P: Joe, this+++ball? Ball+++doggy?

JH: No.

The following transcription shows the confusion even more clearly:

P: Lookit. (He had written his name and wanted JH to look at it.)

JH: Now, Paul.

P: You+++Joe, Okay?

JH: Right. My name is Joe. Do you want me to write down my name?

P: Yeah.

The response shows that JH does not know the relationship between "You+++Joe, okay?"—"You are Joe, okay?" or "You write 'Joe,' okay?" so he responded to both and both were accepted by Paul.

Table 8-2 Predicted two-word utterances based on Taiwanese

Taiwanese + translation	Predicted English Form	Paul's Utterance
NP1 = demonstrative pronoun		
cheh shi dzu cheh dzu	This (is) book.	This kite.	this+++kite
heh shi dzu he dzu	That (is) book.	That baby.	that+++baby
cheh m shi dzu *che m dzu	This not is book.	This not is freeway.	this+++not freeway
heh m shi dzu *heh m dzu	That not is book.	That not is Brent.	that+++not Brent
NP2 = personal pronoun		
ni shi sien-sen *ni sien-sen	You are teacher.	You are Edmond.	you+++Edmond
ngwa m shi sien-sen *ngwa m sien-sen	You not are teacher.	You not are truck.	you+++not truck
NPI = proper noun		
Bun-dao shi ngin-nan *Bun-dao ngin-nan	Bundao is boy.	Bozo is clown.	Bozo+++clown
Bun-dao m shi ngin-nan *Bun-dao m ngin-nan	Bundao not is boy.	Brent not is baby.	Brent+++not baby

* = ungrammatical sentence

Paul quickly moved on from the two-word stage to more sophisticated rules. While a full report of Paul's second language acquisition is beyond the scope of this paper, Table 8-1 gives some notion of this development. Table 8-3 shows one part of his syntactic system: the development of interrogative structures through both imitation and rule formation techniques.

Before discussing Paul's interrogative structures, it might be wise to look at the input of questions asked him by peers and adults. During the first month, few questions were asked him. His responses were cued, as discussed earlier, by intonation, gestures and context. During the second month, he was deluged with "What's this/that?" and "Is this a *Noun*?" questions. He responded to these by nodding or shaking his head, saying yes, no, I don't know, or supplying a noun.

Three other question forms appeared with great frequency.

1. The "do you want" (d'yawana) question:

$$\text{Do you want to} \begin{cases} \text{go home} \\ \text{take off your jacket} \\ \text{make a picture} \\ \text{help us} \\ \text{eat that} \\ \text{fall down} \end{cases} ?$$

2. The "can you" (kə̃nyə) question:

$$\text{Can you} \begin{cases} \text{kick it} \\ \text{button it up} \\ \text{drive a truck} \\ \text{say "teacher"} \\ \text{see K over there} \end{cases} ?$$

It is doubtful if Paul responded to the "do you want" or "can you" signal. He only needed the intonation to know that it was a question. The rest of the utterance was exactly the same as the imperatives that formed the largest part of the language input.

3. The "where's _____?" question. This is labelled as "where's" rather than "where" since it always occurred with the copula contracted

$$\text{"Where's} \begin{cases} \text{the} \\ \text{your} \end{cases} \text{NOUN?"}$$

To these questions, Paul customarily repeated the noun and found it or pointed to it.

"Okay" was used as a tag question during this period, (e.g., "You just listen, okay?").

Table 8-3   Production of question forms

Stage 1

X: Table? This? Walk? Wash hands? Two cat?

A_1 Question repetition
What do you like? How are you doing? What are you doing? What's my name?

B_1 Questions learned via imitation
Are you ready? Are you going too? Hi, how are you? What? What's that? What's your name? Where's Bobby? Which way?

C_1 Rule application. (Q = rising intonation)
This+++slipper? Joe, this+++ball? Ball+++doggy? Okay? Fish+++see?

Stage 2

A_2 Question repetition
Which one? Where are you going?

B_2 Questions learned via imitation
What's this? Whose is this? This one? That one? What now?

C_3 Rule application (Q = rising intonation; where's, what's, whose are question markers, "okay" is a tag question marker)

a   This+++orange? This+++you? This+++not truck? This+++yours book?

b   Where's Kenny? Where's pen? Where's car? Where's Teddy's car? Whose truck?

c   This is my book? This is jacket? This is flower?

Stage 3

B_3 May I be excused?

C   Rule application (addition of can questions, how many, color, and be-inversion)

a   Can K have some juice? Teddy, can I play? Can I write my name? Jim, can you play with the ball?

b   You put the belt on? You see a flag? B is a boy? You want this one?

c   Is this yours house? Are you a good boy? What am I doing?

During the first stage (months 1 and 2) Paul responded appropriately to most questions including less frequent *which, who* and *whose* questions. He also showed that he did not understand the following questions:

> 3/22 If it isn't a balloon, what is it? (no response)
> 3/22 Paul, tell us what you're doing? (no response)

One yes/no question was not understood, though it's not clear whether it was a vocabulary problem with "through" or the question form that he misunderstood (he answered other "are you" questions quickly and accurately).

> 3/1 Paul, are you through now? (looks puzzled)
>   Are you through with the ball? (Through?)
>   Are you through with it? (Yah.)

During the third month (labeled stage 2) Paul continued to be barraged with "What's this/that?" and "Is this a *Noun*?" questions, "do you want" and "can you?" questions. *Who/whose* questions were asked more frequently. The most dramatic increase was in the number of "What are you doing?" questions and the "Are you *verb*ing" prompt. Many of these were in an attempt to see if he had acquired the present continuous verb forms, but they also seemed to occur much more frequently in natural conversations than previously. The "How many" question was also added as Paul quickly learned English numbers.

Questions were responded to appropriately with few exceptions. However, Paul had also learned to evade questions by ignoring them, changing the subject or saying "I don't know.":

> What happened to your face there? (I don't know.)
> What happened? (No.)
> Where are you going? (no response)
> Where are you going? (no response)
> Where did you go? (no response)
> Did you go outside? (No.)

One *why* question, a negative, also appears in the data and it was not responded to: Why don't you go to the fence? Questions asked during this second stage included: yes/no, do-inversion, can-inversion, what-doing, where, who/whose, how many, which, why, and tag questions with "okay."

In the final month, the complexity of all questions increased markedly. For example, *what*-questions included the following:

> What's this/that?
> What's the time now? (It's time to go.)
> What's the baby doing? (Sleep. Sleeping.)
> What are you going to take home? (This and this.)
> What is it that you want? (I want this, please.)

Would questions suddenly increased, largely replacing *can*:

$$\text{Paul, would you} \begin{cases} \text{give me one please} \\ \text{come and sit here} \\ \text{teach her how to write your name} \\ \text{help E} \end{cases} ?$$

Perhaps no one doubted his ability any longer so that *can you* questions no longer seemed as appropriate as *would you*.

With few exceptions, all questions were responded to appropriately. Color questions were new:

> 5/10 Is this whistle black? (no response)
> 5/10 What color is this? (no response)

However, ten days later he could respond to such question forms:

> 5/20 Is this table dirty? (Yes. Dirty.)

5/20 What color is M using? (Yellow)
5/20 What color are you going to use? (I want red.)

Why questions were still not responded to:

E: Why did you give your picture to me? (no response)
Do you want me to keep it? (Yes.)

It is possible that Paul did not understand the why/because relationship even
though he had the concept in his first language. It might also be that he simply
had no definite reason in mind when asked "why" by various peers and adults.

If-then conditionals were responded to with great accuracy, surprisingly
enough:

JH: Ask E if you can have this one.
P: E, can I have this one?
Jim: If I give Paul one and give Joe one then how many will you have?
P: One.
JH: Can you write your name if you don't have a pencil?
P: No.

Turning then to Paul's production of questions, Table 8-3 shows the data
divided into three stages: stage one being months 1 and 2; stage 2, month 3; and
stage 3, month 4.

In stage one, Paul immediately identified rising intonation as a question
signal. Utterances listed under X in Table 8-3 are words repeated from statements
made to him but with rising intonation.

Jim: Take the pencil. (Paul: Pencil?)
Jim: No, Paul, this way, please, this way. (This way?)
JH: Paul, have you washed your hands? (P: Wash hands?)

In the table, A1 utterances are echoed questions which he repeated
immediately after someone asked him the question. Usually he did not understand
the question. Later, however, some of the questions he repeated earlier occur
under B1. That is, he remembered the questions and used them appropriately
later (usually after hearing them in context a number of times).

The utterances under C1 are questions which Paul formed himself. The rule
at stage one is that questions are formed by adding rising intonation to statements: "This+++ball?".

Stage 2 covers the third month of observation. It is difficult to find many
direct imitations of questions. He did mutter "whose? whose?" to himself after
being asked a "whose" question, but "Whose" questions also appeared in his
delayed imitation questions as well (B2). It is also difficult to separate B2 and C2
questions. In addition to the "This+++ball?" question type, Paul added "What's"
and "Where's" questions. He did not go through the "What+++this?" or "Where
+++Bobby?" typical of first language acquisition of English. The copula was
never deleted. Since he heard so many "what's" and "where's" questions, it
appears he learned these by imitation and the 's was not the copula but part of
the interrogative word. While he learned the question form by imitation, he soon

began substituting new nouns freely following the interrogative marker. Evidence that the "where's" question also involved his own rule-formation rather than just straight memorization is the missing article in the questions:

$$\text{Where's} \left\{ \begin{array}{l} \text{pen} \\ \text{car} \\ \text{turtle} \end{array} \right\} ?$$

While he learned to form such questions by a combination of imitation and rule formation, it is clear that they were learned as non-transformational routines. He did not go through a stage of learning to front the interrogative word, then acquire subject-verb inversion, then contract the copula.

The copula began to appear in his "This+++kite" sentences at the very end of this stage. It appeared in both statements and questions:

> This yours book? - - - - - This *is* my school?
> This *is* yours school?

At this point the contracted *'s* on "where's" and "what's" questions was also separated:

> Where's ball? - - - - - Where *is* ball?
> Where *is* my hot-wheel?

Only at this point could we be sure that the *'s* ending was not just part of the interrogative word.

In the final period of the study, the rules of stages 1 and 2 continued. Rising intonation had been the most powerful strategy for question formation up to this point but during the month gradually more and more subject-verb inversion took place.

As mentioned before, *where's, what's, whose* questions were learned as inverted forms to begin with. *Can* questions, with can-inversion, were also learned this way. Again, Paul did not pass through a non-inverted stage. He did not say such things as "I can play?" He had, of course, been subjected to three months of "can you/can I?" questions so again, it is not surprising that this word order was learned via imitation.

Since *can, where's* and *what's* questions were learned in this manner, it is a puzzle why other questions involving inversion were not imitated too. Paul was asked many "do you . . . ?" "Are you . . . ?" "Is this . . . ?" questions daily. He never imitated a "do you . . . ?" question. He persisted in using rising intonation for all questions with *be* or requiring *do*-support:

> You don't want to go?
> This is my name?
> Jim is coming too?

He did imitate "are you . . . ?" questions; in fact, his first question was an imitated "Are you ready?" Yet he did not generalize from his imitated questions with copula inversion. Instead he went through three stages of rules: 1. rising intonation "This+++kite?" 2. copula addition "This is flower?" 3. copula inversion "Is this yours house?"

There seems to be no ready answer as to why some questions were learned by imitation and others were not. Perhaps there is something particularly difficult about recognizing the copula and do-support in English (and not about recognizing *can,* and the interrogative words). Slobin has suggested that grammatical markers carrying some semantic content will be learned earlier than those with little, if any, semantic function. Perhaps this is a possible explanation for slow acquisition of the copula and do-inversion rules.

Again, the production data seems to underrate Paul's ability to communicate with question and response. At the end of the study it appeared that his language was indistinguishable from that of the American children with whom he played. No attempt was made to elicit do-inversion questions from him but he responded to them and to much more complicated question forms with ease.

The question forms show that Paul used two main strategies in learning his second language: imitation and rule formation. It also showed that the two strategies overlapped once he began to recognize segments of sentences which he had originally learned as single units.

Paul's language development differed from that of a child learning a first language in some important aspects. He already had experience with one natural language system and this helped him in the analysis of meaning and of syntax. He was capable, as younger children are not, of imitating amazingly complex sentences almost from the start and to attach a global meaning to them. It took Paul four months to learn as much language as a child would normally learn in two to three years. In 19 weeks Paul learned a second language without formal "language classes." And he learned it with much less exposure to English than first language learners normally get.

At the end of the nineteen weeks, our appreciation of the child's ability to learn language without formal instruction had increased tremendously. We also appreciated how difficult it is to find answers to such questions as: How is a child able to hear, repeat, store and recall sentences of considerable length and complexity with perfect phonetic detail when imitating sentences in the new language? How can he recall these utterances in the appropriate context seemingly without effort? How does he recognize the structure of the new language as different from that of his first language? Why doesn't he simply treat the new language as new vocabulary to be plugged into the syntax he has already created for his first language? Why are some structures in the new language learned by imitation while other similar structures are not? As in most basic research, our knowledge has increased in that we have identified a number of questions for which we have no immediate answer. Much more data will have to be examined in order to find answers and to place the questions in their respective places in the study of second language acquisition.

A Report on the Development

9 of the Grammatical Morphemes

in a Japanese Girl

Learning English as a Second Language

Kenji Hakuta, *Harvard University*

INTRODUCTION

The following study of the Japanese child Uguisu (Nightingale) was presented at the TESOL conference in Denver, 1974. While Hakuta cautions that this report is based on a preliminary analysis of the data (for a full report, see Hakuta, 1975), the preliminary data presented allows us to make some interesting comparisons between Itoh's younger subject, Takahiro, and Uguisu. The difference in age between Takahiro and the little Nightingale makes for a very different profile of language development. Differences in maturation, adjustment to the school situation, and openness to the new language are quite different. Uguisu's language development is much more similar to that of older children, particularly Paul, the Taiwanese child, reported on in this volume.

The study shows that Brown's first language methodology can yield interesting results when used to analyze second language acquisition data. Brown and his students have used the mean length of utterance (MLU) as a way of dividing first language acquisition data into a number of stages. The acquisition of language within each of these stages has certain characteristics which appear to be fairly consistent from child to child. Stage 1 is largely limited to production of a number of nouns and verbs. In the second stage,

a set of little words and inflections begins to appear: a few prepositions, especially *in* and *on*, an occasional copular *am*, *is* or *are*, the plural and possessive inflections on the noun, the progressive, past, and the third person indicative inflections on the

132

verb. All these, like an intricate sort of ivy, begin to grow up between and upon the major construction blocks, the nouns and verbs, to which Stage I is largely limited. However, in the course of Stage II we have only the first sprouting of the grammatical morphemes. Their development is not completed within the stage but extends, for lengths of time varying with the morpheme, beyond II and in some cases even beyond Stage V. (Brown, 1973 p. 249)

Brown has been particularly concerned with the acquisition of the linguistic form and semantics of a set of 14 grammatical morphemes which are described in this paper. The Harvard researchers traced the acquisition order for the 14 morphemes for the now-famous Adam, Eve, and Sara. Jill and Peter de Villiers replicated the acquisition order study with 21 children. These studies have given us information on the order of acquisition of the 14 morphemes for first language acquisition. Hakuta's study is the first attempt to use this methodology with a second-language learner. The result is a comparison of the order of acquisition for first and second language learners. However, the methodology is not an end in itself for this study. Rather, it leads Hakuta to discuss differences between first and second language acquisition and to present the notion of a simplicity principle as one way of accounting for the data produced by a Japanese child learning a second language.

Reprinted with the permission of the author and the publishers of *Working Papers on Bilingualism,* OISE, Toronto, Canada, *4*, 1974, 3, 18-44.

* * *

A five-year-old girl is extracted from her native environment in Japan and is set to re-root in the neighborhoods of Cambridge, Massachusetts. To look at what systems of roots were left in the soils of Japan would be an interesting topic of study. But even more interesting, and perhaps more relevant, is the emergence and growth of new roots in the new environment. To what extent are the strong roots which survived the cultural transplant going to influence the development of the new roots? Among these new roots, we find the interestingly intricate growth of the language of the new environment—a second language. To focus even further, in this paper, we shall look at the acquisition of grammatical morphemes. There are three principal reasons why this particular aspect of language was chosen for study. (1) A methodology for scoring them in terms of percentage supplied in obligatory context as well as a strict definition of full morpheme control has already been established by Brown (1973) and his associates; (2) longitudinal (Brown, 1973) as well as crosssectional (deVilliers and deVilliers, 1973) data have shown a rather remarkable stability in the order of acquisition of these morpehmes in first language children, and this might provide a level of comparison between first language (L1) and second language (L2) learning which MLU (mean length of utterance) does not; and (3) the process is laborious but easily replicable by other researchers of second language acquisition.

There are, of course, countless other areas to be studied in the future, such as the development of the powerful tool of sentence embedding, and this is only a beginning.

THE SUBJECT AND THE PROJECT

The subject studied here will be called Uguisu, "nightingale" in Japanese. She was 4; 11 when she came to the United States in October of 1972 with no previous exposure to English. Her parents come from a highly intellectual background and are visiting Harvard for two years. Uguisu enrolled in a public kindergarten in November of that year, and that was when her exposure to English began. From then until June of the following year, she spent two hours a day in kindergarten. She has many friends, mostly from working class families, and she actively plays with them in the afternoons as well as on weekends. At home, she speaks Japanese with her parents, although they have recently told me that as of late, her amount of English spoken at home has increased.

This project studying the development of her English began in February of 1973, but it yielded so little data as to be useless. Every week, I visited Uguisu's home in North Cambridge and recorded spontaneous speech of her playing with her friends for lengths varying from one to one and a half hours. The very first visit, Uguisu yielded some 11 utterances. The next week, she produced 3. There is definitely a problem in longitudinal studies of L2 acquisition in that the person interacting with the subject cannot be the mother. Whatever, the following week, pictures were used as stimuli and 27 utterances were extracted, literally speaking. From the end of March until the beginning of April, she was not observed. Then on April 12, her English blossomed. She made 114 multi-word utterances in the span of an hour.

According to her parents, Uguisu, while on a trip, was accompanied by an adult with whom she got along well. Very possibly, it was a matter of confidence rather than competence that she started talking.

From that wonderful spring day in April on, Uguisu indeed was a nightingale turned loose, much to my delight. Speech samples were taken quite randomly, although sticking strictly to the rule that at least two hours of speech be collected every two weeks (save a few exceptions), and from October 1973 on, the sampling was reduced to 2 hours every other sample, and 1-1½ hours in the rest. However, little damage has been done to sample size because her rate of output has increased.

Two important events have happened to Uguisu during the course of this project. First, summer vacation from kindergarten, and especially the "going-away-for-the-summer" syndrome of America, has reduced her amount of exposure to active speech with peers, especially between samples 10 and 11. Second, she enrolled in the first grade of public school in North Cambridge, and whatever effects spelling and other forms of instruction may have had on her language is yet to be determined. To give an example, a recent utterance of hers was "They belong together" referring to two different kinds of goldfish, and one can take a reasonable guess where she might have learnt that from.

A final point to make as far as sampling procedures go is that as of sample 7, the interacter was changed from her peer to adults (frequently myself). This was done because an adult who is conscious of the goals of this project tends not to interrupt Uguisu in the middle of an utterance, which frequently occurred in the case of her peers, much to my irritation.

This section cannot be closed without a few anecdotes on Uguisu's metalinguistic awareness, which seems to be relatively strong, at least as far as asking for information goes:

Raggedy-Ann:	Oh, can I stay for a little bit? I'll just watch. Please, please, please, Uguisu?
Uguisu:	I think we can't. Uh, I think we (can).
RA:	We can or can't?
U:	Can't.
RA:	Cant? Why not?
U:	I mean, we can . . .
RA:	Can I stay?
U:	Yeah.
RA:	Yeah?
U:	If we can't.
RA:	Huh?
U:	How do you call "yes"?
RA:	What?
U:	"Yes we can"?
RA:	Yea, "yes we can".
U:	Yes we can, but . . . you, you have to tell your mother.

On another occasion, she said apologetically to an interacter who was not completely familiar to her: "Well, I call it 'like that' because I don't know do you call this plant."

So such is the status of our little co-operative nightingale; let us now see what she has to say about grammatical morphemes.

METHOD

The morphemes investigated include those studied by Brown (1973) and his associates plus several others which proved frequent enough to yield continuous data. They are summarized in Table 9-1 along with examples of how they could be used.

There are several deviances from Brown's (1973) study worth noting. First, in both the case of the copula and the auxiliary for the present progressive, Brown made a distinction between contractible and uncontractible be. However,

Table 9-1   Morphemes scored and examples of usage

Morpheme	Forms	Examples
Present Progressive	-ing ·	My father is reading a books.
Copula	be, am, is, are	Kenji is bald.
Auxiliary (Prog.)	be, am, is, are	She's eating a money.
*Past Auxiliary	didn't, did	Margie didn't play; Did you?; I did.
Preposition *in*	in	Policeman is hiding in Kenji's shoes.
Preposition *on*	on	Don't sit on bed.
*Preposition *to*	to (directional)	He come back to school.
Possessive	's	My father's teacher.
Plural	-s	My hands is dirty.
Articles	a, the	She's in a house.; Gimme the play-dough.
Past Regular	-ed	The policeman disappeared.
Past Irregular	go-went; come-came	She came back.
3rd Person Reg.	-s	This froggie wants more milk.
3rd Person Irreg.	has, does	She has mother, right?
Gonna-aux	am, is, are	I'm gonna died today.

*Morphemes not scored by Brown (1973).

in the case of Uguisu, she has supplied these morphemes to criterion (+90%) from the earliest samples, and so in this study, that distinction would be pointless. A second deviance is that Brown did not distinguish between the auxiliary for the present progressive and the *going to* (or *gonna*) form used to express the future; I found this distinction necessary since *gonna* did not appear in Uguisu's protocols until sample 4, and she seemed to be using the two quite separately. And finally, Brown mentions that the past form of a verb is used also as a hypothetical, but that this form does not appear in the period which he investigated. Uguisu did use hypotheticals in the context of *if . . . then* statements, and this would mark an obligatory context for the past, but such instances were excluded from the count in order to maintain some degree of comparability between the studies.

The morphemes not investigated by Brown are asterisked in Table 9-1. They are: *to* used to express directionality (mostly with *come* and *go*), and the past auxiliary. The latter should not be confused with the past auxiliary for the progressive, as in "He was dying". Rather, it refers to *didn't* used in negation (*I didn't do that*) and *did* or *didn't* as it appears in questions (*Did you steal my dice?*).

Scoring was done according to the rules set by Brown, Cazden and de Villiers. Morphemes were scored *P* for present in obligatory context, *A* for absent in obligatory context, *OG* for overgeneralization (i.e. *That's she's book* for possessive), and *X* for incorrectly supplied (*These are my left hands*).[1] If there were any doubts about whether the morpheme was obligatory or not, it was omitted from the count. Finally, percentage supplied was calculated for those morphemes for which there were 5 or more obligatory contexts in a sample. Acquisition point is defined as the first of three consecutive two-week samples in which the morpheme is supplied in over 90% of obligatory contexts.

RESULTS AND DISCUSSION

The results of this partial scoring are listed in Table 9-2. But before going any further, one obvious but important point to notice is that, in Uguisu as well as in the L1 learners Adam, Eve and Sarah (Brown, 1973), the acquisition of these grammatical morphemes is not a sudden but a gradual one. Figure 9-1 charts out the development of some of the grammatical morphemes by Uguisu. It is quite striking, say, to take the case of the possessive 's, to see that from sample 2 when the morpheme is being supplied 60% until sample 17 when it starts being reliably supplied (+90%), it is a period of 7½ months. Furthermore, an obligatory morpheme is often supplied in one utterance, and in the next breath, the same utterance is repeated, but this time with that morpheme missing. Why such variability exists, even in an L2 learner, remains to be answered, but the appealing explanation of "limited processing span" necessarily loses some wind, since Uguisu is of an older age than an L1 learner.

Table 9-3 maps out the order of acquisition of these morphemes as defined by our criterion. This order is presented alongside those found by Brown (1973) and deVilliers and deVilliers' (1973) cross-sectional study. But before discussing individual morphemes, several general remarks about the rank ordering are in demand.

From sample 1 on, the -ing progressive, the copula and the auxiliary (be) to the progressive are abundantly present, although for none of these has the full percentages been calculated, and they were tied for first rank. From rank order 9 down (past irregular), the morphemes have not reached criterion as of the writing of this paper. Thus, to come up with an order, I took samples 10, 12, 15 and 17 in which full scores for these morphemes were available and summed up the totals, thereby obtaining percentages for each morpheme. They were as follows:

Past irregular	.72	109/155
Plural	.61	104/171
Articles	.54	306/563
3rd P Regular	.35	11/31
Past Regular	.26	10/39
Gonna-aux	.15	19/127

They were added to the rank order list in that order. And finally, the 3rd Person irregular occurred quite infrequently across the samples, and, consequently, the acquisition point is hard to determine. Thus, it was left out of the rank ordering, although the available data is discussed in the section on third person inflections.

Table 9-2   Results of scoring of grammatical morphemes

MORPHEME		1	2	3	4	5	6	7	8	9	10	11	12	13	14	15	16	17	18	19	20
-ing	%							95		100	91										
	n							19		16	23										
cop	%							91		95	95										
	n							78		125	132										
aux	%							93		92	95										
	n							14		13	22										
in	%		(00)	(00)	—	100	(75)	71	61	100	100	100	95	100	89	100	100	100	86	67	
	n		2	3	—	5	4	21	28	27	13	7	22	23	9	12	18	6	7	9	
to	%				45	73	50	82	75	100	100	100	100	95	100	—	85	—	100	71	
	n				11	26	14	22	12	29	20	6	23	19	5	—	20	—	6	7	
past aux	%					—		100	77	94	100	60	94	96	100						
	n					—		8	13	17	12	15	17	25	11						
on	%			(00)	—	(50)		100	80	57	—	—	(67)	100	—	—	100	—	(100)	(67)	
	n			3	—	4		7	5	7	—	—	3	6	—	—	5	—	3	3	
poss	%		60	35	(100)	63	—	75	—	67	—	—	73	85	88	—	59	96	—	100	
	n		15	20	4	24	—	16	—	9	—	—	15	33	8	—	56	27	—	6	
past irr	%					43		72			67		63			94		75			
	n					28		57			88		30			17		20			
pl	%					20		52			57		64			62		58			
	n					36		33			44		74			29		24			
art	%					36		48			44		45			85		65			
	n					107		122			178		196			89		100			
3rd P Reg	%						33	20	8	9	25	00	17	57	—	(100)	55	50	45	—	
	n						6	5	12	11	16	6	6	7	—	3	11	6	22	—	
past reg	%							0			29		14			0		100*			
	n							6			7		21			6					
gonna aux	%				(67)			(100)		00	00	11	17	6		00		33		46	
	n				3			3		15	12	9	52	63		33		30		28	

(n=number of obligatory contexts; blanks indicate samples not yet scored; – indicates 1 or 0 oblig. context.)

*all routines

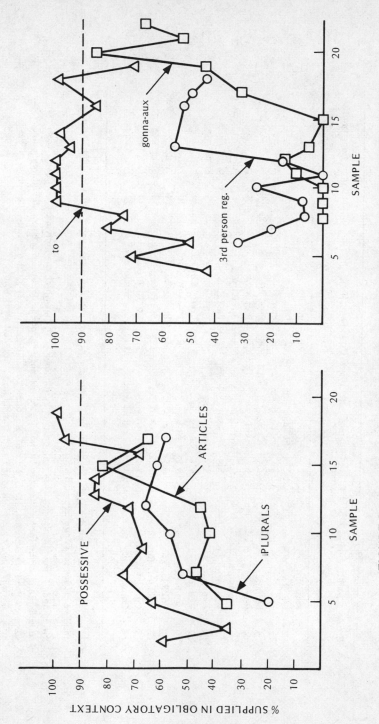

FIGURE 9-1 Acquisition curves for some representative grammatical morphemes

Table 9-3 Order of acquisition found in the various studies of grammatical morphemes compared to the present study

Brown's Longitudinal, 1973[1]		deVilliers and deVilliers' Cross-Sect., 1973[2]				Hakuta's Longitudinal	
Adam, Eve, Sarah		Method I		Method II		Uguisu	
1	Pres. Prog.	2	Pres. Prog.	1	in	2	Pres. Prog.
2.5	on	2	Plural	2	on	2	Copula
2.5	in	2	on	3	Plural	2	Auxiliary
4	Plural	4	in	4	Pres. Prog.	4.5	in
5	Past Irr.	5	Past Irr.	5	Past Irr.	4.5	to
6	Possessive	6	Articles	6	3rd P Irreg.	6	Aux Past (didn't)
7	Uncontr. Cop.	7	Possessive	7	Past Reg.	7	on
8	Articles	8.5	3rd P Irreg.	8	Articles	8	Possessive
9	Past Reg.	8.5	Contr. Cop.	9.	Contr. Cop.	9	Past Irr.
10	3rd P Reg.	10.5	Past Reg.	10	Uncontr. Cop.	10	Plural
11	3rd P Irreg.	10.5	3rd P. Reg.	11	Possessive	11	Articles
12	Uncontr. Aux.	12	Uncontr. Cop.	12	3rd P Reg.	12	3rd P Reg.
13	Contr. Cop.	13	Contr. Aux.	13	Contr. Aux.	13	Past Reg.
14	Contr. Aux.	14	Uncontr. Aux.	14	Uncontr. Aux.	14	Gonna-aux

[1]This is an average rank order; the Spearman rank order coefficients between Adam and Sarah was +0.88, Adam and Eve +0.86, Sarah and Eve +0.87.

[2]In Method I, the morphemes were rank ordered by the lowest MLU at which the individual morpheme was supplied to criterion (n=5, +90%); in Method II, the percentages for each morpheme across all children were summed and then averaged. The Spearman rank order correlations between Brown's study and Method I was +0.84, Brown's study and Method II +0.78, and Method I and Method II +0.87.

Now we are ready to review the nature and behavior of these individual morphemes.

The copula and the auxiliary

When Uguisu says "All the policeman is ghost" or "My hands is sticky", she is lacking number agreement between the subject noun phrase and the *be* verb. I have looked at all utterances in the data which have plural noun phrase subjects with either the copula or the auxiliary, and only .06 (n=4/62) had the proper allomorph of *be*. This is in marked contrast to the copula and auxiliary with the plural demonstrative pronoun *these*, in which case .97 (n=50/52) of the verb *be* agrees with their plural subject. In fact, the two exceptions were the same utterance "What's these?", which means that *are* always followed *these* (when used as a pronoun). Furthermore, in 25 other instances, Uguisu has used *these* to indicate singular referents, but in all instances supplied *are*. The evidence becomes stronger when one looks at examples in which *these* was used as a demonstrative adjective:

M3404	These two girl is good girl.
M3409	These girl is sisters.
R1103	Why these are dirty?
R1104	Why these floor is dirty?
S4508	These card is the policeman.

This suggests strongly that (1) *these are* is, if not a segmentation error since she does use *these* in isolation, two words which have a high probability of occurrences together; and (2) number agreement is practically non-existent (6%) in all other cases. This result is rather surprising, since (1) Uguisu is supplying the copula and auxiliary up to criterion for acquisition (in scoring, cases where *is* was supplied when *are* was required were omitted from the count, since it is not exactly an error of "omitted in obligatory context"); and (2) one of the essential "ingredients" in Brown's (1973) description of the semantics of copulas and auxiliary was "number." It seems like our clever little five-year-old subject has found a way to use these two grammatical morphemes without incorporating the notion of number. With this evidence in mind, we cannot say that she has "full control" of the copula and auxiliary, but we can say that she has "full control without number agreement."

The past tense: regular, irregular and auxiliary

It is surprising to find the regular past towards the very bottom of the rank ordering list. The irregular past is not much further ahead. Then why is it the case that the past auxiliary has been supplied with significant frequency from the earliest samples? There are at least 3 possible explanations, not mutually exclusive: (1) most verbs used by Uguisu, and most children, are irregular, and by definition of the word are not rule-governed; (2) phonologically, the infrequent regular past forms end with a stop, and Japanese does not have words ending with such; and

(3) the past auxiliary form is highly regular. In fact, the two dips in performance in samples 8 and 11 are entirely due to the following utterances:

N3306	Do you saw this rabbit run away?
N4302	What do you do?
O2512	Do you saw three feet?
S0113	Do you bought this too?
S0114	Do you bought this too?
S0204	How do you put?
S0205	Do you put it?

They are all questions, and the other form (in which *didn't* is used for negation), looking at the infrequent occurrences in samples 4, 5 and 6, has always been supplied in obligatory contexts. This, I think, is an important piece of evidence for what we shall discuss later called the *simplicity principle*.

The prepositions: in, on and to

For *in* and *to*, the acquisition points are clear. For *on*, not so clear, perhaps because we have less data.

There is one crucial point to be made concerning obligatory and non-obligatory *in*s. In English, location need not always be expressed by a grammatical morpheme. In these cases, we can say that prepositions are optional. That is, we can either say "The book is there" or "The book is in there" while pointing to a book in an open drawer. Uguisu has used *in* 78 times in these optional cases (I have not yet tabulated non-occurrences of these optional cases), and in 43 cases, they were quite obviously not "contained" in any sense of the word, ie. wrong.[2] In the remaining 35 instances, many were of a doubtful category where the context did not make things too clear.

It is tempting to argue a case for some form of semantic interference from Japanese. Japanese marks locatives by a postposed particle *-ni*, whether containment, support, or simple location is intended. Containment/support is distinguished by saying *cup-inside-ni* (in the cup) or *table-top-ni* (on the table), and we say *point-here-ni* (the point is here), marking it with *-ni* as well. This is decently strong evidence, it seems, for interference.

What of the cases in which prepositions were obligatory? It seems that whenever some preposition other than *in* or *on* was required, *in* substituted (*at* appears occasionally). In 12 instances, *in* invaded the rightful obligatory context of *on*. The misuses of *in* are listed in Table 9-4. Other than *on*, *in* has taken the place of *at*, *out*, *off* and *around*. Could this be the result of interference? Perhaps, but also playing an important role might be the limited lexicon of a child wanting to express more than her linguistic capacities permit.

The possessive and the plural

Little can be said here simply because I have not yet in detail looked at the plural noun inflection, but of the data available, there is one thing to notice: that

Table 9-4   Misuses of the preposition *in* when other prepositions were obligatory

I0306	All children in it this. (?)
R4409	Just seaweed in it this. (around)
R4410	seaweed in here. (around)
N2301	What do you want, put in a salad? (on)
R2709	I saw in a window. (from)
R3315	Put it in here. (bandaid on finger)
S3403	Is she in a floor? (on)
S3404	Is she in a chair? (on)
S3407	(Then) she . . . in . . . ina . . . in that door? (behind)
U2403	You can eat in here. (on table)
U2404	You can eat in here. (on table)
U2909	In this car I just bumped. (instrumental)
U3304	We was waiting in your door. (at)
U3305	She's waiting in your door. (at)
U3309	The policelady was jumping off in a train. (of, from)
U3312	I just jump off in a train. (of, from)
U3404	I'm in here. (out)
U3708	She was waiting . . . in your door. (at)
U5007	She's in a moon. (on)
U5008	She didn't in a moon. (on)
V1009	She's (in) waiting in your door. (at)
V1711	Make believe (there's) some door in it, okay? (?)
V2516	In here. (on)
V3402	I gonna put it in there. (on)
W2117	Can I sit down in your bed? (on)
W3017	We gonna color it in floor. (on)
X1602	In out. (?)
D'27—	Try in night. (at)
D'27—	Try in night. (at)
D'44—	You tell what I said in . . . in a board. (on)

performance is poor on plurals despite the fact that plurals and possessives are homophonous. We cannot attribute any of our results to phonological difficulties, and furthermore, they are both noun inflections. In the English-speaking child (L1), the plural seems to appear before the possessive (Brown, 1973, deVilliers and deVilliers, 1973). Then why is this reversed in Uguisu? Perhaps because the notion of plurality (number) does not exist in the Japanese grammar, whereas possession is expressed by a postponed particle *-no*, and the word order is the same as in English.

Overgeneralization of the possessive *'s* to pronouns is quite frequent. Examples include *you's, she's, he's,* and *that's.* In Japanese, pronouns are inflected for possession, but English L1 children also have overgeneralizations (ie. mines, hims; Brown, 1973, p. 326). This is an ambiguous case between overgeneralization and interference.

Articles: a and the

Articles express the semantic notions of definite/non-definite, and no such exist in Japanese. Obviously, when Japanese want to express definiteness we can resort to "this" or "that", but there is no device which consistently expresses the distinction for every noun. This may account for its low status in the acquisition order.

The third person

Since these grammatical morphemes all occur with third person singular subjects, it is expected that number should once again come to play a role. Looking at the data for the third person irregular from sample 8 on, at which point it becomes rather frequent, out of the 47 instances in which *has* was supplied, .81 (n=38) had either the subject pronoun *she* or *he*. Then could it not be the case that *she has* and *he has* were both learnt as routines, or at least that this consistency has made it easier for Uguisu to acquire? After all, only one verb is concerned, as opposed to the regular form, which involves all other indicative verbs. The latter, as can be seen in Table 9-2, is hovering at about 50%. The crucial evidence may hinge on how long it takes Uguisu to attain criterion in the regular form, which seems to come relatively soon after the irregular form in L1.

Some hypotheses about the determinants of the order of acquisition

We have taken a quick tour of the morphemes involved, and now, what can be said about the determinants behind this order of acquisition? We have several candidates, non-mutually exclusive. First is the presence/nonpresence of that semantic notion expressed in our morphemes in the Japanese grammar. We have seen that number and definite/nondefinite are not expressed in Japanese. Table 9-5 lists all the morphemes dealt with, along with the semantic notions described by Brown (1973, p. 369) plus one of my own (*to*: direction), and indications of whether that notion(s) is expressed in Japanese or not. As seen earlier, the copula and the auxiliary come without number agreement, and therefore "number" has been deleted.

We can make predictions based on the assumption that a morpheme containing a new semantic notion (ie. number, definite/nondefinite) will be acquired later than a morpheme expressing an already-existent notion. Thus the predictions in Table 9-6, with indications of confirmed/disconfirmed. As it turns out, only 3 predictions are disconfirmed, yet this cannot be the only explanation.[3]

Our second candidate for determinant is what Lee Williams (personal communication) has coined the *simplicity principle.* This is similar to one of Slobin's (1973) principles, "Avoid exceptions" and, in a more general sense, what I concluded as a principle "Use whatever you can, but try to make it orderly" in a detailed analysis of samples 1-3 (Hakuta, 1973). What evidence is there that

Table 9-5 Presence/Nonpresence of semantic notions expressed in the grammatical morphemes in Japanese

MORPHEME	SEMANTIC NOTION	PRESENT/ (+) NOT PRESENT (−) IN JAPANESE
-ing	temporary duration	+
copula (w/o number)	earlierness	+
auxiliary (w/o number)	temp. dur., earlierness	+ +
in	containment (location)	+
on	support (location)	+
to	direction	+
aux past	earlierness	+
regular past	earlierness	+
irregular past	earlierness	+
possessive	possession	+
3rd person regular	number, earlierness?	− +
plural	number	−
articles	definite/nondefinite	−

(Based on Brown, 1973)

Table 9-6 Predictions for acquisition order based on semantic presense/non-presence in Japanese

ing	<	3rd p reg	+	to	<	3rd p reg	+
ing	<	plural	+	to	<	plural	+
ing	<	articles	+	to	<	articles	+
cop	<	3rd p reg	+	aux past	<	3rd p reg	+
cop	<	plural	+	aux past	<	plural	+
cop	<	articles	+	aux past	<	articles	+
aux	<	3rd p reg	+	reg past	<	3rd p reg	−
aux	<	plural	+	reg past	<	plural	+
aux	<	articles	+	reg past	<	articles	−
in	<	3rd p reg	+	irreg past	<	3rd p reg	+
in	<	plural	+	irreg past	<	plural	+
in	<	articles	+	irreg past	<	articles	+
on	<	3rd p reg	+	poss	<	3rd p reg	+
on	<	plural	+	poss	<	plural	+
on	<	articles	+	poss	<	articles	+

+ = prediction confirmed   result: 27 confirmed
− = prediction disconfirmed   3 disconfirmed

NOTATION: X < Y means that X will be acquired before Y, the justification being that the semantic notion expressed in morpheme X is also expressed in Japanese, whereas the semantic notion expressed in morpheme Y is not expressed in Japanese.

such a principle exists? As noted earlier in the section on the past tense, the highly regular form of the past auxiliary was acquired quite early, especially relative to the irregular form as well as the infrequent regular form. The simplicity principle can also account quite nicely for the early "acquisition" of the copula and auxiliary, since if number agreement is left out, it works out to a simple system which can be described by the following context-sensitive rules:

be---am/I _____
    are/you, we, they, these _____
    is/he, she, it, this, that, NP _____

or, more concisely, the strategy: IF IT'S NOT *I, YOU, WE, THEY,* OR *THESE,* USE *IS.* Finally, this principle can also account for the relatively early emergence of the third person irregular. And outside of these grammatical morphemes, and this occurs in L1 English as well, there is a strong tendency to pick up regular patterns and use them with a great deal of frequency (e.g. hafta).

    The third candidate for determinants is phonological interference, and the one evidence to date (mostly due to my ignorance in phonology) is the past regular which, as mentioned earlier, would provide certain difficulties to a native Japanese speaker.

CONCLUDING REMARKS

We have looked at the development of grammatical morphemes and tried to hypothesize some determinants of acquisition order. Three possibilities have been discussed: (1) semantic differences between L1 and L2, (2) the simplicity principle, and (3) phonological differences.

    In looking at the data, we must strongly bear in mind that not only are grammatical morphemes one of the many observable aspects of language, it is only one child that has been observed. It would be fruitful to see what the order is in other children as well as adults learning a second language, particularly in those coming from native languages which contain the notions of number and definite/nondefiniteness. More pointedly, is the acquisition order we have seen the result of simply an older child learning a language, or is it the result of the influences of the native language, or is it the result of the interaction of both? The answer would lie in looking at other children as well as the countless other aspects of Uguisu's golden words.

Notes

    1. This last category X is important especially in second language learning, I think, because we would expect more rote memorization as well as segmentation errors to occur. Unfortunately, the figures in this category are not in at the time of this writing, but to give an illustration of what could occur, I have looked at the pluralization of the demonstrative adjectives and pronouns *this/that* and *these/those* in all samples. 68% (n=153/226) were

correctly supplied in obligatory contexts across all samples, but among all instances of *these/those*, only 75% (n=153/202) were correctly used in a plural context. In other words, *these/those* was used with singular referents in 49 instances. This method will be reported in detail in a forthcoming paper.

2. Example: "He was in outside."

3. Merrill Swain has rightfully pointed out to me at the conference that one could very well argue the reverse; that is, the child will pay more attention to those morphemes which express notions *not* present in his/her L1.

10

Two Norwegian Children's Acquisition of English Syntax

Roar Ravem, *University College for Teachers, Norway*

INTRODUCTION

The following brief paper gives us a look at some of the findings of Ravem's study of his two children. The major issue discussed is, again, the L1 = L2 hypothesis vs. contrastive analysis.

For a more detailed discussion of the acquisition of negatives and question forms in English by his two Norwegian speakers, the reader will want to turn to Ravem's dissertation and to the articles in *IRAL* on these children.

One of the interesting issues that can be asked about the data on Reidun is whether forgetting occurs in reverse pattern to acquisition; that is, is 'last learned, first forgotten'? During the early data collection sessions, Reidun did not respond to WHY questions appropriately:

Rune: Why do you put the telephone on the front seat?
Reidun: Yes. (4;1)

When she did acquire the WHY question (around 4;3), the WHY appeared preposed but there was no inversion: *Why that man have got it?* (4;3) *Why you can't eat it?* (4;4). In the following two months, the number of inversions gradually increased. Since Ravem used translations in collecting some of the data, pairs for the eighth and ninth month of observation can be compared:

Why Toto is in his room? (8)
Why is Toto up his room? (9)

Why we don't go to Norway? (8)
Why don't we go in Norway? (9)

When the family did return to Norway, Ravem comments on the regression in question formation for Rune, the older child. His "Why don't you like ice cream?" reverted once again to "Why you don't like ice cream?" That is, perhaps the process of forgetting is the opposite of the learning process, a suggestion which deserves further investigation.

The forgetting phenomenon is mentioned in many studies. Stern & Stern mention a child of German parents born in Sumatra and brought up speaking Malay until age three. He then learned German and when the family returned to Germany, he spoke only German. Within five months he could not understand when Malay was spoken to him. Huang's subject, Paul, who returned to Taiwan with his grandmother immediately after the observational study, had, according to his mother totally forgotten his English when she visited him a few months later. Leopold mentions that at the end of four weeks in Germany, Hildegard had great difficulty in responding to English. She complained about English being spoken to her and said she could not understand (though this was not true). Itoh, visiting her subject, Takahiro, in Japan one month after he left the United States, reports that while he still understood her English questions, he would respond only in Japanese. Tits studied a Spanish child adopted into a Belgium family and schooled in French. She acquired French in school for ten months. After three months at school, she declared she no longer knew Spanish. From all these accounts, it seems that the forgetting rate for the young child may be as fast or faster than the learning rate. Perhaps as much can be discovered about language acquisition from careful 'forgetting' studies as can be learned from acquisition studies.

The following is a summary of the studies of my son, Rune's, and my daughter, Reidun's, acquisition of English as a second language in a naturalistic setting in Great Britain. The studies have been longitudinal-observational and based on tape-recorded interviews and various informal experiments, mainly translation and imitation tasks. They have been conceived within the framework of such first language syntax studies as have been carried out by Roger Brown and his colleagues, particularly by Ursula Bellugi. The structures chosen for special scrutiny have been negatives and interrogatives. In the case of Reidun some atten-tion has also been paid to the development of the auxiliary constituents: modal, progressive, past and perfective.

Rune was 6½ years old when the study began and had a rudimentary knowledge of English from an earlier stay in England. Reidun was 3 years, 9 months old and had no previous knowledge of English. The two studies were undertaken at different times. The study of Rune started in 1966 and lasted for five months. The study of Reidun began in 1968 and lasted for seventeen months with a total of 86, for the most part weekly, recordings, each of approximately forty-five minutes duration. Fifty-four of these, covering the first 10 months of her exposure to English, have been analyzed. In the case of Rune the recording sessions were about twice as long, but undertaken at three to four week intervals.

Both first and second language acquisition in a naturalistic setting have in common that language is acquired in a natural exposure situation. This makes possible a comparison between first and second language acquisition with regard to the product of language acquisition and raises the question whether first and second language learners go through similar developmental stages and make similar syntactic errors. If they do, this would be evidence that similar strategies are employed by L1 and L2 learners. If they do not, this would indicate that L2 acquisition is a different process.

Dulay and Burt (1972) offer two contrasting hypotheses, which make different predictions and which derive from different theoretical assumptions. They are: 1) the contrastive analysis (CA) hypothesis, which rests on the assumption that language learning is habit formation and which predicts interference from first language structures in the learner's second language speech, and 2) the L1 = L2 hypothesis, which predicts that the L2 learner will use the same strategies as the L1 learner and make the same type of transitional errors, e.g., omissions of inflections and minor word classes and overgeneralizations.

With the two hypotheses in mind we can make specific predictions about transitional negative and interrogative structures in the speech of my informants. Of particular interest are those sentences that are transformationally different in English and Norwegian; that is, those sentences that require *do*-support in English, but take a finite main verb in Norwegian.

The CA hypothesis would predict transitional structures of the form *NP MV not NP* and *NP MV Pron not* in sentences such as *He like not the house* and *He like it not*, whereas the L1 = L2 hypothesis would predict sentences of the following form:

$$\text{NP} \left\{ \begin{array}{c} \text{not} \\ \text{don't} \end{array} \right\} \text{MV} \quad \text{NP}$$

(where *don't* is acquired later than *not*, but first as a variant realization of NEG and not as a result of a *do*-transformation). It would yield sentences like *He not like the house* or *He don't like it*. It was this latter prediction that was supported, and my informants' development seems quite closely to have paralleled that of the L1 learner for negatives. In the corpus I have found only one example of a post-verbal *not*. The remaining examples are all of the L1 type: e.g., *I not build the house, I not like it, . . . and you not get off the car, Yes, for you not do it naar* (when) *you going to sleep, I not know it more—I don't know it more, I not know what is edge paa* (in) *Norwegian.*

Nor was the development of *wh*-questions traceable to Norwegian. In sentences requiring *do*-support in English, Norwegian makes use of a finite main verb inverted with the subject noun phrase. The surface structure of these Norwegian *wh*-questions is *WH MV NP?* and of English sentences *WH do NP MV?*

Table 10-1   *Wh*-questions from Rune, times 1-4

Time 1	What is that?
	What are mean? (= what does 'mean' mean)
	What you eating?
	What she is doing?
	Where dem drink?
	Why you say that before? (for)
Time 2	What Jane give him?
(2 weeks later)	Rannveig, what dyou* doing to-yesterday on school?
	What you like?
Time 3	What he's doing?
(3-4 weeks later)	What is he doing?
	What you did in Rothbury?
	What dyou did to-yesterday in the hayshed?
	When dyou went there?
	Why he come for a cup of coffee?
	Why dyou must have table—and chairs?
	Why drink we tea and coffee?
Time 4	What did you more that night?
(3 weeks later)	What did you talk to them?
	What did you do to-yesterday?

dyou was possibly a variant of *you*.

In L1 children's transitional sentences *do* is omitted. An interference hypothesis
would predict sentences like *Where live Tom?*, whereas a prediction based on L1
children's transitional structures would yield *Where Tom live?* Again, there is a
parallel development in my informants' and L1 children's *wh*-sentences. There
are only a few isolated examples of interference from Norwegian. The same lack
of inversion is found also in copular and auxiliary verb sentences, but not
consistently. Tables 10-1 and 10-2 give representative excerpts from Reidun and
Rune.

In *yes/no*-questions Reidun and Rune chose two different strategies. Rune
typically chose inversion of the main verb and the subject noun phrase, in keeping
with Norwegian usage, and produced such sentences as *Know you?, Climb you,
Like you school, Rannveig?* An occasional example of this pattern is found also
in Reidun's speech, but she typically chose a declarative sentence structure with
rising intonation, as do L1 learners. For a long period of time, her favorite
question form was the tag question and only as late as in the eighth month of
exposure to English did she use *do*. The first attested examples were (8:0) *Do you
can—curl it round?* and (8:2) *Does him eat my finger?* From then on, *do* was used
both in *yes/no* questions, tag-questions and elliptical sentences, but not yet in
affirmative *wh*-questions; e.g., (9:0) *When you go to bed?* In negative *wh*-questions
don't was used, probably as an unsegmented negative particle.

Table 10-2   *Wh-*questions from Reidun

Time of Exposure in Months: Weeks	Examples
3:1	What this?
4:4	Whats that?*
5:3	Whats her doing?
	Whats er her doing? (er = is/are)
6:0	What that is?
6:2	Why that man have that on?
	Why uh him have got like that? (a jacket like that)
	Why her don't stand there?
	Whos that?*
	Whos that is?
8:0	Why you can't buy like that shoes?
	Who is that?
	Why him have got a motor?
	Why you can't—why you couldn't take it here? (bring it)
9:3	What are he doing now, then—that man?
	Why isn't that lady in there?
	Why can't you touch with your—with your hand?
	Which color have we got, then?

*whats and *whos* were unsegmented question words.

A further example of a structure which is neither found in the source language nor in the target language and is thus a creation by the child itself is Reidun's use of *do* in affirmative sentences. Starting in the eighth month of exposure to English, *did* + MV became for a period Reidun's favorite means of expressing past tense. She had not yet discovered the regular past tense form, but she did use the past tense of verbs for which she knew the past tense. From then on, the use of *did* became an alternative in these cases, and we even find examples of double specification of past tense.

Examples:
I did bit it. (Why did you bite it?) *'Cause I did want-to. Catherine did make that. My mummy did make lunch for them. I did shut that careful. We did saw that in the shop.*

In all these cases the *did* is weakly stressed, so we are not concerned with an emphatic form. The most likely explanation is that we have a case of overgeneralization in her use of double-marked forms. This spread also to *wh-*questions where the question word functioned as the subject, as in *Whos did drive to Colchester?*

Most of the examples given so far support the notion that the learners "actively organize the L2 speech they hear and make generalizations about its structure as children learning their first language do" (Dulay & Burt, 1972, 236).

The fact that a contrastive analysis explains the occurrence of inversion in *yes/no*-questions in Rune's speech as a case of transfer need not, in my view, destroy this theoretical position, but allowance should be made for the active use of L1 knowledge in the acquisition of a second language. The more closely two languages are related, the more there is which can successfully be transferred. There is much in the development of my informants' English which must be viewed as transfer, in the sense of an active use of L1 knowledge. After an early stage, when the language used was more Norwegian (but with English intonation) than English, Reidun's language became gradually more English. Although she did omit inflections and minor word classes as do first language learners, her English could hardly be characterized as "telegraphese," first and foremost because she could transfer both content words and functors from Norwegian. As an example, the modal auxiliaries were taken over from Norwegian and given a slightly anglicized form. The following are examples of sentences which contain modal auxiliaries and which sounded much more English than they look:

> *Du kan fa play with this one.* (You can get (i.e. permission) to . . .)
> *Du skal have this one.* (You shall)
> *Du kan have this one.*
> *Kan du come i morgen?* (Can you come tomorrow?)
> *She maa lie there.* (must)
> *Vil du have coffee?* (Will you)

The more similar the linguistic means of expressing semantic notions are in the mother tongue and the target language, the more directly the learner's L1 competence will facilitate the acquisition of L2. It is possible, then, that the less related two languages are and the fewer features of the mother tongue can be transferred to the target language, the more telegraphic the learner's early speech will be. It is further likely that both age and personality factors are important variables. The young second language learner does not seem to have the same awareness of the two languages being different as has the more mature learner. Reidun gave no indication that she was really conscious of the fact that her Norwegian-English was not English. She would even, in the beginning, give back the same Norwegian sentence, when asked to say it in English, by a change of intonation and pronunciation only. What she was conscious of was the message to be communicated; the means of expression was subordinated and intuitively governed. Butterworth (1972, 72) says about his adolescent Spanish-speaking informant, Ricardo, that "If he can be said to use any regular strategies at all, it is that he transferred syntax from Spanish and simplified all kinds of other forms. This left him with 'telegraphic' English speech in Spanish syntax." A survey of the data supplied by Butterworth shows that Ricardo made much less use of mother tongue lexical items in his speech than Reidun did and that the general character of his speech was a purer telegraphese. Ricardo was no doubt more conscious of the lexical differences between the two languages than the more subtle syntactic differences.

Although my findings show that the L2 learner does make use of his L1 competence in the acquisition of a foreign language, they also show that a transitional error cannot always be predicted on the basis of a contrastive analysis. That transfer occurs does not imply that we have to accept that language learning is habit formation, with everything that entails. We can still adopt an "active mental organization theory" and view transfer as the learner's active use of his L1 competence—as one of the learner's "processing strategies."

Comparative Studies

11 in Second Language Learning

Judy Wagner-Gough, *University of California, Los Angeles*

INTRODUCTION

Gough presents here part of her analysis of the acquisition of English by the Persian child, Homer. Homer arrived in the States in January, 1973. At the beginning of the study, when Homer was 5; 11, he spoke both Persian and Assyrian, a Semitic language. Assiryian was his native language and the language spoken in his home in Los Angeles. While he had learned Persian from his playmates in Iran, by April he claimed he did not understand questions asked him in that language. Homer was enrolled in a nursery school in mid-January and he attended the morning sessions for three hours each weekday. In addition, data were collected at his home as he played with an American child, Mark.

One of the characteristics of Homer's speech was fluent, if incomprehensible, monologues. Some of his favorite words in these monologues were *do, something,* and *because.* While much of his speech was not understood by adults, Homer's best friend, five-year-old Mark, stated with confidence that he was able to understand *everything* Homer said. Mark frequently 'translated' Homer's speech and at times even patterned his speech after Homer's. One of Homer's favorite expressions was "* my something + NP". Using this expression, Mark, the

American child, planned the morning's next activity—to play with the water hose and Fred's ball:

Mark: I my something this one.
Homer: Come on. On my something.
Mark: Water.
Homer: Yeah.
Mark: Yeah.
Homer: Yeah.
Mark: My something ball.
Homer: Ball.
Mark: Ball əz Fred. (Again, one of Homer's patterns for possessive.)

Unfortunately, the reverse was not true; Homer did not understand everything Mark said. For example, while playing with blocks, Mark demanded that Homer stop building the towers so tall. Homer asked for the meaning of 'so tall' which he pronounced 'sulta.' Rather than explain, Mark simply repeated his command:

Mark: Quit making it so tall!
Homer: What is this sulta! (angry voice)
         What is this sulta!
Mark: Don't make it so tall.
Homer: (whispering to himself) What is this sulta?
         (Then, in Assiryian: I ask what sulta is. He says sulta is something. I
         say there's no such thing as sulta.)

Gough's paper is extremely important because she insists on the need to look at both form and function when asserting the child has 'acquired' a structure in his new language. It has previously been assumed that acquisition of form means acquisition of function and that the concept of the function precedes acquisition of form. The data from several studies suggest this may not always be true. Gough's findings force us to look again at the data on language acquisition, both first and second language papers. Some of our assumptions about the relationship of the acquisition of form and function may be in need of revision.

Reprinted with the permission of the author and ERIC Clearinghouse on Languages and Linguistics, Center for Applied Linguistics, Arlington, Virginia from a portion of *Comparative Studies in Second Language Learning,* CAL-ERIC/CLL Series on Languages and Linguistics, Number 26, June, 1975.

* * *

The order in which English morphemes are acquired has been a subject of much recent discussion and research. Brown (1973) pioneered rank-order studies with his analysis of data from Adam, Eve, and Sarah. Of the 14 grammatical morphemes he examined, the progressive was the first acquired by the three children. Researchers in second language learning have recorded similar findings. Hakuta (1974) has found this his subject, a Japanese child learning English, also acquired the progressive before any other grammatical morpheme.

In her study of ten Spanish children learning English, Adams (1973) noted that the progressive was the first marker of aspect to be learned. Using the Bilingual Syntax Measure with 115 subjects whose native language was either Spanish or Chinese, Dulay and Burt (1974) found that the English progressive was learned early and that it, too, was the first overt marker of aspect. What these studies suggest is that regardless of previous language experience, the progressive is one of the first morphemes to emerge in the speech of children learning English and is the first marker of aspect acquired.

Form of the progressive

The progressive does not usually appear in speech as a fully marked form. Many children initially affix -ing to the verb stem but omit the required be-AUX (Brown, 1973; Adams, 1973).

Some children, however, produce what appear to be progressive constructions that have the AUX, but not the -ing affixed to the verb. In Sarah's data, for example, there were nine sentences with *I'm + verb* such as *I'm play with it.* Cazden (1968) called these forms "reduced catenatives" and suggested they be interpreted as conveying intention, such as *I'm going to play with it.* Adams (1973) also found similar constructions in the speech of second language learners. She noted that one of her subjects omitted *be* before *going to + verb,* and, like Cazden, she suggested that these constructions were "reduced catenatives."

Function of the progressive

While rank order studies have provided us with important data on the relative sequence in which morphemes are acquired, there has been little discussion about the function that the progressive serves in a child's speech. In other words, the relationship of form and function in the emerging progressive has not been explicitly defined.

Two explanations may be offered to account for the widespread interest in form relative to the lack of reference to function. The first is that subjects in the recorded studies may have initially produced the progressive in order to add form to a developed semantic notion. If this were the case, the only variable requiring analysis in the data would be (as it has been) the syntactic form of the developing progressive. Secondly, it is possible that we have falsely assumed function to be a precursor of form, so that the semantic role of the progressive in the learner's speech has remained improperly unanalyzed from the onset of its production.

For determining acquisition of a form, Brown's notion of obligatory contexts is widely used; that is, a form must be produced over a two-week period in 90 percent of the contexts in which it is clearly required. Since Brown's model is constructed to measure the relative sequence in the acquisition of morphemic forms, his production criterion of 90 percent is not suitable for an analysis of the process by which function is learned. For a study of function, we should develop a model that uses a different criterion.

This chapter proposes a criterion for a functional analysis of the progressive as it emerged in the speech of one subject, Homer. All progressives were analyzed in the data, whether or not they were accurately produced in appropriate contexts. In other words, the progressive was analyzed in terms of the function it performed in Homer's speech and not judged for appropriateness in form or function. While meaning was being evaluated, three questions were asked:

1. Is there evidence to suggest that the progressive form emerges as a marker of tense or aspect?
2. Is there evidence to suggest that it occurs in semantic contrast with any other tense in the child's speech?
3. Is there evidence to suggest that it emerges as a new form whose adult function is clear to the child?

A simple report of Homer's progressive verb form as it emerged in his speech does not distinguish it from that of other language learners. As with the children studied by Dulay and Burt, Adams, and Brown, Homer's speech production showed early and pervasive use of the progressive morpheme. Its form was also similar to that used by other children: sometimes the AUX was deleted and only the *-ing* was attached to the verb; sometimes a pronoun with a contracted *be* was produced, followed by *V-ing*. While the frequency of the progressive in his speech steadily increased, at no point did Homer achieve a 90 percent accuracy level for this form during the five-month observation period.

More interesting than an analysis of form is an analysis of the function the progressive served in Homer's speech. Homer used the progressive with reference to present, past, and future time periods. The progressive did not occur in semantic contrast with any other tense in his speech, and, furthermore, it did not seem to emerge as a form whose adult function was clear to him.

In Table 11-1, it is clear that Homer used the progressive with reference to four different time periods: 1) immediate (going to) intentions; 2) intentions of a more distant future, such as tomorrow, next week or sometime; 3) the past; and 4) activity actually occurring at the moment of speech (process-state activity). In addition to these four temporal references, Homer's progressive functioned 5) on occasion as an imperative. Although situations (1), (2), and (4) are cases in which an adult speaker could also use the progressive, we can not assume that Homer's use of this form was in any way related to tense or to aspect, as situations (3) and (5) are ungrammatical in adult speech.

Because the progressive referred to all of these time periods, we can conclude that it did not function as a marker of tense or aspect in Homer's speech. In addition, there is no evidence to suggest that the progressive form occurred in semantic contrast with any other tense form. This statement is further supported by Homer's production of verb stems referring to the same time periods listed in Table 11-1: 1) an immediate intention; 2) a non-immediate future; 3) the past; 4) the progressive and 5) the imperative. Table 11-2 will provide examples of these forms.

Table 11-1

Our criterion for labeling the progressive will be the presence of *-ing* affixed to the verb.

1) *Immediate Intention*

4/23 I my coming. [=I'm going to come to you.]
5/4 I'm going in to all bees inside. [=I'm going to (go to) all bees inside.] (All bees inside meant the classroom. When the teacher wanted them to come in, she would call, "All bees inside.")
5/10 I'm going and found them. [=I'm going to find them or I'm going to go and find them.]
5/11 I'm taking 'nother one. [=I'm going to take another one.]

2) *Intentions of the Distant Future*

4/23 I my tomorrow going /in/ beach. [=I'm going (to go) to the beach tomorrow.] (/In/ had no recognizable semantic function. It may have been a repeated segment from "going" and therefore a double nasal.
4/23 I my dad and then going /in/ beach and then airplane and water like that, like that. See, going /in/ water and then swish and then going /in/ water. [=Dad and I are going (to go) to the beach (tomorrow). The airplane will go in the water (tomorrow).] or [=We're going to throw the airplane in the water (tomorrow).]
5/11 I'm going /in/ give it to Mark. [=I'm going to give it to Mark (sometime).]

3) *Past*

5/10 Mark and Fred going /in/ outside. [=Mark and Fred went outside.]
5/10 I'm playing with that Mark. [=Mark was playing with that.]

4) *Process-State (Progressive)*

4/22 That's a Misty is going, going in there. [=Misty is going in there (right now).]
5/4 It's a sleeping in there a room. [=It's sleeping in the room in there (right now).]

5) *Imperative*

5/11 O.K. Sitting down like that. [=Sit down like that.]

Table 11-2

1) *Immediate Intention*

4/23 I my go my mother. [=I'm going to ask my mother or I'll ask my mother.]

2) *Distant Future*

4/23 I come my brother. [=My brother will come (tomorrow).]

3) *Past*

6/30 Hippies make it. Give it to me. [=Hippies made it and gave it to me.]

4) *Progressive (Ongoing Activity)*

Misty, Misty go in there with it. [=Misty is going in there with it (now).]

5) *Imperative*

5/11 O.K. Sit down over here. Sit down, Judy.

Table 11-3

1) *Immediate Intentions*

   I my coming. I my go my mother. [=I'm going to come to you. I'm going to (ask) my mother.]

2) *Distant Future*

   I don't know Fred a my going, no go. I don't know coming, go. [=I don't know if Fred is going or isn't going. I don't know if he's coming or going.]

3) *Past Tense*

   I'm find it. Bobbie found one to me. [=I found it. Bobbie found it for me.]

4) *Progressive*

   Misty, Misty go in there. Hey Judy, Misty going in there. [=Misty is going in there. Hey Judy, Misty is going in there.]

5) *Imperative*

   O.K. Sit down over here. Sitting down like that. [=Sit down over here. Sit down like that.]

There is nothing in the data to suggest that Homer perceived the relationship between the adult form and its function or selected one verb form over another in an attempt to mark tense. Homer's patterns occurred in semantic free variation, indicating that he had not yet learned the semantic parameters of form. *Going, go, I'm go, I going,* and *I go* functioned as a single semantic unit, meaning movement from one place to another—now, yesterday, or tomorrow.

Table 11-3 provides further evidence supporting the theory of free variation. It contains examples where two different forms of the same verb referred to identical time periods in Homer's speech. All of these utterances were produced either in succession or in very close proximity in Homer's speech.

To summarize what has been proposed so far, syntactically, Homer's progressive developed in a manner similar to that of other children in first and second language studies. Semantically, however, it was not a predictable marker of tense or aspect. It did not contrast with any other tense in his speech, and there is no reason to believe that Homer had analyzed its true function in adult grammar.

Reasons for the progressive's emergence

Speculations on the cause of the early appearance of the progressive in Homer's speech produce interesting explanations of the process of language learning. We could say that Homer was actually testing different verb forms to discover tense limits. However, this explanation is weak in view of the fact that Homer did not use any other time markers in his speech—adverbs or verb affixes—when the progressive emerged. Furthermore, the progressive emerged long before he was asking wh-time questions or responding to those asked of him. The entire concept of time appeared to be unimportant while he was beginning to gather and sort through language data. One might also suggest that Homer was cognitively immature and therefore unable to conceptualize the relationship between syntax and tense. However, we can quickly dismiss this hypothesis since Homer appropriately marked time in his first language.

With the elimination of theories of rule testing and cognitive maturity, we can concentrate on alternative suggestions that may provide a more accurate explanation for the development of Homer's progressive.

Slobin (1973) and Hatch (1974) suggest that perceptual saliency is a language universal important to the acquisition of new forms and that morphemes affixed to the ends of words are the most conspicuous in speech. In addition to being a salient morpheme lacking conditioned phonological variants, -ing occurs at the ends of words. Morphophonemically, it is the easiest affix to learn.

Another important consideration is the frequency with which a form occurs in the learner's environment. The progressive is one of the most pervasive forms in the speech environment of a child. In Brown's count of parental speech samples (1973), the progressive ranked highest in verbal inflections for Eve's parents and second highest in samples from Adam and Sarah's parents. Legun's (1969) study showed that the progressive was the most frequent verb form in the classroom language of kindergarten through third grade.

From this information, we can outline four characteristics of the progressive which are largely responsible for its early appearance in the acquisition of English morphemes: 1) the -ing morpheme is easily recognizable; 2) it is a frequently occurring form in speech; 3) it is phonologically stable; and 4) morphophonemically, it does not affect the base verb form to which it is attached. These features may account for the early production of the progressive pattern.

Reasons for free variation

Although the form is easy to produce, the semantic function of the progressive as it occurs in adult speech is quite complex. Depending on included adverbial time markers or a mutually understood context, it denotes 1) process-state activity; 2) activity of the immediate future; and 3) non-immediate future events. For example:

1. I'm walking to the beach. (A statement made upon meeting a friend while on your way to the beach.)
2. I'm driving, even if I did forget my glasses. (The immediate future.)
3. I'm walking to the beach next Tuesday. (Non-immediate future.)

In addition to marking process-state activity and various future time periods, the progressive can refer to past events of duration. In such cases -ing still remains affixed to the stem, while the AUX changes to either was or were, depending on the subject.

An analysis of Homer's speech suggests that the progressive first emerged as a new verb form but not as a new verb function. Explanations for its early development are the frequency of its occurrence in speech, its perceptual saliency, its phonological consistency, and the manner in which it preserves the phonology of the stem. However, it emerged at a time when Homer was uninterested in marking time and when the semantic function of the progressive was difficult for him to analyze.

Comparison between Homer and first language learners

When comparing Homer's acquisition of the progressive to first language learners, we find that the form emerges early for both learners and—structurally, at least— in the same manner. This is probably due to the linguistic features of the progressive which make it relatively easy to perceive and produce. Moreover, it is a pervasive form in the learner's environment. While there are similarities in both the shape of the progressive and its early appearance, there is a difference in the function it served for Homer compared with its function in the speech of first language learners. Brown (1973) found that first language learners use the progressive to mark process-state exclusively. Even by the study's end, Brown's subjects had still not mastered all of the functions of the progressive. Homer, on the other hand, produced the form with reference to at least four temporal modes.

One explanation for this difference in function is that since first language learners are restricted to their level of cognitive development, they are only able to conceptualize process-state activity at the onset of their production of the progressive. Therefore, there is no possible way for the function of the progressive to be overextended in their speech. Homer, on the other hand, was already mature enough to conceptualize semantic relationships that the Brown children had not mastered at the end of Brown's data collection.

The emergence of form prior to function in Homer's speech may have been due to the fact that his ability to recognize and produce language patterns outstripped his ability to perceive relationships between form and function. Homer was able to refer to all time periods in his native language, yet he lacked the necessary information about English to link its form to its function. Because he was able to recognize similar phonological patterns in his speech environment, however, he grouped these together into one semantic class from which he drew indiscriminately. For example, he knew that *I my, I'm,* and *I am* all belonged to the same general class, and he used them in free variation when referring to himself.

It seems likely that Homer's progressive emerged by the same process: it was a phonological variation of the stem, containing no distinguishing semantic features of its own. For Homer, all verbs denoted action only, whether they occurred in the present tense or past. Later he would discover the range of qualitative semantic differences between the possible forms for each verb; in the initial stages of language learning, he would group according to sound. Thus, *I going, I'm go,* and *I'm going* were grouped together as having one semantic function: Homer's movement from one place to another.

Summary

Although we know that Homer's progressive did not emerge with a semantic function that distinguished it from any other verb form, the emergence of a linguistic form prior to its function has not been treated in the data on second language learning, nor has the question of function been fully explored in first language research. Is the utterance *I'm go*, for example, really a reduced catenative, or could first language learners be grouping this together in their speech with forms such as *I'm going* and *I going* to perform a more general function? The analysis of both the form and function of all verbs, regardless of their appropriateness for a given context, could help to uncover more about the language-learning process and how that process may be similar or different for first and second language learners.

While a description of the language process is the ultimate goal of language researchers, we still have very little information about how the learner formulates his rules, shapes them, and acquires new rules. While it seems that these questions will lead us deeper into the fields of neurolinguistics and psycholinguistics, we still have resources available in language data collected from experimental and observational studies with which to form some hypotheses. By looking at dialogues between Homer and native speakers, for example, there is evidence to suggest that one of his strategies for processing language involved incorporation rules, where the language addressed to him became incorporated into his own speech.

IMITATION AND INCORPORATION RULES

Imitated speech

Homer imitated the speech and behavior of other children. His best friend, Mark, had accused him of being a copier just two weeks after his arrival in Los Angeles. "Don't copy!" Mark warned as Homer successfully recited a full sentence of Mark's. Unintimidated, Homer shouted right back, "Don't copy!"

At nursery school, Homer gave himself away the first week when, during art period, he copied the picture the girl beside him was drawing. This could have passed unnoticed had the teacher not requested that the children put their names on their pictures. Homer's neighbor neatly printed SUSAN on hers; Homer neatly printed SUSAN on his. Thus, it was apparent that one strategy Homer was using to adapt to his new environment was that which Mark called copying, but which language researchers call imitation.

It is true that children do imitate the speech they hear. This may be a way to commit an unanalyzed pattern to memory for some kind of future analysis or it may be a communication strategy where a response is learned which can later be applied to a similar context (Hatch, 1972). Imitation may also give the learner a sense of participation in the conversation, or it may even be a successful teasing strategy, as Homer discovered. Finally, not to be overlooked is the fact that imitation can be sheer fun.

Imitation in Homer's speech

One of Homer's most interesting imitation strategies was his response to yes/no questions. If his answer was affirmative, Homer imitated the question's syntax but changed the direction of the intonation from a rising to a falling pattern. Some examples are listed below:

J: Is Mark at school today?
H: Is Mark school today. [=Yes, Mark is at school today.]
J: Is Misty a cat?
H: Is Misty a cat. [=Yes, Misty is a cat.]

Occasionally he included the affirmative marker, *yes*, in his response, usually after the copula.

J: Is it good?
H: Is it yes good. [=Yes, it's good.]

Negative responses were generated in the same manner with the inclusion of the particle *no* somewhere after the copula.

J: Is this happy birthday?
H: Is no happy birthday.
J: Is this lemonade?
H: Is no lemonade.
J: Is Homer a cat?
H: Is Homer is no. [=Homer isn't a cat.]

This pattern generalized to statements which were not made in response to a previous yes/no question. It also extended to his own yes/no questions. If one were only analyzing yes/no question formation at the time, it would have appeared that he had learned the appropriate inversion rules.

1. J: Got ya.
   H: Is no got ya. [=Don't grab me.]
2. H: Is it bicycle is Judy? [=Is it Judy's bicycle?]
3. Is it Misty?
4. Is Homer. Is something. Is Homer, OK? [It's Homer. I have something for you, OK?]

This resembles the strategy for question formation used by first and second language learners. Questions are initially formed by maintaining SVO word order and changing the direction of the intonation from a falling to a rising pattern. The result is a question such as *This is house?* or *You want ice cream?* Although Homer's sentences contained VSO patterns, his language strategy—simplification—was the same.

When looking at the input data for Homer during this period, it is easy to see why his rules developed the way they did. Most of the input was in the form of yes/no questions beginning with the copula, *is.* Homer, at this point, just one month after his arrival, had still not sorted out word order rules; however, he did recognize question and statement intonation patterns. Therefore, he merely reversed the direction of the intonation pattern for affirmative statements and inserted *no* when the statement was negative. For questions he used the same word order but with rising intonation.

Incorporation rules in Homer's speech

We do not know to what extent imitated speech is analyzed by the child. It is clear that there is no transfer of rules between some imitations and subsequent free speech patterns. For example, a learner may say *My name is Homer* in one breath and *He Fred* in the next, the former being a memorized pattern and the latter the learner's own rule.

While researchers have noted large amounts of imitated speech in their data, it is also true that learners create linguistic rules which systematically approach an adult model of English. During this process, it has been thought that the learner is constantly producing patterns he has never heard before. Such notions may have to be qualified when the total language environment of the learner is examined—input as well as output data.

Traditionally, language research has been organized around the sentence structures produced by the learner and, in a relatively few cases, the sentences produced by the parents or investigators in the study. The latter have been primarily analyzed for effects of frequency (Boyd, 1974; Hatch, 1974; Brown, 1973), and for the effect of parental expansions on the learners' rule formation (Cazden, 1965). While the frequency of a structure combined with other linguistic variables has been shown to influence what the learner acquires (Hatch-Gough, 1974; Boyd, 1974), there has been little research on dialogue patterns and their subsequent impact on the process of rule formation.

An analysis of portions of the dialogues between Homer and native speakers of English reveals that the shape of Homer's utterances is influenced by the patterns addressed to him and that some of his linguistic rules are combined question-response patterns in discourse agreement. In other words, some of Homer's production strategies involve incorporation rules whereby the speech he hears is incorporated into his own language.

Sometimes he immediately incorporated a pattern into his utterance:

1. Mark: Come here.
   Homer: No come here. [=I won't come.]
2. Mark: Don't do that.
   Homer: O.K. Don't do that. [=O.K. I won't do that.]
3. Judy: Where are you going?
   Homer: Where are you going is house. [=I'm going home.]
4. Judy: Where's Mark?
   Homer: Where's Mark is school. [=Mark is at school.]

Sometimes a pattern was not immediately incorporated into the next utterance, but was stored for later incorporation.

   1. Ed: *Which one?*
     Homer: I'll show you.
              I'll show you is that one.
              Which one is that one.

Sometimes a phrase was imitated in isolation before being combined with any other words:

   1. Judy: *What is it?*
     Homer: Aesb. [Assiryian for horse]
              What is this? *What is it?* What is it?
              What is it Jennifer. [=This is Jennifer.]

     Homer's most pervasive language rule involving incorporated speech was his wh-question pattern, based on the question *What is this?* and its response, *This is noun.* The pattern will be analyzed in detail below.

Incorporation rules for wh-patterns

During a 4-week period, from 1/26 to 2/26, Homer produced a number of wh-patterns which looked like these:

     1. What is this sulta?
     2. What is this truck.
     3. What this is Homer.
     4. What this is?
     5. What is this is?
     6. What is this is doot. [a word made up by Mark]
     7. What is it?
     8. What is it Jennifer.

Linguistically and semantically, these phrases differed from adult wh-patterns in at least three ways:

     1. The question word *what* was attached to all phrases, regardless of Homer's intention to pose a question or make a statement.
     2. The position of *be* in the sentence varied, but not in a predictable manner. Sometimes, *be* preceded the subject; at other times it followed. However, semantic interpretation of the sentence was not dependent on word order, but rather on context.
     3. Sometimes either *is* or *this* occurred twice in the same utterance without altering the meaning of the sentence.

Upon examining the nature of the input language addressed to Homer, it becomes clear that his wh-patterns were products of a wh-question and its response in discourse agreement. (I will borrow Miller and Ervin-Tripp's [1964] broad definition of discourse agreement: a question requires a response. Although there are class and verb restrictions placed upon this formal relationship, our interests lie only in the semantic restrictions of discourse agreement. That is, the information required by a *what* question is different from that requested in a *why* or *where* question, and this difference must be respected in the dialogue.)

The process by which Homer produced these wh-patterns is as follows:

1. Homer juxtaposed syntagmatically related units of social discourse— a question and a response pattern—thereby creating his own wh-pattern:

   | Question | + | Response | = | Homer's wh-pattern |

   What is this? This is truck = What is this this is truck.

2. Paradigmatically related units within these two juxtaposed phrases were deleted.

   Homer's wh-pattern + Deletions = Homer's new utterance
   What is this this is truck. [Deletion of *this is* = What *is this* truck.
   What is this this is truck. [Deletion of *is this*] = What *this is* truck.

3. Deletions were randomly applied:
   a. *Is this* was deleted. If this were the case, the amalgamated pattern *What is this this is NP* became *What this is NP*.
      Examples: What this is Homer.
                What this is tunnel.
                What this is airplane.
   b. *This is* was deleted, and the pattern became *What is this NP*.
      Examples: What is this airplane.
                What is this fruga. [Homer's version of the Persian word for airport]
                What is this screaming.
   c. Only *this* was deleted, which shaped the utterance into *What is this is NP*.
      Example: What is this is car.
   d. Homer deleted the NP and either *is this, this is* or *this* when asking a question.
      Examples: What this is?
                What is this?
                What is this is?

Scollon (1974), while studying the language development of a child simultaneously exposed to English, Hawaiian, Creole, and Japanese, noted that the manner in which she constructed her phrases was largely influenced by the nature of the language addressed to her. He has concluded that research on language development should include an analysis of the structures in the input data. In other words, we should extend the data for analysis beyond single utterances produced by the child. Such an extended analysis will result in a more realistic appraisal of why a pattern has been produced, which in turn will provide us with more information about the learning process.

Ruth Clark (1973) found that the data she collected on her son, Adam, while he was learning English as his first language, are rich in incorporated speech. She claims that Adam's earliest two-word sequences were juxtapositions of words mediated by situations. She also argues that children's speech becomes creative through the analysis of the internal structure of sequences which begin as pre-packaged routines, incorporated from the adult's speech before being internally analyzed. Greenfield (personal communication, 1975), too, has seen this same process strategy operating among first language learners who are still at the two-word stage of their language development.

Summary

What these speech samples reveal is that patterns which appear to be highly creative and based on a set of internalized language rules may in fact be patterns from dialogue sets that the learner has lifted from his environment. Homer's wh-question formation, for example, was based on the combined question-answer pattern in social discourse.

These incorporated patterns tell us something about Homer's process strategy for language learning: the rules for both wh-questions and statements were derived from discourse patterns. Homer was focusing on and processing much more than isolated sentence units in speech. Instead, he was sorting through and storing linguistic information he received in language dialogues. This was particularly noticeable in Homer's speech because he was a second language learner and was able to store long utterances. However, this strategy has also been observed in the speech of first language learners as early as the two-word stage.

Therefore, a closer analysis of the dialogue between learner and adult may reveal more about the nature of rule formation than a simple sentence analysis of the learner's speech. Such a conclusion echoes the observation made by Roger Brown in 1968:

> It may be as difficult to derive a grammar from unconnected sentences as it would be to derive the invariance of quantity and number from the simple look of liquids in containers and objects in space. The changes produced by pouring back and forth, by gathering together and spreading apart are the data that most strongly suggest the conservation of quantity and number. The changes produced in sentences as they move between persons in discourse may be the richest data for the discovery of grammar. (p. 288)

Evidence of incorporation rules suggests that an analysis based on a transformational-generative theory is not comprehensive enough to explain the process of rule formation.

INCORPORATION AS A BASIS FOR RULE FORMATION

Transformational theory of wh-question formation

In 1965, Klima and Bellugi described the development of question forms in the speech of the three children studied at Harvard—Adam, Eve, and Sarah. In their analysis they collected the questions posed by each child and found that, allowing for some overlapping, they fell into three successive developmental categories. In Stages 1 and 2, there are four distinct characteristics of the question patterns: 1) the most frequent wh-question words are *what* and *where*, and both appear at the head of the sentence; 2) there is no *do* support; 3) there are no internal inversion rules; and 4) tense is not marked. Questions occurring in the speech of Adam, Eve, and Sarah during Stages 1 and 2 generally look like the following examples:

Where Ann pencil?   What the dollie have?
Where horse go?   What book name?
                           Who that?

In data Hatch (1974) synthesized from over 40 observational studies on second language learning, she found that she could outline a similar pattern for wh-question development: 1) the question word, usually *what, who* or *where*, first appears at the beginning of the sentence; and 2) wh-questions are asked before the copula has been developed, before tense has been marked, and prior to the introduction of *do*-support. Thus, the first wh-questions in the speech of those learning English as a second language look remarkably like those produced by children learning English as a first language.

From the studies of Hatch, Klima, and Bellugi, we can conclude that the developmental process of wh-question formation produces similar wh-patterns in both first and second language learners: 1) there is neither *do*-support nor internal inversion at the onset of production; 2) wh-question words first occur in the initial position of the sentence and 3) wh-questions are produced before the copula is developed and before tense is acquired. Thus, the sequence of wh-question development is similar for those learning English as either their first or second language.

Having described this sequence, a more interesting question to explore is whether the process of wh-question formation is the same among *all* learners of English. There are at least two theories to be further explored, and they are described below.

Klima and Bellugi have described the process by which Adam, Eve, and Sarah acquired wh-question patterns according to the rules of transformational-generative grammar. They treat each utterance as a single sentence unit consisting of a nucleus to which a wh-question marker is preposed. The formula outlining the rules of wh-questions at Stages 1 and 2 is included in their report:

$$S \left\{ \begin{array}{l} \text{Qwhat} \\ \text{Qwhere} \\ \text{Qwhy} \end{array} \right\} \text{-nucleus}$$

Homer's rule formation

This explanation is not generalizable to Homer's question development. His patterns evolved from a process quite different from that of the application of rules to a single sentence nucleus. As has been discussed, Homer's patterns were products of juxtaposed sentences in his speech, resulting in sentences like *What this is Homer!* and *What is this sulta?* While neither of these phrases resembles those recorded for other first and second language learners, the wh-patterns collected after 2/26, Homer's second month in the United States, are similar to those described by Hatch, Bellugi, and Klima. These form the real basis from which to question Bellugi and Klima's interpretation.

If we examine the wh-questions in Homer's speech after 2/26, we find that they, too, resemble those of both first and second language learners described: 1) *what* occurs at the head of the sentence; 2) there is no *do*-support; 3) the copula is not developed; and 4) tense is unmarked. Furthermore, *what* functions only as a question marker, so the wh-question pattern no longer doubles as a statement form. Sentences like these were produced by Homer after 2/26:

1. Judy: Homer, draw a tree.
   Homer: What draw a tree? [=What does *Draw a tree* mean?]
2. Homer: What takta? [=What is the translation for *takta* in English?]
3. Ed: What am I?
   Homer: What what am I? [=What does *What am I* mean?

Assuming that Homer's language-processing strategies did not change significantly, it is possible that *What draw a tree?* is derived from the same process responsible for *What is this truck?* or *What this is Homer.* That is, *What draw a tree?* is a product of two separate sentence units: 1) *What?* (formerly *What is this?*) and 2) *Draw a tree.* Had Homer produced these same questions during the first month of his question development, they would have probably looked like this:

1. What is this draw a tree? or What this is draw a tree?
2. What is this takta? or What this is takta?
3. What is this what am I? or What this is what am I?

After 2/26, Homer may have substituted the question form *What?* for *What is this?* assuming, by his general interpretation of the two forms, that they were paradigmatically related. At least this seems like a possible suggestion since he used both *What?* by itself and *What is this?* to ask for clarification of something he did not understand. It is also possible that Homer recognized the paradigmatic relationship that exists between *This* and *Draw a tree,* noting that one could replace the other.

Considerations for rule development

In trying to account for wh-question development, we have discussed two divergent explanations. Bellugi and Klima couch their explanations of this process in terms of transformational-generative grammar, assuming that wh-question patterns stem from a single sentence nucleus to which transformations are applied. I suggest that Homer's wh-questions reflect a process whereby sentence units are juxtaposed and modified by vertical substitutions and deletions.

The evidence available, however, is not strong enough to support one theory over another. In Homer's data from 1/26 to 2/26, there is very clear evidence to support the theory of juxtapositioning. This same theory can be extended to later sentences by assuming that juxtapositioning continued to be a major process in his language development. Therefore, we can interpret *What takta?* to be a product of two juxtaposed sentence units just as we showed *What this is truck* to be.

In the speech of the Harvard children, there is supporting evidence for either theory, that of Bellugi-Klima or that which I am proposing here. At the same time, there is not enough substantial evidence to discredit either. In other words, by looking at a sentence of the Harvard children, such as *What the dollie have?*, we can describe the process strategy by either theory: juxtaposing rules or transformation-generative rules. We could say that this question is a product of two juxtaposed units, *What is it? + The dollie have (something).* Or, we could say that *What* is preposed and replaces the unknown object of the sentence.

Summary

In the final analysis, we cannot claim to have uncovered any single explanation for the development of wh-questions. Juxtaposing does appear to play a role in the language process, but because of limited data, we can not justify claims that it is responsible for question development among all language learners. Although the utterances of the Harvard children may be interpreted as juxtaposed units, they may also be analyzed as single sentence nuclei with fronted wh-question words. Such flexibility strengthens the position of neither theory but leaves the possibility open for more than one explanation of the data.

From Homer's data, at least, it is apparent that he did attend to discourse sets, which in turn influenced his own sentence formation. An analysis of discourse patterns in the data on other learners may provide valuable information about processing and production strategies in language development.

Second Language Acquisition of Older Learners

Grammatical Problems
12 in Learning English
as a Third Language

Anna U. Chamot, *University of Texas, Austin*

INTRODUCTION

Dr. Chamot's study is unique in that, while her data collection is in the case study format, she uses error analysis as the method for describing the data obtained from her ten-year-old son, who had acquired Spanish and French before learning English. Error tabulations allowed Chamot to look at changes in error patterns for a number of syntactic structures over a one-year period.

One of the interesting, and controversial, aspects of this study is the heavy reliance placed on contrastive analysis to explain 'errors' made by her subject as he acquired English as a third language. Dr. Chamot is, of course, careful to point out that contrastive analysis was more helpful in explaining than in predicting errors. Each 'error' made by the subject was examined to see whether or not it could be accounted for as interference from either French or Spanish, or both, based on an analysis of congruence and difference among the three languages. If an error could *not* be explained by a comparison of the languages, she then turned to first-language learning studies for evidence of parallel examples. These "errors," if they showed similarities to developmental case studies, were then called "non-mastery" errors.

However, since many of the errors attributed to interference also occur in the data of Japanese, Chinese, Iranian subjects as well as in the data of speakers of Romance languages, and occur in developmental studies of first language acquisition, some readers may wish to quarrel with assigning a causal relationship to first language interference. In turn, readers of the Butterworth study of another Bolivian subject may wish to quarrel with arguments against interference given there for data which bear a striking resemblance to Spanish.

The error analysis methodology may be the solution to this problem. It gives us a way of looking for quick extinguishing of developmental-error rules as the learner moves on to acquire more accurate representations. With frequency data over time, we could, for example, compare *it*-deletion (*Is good. No is important.*) in data from many learners and chart how long the form stays in the repertoire of Spanish speakers as compared to speakers of other languages. Young, for example, has suggested that this might be better evidence for "interference" than we have had in many of our research projects in the past.

For similar studies which use error analysis as a methodology for research, the reader is referred to the study of three children by Young, and to the cross-sectional error analysis studies of Duškova, Schachter, LoCoco and Tanka, all of which appear in the abstract section.

The acquisition of English by a ten year old boy bilingual in French and Spanish was studied for nine months. The subject was a coordinate bilingual, having always spoken French at home and Spanish at school and play. At the age of 9; 10 he was moved to Austin, Texas, where both school and play environments were English. French and Spanish were then maintained at home until his competence in English was sufficient for the whole family to converse primarily in this language.

A month after the subject's arrival in the United States, samples of his oral language began to be collected at twice monthly intervals by taping the family dinner table conversation. Twenty-two tapes were made in all, their length ranging from fifteen to thirty minutes.

No special teaching was provided either at school or at home, so that English was acquired in a natural learning situation. Difficulties encountered were classified under two headings: those probably due to non-mastery and therefore developmental in nature, and those probably due to specific interference from one or both of his other languages.

For the grammatical analysis each taped utterance was examined for deviations from the English with which the subject was in contact. For convenience of description, these differences were termed "errors". The language standard used for purposes of determining the deviations was the model heard at home and any items of Central Texas speech which could have been heard at school. The French standard was that of Canton de Vaud (Switzerland) as spoken by the subject's father, and the Spanish standard that of Santa Cruz, Bolivia, where he had lived since infancy.

GRAMMATICAL ANALYSIS

Grammatical difficulties were described in two sections, those dealing with morphology and syntax and those involving sentence formation. The method of approach was essentially error-based. Contrastive analysis of the three languages proved more helpful in explaining than in predicting problems due to interference, which accounted for about two-thirds of the grammatical errors.

This study reveals that during his first nine months of English acquisition, the subject's principal grammatical learning problems in order of frequency were:

> Omission of constituents
> Verb Forms—Present for other tenses
> Sentence Formation—Subordination and embedding
> Article Usage
> Preposition Usage
> Sentence Formation—Complement Pattern
> Sentence Formation—Interrogative
> Sentence Formation—Minor Patterns
> Sentence Formation—Negative
> Verb Forms—Person
> Noun Forms—Number

Some errors were attributed to non-mastery because of their similarity to items found in the acquisition of English as a first language. Other errors seemed to be the result of negative interference, that is, equivalent forms of structures in French and/or Spanish were translated directly into English. Still other errors seemed due to zero interference, that is, they involved completely new items which had no French or Spanish counterparts. Table 12-1 summarizes the attribution of errors.

Obviously there is some overlap in the first and third categories, as some items which are late acquisitions for the young child learning English as his first language do not have equivalents in either of the other two languages.

Table 12-1   Error attribution

Error in Item	Example	Probable Cause
1. Similar to French or Spanish	Omission of copula *be*	Non-mastery
2. Different from French or Spanish	Article usage	Negative Interference
3. Non-existent in French and Spanish	*Do* as AUX in interrogative	Zero Interference

FINDINGS

Error percentages were obtained by counting the number of errors of each kind per taped selection and the number of utterances in which each grammatical type could be found. A ratio between the two amounts gave the error percentage. A numerical value was then assigned to each percentage group, and an error score computed by adding the numerical error values for each error type throughout the twenty-two tapes. The error scores for morphology and syntax and for sentence formation are ranked in Table 12-2.

It is apparent that almost all difficulties encountered in sentence formation were of high incidence, whereas less than half of the problems in morphology and syntax occurred at all frequently. This would seem to indicate that more progress was made or that fewer problems were encountered in the mastery of morphological forms and simple syntactical structures than in more complex sentence formation in the subject's first nine months of exposure to English.

Omission of constituents occurred throughout the tapes, giving a telegraphic character to the subject's speech. The single largest omission was of *it* in both

Table 12-2   Rank order of grammatical errors

MORPHOLOGY AND SYNTAX		SENTENCE FORMATION	
Type	*Score*	*Type*	*Score*
Omission of Constituents	86	Subordination	
Verb Forms:		and Embedding	58
Present for Other Tenses	62	Complement Pattern	43
Article Usage	46	Interrogative	43
Preposition Usage	45	Minor Patterns	39
Redundancy of Constituents	28	Negative	38
Verb Forms: Person	28	Word Order	17
Noun Forms: Number	27		
Adverb Usage	18		
Adjective Usage	14		
Pronoun Forms	13		
Verb Forms:			
Past for Other Tenses	12		
Verb Forms:			
-ING for Other Forms	12		
Noun Forms: Genitive	9		
Verb for Noun	6		
Noun Compounds	6		
Verb Forms:			
Non-Finite for Other Forms	5		
Mass/Count Noun	3		
Noun for Verb	2		

subject and direct object position. As this neuter pronoun does not exist in either French or Spanish, it is understandable that difficulty was encountered. This particular item in the zero interference category was evidently quite difficult to acquire, as there was little improvement in the use of *it* throughout the tapes.

Another frequent omission was of the AUX, in particular the empty carrier *do* in negative and interrogative constructions. Since these patterns are specific to English and are therefore again in the zero interference category, it is not surprising that they present learning problems to the speaker of French and Spanish.

Omissions of the copula *be* occurred mostly in the early tapes and did not seem to be due to interference, but rather to non-mastery; they are typically developmental in that non-insertion of the copula in transformations from deep to surface structure is a feature of early childhood language acquisition.

A less frequent omission was that of the verb particle, an error which showed little improvement. This was probably due to zero interference, as both French and Spanish have separate verbs to express the meanings of many English verb + particle combinations, such as *look at, look for, look up, look like,* etc.

Incorrect verb forms also accounted for a large percentage of errors, most of them due to the use of the present or base form for the past, -ING and past participle forms. Use of the present for past seems clearly due to non-mastery, and whereas this may also be partially true in the use of the present for -ING, it is possible to trace interference from both French and Spanish in the latter case. These languages habitually use the simple present in situations which in English call for the present progressive (AUX:present + -ING). Typical examples are:

> 3:105* Where are we go Sunday?
> 3:37   I eat toast and sardine. (Response to "What are you eating?")
> 11:31   My ears is not hurt anymore.

*Denotes 105th utterance of Tape 3.

In article usage, omission of the required article accounted for the majority of errors, as in the following:

> 14:82   She is nice teacher.
> 11:12   We have lot of soup, right?

These show interference from both French and Spanish, which do not require an article before the names of professions or before the expressions *beaucoup* or *mucho, -a.* Although many omissions of the indefinite article could be attributed to interference, some could not, and neither could omissions of the definite article such as:

> 4:15   Lunch card is for pay for the lunch.
> 20:13   I went to wrong door.

However, redundant use of articles and their use with parts of the body and clothes could be traced to interference from one or both of the other languages, as the following examples show:

>1:61 It is in the stomach.
>3:29 This is the teacher, the Mr. Strinkel.
>5:9 Because the pants [were] short? (Referring to own pants)
>8:112 . . . we cross the eyes . . .

Correct preposition usage proved difficult to master, which was probably due to the fact that the semantic areas covered by English prepositions do not correspond entirely with their French and Spanish equivalents. The most frequent preposition error involved the indiscriminate use of *in*:

>*in bed* for *to bed*; *in Monday* for *on Monday*; *in TV* for *on TV*; *in the school* for *at school*; *in this side* for *on this side*

The last three examples indicate interference from Spanish rather than French, as he seems to be equating the Spanish *en* with *in* (*en la TV, en la escuela, en este lado*). The first two examples seem more likely due to non-mastery, as they do not follow either the French or the Spanish patterns.

To was also used in place of other prepositions such as *on* and *at*:

>*gave to TV* for *gave on TV*; *stay to school* for *stay at school*

These examples show interference from French (*à la TV, à l'école*) rather than Spanish, which would use *en*.

Although redundancy of constituents ranks rather high in percentage of errors, examination reveals that most of these (63.2%) were of a pronoun following the noun it referred to, such as, *Mrs. Cashion she . . . , Bobby he . . . , the kids they . . .* , etc. It was felt that these were not especially significant as they appear to be a fairly typical construction for native speakers of English at this age. Other kinds of redundant items also appeared due to non-mastery.

Errors in morphology due to incorrect person in verb forms occurred in almost all the tapes. The most frequent type was use of the present or base form instead of the third person singular form. There was also some apparent confusion with pronouns such as *somebody, everybody* and *nobody,* with which he generally used the third person plural form. An additional problem was found in interrogative and negative patterns requiring the AUX *do*:

>6:77 She don't tells.
>15:129 . . . so Tim don't listen.

It seems evident that the *-s* ending for the third person singular is known, but that its use has not been mastered. The use of *don't* for *doesn't* was attributed either to non-mastery or to imitation of models heard at school.

Most incorrect noun forms were due to the use of the singular where the plural was required. Although it could be argued that this error might be due to non-mastery, as it is a typical feature of young children learning English as their first language, the fact that virtually no improvement in the mastery of plural forms was evident in the nine month period seems rather to indicate strong negative interference from one or both of his other languages. Regular plural endings in French do not change the sound of a word, and as the subject's French was almost completely oral, it could be that he was unaware of number differences in French nouns. An additional cause for interference may have come from his particular dialect of Spanish in which final [s] becomes a weak aspiration [^{h}]. This speaking and listening habit would also tend to obliterate the difference between singular and plural forms, as the [^{h}] is weak and completely different from the English plural morpheme.

Errors in sentence formation were frequent in all types of sentences involving major transformations. The most frequent was in subordination and embedding. Relative pronouns and word order in embedded clauses were difficult to master, as these examples indicate:

6:93 No, the red one is [what] Joe he gave me.
11:111 I think is for children [who] don't have any money.
12:67 Daddy, do you like the salad what I did?

Omission of the relative pronoun is attributed to non-mastery, as both French and Spanish require one in similar constructions. Use of *what* for *that* is probably due to interference from the *que* of the other two languages. Another typical error in embedding occurred in sentences such as:

3:49 I don't know what is his name.
5:44 I no know what is it.
21:54 I don't know what's the answer.

These relative clause word order errors are apparently due to double interference, as they follow the patterns of both French and Spanish.

Since the complement pattern is a frequent one in English which features various kinds of nominalized verb phrases embedded in sentences, it was considered separately for purposes of error analysis in sentence formation. Equivalent French and Spanish patterns are formed differently, which no doubt accounts for utterances like:

6:35 I want drink my milk.
8:22 Bobby doesn't like come here.
15:54 I want Mrs. Cashion come tomorrow.
19:58 I don't know what you want me say.

These show interference from French and Spanish, which use the pattern V:finite + V:non-finite when the subject of both verbs is identical, and V:finite + *que* + V:subjunctive when the verbs have different subjects as in 15:54 and 19:58.

In the formation of interrogative sentences, many errors involved the use of *do* as an AUX and others were due to the use of declarative word order with an interrogative intonation contour.

> Examples of omission of AUX *do*:
> 1:137 Where you put that?
> 7:56   Why you speak French?
> 13:12 Why you went home?
> 15:173 How many you think?

These show zero interference from French and Spanish, which have nothing in their interrogative formation which corresponds to the obligatory use of the English AUX *do* in the above questions.

> Examples of declarative word order in questions:
> 3:276 You will finish washing the plates? (A direct request to mother)
> 10:118 Where I was?
> 17:19 In how many days it can?

Although the use of intonation alone in questions is an acceptable pattern in English, it was felt that in the contexts in which these examples occurred, the more usual word order would have been AUX + NP:subj + VP. In both French and Spanish, however, the word order used in the examples is not only acceptable but even preferable.

Minor sentence patterns such as transitive receiver (indirect object), indefinite (*there* + *be* + NP) and passive constructions occurred infrequently but with a large proportion of errors. Transitive receiver errors appeared due to interference, difficulties in passives seemed a result of non-mastery, and it was not determined whether the omission of *there* and usually *be* in the indefinite patterns was due to interference or non-mastery.

It was expected that formation of English negative sentences would prove difficult to master because of the different patterns in the other two languages. Considerable improvement in mastery of negative patterns took place. The principal errors involved the use of *no* for the AUX + *not*:

> 2:19   She no look [at] it.
> 6:62   But I no have any book.
> 1:79   This no is chicken.
> 3:210 No, I no finish. (Response to, "Are you finished?")

All of these sentences follow the Spanish pattern, which places the negative *no* before the verb. French requires the addition of *pas* after the verb or AUX. Negative sentences requiring the AUX *do* proved more difficult to master than those with *be* as an AUX, as the latter were mastered from Tape 5 on.

Double negatives following French and Spanish patterns occurred less frequently than had been anticipated. Typical examples were:

7:20   Steve too don't know nothing.
14:88   You can't see her never.
19:139 We can't never finish to study Science.

SUMMARY OF FINDINGS

Table 12-3 shows the percentages of errors in morphology and syntax and their distribution in the twenty-two tapes.

In verb forms, the most acute problem is the use of present for other tenses, which accounts for some of the largest error percentages in nearly every tape. Although it fluctuates widely, a general improving trend is apparent except for the final tape. Although errors in verb person are less frequent, they show little improvement.

Noun forms present fewer problems, and most of these are due to errors involving number. The error percentages fluctuate, showing no permanent improvement.

Omission of constituents accounts for by far the largest percentages of errors in almost every tape. A fluctuating but fairly clear pattern of improvement can be seen, however, as the error percentage is reduced in the final tapes.

Table 12-4 shows the degree of monthly fluctuation of errors in sentence formation. Tapes with very few utterances of the pattern charted were not used, and since the sample of minor patterns was extremely small, no conclusions about progress in this area can be made.

Lack of progress in interrogative patterns indicates not only the inherent difficulty of the construction, particularly when the AUX is *do*, but also that the habit of expressing questions through intonation alone is rarely noticed or corrected because it is on the borderline of acceptable English.

Word order had low error percentages, with no consistent improvement. Substantial improvement was made in the formation of subordinate and complement pattern sentences. The improvement in negative patterns was less dramatic, but caused fewer problems at the start.

CONCLUSION

A case study of the acquisition of English by a ten year old boy bilingual in French and Spanish was conducted over a nine month period. Learning English morphology and syntax posed numerous difficulties, and while progress was evident, some English sentence patterns in particular proved difficult to master

Table 12-3 Errors in morphology and syntax

KEY TO ERRORS	% Errors	0	01-4%	5-9%	10-14%	15-19%	20-24%	25-30%
	Num. Value	0	1	2	3	4	5	6
a Verb Forms	Tape 1	a-4,5,6 b-3,4,5 d,e	a-2,3 b-1,2 c,f,g,i	a-1				h
-1 Present for other tenses								
-2 Past for other tenses	Tape 2	a-2,4,5,6 b-1,2,4,5 c	a-3 b-3 d,e,f,g,i	a-1		h		
-3 ING for other tenses								
-4 Non Fin for finite	Tape 3	a-4,5 b-3,5 c	a-2,3,6 b-1,2,4 c,d	g	a-1 f i			h
-5 N for V								
-6 Person	Tape 4	a-4,5 b-2,3,4,5	a-1,3,6 b-1 c,d,e	i	a-1 f g	h		
b Noun Forms								
-1 Number	Tape 5	a-2,4,5,6 b-2,3,4,5 e	a-3 b-1 c,d,i	f	g			a-1 h
-2 Genitive								
-3 V for N	Tape 6	a-4,5 b-3,4,5 e	a-2,3,6 b-1,2 c,d	f g i		h	a-1	
-4 Compounds								
-5 Mass/Count	Tape 7	a-3,4,5 b-3,4 c	a-2,6 b-1,2,5 d,e,f,i	g		h	a-1	
c Pronoun Forms								
d ADJ Usage								
e ADV Usage								
f PREP Usage								
g ART Usage								

Table 12-3 (continued)

KEY TO ERRORS	% Errors 0	01-4% 1	5-9% 2	10-14% 3	15-19% 4	20-24% 5	25-30% 6
Num. Value	0	1	2	3	4	5	6
Tape 8	a-2,3,4 b-2,3,4,5 d-	a-5,6 c,f,g,i	a-1 b-1 e				h
Tape 9	a-3,4,5 b-2,3,4,5 d	a-2,6 b-1 c,e	f g i		h	a-1	
Tape 10	a-3,5 b-3,5	a-2,4 b-2,4 c,d,e,f	a-1,6 b-1 i	g h			
Tape 11	a-2,3,4,5 c	b-1,2,3,4,5 d,e,f,i	a-6 g		a-1		h
Tape 12	a-2,3,4,5 b-3,5	a-1 b-1,2,4 c,d,e,i	a-6	g	f h		
Tape 13	b-4,5 c,d,e	a-2,3,4,5 b-1,2,3 i	a-7 f g	h	a-1		
Tape 14	a-3,4,5 b-2,4,5	a-2 b-3 c,d,e,i	a-6 b-1 f	a-1 g	h		
Tape 15	a-5 b-2,3,4,5	a-2,3,4 b-1 c,d,e,g	a-6 i	f h	a-1		

h Omission of Constituents

i Redundancy of Constituents

Table 12-3 (continued)

KEY TO ERRORS	% Errors	0	01-4%	5-9%	10-14%	15-19%	20-24%	25-30%
	Num. Value	0	1	2	3	4	5	6
i Redundancy of Constituents (continued)	Tape 16	a-2,3,4,5 b-3,4,5 c	a-6 b-1,2 e,d,i	f	a-1 g h			
	Tape 17	a-2,3,4,5 b-2,4 d	a-1,6 b-3,5 c,e,i	b-1	f,g	h		
	Tape 18	a-2,5 b-2,3,4,5	a-1,3,4 c,d,e,i	a-6 b-1 g	h	f		
	Tape 19	a-5 b-2,5 c,d,	c-2,3,4,6 b-1,3,4 e,i	a-1 f,g,h				
	Tape 20	a-4,5 b-2,3,4,5 c,d,	a-2,3 b-1 e,g,i	a-1 f	a-6 h			
	Tape 21	a-1,2,3,4,5 b-2,3,4,5 c,d,	a-6 e,f,i	b-1 h	g			
	Tape 22	a-2,4,5 b-2,3,5 c,i	a-3,6 b-1,4 d,e,g	a-1 f,h				

Table 12-4 Monthly progress in mastery of sentence formation

Subordination/Embedding

Tape	3	5	6	8	12	15	18	20	22
Sample Size	8	6	6	14	15	26	12	19	13

Complement Patterns

Tape	3	6	8	12	15	18	21	22
Sample size	8	8	9	9	9	12	10	9

Interrogative

Tape	1	4	6	8	11	15	18	21	22
Sample Size	20	18	18	24	33	13	14	33	28

Negative

Tape	2	5	6	8	11	15	18	21	22
Sample Size	17	17	9	15	17	18	6	8	8

Table 12-4 (continued)

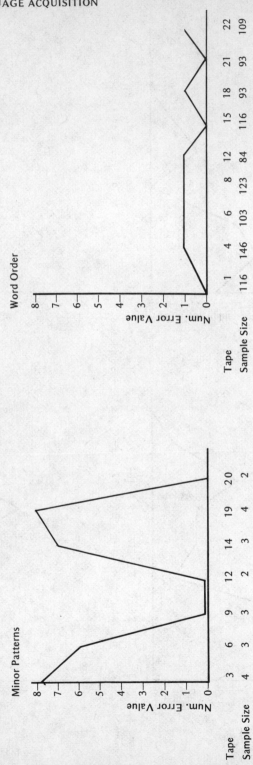

The major problem was in the omission of constituents, and about three-fourths of these omissions were attributed to interference, with the omission of *it* and the AUX *do* accounting for the majority of cases. There was also some omission of the copula *be*, attributed to non-mastery.

Use of the present for other tenses seemed to be a clear case of non-mastery, as simplification of grammatical categories is a feature of first as well as of second language acquisition.

Errors in subordination and embedding were about evenly divided between those caused by interference and those caused by non-mastery. The most persistent error due to interference was the use of interrogative word order in relative clauses; both French and Spanish patterns combined to contribute double interference. Omission of the relative pronoun, however, seemed to be due to non-mastery.

Redundant articles and omission of the indefinite article were found to be due to interference, while omission of the definite article was not. Most preposition errors were due to the use of the wrong preposition, which was expected, given the difference in usage and areas of meaning of equivalent prepositions in the three languages.

In the formation of interrogative sentences the two principal problems were omission of the AUX *do* and declarative word order. It was felt that both were due to interference; in the case of the first because there is no empty carrier like *do* in either French or Spanish, and in the case of the second because both other languages can express questions by intonation alone in many contexts where English prefers interrogative word order.

Difficulties with negative sentence formation were also attributed to interference. Most errors involved the use of *no* for AUX + *not*, and in most cases the AUX omitted was *do*. There was some use of double negatives, but not nearly as much as might have been expected given the French and Spanish patterns.

Errors in verb person were almost all the omission of the inflection -*s* in the third person singular, and were attributed to non-mastery. Errors in noun forms were almost all due to use of singular for plural, and it was felt that this was probably due to phonological interference from the subject's other two languages.

More rapid and complete mastery of the grammatical complexities of English would probably have occurred had the subject received special help in his areas of greatest difficulty. He was expected to pick up English as best as he could from his school and play environments, with some reinforcement at home. This approach could be considered a natural acquisition of English, as it parallels the situation of the young child learning his mother tongue from his environment. In the present case, however, the subject had the impediments of age, which meant that his language acquisition ability at the age of ten was less than in early childhood, and of interference from two related languages, which in some instances produced double interference.

Although he had the advantage of living in an English speaking environment with many models for imitation, the language habits of French and Spanish made it difficult for him to master some aspects of the English grammatical system.

Is Second Language Learning

13

Like the First?*

Susan M. Ervin-Tripp, *University of California, Berkeley*

INTRODUCTION

At the 21st Georgetown Round Table, Susan Ervin-Tripp reiterated the call for studies in language acquisition which Professor Leopold had made at the 5th Round Table meeting:

> Our knowledge of the effects of exposure to second languages in natural situation is limited in many ways. a) We have very little information about the specific kinds of competence children have for the varieties of language in the repertoire of their community. b) We have defined language far too narrowly, omitting just those skills in the social use of language which may have more to do with social acceptability and communicative success than knowledge of school vocabulary. c) We lack well-developed theories of the processing of linguistic information which can account for changes in children's ability to understand, imitate, or produce appropriate speech as they learn. The applied orientation of most work on second language learning has resulted in the lack of a strong theoretical framework for designing empirical studies. On the other hand, many of the theoretical issues and concepts in psycholinguistic work on grammatical processing, and in child language research are relevant to studies of bilingualism. (1970, 313)

The following report is concerned with just these issues, and in particular with an investigation of strategies used by the second language learner which might lead to a theoretical framework for empirical studies.

Using data from American children learning French in Geneva, Ervin-Tripp has made a number of hypotheses about second language learning which she then supports with data from other studies. As in all her work, whether in first or second language acquisition, she presents a sharp analytical look at the data as it relates to the basic questions of language acquisition. The relationship between first and second language acquisition and between age and rate of learning are discussed in detail.

Reprinted with the permission of the author and Teachers of English to Speakers of Other Languages, Washington, D.C. from the *TESOL Quarterly,* 1974, *8,* 2, 111-127.

* * * * *

It has taken surprisingly long for scholars of language learning to envisage the relation between first and second language learning, and to view theories of the human language acquisition system as having a bearing on what they study (Cook, 1973; Corder, 1967; Selinker, 1972). For it has long been believed that there is a fundamental difference between the two, so deep it is pointless to develop a common theory. Why does this belief exist? Some reasons lie in the difference in purpose, method, and focus of the respective research traditions. For example:

1. Research on second language acquisition has generally been applied in purpose, and has until recently been light on basic and general theory; writing on child language, particularly in the Chomskyan tradition, has been more theoretical, and research has been less applied.

2. Child language research, for nearly a century, has used the case study as its primary method, with a focus on stages of development common to various cases. Second language learning studies normally are of large groups, with statistical pooling of information so that individual acquisition patterns are less visible.[1]

3. Research on child language has focused so heavily on learner strategies that the input to the learner was, until recently,[2] almost completely ignored. Research on second language learning has paid primary attention to manipulation of the structure and presentation of teaching materials.

4. With some notable exceptions in which additional instructional milieux were added,[3] research on child language has been limited to the natural settings where language is learned, but not taught, as a by-product of communicative needs. Research on second language learning has almost entirely occurred in classrooms, where language is taught formally and where language structure rather than communicative intent is the focus of attention.

In addition to these differences in research style, there has been a theoretical rationale offered for treating first and second language learning as irreconcilably different; second language learning is, it is argued, built completely upon transfer from the first language, and therefore can tell us nothing more general about language learning (Bever, Weksel, 1965). Now it is certainly the case that the second language learner makes use of prior knowledge, skills, tactics, but it is also true that the first language learner does this. That is, any learning builds on what has happened before, and it remains a major question just how this occurs. A child learning a language at four, whether a first or second language, has knowledge of the world, knowledge of spatial and object relations, knowledge of causality, which a child of one does not have. A child hearing a sentence he has never heard before, at the age of four, can bring to it knowledge of sound groupings, recognition of familiar patterns, expectations about basic syntax-meaning configurations, which a child of one does not have—whether or not he is listening to a new sentence in his mother tongue or a second language. The fact that the second language builds on prior knowledge is not what differentiates it from first language learning.

It has been argued that language-learning is easy for children because the human being is biologically well-prepared to learn languages, a point Chomsky (1965), Lenneberg (1967), and McNeill (1971) have been most noted for making. In addition, it has been argued that there are critical periods for such learning, in order to account for the facts, especially adduced by Lenneberg (1967), or sharp age changes in language acquisition after traumatic aphasia, and for age changes in laterality related to language functions.

If the human brain is especially competent to deal with language learning, there is no reason to suppose this ability would confine itself to the first language. From the standpoint of research, the rejection of second language acquisition as a testing ground for the properties of the Language Acquisition System[4] removes the possibility of studying those very conditions which may account for the repeated observation of age differences. Are the differences due to age? We can readily control age of second language acquisition, but are dependent on social or physical accidents, with attendant confounding circumstances, to study hearing-recovery cases or isolated children, learning a mother tongue late. Are the differences due to the changes in learning circumstances, amount of exposure, the need to communicate, the activity setting, simplicity and semantic obviousness of input, all of which may in natural uncontrolled conditions be greater for the younger language learner? There is certainly a much greater possibility of manipulation of circumstance for second than for first languages, for ethical reasons.

The research reported in this paper concerns an initial study asking two questions: Is second language learning like first language learning? Is there a change in learning rate or process with age? If it is the case that second language learning appears to draw on skills and processes similar to those available during first language learning, then the answer to the second question may be generalizable to first language acquisition. If the process is similar, then also we can manipulate the functional, social, and structural circumstances in which learning occurs and have a much broader knowledge of the learning system than is now available.

Method and subjects

The small study to be reported here was conducted in Geneva, Switzerland, and involved the testing of all English-speaking children in that area between the ages of 4 and 9 who were in school where French was the instructional medium, and who had not been exposed to French for more than nine months. There were thirty-one children in the study, with heavier age concentrations at the younger ages. The subjects are in no sense a random sample of second language learners; the social circumstances were such that English speakers in Geneva are unusually well-educated, and those who chose to send their children to French rather than bilingual or English schools tend to be almost entirely professionals. The diminution in numbers available at 8 and 9 probably is related to the preference for English schools as curricular complexity increases, since some people were on one-year visits.

Comprehension tests

Most of the tests employed involved the comprehension of syntax and morphology, rather than production, in order to avoid shyness, perfectionism, and other factors which might mask knowledge of the second language by performance inhibition. The most elaborate comprehension tests were of 24 sentences with passives, actives, reversed anomalous passives (e.g., the boy was eaten by the carrot), indirect objects, and telegraphic sentences (box open boy), in which the children acted out the situation with dolls or animals. These were given in both English and French, since the younger children had not mastered these sentence types in their mother tongue. Mastery of French pronouns for number and gender (for animate referents only) was assessed through two tests: a story in which sentences about dolls were interspersed with sentences using anaphoric pronominal reference (e.g., *il la lave*), and a picture-comprehension test using demonstrative and adjectival cues (*ces petites amies, ce petit camarade, cette petite camarade, ces petits amis*).

Imitation was employed with the children of five to nine. The sentences had two purposes. One was the inclusion of phonological features, with contrasted pairs where possible in a given sentence. The other was testing the relative accuracy of pronominal imitation as a function of initial, medial, or final location in a sentence, or of phonological features, e.g.,

> Lui il a répondu: "Cachez-la."
> Il lui a répondu: "Cachez-la."
> Il a répondu: "Cachez-la-lui."
> Papa t'apportait le train.
> Papa m'apportait le train.
> Papa supportait le train.
> Papa y apportait le train.

Translations were elicited for key structures such as simple sentences, interrogation, and various kinds of indirect and direct objects.

Case material. Diary records and taped natural conversation of a five year old and a six and a half year old child added details to the knowledge obtained from tests, with a production emphasis. In addition, in the discussion below we shall refer to studies of case development by students of Evelyn Hatch, who have studied natural acquisition of English by children.

Social milieu. The logic of the study required that the acquisition of French be in situations like those in which children acquire their mother tongue. Since the study was done during the school year, we were limited to children who were exposed to French in school. There were basically three sources from which they acquired French: peers, school, and home. All learned from peer interaction in the school and often outside of school. All learned in the classroom. The majority of them were in classes where each was the only anglophone, and where the teacher knew little or no English. Many of the children also learned French at home, since their parents, and often an *au pair* girl spoke to them. In some families, sibling interaction began to occur in French in the course of the year. We have no control over the amount of home exposure. In addition, television and assorted interaction in shops provided miscellaneous exposure. It was clear that in terms of hours, the school training was important. The children spent between 22 and 26 hours a week in class; nursery schools were on half-days. The children heard only French in school. There is more time given to memorizing songs and poetry than here, and playground activities tend to be highly structured, with language involved in instructions and teacher control of activities. The classroom interaction is formal and teacher-centered.

We do not know how much of the classroom instruction was specifically focused on language. At the age of six, primers were used which are in some ways optimal initiation into second language. The impact of schooling was evident in the spelling pronunciations which sometimes appeared in the imitation tests—such as "grenouille" pronounced with a final /l/ instead of a semi-vowel. Presumably the content of the curriculum dealing directly with French structure varied with the grade level. A good deal of formal instruction in French schools perforce deals with gender and with conjugation, since the cues for some of the contrasts are different in the written and oral forms of the language.

A few children had a little supplementary FSL instruction in their schools, but as far as we could learn the focus was on vocabulary, not on the syntactic features of this study.

RESULTS

Similarity to child language

1. Learning by children occurs first for the material which is predictable, and for which the meaning is apparent. We did not have diachronic comprehension tests,

so our evidence on this point comes from the diary material. Some of the children said nothing for many months, so we do not know what they were learning. My own children began speaking six and eight weeks after immersion in the school setting. Their earliest utterances included greetings: "au revoir," "salut," "bonjour, Madame;" operational terms dealing with interaction: "regarde," "tiens," "allez-y," and claims related to the self: "moi bébé," "moi sanglier."[5]

Evelyn Hatch mentioned that a Chinese five year old learning English after two weeks of exposure imitated "get out of here" with full comprehension, as indicated by a correct translation. Three months later this phrase survived in expansion sets like "Let's go. Get out of here. Let's get out of here."

In the Geneva study, the first phrase memorized by the two children in the case study was "Peut-je jouer avec Corinne?" They knew its meaning. It referred to a child in a hotel they occupied for two weeks. This phrase, without overt practice, was recalled two months later. As in the Huang example, the size of the unit stored is impressive, since at the time it must have been stored as a lexical simplex.

Second language learners, like children, remember best the items they can interpret.

2. Meaning recurrences provide basic categorization devices for mapping of forms. Two examples can be seen in the texts in Table 13-1. When the child said "moi sanglier," with the meaning of "my boar" (boars being major figures in a favorite French comic strip), he was corrected: "mon sanglier." He resisted complicating the system by having inflected pronouns, and persisted for some time in using "moi" as the form both for "my" and "me." The resistance to correction when the system would be complicated is familiar in child language studies. In this case it cannot be attributed to mother tongue interference.

The child reported that a new word learned at school was "Assieds-toi" (sit down), pronounced as a single word [asi´ɛtə]. The next day he reported that this was a mistake, he had heard wrong, the word was "asseyez-vous." The situations appeared identical to him, requiring a single form.

Most of the 31 children regularly treated "le" (masculine article) and "la" (feminine article) as synonyms, perhaps because they appeared to have identical meanings. In the imitation test, though they never confused [a] and [ɨ] otherwise, they regularly failed to differentiate these articles and pronouns. In songs they confused them. In the pronoun comprehension test, differentiation of gender for direct object pronouns "le" and "la" was quite late. In texts, the existence of arbitrary gender created ambiguous cues for marking the meaning of the forms. In the case of number, this ambiguity did not exist, so number contrasts for articles and pronouns were correctly imitated and understood much earlier, while gender still was random.

E. Hernández studied a Chicano child who in learning English rejected double vocabulary, noting that "it's not wolf, but *lobo*!" in a bilingual environment. *The basic preference of the child at first is for a principle of one meaning-one form, and he rejects two forms for what appears to be an identical meaning or referential situation.*

Table 13-1   First spontaneous speech samples of two Anglophones at home. French

Weeks in Geneva		6.7 year old child
6	moi sanglier	(me boar) [claiming animal from comic book]
	au-revoir	goodbye
	je-ne-comprends	(I don't understand)
	à moi, lait, moi	(mine, milk, me) [gestures he wants milk]
	allez-y	(hurry up, get going)
	tour de vélo	(bike trip) [wants to go biking]
	assieds-toi	(sit down)
	asseyez-vous	(sit down)
8	Nicholas dit non.	(Nicolas says no)
	Nicolas dit pourquoi.	(Nicolas says why)
	pousse-moi	(push me)
	ferme la porte	(close the door)
	toi nez rouge	(you nose red)
	petit couteau	(little knife)
	ça Nicolas vélo	(that Nicolas bike)

		5 year old child
8	regarde [lə'gaʁd]	(look)
9	regarde, escargots	(look, snails) [saw snails for dinner]
	moi bébé	(me baby) [playing she is baby]
	moi poupee	(me doll)
	moi princesse	
	Thérèse, tiens	(Therese, take)
11	regarde, Anna	(look at Anna)
	le crayon bleu, c'est là-bas	(the blue pencil, it's over there)
16	pas moi, toi, moi là	(not me, you, me there) [directing play locations]
	ça moi, ça Alexandre.	(that's me that Alexander.) [possessions]
	moi, c'est grand	(me, it's big) [=mine's big]
	ça va, ça va pas, Eric?	(that's okay, that's not okay, Eric?)
	pas lait là, pas lait, milk.	(not milk there)

3. *The first features of sentences to be used in comprehension rules are those which survive in short term memory best.* We have argued elsewhere (Ervin-Tripp, 1973a, b) that it is plausible to extend findings from word list studies to the learning of initially unfamiliar sentences. In these studies first and last position survive best in memory. In the Geneva study, medial pronouns were far less often imitated than initial or final pronouns. The order of items is relatively easy to recall, and appears to be very strong in imitation examples, from the beginning.

Young children also learn the relation of order to meaning relatively early. In permuting languages like Finnish, they learn the relative hierarchy of frequency of subject-verb-object order and other permutations. In fixed order languages, they learn simple order strategies at an early age, such as English possessor + possessed, quantifier + quantified, attribute + head. Paul Huang's studies of a Chinese child learning English showed sentences much like native speaker English: "This kite," "Two cat," "No candy," "No more truck." Although in both Norwegian and French the negator follows the main verb, Ravem (1968), studying a Norwegian child learning English, and Kesselman studying French children (personal communication) found that in English they placed the negator before the verb.

The most thoroughly studied of these order strategies is the so-called NVN or SVO strategy, which in its basic form identifies the first noun as an agent, and the second as direct object of a transitive action (Bever, 1970, 1971). Developmentally, this begins with a rule that the noun just before the verb is the agent (sometimes with semantic restrictions that it be animate or a vehicle). Later the order of nouns alone signals the meaning (Sinclair-de Zwart, 1973).

In my research, half of the four and five year olds interpreted the first noun in an English NVN sequence, even a passive, as the agent. Thus in "The bear is pushed by the giraffe" it is the bear who pushes. This strategy remains later for word sequences which are telegraphic, such as "box open boy." Sinclair-de Zwart (1973) found that 37% of the seven year old francophones try to make the box open the boy when they hear "boite ouvrir garçon." The general principle of this rule also causes errors of comprehension for indirect objects in English. In response to "The bear gave the giraffe the monkey" many children, even at later ages, move the giraffe to the monkey.

After five the children begin to interpret the morphological information in passives well enough to by-pass this rule, but they may not do so if semantic plausibility counteracts. For example, if the first noun is animate and the second both inanimate and a common object of the verb, an active interpretation is almost inevitable, as in a sentence like "the boy was eaten by the carrot." The same children who stumbled over this sentence might correctly interpret "the boy was pushed by the dog."

We might expect, on the transfer hypothesis, that English-speaking children learning French would simply interpret the sentences as if they were English. But they don't. In the early stages of learning French, regardless of age, the children reverted to the unmodified SVO strategy and systematically misunderstood passives. The older children, who in English correctly understood anomalous passives, regressed on the French version.

In French, the indirect object sentences are easy since they are marked by a preposition, but if we used the English order, the children often ignored the prepositions and interpreted the noun following the verb as the patient, regardless of its form. Thus they continued to use an SVO strategy in spite of the cue from the preposition.

Table 13-2   Examples of English to French translations

Stimulus	5 year old Geneva since birth English only at home	5½ year old Geneva 9 months E, F at home	7 year old Geneva 9 months, E, F at home
I see her.	Je vois elle.	Moi je vois elle.	Je elle vois.
She sees them.	Elle voit eux.	Elle regarde eux.	Elle les voit*
Why does she eat them?	Pourquoi elle mange le?	Pourquoi il mange ça?	Pourquoi elle les mange?†
He gave her the carrots.	Il a donné une carotte.	Il a donné les carottes.	Il a donné à elle les carottes.†
Who is she waiting for?	Où est-elle attend pour?	Qui elle attend pour?	Elle attend pour qui?
She's waiting for them.	Elle attend pour eux.	Il attend pour eux.	Elle les attend.*
What pushed the door?	Quoi poussait la porte?	Quoi il poussait la porte?	Qu'est-ce qui a poussé la porte?*
What fell down?	Quoi-t-il a tombé?	Quoi il a tombé?	Qu'est-ce qui a tombé?
Why is he pushing her?	Pourquoi il pousse elle?	Pourquoi il pousse elle?	Pourquoi il elle pousse?
Where is the dog going?	Où es le chien, il va?	Où le chien il va?	Où va le chien?*
Where is he going?	Où est-ce il va?	Où lui il va?	Où ils'en va.† Il s'en va où?†

* Correct.   † Colloquial, possible in native speaker's usage.

By chance, we encountered two American children who were losing English after nine months living with their Swiss mother and grandparents in Geneva. Their family language had been English until then, but their father was absent in the Air Force. They were extremely reluctant to respond to English speech, and when they did, used comprehension patterns similar to those of the other children after three months exposure to French. That is to say, they interpreted English passives, but not French passives, as if they were active. They had regressed to a simpler sentence processing heuristic in which the cue from the function words and suffixes was inoperative, and the primary pattern, NVN = SVO, reappeared. Other studies of language loss may show patterned deterioration of syntax, too.[6] We would expect that the general syntactic rules which are qualified by special rules would take over and the special rules would be the first to be lost; also that over-generalizations would take over, in morphology.

Translations were our only systematic data on sentence production, other than the diary and taped material, which only exist for a few children. At first glance, many of the translations (Table 13-2) look as if they were word-for-word. We would expect to find such translations if the general production pattern for the children was mapped onto English syntax rather than onto a newly developing French syntax, or if the child solved the particular challenge of the task by a word-for-word mapping onto the surface of the sentence. But these appeared to be the strategies used in only a small residual of sentences. The basic patterns seemed rather to be as follows:

a. In declarative sentences, use SVO order. Very few children had progressed to a separate rule for pronominal objects. The result of this rule was sentences like:
    "I see her"   Je vois elle
b. In question word sentences, give the question word, then the nuclear order, either SVO or SVL. (Older children displaced the question word to preserve nuclear order.)
    "What can she see?"
        Quoi elle peut voir. (What can she see.)
        Elle peut voir quoi. (She can see what.)
    "Why is she there?"
        Pourquoi elle est là. (Why she is there.)
    A word-for-word translation would lead to inversion of these sentences, but inversion was rare. It is not surprising that Dato (1970) found inversion errors to be rare in anglophones learning Spanish.
c. Word-for-word translations were a small residual and were most frequent in the youngest children. These were to some extent lexical, as in:
    "Who is he waiting for?"
        Qui elle attent pour? (Who she waits for.)

A particularly interesting example is the sentence "Where is the dog going?" which produced some of the most amusing translations. The older children had, in many cases, learned the French inversions or an acceptable apposition:

> Où va le chien? (Where goes the dog?)
> Où il va, le chien? (Where he goes, the dog?)

Or they employed the second rule, with results like this:

> Où le chien il va. (Where the dog, he goes.)
> Le chien va où. (The dog goes where?)

The smallest children had more trouble, and revealed segmentation errors arising from the very high frequency, familiar question "Où est le chien?" which was one of their first question structures. Its alternative form is "Où il est, le chien?" The result of the alternation is that "Où-est" = "Où il-est" and they are in free variation for the little speakers. My two year old, months after our departure, still alternated "Où-il-est Daddy" and "Où-est Daddy." The translations employed these forms, which of course are inappropriate for a main verb sentence.

Où-il-est	le chien	aller.
Où-il-est	le chien	il-va.
Où-est	le chien	va.

"Where did the dog go" also elicited the same forms, so we cannot account for them entirely as word-for-word translations. They may also reflect the question-forming rule Q-S-V, but with a different segmentation for the components, just as we find in early child English free variation of "there's," "there's a" and "there" in sentence-initial position (Ervin-Tripp, in press).

In sum, we found many similarities between the sentence forms produced and understood by children learning their mother tongue and children learning a second language. In the most carefully studied example, the SVO strategy, it appeared that this clause-analysis heuristic is either relearned again in the early stages of the acquisition of French, or that the detailed subrules which govern indirect objects and passives are ignored in early comprehension of French, just as they seem to be lost as mastery of English disappears. Obviously, the best test of these alternatives would be the study of a language in which the rules of simple clause analysis are quite different in mother tongue and second language.

Most of the evidence showing mother-tongue interference in the learning of syntax has had two peculiarities: It has come from learning conditions in which the second language was not the language of the learner's larger social milieu so that the learning contexts were aberrant both in function and frequency of structures. Further, both the learning and the testing often occurred in situations where the milieu and the addresses were not overwhelmingly connected with the second language. Yet we know that learners are extremely sensitive to such nuances.

If it is the case that second language learners recapitulate mother tongue acquisition, why do we have the impression that the second language learner is severely handicapped by first language interference?

Let me speculate a little on this question. We do not at the moment have good models of speech production, even for monolinguals, so we have very little knowledge of how interference occurs. In the free speech observed by Evelyn Hatch's students, and in my own tape recordings, there is only partial evidence of word-for-word translations. Most of the first sentences are either learned as units or generated from very simple order rules, such as those we find in early child language. The older learner, as Hatch has persuasively shown, has a very good capacity to repeat long sequences, compared to two-year olds, so more idiomatic material could occur of deceptively long sequences.

I would suppose that if we push a child to generate sentences about semantically difficult material or concepts unfamiliar in the new culture, he may use somewhat different production patterns. Some years back, there was an argument over whether speech was degenerate and full of errors and false starts; the evidence from conferences suggested that it was, the evidence from family speech to small children that it was not (Bever, Fodor and Weksel, 1965; Pfuderer, Drach and Kobashigawa, 1969). I am suggesting that the simpler the semantic task, and the simpler the relation between meaning and form (e.g., description vs. interference), the less the likelihood the speaker will have recourse to other-tongue formations.[7] This notion might lead us to predict the kinds of speech situation which should produce most and least interference. It may also be the case that we normally make greater semantic demands in testing older learners, and that they may, in free speech, make attempts at more complex communication than younger children do, leading to more apparent interference.

Age and rate of learning

It is a common belief that the older the learner is, the more burdened he or she may be with overlearned habits. My reasoning supports a different prediction, on the following grounds:

1. Oral languages are alike more than they are different. The older learner has already discovered some basic principles of phonology. If he has learned to read a syllabic or morphophonemic written language he has acquired a fairly abstract knowledge of oral language phonology.
2. Languages tend to have similar semantic content. By and large the major changes we find in acquisition of the mother tongue with age are related to semantic development. The older child has a fuller semantic system, so he merely needs to discover a new symbolic representation. There will of course be errors in the cases where the semantic properties differ, but these are minor compared to the burdens of a child learner at a similar stage of syntax.
3. The older child has more efficient memory heuristics, related to his greater knowledge. Because he can learn both strings and single items faster, he may map new vocabulary into storage too quickly, before he has enough text to discover the semantic and structural distribution, in those cases where there is a slight difference.
4. The older learner is smarter. The child's capacity to solve problems, to make sub-rules, to carry in mind several principles increases with age. We would expect rule learning to be faster with age in both phonology and syntax.

Another way to think about age is to examine the principle that we learn our mother-tongue throughout life, but that different components of our Language Acquisition System are most activated at various ages. For most people, the prime activation of phonology learning is in the first five years, and then again at six in relation to reading, where different segmentation is required than in speech. Only if we travel in different dialect areas or learn to understand quite different phonological registers do we tamper much with phonology in later years.

For most people the prime period for the learning of syntax may be from two to ten or so, and only recondite aspects of register are of issue later. For all of us, vocabulary learning goes on throughout life, unless we lead very isolated and humdrum lives. Even in village cultures, the social nuances of certain vocabulary continue to be elaborated throughout life.

Thus adults learning a second language tend to pay most attention to vocabulary, but I would suppose that children well into their teens may still be good learners of syntax (Asher and Garcia, 1969). I have assumed that for phonology, the optimal learning stage might be around seven or eight, after the learning of reading. In these predictions, the assumption is that learning strategies can fall into relative disuse. There is, of course, another set of predictions, based on biology, which would be generated by lateralization and aphasia research (Bever, 1971). However, testing such generalizations would require a later time range than this study included.

Phonology. For most features of segmental phonology, the children above seven learned faster than the younger children. The samples are fairly small in the higher age ranges, however. This finding is consistent with the experiment of Olson and Samuels (1973).

The most interesting finding is accidental. My six and a half year old son, who could read English and was learning to read French, playfully pronounced an American name with a French accent a month after our arrival. Of course I rapidly tested both the children on this skill and developed a test for the other children in the study, but at a much later stage. The evidence in Table 13-3 will show you responses of two children who had been in a French milieu only a month. The younger child could not read, and had much simpler rules. However, it is very clear that the children had mapped the two phonological systems onto each other and had discovered some general principles.

The younger child reduced all words to a single syllable, and deleted most final consonants. She converted nasal segments to nasalized vowels, and partially

Table 13-3   Phonological translations after five weeks

English Stimulus	5 year old	6½ year old
knife [naɪf]	[naɪ]	[nif]
ride [raɪd]	[raɪt]	[ʁad]
fan [fæn]	[fæn]	[fã]
fast [fæst]	[fæs]	[fɑst] "British"
bent [bɛnt]	[bɛ·]	[bant]
cones [konz]	[kõ]	[kõz]
bones [bonz]	[bõ]	[bõz]
finger [ˊfɪŋgr]	[fɪŋ]	[fɪŋˊgøʁ]
winter [ˊwɪntr]	[wɪn]	[wɪnˊtiʁ]
ladder [ˊlædr]	[læt]	[ləˊtir]
hungry [ˊhəŋgri]	[həŋg]	[hənˊgʁi]
birthday [ˊbrθdeɪ]	[brθ]	[ˊbɪθdeɪ]
umbrella [əmˊbrɛlə]	[bʁɛl]	[pɑʁaˊplyi]

replaced apical or retroflex with uvular R. Her older brother had more complex rules, including more complete R replacement, a shift of stress to second syllables, vowel changes to the French vowel values—even including a rounded front vowel, and of course nasalization.

* The dramatic evidence from this example and the other cases is that children can make such correspondences well before they comprehend much. Eduardo Hernandez-Chavez and others have told me that anglophone children spontaneously "speak Spanish" by adopting Spanish phonological features, with either English words or nonsense. Ronjat (1913) in his elegant description of his child's Franco-German bilingualism from birth, reported that the child tried words out in both systems before settling on the right one, as though he stored them abstractly and had corresponding production rules. So there is apparently a phonological mapping, much like lexical mapping, onto an existent analysis. The children did, however, have a strong sense of the appropriate system in speech and did not recognize, or correct, proper French names if they were anglicized.

Morphology. The older children learned number and gender more rapidly than the younger children. The youngest learner was a very bright six year old. Both number and gender exist in English and are usually semantically mastered by the ages in this study. The assumption made here is that French gender for inanimate nouns creates "noise" in acquisition, and retards the discovery of systematic correspondences between form and meaning. Number was correct before gender.

In an analysis of the acquisition of English plurals in two Malayan children, Arfah Aziz has shown in a term paper than an eight year old uniformly learned to use suffixes (although with some phonological problems) when the four year old had not. The four year old more often added numerals, which is the most general of the Malay pluralizing devices which could be extended to English. These findings confirm the age difference in rate of acquisition, and suggest that the child might (as in the Israeli example) at first overgeneralize patterns which look common to the two languages.

Syntax. Syntax was learned faster by the older children. On virtually all the tests the nine year olds were always correct in French, including a child in Geneva for only six months. Age gave enough of an advantage to overcome even a relatively short exposure.

The most complex syntactic tasks were relative clauses, with the purpose of finding changes at later ages, when internal clause structure might be stabilized. The measure of comprehension was acting out of two actions in the two clauses. In each of 12 sentences there were three nouns and two verbs. Table 13-4 shows the sentence types, and relative success at various ages. In the first three of the sentences the order was NVNVN or NVNNV. In these sentences, the children could draw on the NVN = SVO strategy to interpret agent and patient in the clauses. In the last, which proved much harder, they could not, since the order was NNVVN.

Table 13-4   Relative clause comprehension*
(percent with correct patients
and agents)

Age	English		French	
	4-6	7-9	4-6	7-9
	%	%	%	%
SS	78	79	38	55
OS	24	68	35	60
OO	38	92	52	72
SO	15	57	27	64
N	19	12	19	12

SS   The dog who pushed the cat carried the bear.
OS   The dog pushed the cat who carried the bear.
OO   The dog pushed the cat that the bear carried.
SO   The dog that the cat pushed carried the bear.

*There were three sentences of each type in French,
two in English.

In the first three sentences, the children easily interpreted the first NVN sequence, but had trouble finding the missing noun complement in the second clause. The younger subjects tended often to keep the same agent for both actions. This solution leads to success for sentence SS but error on sentence OS, which were treated indiscriminately by children 4 through 6, in English.

A second common solution, found at all ages, was to interpret NV sequences as agent-action. This solution produced errors on SS but success on OS and OO. A third strategy appeared on the OO sentence, where the problem was to find a patient. Many subjects went back to the first noun of the sentence for that patient—possibly a random guess. The English findings are similar to those of Amy Sheldon (1972).

I have mentioned earlier that children had available to them in French an SVO clause interpretation strategy, so they had no problems with the first clauses of these sentences (at least the first three). The surprising finding was that they generally used solution strategies in French for the second clause like those in English. Age, rather than language, seemed to dictate their solutions. In both languages, for each sentence type, the older children were more successful and more likely to take into account the location of the relative pronoun.

Only for the most recent learners, who knew little French, was there a distinct advantage in interpreting the English sentences. This was true of the passives, too, but in the case of the passives, the new learners used a simplifying, earlier strategy still available to them. In the relative clauses, there is no evidence of such return to a simpler, earlier strategy.

For the younger newcomers, there was a reduced tendency in French to use the first noun in the sentence to complement the second verb. The result was that in French they had fewer errors on the second and third sentence in French than in English and more on the first sentence. Perhaps their short term memory was briefer in French so the first noun was less salient.

In brief, learners of transitive clauses in French appeared to recapitulate the stages of acquisition the first language learners traverse. But in interpretation of relative clauses they do not. Perhaps the interpretation of relative clauses is less a function of surface structure heuristics and more related to the stage of cognitive maturity than is comprehension of simple sentences.

The first question of this paper was whether the process of second language acquisition looks like the first. We found that the functions of early sentences, and their form, their semantic redundancy, their reliance on ease of short term memory, their overgeneralization of lexical forms, their use of simple order strategies all were similar to processes we have seen in first language acquisition. In broad outlines, then, the conclusion is tenable that first and second language learning is similar in natural situations. However, if children come to the task with some knowledge already available, there may be very accelerated progress in some respects, so that the rate of development will not look the same for all details. In every respect, we found that in the age range of four through nine the older children had an advantage and learned faster.

The first hypothesis we might have is that in all second language learning we will find the same processes: overgeneralization, production simplification, loss of sentence-medial items, and so on. More detailed studies will be needed to find which aspects of acquisition change with age when learning contexts are identical, and which are sensitive to structural dissimilarities between L_1 and L_2, or differences in social milieu.

The most difficult problem in generalizing the results of this study is the high degree of syntactic similarity between French and English. For the syntactic patterns studied in the simple and complex sentences the languages are word-for-word translations of each other. Therefore, in this particular study, we cannot fully differentiate the two interpretations, which I have used interchangeably: (a) The children in learning a second language recapitulate learning, and go faster through essentially the same stages, as a child learning French as a mother tongue, (b) because they lack knowledge about, for example, the morphemes identifying passives in French, they "regress" to a processing strategy still available to them for use under certain conditions in English. Only studies of structurally dissimilar languages can disambiguate these interpretations. But we can reject, at least, the hypothesis that children's interpretations of second-language sentences are directly processed through a translator. For interpretation tasks and translations both, direct word-for-word translations did not account for the evidence as well as did learner strategies quite like those mother-tongue learners employ.

Notes

*The research was supported by an NIMH grant to the Language-Behavior Research Laboratory at the University of California, Berkeley. We owe a great deal to the advice, stimulation, and practical aid of Hermine Sinclair-de Swart in Geneva, and to the assistance of Leo Barblan, Marie-Claude Capt, Gwen Bianco, Edith Kleibaer, and Shira Milgrom. Herbert Simon contributed some bibliographic ideas.

1. There have of course been exceptions, such as the work of Evelyn Hatch's students (Huang, 1971), Ravem (1968), and Malmberg (1945, 1964).

2. Findings by a group of students concerning input to English-speaking children (Pfuderer, Drach, and Kobashigawa, 1964).

3. Cazden (1965), and numerous Russian studies.

4. In Ervin-Tripp (1973b) we have argued that a Language Acquisition System (LAS) is composed of component processors whose properties were discussed generally there. Some of these may be highly limited and specific to language acquisition, as proposed by Chomsky in his discussion of an hypothesis-testing Language Acquisition Device (1965). It has been shown convincingly by Braine (1971) that an hypothesis-testing device requires corrective feedback which does not exist in natural conditions. Levelt (1973) cites studies showing that learning must involve interaction, or at least have very special text properties, for even quite weak grammars to be learned.

5. These sentences and phrases are parallel to those observed by others. Benjamin Chen, keeping a record of his two-year-old son's first utterances in English as a second language for a term paper found "Thank you," "you are welcome," "Ya," "Good night," "Pleasant dreams," "no," "Good-bye," "Bad boy," "Like that," "Wait here," "It's mine," "Like you," "Stand up," "Sit here," and "want that," in that order. He pointed out that the child did not map the meanings onto already known Hebrew forms such as the equivalent of "Good night." Instead, he overgeneralized: Whenever his father kissed him, even in the morning, he said "good night, pleasant dreams." As Chen points out the first forms are not nouns but functionally significant reflections of interactive milieux.

6. In a study of language loss of Israeli-speaking children in the United States, Shaltiel (personal communication) noted that the irregular forms were particularly vulnerable, as if the over-regularization stage of child language may recur. In two years, during which Hebrew was the home language, the six year old lost the ability even to say "I want to go home" which has two irregular forms.

7. There is some evidence that in formulating simple order rules, children sometimes draw on mother-tongue formulations if (a) there is some second language support for the rule, i.e. partial overlap or (b) the mother-tongue rule is much simpler. An example appears in Ravem's (1968) data. The children employed the English order rule for negation, because it was simpler than the Norwegian and did not differentiate between modal and main-verb sentences, but always puts the negator before the main element in the verb phrase. But the children retained the Norwegian question-inversion rule, for main verbs at first. The implication, which needs testing through studies of comprehension, is that verb-first sentences are highly marked and the salience of the verb was important to major interrogation-forming rules in Norwegian and were carried over into English.

Shira Milgrom, studying Israeli acquisition of English in a term paper, found that children, but not adults, went through a stage which evidently was influenced by Hebrew. In Hebrew, there is a Y/N interrogation morpheme that is sentence-initial. Children created a syntactic class of preposed auxiliaries, rather on the model of tag questions, as in:

Is I am going to be a rich man?
Is it he is singing a song?
Is she is crying?
Do I'm am going to be a fortune teller?
Do you can tell me what is the time?

The Acquisition

14

of English Negatives and Interrogatives

by Native Spanish Speakers

Herlinda Cancino, Ellen J. Rosansky, John H. Schumann, *Harvard University*

INTRODUCTION

Cancino, Rosansky & Schumann studied the acquisition of English as a second language by six Spanish speakers: two children, two adolescents and two adults. Theirs is the first observational-longitudinal study that looks specifically at age differences in the rate of acquisition of language forms. Because their study is longitudinal, they are able to talk about *acquisition* of forms while the large cross-sectional studies can only work with *accuracy* of forms in the speech data.

This paper is concerned with the acquisition of negation and questions. Milon (abstract section of this volume) compared negation in the speech of his second-language learner, Ken, with that of first-language learners. He found strong similarities. Cancino, Rosansky & Schumann question those findings (as well as those of researchers in first language acquisition) in terms of the reality of Stage 1 negation. Perhaps the only strong evidence for Stage 1 negation in second language learning is to be found in Murrell's study of Sandra, a two year old learning three languages. Her output is especially interesting since it shows virtually free word order with negation usually in sentence initial position for English. Certainly free word order is atypical of most children learning first and second languages though it was also characteristic of the data collected by Bowerman for acquisition of Finnish as a first language. Finnish is one of the three languages with which Sandra had contact.

The second part of this chapter concerns question formation. The authors draw further contrasts and parallels with first and second language learners.

The figures presented in this chapter give us an easy way of comparing the progress made by each of the six subjects. The least progress, obviously, is that made by Alberto, the thirty-three year old. The reader may wish to follow this chapter with a reading of Schumann's report on Alberto and the reasons for his minimal progress in the second language.

This paper describes the natural, untutored acquisition of English negatives and interrogatives by six native Spanish speakers: two children age five, two adolescents ages 11 and 13, and two adult subjects, whom we visited approximately twice monthly for an hour over a period of ten months. All of the subjects had been in this country less than three months when we began. The data were collected in the following ways:

1. Spontaneous speech recording in which the experimenter engages the subject in conversation;
2. Experimental elicitations in which the subject is asked to do such things as imitate or negate a model utterance;
3. Pre-planned socio-linguistic interaction in which subjects are taken to parties, restaurants, museums, sports events, etc., in order to collect speech in varied natural situations.

All of the data were taped and in addition to the investigator, a bilingual transcriber was always present, taking notes. The transcribers then transcribed (and where necessary, translated) the tapes in a standard format along the lines suggested in the *Slobin Manual.*

The six subjects discussed are Marta, Cheo, Juan, Jorge, Alberto, and Dolores. Marta (5 years old) is an upper middle class Puerto Rican. Cheo (5 years old) is an upper middle class Colombian from Cali. Juan (11 years old) and Jorge (13 years old) are upper middle class Colombians from Bogota. Alberto (33 years old) is a lower middle class Costa Rican, and Dolores (25 years old) is a middle class Peruvian. In addition to age and socio-economic differences among our subjects, there are some differences in the nature of their exposure to English. While Jorge, Juan, Marta and Cheo were all exposed to English through peer speech in public schools (with practically no ESL instruction), Alberto worked in a factory where some of his input is from other non-native speakers of English. Dolores was a babysitter for English speaking children. All of the subjects spoke Spanish in the home.

THE NEGATIVE

Acquisition of the negative has been treated extensively in the first language acquisition literature. Klima and Bellugi (1966) found three stages in the development of the negative in a study of three children, Adam, Eve and Sarah. In the first stage the negative particle is sentence-external: *no singing song, no the sun shining.* In the second stage the negative is placed within the sentence and *don't* and *can't* appear: *He not little, he big; He no bite you; I don't want it; We can't talk.* The third stage is characterized by full realization of the auxiliary. Auxiliaries begin to appear in declaratives and interrogatives and therefore are no longer simply part of the negative element in the sentence: *No, it isn't; That was not me; Paul didn't laugh; I am not a doctor.*

Most discussion concerning the development of the negative centers around whether or not Klima and Bellugi's stage one exists. Bloom (1970) in a study of three subjects found that the negative element occupied the first position in the early negative utterances of her subjects, but she asserted that this structure was the result of the deletion of sentence subjects. Hence, she did not find Klima and Bellugi's stage one. Lord (1974) also failed to find evidence for stage one-type utterances in a study of the acquisition of the negative by her daughter.

In the second language acquisition literature, Milon (1974) in a study of the acquisition of English by a 7-year-old Japanese boy found a developmental pattern similar to that described by Klima and Bellugi for first language learners. Gillis (1975) studied the acquisition of English by two Japanese children ages seven and eight and found that her subjects showed a developmental pattern that corresponds only to Klima and Bellugi's stages two and three. One of the subjects had utterances which appeared to be a residue of Klima and Bellugi's stage one, but the other had no utterances representing this stage. In a preliminary analysis (Cancino, Rosnasky and Schumann, 1974) of negatives in three of our subjects (Marta, Jorge, Alberto) over a three month period we did not find convincing evidence for the stages described by Klima and Bellugi.

In describing our data, we did not write grammars *per se.* Brown and Fraser (1963) indicated the difficulties in writing traditional grammars for child speech. The concept of writing grammars derives from linguistics which uses grammar writing as a descriptive tool for presumably static grammars. Writing "grammars" for a dynamic system, however, is not only difficult, but is also not suitable as a developmental descriptive technique.

We did, however, think that perhaps traditional grammatical descriptions in the form of rules could be made of such linguistic subsystems as negative, interrogative or auxiliary. Our attempts to write rules for the negative proved fruitless. The constant development and concomitant variation in our subjects' speech at any one point made the task impossible. The technique to which we turned was to catalogue the various negating devices (*no, don't, can't, isn't,* etc.) and for each sample to determine the proportion of each negating device to total number of negatives (including negated adjectives, nouns, adverbs, etc.) used by our subjects. We limited our analysis, however, to proposition negating utterances. By this we mean the negative of a verb within an utterance. Thus we are concerned with the use of the negative particle and its relation to the auxiliary system, but not with the indefinite and indeterminate forms of the negative.

For all subjects, we have eliminated the expression "I don't know," which seemed to be a memorized whole (or, using Evelyn Hatch's term, a "routine formula"). In addition and for the same reason, "I don't think so" is excluded from the tally of Marta's *don't V* constructions.

The "cataloguing" approach produced the following results:

1. The subjects began negating by using *no V* constructions.

Marta:	I no can see.
	Carolina no go to play.
Cheo:	You no walk on this.
	You no tell your mother.
Juan:	Today I no do that.
	No, I no use television.
Jorge:	They no have water.
	But no is mine is my brother. (=It's not mine; it's my brother's.)
Alberto:	I no understand.
	No like coffee. (subject deletion)

This form is found in the early speech of English speaking children. It is also very similar to the way the negative is formed in Spanish (e.g., (yo) no entiendo; (yo) no tengo agua).

2. At the same time or shortly after the *no V* constructions appear, the subjects began to negate using *don't V* constructions. Examples of *don't V* utterances are:

Marta:	I don't hear.
	He don't like it.
Cheo:	I don't understand.
	I don't see nothing mop.
Juan:	I don't look the clock at this time.
	Don't have any monies. (subject deletion)
Jorge:	My brother and I don't have more class.
	That don't say anything.
Alberto:	I don't can explain.
	I don't have a woman.

3. Next the subjects used the *aux-neg* constructions in which the negative is placed after the auxiliary. In general the first auxiliaries to be negated in this way were *is* and *can*.

Marta:	Somebody is not coming in.
	You can't tell her.

Cheo: It's not danger.
             He can't see.

Juan: I haven't seen all of it.
             It wasn't so big.

Jorge: No, he's not skinny.
             But we couldn't do anything.

Alberto: Ø

4. Finally, they learned the analyzed forms of *don't* (do not, doesn't, does not, didn't, did not):

Marta: It doesn't spin.
             One night I didn't have the light.

Cheo: I didn't even know.
             Because you didn't bring.

Juan: We didn't have a study period.
             It doesn't make any difference.

Jorge: She didn't believe me.
             He doesn't laugh like us.

Alberto: Ø

Dolores: My father didn't let me.
             It doesn't matter.

The relative frequencies of these negating devices can be seen in figures 14-1-6. The vertical axes indicate each taping session. In interpreting these graphs it is necessary to consider the span and height of each curve in relation to the other curves. In this way one can determine when each negating device is first used and to what extent it is used in relation to the other negating devices. The orders in which the curves appear and/or peak on the graphs indicate the learners' successive interim hypotheses about the construction of the English negative. An analysis of the curves also indicates when negated *do*-forms begin to be inflected.

Marta (fig. 14-1) has a clear *no V* negating system until tape 6. The slight *don't V* and *aux-neg* peaks at tape 3 are accounted for by four utterances out of a relatively small total negative sample (14). At tape 6 *don't V* becomes the dominant negating strategy and *no V* is radically diminished. At tape 8 Marta begins to use the *aux-neg*, and by tape 9 it reaches the same level as *don't V*. Also at tape 9 analyzed *don't* begins to appear and after some fluctuation it seems to be increasing by tape 15.

Cheo (fig. 14-2) went through a silent period and did not begin to speak English until the third tape. At that point his negation strategy was *no V*. At tape four he adopted *don't V* and used it simultaneously with *no V* until tape 8, where *aux-neg* seems to be an additional firmly established negation strategy. At tape 9 he begins using the analyzed forms of *don't* and by tape 10 he appears to have abandoned *no V*.

Although at tape 1 Juan (fig. 14-3) appears to have all four negating strategies, *no V* is clearly attenuating and *don't V* is the dominant negation strate-

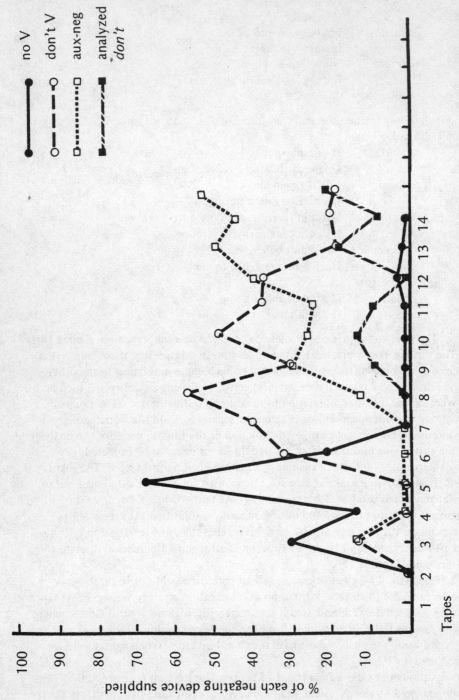

Figure 14-1 Development of negation in Marta showing proportion of each negating device to total negatives in each sample

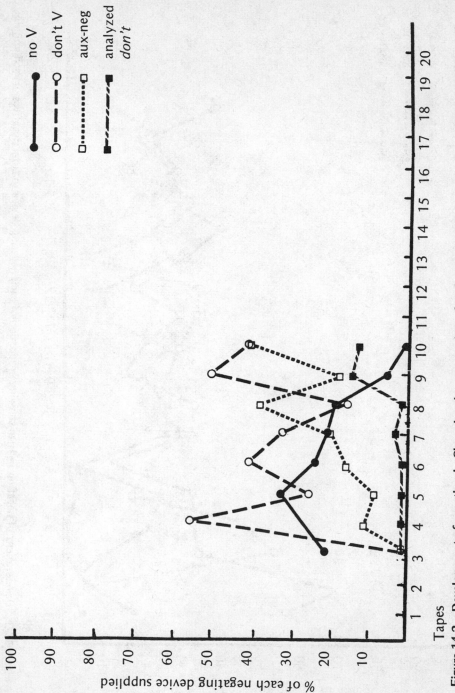

Figure 14-2 Development of negation in Cheo showing proportion of each negating device to total negatives in each sample

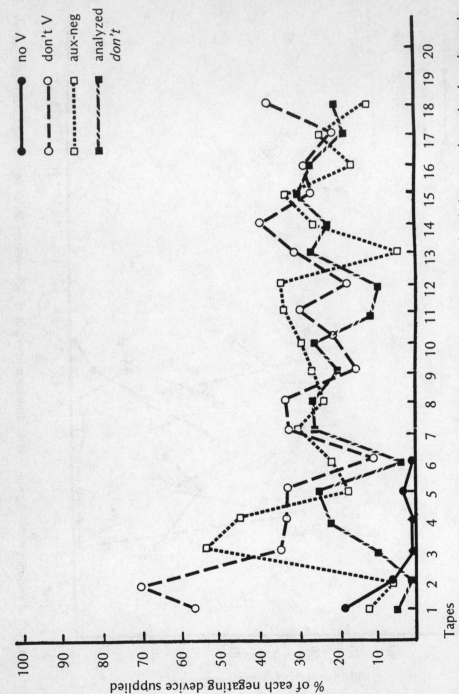

Figure 14-3 Development of negation in Juan showing proportion of each negating device to total negatives in each sample

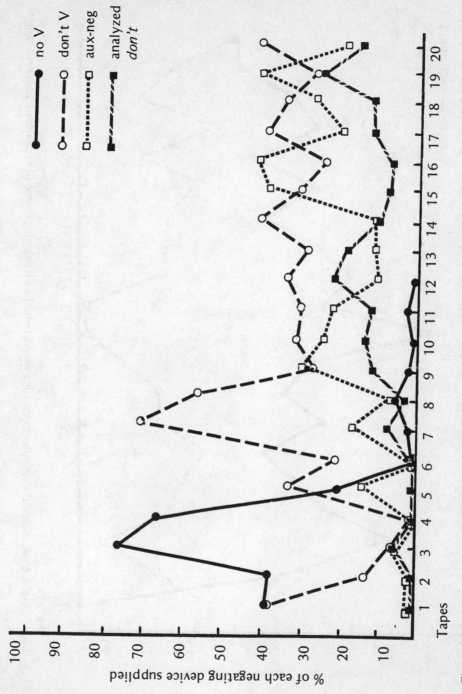

Figure 14-4   Development of negation in Jorge showing proportion of each negating device to total negatives in each sample

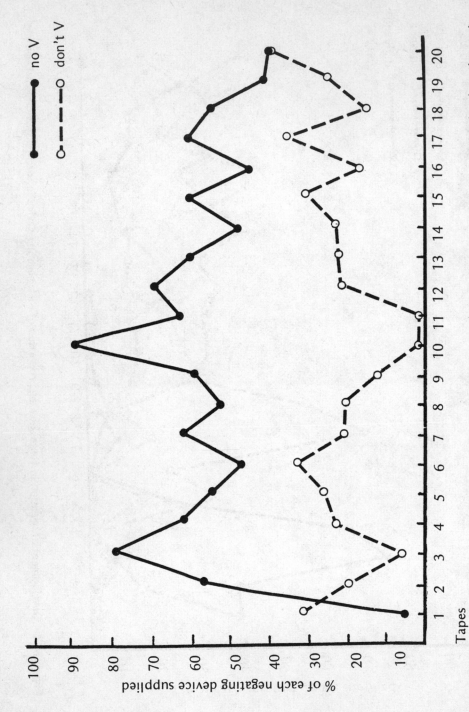

Figure 14-5   Development of negation in Alberto showing proportion of each negating device to total negatives in each sample

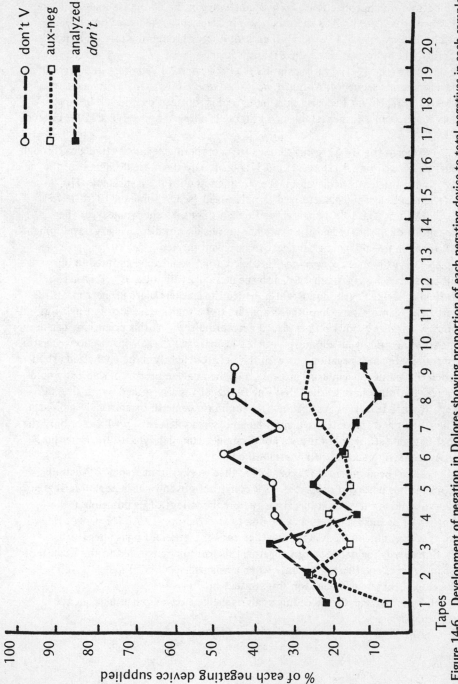

Figure 14-6 Development of negation in Dolores showing proportion of each negating device to total negatives in each sample

gy. It would appear that *no V* is dropping off in Juan's speech at the point where we begin our data collection. *Don't V* continues in the dominant role until tape 3, when *aux-neg* exhibits a sharp increase in frequency. Analyzed don't seems established by tape 5. In general, Juan progressed through the interim hypotheses rapidly and by tape 7 his negative is fully formed.

Jorge (fig. 14-4) clearly exhibits the *no V, don't V, aux-neg,* analyzed *don't* developmental sequence. Although *no V* and *don't V* appear simultaneously at tape 1, by tape 3 *no V* clearly dominates and is replaced by *don't V* in tape 7. *Aux-neg* becomes firmly established in tape 9 followed by analyzed *don't* in tape 12.

Alberto (fig. 14-5) seems to have two competing negation strategies throughout: *no V* and *don't V*. However, *no V* is obviously the more dominant of the two and consistently achieves a higher frequency until the last sample. His interlanguage can be characterized as pidginized (see Schumann, 1974, 1975).

Dolores (fig. 1406) knew more English than the other subjects at the beginning of the study and therefore her graphs do not display early development. All that can be said is that her negatives are well formed.

The *no V, don't V, aux-neg,* analyzed *don't* sequence exhibited in our subjects' speech suggests that Spanish speakers' first hypothesis is that negation in English is like negation in Spanish, hence the learners place *no* in front of the verb. The learners' next hypothesis appears to be that the negator in English is not *no*, but *don't*, and *don't* is placed before the verb. At this point, one can argue that *don't* is simply an allomorph of *no* and that *don't verb* constructions are still essentially Spanish negation but with the negator slightly more anglicized. Then when the learners begin using *aux-neg*, and the analyzed forms of *don't* it would appear that they have learned that English negatives are formed by putting the negative article (n't, not) after the first auxiliary element. Interestingly, in Marta, Cheo, Juan and Jorge, the two children and two adolescents, *no V* is not only the first negating strategy but it does not disappear completely until the time that analyzed *don't* becomes firmly established.

It has been observed (Clyne, 1975) that worker immigrants to Australia from various parts of Europe use *no V* constructions in English negation. It is not clear how long they retain this strategy, but the extent of its duration in the English of Spanish speakers may be due to two factors: 1. All learners of English, we theorize, quickly come to know that *no* is the general English negator. 2. Since *no* is the only Spanish negator, this form is transferred to the English of Spanish speakers. Hence, it is only when a Spanish speaker's English is well developed that he will abandon this strategy entirely.

Summarizing, the preceding analysis yields a developmental sequence of negating devices:

1. *no V*
2. *don't V*
3. *aux-neg*
4. analyzed *don't*; disappearance of *no V*

THE INTERROGATIVE

Interest in the development of the interrogative in studies of first language acquisition was initially motivated by the desire to see whether the acquisition sequence reflected the rules, presented in a transformational analysis of adult English grammar. For our purposes here, the transformational rules for *wh-questions* (Who, What, Where, When, How) can be summarized as follows:

1. Base (or what we'll call the base), can be exemplified by the sentence:
   He — is — going — where (someplace)
2. PREPOSING: Where — he — is — going
   (Wh- word is moved to the front of the string)
3. INVERSION: Where — is — he — going?
   (Aux is moved in front of the subject)

Brown (1968) hypothesized the existence of both the base form and the preposed form in the early development of children's interrogatives. Whereas he found no evidence for the base in his subjects' speech, he did find realizations of the second derivation involving preposing without inversion. In addition, Klima and Bellugi (1966) in an analysis of some of the same data describe a stage (C) in which children are inverting in *yes/no questions* but not in *wh- questions.* Ingram (1973) in a study involving 21 children questions Klima and Bellugi's result. He found a gradual increase in inversions in *yes/no* and *wh- questions,* but found no evidence for a period in which subjects invert in *yes/no* but not *wh- questions.*

In the second language acquisition literature Ravem (1970) studied the acquisition of English by two Norwegian children. He found preposing without inversion in *wh- questions,* thus reflecting Brown's (1968) results. Hatch (1974) examining the data from fifteen studies of 40 second language learners, found: *wh-questions* begin with wh-fronting without inversion (frequently before the copula has developed); modal inversion (can) is prior to inversion with other auxiliaries; and *be* inversion occurs before *do* inversion.

With this literature in mind we examined our interrogative data by asking the following questions:

1. Do *wh- questions* appear in the uninverted form?
2. Do uninverted *wh- questions* appear prior to inverted *wh- questions*?
3. Do *y/n questions* appear in the uninverted form?
4. Do uninverted *y/n questions* appear prior to transposed *y/n questions*?
5. Does Klima and Bellugi's "Stage C" exist for our second language learners?
6. Is there a stage for our second language learners which is the exact opposite of "Stage C," i.e., where *wh- questions* are inverted and *y/n questions* are not?

The examination of the data indicated that:

1. *Wh- questions* appear in the uninverted form for all subjects.
2. Uninverted *wh- questions* do not necessarily appear prior to inverted *wh-questions.*

3. All subjects use uninverted *y/n questions.*
4. Uninverted *y/n questions* consistently appear prior to inverted *y/n questions.*
5. There is no evidence for Klima and Bellugi's "Stage C" for our second language learners.
6. With the exception of Jorge, there is no stage for our subjects where *wh-questions* are inverted and *y/n questions* are not.

The development of the interrogative seems to unfold in the following manner: Both *y/n* and *wh- questions* appear in the uninverted form, but there is no stage in which the uninverted form consistently appears and the inverted is not present. Inverted *y/n questions* do not precede inverted *wh- questions* or vice versa.

Order of appearance of inverted auxiliary. In *wh- questions* inversion is always obligatory: *What are you doing?* *What you *are doing?* However, this is not the case with *y/n questions*: *Are you going? You're going?* Therefore, in order to determine the order of appearance of inverted auxiliaries, only the auxiliaries in *wh- questions* were considered. *Is*-copula is inverted at 100% from the very beginning for most of the subjects: *What is it?* However, there are a number of reasons for questioning whether Wh + *is* (cop) really involves inversion. First, as Ingram suggests, Wh + *is* (cop)—e.g., what's where's—might simply be learned chunks. In addition, in our data, the early appearance of *is* (cop) before subject NP's in *wh- questions* could be simply a direct translation from Spanish, which does not have inversion but nevertheless yields a word order similar to English *"is (cop)" wh- questions.*

> What is? = ¿Qué es?
> Who is? (it) = ¿Quién es?
> Where is? (it) = ¿Dónde está?
> How is? (it) = ¿Cómo es?
> When is? (it) = ¿Cuándo es?
> Why is? = ¿Por qué es?

The other auxiliaries which are inverted early are *can* and *do.* However, *can* is inverted more consistently than the others, often reaching 100%. This may be due to the fact that in adult English *can* in an uninverted *yes/no question* generally carries the notion of *ability* (*You can swim?*) whereas in inverted *yes/no questions* it can mean either *request* or *ability* (*Can he play soccer?*). Thus the learners may sense that when they *request* with an uninverted form they are somehow doing something semantically inappropriate.

Do. Do differs from other auxiliarites in that it is not usually present in declarative sentences: *He goes to school?* In a transformational analysis, *do* must first be inserted in to the declarative sentence and then be moved in front of the subject in order to form a question, e.g.: *Does he go to school?* Other auxiliaries are already present in the declarative form. According to the analysis, questions with *do* involve two operations whereas only one operation is required for other auxiliaries. Consequently *do* inversion might be expected to appear late. However, in general, *do* appears irregularly in the inverted form from the very beginning for most of the subjects: *You speak Spanish?, Do you live in Boston?*

"Inversion Look" of Do. What seems to be the early inversion of *do* may not be inversion at all. In *yes/no questions* of our subjects *do* may be simply placed in front of the declarative utterance as a question marker: *You have children., Do you have children?* Another explanation for the "inversion look" of *do* may be that certain constructions such as *Do you like, Do you have, Do you want* are "memorized chunks." In general, however, the constructions which are preceded by *do* also appear without *do*: *you like, you have, you want.* Perhaps the best explanation is the former: that *do* is irregularly placed before declarative utterances in which the verb is in simple present tense in order to make the utterance into a question. Here the learners may be responding to the nature of the input which is also variable with respect to inversion since inversion is largely optional in *yes/no questions*:

> You go to school?
> Do you go to school?

Of course, inversion is obligatory in *wh-* *questions*. Thus, if the input is consistently inverted in *wh-*, one would expect that the frequency of inversion in our subjects' *wh-* *questions* would be higher than it is in *yes/no questions* and that over time the frequency would increase, reflecting a closer approximation to the target input. We do find that *do* is inverted more frequently in *wh-* than in *yes/no* but with the exception of Jorge and Juan, who reach 100% inversion, the other subjects' *do* inversion in *wh-* remains variable. An explanation for this variability might still lie in the input, however, if we consider the *wh-* input to include not only *wh-* *questions* which are inverted but also embedded *wh-* *questions* which are correctly uninverted. Thus the *wh-* input to which the subject is exposed may well appear to the subject as variably inverted although the overall frequency of inversion in the *wh-* input is greater than in *yes/no* since embedded questions probably do not comprise a great percentage of all *wh-questions* in normal conversation.

Embedded Questions. However, if we consider all *wh-* *questions* (both embedded and simple) as forming the same input pool to the learner, then the learner's first hypothesis about *wh-* *questions* might be that, like *yes/no questions,* they are sometimes inverted and sometimes uninverted:

> simple: Where are you going?
> embedded: I know where you are going,

but with the inverted form being more frequent (since simple *wh-* *questions* are probably more frequent in the input). The learner is thus exposed to English input that indicates that *wh-* *questions* are variably inverted. If the learner chose the simpler of the two forms, the uninverted form, he might produce mostly uninverted *wh-* *questions* in the beginning (see explanation below) with inversion increasing over time. This situation would also account for inversion in embedded *wh- questions.* Finally, the learner should begin to differentiate between simple *wh- questions* and embedded *wh- questions* and invert in the former, but not in the latter. This differentiation may be difficult for Spanish speakers since no such differentiation occurs in their native language.

Hence the following developmental pattern should emerge:

Stage I—Undifferentiation: Learner does not distinguish between simple and embedded *wh- questions.*

a.   uninverted: Both simple and embedded *wh- questions* are *uninverted.*
     simple: *What you study?*;
     embedded: *That's what I do with my pillow.*

b.   variable inversion: Simple *wh- questions* are sometimes inverted, sometimes not.
     inverted: *How can you say it?*;
     uninverted: *Where you get that?*

c.   generalization: increasing inversion in *wh- questions* with inversion being extended to embedded questions.
     simple: *How can I kiss her if I don't even know her name?*;
     embedded: *I know where you are going.*

Stage II—Differentiation: Learner distinguishes between simple and embedded *wh- questions.*
     simple: *Where do you live?*;
     embedded: *I don't know what he had.*

As explained earlier, simple *wh- questions* involving *is (cop)* may not involve inversion at all and may simply be translations from Spanish which would inflate the percentage of inverted questions and make them look more "correct." In embeddings, *is (cop)* also inflates the percentage of inversions and thus makes them appear less "correct." Thus we decided to remove all *is (cop)* constructions from the analysis. When we did so, the developmental pattern described above appeared. See figures 14-7-11. In the following discussion, the subjects are described in developmental order.

Cheo (fig. 14-7) goes through Periods "a" and "b" in Stage 1. In tapes 4-7 there is no inversion in either simple or embedded *wh- questions.* After tape 7, he enters Period "b" where there is a slight increase in inversion in simple *wh-questions* and where embeddings continue to be uninverted.

Marta (fig. 14-8) also moves through Periods "a" and "b" in Stage I. However, her inversion in Stage Ib is at a higher frequency than Cheo's.

Jorge (fig. 14-9) progresses through Periods "a," "b" and "c" of the undifferentiated stage. Until tape 3 he is in Period "a"; from tapes 3-8 he is in Period "b" where he shows variable inversion in simple *wh- questions* and his embeddings remain uninverted. After tape 8 we see generalization with variable inversion in both simple and embedded *wh- questions.*

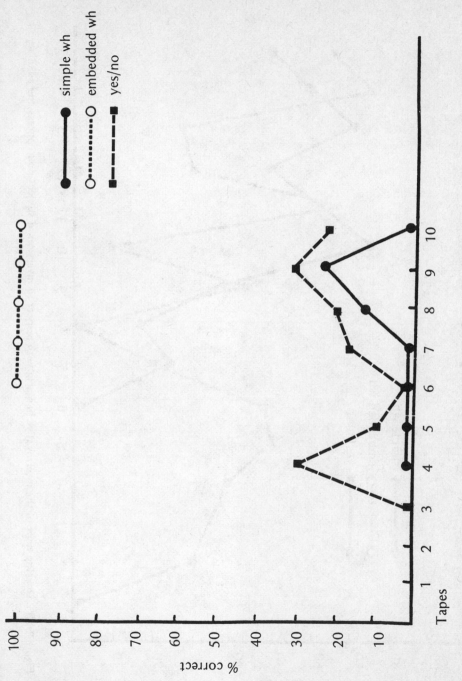

Figure 14-7   Development of the interrogative in Cheo with respect to inversion of subject noun phrase and auxiliary

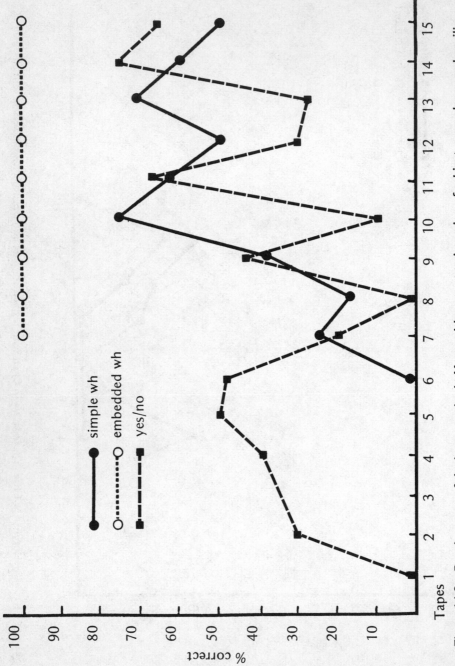

Figure 14-8   Development of the interrogative in Marta with respect to inversion of subject noun phrase and auxiliary

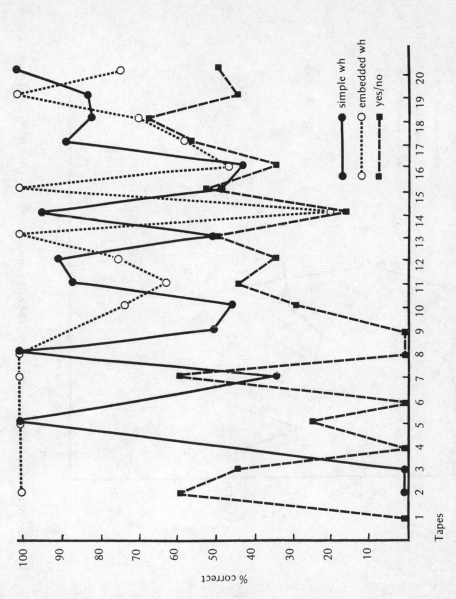

Figure 14-9 Development of the interrogative in Jorge with respect to inversion of subject noun phrase and auxiliary

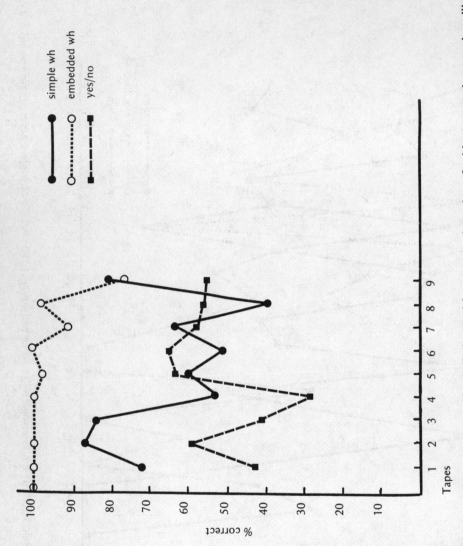

Figure 14-10   Development of the interrogative in Dolores with respect to inversion of subject noun phrase and auxiliary

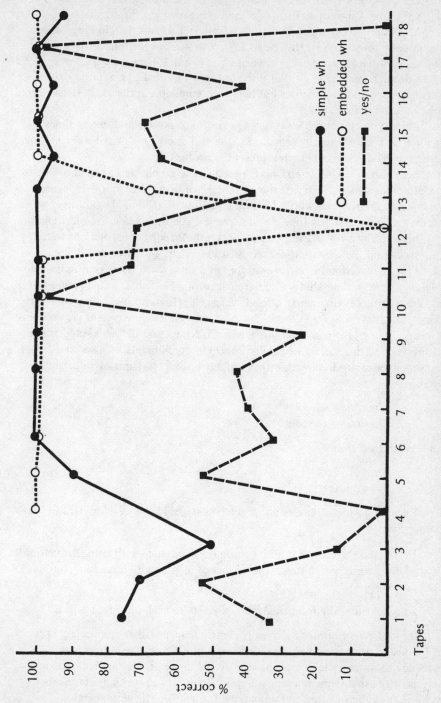

Figure 14-11 Development of the interrogative in Juan with respect to inversion of subject noun phrase and auxiliary

Dolores (fig. 14-10) starts in Period "b" of the undifferentiated stage (tape 1-4). After tape 4 she enters Period "c" and remains there through tape 9.

Juan (fig. 14-11) begins in Period "b" (tape 1-4) and then in tape 5 seems to go directly into Stage II. However, due to Christmas vacation, no data were collected on Juan for six weeks between tapes 4 and 5. He may well have progressed through Period "c" at that time. In tapes 12 and 13 he appears to be inverting in embedded questions but here the depression in the graph is accounted for by only two errors.

Alberto inverts only eleven times in *yes/no questions* and twelve times in *wh- questions.* He essentially remains in Stage I, Period "a" for the whole period of research. Therefore, no graph is presented for him.

Inversion in yes/no questions. On each of the graphs described above there is a dotted line which represents the percentage of inversions found in *yes/no questions.* In the subjects who evidenced a Period "a" (Cheo, Marta, Jorge) we find that *yes/no questions* appear to be inverted at a time when *wh- questions* are not. This result was not evident (see p. 222) until *is (cop)* constructions were eliminated from the *wh- questions.* As mentioned earlier, Klima and Bellugi (1966) found inversion in *yes/no questions* at a time when there was no inversion in *wh-questions* in their study of children acquiring English as a first language and labelled this developmental period "Stage C." However, we believe that our subjects only have a Stage C "look" because most of their inversions are accounted for by *do* (e.g., *Do you have one?*), whereas Klima and Bellugi's subjects had had inversion with a variety of auxiliaries. *Do* in our subjects, as discussed earlier, may simply be a question marker that variably appears in front of a declarative sentence:

> You go to school?
> Do you go to school?

or a "memorized chunk":

> Do you want?
> Do you like?

Excluding early *do*-inversion we see two stages in the development of *yes/ no questions*:

i) In the first stage there is no inversion (i.e., sentence with rising intonation);
ii) in the second period there is some inversion gradually increasing, but with variability.

In conclusion, the foregoing analysis yields several important points:

1. *is (cop) wh- questions* behave differently than do other auxiliaries. They do not involve inversion and may be either translations from Spanish or high frequency habitual patterns conditioned by the input. If they are included in the analysis, the best statement about *wh- questions* that can be made is that they appear in both the inverted and uninverted forms from the very beginning.

2. The input to the learner for *wh- questions* is likely to be both inverted and uninverted such that the learner does not differentiate between simple and embedded *wh- questions* at the outset.

3. If *is (cop) wh- questions* are eliminated from the data and simple and embedded *wh- questions* are regarded as a single input pool to the learner, a two-stage developmental pattern evolves. In stage I the learner does not differentiate between simple and embedded *wh- questions*. This stage can be described as having three periods. In period "a" both simple and embedded *wh- questions* are uninverted. In period "b" simple *wh- questions* are sometimes inverted and sometimes not. Period "c" is characterized by increasing inversion in *wh- questions* with inversions being extended to embedded questions. In Stage II the learner differentiates between simple and embedded *wh- questions* such that he inverts at least 80% of the time in simple *wh- questions* and does not invert in *wh- embeddings*.

4. There is a Stage C "look" in three of the subjects. But the *yes/no questions* which are inverted prior to inversion in *wh- questions*, are with the auxiliary *do*. We speculate that *do* may simply be a question marker, a memorized chunk, or a production pattern observed in the input. Excluding "*do* question markers" as inversion, then two stages emerge in the development of *yes/no questions*:

i)   sentence with rising intonation;
ii)   inversion—gradually increasing but with variability.

SUMMARY

Negative. The purpose of this project was to establish developmental sequences in the acquisition of English by Spanish speakers. We examined the negative and interrogative.

The general sequence in the development of the negative evidenced by our six subjects is as follows:

     i. *no V* (I no understand)
     ii. *don't V* (He don't like it)
     iii. *aux-neg* (You can't tell her)
     iv. analyzed *don't*; disappearance of *no V* (He doesn't spin)

The above sequence became apparent after the various negating devices (*no, don't, aux-neg,* and the analyzed forms of *don't*) were analyzed in terms of the frequency of each negator relative to the total number of negatives (including negated adjectives, nouns, etc.) in each tape sample. When these relative frequencies were graphed and compared across subjects the above sequence emerged. Although all of the subjects did not necessarily reach step iv in the sequence, they all followed the same developmental pattern.

Interrogative. In examining our interrogative data we were interested in the development of inversion. We discovered a developmental sequence in the acquisition of *wh-* questions and *yes/no questions.*

In *wh-* questions the following sequence emerged:

Stage I—Undifferentiation: learner does not distinguish between simple and embedded *wh-* questions.

    a. uninverted—both simple and embedded *wh-* questions are
       uninverted
    b. variable inversion—simple *wh-* questions are sometimes inverted,
       sometimes not
    c. generalization—increasing inversion in *wh-* questions with inversion
       being extended to embedded questions.

Stage II—Differentiation: learner distinguishes between simple and embedded *wh-* questions, reaching criterion inversion (80%) in simple *wh-* questions and uninversion in embedded *wh-* questions.

In *yes/no questions* an acquisition sequence was also observable, after the exclusion of the early *do* inversion (considered to be an "inversion-look"):

    i. sentence with rising intonation
    ii. some inversion, gradually increasing, but with variability from
       session to session.

Note

The research reported herein was performed pursuant to a grant (No. NE-6-00-3-0014) with the National Institute of Education, U.S. Department of Health, Education and Welfare. Contractors undertaking such projects under Government sponsorship are encouraged to express freely their professional judgment in the conduct of the project. Points of view or opinions stated do not, therefore, necessarily represent official National Institute of Education position or policy. We want especially to thank Courtney B. Cazden for her most helpful and generous guidance at every stage of the project. Without her interest and expertise this research would have been impossible.

A Spanish-speaking Adolescent's Acquisition

15

of English Syntax

Guy Butterworth and Evelyn Hatch, *University of California, Los Angeles*

INTRODUCTION

The previous chapters of this book have been concerned with the acquisition of a second language by young children. The following study, conducted by Guy Butterworth in 1972, is our first look at adult second-language learning.

There are, of course, vast differences between child and adult learners. The adult wishes to converse about a much wider and more sophisticated range of topics. The language input to an adult is also quite different from the language input to a child. But, beyond that, we have been told that after some set time in maturation, usually 11 to 13 years, languages must be taught, not just acquired. At the point of physical maturation we are told that interference becomes a dominant force in the learner's language development. The optimal age hypothesis (based on completed lateralization of the brain, the appearance of accents, and on the non-restoration of language in certain aphasiac cases) has been suggested (Penfield & Robert, 1959; Lenneberg, 1967; Scovel, 1969) as a way of accounting for the less successful attempts of adults at second language learning. One must, according to the hypothesis, learn language before puberty in order to learn it 'naturally' or to acquire native-like use of the language. Some of the evidence for the optimal age hypothesis has recently been discounted. Krashen (1972) has documented lateralization as occurring not in the 11 to 13 year age range but rather by age 5. This would mean that second language acquisition after age 5 should be as difficult as after 13 if lateralization were the primary evidence. Foreign accent development also seems to be important in the data of some children as well as for some adults. Hill (1970) has shown evidence from various culture groups where second language learning to native-speaker competence levels for adults is an expected fact, necessary for marriage and/or business. Waterhouse (1965) has written of groups where second-language acquisition is part of the expected transition from child to adulthood. Obviously, people do learn languages late in life.

As Butterworth cautions, this is a study of only one adolescent; the findings may be typical or idiosyncratic for Ricardo's age group. Certainly the study revealed the problems of at least one teenager in adjusting to a new language environment. It is difficult to know whether Ricardo's adjustment problems were due to his slow acquisition of English or whether his problems with English were due to his adjustment difficulties. The work of Cazden, Cancino, Rosansky, & Schumann, comparing child, adolescent and adult subjects, and of Helen Tebble, who has a parallel study in progress with a Portuguese-speaking adolescent, as well as experimental work by Snow, should help us to make stronger statements about the similarities and differences between child and adult learners. Perhaps the differences between adolescents and adults will prove to be as great (or as minimal) as those between children and adults.

Previous studies of second language acquisition (Ravem, 1968; Dato, 1970; Huang, 1971; Cathcart, 1972) have focused on four, five, and six-year-old children as they learned a second language. The native language these children possessed was, in most cases, still not fully matured or adult in form. This, it seemed, might make second-language learning different, easier, or less "conscious" for the child than for an adult.

The research reported here is on second-language learning of an adolescent/ adult. The questions to be considered were what an adolescent learns of a second language in a predominantly "natural" environment and how he learns what he learns. We hoped also to test whether or not the techniques used for observing language development in young children could be successfully applied to older subjects.

Because the data comes from only one subject, the discussion of the data must be highly speculative. This study must be considered a first step rather than the basis for even weak generalizations about language learning in adults. Nevertheless, first studies are valuable to our understanding of the language learning process.

INFORMANT

Ricardo, a thirteen-year-old Spanish-speaker from Colombia, arrived in the United States at the end of October, 1971. On November 11, he entered a junior high school which served an upper middle-class area of Laguna Beach, California. Ricardo's peers at the school were generally privileged, aware, and free of many prejudices common among Anglo students toward foreign students.

At the first meeting, one month after he began school, Ricardo appeared outgoing, pleasant and willing to take part in the project. At this session, it was obvious that, despite having studied English by a grammar-translation method in Colombia, he had very limited facility for either understanding or producing English. He did know and use a few memorized formulas (e.g.: What's your name? Where are you from? What time is it, please?). Although his knowledge of English was extremely limited, he had created an initially favorable impression on teachers and students because he was bright, engaging, and because of his interests—in particular, chess, soccer, and girls.

Ricardo is from an upper-middle-class Colombian family of some promi-nence. He continually expressed pride in Colombia and things Colombian. He spoke Spanish with his mother who had married an American national, and English with his stepfather. He watched English and Spanish television programs, but did not listen to the radio. Monday through Friday from 8:00 to 2:30, he attended classes with English-speaking students. He spoke English with teachers and students who were not bilingual. When the Spanish teacher or the other Spanish-speaking student at the school were present, he used Spanish, forcing the bilingual to translate for him.

For two fifteen-minute periods each week Ricardo worked with a speech therapist. These periods consisted of reading, pronunciation exercises, and vocabulary work. In the reading and pronunciation exercises, the speech therapist corrected articulation errors but did not correct either stress or intonation. The therapist concluded (and Ricardo agreed) that he had a minor speech defect, a slight lisp. In reviewing the tapes, little if any evidence of a lisp was found. It is probable that the perceived lisp was dialectal in his Spanish, not a speech defect detectable elsewhere.

The therapist gave Ricardo a small workbook containing common English words in alphabetic order as an aid to increased vocabulary. Ricardo wrote Spanish translations next to the English words. Included in the workbook were different forms of the same word (e.g., plural and tense inflections, irregular verb forms, etc.). These two fifteen-minute periods were the closest thing to English language instruction that Ricardo received.

Though it was impossible to do a detailed study of language exposure, it was apparent that Ricardo heard a large amount of English during the school day and at home on television. With the exception of speech therapy, there was no language instruction in the second language. The question remains as to how much of the English he heard constituted more than just background noise for Ricardo.

DATA COLLECTION

Data collection began the week of January 9, 1972 when Ricardo was 13:1 and had been in school two months. It continued for a three-month period through the week of April 2, 1972.

Five types of data were acquired: 1) spontaneous speech, 2) negation tests, 3) elicited imitations, 4) morphology tests, and 5) translation data.

The spontaneous speech data were recorded at school. Daily schedule changes prevented pre-planning the sessions. The volume of samples varied from week to week, reflecting restrictions on both time and interest of one or the other participant. At least one, and usually several, sessions were recorded each week with the exception of weeks 8 and 12. The tapes were then transcribed, glosses were supplied where meaning was not clear, and notes on context were given. Intuition as to glosses may in some instances have been defective; he may have actually tried to say something quite different. There were also some examples of ambiguous utterances, the intent of which could not be reconstructed.

The negation test was devised because there were so few examples of negation in the early spontaneous speech samples. This test was given in weeks 3, 4, 5, 6, 7, 9, 10, 11 and 13. The elicited imitations provided another way of getting at structures which did not occur in the spontaneous speech data. The final sessions for the elicited imitations concentrated on sentences with AUX development since tense and aspect had not yet emerged in the spontaneous speech data. The morphology test was an adaptation of the Berko English morphology test; it was given in weeks 2, 4, 7, 9, 11 and 13. The translation test was added because it had been so successfully used by Ravem. It was given in weeks 5, 7, and 13. Indirect statements were written on cards in Spanish. The cards were shuffled so that the order of items in each administration of the test were randomized. Ricardo had to use English to express what was written on the cue card.

RESULTS

The first impression of Ricardo as a very good subject was misleading. By week 8 he was having problems adjusting to America, Americans, and the school, which adversely affected the ease of data collection. We had hoped for a close friendly relationship so that observational data could be collected on a wide variety of topics. This did not happen. Instead, a student-teacher relationship developed and the interviews were, indeed, interviews rather than conversations between friends. It became quite apparent that he considered many of the activities onerous tasks. Unlike younger children who often see the investigator as play-mate, Ricardo was quite aware of the purpose of the visits because he had been told what we hoped to do. He did not like the formal activities that the tests imposed on him. The combination of unhappiness with school and frustration with some of the collection techniques may have had serious, but undetermined, effects on the data.

Conversations were pleasurable since they gave him the chance to guide the context to areas about which he was concerned, especially to topics about sports and girls. On topics of his own choice, he could overcome his limited knowledge of English syntax in a variety of ways.

One of his best communication devices was the use of gestures. Gestures filled in blanks for unknown or unremembered English words. For example, "One person in Homeroom (gesture), is good (gesture)." In this example, the gesture was filled in when Ricardo stood up and imitated a left-footed soccer player. We had been talking about soccer, so the gesture easily supplied the missing vocabu-lary. Gestures also assisted in clarifying constructions which contained appropriate or nearly appropriate vocabulary. At other times, Ricardo would write figures or draw pictures to accomplish the same thing. Gestures helped the investigator as well. Whenever we used a word or expression with which he was unfamiliar, a gesture or two would fill in meaning.

Sentences with simple structure also aided the communication process. In fact, there was almost a compulsion to use uncomplicated syntax. Phrases, key words, or whole sentences would be repeated. After a statement, Ricardo then would indicate either by facial or verbal expression whether he had understood. Lack of immediate understanding would trigger another repetition. The repetition was seldom exact but rather it might be a near, but more simplified version of the original utterance. While not consciously producing ungrammatical utterances, it was inevitable that, in the process of simplifying, a point might be reached where ungrammatical forms of adult English would appear. Speech became "telegraphic" as determiners, inflections, etc. were deleted. What remained were sentences that did not resemble adult utterances and which contained a high percentage of stressed content words. Tape recordings of other teachers speaking with Ricardo did not reveal this same sort of simplification of speech directed at Ricardo; rather they seemed to expect Ricardo to understand very complex syntactic structures.

When asked in Spanish what he did to process the English he heard, Ricardo said that he did not try to understand everything. He listened for a few key words. He applied what he could understand to the immediate context and responded appropriately. His responses reflected a process of simplification similar to that of his comprehension. The process looks very similar to that proposed by Schumann in his paper on similarities between second-language learning and the pidginization process (1975).

The data obtained in the sessions could be described in a number of ways. In order to compare it with that of children learning a second language, the following categories (discussed in those studies) are presented: copula, tense/aspect development, pronouns, negation and question formation, and the development of noun phrases.

Copula

Ricardo's attempts at producing equational constructions resembled those produced by Huang's subject (1971) as well as Spanish and English constructions. Throughout the 13 weeks of taping, Ricardo had three ways of expressing equational relationships:

1. Is man.
   Is boat.
2. He champion.
   This Cisneros.
3. This is dictionary.
   He is Pachon.

The first examples above demonstrate the influence of the Spanish pattern on Ricardo's English. When the subject of a Spanish copula construction is understood from context, it is usually deleted, though still reflected in the verb ending (e.g., Está aquí (*ella* deleted); Es frío (*el hielo* deleted)). Rosansky (personal correspondence), in looking at her data for child, adolescent, and adult learners of English (a study involving Spanish-speaking subjects) found that Type 1 sentences of her subjects usually were due to a missing pronoun *it*. She further suggests that the "is" is not clearly pronounced as an English "is" but rather as some sort of amalgam of "es," "is" and "it's." A check of the transcribed tapes does not indicate that the *is* form in Type 1 sentences was used primarily when *it* would have been the subject; however, *it* was deleted more frequently than any other pronoun.

The third type of sentence in the examples above might also be traced to Spanish (this time as positive transfer). The result looks like English syntax but lacks the contractions customarily used in spoken English. *Cindy is good* seems to correspond to the Spanish pattern, *Ella está bonita*.

The second type of copula utterance bears a close resemblance to those seen in child language studies.

Ricardo had all three of these constructions in just about free variation. (See Table 15-1.) Since three kinds of predicates are possible with equational sentences, the three patterns were investigated to see if any of the three types was more frequent than the others depending on the predicate following the copula. It appeared that for copula sentences with an adjective predicate, the "Is ADJ" pattern perdominated. But looking at the data week by week, the difference between the three types is minimal; the Spanish pattern does not overshadow the others. For copula sentences with a Noun Phrase predicate, there is a gradual increase in the number of *NP is NP* (type 3) forms. One might think that Ricardo was gradually acquiring the form in sentences where the predicate was a noun phrase. Unfortunately, this progress may be deceptive since at week 4, Ricardo began to use "This is + NP." The "This is" seemed to be a formula, an unanalyzed

Table 15-1   Copula data by predicate form

		Week									
Type	Example	1	2	3	4	5	6	7	9	10	Total
Pred ADJ											
1	Is nice	.37	.45	.43	.46	.32	.23	—	.33	.72	.42
2	Me thin.	.50	.46	.36	.15	.32	.46	—	.33	.05	.31
3	Wood is good.	.13	.08	.21	.38	.35	.30	—	.33	.22	.27
Pred NP											
1	Is man.	.57	.44	—	.15	.12	.00	.25	.18	.12	.19
2	He champion.	.43	.22	—	.23	.46	.37	.25	.13	.24	.28
3.	This is map.	.00	.33	.62	.72	.43	.63	.50	.69	.65	.55
Pred Locative											
1	Is here.	—	—	—	.07	.00	.00	—	.05	.10	.07
2	She over there.	—	—	—	.00	.27	.71	—	.50	.60	.38
3.	He is in ocean.	—	—	—	.93	.73	.29	—	.45	.30	.54

unit. These account for a large portion of the *NP is NP* sentences. If the "This is + NP" sentences are not counted, the distribution over the three forms would again be close to free variation. The few utterances which had a locative predicate seemed to follow the *NP is NP* pattern somewhat more consistently.

If one wished to make the strongest possible case for Spanish interference, one could say that in cases (such as the locative) where the first NP in the sentence is not clear, both NP's appear. Since such sentences require the copula in Spanish, it too is used. If the first NP is clear from the context, the first Spanish pattern (Type 1) is used. This leaves a few instances (approximately one-third of the utterances) which cannot be accounted for as Spanish interference and these are similar to those of both first and second language learning of children. In fact, however, as strong a case could be made for similarity to child language acquisition. Type 2 and 3 sentences are like those in child language data (see previous studies in this volume). This leaves only Type 1 sentences, which account for ¼ of the data, to be attributed to Spanish interference.

AUX and VP development

In the spontaneous speech data, and in the more formal tasks, there is little, if any, evidence to show that Ricardo developed either tense or aspect. The modal system, with few exceptions, was not developed. While it is possible to say that this is due to a mismatch between the two language systems, it seems much more plausible that in dealing with a great variety of language input and trying to deal with the communication demands put on him, Ricardo simply ignored a system which had parallels in his own first language. Intonation, stress, and word order appeared to be much more important than the presence or absence of inflections for Ricardo.

It is quite clear that Ricardo did not develop tense. Seventy-five percent of his verbs were in base form (uninflected regardless of time referrant), in 21% of his utterances requiring verbs other than *be*, the verb was omitted; 3% showed an -s ending (usually inappropriately used), 1% used an *-ing* ending without the *be*, and less than 1% used *be + ing* (though again this should not be taken to mean he marked progressive aspect). Finally, a few of his utterances included the modal *gotta* (I gotta go. I gotta go 9:15.), and there was one example for *can* from the translation task. In week 7, when directed in Spanish to ask me if I could swim, he responded by asking the question two ways: "You understand swim?" and "Can you swim?" *Can* never appeared again in the data except as an immediate imitation.

The data on lack of tense/aspect was similar, then, to those of children in the earliest stages of first or second language learning. They are different from child production in that there was no progress toward acquisition of the forms over comparable observational periods.

Negation

If one looks at first language data (cf. Klima and Bellugi, 1966), the beginning stage of negation has a NEG placed externally to a sentence nucleus: "*no* play that." In the second stage, the NEG appears inside the utterance: "I *no* taste that." Ricardo's spontaneous speech data shows this same pattern: "*No* play that"; "Me *no* ski." However, it is also possible that these patterns are not developmental but rather examples, again, of Spanish interference. Looking first at negative copula utterances, there are three major negative forms. One has the negative in pre-copula position: *no* is professional; *no* is good. The second shows the NEG within the utterance between the first NP and the predicate: Me *no* bad. The third moves the NEG inside the utterance before the predicate: Plays is *no* professionals. I am *no* hungry. The second and third are more interesting since they do not seem to be derived from Spanish. Type 3 utterances show English word order but lack other English characteristics such as contraction. Percentage tabulations show that 20% of the negative utterances with *be* are definitely Spanish patterns while at least 52% are similar to child language patterns. (See Table 15-2.)

The negative pattern in sentences with *be* was definitely in flux. Perhaps the clearest example of Ricardo's trials of several different forms occurred during a Spanish translation task. Ricardo, reading a Spanish cue card, protested that the Spanish was not correct. He protested this several times in the following ways: Is *no* correct. *No* correct. *No* is correct. This is *no* correct.

With verbs other than *be*, the negation pattern can be claimed, once again, to be similar to first language acquisition: Klima and Bellugi show stage 1 and 2 examples like: *Me no go. No go.* Ricardo said: *Me no ski. No understand.* But

Table 15-2   Negation patterns

Negation with Copula					Verbs other than BE	
(X) no $\left\{\begin{array}{l}\text{ADJ}\\\text{NP}\end{array}\right\}$	.52	X no is.		.02	(X) no VERB	.67
No is $\left\{\begin{array}{l}\text{ADJ}\\\text{NP}\end{array}\right\}$	.20	(X) not $\left\{\begin{array}{l}\text{ADJ}\\\text{NP}\end{array}\right\}$		.02	I don't know.	.25
X is no $\left\{\begin{array}{l}\text{ADJ}\\\text{NP}\end{array}\right\}$	.12	X no.		.02	No NP VERB	.04
Is no $\left\{\begin{array}{l}\text{ADJ}\\\text{NP}\end{array}\right\}$	.04	(X) (is) nothing.		.02	No Ø verb	.04
X is $\left\{\begin{array}{l}\text{NP}\\\text{ADJ}\end{array}\right\}$, no?	.04					

here, again, the negative utterances could as well be accounted for by transfer of the Spanish structure. Since he knows the Spanish form, he may simply transfer that form to English, substituting English words. Since there is no *do* for these forms in Spanish, one could say he either avoids it or is unaware of it in English. Of course, the studies of child first and second language acquisition all share this late acquisition of *do* as tense carrier in negatives. The function of *do* is not clear to children learning English and, as English language teachers are well aware, it is difficult to teach *do* to most adults learning English as well. Whether this is because of its lack of evident semantic value is not clear.

To say that Ricardo is totally unaware of *do* may not be completely accurate. He did have the formula: *I don't know.* He used it over and over again. He expanded it to: I don't know you name. I don't know "comics." I don't know "blank." At the same time that he said *I don't know,* he also used *I no understand,* frequently saying one right after the other. This leads one to suspect that his *I don't know* utterances were unanalyzed units.

Once, on reading from one of the programmed readers, Ricardo came to the sentence "Did the man sit on the mat?" He read the sentence aloud with rising intonation. He answered an accompanying question correctly. Then, he pointed to *did* and asked what it meant. The answer, however, was not sufficient to cause him to start attending to *do*; there were no further examples of *do* in the natural data.

Question forms

The interrogative structures also reflect both similarities to first language learning data and to Spanish interference. Ricardo, as other language learners, paid attention immediately to question intonation. In order to comprehend questions

Ricardo needed only to attend to stressed content words and to intonation. To produce questions, he simply added rising intonation to his utterances:

You come by Friday? (1)	He understand chess? (7)
You watch Alvaro? (2)	You like Los Angeles? (10)
This is Costa Mesa? (5)	You no understand? (3)

These are similar to the data from children learning English as a first or second language; they are also possible examples of Spanish interference. In Spanish, changes in intonation (Ellos van a salir manana. → ¿Ellos van a salir manana? La muchacha es bonita. → ¿La muchacha es bonita?) change the sentences to questions. It is not the same in English where such changes usually signal an echo of, or disbelief in, a previous statement rather than a question asking for a yes/no answer (He's here. → He's here?). Unfortunately, it is impossible to determine if rising intonation in Ricardo's questions is the result of transfer or of language learning strategies similar to the child's, or a combination of the two.

For the Wh-questions, Ricardo had a number of formula questions: What's your name? What time is it, please? How old are you? How do you say X? When he tried to extend these, the results were not always grammatical: "What's your name teach history?" He did not, in the first sessions, understand all the WH-words. He acquired *what, where,* and *who* quickly, but when asked, "When did you eat breakfast?" he replied, "Coffee, egg, bread." He used *what time* in place of *when.*

WH-words were sometimes placed within the sentence rather than preposed:

Today is *what*?	This is for *what*?
You watch *where*?	He is *who*?
You watch in television *what*?	

While these might seem to support Brown's (1968) suggestion of intermediate psychological realities to support transformational rules, they did not have either rising intonation or primary stress as do the "occasional questions" described by Brown. However, most of Ricardo's WH-questions were simple WH-preposed forms with following regular declarative word order:

> What (when) you eat you dinner yesterday?
> Why you no sleep in UCLA?

There were a few examples of subject-verb inversion similar to those Ravem noted for Rune:

> Who like more you, Japan or German country?
> What city like you more?
> What time come by you San Francisco?

Just as Ravem could attribute these kinds of questions to Norwegian interference, so Ricardo's examples could be attributed to Spanish interference:

> ¿Tomaron ellos unas cervezas anoche? → ¿Qué (cervezas) *tomaron ellos* anoche?
>
> ¿Mató Juan un toro ayer? → ¿Qué (toro) *mató Juan* ayer?

However, these subject-verb inversions examples were exceptional rather than typical of his question formation.

Pronouns

Acquisition of English pronouns appeared to be similar to that of child language learning. There are some differences, however. At the beginning of the study, Ricardo used both *me* and *I* for subject pronoun, first person. While *me* and *my* were used correctly for accusative and possessive cases throughout the study, the *I/me* variation continued uncorrected over the three months. Figure 15-1 shows the variations in frequency for the two forms.

You and *he* were used correctly but not marked for case (you girlfriend; he car). There were fewer examples of *she*, again unmarked by case (she hair); *he* was frequently substituted for *she*. *We, it* and *they* were frequently omitted or circumvented by substituting *he*, sometimes in the plural (e.g., *he is and he is* for *they are*). Over the three months there were only two examples of *we* and four of *they*.

From the preceding sections it might appear that Ricardo made no progress in English over the three months. Yet his MLU (mean length of utterance) increased from 2.9 in the first two sessions to 4.78 in the last two sessions. If his data did not show the usual marks of increasing complexity (tense, aspect, morphological endings), what happened to account for increased utterance length?

First, he had learned to develop the noun phrase in interesting ways. As in child language acquisition, Ricardo's NP development occurred almost always in the second NP of the sentence. The subject NP would always be a single noun or pronoun (He is new XXX (teacher) for school. Me good player.). In contrast, he developed the predicate NP in a variety of ways. One of the most interesting was the use of *for* patterns (see Table 15-3). Native speakers of Spanish will recognize many of the uses of *for* as transfers from Spanish *por* and *para*. But the interesting fact is that Ricardo transferred a pattern from Spanish and then expanded it in ways not acceptable in Spanish (or in English).

While the resulting utterances sound strange to native speakers of English, they can be understood both from context and from the way in which they express concepts through structure. Such nominalizations as "shoes for water ice" (ice skates) are probably transferred Spanish syntax. But transfer cannot fully explain "He cleans for floor, for carpet" because Spanish only allows the use of *para* with inanimate nouns. Other examples that cannot be traced easily to Spanish are the conjunction uses of *for*; the contexts in which Ricardo said these

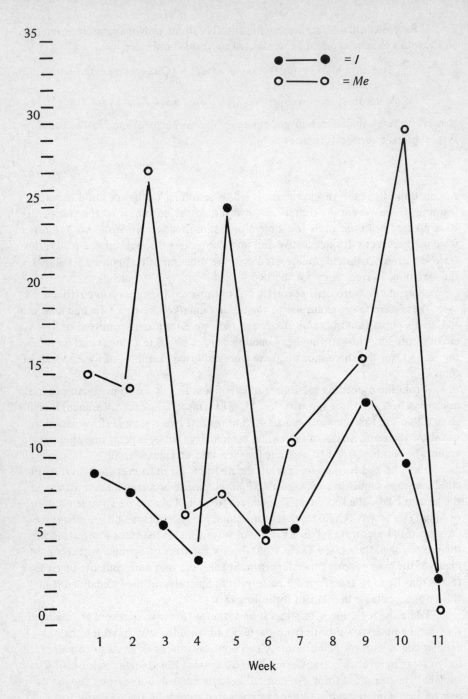

Figure 15-1. Frequency of *I* and *Me* as Subject Pronoun

Table 15-3   *For* examples

A.   Nominalizations
   (1)* He for selling. (He's a salesman; he sells)
   (3)   In house one machine for hot. (space heater)
   (3)   One man is clean for clothes. (laundryman)
   (3)   He is for school. (teacher)
   (4)   This machine for envelopes for newspaper. (printing press)
   (4)   These is shoes for water ice. (ice skates)
   (5)   He champion in France for world. (world champion)
   (5)   This shoes for skiing. (ski boots)
   (6)   Beds, rooms for sleep. (dormitory)
   (7)   He's for English. (an English teacher)
   (7)   One peoples cleans for floor, for carpet. (janitor)
   (9)   One animal go for eye, for hair. One animal go for ear. (a bug)

B.   In direct object position
   (1)   My father me go for lobster. (We fish for lobsters)
   (3)   I do soap for clothes. (? I wash clothes. I do the washing)
   (6)   He for long hair ties it. (He ties back the long hair.)
   (7)   Maybe for Mr. Nixon pow! (Maybe someone will pow Mr. N.)
   (8)   Maybe me for he one. (Maybe I'll hit him.)
   (10) He clean for teeth. (He brushes his teeth)

C.   In indirect object position or benefactive
   (6)   Coffee for he. (They bring him coffee)
   (7)   One hits him for he. (Someone hit him for somebody else.)
   (9)   Go for peoples for drink.

D.   As preposition (to/into/near/down/on)
   (2)   In U.S. people go for San Silvestre. (to)
   (3)   Go for sands in car. (down the sand . . . a dune buggy)
   (5)   Maybe go for Los Angeles. He go for Cali. (to)
   (4)   He is for bicycle. (on the bicycle team)
   (4)   Smoke for you face. (Blowing smoke away from GB)
   (6)   He go for cafe. (into)
   (7)   You go for one girlfriend. (to)
   (10) Me everydays go my dictionary for my house. (take it home)

E.   Duration (many examples)
   (3)   Me working for 40 hours a week.
   (10) A ticket for one month.
   (10) Maybe 50 kilometers for hour.

F.   Conjunction
   (3)   You for me. (and)
   (4)   You for me maybe? (We will play chess?)
   (6)   Father for son. (and)
   (6)   Me for you? (and)
   (10) My mother me go for my mother watch. (so that)

---

*Week in which the example appeared.

sentences demanded the conjunction *and*. The reason for the productiveness of the *for* structures seems to be two-fold. First, they were almost always circumlocutions, a way of expressing vocabulary which he did not have. This is particularly true of the nominalizations. In fact, it seems a fairly good way of eliciting vocabulary from the listener. His *for* structures were always understood. Second, they provided a means of obtaining some fluency for his speech without demanding that he attend to and learn new English structures or more difficult syntax. The question is, then, why he did not try to transfer more elements of Spanish syntax, extending such structures for English production. It seems possible that Ricardo was having enough difficulty just attending to word order and learning vocabulary; perhaps these are the essentials for the adult learner confronted with a wide variety of language input. A small number of syntactic devices like the *for* patterns enabled Ricardo to establish more complicated relationships (those beyond equation, description and actor-agent) and to give some feel for fluency in a relatively easy way.

DISCUSSION

Three months seemed a long enough period of time for us to expect that acquisition patterns would be evident in Ricardo's language. Both Ravem and Huang were able to describe several stages in linguistic maturation for their young subjects over a similar time period. First language learners do not show much change in three months, but they lack prior cognitive requisites. The adult should be aided by his prior learning of a language, his greater memory span, his full cognitive development, and a predisposition to analyze new information.

Why doesn't all that facilitate learning? Some of the data which have not been studied in depth support the notion that the language-learning context—even "total immersion" contexts—is important. The data suggests that the adult wants to enter into a wide range of topics and communication situations; the child satisfies himself with very immediate and concrete wants. Adults want to, and even unconsciously may be expected to, communicate far more numerous and abstract ideas. Several first-language studies (Snow, 1972; Drach et al, 1969) of adult-child and adult-adult speech show that there are significant differences between the quality of the two. In a second-language situation, the native speaker usually tries to adjust his language to accommodate the learner while simultaneously trying to maintain an adult level of communication. Even a cursory comparison of Huang's data for the five-year-old and our data shows that Ricardo liked to talk of more things and of things which were not in his immediate surroundings. Huang's child subject does not show that breadth or depth. The expectations of researcher and subject may be much narrower when studying the child.

In addition, it may be that the child has fewer social pressures on him about the speed of his language learning. Ricardo was under tremendous pressure in this regard. Even with the assistance his language, memory span, and cognitive development gave him, he still wanted to say more than he had language to express. Of necessity, an adult may then employ his native syntax or construct rules based on the native language for his second-language utterances. When adult communicative expectations and adult concepts of learning join, the result may be a heavily burdened language-learning context.

From the data it appears that Ricardo's predominant strategy was one of simplification or reduction of both input and output. He makes very little structure cover a lot of contextual ground. He ignored the AUX system (tense, modals, be + ing, have + en, do) except in imitations. He did not acquire the morphological endings for plurality, possessives, etc. either in spontaneous speech or in the morphology tests. If he knew the verb, he used it; if he didn't, he let the context supply it. The use of the copula seemed to be optional. Function words of all kinds were omitted, or a few made to carry the burden of many expressions (his *for* expressions). He created all kinds of circumlocutions when he could not remember a word. He repeated words to indicate intensity. And, he used gestures of all sorts to clarify meaning.

Interference from the first language was obvious. However, it was not always clear whether it was more important as a force in his language learning than were the similarities to developmental errors of child first and second-language learners. If interference were a dominant force, why should it appear only in certain instances and not others? For example, both languages have plurals, but Ricardo did not learn plurals. Both languages have similar pronoun systems marked for case, but Ricardo did not mark his pronouns for case. In some instances, particularly the WH-questions, the errors do not resemble Spanish syntax at all but, rather, the developmental errors of children learning English. Nevertheless, the influence of Spanish on his language cannot be denied.

Despite the importance of first language interference, teaching experience makes us aware that the adolescent-adult learner from any language background seems to attack the acquisition process in similar ways. In Viet-Nam a student would say, "Me go Saigon tomorrow," and in Laguna Beach, Ricardo might say, "Me go Dana Point tomorrow." From distinct language backgrounds, they both reduce English to what they consider manageable proportions. They draw on their native languages to provide them with help when the demands of communication exceed their knowledge of English. The simplification process may be more apparent in adult data than it is in child language and it may be more resistant to change, but the data also show that learning does take place. The specifics of that process have yet to be discovered.

The Non-learning

16 of English:

Case Study of an Adult

Rina G. Shapira, *University of California, Los Angeles*

INTRODUCTION

Shapira, herself a multilingual, undertook the following study to give us more
information on adult second language learners. Her study, along with those of
Schumann, Butterworth, and Hanania, leaves us with a depressing picture of adult
language learning. However, if we look at *other* than morpheme development and
AUX development in negation and question formation, the picture changes
radically. In terms of communicating, her subject, Zoila, gets along very well in
her limited sphere of contact with English speakers. She is a *fluent* speaker of
English, albeit her production of morphemes leaves much to be desired.

One of the notions of conversational analysis in second language research is
that learners are sensitive to input and to correction. But while Zoila is sensitive
to almost everything else in conversation, she is not sensitive to the language
model, as can be seen in these adjacent pairs:

Shapira: It makes no difference.
Zoila: Anyway, it no making difference.

Zoila: . . . very /sɛnsər/.
Shapira: Sincere?

Zoila:	Sincero. Sincero?
Shapira:	Sincere.
Zoila:	Yeah.

On the other hand, Shapira is an excellent language learner and she, in fact, modifies her speech to 'learn' the language of her subject:

Zoila:	Do you think is ready?
Shapira:	I think is ready.
Zoila:	Why she's very upset for me?
Shapira:	S. is upset for you?
Zoila:	Yeah, is.

Perhaps the study, had it been of Shapira herself rather than of Zoila would have given us a bright picture of second language learning by adults.

This study is a report of a longitudinal study of one adult Spanish speaker learning English as a second language without instruction. Answers were sought to the following questions: 1) Is there evidence for language acquisition in the traditional sense of acquisition of grammar? 2) If so, what is the order of acquisition of English morphemes for this adult. If not, why not?

The subject, Zoila, is a 25-year-old Guatemalan woman and a native speaker of Spanish. She came to the United States when she was 22. Her formal instruction in English prior to her arrival here was very limited and dated back about eight or nine years. Zoila has a basic elementary education (eight years of public school) plus two years of vocational training in bookkeeping. She held a position of bookkeeper's aid in an embassy in Guatemala.

In the United States, Zoila has been working as a housekeeper in homes where English is spoken among the members of the household and to her as well. She has not attended formal English classes due to the nature of her job. She was supplied with "teach yourself" type books and records, but has not used them. She socializes with Spanish-speaking people, watches Spanish T.V., reads Spanish, and listens to Latin-American music.

The data were collected in the form of a conversation-interview. Spontaneous speech samples were recorded in November, 1973, May, 1974 and April, 1975. The three sessions were preplanned and took between thirty and forty-five minutes each.

The transcribed data were then studied for the acquisition of ten grammatical morphemes and syntactic structures: the plural morpheme -s; third person, singular -s; plural NP subjects followed by the verb BE; BE copula; BE + V-ING; negation of sentences with BE; negation of sentences with verbs other than BE; Yes/No questions; WH-questions; the possessive -s. These particular morphemes and structures were selected for analysis since they had been described in other second-language learning studies; comparison of progress with other learners could be made.

The analysis was based on grammaticality, which was determined on the basis of the presence or absence of morphemes in obligatory environments, or on the success or failure in the application of rules in obligatory environments. A morpheme or rule is considered acquired if it is grammatically applied in 80-85% of all obligatory environments. (The percentage depends on sample size; the cutoff point has been adopted from several other studies of second language acquisition.)

In order to account for the source of errors, the surface structures of the ten grammatical morphemes and syntactic structures of English were contrasted with their Spanish equivalents in the form of a simplified linguistic representation (see Table 16-1). It was hoped that this would allow us to classify errors as resulting from transfer of the grammar of L1 as interference errors, or as possible developmental errors. These classifications are not mutually exclusive; thus an error could be the result of both.

The data is displayed in Table 16-2 to allow us to compare the findings over the time period and to point out the areas in which progress toward acquisition might be detected. There is a considerable difference in sample size which, one could claim, might have influenced the shape of the data to some degree. The true picture, however, is not distorted, since all calculations are based on the number of occurrences of grammatical and ungrammatical instances of each category throughout the observational study.

During the 18-month observation period, there appears to have been little, or quite insignificant, development in the acquisition of any of the ten grammatical categories studied. The use of the plural -s morpheme is grammatical in a great majority of the occurrences throughout the study (84%; 70%, 82%). No real change is observed since the slight drop in Set 2 is not significant. Examples of her correct and incorrect plural usage are: *They have too many trophies. The no rich people have tamales. In two year more. Liking many girl.*

The third person -s morpheme is consistently omitted (0%, 0%, 5%): *Mrs. L tell me. She go in one home. He work in the bookkeeper.* All the categories in which BE is involved show that Zoila has not acquired its various forms. She uses almost exclusively the "unmarked" form *is.* This may result from the phonological similarity between "is" and the Spanish *es.* However, in most cases, she simply omits the copula: *Everybody sad. Maybe you angry for one year. Is very well. The water hot is ready.* "Is" is also the most frequent BE form in the recorded input data. Consequently, "is" shows up in wrong environments, e.g., after plural NP's: *My bones is hurt. Tamales is more better, is best.* Copula BE, then, appears as "is" or is deleted. The proportion between "is" and $\emptyset$ does not change over time ($\emptyset$ = 31%, 31%, 27%; IS = 69%, 69%, 73%) in sentences where BE should appear before the predicate phrase.

Another category where BE is involved is the progressive. Zoila very consistently deleted BE: *I liking snow. My family needing money.* She seems to use the progressive in free variation with the simple present. She has analyzed neither the structure nor the function of the progressive, and she uses verbs such as "like" and

Table 16-1   Contrasts of 10 structures, English & Spanish

	ENGLISH	SPANISH
1. NP_{pl}	NP + S	NP + S
2. 3rd Person	V + S	V
3. NP_{pl} + BE	NP_{pl} + BE_{pl}	(NP_{pl}) + $\left\{ \begin{array}{c} SER \\ ESTAR \end{array} \right\}_{pl}$
4. Cop. BE	NP + BE + PRED.	(NP) + $\left\{ \begin{array}{c} SER \\ ESTAR \end{array} \right\}$ + PRED.
5. Progressive	NP + BE + V-ING + . . .	(NP) + ESTAR + V-IENDO
6. Neg. of BE	NP + BE + NEG + PRED.	(NP) + NEG + BE + PRED.
7. Neg. of V	NP + DO + NEG + V + . . .	(NP) + NEG + V
8. Yes/No Q	DO + NP + V + . . .	Statement [+ rising intonation]
9. WH-Q	WH + $\left\{ \begin{array}{c} BE \\ DO \end{array} \right\}$ + NP + $\left\{ \begin{array}{c} V\text{-ing} \\ V \end{array} \right\}$ +	WH + (NP) + V +
10. POSS.	N'S N	NP de NP

"need" in the ING form even though they belong in a group of verbs which do not take this morpheme.

As a direct result of the above, negative sentences with BE are also a problem area. The negation of BE sentences is divided between Zoila's utterances with BE (40%, 28%, 38%) and those without BE (60%, 72%, 62%). When Zoila uses BE, the sentence negation is correct (if we disregard her lexical borrowing from Spanish of the negating word *no*). The ungrammatical sentences are faulty mainly because of BE deletion. For example, *Is no good anymore. She no old. When you no home, fold the bed.* Development toward grammaticality in these sentences, therefore, depends on the mastery of BE.

Zoila has not acquired DO-support and, therefore, her negation of sentences with verbs other than BE are also ungrammatical; the negation word *no* is inserted between (optional) subject and verb (75%, 86%, 73%): *He no call me Saturday. You no understand. Why she no think before come here?* Zoila seemed to have one formula for negation *I don't X* which she first used with the verb *know.* We can speculate that she acquired this specific sentence because of the phonological problems with *"I no know."* However, in a few instances Zoila tries to apply her NO + VERB rule even to the verb *know.* The recordings document how she struggles with *no* and *know,* and finally ends up saying only one attenuated *no,* which means she doesn't know. In the final data collection session, she extended the use of *I don't* to a few additional verbs such as *think, wanna, need,* and even *are.* But in no way can we argue at this stage that this is becoming a productive process.

Table 16-2   Summary table of observational data

Category/ Sample Sizes	Ungrammatical Structure Used	Pct.	Mean	Grammatical Structure Used	Pct.	Mean
1 -S PLURAL 19, 27, 34	N+∅	16%, 30, 8	21	N+S	84%, 70, 82	79%
2 -S THIRD PERSON 19, 28, 37	V+∅	100, 100, 95	98	V+S	5	2
3 PLURAL +BE 3, 5, 3	NP$_{pl}$+is	100, 100, 100	100			
4 BE + COPULA 52, 80, 147	NP+∅+Pred.P.	31, 31, 27	30	(NP)+BE+Pred.P.	69, 69, 73	70
5 V + BE -ING 12, 16, 61	NP+∅+V-ING / NP+BE+V-∅	100, 88, 95 / 2	95	NP+BE+V-ING	12, 3	5

Table 16-2 (continued)

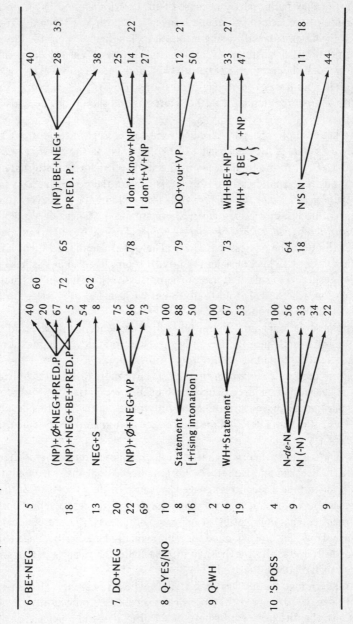

6 BE+NEG — 5

  18   (NP)+Ø+NEG+PRED.P.   40 20 67 5 54 / 60 72 / 65 → 40 28 35
         (NP)+NEG+BE+PRED.P.
  13   NEG+S   8 62 → (NP)+BE+NEG+PRED. P. → 38

7 DO+NEG — 20 22 69

    (NP)+Ø+NEG+VP   75 86 73 / 78 → I don't know+NP   25 14 22 27
                          I don't+V+NP

8 Q-YES/NO — 10 8 16

    Statement   100 88 50 / 79 → DO+you+VP → 12 50 / 21
    [+rising intonation]

9 Q-WH — 2 6 19

    WH+Statement   100 67 53 / 73 → WH+BE+NP   33 47 / 27
                           WH+ { BE / V } +NP

10 'S POSS — 4 9 9

    N-de-N   100 56 33 34 22 / 64 18 → N'S N → 11 18 / 44
    N (-N)

As sentence types become more and more complicated with respect to the number of obligatory morphemes and rules they call for, so Zoila's sentences become more ungrammatical. This is the case with her interrogative structures. Not only are they faulty partly because of BE deletion and no DO-support, but also because of the lack of subject-verb inversion. Both Yes/No and WH-questions are basically statements with rising intonation. The figures seem to show improvement, but close study reveals that in the case of Yes/No questions, Zoila has acquired another formula: *Do you + VP?* and in the case of WH-questions she has acquired a number of formulae expressions: *How is NP? How are you?*, etc. Again, these are not extended to other contexts and should not be considered productive.

Zoila does not appear to have acquired the possessive structure *N's N*. She generally uses *N de N* for possessive (100%, 56%, 34%): *The car de Carlo . . . The son de Mrs. P. . . .* In the final weeks of the study she added an alternate form, *N N*, which might be an indication of progress toward the possessive: *. . . same Jody books, you know. . . . in the Queen Arms* (= a restaurant). However, all examples are names of books, movies or places. There are also instances of *N's N*: *I wait for Gallo's brother he call. I forget in Gallo's room.* The use of this structure is extremely limited; the possessor is always Gallo, her friend, and the possessed has something to do with his house and family. It seems likely that she has had a good deal of exposure to this limited use of the possessive structure in instructions given her on her job, where she is told to do things with so-and-so's sister, mother, etc., or to clean so-and-so's room.

The observational data, then, shows little evidence for progress in the acquisition of specific morphemes and syntactic structures. The question still remains as to why Zoila did not improve in these areas.

It is a common assumption that adults have more difficulties in learning a second language than children. There have been several attempts to discover what role age plays in language learning. I will only mention the theories developed around this issue. For a detailed discussion, see Schumann, 1975, and Krashen, 1973, 1974.

A very common theory is that of biological development. This theory, first suggested by Penfield and Roberts (1959) maintains that the reason adults have difficulty in learning a second language is because of the process of cortical lateralization in which language functions localize in the left cerebral cortex. This development reaches completion at puberty, which was, therefore, considered the critical age. However, the evidence for a biologically based critical age for language learning was found faulty by Krashen (1973). Thus the validity of this theory is still very much an open question.

An alternative theory was suggested, in which researchers (Rosansky 1975; Hale & Buder, 1970) suggest that a critical period based on cognitive development accounts for the difficulty adults have in learning a second language.

"Within this framework the cognitive and social changes brought on by the onset of formal operations are seen to cause adult language learning difficulties." (Schumann, 1975, p. ix.)

Still another theory relating critical age with the difficulties adults have in learning a second language involves affective factors.

> It is here that age intersects with the notion of psychological distance. The affective argument maintains that as a person gets older language shock and culture shock are likely to be more severe, the development of an integrative motivation is likely to be greatly reduced. These factors make adults more psychologically distant than children from speakers of the target language. (Schumann, 1975, p. ix.)

Zoila is an adult learning a second language. She was well past the "critical age"—be it based on biological, cognitive or affective factors—when she started learning English. She did not and still has not had any formal instruction in English. Thus, she is totally dependent on the English she hears from her environment. Being past the age when learning by exposure to natural speech is conducive to language learning she has difficulties learning the language.

In spite of these difficulties, language acquisition is expected to occur, at a slower pace. These expectations do not seem to have materialized in Zoila's data. After three years in the U.S. there is practically no evidence for progress in her acquisition of English grammar. The only area in which learning can be observed is fluency.

It seems that in addition to the theory of critical age, something else is involved. I feel very strongly that had Zoila really wanted to learn grammatical English, she could have made much greater progress, even with no formal instruction. Here is where the issue of affect plays a decisive role.

Zoila did not come to the U.S. out of choice. She was practically driven away from home and had no other place to go. The circumstances of her arrival may have built up negative feelings about her being in the U.S., about the U.S., and all things American. Under these circumstances it may be likely that she developed a negative attitude to learning English beyond the level of communication. Having an instrumental, rather than an integrative, motivation, her performance has not improved beyond a certain point which satisfied her needs. Zoila set herself a goal—to learn how to communicate in English so that she could survive and settle down again. Communication, as we have seen earlier, is a rather elementary stage in the process of language acquisition, and relatively easily acquired. Once Zoila reached this goal she aspired no further. In time her attitude changed. She does not have negative feelings about the U.S. anymore and she even likes her life here. By this time, however, Zoila has developed fluency in English to a level that enables her to understand all she is interested in, and to make herself understood. She interprets her development as evidence of progress in the acquisition of English. Her daily interaction with English speakers constantly reinforces her feeling that her English is good enough since it is accepted, i.e., understood. Most, if not all, native speakers Zoila is in contact with are sympathetic and tolerant of her language problems.

Zoila seems to focus her attention on those elements in speech which convey content. She ignores non-informative elements; she reduces and simplifies the speech she "intakes" probably even before the decoding stage. The less grammatical information loaded on the decoding system the easier it seems for her to process it.

In the following dialogue between Zoila and myself, she candidly reveals the method she uses for communication in English. This exchange took place at one point during the administration of the imitation task.

Zoila: I never . . . I never listen, you know the . . . the words little, uh, small words for continue my conversation.

Rina: What, like what?

Zoila: The /fras/, you know *frase*?

Rina: Sentence.

Zoila: The sentence, sentence. In the sentence I never using this little, little words.

Rina: Like what?

Zoila: Ah, "and," and "that," /ʌm/ /ipidit/ (=examples of "little" words as observed by Zoila). You know? If /bin/ /it/ sometimes . . . (unintelligible) . . . Well, maybe because I no study . . . never, and only hear the people and . . . and talking.

Rina: Yeah, but people talk with these words.

Zoila: Yeah, *pero* /əs, əh/, I'm . . . hear and put more attention the big words. You know and . . . something "house." I know "house" is the *casa* for me. And /əsəs/ and little words is no too important for me.

This piece of her mind which Zoila volunteered sums up very simply how she learned what she knows in English, "only hear the people . . . and talking"; what she considers essential for communication, ". . . put more attention the big words . . . little words is no too important for me"; and the fact that she relies a good deal on translation equivalents, "I know 'house' is the *casa* for me." As a matter of fact, Zoila does use "little words" in her speech. Thus, I suspect what she really means by the distinction "big words" and "little words" is not so much the traditional dichotomy content vs. function words, bur rather communicative utterances vs. redundancies. This impressionistic observation calls for verification through further research.

In concluding this study, an attempt will be made to determine what we can learn about language acquisition by adults from a single-case study.

Zoila's speech is simplified and reduced to the essentials. It seems that a great many of her speech patterns follow "universal" patterns, or developmental, interim surface structures common to learners of English as a second language with different language backgrounds. There is a considerable amount of transfer from Spanish, too, in syntax as well as in vocabulary.

There seems to be a process of "replacement" of transferred vocabulary by English equivalents. While a considerable number of function words, for example, occur in the first set of the observational data (*pero, de, ya,* etc.), they are slowly being replaced by English "but," "of," "already," etc., respectively.

As far as syntactic structures are concerned, a process of "replacement" of structures transferred from Spanish is not at all clear. Zoila used the same basic structures in April, 1975, as she did eighteen months earlier in November, 1973.

However, there is evidence that she is adding a number of alternate structures—in a few cases—which she uses in usually highly controlled environments. These added structures are unanalyzed phrases, or formulae, learned as a unit, through constant exposure. These formulae are used in only those environments which match their surface structure. "Don't" from the formulae "I don't know" occurred only in this environment in the second set of the observational data. However, in the third set, this formula was a little more flexible, allowing some variation on the verb. Out of a total of 27 occurrences of "I don't V," V = "know" in 19 examples, and in the remaining eight examples, V = "see," "care," "do," "think" and "say," all of which are high frequency verbs in everyday speech.

The fact that Zoila's acquisition of English seems to be restricted to formulae may have significant implications about the way adults learn a second language through exposure rather than instruction.

First language learning and second language learning by children or pre-adolescents can be characterized as learning by rule-formation. Rules are generated from speech (= data) learners are exposed to in natural environments. An adult in the same environment—in our case, Zoila—does not go through the same linguistic development. Zoila does not generate transformational rules from the speech she is exposed to. Rather, she acquires certain surface structures—formulae—which she uses in their restricted environments without even using analogy to expand their application. This case study could, thus, serve as evidence for the claim that there is a fundamental difference in learning strategies between children and adults.

Second Language Acquisition:

17

The Pidginization Hypothesis

John H. Schumann, *University of California, Los Angeles*

INTRODUCTION

The following paper presents a case study of an adult learner, comparable in many ways to Shapira's study of Zoila. The subject is a 33-year-old Costa Rican named Alberto. During the ten-month period of study, little linguistic growth was observed; Alberto's speech, like that of Zoila, showed evidence of pidginization. To explain the pidginization process, Schumann claims two factors must be considered primary: social and psychological distance.

In the 1920s, Delacroix (*Le langage et la pensée*) called the psychologists to task:

> There can be no psychology of language without recourse to linguistics. Without it one could, of course, study certain aspects of the speech of one individual. There are numerous psychologists, . . . who believe it is possible only by psychological observation to determine the nature of language acquisition, of inner language, of external forms of expression, and of language pathologies. But a reading of their works reveals their incompleteness. They give general viewpoints and schemes, while quite obviously neglecting considerable facts that condition what they attempt to explain. They are led inevitably to ask useless questions, to forget essential questions, to misconstrue the actual facts, to misinterpret established facts. . . . If they had ignored the structure of language less, they would not have misconceived the conditions of speech for such a long time. (Delacroix, p. 7; see also Blumenthal, 1970, p. 114)

Schumann, in this article, gives us the other side of the coin. We have looked only at linguistic forms; we have perhaps believed that "it is possible only by *linguistic* analysis to determine the nature of language acquisition, of inner language, of external forms of expression, and of language pathologies." We, too, have neglected essential questions because we have failed to look at the more global picture of second language learning. In a sense, then, there can be no psychology of language without recourse to psychology and sociology.

Reprinted with the permission of the author and the University of Michigan Press from *Language Learning*, 1977, *26*, in press.

* * *

In the fall of 1973 a research project (Cazden, Cancino, Rosansky and Schumann, 1975) was undertaken to make a ten-month longitudinal study of the untutored acquisition of English by six native speakers of Spanish—two children, two adolescents and two adults. Data collection involved the recording of both spontaneous and experimentally elicited speech. This report is a case study of one of the six subjects, a 33 year-old Costa Rican named Alberto, who evidenced very little linguistic development during the course of the project. It was felt that by attempting to account for his lack of learning, significant insight could be gained on what is involved in successful second language acquisition in general.

DEVELOPMENTAL PATTERNS IN THE NEGATIVE, INTERROGATIVE AND AUXILIARY

The research focused on the subjects' acquisition of negatives, wh- questions and auxiliaries. The analysis revealed several clear patterns of development. In the negative all subjects began with *no + verb* (*no V*) constructions in which the negative particle, while internal to the sentence, was external to the verb: *I no can see, But no is mine . . . , I no use television.* Simultaneously or shortly afterwards the subjects started using *don't + verb* (*don't V*) constructions. Here *don't* did not consist of *do + not*, but was simply an allomorph of *no* which was also kept external to the verb: *I don't hear, He don't like it, I don't can explain.* In the third stage, *auxiliary + negative* (aux-neg.), the subjects learned to place the negative particle after the auxiliary. In general, the first auxiliaries to be negated in this way were *is* (isn't) and *can* (can't). In the final stage (*analyzed don't*), the learners acquired the analyzed forms of *don't* (do not, doesn't, does not, didn't, did not): *It doesn't spin, Because you didn't bring, He doesn't laugh like us.* At this point *don't* was no longer a negative chunk, but actually consisted of *do* plus the negative particle. The stages in this sequence were not discrete and there was a good deal of overlap among them. Each stage was defined by the negating strategy that was used predominantely at that time.

The analysis of the acquisition of wh- questions revealed a developmental pattern which consisted of two stages (undifferentiation and differentiation). The first stage involved three periods (uninverted, variable inversion and generalization). This developmental sequence is summarized below:

> Stage I—Undifferentiation: Learner did not distinguish between simple and embedded *wh- questions.*
> a. uninverted: Both simple and embedded *wh- questions* were *uninverted.*
>   simple: *What you study?*;
>   embedded: *That's what I do with my pillow.*
> b. variable inversion: Simple *wh- questions* were sometimes inverted, sometimes not.
>   inverted: *How can you say it?*;
>   uninverted: *Where you get that?*
> c. generalization: increasing inversion in *wh- questions* with inversion being extended to embedded questions.
>   simple: *How can I kiss her if I don't even know her name?*;
>   embedded: *I know where are you going.*
> Stage II—Differentiation: Learner distinguished between simple and embedded *wh- questions.*
>   simple: *Where do you live?*;
>   embedded: *I don't know what he had.*
> (from Cazden, Cancino, Rosansky and Schumann, 1975, p. 38).

In the analysis of the acquisition of auxiliaries we found that *is (cop)* was acquired first by all the subjects and that generally *do* and *can* followed shortly afterwards. The other auxiliaries appeared in a highly variable order.

ALBERTO'S DEVELOPMENT

As mentioned above, one of the adult subjects, Alberto, showed very little linguistic development during the course of the study. Whereas four stages were found in the acquisition of the English negative (*no V, don't V, aux-neg, analyzed don't*); throughout the study Alberto remained in the first stage. Two stages were found in the acquisition of English wh- questions (undifferentiation and differentiation); throughout the study Alberto remained in the first period of the first stage. In addition, in yes/no-questions he inverted considerably less frequently than the other subjects. The four inflectional morphemes (possessive, past tense, plural and progressive) which were studied showed little or no growth over time. In terms of auxiliary development, *am (cop), can* and *are (cop)* could be classified as appearing in his speech (i.e., they were supplied 80% of the time in three consecutive samples), but only *is (cop)* approaches the criterion for acquisition (correctly supplied in 90% of obligatory contexts for three successive samples). In general then Alberto can be characterized as using a reduced and simplified form of English:

    a. in which the negative particle remains external to the verb and is not placed after the first auxiliary element as required in well-formed English;

    b. in which inversion is virtually absent in questions;

    c. in which no auxiliaries [except possibly *is (cop)*] can be said to be ACQUIRED, and using a less stringent criterion only four auxiliaries [*is (cop), am (cop), can* and *are (cop)*] can be said to have APPEARED;

    d. in which the possessive tends to be unmarked;

    e. in which the regular past tense ending (ed) is virtually absent;

    f. in which positive transfer from Spanish can account for the plural inflection being supplied 85% of the time, for *is (cop)*'s being correctly supplied to a greater extent than other auxiliaries and for *am (cop), are (cop)* and *can* reaching criterion for appearance;

    g. and in which the progressive morpheme (*-ing*) is supplied only about 60% of the time.

REASONS FOR ALBERTO'S DEVELOPMENT

Now the question becomes what accounts for the lack of development in Alberto's speech. Three explanations are considered: ability, age and social and psychological distance from speakers of the target language.

ABILITY

Performance on a Piagetian test of adaptive intelligence (Feldman, *et al,* 1974) indicated that Alberto had no gross cognitive deficits that would have prevented him from acquiring English more fully. Therefore, lack of ability does not seem adequate to explain his acquisition pattern.

Age

It was once thought that the completion of cortical lateralization at puberty was the cause of adult difficulties in acquiring second languages. However, Krashen (1973) has demonstrated that the lateralization process which gradually locates language functions in the left hemisphere of the brain is completed by the age of five. Therefore, since we know that six, seven and eight year olds learn second languages without great difficulty, we are left with no age related biological or neurological explanation for Alberto's lack of development in English.

Pidginization[1]

Alberto's essentially reduced and simplified English contains several features that are characteristic of pidgin languages. A pidgin language is a simplified and reduced form of speech used for communication between people with different languages. The grammatical structure of pidgins is characterized by a lack of inflectional morphology and a tendency to eliminate grammatical transformations. Alberto's English shared the following features with other pidgin languages:

a. He used the uniform negative "no" for most of his negative utterances as in American Indian Pidgin English (AIPE) (Leachman and Hall, 1955) and English Worker Pidgin (EWP) (Clyne, 1975).
b. He did not invert in questions as in Neo-Melanesian Pidgin (N-MP) (Smith, 1972) and EWP.
c. He lacked auxiliaries as in EWP.
d. He tended not to inflect for the possessive as in AIPE.
e. He used the unmarked form of the verb as in English-Japanese Pidgin (E-JP) (Goodman, 1967), AIPE and EWP.
f. He deleted subject pronouns as in EWP.

Since Alberto's English appears to be pidginized, we want to answer the question, "What causes pidginization?" The answer lies in the functions which a pidginized language serves. Smith (1972) sees language as having three general functions: communicative, integrative and expressive. The communicative function operates in the transmission of referential, denotative information between persons. The integrative function is engaged when a speaker acquires language to the extent that it marks him as a member of a particular social group. That is, his speech contains those features (such as correct noun and verb inflections, inversion in questions, and correct placement of the negative particle) that are unnecessary for simple referential communication, but which are necessary in order to sound like a member of the group whose language contains these features. The expressive function goes beyond the integrative in that through it, the speaker becomes a valued member of a particular linguistic group. In other words, he displays linguistic virtuosity or skill such that he becomes an admired member of the community. Examples of such people are storytellers (especially in non-literate societies), comedians, orators, poets, etc. Since many native speakers do not command the expressive functions of their language, in order to be considered a fluent speaker of a language, one need only master the communicative and integrative functions. According to Smith, pidgin languages are generally restricted to the first function—communication. That is, their purpose is merely to convey denotative, referential information. Since pidgins are always second languages, the integrative and expressive functions are maintained by the speakers' native languages. As a result of this functional restriction, pidginization produced an interlanguage which is simplified and reduced.

The next question to be answered then is, "What causes restriction in function?" Martin Joos (1971) suggests that "the skeletonizing/skeletonized pattern of pidgin-formation . . . emerges automatically from lack of actual/ prospective SOCIAL solidarity between speaker and addressee" (p. 187) (emphasis mine). To this I would also add the lack of actual or prospective psychological solidarity between the two parties. If we turn this formulation around, restriction in function can be seen as resulting from social and/or psychological distance between the speaker and addressee. Placing this notion within the framework of second language acquisition, we would argue that the speech of the second language learner will be restricted to the communicative function if the learner is socially and/or psychologically distant from the speakers of the target language. The extent and persistence of the pidginized forms in the second language learner's speech will result automatically then from the restriction in function.

Social distance pertains to the individual as a member of a social group which is in contact with another social group whose members speak a different language. Hence social distance involves such sociological factors as domination versus subordination, assimilation versus acculturation versus preservation, enclosure, size, congruence and attitude. Psychological distance pertains to the individual as an individual, and involves such psychological factors as resolution of language shock, culture shock and culture stress, integrative versus instrumental motivation and ego-permeability. In the following two sections each form of distance will be discussed.

Social distance[2]

The following notions about social distance (Schumann, 1976) evolve from the literature on bilingualism, second language acquisition, sociolinguistics and ethnic relations. They represent societal factors that either promote or inhibit social solidarity between two groups and thus affect the way a second language learning group (2LL group) acquires the language of a particular target language group (TL group). The assumption is that the greater the social distance between the two groups the more difficult it is for the members of the 2LL group to acquire the language of the TL group. The following issues are involved in social distance: In relation to the TL group is the 2LL group politically, culturally, technically or economically DOMINANT, NON-DOMINANT, or SUBORDINATE? Is the integration pattern of the 2LL group ASSIMILATION, ACCULTURATION, or PRESERVATION? What is the 2LL group's degree of ENCLOSURE? Is the 2LL group COHESIVE? What is the SIZE of the 2LL group? Are the cultures of the two groups CONGRUENT? What are the ATTITUDES of the two groups toward each other? What is the 2LL group's INTENDED LENGTH OF RESIDENCE in the target language area? The above terms are defined as follows:

1. Dominant—2LL group is politically, culturally, technically or economically SUPERIOR to the TL group.
2. Non-dominant—2LL group is politically, culturally, technically and economically EQUAL to the TL group.

3. Subordinate—2LL group is politically, culturally, technically and economically INFERIOR to the TL group.
4. Assimilation—2LL group gives up its own life style and values and adopts those of the TL group.
5. Acculturation—2LL group adapts to the life style and values of the TL group, but at the same time maintains its own cultural patterns for use in intra-group relations.
6. Preservation—2LL group rejects the life style and values of the TL group and attempts to maintain its own cultural pattern as much as possible.
7. Enclosure—The degree to which the two groups have separate schools, churches, clubs, recreational facilities, professions, crafts, trades, etc.
8. Cohesiveness—The degree to which members of the 2LL group live, work and socialize together.
9. Size—How large the 2LL group is.
10. Congruence—The degree to which the cultures of the two groups are similar.
11. Attitude—Ethnic stereotypes by which the two groups either positively or negatively value each other.
12. Intended length of residence—How long the 2LL group intends to remain in the TL area.

It is argued that social distance and hence a bad language learning situation (see columns A and B in Table 17-1) will obtain where the 2LL group is either dominant or subordinate, where both groups desire preservation and high enclosure for the 2LL group, where the 2LL group is both cohesive and large, where the two cultures are not congruent, where the two groups hold negative attitudes toward each other and where the 2LL group intends to remain in the target language area only for a short time. It is also argued that social solidarity and hence a good language learning situation (see column C in Table 17-1) will obtain where the 2LL group is non-dominant in relation to the TL group, where both groups desire assimilation for the 2LL group, where low enclosure is the goal of both groups, where the two cultures are congruent, where the 2LL group is small and non-cohesive, where both groups have positive attitudes toward each other, and where the 2LL group intends to remain in the target language area for a long time.

In comparing Alberto's social distance from Americans with that of the other subjects in the Cazden, Cancino, Rosansky and Schumann (1975) study, Alberto can be regarded as belonging to a social group designated as lower class Latin American worker immigrants, and the other four subjects can be classified as children of upper-middle class Latin American professional immigrants. There was insufficient background on the second adult subject to include her in this classification.

Latin American worker immigrants (see column D in Table 17-1) are subordinate in relation to Americans since they represent an unskilled labor group whose modal socio-economic status is lower than that of Americans in general. This view is probably shared by both the worker immigrants and the Americans. The worker immigrants probably fall somewhere between preservation and acculturation with regard to their desired integration into American society. American society in general expects them to assimilate as it does all immigrants, but it does not necessarily make the assimilation easy. In terms of enclosure the Latin American workers have access to American institutions, but generally live in immigrant neighborhoods where they share schools, churches and associations with other immigrants having the same socio-economic status and usually having the same language and culture. This enclosure by neighborhood fosters cohesiveness, particularly in Alberto's case where Costa Rican immigrants are a small minority within a Portuguese minority area. The culture of the Latin American worker immigrants is relatively congruent to that of the Americans (both being Western and Christian), but since the Latin American workers may represent the "culture of poverty" more than does the modal American culture, there may also be an element of incongruence between the two cultures (indicated by the arrow, ↓, in Table 17-1). The attitudes of the two groups toward each other would have to be measured before accurate judgments could be made. It is also difficult to assess the intended length of stay in the United States by Latin American workers.

Upper-middle class Latin American professional immigrants (see column E in Table 17-1) are probably viewed by Americans and also view themselves as non-dominant in relation to the English-speaking TL group because their educational background and socio-economic status more closely match that of Americans in general (particularly in the Boston/Cambridge area). The Latin American professionals are solidly acculturative in their integration pattern. They have to be able to demonstrate culturally appropriate behavior in their relationships with American colleagues and therefore must adapt to American life styles and values. But since their length of residence in the United States is often confined to a period of postgraduate education, they generally do not choose to assimilate. The professionals are generally integrated into the university and professional communities and do not live in immigrant neighborhoods. Therefore, their enclosure is low and they are less cohesive than the worker immigrants. The size of the professional group is likely to be smaller than that of workers, and the congruity of the two cultures is relatively high. Once again attitudinal orientations would have to be empirically assessed in order to be correctly classified.

When both profiles are considered we find that the Latin American worker immigrant group is at a considerably greater social distance from Americans than are the professionals. Thus, we would expect the workers' use of English to be functionally restricted and to pidginize. This is precisely what we find in Alberto.

Psychological distance[3]

As the classification of the 2LL group in either the good or bad language learning situations becomes less determinant (i.e., if a group stands somewhere between the bad and good situations), then success in acquiring the target language

Table 17-1. Analysis of social distance characteristics for good and bad language learning situations and for worker vs. professional immigrants from Latin America to the United States
(Corresponding √'s and X's indicate similarity of situations)

	A — Bad language learning Situation I	B — Bad language learning Situation II	C — Good language learning Situation	D — Latin American Workers	E — Latin American Professionals
political economic technical cultural					
TLgp views 2LLgp					
dominant	*				
—dominant			X		X
subordinate		√		√	
2 LLgp views itself					
dominant	*				
—dominant			X		X
subordinate		√		√	
culture					
TLgp desires of 2LLgp					
assimilation			X		
acculturation					X
preservation	*	√		√	
2 LLgp desires for itself					
assimilation			X		
acculturation					X
preservation	*	√		√	
structure					
TLgp desires for 2LLgp					
high enclosure	*	√			
moderate enclosure				√	
low enclosure			X		X
2 LLgp desires for itself					
high enclosure	*	√			
moderate enclosure				√	
low enclosure			X		X

Table 17-1 (continued)

	A	B	C	D	E
	Bad language learning Situation I	Bad language learning Situation II	Good language learning Situation	Latin American Workers	Latin American Professionals
2 LLgp's cohesiveness					
cohesive	*	√		√	
—cohesive			X		X
Size of 2 LLgp					
large	*	√		√	
small			X		X
Culture of 2LLgp					
congruent with TLgp			X	√↓	X
—congruent with Tlgp	*	√			
Tlgp's attitude towards 2LLgp					
positive			X		
negative	*	√			
2LLgp's attitude towards TLgp					
positive			X		
negative	*	√			
2 LLgp's intended length of residence in TL area					
short	*	√			X
long			X		
Social distance					
great	*	√		√	
little			X		X

attitudes (bracket spanning: Tlgp's attitude towards 2LLgp / 2LLgp's attitude towards TLgp) becomes more a matter of the individual as an individual rather than of the individual as member of a particular social group. In addition, in either a good or a bad language learning situation, an individual can violate the modal tendency of his group. Thus, an individual might learn the target language where he is expected not to, and not learn the language where successful acquisition is expected. In these cases it is PSYCHOLOGICAL DISTANCE (Schumann, 1975b) or proximity between the learner and the TL group that accounts for successful versus unsuccessful second language acquisition. The factors which create psychological distance between the learner and speakers of the target language are affective in nature and involve such issues as the resolution of language shock and culture shock, motivation and ego permeability.

In experiencing language shock (Stengal, 1939), the learner is haunted by doubts as to whether his words accurately reflect his ideas. In addition, he is sometimes confronted with target language words and expressions which carry with them images and meanings which he interprets differently than do native speakers of the target language. Also, the narcissistic gratification to which the learner is accustomed in the use of his native language is lost when he attempts to speak the target language. Finally, when speaking the second language the learner has apprehensions about appearing comic, child-like and dependent.

The learner experiences culture shock (Smalley, 1963; Larsen and Smalley, 1972) when he finds that his problem-solving and coping mechanisms do not work in the new culture. When they are used they do not get the accustomed results. Consequently, activities which were routine in his native country require great energy in the new culture. This situation causes disorientation, stress, fear and anxiety. The resultant mental state can produce a whole syndrome of rejection which diverts attention and energy from second language learning. The learner, in attempting to find a cause for his disorientation, may reject himself, the people of the host country, the organization for which he is working, and even his own culture.

Motivation (Gardner and Lambert, 1972) relates to the goals of second language learning. In terms of psychological distance, the integratively motivated learner would seek maximum proximity in order to meet, talk with, and perhaps even become like the speakers of the target language. An instrumentally motivated learner would achieve a level of psychological solidarity that would only be commensurate with his instrumental goals. Consequently, if the learner's goal were mere survival, he might maintain a good deal of psychological distance between himself and the speakers of the target language.

Another source of psychological distance may be the relative rigidity of the learner's ego boundaries (Guiora, 1972). Some experimental evidence indicates that people who have ego permeability, i.e., the ability to partially and temporarily give up their separateness of identity, are better second language learners. This essentially psychoanalytic concept is intuitively appealing and provides another perspective from which the concept of psychological distance can be understood.

In sum then, factors causing psychological distance, like those causing social distance, put the learner in a situation where he is largely cut off from target language input and/or does not attend to it when it is available. The language which is acquired under these conditions will be used simply for denotative referential communication in situations where contact with speakers of the target language is either absolutely necessary or unavoidable. The learner's psychological distance will prevent him from identifying with the speakers of the target language such that he will not attempt to incorporate into his speech those linguistic features that would help to identify him as a member of the TL group. Hence, his use of the target language will be functionally restricted and, therefore, we would expect it to pidginize.

In order to get some assessment of Alberto's psychological distance from English speakers, at the end of the study, he was asked to fill out a short questionnaire which elicited information concerning his attitude and motivation. In terms of this questionnaire, he seemed to have a positive attitude and good motivation, and hence little psychological distance. However, there is some question as to whether he was entirely candid in his answers. Alberto tended not to like to displease and therefore his answers may reflect what he thought the experimenter wanted to hear.

There are several aspects of Alberto's life style that appear to contradict the positive attitude and motivation expressed in the questionnaire. First of all, he made very little effort to get to know English-speaking people. In Cambridge he stuck quite close to a small group of Spanish-speaking friends. He did not own a television and expressed disinterest in it because he could not understand English. On the other hand, he purchased an expensive stereo set and tape deck on which he played mostly Spanish music. Also, he chose to work at night (as well as in the day) rather than attend English classes which were available in Cambridge.

The other subjects were not given the attitude and motivation questionnaire, but in general they seemed to be psychologically much closer to Americans. All the children attended American schools and had American friends. The second adult baby-sat for American children, studied English on her own and tried to get to know and speak with Americans.

The effect of instruction

From the point of view of the pidginization hypothesis we would argue that Alberto did not seek out instruction in English because his pidginized speech was adequate for his needs. Nevertheless, it might be argued that with instruction his simplified linguistic system might have reorganized and come to conform more closely with the target language. The opportunity to test this idea presented itself after the study was completed. At the end of the ten-month project, twenty, one-hour speech samples had been collected. As mentioned earlier, throughout this period Alberto had maintained essentially a *no V* negation system.

The experimenter then undertook to teach him how to negate in English to see if this intervention would cause him to alter his pidginized system of negation. Extensive instruction was provided during the collection of speech sample 21 and then intermittently in samples 22 through 32. This program covered a seven-month period. At the same time in samples 22-30 Alberto was given extensive sets of positive sentences which he was asked to negate. These elicited negatives were then compared with the negative utterances in his spontaneous speech. In elicited speech after instruction, Alberto's negatives were about 64% (216/335) correct. His spontaneous negatives, however, were only about 20% (56/278) correct i.e., 222 *no V* utterances (incorrect) and 56 *don't V* utterances (correct). The latter are correct only by coincidence simply because *don't*, as an allomorph of *no,* was occasionally used in the appropriate linguistic environment. Therefore, we see that instruction influenced only Alberto's production in a test-like, highly monitored situation; it did not affect his spontaneous speech which he used for normal communication. This result is even more striking when we compare it with spontaneous and elicited negatives prior to instruction. In samples 16-20, Alberto's spontaneous negatives were 22% (23/105) correct and his elicited negatives were 10% (7/71) correct. This indicates that instruction has radically improved his performance in an artificial, highly monitored elicitation task, but that it had virtually no effect on his spontaneous speech which he uses in normal communication with native speakers of English. Hence we can conclude that instruction is evidently not powerful enough to overcome the pidginization engendered by social and psychological distance.

COGNITIVE PROCESSES IN PIDGINIZATION

The social and psychological forces that cause the persistence of pidginization in a second language learner's speech have been discussed. The term "persistence" is used because, as predicted in Schumann (1974a and b), pidginization appears to be characteristic of early second language acquisition in general. What has been described as pidginization in Alberto's speech corresponds to the early stages of the acquisition of English by all six learners. Alberto remained in stage one of negation (the *no V* stage) and in stage one, period *a* of interrogation (uninversion in both simple and embedded wh- questions). Since it is reasonable to assume that, as with Alberto, inflectional marking tended to be absent in the early speech of the other five subjects (this was not specifically examined in Cazden, Cancino, Rosansky and Schumann, 1975), evidence exists that pidginization may characterize all early second language acquisition and that under conditions of social and psychological distance it persists. Since pidginization may be a universal first stage in second language acquisition, it is important to explore what cognitive processes either cause or allow the pidginization to occur.

Kay and Sankoff (1974) believe that contact vernaculars such as pidgins and other varieties of incomplete competence such as child language, second language acquisition, bilingualism and aphasia are all potential areas for examining linguistic universals. Referring to contact vernaculars in particular they state that "since the communicative functions fulfilled by contact vernaculars are minimal, these languages may possibly reveal in a more direct way than do most natural languages the universal cognitive structure and process that underlie all human language ability and use." (p. 62)

Smith (1973) notes that the early speech of children is largely unmarked (hence the term telegraphic speech) and that in the process of socialization the child learns to mark his language with those features which characterize his speech community. The result of this development is that adult speech is naturally and normally marked (p. 3). However, pidgin languages which are spoken by adults are characteristically unmarked. Smith attempts to account for the fact that pidginization produces a generally unmarked language by viewing unmarking and marking as part of the same process. The child at one point in his development has had the ability to unmark. Smith speculates that this ability is not lost and can be retrieved under certain social conditions. One of these conditions is the pidginogenic social context where the function of the language is restricted to communication of denotative referential information. Both the child in early native language acquisition and the pidgin speaker reduce and simplify the language to which they are exposed into a set of primitive categories which undoubtedly are innate (p. 11). These primitive categories emerge in speech as utterances relatively unmarked by inflections, permutations and functors. Within this framework unmarking is not seen as a deficiency, but as a positive cognitive strategy to which a language learner turns at certain development stages and under certain social conditions.

Corder (1975) maintains a similar position, but argues that "simple codes" spoken by children, neophyte second language learners, pidgin speakers, and adults using baby-talk or foreigner talk are not "simplified," i.e., they are not reductions of a more complicated and expanded code. Instead they represent a basic language which, in the process of learning, is expanded and complicated. Following Kay and Sankoff (1972), Corder suggests that simple codes "are nearer, in some sense, to the underlying structure or 'inner form' of all languages. i.e., more overtly reflect semantic categories and relations." (p. 4). He goes on to speculate that this basic language, and all intermediate linguistic systems between basic and complex, once learned are never obliterated. These approximative systems remain "available both for special communicative functions in the mother tongue [baby talk, foreigner talk] and as an 'initial hypothesis' in the learning of second language." (p. 9).

Within this framework, pidginization in second language acquisition can be viewed as initially resulting from cognitive constraints and then persisting due to social and psychological constraints. Hence, early second language acquisition would be characterized by the temporary use of a non-marked, simple code resembling a pidgin. This code would be the product of cognitive constraints engendered by lack of knowledge of the target language. The code may reflect a regression to a set of universal primitive linguistic categories that were realized in early first language acquisition. Then, under conditions of social and/or psychological distance, this pidginized form of speech would persist.

CONCLUSION

The pidginization hypothesis predicts that where social and psychological distance prevail we will find pidginization persisting in the speech of second language learners. There are several experimental and several clinical studies that could be undertaken to further explore this hypothesis. In order to experimentally test the social distance aspect of the hypothesis, one might choose a population of worker immigrants in the United States and compare its success in the acquisition of English to the success in the acquisition of English experienced by a group of professional immigrants. To experimentally test the psychological distance aspect of the hypothesis one could make an intensive examination (using questionnaires, interviews, etc.) of those worker immigrants who DO successfully learn English and the professional immigrants who fail to learn it.

To clinically examine social distance phenomena, a questionnaire might be developed which would be filled out by experimenters doing research in second language acquisition. In it they would attempt to classify the subjects with whom they were working (either groups or individuals) on social distance dimensions. The questionnaire would be designed to permit the researcher to rate a particular 2LL group's dominance, cohesiveness, enclosure, etc., on a numerical scale, to compute a social distance score for the group and then to relate that score to the extent of pidginization found in his subject(s)' speech.

Psychological distance might receive clinical examination by studying a small group of subjects (six to ten) who will be living in a foreign language environment for a fairly long period of time. The subjects might be a group of Peace Corps Volunteers or foreign service personnel who have a good opportunity to become bilingual as a result of training in and exposure to the target language. At the beginning of the study the subjects would be assessed on as many relevant variables as possible, including: language learning aptitude, attitude, motivation, ego-permeability (assuming a valid measure is available), experiences in learning other second languages and general social adjustment. The subjects would be asked to keep diaries in which they would describe daily exposure to the target language, efforts to learn the language, and feelings about language learning and the new culture. In addition, the subjects would be interviewed once every two weeks in order that the researchers could probe the same issues verbally. Finally the subjects' achievement in the second language would be tested monthly by means of an oral interview which could then be analyzed for aspects of pidginization. The object of this approach would be to develop several case studies in which an individual's pattern of second language acquisition could be related longitudinally to factors involving his psychological distance from speakers of the target language.

Such research strategies could shed light on the interaction between the phenomena of social and psychological distance; uncover new factors contributing to both phenomena and perhaps indicate ways in which social and psychological distance can be overcome and thus free those affected to become bilingual.

Finally, by studying the second language speech of learners affected by social and/or psychological distance in a variety of contact situations (e.g., Chinese-English, English-Persian, Italian-French, etc.) a further contribution could be made to our knowledge of the linguistic aspects of pidginization and the processes of simplification and reduction in natural languages in general.

Notes

1. The type of pidginization referred to here is secondary hybridization, not tertiary hybridization. The position taken in this paper is that secondary hybridization is legitimate pidginization. For a discussion of this issue see Whinnom (1971).

2. For a detailed discussion of social distance see Schumann (1976).

3. For a detailed discussion of the factors involved in psychological distance see Schumann (1975b).

Part II
 Experimental
Studies

Multiple Measures

Methodology

18

for Examining

Second Language Acquisition

Marilyn Adams, *University of California, Los Angeles*

INTRODUCTION

As more and more observational studies appear on second-language acquisition, we have begun to realize that there is a great deal of data missing that we would like to have. This is partly because the questions we want to ask are changing and partly due to the nature of observational studies. Unless everything is recorded— the input data, glosses and context—it is difficult to reanalyze data for answers to new questions we wish to ask. In observational studies of second-language acquisition it is extremely important that the observations be frequent; they cannot be once every two weeks or once a month as in first language acquisition. Most subjects learn much too quickly for such a schedule. If the observer is not present a good deal of the time, one cannot accurately talk about the acquisition process. Too many gaps occur in the data to allow us to be sure of much.

Even when a great deal of data are collected, it is limited by the context in which it is collected. If various structures do not occur in the data, we are not sure whether the child does or does not have those structures, only that he did not use them during the periods when we observed. In addition, some children are shy and reticent in their language production. Yet we would like to have as much data on their language acquisition as we have from more verbal, out-going children. Experimental techniques, then, are frequently necessary to elicit additional information about the child's language learning process, to answer the questions that we have.

The Adams study, conducted in 1971, shows how elicitation techniques can test the child's comprehension and production of structures which may not appear in the observational data. They also show how such techniques allow one to corroborate the sometimes sketchy data obtained in spontaneous speech recording. Ideally, whenever the researcher notices a new form developing or an old form fading out of his subject's speech, he could quickly devise elicitation "tests" for that particular feature of the language. This would give the investigator the kind of data he needs to feel confident in reporting developmental trends in the second language learning process.

Similar elicitation techniques have been used by several of the investigators in this volume: morphology tests, imitation tests, and translation tests. The care with which Adams constructed tests which would appeal to the child and thereby elicit his best production, however, is unusual. Since her paper is on AUX development, her tasks directly elicited examples of tense, modal, progressive and perfective in English from her 10 Spanish-speaking children. She then charted spontaneous speech data alongside translation and imitation data. The experimental and observational data support each other so that, in combination, the methodology allowed her to feel certain about the claims she has made for AUX development in English as a second language.

There is evidence to suggest that individual children go through strikingly similar stages of development when learning their native language (Slobin, 1971). Moreover, recent studies indicate that young children follow a similar process when acquiring a second language if it is learned in a natural situation such as that provided in a classroom where the second language is used as the medium of instruction but with no direct teaching of that language (Lambert, Just and Segalowitz, 1970).

The purpose of this study was to describe the stages ten Spanish-speaking children would go through in such a natural situation in acquiring part of the English language, the auxiliary system (the AUX in transformational terminology). As the research progressed, however, it became evident that it would not be possible to obtain sufficient data (with the method of data collection being used) to allow one to draw valid conclusions. This led to a consideration of alternative methodologies.

Much of the information available about the competence of adult speakers of a language has come from the linguist's introspection and his questioning of other mature speakers of the language. He can ask adults questions such as *does 'X' mean the same thing as 'Y'?* or *can I say . . . ?* Unfortunately, when appealing directly to the linguistic intuition of the young child, this does not work so well, as the following example from Brown and Bellugi (1964) attests:

Interviewer: "Adam, which is right, 'two shoes' or 'two shoe'?"
Adam: "Pop goes the weasel!"

Since this inquiry technique has not proven successful with children, other methods have been developed. One might observe the child's spontaneous speech, record what is heard, and write rules that would generate sentences similar to those in the data. These rules would be based on the S's performance which may be quite different from his actual competence in the language. Children, like adults, make mistakes in their performance for a variety of reasons, including memory, distraction, perception, etc. Rules written from such production data can distort our picture of the S's actual competence.

Rather than write rules to account for *all* of the obtained data, Bloom (1970) determined regularities of performance that could be used as evidence for inferring the child's language system. This involved defining a standard of "productivity" and accounting for structures that were productive in the child's linguistic system at a given time. Productivity of a structure was judged on the basis of its use with different formatives in different situations, the frequency and consistency with which it was used, where it had occurred before, and might therefore have been expected to occur again. Generally, she classified a structure as "unique" if it occurred only once in a speech sample, "marginal" if it occurred fewer than five times, and "productive" if it occurred five times or more. Such a description allows us to avoid writing misleading or unproductive rules.

Since we want to know how children acquire a second language, one could follow the development of an individual child from one specific point in time to another. Such *longitudinal case studies* can provide a fairly complete detailed description assuming enough data have been collected at frequent intervals. There are, however, at least two disadvantages in this research design: 1) it takes a long time to obtain the data, and 2) a single case study does not permit us to know what is universal, language specific, or child specific.

A different approach is a *pseudo-longitudinal study* which is designed so that one may work simultaneously with children of different language-experience groups, each having utterances representing various levels of development: a composite picture of different levels simultaneously. While this design reduces the time necessary for collection, it is possible that the composite description of each language experience level may not reflect with complete accuracy the actual language competence of any one subject.

A third design which Dato (1970) used to study the acquisition of Spanish as a second language among a group of native English-speaking children is a combination of the single case and the pseudo-longitudinal studies. Here is an example of how one might set up groups for observation:

Group	Time 1	Time 2	Time 3	Time 4
a	1 month	2 months	3 months	4 months
b	2 months	3 months	4 months	5 months
c	3 months	4 months	5 months	6 months

If we compare the stages represented in the column *Time 1*, we get a composite picture, a *pseudo-longitudinal* study; when we compare the stages horizontally, we have a *longitudinal* case study. By using both analyses we arrive at a more complete description in less time and can better justify the generalizations we make.

Assuming that we have collected a large enough speech sample for each group at each time, the next step would be to write the rules necessary to generate the "productive" utterances recorded in each cell. Next we could look to see if the structures were learned in any definable sequence through time (compare group *a*'s grammar for month *1* with its grammar for month *2, 3,* and *4*). Once we had determined the sequence of structural development of each group, we would need to compare their sequencing to find out if the order of acquisition of grammatical rules was similar across groups.

In my study the observation groups were set up as closely as possible to those described in the third design above.

Subjects

Ten native-Spanish-speaking children enrolled in a public school in the Los Angeles area were selected for observation. There were 4 boys and 6 girls, ranging in age from 4:11 to 5:9 at the beginning of the study (September, 1971). At that time several of the *S*s were able to express themselves in English with little observable difficulty while others only used Spanish in the classroom and depended on their classmates' interpretation of the teacher's instructions. During the two years of observation the children received no formal language instruction. No tests of English proficiency were given to place *S*s in the appropriate design cell, but I felt it was possible to rate each child accurately on a scale from least to most fluent based on my observations of his ability to follow instructions; his other comprehension responses; if other *S*s had to translate for him or if he served as interpreter for others; and the level of his apparent structural development—i.e., no production in English, the "two or three word stage," or advanced structural development.

I then collected spontaneous speech of the children over a two-year period using the conventional first language acquisition approach.

SPONTANEOUS SPEECH

Materials and procedure

A minimum of 12 hours per week was spent in the classroom to record the free speech data on the 10 *S*s. Due to the noise level of the classroom and the movements of the children, it was impossible to tape record the data. I wrote down as many of their utterances as possible in a journal. At first the children were curious about my notebook, but they accepted my explanation that I was learning how to teach and needed to keep track of class activities. They frequently reminded me to get my notebook, even to take it out to recess.

Results

A chart mapping AUX development was drawn for each *S*. In the sample chart (see Table 18-1), each column summarizes all the AUX data collected over a one-month period. As can be seen from the sample, there are empty cells and cells with descriptions based on very few and sometimes only one utterance. As a result, I could not apply Bloom's standard of productivity. Instead, I measured the increased use (or phasing out) of a pattern over time. A plus sign in front of a word or morpheme means that the *S* used it correctly; whereas a minus indicates he omitted it when it would have been required in adult speech. An arrow indicates the *S* used the form following it where the one preceding the arrow would be the form used by a mature speaker of English.

Notice that this *S* over-generalized the rule for past tense, saying "bringed" for "brought." She was given credit for knowledge of the allomorph /-d/. Where there is a minus and an item in parenthesis (e.g. "can" or "does"), that item would be the acceptable form in adult language but was omitted by that *S*. If the *S* only produced one example of a certain form in one period but in the following periods proceded to use it in the same way, I credited him with a productive rule when it first appeared.

After writing descriptions for the individual *S*s, these were compared (along the lines of Dato's combination of the case and pseudo-longitudinal study) in order to find similarities across children.

The generalizations reported below are based on a pooling of data from the 10 *S*s. Not all *S*s had, however, examples of every pattern. I have not made any generalizations from the data of only one subject in the areas where the observations were scanty.

Affirmative sentences

Of the three verb inflections, the progressive (-ing) appeared first. Although several of the *S*s occasionally used the copula in present tense at that time, they omitted the AUX *be* when expressing the progressive. The omission of auxiliary *be* continued for a long time (4-15 months); but when the progressive finally did include *be*, there was still one case where *be* was omitted: be + going to + verb, conveying intention rather than on-going action.

The inflection for progressive was also the first verb inflection to emerge in the three *S*s studied in first language acquisition by the Brown group (Cazden, 1968). Interestingly, two of the Brown *S*s (Sarah and Adam) occasionally used a form of *be* without *ing*. In Sarah's speech there were nine instances, all containing *I'm* plus verb, such as "I'm play with it" and "I'm twist his head." These constructions are probably reduced catenatives (I'm going to play with it) conveying intention. (It is also possible that *I* and *I'm* were variants—*I'm play* a variant of *I play*.) The other *S*, Adam, produced only one utterance without *-ing* but many instances of *it's* plus verb: "It's go up" and "It's went away." Adam's use of "it's" was analyzed as a temporary segmentation error with "it's" as a

Table 18-1 Sample chart summarizing AUX data of one S collected over four months

Month	12/72	1/73	2/73	3/73
T + be	+ is (2 ex.) + was (2 ex.)	+ is (1 ex.) − is (1 ex.)	+ am (2 ex.) + is (9 ex.)	am →is (1 ex.) + is (4 ex.) + was (3 ex.)
T pres + V		+ /-z/ (1 ex.) needs − /-z/ (1 ex.) go	− /-z/ (1 ex.) go	+ /-z/ (4 ex.) goes, *says − /-z/ (2 ex.) say, swim + /-s/ (2 ex.) likes, *gots
T past + V	− irreg: win	− /-s/ (2 ex.) work has →have (1 ex.) + /-d/ (1 ex.) *bringed + irreg: went − irreg: go, get, do	+ irreg: did, got, brought − irreg: do	− /-t/ (2 ex.) erase, practice + irreg: went, said, brought − irreg: get, do, have
Modals	"no can" (2 ex.)	"no can" (1 ex.) + can (2 ex.)	+ can't (4 ex.) + can (3 ex.) − should (1 ex.) − will (1 ex.) won't→don't (1 ex.)	+ can't (3 ex.) + can (1 ex.) − should in Q-y/n (1 ex.) + could in Q-y/n (4 ex.)
be + ing		− is (1 ex. in Q-wh) are−is (1 ex. Q-wh) am are } → ∅ / ___ gonna + V	+ is (2 ex.) + are (1 ex.) + was (1 ex.) am → ∅ / ___ Ving (1 ex.) / gonna (5 ex.) + am/___ gonna (1 ex.)	+ am (2 ex.) + was (3 ex.) } / ___ Ving + is / ___ gonna + V (2 ex.)

Table 18-1 (continued).

have + en	no/__ can (3 ex.) __ was (1 ex.) don't / __ V 1 ex. routine		have seen → "see" (1 ex.)
T neg	no/__ can (1 ex.) __ V (3 ex.) doesn't (1 ex.) – don't/__ V don't (3 ex.)	not/__ gonna (1 ex.) + can't (3 ex.) + don't (6 ex.) + doesn't (1 ex.) didn't (1 ex.) won't (2 ex.) imperative–don't (4 ex.)	not/__ gonna (1 ex.) + can't (3 ex.) + don't (6 ex.) + doesn't (1 ex.) ___ don't + didn't (1 ex.) + didn't (1 ex.) imperative–don't
T yes/no	+ be inversion (cop. "is" 1 ex.) + M inversion (can, 1 ex.) + do support (do, 2 ex.) – do support (do, 5 ex.) + is copula (inverted, 2 ex.) – are copula (1 ex.) – is prog (1 ex.) are–is/How many __ Ving (1 ex.)	– M inversion (can, 1 ex.) + is copula (inverted, 2 ex.) – is copula (1 ex.) + are prog. (invert 1 ex.)	do you + can (1 lex.) want (1 ex.) brought (1 ex.) got (4 ex.) + M inversion (could, 4 ex.) – do support: (do, 1 ex.), (did, 1 ex.) (can, 1 ex.) + be inversion is ―is are ―is
T wh		– M (should, 1 ex.) – do support: (do, 2 ex.) (does, 1 ex.) NP & VP inverted (does, 3 ex.)	+ do support (do, 1 ex.) – do support: (did, 1 ex.) (does, 2 ex.)

variant of "it" presumably because in his mother's speech "it" was followed much more often by "is" than by a main verb (Brown, Cazden, and Bellugi, 1969). Although my Ss' speech contained reduced catenatives, the omission was always *be* instead of the *-ing* inflection.

In the data, all Ss used the copula before they used any tense marking on the main verb though copula usage was sporadic. Tense with main verbs began to emerge before copular *be* became stable. The sequence of acquisition for regular past and present was less consistent than the progressive. The first observation of tense on main verbs occurred for present with 4 of the Ss, for past with 3 of the Ss, one S had occurrences for past and present simultaneously, and 2 Ss failed to produce present or past inflections throughout the two years of data collection. Brown's first language Ss showed the same inconsistency. By period V, Sarah had attained the criterion of 90 percent accuracy on both present and past, Eve had attained only the past, and Adam only the present indicative.

Negative sentences

The following generalizations on negative development are based on data taken from all 10 Ss. However, some of the Ss had already passed the initial stages of negative development when observation began. By the end of the two years of observation, the least advanced Ss had not yet reached the last level described below.

In the first period there were no negatives within the utterances, nor were there auxiliary verbs (modals, *have,* or *be*); the Ss used "no" to signal negation and it either preceded or followed the rest of the utterance: "no dis one no." This initial period was very short; very few examples were observed.

In the second period, the negative element is within the sentence: "no" directly precedes the main verb (there is no tense marker present) and "not" precedes the predicate in sentences with a copula as required in adult speech (the copula is often omitted at this stage). "Not" never occurred with a main verb. One S didn't even use "not" in sentences with a copula. Her productive rule for negation was more general: place "no" immediately before main verbs, modals, and even before forms of *be*, for example "I no wanna play," "We no can go on the bars," and "He no was there." The only case where the do-support occurs is in memorized expressions such as "I don't know" and with negative imperatives with "don't" plus verb.

In the third period there was a gradual increase in the use of "don't" plus main verb as the "no" plus main verb pattern subsided. In fact, "don't" was over-generalized and used as a negative filler in place of other forms (i.e., for *doesn't, won't, can't, haven't*). "Not" is still used with auxiliary *be* and copula. Toward the end of the third period the use of "don't" as a negative filler became more limited and the modal auxiliaries began to emerge. *Can't* and *won't* were the first to appear. At this time the do-support was used to carry tense (i.e., a distinction was made between *don't, doesn't* and *didn't*), but double marking of tense was common: "didn't found," "doesn't wants." In this period the indeterminates start to appear, also with frequent doublemarking: "don't want nothing," "ain't gonna never," "nobody won't," "doesn't have no crayons."

At the end of the two years, most of the *S*s still hadn't produced any sentences with the AUX element have + en. The two who were starting to acquire this construction made errors such as "haven't do" for "haven't done" and "hadn't stayed" for "didn't stay."

Studies in first language acquisition report the auxiliary verb to emerge first always associated with negatives (don't, can't) (Ervin-Tripp, 1963; Klima and Bellugi, 1966). Later the modals and "do" appear inverted in Q-yes/no. At the same time, the modals but not "do" emerge independent of interrogatives and negatives. Not until the next period does the inversion of auxiliary verbs extend to questions introduced by an interrogative word.

My data also indicate that "do" appears first as a negative element, then inverted with the subject in Q-yes/no, and finally in Q-wh. The modals, however, did not parallel "do" development. In most cases my *S*s first used modals in the affirmative, next inverted in Q-yes/no, next in negative sentences, and near the end of the observation period there were a few examples of inversion in Q-wh.

Yes/No questions (Q-yes/no)

The development of Q-yes/no rules can be divided into three main stages. In the first one, declarative sentence word order is used and rising intonation is the only signal for the question. Many of the earliest utterances did not include the subject NP: "Is good?", "Play blocks?", "Wanna see something?". Main verbs other than *be* were not marked for tense.

In the second stage, rising intonation was still the most common way to signal yes/no questions when none of the optional AUX elements was present. There were only a few routine expressions where "do" occurred: "Do you got _____?" "Do you have _____?", "Do you know?", etc. One *S* used *d'you* as a variant of *you*, but she did not segment *d'you* into *do* plus *you* since there were no occurrences of *do* independent of *you*. The modal *can* appeared in stage two inverted with the subject NP.

One might expect the *S*s to over-generalize the English rule for inversion and extend it to the sentences containing only tense plus verb since this is the rule for forming yes/no questions in Spanish: ¿Quiere usted cafe? (*Want you coffee?). There were no examples of this in their English.

The use of *be* was not stable at stage two. Sometimes it was omitted in yes/no questions; sometimes it was present but occurred after the subject NP as in declarative statements; other times it was inverted correctly.

There was one interesting exception to stage two Q-yes/no formation in the data of the same *S* who had the simplified set of rules for negation in stage two. All the following examples are yes/no questions she produced in stage two:

1. Could I borrow white?	6. Do you wanna play bingo?
2. Could I go to the bathroom?	7. Do you brought your lunch?
3. Could you do it?	8. You put three?
4. Do you can bring it?	9. I did good?
5. Do you got any 'b'?	

These utterances show a coexistence of rules from stage one and a new system. The *S*'s most productive pattern at this stage was "do" plus declarative sentence word order (No. 4-7). No other *S*s used "do" with modals. Examples 8 and 9, with rising intonation, represent an earlier phase of development. Although the *S* did not invert *can* in example 4, she did in three examples with *could*. *Could* appeared to be a memorized form since it only occurred in Q-yes/no, yet it also reflected an emerging pattern for stage three.

By the third stage *be* inversion stabilized for all *S*s; and more modals began to appear (*will, could, should*) inverted for the question. *Do you* + verb emerged before *does* or *did*. Throughout the two years of observation, first and second person singular were by far the most frequent in the speech of all the *S*s.) When the *S*s did start to use tense in sentences with do-support, they often included double tense markings such as "Did you saw _____ ?" for "Did you see _____ ?"

The *S*s acquisition of Q-yes/no parallels Klima and Bellugi's description for first language acquisition with a few exceptions during the second period. In the first language acquisition data, modals and do-support were associated with negative and never occurred in affirmative statements or questions. The copula was not present in questions either. Q-yes/no was only signaled by rising intonation imposed on an utterance with declarative sentence word order. In contrast, all my *S*s had acquired at least one modal (*can*) in the second period and were using it in affirmative and/or yes/no questions. In Q-yes/no the modal was inverted. Whereas *be* was absent from the first language data, it was unstable in mine. When a form of *be* was present, it was inverted only part of the time. *Do* was first associated with the negative in my data as it was in the first language studies, and in period two the do-support was present only in a few yes/no questions which were classified as memorized expressions.

Wh-questions (Q-wh)

The development of Q-wh can be divided into three main periods. In the first, the interrogative word preceded the rest of the sentence which had declarative word order: wh-NP-VP. All of the examples observed for this time contained a subject NP which was either *you* or *I*, thus the verb had no overt tense marker in the present. Since there were no examples where a past tense would have been required, I cannot determine whether or not they would have used it given the appropriate situation. No claims can be made about the use of *be* in wh-questions because there were not enough examples. No modals were included in wh-questions nor did there seem to be any sentences observed where a modal would have been necessary.

By the second period there were still no modals present in wh-questions. *Be* (both as copula and auxiliary) was generally used in this period and, more often than not, it was inverted correctly. The transporting rule was over-extended to sentences with *be* in embedded questions producing a number of examples such as "I don't know where *is* mines." There is no discussion of embedded questions in first language studies, but I have noticed many similar utterances in the speech of Anglo nursery school children.

In the second period the most common word order for Q-wh containing a simple verb was *Wh* plus declarative sentence: "When you go to your house?" There were, however, four *S*s who occasionally extended the transposing rule to wh-questions with a simple verb: "What say that?" In Spanish, if the subject NP is expressed independently from the verb (which it need not be since the verb is inflected for person), there are two ways to signal a yes/no question: by imposing rising intonation on a sentence with the normal NP+VP word order or by inverting the subject and verb ("¿Ustedes vienen a las ocho?" or "¿Vienen ustedes a las ocho?"). With Wh-questions, however, inversion is obligatory: "¿Cuando vienen ustedes?" but never *"¿Cuando ustedes vienen?" These *S*s may have tried to apply the Spanish rules. This would affect Q-wh formation more than Q-yes/no since there is an optional Q-yes/no in Spanish which comes closer to the English one than does the Q-wh.

Although this is a reasonable explanation for their errors, one could just as easily account for the verb-inversion in terms of normal language development in English. Over-extension of the inversion rule in Q-wh occurs in first language acquisition data as well (Miller and Ervin, 1964).

By the third period, *be* (both auxiliary and copula) was used correctly in Wh-questions. There were only a few examples of modals in Wh-questions; those recorded were correctly inverted. The do-support appeared in yes/no questions first. Shortly after its appearance there, it began to emerge in Q-wh. Again, tense was often doubly marked: "Where did he found it?" and "Where's this one belongs?"

From the previous discussed it appeared that the *S*s of this study went through stages in AUX development quite similar to those described in first language acquisition studies. These results, however, could not be considered conclusive. Additional means of data collection needed to be used for a more complete picture. Since I was not satisfied with the spontaneous speech corpus, I decided to try two additional techniques (elicited imitation and translation from Spanish to English) to see if they would reflect patterns similar to those observed in the spontaneous speech production collected during the same period. Data obtained by these techniques could be compared with the free speech data to give a more accurate picture of AUX development.

ELICITED IMITATION

Studies of imitation have been used to learn about first language acquisition (Slobin and Welsh, 1973; Menyuk, 1963; Fraser, Bellugi, and Brown, 1963). Recently, imitation tests have also been used to study second language acquisition (Butterworth, 1972; Cathcart, 1972; Swain, Naiman, and Dumas, 1972). These examiners suggest that the child has to filter the model sentences through his own productive linguistic system; by doing so he will make alterations in his imitation of the modeled sentences if his grammar differs from that of the model.

There are at least three advantages of using the elicited imitation technique over freer test forms. First, by controlling the input or modeled structure, the S is forced to use a certain form unless his grammar differs from the model. If the same model is used for more than one S, a comparison can be made across Ss. For shy children that produce little free speech data, the imitation task gives them the security of having a model.

Materials and procedure

A pilot imitation task had been administered during the kindergarten year, and it was found that the Ss attention span was extremely short when the model sentences were unrelated and there were no visual aids. To maintain the Ss' interest, the sentences for the test formed a story which was illustrated with a set of pictures. To make it more realistic, there were also sound effects to imitate: yawning, sniffing, tweeting like a bird, and knocking on the table. There were fifty-two sentences to be imitated, including the AUX areas outlined on the sample chart (see Table 18-2).

First, the E told the S the story using the pictures. Then she told the S that she would teach him the story by having him repeat each sentence after her. If the S's first attempt was not acoustically clear, he was given a second chance and the best one was used. The modeled sentences and the Ss' imitations were tape recorded. The procedure took about fifteen minutes for each child.

Results

The results of this test were charted against the observations made of the S's free speech as shown in the columns of Table 18-2. The sample is taken from the same S whose free speech data appear in Table 18-1. Note that the S was given credit for knowledge of the rules for present and past tense formation if he made over-generalizations such as "haves," "gots," and "sayed." A plus sign in front of a word or morpheme means that the S used it correctly; whereas a minus indicates that he omitted it when it would have been required in adult speech. An arrow indicates that the S used the form following it in place of the one preceding the arrow which would be the form used by a mature speaker of English.

A comparison was made between each S's free speech collected in March and his own responses on the imitation test. Unfortunately, there were some areas where the free speech and imitation data did not overlap, usually due to gaps in spontaneous production. The items where there was no overlap will not be discussed. Where the data overlapped it was found that there were many AUX forms used correctly in both free speech and imitations.

If the Ss had repeated all of the modeled sentences exactly like the model, it would not necessarily mean that the Ss had a productive rule for each AUX item; the child could have been parroting without comprehension. However, the S's imitations did *not* follow the model exactly and they made the same deviations from the adult grammar as found in their free speech. When in his free speech sample the S formed Q-wh by fronting the Wh-word and using statement word order, he made the same alterations in imitation. For example, in his spontaneous speech one S said "What it say there?" and in imitation he changed the model sentence "What does your dog like to eat?" to "What your dog like?" Another S had a productive rule for forming Q-yes/no by placing *do* in front of the subject when it was *you*. Thus in her March free speech she produced questions such as "Do you can bring me a book?" and "Do you brought your lunch?" Similarly, when imitating the model sentences "Can you really take us back home?" and "Can you smell the flowers, Peppy?", she altered them to agree with her own grammar: "Do you really can take us to home?" and "Peppy, do you can smell the flowers?" Another consistent variation from AUX formation with have+en was to use only the past participle of the main verb and omit the *have*: in free speech one S said "She already done it" for "She has already done it" and in her imitation of "I've gone too far from my home" she again omitted the *have*.

Although most of the imitations of each S did correspond to his free speech production, there were a few cases where differences existed between the two. In most of these a slightly more advanced stage of AUX development was reflected in the spontaneous utterances. Compare the following samples taken from several Ss:

Free Speech	Imitation
1. It goes all the way down my foot.	She need some dinner, said Mr. Jones.
2. I finished, Mrs. Blumberg.	Mary Jane knock on the door.
3. Do you know where is there is more?	You see a butterfly, puppy?
4. What is that three words? What is this word?	Where we are?
5. How does it look?	What your dog likes to eat?

In Examples 1 and 2 the imitation lacks the tense marker. The third imitation omits the do-support, and in the fourth the S failed to invert the subject and copula. The fifth imitation shows that the S is conscious of tense, but his utterance does not contain the do-support.

Table 18-2   Sample chart taken from one S: Comparison of AUX data collected in the same period by three different means

Data Source	Free Speech	Imitation	Translation
T + be	+ is (4 ex.) + was (2 ex.) am →is (1 ex.)	+ am (2 ex.) + are (1 ex.) + was (2 ex.)	+ is (1 ex.) is →gots/___ years old + are (2 ex.) + was (1 ex.)
T pres + V	+ /-z/ (3 ex.) goes, says − /-z/ (2 ex.) way, swim + /-s/ (2 ex.) *gots, likes	+ /-z/ (2 ex.) needs, *haves + /-s/ (1 ex.) likes + /-ǝz/ (1 ex.) watches	− /-z/ (2 ex.) live, play + /-s/ (2 ex.) likes, *gots (for *is* ref: age) has → got
T past + V	− /-t/ (2 ex.) practice, erase − irreg: get, have, do + irreg: went, said, brought	+ /-d/ (2 ex.) followed, *sayed − /-d/ (2 ex.) live − /-ǝd/ (1 ex.) want + irreg: went − irreg: take, get	− /-t/ (2 ex.) help, promise + /-t/ (2 ex.) looked, walked + /-d/ (1 ex.) *sayed − /-d/ (3 ex.) live, call, stay − /-ǝd/ (1 ex.) wait + irreg: thought − irreg: get, go, give, have, say
Modals	+ can (1 ex.) + can't (3 ex.) + could in Q-y/n (4 ex.) − should in Q-y/n	+ can (2 ex.) + can't (1 ex.) can−could (1 ex.) in Q-y/n + will (2 ex.) − would (1 ex.) − should (1 ex.)	can → could (5 ex.) in Q-y/n + can't (1 ex.) + could (1 ex.) + will (1 ex.), will → can (1 ex.) − will (1 ex.) won't−don't
be + ing	+ am (2 ex.) + was (3 ex.) } /___ Ving + is/___ gonna + V	+ am, is, are (was/were) → was } /___ Ving	am → ∅ (was/were) → was } /___ Ving

Table 18-2 (continued)

	unmarked simple verb	unmarked simple verb	unmarked simple verb
have + en			
T neg	+ can't (3 ex.) + not/am___ gonna (1 ex.) don't (6 ex.) doesn't (1 ex.) } →don't___V didn't (1 ex.) + didn't (1 ex.) imperative →don't (1 ex.) + M inversion "could" (1 ex.)	+ can't (1 ex.) don't doesn't } →don't didn't won't won't → { don't never / will never + M inversion "could"	+ can't wasn't—don't wasn't don't doesn't } →don't didn't won't "Me either" →"I never don't find it too." + M inversion "could"
T yes/no	Do you + { can + V (1 ex.) / got (any) (4 ex.) / brought / wanna } − do (1 ex.) "You put 3?" − did (1 ex.) "I did good?"	Do you + { can . . . (2 ex.) / V simple (2 ex.) } does → [I] + { anybody / nobody + V . . . ? / somebody }	+ do (1 ex.) "Do you wanna . . . ?"
T wh	What is + { NPsing (1 ex.) / NPpl. (1 ex.) } How many do NP . . . ? What you said? (—did) What says . . . ? (—does)	Where NP are? Who are NP? What are NP going to V? What NP V? (—do) What's NP V? (+ does) Where do NP V? (did—do)	Where NP are? Wh NP V? { ("Where do you live?" / "Where do you go?" for / "Where are you going?") How *do you can* V . . . ? for How *did* . . . ?

TRANSLATION TASK

Although the results on the imitation test probably reflect the child's competence in English as well as his spontaneous production does, there is a slight possibility that a child could have imitated the sentences without comprehension. Therefore another method was tried to see if it would produce similar results, a translation task from Spanish to English.

Materials and procedure

Like the elicited imitation task, the translation task was centered around a simple story. In order to keep their interest, I wanted to make sure that the children would not be familiar with the story they were to translate. The easiest way to be assured of this and at the same time control for structural complexity and for vocabulary was to write my own. The story was written in English, then translated into the Spanish version which ideally would have given back the English AUX elements in question if retranslated. The story was recorded in Spanish with pauses between each sentence.

I explained to each S that I had a good story on my tape recorder, but it was in Spanish and the lady who recorded it spoke too fast for me to understand. I told them I would draw some pictures to complement the story if they could tell me, in English, exactly what the lady said. The Ss' translations were taped on another recorder. The procedure took about 20 minutes for each S.

The children were delighted to help and proud to show me how skillful they were at a task which I was presumably incapable of performing. They were allowed to hear the Spanish sentence more than once if they were not satisfied with their own translation after the first try. Occasionally I pretended to recognize a word such as *mamá* (mother or mama), *adiós* (goodbye), or *gracias* (thank you) so that they would really believe I was paying attention and they were teaching me. When I could pick a word out of the stream of speech, they congratulated me as though I had said my "first word."

Results

In translating most of the Ss made comments such as "What's años?" or "I don't know how you say it." when they had difficulty expressing the English equivalent of a certain word or phrase. These additional sentences were classified as free speech and included in the corpus of observational data collected in the same month.

After the data had been transcribed, the AUX elements of each sentence were arranged on a chart so that they could be compared with those present in their free speech data and with their responses on the elicited imitation task (see Table 18-2).

Before looking at the comparisons, I would like to mention some of the unpredicted alterations that occurred in translation and the importance of interference from Spanish in the task. The Ss were instructed to translate exactly what was said on the tape in order to force them to use each AUX form. Some of them, however, changed the modeled sentences from direct to indirect speech and vice versa: "Voy al parque mamá." (I'm going to the park, Mama) was translated as "He's going to the park." Others simplified complex sentences by making the embedded clauses into independent clauses or sentences. For example, "¿Quieres ir al parque a jugar con mi pelota nueva?" (Do you want to go to the park to play with my new ball?) was broken down into "You want to play in the park? . . . pause . . . my ball is new."

In a study of English-speaking five-year-olds learning French as their second language (Swain, Naiman, and Dumas, 1972) a translation test was given in which the Ss were asked to translate modeled sentences from their second language into their native language, the reverse of my procedure. Surprisingly, the children maintained French word order in their translated sentences; one would not expect such strong influence of the second language on the Ss' production in their first. Another interesting finding from their translation data was that frequently the English word given, although not a lexical equivalent of the French word, was a member of the same semantic category. For example, water, milk, and coffee were given as translations of "le lait," thus maintaining the semantic category of something to drink.

These two cases (preservation of word order in translation and word substitution based on semantic relationships) were also prevalent in my data. "La mamá de Carlos" was translated with Spanish word order as "the mother of Carlos." In English a descriptive adjective precedes the noun it modifies; it is the reverse in Spanish. Several of my Ss produced "ball new" as the translation of "pelota nueva." Probably the most amusing example came from the child who was nearly a balanced bilingual. She translated "muchas gracias" (thank you very much) into "very thank you." In the two years of free speech observation, there was never an error with this common expression, even by the least fluent child.

Not only did the model sentences have an influence on the Ss' word order in translation, but there were cases of mixing and word for word translation. "Tu papa no quiere que vayas al centro solo (Your father doesn't want you to go downtown alone) was translated by one as "Your dad don't want you to go to the . . . to a store sin anybody." Sin is the Spanish word for without. Another S made a word for word correspondence to "todos los dias" by saying "all the days" instead of "every day." Spanish-speaking students in the initial stages of learning English usually have trouble with the distribution of the verbs be and have because their word for have (tener) functions in a few cases where English would require a form of be. Tiene, in "Carlos tiene siete años y su amigo Pablo tiene seis" (Carlos is seven and his friend Pablo is six) was translated a number of ways: have, haves, got, and gots. The correct form, is, was only whispered by a few as if they were thinking out loud, but quickly changed to one of the above forms. Although at one time many of the Ss did use some form of have or got in place of be with reference to age, by the time the translation task was given, be was definitely the most frequently produced in spontaneous speech. Obviously, caution must be taken when using data derived from translation because there is interference from the Ss' first language which is not normally observed in their spontaneous speech.

Lexical substitutions were abundant and diverse. As in Swain's data, my Ss used a member of the same semantic category. "Una señora vieja" (an old lady) was changed to "a mother," "a old girl," and "a grandma." One S corrected herself in her translation of "está lejos de aquí" (It's far from here) by quickly changing "low" to "far."

In spite of an attempt to control for vocabulary, there were a few words that the Ss either did not know in English or could not produce at the time. When they tried to describe the concept instead of substituting a word, it affected their translation of the whole sentence. In the following examples, notice how the word in italics was defined by the S.

1. "Miraron el *semáforo* y esperaron la luz verde." (They watched/ looked at the *stoplight* and waited for the green light.)
   S: "I don't know what's the last word . . . it stop all the car . . . all the people on the other side go . . . you know, when a car's like that and another car's right here like that, and the red light. . . .
   E: "A stoplight?"
   S: "Um . . . they look up the stoplight and waited for the green light."
2. "Creo que estamos *perdidos.*" (I think we are *lost.*)
   S: "We think we are um . . . what is when you are . . . when you don't know where's your house and everything?"
   E: "Is that lost?"
   S: "Yeah, we are lost."
3. "No veo la *entrada* de Disneylandia." (I don't see the *entrance* to Disneyland.)
   S: "He didn't see the stuff where you go inside of Disneyland."

After comparing the Ss' translation of the sentences to the predicted translation of the model sentences, I realized that a one to one correspondence could not be the criterion for correctness. The following examples will help clarify my point. The sentences in parenthesis are the expected English translations. The AUX elements in question have been italicized.

1. (*Do* you *want* to go to the park to play with my new ball?)
   S: "He said does he wanna go to the park and play with his new ball."
2. (I'*m going* to the park, Mom.)
   S: "He's going to the park."
3. (They *saw* a policeman on the other side of the street.)
   S: "There was a policeman in the other street."

4. (We *have come/came* here to look for Disneyland.)
S: "We want to go to Disneyland."
5. (When Carlos *told* her how he *had helped* a lady in the park, his mother *promised* to take him to Disneyland the next weekend.)
S: "Carlos *explained* to his mother how he *helped* a little woman get his cat and then his mother promise que she would take him to Disneyland."

The Ss had not followed my translation exactly, but they conveyed almost the same information. Instead of asking if a S could translate *conto* to *told* (example 5) and rating him with a plus or minus, I found that a more accurate description could be achieved by noting how the S did express the idea contained in the model sentences. The S's translation of example 5 demonstrated his knowledge of past tense inflections even though he did not use the irregular past of *tell* which I had hoped to elicit.

Comparing the spontaneous speech data collected in March with that obtained through translation, it was found that there were no significant differences between the two where there was an overlap. Where there was no overlap, much more data were available from responses given on the translation task. The translation test, then, turned out to be more of a stimulus for free speech production than one of rigid control like the elicited imitation task. By accepting it as such, it proved to be a rich source of information which paralleled that gathered as spontaneous speech.

CONCLUSIONS

The purpose of this study was to describe the order in which Spanish-speaking children acquired the English auxiliary system. It was assumed that this information could be gathered through observation of the Ss' spontaneous speech. This was not the case so other methods of data collection were devised. Each method had its advantages and disadvantages.

For observational data, if the S proved to be talkative, a great deal of information could be acquired; but if the S was shy, he did not demonstrate his full competence. This made it difficult to compare data across Ss. The level of classroom noise made it impossible to use a tape recorder. Relying on manual transcription became frustrating if the observer was suddenly faced with a burst of verbal activity and could not write it down fast enough. A personal disadvantage to observation was the amount of time involved both in data collection and in sorting out the corpus.

The elicited imitation test had the advantage of controlling the sample, making it easier to do comparisons across Ss. By designing the model sentences to bring out certain patterns, it forced the S to demonstrate his knowledge of those forms. However, since the sample sentences were controlled, the Ss' full scope of language competence could not be recorded, only that which was included in the model. To keep the Ss' attention and elicit their best production, isolated sentences could not be used. Centering the test around a story and including pictures, meant many hours of test preparation but the results made it worthwhile.

The model sentences for the translation task were also built around a story, which meant there was some control of the possible responses that the S could give. The responses turned out to vary more than expected, primarily due to the individual's choice of words and his narrative style. There was obvious interference from Spanish which was rarely found in the Ss' free speech. Nevertheless, with respect to AUX forms, there did not appear to be any significant interference from Spanish. Where the data overlapped with that collected by observation, the Ss made the same alterations in the AUX forms.

Where the data overlapped from the three methods, the same results were found for acquisition of the English AUX system for the 10 Ss. Differences between Ss were also revealed by using the three methods. I am convinced that multiple measures are useful in studying second language acquisition. For a thorough study, each method supplements the others, giving us a more complete picture of each child's language acquisition.

19

of the Learning of French

by English-speaking Five-year-olds

Merrill Swain, Neil Naiman and Guy Dumas, *Ontario Institute for Studies in Education*

INTRODUCTION

Diary studies have given us many observations, important observations about the second language learning process. However, such long-term data gathering, as Adams pointed out, is neither efficient nor reliable if one wishes to make strong arguments for any of the findings. The diary observations need to be reformed and tested as hypotheses in experimental work.

The Swain, Naiman & Duman report, first presented at the AILA Conference, Copenhagen in 1972, is a move in that direction. While they use measures similar to those devised by Adams (a morphology test, an imitation/repetition task, and a translation task), they were able to compare results on three tests much more directly. This was possible since each task was set up to test the acquisition of certain morphological markers.

The elicitation process used in this study is easily replicated; the tasks are simple to administer and, conveniently, fairly easy to analyze.

The research team at OISE has been primarily concerned with finding efficient and reliable ways of evaluating bilingualism of English-French children in Canada. For that reason they have now moved toward hypothesis testing in large cross-sectional studies. In a sense, then, this study forms a bridge between longitudinal or pseudo-lingitudinal studies on the one hand and large-scale experimental research on the other.

Although Canada's two official languages are English and French, a large proportion of its population are speakers of only one of these languages. Of those who are fluent speakers of both English and French, in the majority of cases it has been the French-speaking people who have learned English rather than the English-speaking people who have learned French. Why this has been so is a long story and is certainly beyond the scope of this paper. Within the last few years, however, a reversal of this trend has been noted in certain sectors of Canada's English-speaking population. Where before, English-speaking parents and educators were satisfied that French was taught as a subject in school, many are now considering such programs as unsatisfactory because the students have not obtained a native-like command of French.

The problems of creating fluent French speakers in a basically English-speaking community has led to the establishment in Ontario of several experimental programs in bilingual education. One such program begins at the kindergarten level with the presentation of the entire curriculum in French. French continues to be the only language of instruction through grade one. This means that the children first learn to read and to write in their second language. At the grade two level a certain period of time is allotted each day for the teaching of English language skills. With each successive year, more of the curriculum is taught in English until approximately 50% of the curriculum is taught in English and 50% in French.

This paper is concerned with certain aspects of the linguistic behavior of children attending the kindergarten year of a program like that described above. The study reported here is a small part of an extensive long-term study being undertaken by the Bilingual Education Project at the Ontario Institute for Studies in Education to evaluate the linguistic development and the academic achievement of children in such French "immersion" classes.

In initiating this part of the study, which was considered entirely *exploratory* in nature, our specific intentions were two-fold. The first goal was to describe the order in which certain French grammatical rules were learned by these English-speaking children. Because the language learning environment was more natural in that French was used as a medium of communication rather than as a subject to be taught, it was considered that the acquisition sequence observed would approximate rather closely that of children learning French as a second language in a natural language learning environment. Our second goal was to determine if there was any effect on English language structures resulting from French structures already learned. Additionally, we hoped that some of the observations made would be of some relevance in the more general field of second language acquisition in children.

METHOD

Test materials

In reviewing the literature in search of tests and documentation of native language acquisition, it became evident that most tests of native language acquisition were not suitable for the present conditions. This was the case because most of these tests were either for children much younger, or if they were for children about five years of age, the rules they were testing were suitable for more complex language development than was possible to test in French with children in the initial year of a French immersion program. The present situation was unique in that there was an attempt to test children of kindergarten age for language structures that would be acquired by native speakers at a much younger age. What was needed was a test that would not only test for structures already possessed in English, but that would also be able to trace the development of similar structures in French. The test which seemed the most suitable for this situation was the one developed by Jean Berko (1958).

Berko's test is an ingenious one intended to measure a child's knowledge of certain morphological rules of his language. By having children complete sentences about pictures that she showed them, Berko was able to test their mastery of morphological rules such as plurality and tense markings. To ensure that the child knew these rules, she had the child attempt to apply them to nonsense syllables: the child's correct response could not be attributed to familiarity with the specific items, but could be seen as an application of a learned rule to a new item.

It was necessary to adapt the original Berko test so that relevant and comparable structures in both French and English could be examined. An English and French version of the test was prepared and used in a pilot study. A few revisions were made to the test based on observations of some of the difficulties encountered by the children with the French version of the test. The revisions were also motivated by a desire to standardize all of the items in terms of the number and length of sentences used in each test item, and the number of times the nonsense word was repeated. In each item of the final version of the test, there are two sentences and the nonsense word is given only once. Henceforth, this final form of the test will be referred to as Berko$_E$ or Berko$_F$ depending on whether the English or French subtests respectively are being discussed.

The items in Berko$_E$ or Berko$_F$ were designed to measure the child's ability to produce some of the grammatical correlates of gender, plurality, and tense. Each testing session consisted of giving five items in either English or French. The first items tested the child's ability to pluralize a noun. For example, a picture of a bird-like animal would be shown and the experimenter would say, *Here is a lep.* Then a picture of two bird-like animals would be shown and the experimenter would say, *Now there are two . . . ,* and the child was expected to respond with the word *leps.*

The second and fourth items tested the child's ability to form the past and future tenses respectively by showing a picture of someone performing a nonsense action and saying in the case of the former, *Here is a man who is ricking. Yester-*

day he . . . and in the case of the latter, *Here is a man who is dobbing. Tomorrow he is going to* . . . The third item tested the child's ability to form a masculine adjective when presented with a feminine one, and the fifth item tested the child's ability to form the present tense. (Appendix A lists some sample items of Berko$_E$; Appendix B lists some sample items of Berko$_F$.)

The nonsense words used in Berko$_E$ and Berko$_F$ were ones that sounded similar to English words as judged by a native speaker of English, and to French words as judged by a native speaker of French. (See Appendix C.) Pictures were drawn which illustrated items or actions for which the child would likely have no single word in his vocabulary to express that item or action. A new set of pictures and words was used each time the test was administered.

In addition to the Berko test, an imitation test was also developed. Slobin and Welsh (1973) argued that one valid way of examining a child's grammatical competence is to have him imitate sentences containing relevant structures. The child, in repeating a sentence, must filter it through his own productive system. The sentences produced tended to contain systematic errors. Thus a number of French sentences were prepared in which each sentence contained at least one example of a grammatical structure tested in Berko$_F$. For example, sentences to be imitated corresponding to the child's ability to form the future tense included *Demain il va manger un biscuit* and *A Pâques Jean va acheter un lapin.* (A sample of the sentences used for imitation is listed in Appendix D.) The words used in these sentences were ones used frequently in the classroom and therefore likely to be understood by the students. In order to verify this, during the last few testing sessions, each child was asked to translate into English the same sentences he had earlier imitated in French.

SUBJECTS

The *S*s were English-speaking students in one of two kindergarten classes in Toronto in which from the first day of school, they were spoken to in French by their teacher and her assistant. However, at the beginning of the term they were not obligated to speak French either to their teacher or among themselves. After Christmas, they were encouraged to speak French in response to their teacher and were even required to do so when asking the teacher for certain things they wanted. However, at the end of the school year, they still did not spontaneously use French among themselves.

Their exposure to French was limited to about one-half hour at the beginning and at the end of each class during which time their teacher spoke to them as a group. During the other hour of class time, they played among themselves hearing French only when their teacher or her assistant talked to them individually or in small groups, or when they listened to French records.

Each kindergarten class consisted of 25 students. From these students, eight were selected—four from one class and four from the other. Two of the children selected from each class were female and two were male. Their average age in

November, 1971 was five years, seven months. Seven of the Ss were native speakers of English. The other S was a native speaker of Estonian, but appeared quite at ease in English. In selecting the eight Ss, we chose children who appeared both cooperative and verbal based on our observations of them in the classroom and on our discussion with their teacher.

Procedure

Before the commencement of the testing sessions in December, the experimenters spent several weeks in the classroom so that the children would feel comfortable in their presence. There were two experimenters—one, a native speaker of English (E_E), and the other, a native speaker of French (E_F).

On the first day of testing, E_E asked one of the Ss if he wanted to play a game, and subsequently took him to a small room. E_E explained to the child that she was going to show him some pictures and to tell him something about the pictures. The child was to finish telling about the pictures. The child was then given two sample items which used words and pictures with which he was familiar. This procedure was repeated with the remaining three Ss in the kindergarten class. One week later, the four Ss of the other kindergarten class were treated in the same manner.

Two weeks following the initial testing session, each S was again asked by E_E if he wanted to play the game again. As he was taking to the testing room, E_E explained to S that this time he would be playing the game in French with E_F whom he knew. E_E reminded him how the game was played, and left him with E_F who spoke to him only in French, but otherwise followed the same procedures as in the administration of Berko$_E$. With Berko$_F$, a tape recorder was used to record the children's responses, although Ss were not aware of being recorded.

As our intent was to look for changes in language production during the school year, the same general procedure described above was repeated six times during the period from January to June with the several exceptions given below.

Beginning with the second testing session in French, the imitation task was initiated. After S completed Berko$_F$, he was asked if he wanted to play another game. E_F explained that S was to repeat, as best he could, the sentence that was given to him. He then gave several examples to be sure that S understood the task. Following the examples, five sentences were given one at a time to S. The responses were tape-recorded. A different set of five sentences was given at each subsequent testing session in French.

Beginning with the fourth testing session in French, the translation task was initiated. After S completed imitating the five sentences, E_F asked S to tell him in English what the sentence said. He gave S an example and then one by one repeated the five sentences that had just been given in the imitation task asking S after each to say the sentence in English. These data were also recorded on tape.

Beginning with the sixth testing session, the use of the Berko test was eliminated. (The full testing schedule is given in Appendix E.)

If an S was absent for a particular testing session, no attempt was made to administer that testing session at a later time.

RESULTS

The results are summarized in Figures 19-1 through 19-5. The percentage of correct responses marked on Figures 19-1 to 19-5 show the average score of the first two times and the average score of the last two times any particular test was administered.

Looking first at the results of the Berko$_E$ test, we see that the scores are high but by no means perfect. With one major exception, there was some improvement over time in the children's performance. The exception is seen in Figure 19-4 where performance shows a marked decrease over time. The errors made by the children were all the same—they did not pronounce the 's' sound at the end of the word. This is, of course, correct in French but not in English. The decline in performance is therefore interpreted as an indication of interference from the second language on the first.

Turning now to the results of the Berko$_F$ test, we see that Ss never correctly produced either the future tense or the past tense (Figures 19-2 & 19-3), yet they scored perfectly when required to form the plural of a noun (Figure 19-4). In both the formation of the present tense (Figure 19-1) and the creation of a masculine adjective from a feminine one (Figure 19-5), some improvement in performance occurred over time.

The vast majority of the errors made in Berko$_F$ were the result of simply repeating the nonsense word as it was given in the first sentence of the test item. This repetition coincided with the correct answer in the case of the formation of the plural. This makes the perfect score obtained on the pluralization task somewhat ambiguous. However, if we consider these results in relation to what happened in Berko$_E$ when Ss pluralized a noun, it would seem that what the children have learned is that a plural noun need not necessarily be marked with an 's' sound.

Because the scores on the Berko$_F$ test were so low with the exception of the items concerned with pluralizing the noun, the results must be interpreted with caution. However, the general trend seems to indicate an order of acquisition of the rules being tested which, we shall see, corresponds to that indicated by the imitation and translation data: first learned was the pluralization of a noun; second was the formation of the present tense and of a masculine adjective; and third was the formation of the past and future tenses. Based on the children's performance on Berko$_E$, we can assume that the children had the cognitive capacity to deal with the concepts represented by these grammatical forms. Thus, we might assume that the order of acquisition seen in the results from Berko$_F$ is related to the linguistic characteristics of the forms being learned. And, in fact, of the forms we examined, the first to be acquired were those which linguistically were the simplest, that is, the stem form.

Looking now at the results of the imitation task, we see that with one exception, there is an improvement in performance over time. In the imitation task, to be considered correct, all the correlates of any particular grammatical rule

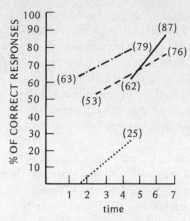

Figure 19-1   Present Tense

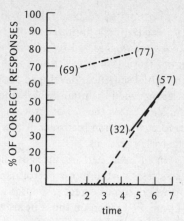

Figure 19-2   Future Tense

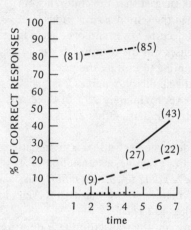

Figure 19-3   Past Tense

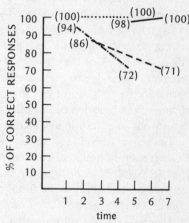

Figure 19-4   Pluralization of Noun Phrase

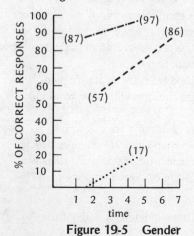

Figure 19-5   Gender

had to be imitated correctly. For example, in order for pluralization to be considered correctly imitated in the sentence *Nous allons dessiner des nuages,* both *des* and *nuages* had to be imitated correctly. The decrement in performance seen in Figure 19-4 is an artifact of the task and the criteria for correctness we set. In the initial sentences developed for the imitation task, numbers rather than articles preceded the noun, whereas in the later sessions, articles preceded the noun. Very often the *des* or *les* was changed to *de* or *le* in imitation and was therefore considered incorrect. There was no opportunity for this error to occur in the earlier sessions.

In all cases, performances on the imitation task were better than on the Berko$_F$ test. Furthermore, performance on the imitation task was better on those items where some correct responses were given on the Berko$_F$ test (Figures 19-1, 19-4 and 19-5) than on those items where no correct response was ever given (Figures 19-2 and 19-3).

The data collected from the imitation task suggest that the children were not simply parroting the sentences. They changed the sentences in various systematic ways. For example, one change that occurred over and over again in repeating sentences using the past and future tenses was the deletion of the auxiliary. Over 50% of the errors made in attempting to imitate the past and future tenses were due to the omission of just the auxiliary, whereas less than 3% were due to the omission of just the main verb. Approximately 20% of the errors were due to the omission of both the verb and its auxiliary. Other types of changes made in imitation will be discussed later.

In the translation task, an item was considered correct if it was grammatically correct even though not lexically correct. For example, a translation of *A Pâques Jean va acheter un lapin* to *At Easter we're going to catch a rabbit* was considered correct because the future tense was marked in the translation even though *acheter* was realized as *to catch* rather than as *to buy*.

Figures 19-1 to 19-4 show that performance on the translation task improved over time and was consistently better than on the imitation task. If it is assumed that translation is an indication of the children's comprehension of the sentences they attempted to imitate, then the gap between performance on the translation task and performance on the imitation task can be considered as an indication of the extent to which comprehension exceeds production skills.

In addition to these results, the data gathered from the imitation and translation tasks contained some other interesting findings which we would like to turn to now.

As mentioned before, in the imitation task children were not simply parroting the sentences they heard. They made certain changes—changes which involved substitution, deletion, and insertion of semantic or syntactic elements.

The following statements describe some of the changes that were made by the children in the imitation task.

> When *nous* was an indirect object, it was deleted by 80% of the children responding.

The subordinate conjunction *que* was deleted by 100% of the children responding.

The coordinate conjunction *mais* was either deleted or changed to *et* by 80% of the children responding.

When substitution occurred, the substituted item very frequently belonged to the same semantic and syntactic category. For example, the adjective *jolie* was substituted for *belle*; the noun *chat* was substituted for *chien*; and the preposition *de* was substituted for *pour*.

An unexpected finding turned up in the translation data. The word order within the sentence to be translated had an overwhelming effect on the translation that was given. Two examples will suffice to illustrate this point.

In expressing possession in French, the first noun represents the possessed object and the second noun represents the possessor of the object, whereas the reverse order is typically the case in English. Thus, in French one would say *La chemise de papa* whereas in English one would usually say *Daddy's shirt*.

In translating the possessive structure into English, 88% of the translations given retained the French word order. The *S*s used several strategies—some resulting in a correct English structure, some not. For example, in translating *Le pantalon de David est blue, the pants of David* was given three times, *the pants to David* was given three times, *the pants that David has* was given once, and *David's pants* was given once. We were surprised to see that a child would introduce a relative clause as in the case of *the pants that David has*, rather than change the word order.

This same phenomenon occurred in the translation of noun phrases containing adjectives. In French, the adjective often follows the noun whereas in English, the adjective usually precedes the noun. We found that where English and French word order differed, in over 80% of the cases the word order of the French noun phrase was preserved in the translation. For example, as a translation of *belle robe jaune,* five children gave *nice dress yellow,* one gave *beautiful dress rouge,* one gave *beautiful dress that was yellow,* and one gave *nice dress.*

We are somewhat hesitant to try to interpret these data at this point. It may be that the children were simply translating word for word. If this was the case, then it would be a rather striking demonstration of children's capacity to analyze sentences into words and form a one to one correspondence between them. However, this interpretation would not account for the use of the relative clause in the translations. We do know that word order is one syntactic way of signalling meaning and that it plays an important role in the early stages of first language acquisition (Slobin, 1970). The preservation of word order in translations may have been the children's syntactic way of preserving meaning in the translation.

Another interesting finding from the translation data was that frequently the English word given, although not a lexical equivalent of the French word, was a member of the same semantic category. For example, *water, milk* and *coffee* were given as translations of *le lait* thus maintaining the semantic category of something to drink. Similarly, *jar, box, plastic jar* and *little package* were given as translations of *la boîte* thus maintaining the semantic category of container.

DISCUSSION

We began this exploratory study with the intention of investigating some aspects of the growing competence of a child in a second language, and the effects of that developing competence on the first language. We adapted techniques that have been used in the investigation of first language acquisition, and found evidence in the data to encourage their continued use. Through their combined use we were able to isolate instances of interference, suggest an order of acquisition of certain grammatical rules in the second language, and reconfirm that the ability to comprehend an utterance tends to be slightly greater than the ability to repeat an utterance which in turn tends to be greater than the ability to produce a novel utterance.

We also found evidence in the translation data to suggest that translation *per se* might serve as a useful tool to probe the strategies of semantic and syntactic storage and retrieval.

Two studies have followed up this initial exploratory work (Dumas and Swain, in press; Naiman, 1975). The Dumas and Swain study examined the spontaneously produced French utterances of children in the French immersion program at the end of grade one. The data suggest that the vocabulary and pronunciation of the children were predominantly French while the structure of their language was basically that of English, their first language. There was a tendency to ignore or incorrectly use gender and tense markings in spontaneous speech, although tests of French comprehension demonstrated that they understood them.

Naiman extended and expanded the present study to include children in grades one and two of the French immersion program. In his study he used an imitation task in conjunction with two translation tasks as measures of language competence—translation from English to French was used as a measure of second language production and translation from French to English was used as a measure of second language comprehension. Many of the errors in language production made by the kindergarten children in the present study were also made by the grade one and two children of the Naiman study, but to a lesser extent. For example, by the end of grade one the children rarely omitted the auxiliary in the past tense verb form in imitation. Grade one children still tended to translate the genitive and the adjective noun phrase in a word-for-word fashion both when translating from English to French and from French to English. By grade two, however, this tendency was much less evident. When errors were made in the imitation of a model sentence, similar errors were evident in the second language production of the children. Overall, the results of his study suggest that accurate imitation of sentences in the language being learned depends upon the ability to both decode and encode the syntactic structures.

In the future, we hope to collect data from a sample of French native speakers at a much younger age, so that we can compare the order of acquisition of certain grammatical rules by those learning French as a first language to those learning French as a second language. Perhaps then we can begin to speculate on the relationship between the strategies of first and second language learning.

APPENDIX A

Sample items of Berko$_E$

1. *Plurality*
   (a picture of first, one bird-like animal, then two of them)
   Here is a lep. Now there are two . . .
2. *Past Tense*
   (a man swinging a funny-shaped object)
   Here is a man who is ricking. Yesterday he . . .
3. *Gender*
   (a picture of a girl with spots all over, and then a picture of a boy also covered with spots)
   Here is a girl who is pif. Here is a boy who is also . . .
4. *Future Tense*
   (a picture of a man doing some type of exercising)
   Here is a man who is dobbing. Tomorrow he is going to . . .
5. *Present Tense*
   (a picture of a man about to go down a set of stairs, then a picture of a man half-way down the stairs)
   Here is a man who is going to gling. Now he . . .

APPENDIX B

Sample items of Berko$_F$

1. *Plurality*
   (a picture of first, one frog-like animal, then another one)
   Voici un gof. Maintenant voici deux . . .
2. *Past Tense*
   (a man balancing a pitcher on his head)
   Voici un homme qui pole. Hier il a . . .
3. *Gender*
   (first, a picture of a very tall and skinny girl, then a similar picture of a boy)
   Voice une fille qui est cherte. Voici aussi un garçon qui est . . .

4. *Future Tense*
   (a picture of a man arms extended with a large box balanced on his arms)
   Voici un homme qui dape. Demain il va . . .
5. *Present Tense*
   (first, a picture of a man about to go up a set of stairs, and then a picture of a man about half-way up the stairs)
   Voici un homme qui va tifer. Maintenant il . . .

APPENDIX C

List of nonsense words used in Berko$_E$ and Berko$_F$

English

1.	lep	zib	lub	bim	tup
2.	rick	tor	bof	tig	mig
3.	gam	tassy	pif	sull	spag
4.	dob	hif	dev	lud	pab
5.	gling	mot	hod	mog	gar

French

1.	tef	bri	plo	gle	cine
2.	lime	danfe	chale	rafe	louse
3.	cherte	muve	botte	vette	gatte
4.	boque	vanne	sife	fique	dare
5.	dipe	chime	vope	ploffe	life

APPENDIX D

Sample of French sentences for imitation

Voilà quatre pommes sur la table.
Hier Paul a trouvé un chat.
Voici un petit cadeau pour maman.
Demain il va apporter un livre.
Papa ours mange un biscuit maintenant.

Les enfants aiment les pommes et les pêches.
Hier maman a fait un gâteau.
Suzanne porte une robe verte aujourd'hui.
Demain Paul va apporter un livre.
Pierre joue dans la salle de classe maintenant.

Dans la boîte il y a trois crayons.
Paul a dessiné une petite fille.

Hélène a fait une grande maison verte.
A Pâques Jean va acheter un lapin.
Pierre aime beaucoup faire de la peinture.

Le papa de Pierre a cinq chandails.
Dimanche Michel est allé au zoo.
Hier Anne portait une belle robe jaune.
Les enfants vont manger des biscuits.
Aujourd'hui Anne porte un chapeau rouge.

APPENDIX E

Testing schedule

	Session 1	Session 2	Session 3	Session 4
English	Berko$_E$	Berko$_E$	Berko$_E$	Berko$_E$
French	Berko$_F$	Berko$_F$ Imitation	Berko$_F$ Imitation	Berko$_F$ Imitation Translation

	Session 5	Session 6	Session 7
English	Berko$_E$		
French	Berko$_F$ Imitation Translation	Imitation Translation	Imitation Translation

Age Comparisons

Comprehension and Production

20

in English as a Second Language

by Elementary School Children

and Adolescents

Arnulfo G. Ramírez and Robert L. Politzer, *Stanford University*

INTRODUCTION

The issue of adult vs. child success in learning second languages is one of the basic issues in second-language research. The observational studies of Schumann and Shapira show us adults for whom fluency in communication, rather than grammatical accuracy, seems the prime goal. These adults gave little attention to what Zoila called 'the little words' of morphology. Other reports, for example Hill (1970), claim that adults can, in fact, learn second languages but that differences might be due to the social expectations of particular societies.

Our basic assumption of age differences, however, needs empirical examination. The following two studies use an experimental rather than a case study approach in asking whether there is a direct correlation of age and proficiency in second language learning. If there is not, is the youngest child the best learner; is the mature child better than the infant at learning languages; or is the adult the 'best learner' (when all other factors—motivation, exposure time, etc.—are kept equal)?

The Ramírez and Politzer study looks at an age range of children in grades kindergarten, 1st, 3rd and 5th and two older groups of adolescents—newly-arrived junior and senior high students and students from the same grade range who had been in school in the States for one year. Both comprehension and imitation data were collected to test progress on a variety of English structures. The problem, as the authors point out, is in devising measures which truly tap language progress separate from other factors, such as short term memory. Of course, if an advantage in such factors improves learning, then surely they are also important in any discussion of language learning capacities over age groups.

The results of the following study should be compared with those found by Snow. Secondly, since many of the same morphemes are studied in this experiment as are elicited by the Bilingual Syntax Measure, the reader might wish to compare the findings of this study with those presented by Dulay & Burt, Larsen-Freeman, and Bailey, Madden & Krashen.

The research reported in this article was undertaken as part of a project on "Second Language Acquisition in Unstructured Contexts" sponsored by the Stanford University Research Development Fund. Some of the data utilized in this article are also found in the main report concerning this project: J.A. Chun & R.L. Politzer: *A Study of Language Acquisition in Two Bilingual Schools,* Stanford, California: Stanford University, School of Education, 1975.

* * *

In conjunction with a research project dealing with language acquisition in two bilingual schools (Chun & Politzer 1975) a Comprehension and Production Test based on the model of similar ICP (Imitation Comprehension Production) tests utilized in first language acquisition (e.g., see Slobin, in Ferguson & Slobin 1973) was developed. The test consisted of 14 grammatical categories presented in minimal pairs (e.g., affirmative vs. negative). On each test (Comprehension or Production) each category was represented by 2 items. Since items were scored according to errors, the score of each subject in each category could thus range from 2 (2 errors) to 0 (both items correct). Total test scores in either C or P could range from 28 (all items incorrect) to 0 (all items correct).

Categories chosen for the test were, perhaps somewhat arbitrarily, selected from those used in first language acquisition research and in some studies dealing with bilingual (Kessler 1971) and second language (Ervin-Tripp 1974) learning. A sample item illustrating each of the 14 categories is reproduced below.

Category I.	(Singular/Plural): The girl writes/the girls write
Category II.	(Present/Past): The girl is eating/the girl ate.
Category III.	(Present/Future): The boy is writing/the boy is going to write.
Category IV.	(Affirmative/Negative): The donkey is walking/the donkey is not walking.

Category V.	(Mass/Count):
	Some chicken/a chicken.
Category VI.	(Singular Possessor/Plural Possessor):
	Her cat/their cat.
Category VII.	(Masculine Subject Pronoun/Feminine Subject Pronoun):
	He is writing a letter/she is writing a letter.
Category VIII.	(Masculine Object Pronoun/Feminine Object Pronoun):
	The dog is biting him/the dog is biting her.
Category IX.	(Direct Object/Indirect Object Reversal):
	The boy is showing the dog the cat/the boy is showing the cat the dog.
Category X.	(Active Sentence: Agent/Patient Reversal):
	The truck is pushing the car/the car is pushing the truck.
Category XI.	(Passive Sentence: Agent/Patient Reversal):
	The girl is hit by the boy/the boy is hit by the girl.
Category XII.	(Embedded Relative Clause: Agent/Patient Reversal):
	The boy that the girl hit fell down/the boy that hit the girl fell down.
Category XIII.	(Word order change: Relative Clause/Main Clause):
	The bird he caught/he caught the bird.
Category XIV.	("look & prep"):
	The boy is looking at the book/the boy is looking for the book.

Each of the test items is illustrated by 2 pictures corresponding to the contrast being tested. For the Comprehension task subjects are shown the 2 pictures, listening twice to the sentences associated with the picture. As they listen to the sentence the second time, they point to the picture to which each sentence refers. For the Production task, the examiner points to each picture while uttering the sentence referring to it. Then using the picture as a cue he asks the subjects to reproduce the appropriate sentence. In scoring the Production tests only errors affecting the particular grammatical contrast which is the object of the item are taken into consideration. In the Comprehension task a correct answer consists in the subjects pointing at the particular picture illustrated by each of the two sentences. For each test administration the order of presentation of items, as well as the sequence of Comprehension and Production, was randomized within each group of subjects. (cf., Chun & Politzer, 1975).

For the purpose of comparing language acquisition in two different bilingual schools, the CP (Comprehension-Production) test was administered in English in a Spanish/English Bilingual Education Program to kindergarten, first, third, and fifth grade children in November/December of the school year. According to available records, all the subjects chosen for the study had entered school at the kindergarten level as monolingual or practically monolingual speakers of Spanish. At approximately the same time, the tests were also given to two groups of junior and senior high school students (ranging from age 13 to 17). The first group

(group A1) was made up of pupils who had recently arrived in the U.S.A. and who were, at any rate, in their first year of immersion in an English school program. The second group (group A2) had a similar background to the A1 group, but was already in its second year of schooling in the U.S.A. The native language background of the high school student group was primarily Spanish, but a sprinkling of other backgrounds was also included (1 Portuguese, 1 Armenian, 1 Hebrew). The main purpose of this study is the comparison of the performance of the CP test on the part of the two groups of secondary school students with that of the primary grade pupils in the Bilingual Education Program.

The exact numbers and distribution of subjects on which this report is based are shown in Table 20-1. Analysis of variance of total test scores for sex showed a significant sex difference only in one isolated case in 1st grade in which there is very small unevenly distributed N (male 2, female 5, see Table 20-2).

Since the group of adolescents included in this study was made up of students from 2 junior and 1 senior high school, the main dependent variables, namely total Production and Comprehension scores, were also analyzed for school differences. No significant differences were found between the two Junior High Schools (C Test, d.f. 8, 1, f=2.26, p=0.17; P Test, d.f. 8, 1, f=0.73, p=0.57). The differences between the Junior High and Senior High pupils performance also had mixed significance levels (C Test, d.f. 22, 1, f=2.92, p=0.10, P Test, d.f. 22, 1, f=3.51, p=0.07), but High School students appeared to perform better than Junior High School students (C Test: Junior High School mean 7.00, Senior High School mean 4.61; P Test: Junior High School mean 14.20, Senior High School Mean 9.08).

Tables 20-3A and 20-3B show the mean scores (i.e., number of errors) achieved by all six groups (A1, A2, kg, 1st, 3rd, and 5th grade) in C and P on each of the 14 categories as well as on the total tests which, on the basis of the data obtained in the bilingual school program above, showed a reliability of Cronbach α .86 for C and α .94 for P.

Figure 20-1, a graph which compares the mean total test scores for the six groups, summarizes the main findings of the investigation. The result is somewhat surprising. As expected C scores show fewer errors (i.e., are better) than P scores. As expected there is an obvious progression of improvement from kg to 1st to 3rd

Table 20-1   Subjects used in the study

	Male	Female	Total
Group A[1]	6	6	12
Group A[2]	5	4	9
Kg	10	7	17
Grade 1	2	5	7
Grade 3	6	4	10
Grade 5	6	6	12

Table 20-2   Analysis of variance of total test scores in comprehension (C) and production (P) by sex of subjects

			N	$\bar{x}$ S.D.	f ratio
Group A1	C	Male	5	5.80	0.18
		Female	7	4.85	
	P	Male	5	9.40	0.51
		Female	7	12.28	
Group A2	C	Male	5	7.40	0.37
		Female	4	6.00	
	P	Male	5	13.20	1.06
		Female	4	8.50	
Kg	C	Male	10	12.40	0.28
		Female	2	14.00	
	P	Male	10	21.50	0.72
		Female	2	18.50	
1st Grade	C	Male	2	14.00	12.35*
		Female	5	7.40	
	P	Male	2	19.50	p=5.61 (p=0.06)
		Female	5	14.00	
3rd Grade	C	Male	6	4.67	f=0.37
		Female	4	6.00	
	P	Male	6	10.17	f=0.05
		Female	4	9.75	
5th Grade	C	Male	6	1.67	f=0.04
		Female	6	1.83	
	P	Male	6	3.17	f=2.59
		Female	8	6.33	

*$p < .05$

to 5th grade in the Bilingual Program. What is surprising, however, is that there is almost no difference at all between the score of the A1 and A2 groups. In spite of the A2 group having had some 12 months more exposure to English than the A1 group, A1 and A2 perform at about exactly the same level, which appears to be the general level of the 3rd graders who are in their 4th year of immersion into an English program. Both groups perform far better than kg group (whose exposure to English is approximately the same as the A1 group) and somewhat better than the first graders (whose exposure of English is roughly equal to that of the A2 group).

An analysis of variance of test scores of groups A1 and A2 revealed what one would expect from the inspection of the data. There is not a single significant difference between A1 and A2 in either total scores on the C and P scores in any

Table 20-3A Mean scores and standard deviation for 14 categories and total tests in C (comprehension) and P (production) for group A1, A2 and Kg

Category		Group A1 $\bar{x}$	S.D.	Group A2 $\bar{x}$	S.D.	Kg $\bar{x}$	S.D.
I	C	0.33	0.65	0.56	0.73	1.08	0.79
	P	0.92	0.90	1.00	0.71	1.50	0.52
II	C	0.17	0.39	0.22	0.44	0.67	0.78
	P	0.83	0.83	1.00	0.71	1.08	0.67
III	C	0.17	0.39	0.33	0.50	0.33	0.49
	P	0.92	0.90	0.56	0.72	1.42	0.79
IV	C	0.00	0.00	0.11	0.33	0.58	0.79
	P	0.17	0.58	0.30	0.71	0.91	0.67
V	C	0.75	0.75	0.60	0.71	0.83	0.71
	P	0.83	0.72	0.44	0.53	1.08	0.79
VI	C	0.00	0.00	0.22	0.67	0.58	0.51
	P	0.42	0.79	0.33	0.50	1.58	0.66
VII	C	0.00	0.00	0.00	0.00	0.66	0.49
	P	0.08	0.29	0.44	0.88	1.42	0.51
VIII	C	0.25	0.62	0.44	0.73	1.33	0.89
	P	0.50	0.67	0.56	0.88	1.25	0.62
IX	C	0.83	0.72	0.78	0.67	1.08	0.29
	P	1.25	0.87	1.55	0.73	1.75	0.45
X	C	0.17	0.39	0.00	0.00	0.67	0.65
	P	0.58	0.79	0.22	0.44	1.42	0.79
XI	C	1.00	0.74	1.22	0.97	1.33	0.79
	P	1.00	0.85	1.33	0.87	1.83	0.39
XII	C	0.67	0.89	0.67	6.50	1.42	0.67
	P	1.58	0.67	1.33	1.00	2.00	0.00
XIII	C	0.33	0.49	0.60	0.71	1.25	0.87
	P	0.67	0.89	0.78	0.83	1.83	0.39
XIV	C	0.58	0.52	0.88	0.78	0.83	0.58
	P	1.73	0.78	1.22	0.97	1.92	0.29
Total	C	5.25	3.57	6.78	0.31	12.67	3.73
	P	11.08	7.01	11.11	6.83	21.00	4.52

Table 20-3B   Mean scores and standard deviation for 14 categories and total tests in C (comprehension) and P (production) for 1st, 3rd and 5th grades

Category		1st grade $\bar{x}$	S.D.	3rd grade $\bar{x}$	S.D.	5th grade $\bar{x}$	S.D.
I	C	0.71	0.49	0.40	0.52	0.08	0.29
	P	1.85	0.38	1.40	0.70	0.75	0.00
II	C	0.29	0.49	0.10	0.32	0.00	0.00
	P	1.00	0.58	0.80	0.63	0.17	0.39
III	C	0.29	0.49	0.00	0.00	0.00	0.00
	P	0.85	1.07	0.40	0.70	0.17	0.39
IV	C	0.29	0.76	0.10	0.32	0.00	0.00
	P	0.29	0.49	0.10	0.32	0.08	0.29
V	C	1.57	0.54	0.70	0.83	0.50	0.52
	P	0.86	0.69	0.30	0.48	0.08	0.29
VI	C	0.43	0.54	0.20	0.63	0.00	0.00
	P	0.43	0.54	0.50	0.85	0.08	0.29
VII	C	0.43	0.79	0.00	0.00	0.00	0.00
	P	0.43	0.53	0.10	0.32	0.08	0.29
VIII	C	0.29	0.49	0.10	0.32	0.00	0.00
	P	0.57	0.54	0.50	0.71	0.00	0.00
IX	C	1.00	0.58	1.10	0.74	0.33	0.49
	P	1.14	0.90	1.20	0.79	0.58	0.51
X	C	0.14	0.38	0.00	0.00	0.00	0.00
	P	0.57	0.79	0.10	0.32	0.16	0.39
XI	C	1.14	0.90	0.60	0.70	0.08	0.29
	P	2.00	0.00	1.20	0.92	0.42	0.67
XII	C	0.29	0.49	0.30	0.48	0.33	0.49
	P	2.00	0.00	1.90	0.32	1.25	0.87
XIII	C	1.43	1.79	1.10	0.74	0.33	0.49
	P	1.71	0.49	1.20	0.92	0.75	0.07
XIV	C	1.00	0.82	0.50	0.71	0.08	0.28
	P	1.86	0.38	0.00	0.84	0.17	0.39
Total	C	9.29	3.82	5.20	3.43	1.75	1.42
	P	15.56	7.29	10.30	6.15	4.75	3.56

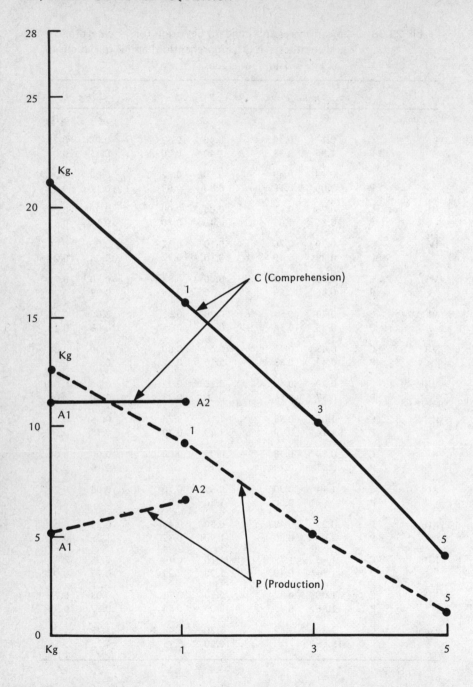

Figure 20-1   Graph Showing Total Comprehension and Production Scores
for Kg, Grades 1, 3, 5, and Groups A1, A2

of the 14 categories (e.g., significance of differences between A1 and A2 in total C scores: d.f. 20.1 f=1.001; difference between A1 and A2 in total P scores: f=-.001). The significant differences between A1 scores and each of the grade levels of the Bilingual Program are shown on Table 20-4. Table 20-5 gives the parallel information for the differences between the Bilingual Program and group A2. The information conveyed by the table may be summarized as follows (the symbol > is used to indicate "better than" = "significantly fewer errors").

Groups A1, A2 and Kg
     A1 > kg
Cat. I.   C P   (Singular/Plural)
Cat. II.   C   (Present/Past)
Cat. IV.   C P   (Affirmative/Negative)
Cat. VI.   C P   (his, her/their)
Cat. VII.   C P   (he/she)
Cat. IX.   P   (Direct Object/Indirect Object Reversal)
Cat. X.   C P   (Active Sentence: Agent/Patient Reversal)
Cat. XI.   P   (Passive Sentence: Agent/Patient Reversal)
Cat. XII.   C P   (Embedded Relative Clause: Agent/Patient Reversal)
Cat. XIII.   C P   (Word order change)
Cat. XIV.   C P   (look & prep)
Total Comprehension Score
Total Production Score

     A2 > kg
Cat. I   C P   (Singular/Plural)
Cat. III.   P   (Present/Future)
Cat. IV.   P   (Affirmative/Negative)
Cat. V.   P   (Mass/Count)
Cat. VI.   P   (his, her/their)
Cat. VII.   C P   (he/she)
Cat. VIII.   C P   (him/her)
Cat. X.   C P   (Active Sentence: Agent/Patient Reversal)
Cat. XIII.   P   (Word order change)
Cat. XIV.   P   (look & prep)
Cat. XII.   C P   (Embedded Relative Clause: Agent/Patient Reversal)
Total Comprehension Score
Total Production Score

     The above summary gives, of course, some indication as to where the kg children seem to attain scores similar to the adolescents. No significant difference between the kg and A groups were found on 14 of the 20 measures in C. Thus the kg children seem to have a better chance of equalling the teenagers in Comprehension rather than Production. This is most likely due to the adolescents' better short term memory span which would give them an obvious advantage insofar as

Table 20-4 Significant differences in comprehension (C) and production (P) between group A1 and Kg, 1st, 3rd and 5th grades in 14 categories and total test scores

Category		Kg	1st grade	3rd grade	5th grade
I	C	d.f. 23.1 f=6.41*	NS	NS	NS
	P	d.f. 23.1 f=3.79 (p=0.06)	d.f. 18.1 f=6.80*	NS	NS
II	C	d.f. 23.1 f=3.96 (p=0.06)	NS	NS	NS
	P	NS	NS	NS	d.f. 23.1 f=6.29*
III	C	NS	NS	NS	NS
	P	NS	NS	NS	d.f. 23.1 f=7.02*
IV	C	d.f. 23.1 f=6.49*	NS	NS	NS
	P	d.f. 23.1 f=8.65**	NS	NS	NS
V	C	NS	d.f. 18.1 f=6.37*	NS	NS
	P	NS	NS	d.f. 21.1 f=4.00 (p=0.06)	d.f. 23.1 f=11.28**
VI	C	d.f. 23.1 f=15.40**	d.f. 18.1 f=8.05*	NS	NS
	P	d.f. 23.1 f=15.18***	NS	NS	NS
VII	C	d.f. 23.1 f=22.00**	NS	NS	NS
	P	d.f. 23.1 f=61.22**	d.f. 18.1 f=3.41 (p=0.08)	NS	NS
VIII	C	d.f. 23.1 f=11.99**	NS	NS	NS
	P	d.f. 23.1 f=8.03**	NS	NS	d.f. 23.1 f=6.60*

Table 20-4 (continued)

Category		Kg	1st grade	3rd grade	5th grade
IX	C	NS	NS	NS	d.f. 23.1 f=3.96 (p=0.06)
	P	d.f. 23.1 f=3.14 (p=0.08)	NS	NS	d.f. 23.1 f=5.25*
X	C	d.f. 23.1 f=5.21*	NS	NS	NS
	P	d.f. 23.1 f=6.62*	NS	NS	NS
XI	C	NS	NS	NS	d.f. 23.1 f=16.04**
	P	d.f. 23.1 f=9.48**	d.f. 18.1 f=9.40**	NS	d.f. 23.1 f=3.48 (p=0.07)
XII	C	d.f. 23.1 f=5.47*	NS	NS	NS
	P	d.f. 23.1 f=4.66*	NS	NS	NS
XIII	C	d.f. 23.1 f=10.16**	d.f. 18.1 f=14.13**	d.f. 21.1 f=8.47**	NS
	P	d.f. 23.1 f=17.39**	d.f. 18.1 f=8.17*	NS	NS
XIV	C	NS	NS	NS	d.f. 23.1 f=8.61**
	P	d.f. 23.1 f=5.92*	NS	d.f. 21.1 f=4.49*	d.f. 23.1 f=21.56**
Total	C	d.f. 23.1 f=24.79**	d.f. 18.1 f=5.38*	NS	d.f. 23.1 f=9.96**
	P	d.f. 23.1 f=16.97**	NS	NS	d.f. 23.1 f=7.71*

Table 20.5 Significant differences im comprehension (C) and production (P) between group A2 and Kg, 1st, 3rd and 5th grades in 14 categories and total test scores

Category		Kg	1st grade	3rd grade	5th grade
I	C	NS	NS	NS	d.f. 20.1 f=4.24*
	P	d.f. 20.1 f=3.49 (p=0.07)	d.f. 15.1 f=8.34*	NS	NS
II	C	NS	NS	NS	NS
	P	NS	NS	NS	d.f. 20.1 f=11.98**
III	C	NS	NS	d.f. 18.1 f=4.47**	d.f. 20.1 f=5.43*
	P	d.f. 20.1 f=6.51*	NS	NS	NS
IV	C	NS	NS	NS	NS
	P	d.f. 20.1 f=3.73 (p=0.07)	NS	NS	NS
V	C	NS	d.f. 15.1 f=7.90*	NS	NS
	P	d.f. 20.1 f=4.36*	NS	NS	NS
VI	C	NS	NS	NS	NS
	P	d.f. 20.1 f=22.07**	NS	NS	NS
VII	C	d.f. 20.1 f=16.28**	NS	NS	NS
	P	d.f. 20.1 f=10.11**	NS	NS	NS
VIII	C	d.f. 20.1 f=5.99*	NS	NS	d.f. 20.1 f=4.57*
	P	d.f. 20.1 f=4.50*	NS	NS	d.f. 20.1 f=4.85*

Table 20-5 (continued)

Category		Kg	1st grade	3rd grade	5th grade
IX	C	NS	NS	NS	NS
	P	NS	NS	NS	d.f. 20.1 f=12.94**
X	C	d.f. 20.1 f=9.31**	NS	NS	NS
	P	d.f. 20.1 f=16.46**	NS	NS	NS
XI	C	NS	NS	NS	d.f. 20.1 f=14.96**
	P	NS	d.f. 15.1 f=4.08 (p=0.06)	NS	d.f. 20.1 f=7.52*
XII	C	d.f. 20.1 f=7.95**	NS	NS	NS
	P	d.f. 20.1 f=5.43*	NS	NS	NS
XIII	C	NS	d.f. 15.1 f=4.15 (p=0.06)	NS	NS
	P	d.f. 20.1 f=15.08**	d.f. 15.1 f=6.92*	NS	NS
XIV	C	NS	NS	NS	d.f. 20.1 f=10.92**
	P	d.f. 20.1 f=5.56*	NS	NS	d.f. 20.1 f=11.81**
Total	C	d.f. 20.1 f=14.11**	NS	NS	d.f. 20.1 f=22.50**
	P	d.f. 20.1 f=16.01**	NS	NS	d.f. 20.1 f=7.62*

the Production task of the test is obviously aided by possible retention of the
sentence in short term memory. One could also argue that a sequence of C before
P in language acquisition might make for more likelihood of the kg subjects
"catching up" with the teenagers in C rather than in P.

Group A1, A2 and 1st grade
    A1 > 1st grade
Cat. I   P (Singular/Plural)
Cat. V.   C   (Mass/Count)
Cat. VI.   C   (his, her/their)
Cat. VII.   P (he/she)
Cat. XI.   P (Agent/Patient Reversal, Passive Clause)
Cat. XIII.   C P (Word order change)
Total Score

    A2 > 1st grade
Cat. I   P (Singular/Plural)
Cat. V.   C   (Mass/Count)
Cat. XI.   P (Agent/Patient Reversal, Passive Clause)
Cat. XIII.   C P (Word order change)

By the first grade the bilingual school children appear to have reached the
same level as the two groups of adolescents in most categories. No clear picture of
the reasons for the superiority of the A1/A2 group over the 1st graders appears
to emerge from the categories in which A1, A2 > 1st grade. All of the five A2 >
1st grade instances are also found among the A1 > 1st grade group. C and P are
fairly equally distributed. Some of the categories in which A1 or A2 > 1st grade
offer primarily semantic problems (e.g., cat. V, XI, XIII); others contain difficulties that seem mainly associated with surface structure (cat. I, VI). It should also
be noted that A1, A2 > 1st grade in cat. V is associated with a deterioration in
performance from kg to grade 1 (Mass/Count distinction is evidently more
confusing to the 1st graders than to the kg pupils!).

Group A1, A2 and 3rd grade
    A1 > 3rd grade
Cat. XIII.   C   (Word order)

    3rd grade > A1
Cat. V.   P (Mass/Count)
Cat. XIV.   P (look & prep)

    3rd grade > A2
Cat. III.   C   (Present/Future)

At the third grade there are only a few significant differences between the primary school children and the A1, A2 groups. Only one of the differences (C XIII) is in favor of the A1 group. The others are in favor of 3rd grade over either A1 (P V, P XIV) or A2 (CIII).

Group A1, A2 and 5th grade
    A1 > 5th grade
Cat. II.   P (Present/Past)
Cat. III.   P (Present/Future)
Cat. V.   P (Mass/Count)
Cat. VIII.   P (his/her)
Cat. IX.   C P (Direct Object/Indirect Object Reversal)
Cat. XI.   C P (Agent/Patient Reversal in Passive Clause)
Cat. XIV.   C P (look & prep)
Total C P Test Score

    A2 > 5th grade
Cat. I.   C   (Singular/Plural)
Cat. II.   P (Present/Past)
Cat. III.   C   (Present/Future)
Cat. VIII.   C P (him/her)
Cat. IX.   P (Direct Object/Indirect Object Reversal)
Cat. XI.   C P (Agent/Patient Reversal in Passive Clause)
Cat. XIV.   C P (look & prep)
Total C P Score

At the 5th grade all the significant differences are in favor of the 5th graders over the A1, A2 groups. There is an expected large overlap between the 5th grade > A1 and 5th grade A2 categories. Categories III (Present/Future), V (Mass/Count) and XIV (look & prep), which were already favoring the primary school children at the third grade, continue to be in the primary school > A1, A2 column. The difference in total C P scores between 5th grade and both A1 and A2 groups are also significant ($p < .05$ for P, $p < .01$ for C).

Table 20-6 summarizes the significant and near significant differences (up to $p=0.05$) that occur between the grades (kg/1st, 1st/3rd, 3rd/5th) of the elementary school. The intervals 1st/3rd grade and 3rd/5th grade are, of course, approximately equivalent to two years of language exposure. Therefore, the most relevant and interesting comparisons that can be made between the A1, A2 groups on the one hand and the elementary school on the other are the ones between the lack of progress from A1, A2 and the progress from kg to grade 1 and between the categories in which 1st graders and the A1, A2 groups show progress over the kg pupils. The first of the comparisons has already been made and illustrated in Figure 20-1. Table 20-6 merely adds the information that progress on total C scores from kg to grade 1 is in fact nearly significant ($p < .07$) and that progress on total P scores is significant at the $p < .05$ level.

Table 20-6 Significant differences between Kg/1st grade, 1st grade/3rd grade and 3rd grade/5th grade in comprehension (C) and production (P) in 14 categories and total test scores

Category		Kg/1st grade	1st grade/3rd grade	3rd grade/5th grade
I	C	NS	NS	d.f. 21.1 f=3.30 (p=0.08)
	P	NS	NS	d.f. 21.1 f=3.64 (p=0.07)
II	C	NS	NS	NS
	P	NS	NS	d.f. 21.1 f=8.31**
III	C	NS	d.f. 16.1 f=3.53 (p=0.07)	NS
	P	NS	NS	NS
IV	C	NS	NS	NS
	P	d.f. 18.1 f=4.72*	NS	NS
V	C	d.f. 18.1 f=5.55**	d.f. 16.1 f=6.00*	NS
	P	NS	d.f. 16.1 f=3.87 (p=0.07)	NS
VI	C	NS	NS	NS
	P	d.f. 18.1 f=15.11**	NS	NS
VII	C	NS	NS	NS
	P	d.f. 18.1 f=15.85**	NS	NS
VIII	C	d.f. 18.1 f=8.17*	NS	NS
	P	d.f. 18.1 f=5.80*	NS	d.f. 21.1 f=6.06*

Table 20-6 (continued)

Category		Kg/1st grade	1st grade/3rd grade	3rd grade/5th grade
IX	C	NS	NS	d.f. 21.1 f=8.47**
	P	d.f. 18.1 f=3.90 (p=0.06)	NS	d.f. 21.1 f=4.87*
X	C	d.f. 18.1 f=3.73 (p=0.07)	NS	NS
	P	d.f. 18.1 f=5.05*	NS	NS
XI	C	NS	NS	d.f. 21.1 f=5.48*
	P	NS	d.f. 16.1 f=5.20*	d.f. 21.1 f=5.35*
XII	C	d.f. 18.1 f=15.15**	NS	NS
	P	NS	NS	d.f. 21.1 f=5.04*
XIII	C	NS	NS	d.f. 21.1 f=8.47**
	P	NS	NS	NS
XIV	C	NS	NS	d.f. 21.1 f=3.50 (p=0.07)
	P	NS	d.f. 16.1 f=13.45**	NS
Total	C	d.f. 18.1 f=3.57 (p=0.07)	d.f. 16.1 f=5.34*	d.f. 21.1 f=10.16**
	P	d.f. 18.1 f=7.25*	d.f. 16.1 f=4.07 (p=0.06)	d.f. 21.1 f=6.91*

**p <.01   *p <.05

The other instances of significant or near significant superiority of 1st graders over kg are the following:

1st grade > kg

Cat. IV   P   (Affirmative/Negative)
Cat. VI.   C   (his, her/their)
Cat. VII.   P   (he/she)
Cat. VIII. C P   (him/her)
Cat. IX.   P   (Direct Object/Indirect Object Reversal)
Cat. X.   C P   (Active Sentence: Agent/Patient Reversal)
Cat. XII.   C   (Embedded Relative Clause Agent/Patient Reversal)

There is one category, namely C X (Mass/Count) in which first grade performance deteriorates over performance at the kg level.

The following are thus the categories in which the A1 and A2 groups of adolescents are significantly or nearly significantly better than the kg children while 1st graders are not:

A1 > kg but 1st = kg

Cat. I.   C P   (Singular/Plural)
Cat. II.   C P   (Present/Past)
Cat. IV.   C   (Affirmative/Negative)
Cat. VI.   C   (his,her/their)
Cat. VII.   C   (he/she)
Cat. XI.   P   (Passive Sentence: Agent/Patient Reversal)
Cat. XII.   P   (Embedded Relative Clause: Agent/Patient Reversal)
Cat. XIII. C P   (Word order change)
Cat. XIV.   P   (look & prep)

A2 > kg but 1st = kg

Cat. I.   P   (Singular/Plural)
Cat. III.   P   (Present/Future)
Cat. V.   P   (Mass/Count)
Cat. VII.   C   (he/she)
Cat. XII.   P   (Embedded Relative Clause: Agent/Patient Reversal)
Cat. XIII.   P   (Word order change)
Cat. XIV.   P   (look & prep)

The "A1 > kg 1st = kg" differences are rather evenly distributed among C and P tasks (6C, 6P). In the "A2 > kg, but 1st = kg" group the P tasks dominate (1C, 6P). In terms of improvement over the kg group, the adolescents have the edge over the first graders in some tasks that seem relatively simple and "straight forward" both in terms of surface structure and semantics (e.g., categories I, II, VI, VII) as well as in the categories which appear to be more complex from both the semantic and/or surface structure point of view (e.g., categories XIII, XIV). One would suspect that both a better memory span and more fully developed ability to handle some difficult semantic distinctions in L_1 account for the relative superiority of the high school students.

As mentioned previously there is one comprehension task (C V, Mass/Count) in which 1st grade performance deteriorates over kg's. A2 is significantly superior to kg in the corresponding production task, but interestingly neither A1 nor A2 is superior to kg in the same task, though the adolescents' performance is at least not significantly lower. A look at Tables 20-3 and 20-6 shows that in the C cat. V task the "progress" from kg to grade 5 consists, in fact, in a deterioration from kg to 1 which is then reversed in the step from 1 to 3. The some/a contrast is evidently difficult to grasp (part of the difficulty may be caused by possible ambiguity in illustration). The small sample of 1st grade pupils used in this study does not justify a great deal of speculation as to what may be the specific cause for the deterioration of performance in grade 1 (e.g., a possible cause may be increased reliance on semantic rather than strictly surface structure cues which may, initially at least, increase the possibility of confusion, see Slobin 1966).

There is finally one single task, namely P cat. IX (Direct Object/Indirect Object Reversal) in which 1st grade > kg (p=0.06) but A2 = kg. Since A1 > kg in the same task no particular generally significant explanation need or can be advanced for this statistically significant kg/1st grade difference. As Table 20-6 indicates, the really important significant step toward improvement in category IX occurs in the interval grade 3/grade 5.

The information concerning the significant differences between grade 1 and 3, and 3 and 5 (Table 20-6) is of interest insofar as it shows that in some categories (like cat. IX mentioned above), the significant steps toward improvement occur rather late, namely in the interval from grade 3 to 5. This comparatively late improvement is somewhat surprising in what seem rather simple and highly frequent tasks (like cat. I, Singular/Plural, cat. II Present/Future). It is to be expected in the categories which appear to be either semantically more difficult (cat. XIII Word order, cat. XII Embedded Relative Clause, cat. IX Direct Object/ Indirect Object Reversal) or structurally confusing (cat. XIV, *look* & prep).

In conclusion, it appears that this investigation shows both superiority as well as possible advantage of the high school age L_2 learner compared with the kindergarten beginner. The superiority is probably connected with better memory storage capacity as well as a more fully developed conceptual system. The high school subjects of the A1 group of this study reached in approximately half a year the level of the third graders who had started L_2 English at the kg level. The comparison of the first year progress of kg to 1st grade, as opposed to that of the high school students, documented a steady progress from kg to 1st grade but total levelling off for the high school subjects.

The relative advantages or disadvantages of older L_2 learners over small children has been a hotly debated subject for a long time. Some (e.g., Stern 1963) see both advantages and disadvantages for either groups. Others are partisans for the young child (e.g., Andersson 1969) and others for the adult learner (e.g., Ausubel 1964). A recent study in England and Wales reported in the *Report in*

Education Research (6, 26, 1974) casts considerable doubt on the advantages of the early start in L_2 learning in a school environment. We do not propose to have found a definite answer for the complex problem. The tests used do not measure pronunciation or any kind of natural speech but are very specific types of Comprehension and Production (quasi imitation) tasks in which adolescents may have several advantages over smaller children. The levelling off effect shown by the adolescents may, to some extent at least, also be an artifact of the instruments which combine some very easy tasks and some rather difficult ones. After the first year of L_2 exposure, the A2 group may have thus been tested at exactly the moment at which performance in the easy task was no longer significantly better than it was after about a half a year while the very difficult tasks (e.g., cats. IX, XI, XII, XIII, XIV) were still not within the competence of most subjects. An instrument including more tasks of intermediary types of difficulty may have revealed some progress from A1 to A2. Still the overall conclusion of the study strongly suggests that the advantage of the adolescent over the adult as L_2 learner consists in initially greater speed of L_2 acquisition. This impression of an initial advantage of age is also reinforced by the near significant difference favoring senior high school over junior high school students on the total C and P scores. But there is also some evidence that the greater speech associated with maturation may be followed by a rather marked and possibly prolonged levelling off period.

Age Differences

21 in Second Language Acquisition*

Catherine E. Snow and Marian Hoefnagel-Höhle, *University of Amsterdam*

INTRODUCTION

Snow's approach to age difference in second language acquisition is to first dispel the notion of language acquisition as a monolithic process. All of us have had students who excel in acquisition of various aspects of the language system. Some seem to develop amazing vocabularies, others perfect pronunciation but suffer from limited vocabulary development. Others develop beautiful segmentals but are absolutely incomprehensible because the intonation system has not been acquired, thereby throwing off stress and even segmental values in the total speech stream. Some learners read well but cannot understand the spoken language. Snow's question is whether or not these skills are differentially acquired over an age range.

To answer this question, Snow and her associates have undertaken a large scale investigation of second language learning. The preliminary report given here presents only the first findings from that project.

Once we agree that acquisition is not a monolithic process, we will have committed ourselves to an investigation of the literature in neurolinguistics, a literature which relates to stages of language development as well as differential impairment of language skills in aphasia and other language pathologies. Pidginized second language data, for example, can be related on the continuum from normal speech to non-fluent (Broca's aphasia) data. The telegraphic, agrammatic syntax of non-fluent aphasia patients looks much like that of many adult learners. If one looked at the following data of a subject describing a picture, one would be hard pressed to say whether the description was from Broca's data or from that of a second language learner: "Here . . . cookie jar . . . boy fall . . . uh, oh, fall . . . wife spill water . . . uh dishes . . . and uh cup and saucer and uh plate . . . I uh . . . no . . . done." The circumlocutions in conduction aphasia data look much like that of an adult second language learner trying to retrieve the right vocabulary word and not being able to: "The boy's falling down his . . . I mean his uh whatever you call it . . . his whatever he may be . . . oh whatever it is." The data on quick acquisition and retention of concrete nouns as compared to verbs or even abstract nouns for second language learners is comparable to that of first language learners and to data on retrieval by aphasia patients. Each of the skills that we wish to differentiate has been discussed in neurolinguistic terms, in terms of what we know about language and the human brain. While data on bilingual aphasia is interesting and important to our field, a basic understanding of the work that has been done on the differentiation of languages skills and brain organization is even more important in understanding the uneven acquisition of skills by the second language learner.

Together, the fields of neurolinguistics, psycholinguistics, child language and second language acquisition can contribute valuable supporting data for all the postulated components of theoretical linguistics. Second language data can be as useful as that from any of the other fields of inquiry in giving evidence in support of competing linguistic models.

This research was supported by The Netherlands Foundation for the Advancement of Pure Research (ZWO). Preparation of the paper was carried out while the first author was at the Unit for Research in the Medical Applications of Psychology, University of Cambridge.

* * *

The question whether there are age differences in the ability to acquire a second language is relevant to two issues of interest to psycholinguists, one of applied and one of primarily theoretical importance. If there are age differences, these should be taken into account in planning second language education programs, so that the period of fastest and easiest acquisition is the period when second language training is offered. If there are no age differences, then our ideas about the nature of first language acquisition must be somewhat modified. First language acquisition has traditionally been seen as a unique process which occurs during a period of optimal brain plasticity and which is different in nature from later language acquisition or from the other kinds of learning that young children undergo. If second language acquisition occurs equally quickly and effectively in very young children and in older children and adults, this would suggest that young children have no particular facility for language acquisition, and that first language acquisition therefore might be quite similar to the acquisition of any complex skill.

It is, of course, a mistake to think of language acquisition, either first or second, as a single, monolithic process. Speaking a language involves several, separate skills, and there is no a priori reason to assume that all those skills are acquired equally easily by any individual. Second language teachers are constantly confronted with students who do quite well in some aspects of the training, e.g., learning vocabulary, but who never achieve great success in other aspects, e.g., correct word order, or accent. Such individual differences in the profile of component abilities are probably present for one's first language as well, but are less noticeable because of the generally higher level of achievement in all component skills.

Pronunciation is one component of second language skill which is most commonly cited as showing age differences, and receptive control of the second language's phonological system is often thought of as having a critical period as well. A complete test of the hypothesis that there are no age differences in second language acquisition requires separate tests for all the separate identifiable components of language skill—receptive and productive control of morphology, syntax, vocabulary and fluency skills as well as phonology.

Besides looking for age differences in speed or effectiveness of acquisition of the various component language skills, one might also wish to test the strongest form of the hypothesis that there are no age differences by looking for age differences in strategies of acquisition. Various researchers have recently stressed the similarities between first and second language acquisition (Corder, 1974; Hansen-Bede, 1975; Holley and King, 1974; Macnamara, 1973), pointing out that errors typical of first language acquisition, such as overgeneralization, also occur in second language acquisition (Ravem, 1974; Richards, 1974; Snow, 1974), and that interference is of limited importance (Buteau, 1974; Wardhaugh, 1974). These conclusions disagree with the traditional view based on contrastive analysis, concerning the prevalence of interference errors. One possible explanation for the disagreement is that interference errors may be more typical of those who have gone through second language training, whereas those who learn a second language in an unstructured, "picking-it-up" situation may use strategies more similar to those of the first language learner.

We have attempted to test the strong version of the hypothesis that no age differences in the ability to acquire second language exist by studying acquisition in a natural situation, by assessing achievement with a large battery of tests, and by performing error analyses as well as quantitative analyses on the results. Because of limitations on length, only quantitative analyses on only the most important tests from the battery will be discussed in this paper. Further results will be treated in forthcoming reports.

PROCEDURE

Subjects

Native speakers of English who were living in Holland were recruited as subjects. Forty-two of the subjects had arrived within three months before the first test session; almost all the school children in this group had received their first real exposure to Dutch at the start of the school year, within a month before the first test session. This group, called the Beginners, was divided into five age groups: Seven 3-5 year olds, eight 6-7 year olds, ten 8-10 year olds, six 12-15 year olds, and eleven adults. These subjects were tested three times at 4½ month intervals, to assess their progress in speaking Dutch. Another twenty-seven native English speakers who had been in Holland at least a year, and all of whom were functioning as adequate bilinguals, were also tested once. These Advanced subjects fell into four age groups: Six 6-7 year olds, six 8-10 year olds, six 12-15 year olds, and nine adults. In addition, some of the tests from the test battery were administered to eight 6-7 year old and eight 12-15 year old native Dutch speakers, to provide some norms for assessing the level of achievement of the English speakers.

Test Battery

Only those tests to be discussed in the results section will be described here. A fuller account of the test battery can be found in Snow (1974).

Pronunciation

Eighty pictureable words were chosen which contained problematic Dutch phonemes in initial, medial, and final position. The subjects pronounced each of these words directly imitating a native speaker, and then again a few minutes later named the pictures without an immediate auditory model. These productions were individually scored on a six point scale (0 = English word produced instead of Dutch; 2 = very strong English accent in Dutch word; 5 = perfect native-like pronunciation) by a native speaker. The judge scored all productions on two separate occasions and achieved high reliability. A second judge also scored a portion of the productions, and achieved acceptable levels of agreement with the first judge. The individual subject's score is given as a mean of the score achieved on all the words attempted in the spontaneous production condition, and on all the words in the imitation condition.

Auditory discrimination

Pictureable words representing minimal pairs for Dutch phoneme distinctions not present in English were chosen. These words were spoken in a random order by a native speaker, and the subject was instructed to point to the correct picture. Some errors on this test reflected vocabulary—some of the subjects simply did not know all the test words. The errors which reflected true auditory confusions were divided by the total number of correct answers plus auditory confusions, to give a subject's score.

Morphology

Knowledge of morphology was tested with an adaptation of the Berko (1958) wug test, in which nonsense words are presented with pictures in order to elicit the desired morphological changes. Tests for plural, agentive, diminutive, past tense, and past participle were included, as well as a sub-test for final devoicing when forming the singular from the plural.

Peabody Picture Vocabulary Test

The PPVT (Dunn, 1959) was administered in English at session 1 and in Dutch at all sessions. The standardized Dutch translation (Manschot and Bonnema, 1974) was used up to item 100 (as far as it goes), and our own translation for items 100-150.

Sentence repetition

Thirty-seven sentences of increasing length and syntactic complexity were read one-by-one by a native speaker to each subject, who was asked to repeat them. The number of words correctly repeated from the model sentences was taken as each subject's score.

Translation

Sixty sentences of increasing difficulty were given in English, and the subjects were asked to translate them into Dutch. Help was given with any content words the subject did not know. The translations were scored structure by structure; the quantitative scores presented here represent each subject's total points correct (maximum 325).

These and other tests in the battery were administered individually to the subjects at home or at school in a relaxed test session lasting about an hour and a half. The numbers of subjects reported on for each test vary slightly because some subjects were added to the sample too late to be scored for all tests, and because some of the younger subjects refused to do some tests. In addition, some of the beginners were lost between sessions 1 and 2. The third test session is not yet completely analysed, and only the first and second will be discussed here.

RESULTS

Significant improvement was made by the Beginners as a group on all six tests between session 1 and session 2 (tested in all cases with Wilcoxon signed-ranks test for those subjects available at both sessions). This improvement indicates that the tests used were sensitive to level of achievement, and that considerable acquisition was occurring for our subjects. The improvement will not be discussed for each test separately.

The statistical analysis was essentially the same for all six tests, and will not be described in each section. Age differences were tested with the Kruskal-Wallis nonparametric one-way analysis of variance. Differences between the Beginners at session 2 and the Advanced groups, and between the Advanced groups and the Native Speakers, were tested for each age group separately with the Mann-Whitney U. Outcomes of the specific tests are given in the relevant tables.

Pronunciation

The pronunciation test showed only marginal age differences. There was a significant age difference for spontaneous production at session 1 (see Table 21-1), with the older subjects performing better. The younger subjects showed significantly greater improvement, such that no age differences existed by session 2. The Advanced subjects showed no age differences. By session 2 the performance of the Beginners was no longer significantly worse than that of the Advanced subjects, tested for each age group separately. However, none of the Advanced subjects had achieved perfect, native-like pronunciation on all words. Imitation was significantly better than spontaneous production (Wilcoxon signed-ranks test), but this difference decreased in session 2 and had almost disappeared in the Advanced subjects.

Table 21-1 Results of the phonology test. Medians for the various age groups on Imitation (Imit) and Spontaneous Production (Spon) of 80 test words. 5 represents a perfect native-like pronunciation.

| | | BEGINNERS | | | | | ADVANCED | | |
| | | session 1 | | | session 2 | | | | |
Age	n	Imit	Spon[1]	n	Imit	Spon	n	Imit	Spon
3-5	7	3.80	2.00	7	4.20	4.20			
6-7	8	4.05	2.80	4	4.75	4.30	5	4.60	4.60
8-10	10	3.95	3.10	5	4.55	4.40	4	4.70	4.50
12-15	6	4.30	3.55	6	4.55	4.30	3	4.67	4.50
adult	11	4.28	3.73	10	4.35	4.05	2	4.25	3.90

[1]Significant age difference for the column indicated, tested with the Kruskal-Wallis one-way analysis of variance (H = 10.70, p < 0.05).

NOTE: Improvement from Time 1 to Time 2, tested with the Wilcoxon signed-ranks test, was highly significant for both imitation (T = 56.5, Z = 3.88, p < 0.0001) and for spontaneous production (T = 0, Z = 4.94, p < 0.0001). There were no significant differences between the beginners at session 2 and the advanced subjects of the same age (tested with the Mann-Whitney U).

Table 21-2   Results of the Auditory Discrimination Test. Median
percentage incorrect answers in each group are
presented.

Age	n	Beginners session 1	n	session 2	Advanced n		Native Speakers n	
3-5	7	22.2	7	17.8				
6-7	8	23.6	5	17.6	5	3.9	8	1.8
8-10	10	20.3	7	12.2	6	4.8		
12-15	6	7.3	6	4.5	6	2.8	8	1.8
adult	11	15.9	10	16.1	8	7.7		

NOTE: There were no significant differences due to age. The improvement
from session 1 to session 2 was significant (Wilcoxon signed-ranks test T =
152.5, Z = 2.66, p < 0.01). There were no significant differences between the
Advanced subjects and the Beginners at session 2. The native speakers were
significantly better than the Advanced subjects in both the 6-7 (Mann-
Whitney U = 9.0, p < 0.05) and the 12-15 (U = 9.0, p < 0.05) year old groups.

Auditory discrimination

There were no significant age differences in Auditory Discrimination. The Beginners in the second session were no longer significantly worse than the Advanced
groups, though their median performance was still considerably lower (see Table
21-2). The Advanced subjects were significantly, though not greatly, worse than
their age mates who were native speakers.

Morphology

The morphology test showed enormous age differences in favor of the older
subjects (see Table 21-3). These differences were so great that the test could not
even be successfully administered to anyone in the two youngest groups at the
first session. At the second session, the youngest children did all attempt the test,
though they still produced very few correct answers. The Advanced subjects
showed no age differences. The three oldest groups of Beginners achieved the
level of the Advanced subjects by session 2, but the Advanced 6-7 year olds were
significantly better than the 6-7 year old Beginners at session 2. The 12-15 year
old native speakers were significantly better than the Advanced 12-15 year olds.

The pattern of increase with age on the Morphology Test deserves special
mention, as it recurs in the rest of the tests to be discussed. Steady increase with
age is seen up to the teenagers; the adults scored at or a bit below the teenage
level, but still better than any of the younger groups. This age difference decreased
by session 2, and had disappeared for the Advanced subjects.

Table 21-3   Results of the Morphology test. Median number of correct responses per group are presented (maximum possible score was 82).

Age	n	Beginners session 1[1]	n	session 2[1]	Advanced n		Native Speakers n	
3-5			7	1.0				
6-7			4	13.5	4	46.5	8	50.0
8-10	10	20.0	5	38.2	6	52.5		
12-15	6	36.5	6	43.0	5	43.0	8	69.0
adult	11	33.0	10	42.0	9	48.0		

[1]Significant age effect for the column indicated, as tested with Kruskal-Wallis one-way analysis of variance. For session 1, $H = 11.2$, $p < 0.01$; for session 2, $H = 22.9$, $p < 0.001$.

NOTE: Improvement from session 1 to session 2 was significant (Wilcoxon signed-ranks test, $T = 7$, $p < 0.01$). The Advanced 6-7 year olds were significantly better than the Beginners at session 2 (Mann-Whitney $U = 0$, $p < 0.02$), as were the 12-15 year olds (Mann-Whitney $U = 2.5$, $p < 0.01$).

Vocabulary

The Dutch PPVT showed an age effect very similar to that described for morphology: steady significant increase up to the teenage group, with the adults scoring slightly worse than the teenagers (see Table 21-4). The age pattern was more persistent on the PPVT, as it was still marked at session 2, and even for the Advanced subjects. That this "teenage ceiling" is typical only for second language acquisition can be seen from the scores on the English PPVT, which show the expected steady increase with age continuing through adulthood.

There were no significant differences between the Beginners at session 2 and the Advanced subjects, but both groups of native speakers were significantly better than the Advanced groups of the same age.

Sentence repetition

Significant age differences, conforming to the teenage-ceiling effect, were present at both sessions for the Beginners, but were much decreased in size by session 2 (see Table 21-5). Interestingly, the native speakers also showed a significant age effect, though the Advanced English speakers did not. The Advanced subjects were as good as the native speakers, and the Advanced 6-7 year olds and adults were significantly better than the Beginners.

Table 21-4   Results of the Peabody Picture Vocabulary Test. Maximum possible score for the Dutch version was 50 for the 3-7 year olds, and 100 for the older subjects. Subjects were tested to ceiling in the English version.

Age	n	Beginners session 1		n	session 2	n	Advanced		n	Native Speakers
		English[1]	Dutch[1]		Dutch[1]		English[1]	Dutch[1]		Dutch[1]
3-5	7	45.2	24.8	7	30.0					
6-7	8	50.3	29.5	4	41.0	6	44.0	45.5	8	49.9
8-10	10	79.5	56.1	5	68.0	6	73.0	80.5		
12-15	6	108.0	71.5	6	80.0	5	82.0	86.7	8	94.5
adult	11	140.5	68.0	10	74.0	9	136.0	87.0		

[1]Significant age effect for the column indicated, as tested with the Kruskal-Wallis one-way analysis of variance. Beginners, English $H = 34.8$, $p < 0.0001$; Beginners, Dutch, session 1, $H = 36.0$, $p < 0.001$; Beginners, Dutch, session 2, $H = 25.7$, $p < 0.001$; Advanced, English, $H = 21.3$, $p < 0.001$; Advanced, Dutch, $H = 14.1$, $p < 0.01$; Native Speakers, Mann-Whitney $U = 0$, $p < 0.01$.

NOTE: Significant improvement occurred between session 1 and session 2 (Wilcoxon signed-ranks test, $T = 5$, $Z = 4.76$, $p < 0.0001$). There were no significant differences between the Beginners at Time 2 and the Advanced subjects. Both groups of native speakers were significantly better than the Advanced subjects (for 6-7 year olds, Mann-Whitney $U = 7.0$, $p < 0.01$; for 12-15 year olds, $U = 1.5$, $p < 0.01$).

Table 21-5   Results of the Sentence Repetition Test. Median number
of words correctly repeated per group are presented.
Maximum possible score was 238.

Age	n	Beginners session 1[1]	n	session 2[1]	Advanced n		Native Speakers n	
3-5	7	54.0	7	178.0				
6-7	8	87.5	5	172.0	6	213.5	8	220.0
8-10	10	134.5	7	211.0	6	233.0		
12-15	6	204.0	6	225.0	5	234.0	8	234.0
adult	11	171.0	10	190.5	9	229.3		

[1]Significant age effect for the column indicated, as tested with a Kruskal-Wallis one-way analysis of variance (for session 1, $H = 21.4$, $p < 0.001$; for session 2, $H = 13.9$, $p < 0.01$). Improvement between sessions 1 and 2 was highly significant (Wilcoxon $T = 1$, $Z = 5.15$, $p < 0.0001$). The 6-7 year old Advanced subjects were significantly better than the 6-7 year old Beginners at session 2 (Mann-Whitney $U = 3.0$, $p < 0.02$), and the Advanced adults were better than the adult Beginners ($U = 6.0$, $p < 0.001$). The Advanced subjects were not significantly different from the native speakers.

Translation

As for Sentence Repetition, large significant age differences for the Beginners at session 1 and smaller but still significant age differences at session 2 were found for the translation test (see Table 21-6). The teenagers scored the best, and the adults scored slightly better than the 8-10 year olds. There were no age differences for Advanced subjects, who in all age groups except 12-15 were significantly better than the Beginners at session 2.

DISCUSSION

To summarize the results:
1. Considerable improvement occurred in all aspects of knowledge of Dutch for subjects of all ages. However, this improvement occurred at different rates for the different aspects and the different age groups.
2. Older learners seemed to have an advantage over younger learners in acquiring the rule-governed aspects of a second language—morphology and syntax. This advantage of age was, however, limited, as the teenagers did better than the adults, and reflected simply rate of acquisition, not an upper limit on ability, since age differences on these tests diminished and disappeared with longer residence in Holland. It also seemed to be possible to attain native levels of performance on these tests within a couple of years of exposure to the second language.

Table 21-6   Results of the Translation Test. Medians are
presented per group. Maximum possible
score was 325.

Age	n	Beginners session 1[1]	n	session 2[1]	Advanced n	
3-5	7	6.0	7	82.0		
6-7	7	30.0	4	135.0	4	267.5
8-10	10	153.5	5	234.0	5	288.0
12-15	6	242.5	6	273.5	5	292.0
adult	11	185.0	10	234.0	9	281.0

[1]Significant age effect for the column indicated, as tested with
Kruskal-Wallis one-way analysis of variance (for session 1, $H =$
23.7, $p < 0.001$; for session 2, $H = 17.5$, $p < 0.01$). The Advanced
subjects in all age groups except 12-15 were significantly better
than the Beginners at session 2 (for 6-7, Mann-Whitney $U = 0$,
$p < 0.03$; for 8-10, $U = 1$, $p < 0.02$; for adults, $U = 13$, $p < 0.01$).

3. There were no or very small age differences for tests reflecting control of the
phonetic system, and the native level of performance was not achieved by non-
native speakers on these tests.

These results are fairly clearcut; their interpretation, however, is somewhat
less clear. This pattern of results is consistent with a number of different possible
realities as to the existence of age differences in the ability to acquire a second
language. It might be the case that the underlying reality is reflected directly in
the results—that teenagers really are better at second language acquisition than
any other age group. This seems unlikely, however, since it does not accord with
any known psychological age functions. The oldest adult in the study was in his
fifties, and most were in their twenties or thirties, so they were not suffering
from any geriatric decline in learning ability. One would normally expect a steady
increase with age up to age forty at least for "learning how to learn" abilities.

The second possibility is that the ability to acquire rule systems does in
fact increase steadily with age, or reaches an asymptote in the teens, but that the
adults did worse than the teenagers because of differences in their situations. It is
possible that the adults found themselves in a much less adequate second language
environment, that less severe communicative demands were made upon them, that
less support was given them in learning Dutch, that the kind of Dutch they heard
was less appropriate as a basis for learning the language, etc. All the nonadults in
this study were learning Dutch primarily in school, from teachers and from
classmates. The adults were quite varied in their contacts, but it was probably the
case that none of the adults encountered very many situations in which knowledge
of Dutch was absolutely crucial to effective communication. This was not the
case for the school children, and may well explain why adults do worse than
teenagers in acquiring Dutch. This explanation receives some support from the

fact that the adults scored only at the teenage level on the vocabulary test as well as on the morphology and syntax tests, though acquisition of vocabulary in one's first language continues into adulthood (as shown by the scores on the English version of the PPVT), and thus cannot be subject to any age limitation.

The third possibility is that acquiring rule systems is in fact equally difficult for all ages, and that, in conformity with popular belief, acquiring the phonetic system gets progressively more difficult with age. The pattern of results obtained in this study could then be explained as a result of increasingly appropriate second language learning environments as the children get older, which offset the inherent advantage of the younger children. This possibility is not counterintuitive to anyone who has observed the language environment of and communicative demands made in various classrooms. Kindergarten children whom we tested and observed seemed to be able to function fairly well in the school situation without any specific linguistic interaction with either classmates or teacher, whereas most of the teenagers were attending quite demanding academic high schools and required a fair command of Dutch in order to keep up with their studies.

It is clear that this kind of naturalistic study is only a first step in answering the questions whether there are age differences in the ability to acquire a second language. It is inadequate in precisely the same way that the 1960's studies of first language acquisition were inadequate—in that both ignored the linguistic environment and the communicative needs of the language learner. A fuller answer can come either from a study of second language acquisition under precisely controlled input conditions or from a detailed, ecological study of second language acquisition, including observations of the acquisition process as well as measurements of the achievements. Both these approaches have their problems. Controlled input conditions imply nonnatural second language learning—a second language classroom situation, or an unmotivated learning experiment approach. Neither of these could be said to be highly relevant to the question of language acquisition. The ecological approach, in which extensive observations are made relevant to all the complex factors which might be hypothesized to influence success of second language acquisition, is time-consuming, intrusive, and probably impossible to achieve completely.

Precisely because neither of these approaches is by itself entirely satisfactory, we have decided to use both of them in attempting to sort out the reality underlying our findings on age differences in second language acquisition. We are currently starting two studies, one a study of age differences in the ability to pronounce foreign sounds in a controlled input situation, and the second a study of the language environment of a new set of English speakers learning Dutch in a natural situation. We hope that these two approaches in combination will give us considerably more basis for interpreting the very striking age differences we have found in second language acquisition.

Note

1. Paper presented at the 4th Congress of the International Association of Applied Linguistics, Stuttgart, August, 1975.

Natural Sequence Order of Morphemes

Natural Sequences in Child Second Language Acquisition

22

Heidi C. Dulay and Marina K. Burt, *State University of New York at Albany*

INTRODUCTION

Rather than record observational data on a small number of subjects in a longitudinal study, Dulay and Burt have turned directly to large numbers of subjects at one period of time using a cross-sectional approach.

To elicit speech samples from children, Dulay and Burt created the Bilingual Syntax Measure which they administered to 55 Chinese and 60 Spanish-speaking children in the 6 to 8 year old range. With the Bilingual Syntax Measure, the experimenter uses a series of questions to elicit the child's response to picture stimuli. The speech samples for the children in this report were then analyzed for production of 11 morphemes (similar to those identified in first-language research by Brown, deVilliers & deVilliers, and others).

The basic question asked in the study is whether children from two dissimilar first languages would show the same sequence of acquisition of the 11 morphemes. In order to answer this question, they needed to reexamine data analysis procedures used in previous studies. Using more than one scoring method and then testing for differences with statistical procedures allowed them to feel confident in their statements on sequence of acquisition for the two groups. The sequence of structures provided by these procedures does give evidence to support the notion of universal child language learning strategies.

The study is particularly important because it gives the research person another strategy for eliciting data from a large number of subjects. The same test has since been used both in case studies and also in cross-sectional studies for a wide variety of age and language groups.

Reprinted with the permission of the authors and the publishers of *Language Learning,* 1974, *24,* 1, 37-53.

* * *

BACKGROUND AND RATIONALE

The present study is the third "episode" in our on-going efforts to discover the universal regularities in child second language acquisition. The first episode (Dulay and Burt 1972; Dulay and Burt 1974) summarized and added to the growing amount of evidence for the existence of second language learning strategies common to all children. These studies are for the most part error analyses which strongly indicate that regardless of first language background, children reconstruct English syntax in similar ways. Specifically, the types of errors in English that Spanish-, Chinese-, Japanese-, and Norwegian-speaking children make while still learning English are strikingly similar. This similarity of errors, as well as the specific error types, reflect what we refer to *as creative construction,* more specifically, *the process in which children gradually reconstruct rules for speech they hear, guided by universal innate mechanisms which cause them to formulate certain types of hypotheses about the language system being acquired, until the mismatch between what they are exposed to and what they produce is resolved.* The child's construction of linguistic rules is said to be creative because no native speaker of the target language—whether peer, parent, or teacher—models the kind of sentences produced regularly by children who are still learning the basic syntactic structures of a language.

The second episode (Dulay and Burt 1973:251-256) was a pilot investigation of natural sequences in the acquisition of eight English grammatical strucutres by Spanish-speaking children. We found that for three different groups of children— Chicano children in Sacramento, California; Mexican children living in Tijuana, Mexico, but attending school in San Ysidro, California; and Puerto Rican children in New York City—the acquisition sequence of the following eight structures was approximately the same: plural (-s), progressive (-ing), copula (is), article (a, the), auxiliary (is), irregular past (ate, took), 3rd person singular (-s), and possessive (Noun-'s).

The rationale for this pilot study was the same as that for the study we will report in this paper. Namely, if the creative construction process does play a major role in child L2 acquisition, then we should find a common sequence of acquisition of grammatical structures across diverse groups of children learning the same language. In other words, if it is true that universal cognitive mechanisms (or strategies) are the basis for the child's organization of a target language, and if it is the L2 system rather than the L1 system that guides the acquisition process, then the general sequence in which certain English syntactic structures are acquired by children of different language backgrounds should be the same, with only minor individual variation.

To test this hypothesis we compared Chinese- and Spanish-speaking children's acquisition order for 11 English "functors"—the little function words that have at best a minor role in conveying the meaning of a sentence: noun and verb inflections, articles, auxiliaries, copulas and prepositions. We chose to study functors (for the time being) as they are easily elicited—almost any verbal utterance contains several, and it is also fairly easy to determine whether or not they are used correctly. Moreover, Brown's (1973) important methodological insights in functor acquisition research for first language learners permitted us to develop rigorous methods of analysis. The functors included in this study were those that were regularly elicited by an expanded version of the *Bilingual Syntax Measure* (Burt, Dulay and Hernández 1973), the instrument we used to collect *natural* speech. It is briefly described below. The functors include the original eight in the pilot study just mentioned, plus pronoun case (nominative and accusative), regular past (*-ed*), and long plural (*-es*, e.g. hous*es* as opposed to the "short" plural door*s*). These are also described in detail below.

METHOD

Our original plan had been to use a longitudinal research design, as Brown had done for first language acquisition. This would have involved collecting large amounts of speech at weekly intervals from a small number of children (about three Chinese and three Spanish) over a one-year period. Coincidentally, however, at the time we were looking for children who were likely to stay in the area for a nine-month data collection period and whose parents and teachers would permit us to spend several hours every week or two with them, we became involved in the evaluation and diagnosis of the language development of children in two bilingual programs. This involvement resulted in 1) access to nearly 1,000 children who were acquiring English as a second language and 2) the development of the *Bilingual Syntax Measure* (BSM), which successfully elicited natural L2 speech from young children. Thus, instead of pursuing the oiriginal longitudinal plans, we decided on a cross-sectional design, using small corpuses of natural speech collected from large numbers of children by means of the BSM.

Subjects

The subjects in this study were 60 Spanish-speaking children, from seven schools in the Brentwood, Long Island school district in New York, and 55 Chinese-speaking children in Public School No. 2 in Chinatown, New York. The distribution of children by age and ethnic background was as follows: of 38 six-year-olds, 18 were Chinese and 20 Spanish; of 39 seven-year-olds, 18 Chinese, 21 Spanish; of 38 eight-year-olds, 19 Chinese and 19 Spanish. Both groups of children were in schools where many of their peers, of both their own ethnic group and of Anglo-American background, were native speakers of English. Our subjects all received some ESL instruction and some subject matter instruction in English.

Data collection and instrument

All of the data were collected using an expanded version of the BSM to elicit speech. The BSM is designed to measure children's acquisition of English and/or Spanish grammatical structure while they are in the process of becoming bilingual. It consists of seven color cartoon-type pictures and a set of 33 questions in English and Spanish. Each version—either the English or the Spanish—can be used alone—to measure proficiency in one of the two languages. For this study, the English version was used alone, to which two pictures and six questions were added to increase the opportunities for the children to use certain functors as required by the research methods used in this study.

The administration of the BSM is like chatting with a child about some pleasant pictures. There are no "correct" answers in a conversation of this kind. Different answers to the same questions are expected since children have different backgrounds and perceive the pictures differently. For example, in answer to the question "Which one is he?" one child might say, "He's the fat guy"; another might say, "The big man"; another "The father"; or even, "She's the mother." These are all recorded as the child says them. In effect, the BSM only looks at the degree of proficiency with which the child uses the structures he offers in response to the questions. The questions are constructed so that certain structure types will be almost unavoidable in the child's responses. For example, pointing to a very fat cartoon character, the investigator asks: "Why is he so fat?" Most children offer some form of "Because (s)he eat(s) too much." Thus, one can look to see how the child forms simple finite clauses (word order, gender, number and case for the pronoun, agreement for the verb, the form of the qualifier, etc.). However, less common responses such as "He no do exercise" are also valid data and are coded for the structures the child offered. The aim of the BSM is to elicit natural speech from children, not specific responses.

Having personally administered the BSM to some 800 children, we can confidently report that the children became so absorbed with the content of the "BSM conversation" that even those who could produce only a minimal amount of L2 speech were eager to express their thoughts and opinions about the pictures.

The BSM was administered in the schools, usually in an empty classroom, sometimes in a quiet corner of the regular classroom. The "conversations" were taperecorded, and in addition, the child's responses were written down along with the child's non-verbal gestures that were relevant to the meaning of the utterances. All the written responses were checked against the tape recordings.

Scoring procedures

The 11 functors regularly elicited from the children appear in Table 22-1.

Pronoun case: Regularly elicited were the pairs *he-him, they-them,* and less frequently, *she-her*. These were scored for case whenever they appeared, i.e. in subject position, in indirect or direct object position, and immediately following prepositions. Nominative or accusative pronouns were not scored separately. However, the number of occasions for both forms were about the same. (*It* and *you*, of course, cannot be scored for case as the form remains the same in all positions.)

      Pronoun number and gender were also scored, but they were eliminated from this study for the following reasons. For pronoun number in English, one deals only with singular or plural. As it turned out, the singular pronouns *he-him, she-her,* and *it* were much more frequent than the corresponding plural pair *they-them* (*we-us* not elicited). Since we did not keep a separate tally of singular and plural, but lumped them together under "pronoun number," the data could not be used to make any conclusions about the acquisition of pronoun number.

      Pronoun gender includes masculine (*he-him*), feminine (*she-her*), and neuter (*it*). However, the masculine pronouns were more frequent than the feminine and

Table 22-1   The 11 functors

Functors	Structures	Examples
Pronoun case	Pron-(Aux)-(Neg)-V-(Pron)	*He* doesn't like *him*
Article	$(Prep)\text{-}Det\text{-}(Adj)\text{-} \left\{ \begin{array}{c} N \\ Pron \end{array} \right\} \left\{ \pm \right\} Poss \right\} (N)$	in *the* fat guy's house
Singular Copula	$\left\{ \begin{array}{c} NP \\ Pron \end{array} \right\} \text{-}(be)\text{-} \left\{ \begin{array}{c} Adj \\ NP \end{array} \right\}$	*He's* fat
-ing	$\left(\left\{ \begin{array}{c} NP \\ Pron \end{array} \right\} \right)\text{-}(be)\text{-}V_{+ing}$	(He's) mopp*ing*
Plural	NP_{+pl}	window*s*
Singular Auxiliary	$\left\{ \begin{array}{c} NP \\ Pron \end{array} \right\} \text{-}be\text{-}V_{+ing}$	She*'s* dancing
Past regular	$\left\{ \begin{array}{c} NP \\ Pron \end{array} \right\} \text{-}(have)\text{-}V_{+pst}\text{-} \left\{ \begin{array}{c} NP \\ Pron \end{array} \right\}$	He clos*ed* it
Past irregular	$\left\{ \begin{array}{c} NP \\ Pron \end{array} \right\} \text{-}V_{+pst}\text{-}\left(\left\{ \begin{array}{c} NP \\ Pron \end{array} \right\} \right)$	He *stole* it
Long plural	NP_{+pl}	house*s*
Possessive	$Det\text{-}(Adj)\text{-}N_{+poss}\text{-}(N)$	the king*'s*
3rd person singular	$\left\{ \begin{array}{c} NP \\ Pron_{+sing} \end{array} \right\} \text{-}V_{+tns}\text{-}(Adv)$	he eat*s* too much

neuter pronouns combined, and since masculine, feminine, and neuter were not tallied separately this information could not be used to make conclusions about the acquisition of pronoun gender in general.

Article: Following Brown, both *a* and *the* were combined under the general category "article." The linguistic context in which the articles were most often elicited were prepositional phrases, noun phrases, and adjective and possessive NP constructions.

Copula: Singular and plural copulas were tallied separately, but present and past were lumped together under these categories. (Past copulas were very infrequent). As it turned out, the plural copula was elicited too infrequently to be used in this study. Therefore we used only the singular copula. In scoring, it became very important to note *back-to-back* "s's." In such cases it is impossible to tell where the "s" belongs. For example, in "He's so fat" one cannot be sure whether the copula is present or not in conversational speech. Thus, all cases of *back-to-back* "s's" were omitted from the tally.

-ing: -ing was tallied for any progressive tense, whether it was present, past, or future progressive. Gerunds were not included in the tally.

Plural: Under this category only the "short plural" was included, the *-s* (both /s/ and /z/ allomorphs) attached to nouns such as *door-s, window-s*. The short plural was tallied separately as there is evidence that it is acquired well before the long form (*-es*), (D.C. and L.F.S. Natalicio 1971). Here again, cases of back-to-back "s's" were eliminated from the tally (e.g. "He have windows *so* he can see").

Auxiliary: As in the case of the copula, the singular and plural were tallied separately, but present and past were combined under each category. As with the copula, the plural auxiliaries were infrequent and thus only the singular auxiliary was included in this study. Back-to-back "s's" were eliminated (e.g. *He's sleeping.*).

Past regular: All allomorphs of the past regular (/t/, /d/, and /əd/) were included. In addition to scoring *-ed* on weak verbs when it was required, *-ed* was also scored as correct when it appeared on strong verbs, such as *eated, tooked,* etc., as it showed clearly that the child had acquired the past *-ed* rule, and was simply applying it to exceptional cases. (See Past Irregular below.) The *-ed* was disregarded in cases of back-to-back stops, for the same reason back-to-back "s's" were disregarded. For example, in "He clos*ed the* door" it is not possible to tell where the stop belongs—on the end of "close" or the beginning of the article.

Past irregular: These included only main verbs, such as *ate, stole, bit,* and *fell.* Auxiliaries (*were, was,* etc.) were not included in this tally, and neither were past participles such as *gone.* In cases where a child offered "eated," past irregular was scored as a misformation, and past regular was scored as correct.

Long plural: These included all cases where the plural allomorph /əd/ was required, e.g. *houses, noses,* and *fishes.*

Possessive: Only the possessive marker *'s* on nouns was included in this tally, even though we had originally also tallied for possessive pronouns separately. However, the problem of distinguishing *he's* from *his,* since some children pronounced both the same, prohibited use of this data. Occasions of *hers* were too infrequent to permit any analysis.

3rd person singular: These were scored whenever a singular noun or pronoun appeared in subject position immediately followed by a main verb (*does* and *has*) used as main verbs were not included in the tally. Again, cases where back-to-back "s" obtained were disregarded from the tally (e.g. "He eats so much").

Data analysis

So far, there have been no cross-sectional studies of natural sequences of L2 acquisition. Consequently we developed new methods of analysis appropriate both for a cross-sectional design, and for L2 speech. In this study we used three different methods of analysis to arrive at a single acquisition sequence. The use of three methods permits us to report our results with confidence.

These methods are described in some detail below, and readers who are more interested in the results than in the methods used to obtain them should disregard the statistical detail in those descriptions.

All our methods of analysis include two core notions adopted from Brown's L1 research: 1) "obligatory occasion" and 2) the scoring of each obligatory occasion as a test item.

Obligatory occasions: Most verbal utterances that consist of more than one morpheme create occasions where certain functors are required. For example, in the utterance "She is dancing" a mature native speaker of English would never omit the functor *-ing*, because it is obligatory that *-ing* be attached to any verb in English when expressing a present progressive action. When a child speaks a language he is still learning, he will create *obligatory occasions* for functors in his utterances, but he may not furnish the required forms. He may omit them, as in "he like hamburgers," where the 3rd person present indicative is missing, or he may misform them, as in "They do hungry," where something was supplied for the copula, but it wasn't quite the right "thing."

Scoring of obligatory occasions: Given this notion of "obligatory occasions," one can use the natural utterances children offer, and at the same time precisely quantify the degree of functor acquisition:

> . . . one can set an acquisition criterion not simply in terms of output but in terms of output-where-required. Each obligatory context can be regarded as a kind of test item which the child passes by supplying the required morpheme or fails by supplying none or one that is not correct. This performance measure, the percentage of morphemes supplied in obligatory contexts, should not be dependent on the topic of conversation or the character of the interaction (Brown 1973:255).

Treating each obligatory occasion for a functor as a "test item," each item was scored as follows:

no functor supplied	= 0 (She's dance___)
misformed functor supplied	= 1 (She's dan*ces*)
correct functor supplied	= 2 (She's danc*ing*)

Group score method

The method bears this label because the group of children for whom an acquisition sequence is to be determined, e.g. the 55 Chinese children in our sample, receives one single score for each grammatical morpheme. The group score for a particular functor is obtained by computing a ratio whose denominator is the sum of all obligatory occasions (where each occasion is worth two points) for that morpheme across all the children in the group, and the numerator is the sum of the scores for each obligatory occasion of that morpheme across all children (see paragraph on scoring obligatory occasions above), and multiplying the resulting quotient by 100.

To illustrate the method, let us take five utterances produced by three children and compute the group score for the Past Irregular.

	Past Irregular	
	Raw Score	Occasion
Child 1: He *eated* it.	1	2
This man *taked* it away.	1	2
Child 2: He *bite* it.	0	2
Child 3: He *stole* it.	2	2
The dog *took* it.	2	2
	6	10

$$\text{Group Score} = \frac{6}{10} \times 100 = \underline{\underline{60}}$$

The functors were then ranked according to *decreasing group score* to yield a sequence of acquisition. Sequences of acquisition were obtained for the Chinese and for the Spanish children separately. The comparison of these two sequences was determined by a Spearman rank order correlation and is illustrated in Figure 22-1.

The advantage of this method is that even a child who has just one obligatory occasion for a morpheme in his speech corpus is admitted into "the group." The assumption made is that the error introduced in using only one obligatory occasion from a child whose performance may be variable, will be minimized by the size of the sample. For example, a child may have one occasion for a functor and miss it, but another child might only have one occasion and provide it. In both cases, the children might be in the process of acquiring the functor in question, meaning that they sometimes supply it, and sometimes not. However, their scores should tend to "even out" when the sample is large enough.

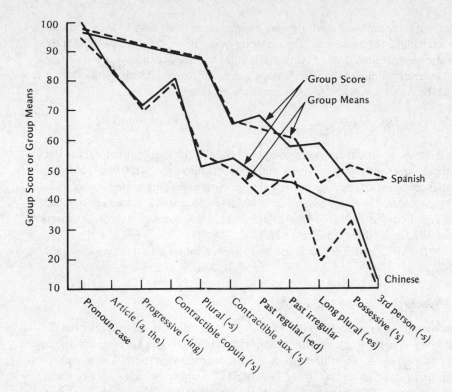

Figure 22-1. Comparison of L2 sequences obtained by the group score and the group means methods.

The potential weakness of the method is that variable performance is indeed a fact in syntax acquisition. When a functor is not yet fully acquired, the child sometimes supplies it and sometimes not. Thus the contribution of only one obligatory occasion by a child to the group corpus may not accurately reflect that child's degree of acquisition, and the statistical assumption that a large sample would in the end iron out that inaccuracy is still a real risk. Thus, the Group Means Method was designed to correct for that weakness.

Group Means Method

To reduce the effect of variability, the children who had fewer than three obligatory occasions for the morpheme in question were eliminated from the sample on which a functor score for that morpheme was computed. For example, if a child had two obligatory occasions for the long plural, but three or more for the other ten morphemes, that child would be excluded from the long plural computation, but not from the others. For each child who had three or more obligatory occasions of a functor, a functor score was computed. (For a similar procedure see J. and P. de Villiers 1973.) The functor score, like the group functor score, is obtained by computing a ratio whose denominator is the sum of the child's scores for each obligatory occasion. The resulting quotient was multiplied by 100 to yield a whole number. For example, if a child had six occasions for the copula and correctly supplied the copula three times, misformed it twice and omitted it once, his functor score would be computed as follows:

$$\text{functor score}_{cop} = \frac{2+2+2+1+1+0}{12} = \frac{8}{12} = .67 \times 100 = 67$$

Mean functor scores were computed for each of the 11 functors, for the entire sample, and for the Chinese and Spanish children separately. Acquisition sequences were obtained by ranking the functors according to *decreasing mean functor scores*. The comparison of the Chinese and Spanish sequences obtained by both methods for each group were determined by Spearman rank order correlations and are illustrated in Figure 22-1.

The sample sizes for each method for each functor are tabulated in Table 22-2.

The Syntax Acquisition Index (SAI)

This method is a variation on one used in first language acquisition research (J. and P. de Villiers 1973). For the reader who is familiar with L1 research, the SAI is a variation of the de Villiers' Method I for ordering functors: "The morphemes were first ranked according to the lowest MLU sample at which each morpheme first occurred in 90% or more of the obligatory contexts. When more than one morpheme reached this criterion at the same MLU, the ranks were tied" (J. and P. de Villiers 1973). The SAI replaces MLU as an acquisition index, while the 90%

Table 22-2   Samples for group score and group means methods

Functor	3 or more oblig. occasions (Group Means Method)	1 or 2 oblig. occasions	Totals (Group Score Method)
	Number of children who had:		
Pronoun case	115	0	115
Article	115	0	115
Progressive -ing	103	12	115
Copula	92	20	112
Plural	115	0	115
Auxiliary	40	54	94
Past regular	35	55	90
Past irregular	106	9	115
Long plural	41	70	111
Possessive	67	48	115
3rd person	52	50	102

acquisition criterion is retained, with the refinement of giving the child "half credit" for a misformed functor. MLU was not used as the acquisition index as it is inappropriate for older children learning a second language.

The SAI is an acquisition index borrowed from the experimental BSM scoring system. It is based on the assumption that it is relatively easy to tell what structure the child offered within the context of the "BSM conversation," even when part of it is absent or misformed. The questions are not only highly structured and specific, but the pictures to which the investigator points suggests the questions in many cases. We found that children who were just beginning to speak relied heavily on gesturing and pointing to the pictures while communicat-ing. For example, to "Why does he live there?" one child pointed to the picture of the fat man and that of the fat house and said "He in here." And whether this is interpreted as "He lives/goes/belongs in here," the structure is still the same. There are times, however, when it is impossible to determine what structure the child offered—as in "He who the fat skinny." Such cases are omitted from consideration altogether. In the event that there is more than one grammatical option available when interpreting a child's response, the shorter option is always chosen in an attempt to stay as close as possible to what the child said so as to

Table 22-3   Syntax-acquisition-index method to determine order of acquisition

SAI	Case	Art	Ing	Cop	Plu	Aux	Pastr	Pasti	Pos	LPlu	3rd
100-96 +acquired	9	7	7	7	9	3	5	8	3	3	1
−acquired	0	2	0	0	0	0	1	0	1	5	2
95-90 +acquired	26	23	20	21	20	6	(5)	7	8	(3)	(5)
−acquired	0	3	5	2	6	2	9	19	8	10	6
89-85 +acquired	18	13	14	12	12	1	0	0	2	0	0
−acquired	0	5	2	2	6	4	3	18	11	7	9
84-80 +acquired	13	7	9	7	4	3	0	(1)	(1)	0	0
−acquired	1	8	4	6	11	2	3	13	6	6	8
79-75 +acquired	17	12	4	7	(3)	1	0	0	0	0	0
−acquired	0	5	11	9	14	5	1	16	12	6	8
74-70 +acquired	10	4	2	2	0	(1)	0	0	0	—	0
−acquired	0	6	7	7	10	5	3	10	8	—	6
69-65 +acquired	9	2	4	0	0	0	0	0	0	0	0
−acquired	0	7	4	6	9	4	3	7	4	1	4
64-60 + acquired	2	(2)	0	(1)	0	0	0	0	0	—	0
−acquired	2	3	5	2	5	3	2	4	0	—	3
59-55 + acquired	1	0	(1)	—	0	—	—	0	0	—	—
−acquired	0	1	0	—	1	0	—	1	1	—	—
54-47 +acquired	(3)	0	0	0	0	—	—	0	0	—	—
−acquired	0	5	3	1	5	—	—	2	2	—	—
Total	111	115	103	92	115	40	35	106	67	41	52

give him the benefit of the doubt. For example, the response "For he fat" (to "Why does he live there?") is interpreted as "because he's fat" rather than as "because he's a fat man."

Given that the grammatical form of a child's utterance can be determined for the BSM corpus (following the conditions specified above), it became feasible to think of an overall syntax acquisition index in terms of *how much of the grammatical structure that the child offered in his utterance was wellformed*. The quantification of this notion consists of 1) assigning points to the grammatical version of the child's response and 2) subtracting points from this grammatical form to reflect the still "developing" parts of the child's utterance to obtain a value for it. A system of weighted morphemes is used to assign point values to utterances. The syntax acquisition index is the quotient resulting from computing a ratio whose numerator is the sum of the values of all the utterances of the child and whose denominator is the sum of the values of all the corresponding grammatical forms, multiplied by 100. For example, if the child response value is 80 and the grammatical form value is 120, the SAI would equal (80/120) (100), or 67.

The SAI's for our sample ranged from 47-100. These indexes were arbitrarily divided into 5-point ranges for this analysis, except for the lowest range. Then, the number of children who had acquired a particular functor were tallied for each 5-point range and for each functor. The criterion of acquisition was as follows: the functor is acquired if it is used 90% correctly in occasions where that particular functor was required (see Group Means Method above for description of computation).

The last step in this analysis is to determine the lowest SAI range in which at least one child had acquired a given functor. The functors were ranked according to the lowest SAI range within which each functor was first acquired by at least one child. For example, to determine the sequence of Copula, Auxiliary, and Past Irregular, the first step is to assign each functor the value of the lowest SAI range within which it was first acquired by at least one child, using the following data:

Number of children

SAI range	Copula	Auxiliary	Past irregular
84-80 acquired	.	.	1
not acquired			13
79-75 acquired	.	.	0
not acquired			16
74-70 acquired	.	1	0
not acquired		5	10
69-65 acquired	.	0	0
not acquired		4	7
64-60 acquired	1	0	0
not acquired	2	3	4

Table 22-4   L2 rank orders (sequences) obtained

Group Score Method	Group Means Method	SAI Method
1 case	1 case	1 case
2 Article	2 Article	2 Copula
3 Copula	3.5 { Copula	3.5 { Article
4 -Ing	{ -Ing	{ -Ing
5 Plural	5 Plural	5 Auxiliary
6 Auxiliary	6 Auxiliary	6 Plural
7 Past-reg	7 Past-reg	7.5 { Past-irreg
8 Past-irreg	8.5 { Past-irreg	{ Possessive
9 Long Plural	{ Possessive	{ Past-reg
10 Possessive	10 Long Plural	10 { Long Plural
11 3rd Person	11 3rd Person	{ 3rd Person

Thus, Copula = 64.60, Auxiliary = 74.70, Past Irregular = 84.80, and the resulting sequence is Copula-Auxiliary-Past Irregular. All 11 functors were ranked in this manner. The resulting L2 sequence is compared with the sequences obtained by the other two methods, again using Spearman's rank order correlation. Rank orders for each method are reported in Table 22-4.

RESULTS

We have waited long and labored patiently to answer the question: Is there a natural sequence of L2 acquisition common to children of diverse backgrounds, in particular to Chinese and Spanish-speaking children learning English? The results of our efforts are most rewarding.

1. *The sequences of acquisition of 11 functors obtained for Spanish and Chinese children are virtually the same.* Using two methods—the Group Score and the Group Means methods—acquisition sequences were obtained for 60 Spanish children and 55 Chinese children separately. The results are illustrated in Figure 22-1.

As Figure 22-1 illustrates, the contours of the Spanish and Chinese children are strikingly similar, for both methods used in the comparison. Statistically, the similarity is shown by almost perfect Spearman rank order correlations ($p < .001$) for the sequences obtained:

Spanish with Chinese (Group Score Method)	+.95
Spanish with Chinese (Group Means Method)	+.96
Group Score Method with Group Means Method (Chinese)	+.98
Group Score Method with Group Means Method (Spanish)	+.96

These extremely high correlations surpassed the expectations of even those of us who did expect a similarity of sequence (as predicted by the creative construction account of L2 acquisition).

2. *The same sequence of acquisition of 11 functors, obtained by three different methods, provides strong evidence that children exposed to natural L2 speech acquire certain structures in a universal order.* The similarity of sequences reported above justified the use of a third method—the SAI Method described in the previous section—which combined both Chinese and Spanish children to obtain a single sequence for the entire sample. The results of the SAI analysis are reported in Table 22-3, where the direction of the circles from the lower left hand corner to the upper right illustrate the order of acquisition obtained. In order to compare this sequence with that obtained by the Group Score and Group Means methods, the group score and the group means for each functor was obtained for the entire sample also. The resulting rank orders for the 11 functors are given in Table 22-4.

The correlation of the three rank orders are, again, remarkably high, as shown by the following Spearman correlation coefficients ($p < .001$):

Group Score with Group Means	+.98
Group Score with SAI	+.89
Group Means with SAI	+.91

In sum, the sequences of acquisition of 11 English functors for native Chinese- and Spanish-speaking children are virtually the same, as determined by three different methods of analysis.

CONCLUSION

It is difficult to write a conclusion for an investigation that has by no means ended. We have studied a small part of the L2 acquisition of English syntax—11 functors—in an effort to further display the creative construction process in child L2 acquisition. We have found that both Chinese- and Spanish-speaking children exposed to natural English peer speech acquired 11 functors in approximately the same order. Although only a fragment of English was studied, the results of this study provide a strong indication that universal cognitive mechanisms are the basis for the child's organization of a target language, and that it is the L2 system, rather than the L1 system that guides the acquisition process. The grammar of the 11 functors is wildly different in Chinese and Spanish, and both differ from English in certain ways. For example, Chinese does not express Copula at all, while Spanish does, yet both Chinese and Spanish children acquire Copula at about the same point in the sequence. Spanish plurals are expressed exactly as plurals are expressed in English, yet Plural appears midway in the acquisition sequence, not first, as one would expect if the child's L1 grammar were guiding the L2 process.

The obvious question—which we will not attempt to answer yet—now arises: What is the specific nature of the creative construction process? In other words, what characterizes universal language processing strategies? It would be very tempting to formulate strategies based on the acquisition sequence we obtained. However, we believe that "universal strategies" should be sufficiently abstract and comprehensive so as to predict acquisition orders based on different types of language input, such as languages other than English, or types of speech exposure other than natural speech. For example, if a child is exposed only to a list of vocabulary words and one or two syntactic structures, the resulting product— acquisition sequence—would be quite different from the sequence resulting from exposure to the entire basic framework of the target language, as in exposure to natural speech. Although the language processing strategies available to the child are the constants in the language acquisition process, the language data to which the child is exposed may vary. As the speech product is the result of the interaction between the child and the input language, the product should reflect both, i.e. the product should not be constant if the language input varies significantly. Thus, acquisition sequences and error types should vary to the extent that the language input varies significantly; and "universal strategies" should predict all of those variations.

Realizing this, a major purpose of this study has been to stimulate the much needed research that is required before we can formulate L2 acquisition strategies with any confidence. For this reason, the research methods that have proved productive in our investigations were described in detail. Using these and other tools, it may become possible to systematically and efficiently explore the process of acquisition of different "second languages" in diverse learning environments. Such a research program is an enormous undertaking, but its potential for both theory and practice is even greater. It would bring us a little closer to deciphering the structure of a child's mind and in so doing, would provide the basis for the development of second language curricula that closely follow the child's own strategies for language acquisition.

Is There a 'Natural Sequence'

23

in Adult Second Language Learning? *

Nathalie Bailey, Carolyn Madden and Stephen D. Krashen,

*English Language Institute and Linguistics Department, Queens College and the
Graduate Center, City University of New York*

INTRODUCTION

Our literature on adult second language learners seems to show major, and dis-
quieting, differences. The diary studies reveal slow, if indeed any, acquisition of
grammatical morphemes, or semi-fossilization at various stages in the acquisition
process. Fluency, on the other hand, is eventually attained even without the
development of various grammatical markers. In the experimental studies, Snow's
findings allow us to paint a more optimistic picture of adult language learning.

It is easy to understand, then, the importance of the Bailey, Madden, &
Krashen study as the first large-scale experimental study of the adult learner's
acquisition of morphemes. Replicating the procedure used by Dulay & Burt for
child learners, Bailey, Madden & Krashen were able to directly compare the order
of acquisition of grammatical morphemes for adult and child learners.

This study has since served as valuable data in other ways as well. Not the
least is the evidence it has given Krashen in support of his model of adult second
language learning. While the Monitor Model is still in the development phase, the
substantial preliminary papers have stimulated a variety of studies on the ability
of adults to monitor their language production (see Krashen & Pon, 1975;
Stafford and Covitt, 1976).

Perhaps the differences shown in the experimental studies as compared with the diary studies can be directly related to formal language instruction. However, for a larger theoretical framework in which to consider these differences, the reader is referred once again to Schumann's paper on social and psychological distance factors as well as to the brief description of the Krashen model in the *USC-UCLA Second Language Acquisition Forum Report*.

Reprinted with the permission of the authors and the publishers of *Language Learning*, 1974, *24*, 2, 235-243.

* * *

On the basis of intensive analysis of the speech of three children as well as the study of available literature on child language acquisition, R. Brown (1973) concluded that the order of acquisition of certain functors (or grammatical morphemes) in English is invariant; despite differing rates of first language acquisition, there seems to be a surprisingly uniform developmental course that all children take in learning English. Brown analyzed the speech of three children longitudinally, and noted the presence or absence of each functor in each "obligatory context," that is, in each locus where adult syntax would require the presence of the functor. A functor was considered acquired when it was supplied in 90% of obligatory contexts for three successive recording sessions. A slightly different method was used by de Villiers and de Villiers (1973) in a cross-sectional study; they simply ranked functors according to relative accuracy in obligatory contexts. This alternative method correlated significantly with Brown's results.

Dulay and Burt (1973), studying a subset of the 14 functors Brown dealt with, presented evidence that 5 to 8 year old children learning English as a second language also show a high degree of agreement with each other with respect to degree of accuracy of functors. Dulay and Burt concluded that "there does seem to be a common order of acquisition for certain structures in L2 acquisition" (p. 256); however, the actual difficulty ordering found by Dulay and Burt was not the same as that found in first language acquisition studies (see Table 23-1).

To explain this difference, Dulay and Burt note that the order of acquisition posited for older learners is not affected by the cognitive and conceptual development the first language learning child undergoes while learning his first language.

Dulay and Burt's findings are consistent with another observation reported in the same paper (Dulay and Burt 1973); the overwhelming majority of errors made by children in learning English as a second language are "developmental" rather than "interference," that is, they are similar in kind to errors made by children learning English as a first language and not the result of interference from the learners' first language habits. Dulay and Burt conclude from these results that first and second language learning in children involves similar kinds of processing of linguistic data. Specifically, the process of learning English as a

Table 23-1   Difficulty order of functors [1,3]

First language learners (de Villiers and de Villiers, 1973)	Second language learners (Dulay and Burt, 1973)[2]
1. plural (-s)	1. plural (-s)
2. progressive (-ing)	2. progressive (-ing)
3. past irregular	3. contractible copula
4. articles (a, the)	4. contractible auxiliary
5. contractible copula	5. articles (a, the)
6. possessive ('s)	6. past irregular
7. third person singular (-s)	7. third person singular (-s)
8. contractible auxiliary	8. possessive ('s)

[1] de Villiers and de Villiers (1973) studied 14 functors in all; included here are the eight functors covered in both studies.

[2] Taken from Dulay and Burt's largest sub-group ("Sacramento").

[3] Difficulty orders from the two studies do not correlate significantly (rho = .59, n.s.).

second language must involve the "creative construction" and testing of hypotheses about the target language.

Recent studies have emphasized that errors made by adults in second language learning are to a large extent (1) common to learners with different mother tongues, and (2) analyzable as incorrect hypotheses about the target language (Richards 1971a, 1971b, Buteau 1970, Duskova 1969, Bailey and Madden 1973). Such results encourage the hypothesis that adult second language learning may also involve a natural sequence of acquisition. One would not expect the adult sequence to match that of the child's learning of his first language. Rather, since adults are more similar to 5 to 8 year olds with respect to cognitive maturity, the adult order should be closer to that of the older child learning English as a second language. In this study, the following two hypotheses will be tested:

(1) adults learning English as a second language will show agreement with each other in the relative difficulty of functors in English.

(2) the adult rankings will be similar to that of the child learning English as a second language, rather than to that of children learning English as a first language.

PROCEDURE

Seventy-three adult subjects (ages 17 to 55) were tested. The subjects were members of eight classes in ESL (the first four levels of each of two programs) at Queens College, New York. One program, the English Language Institute program, is an intensive, all day program for foreign students preparing to study in American colleges, and the other, the Continuing Education program, is a four hour per week adult education course. Generally, the adult education subjects had more exposure to English outside the classroom. The subjects were also classified as Spanish or non-Spanish speaking. The Spanish speaking group consisted of 33 students and the non-Spanish group consisted of 40 students representing eleven different mother tongues (Greek, Persian, Italian, Turkish, Japanese, Chinese, Thai, Afghan, Hebrew, Arabic, and Vietnamese).

As in Dulay and Burt's (1973) study, language data was elicited with the Bilingual Syntax Measure (BSM) (Burt, Dulay, and Hernández 1973). Despite the fact that the Bilingual Syntax Measure was originally designed for children it was successfully used with adults here. The BSM consists of seven colored cartoons accompanied by preliminary questions and testing questions. The preliminary questions are designed to insure the subjects' knowledge of lexical items. The testing questions are designed to elicit the use of the eight selected English functors listed in Table 23-1.

Each subject was tested individually by a team of two undergraduate students from the Queens College Linguistics Department. One E showed a picture to the S, asked the pertinent preliminary questions, then proceeded to the test questions. The second E recorded the S's answers to the test questions on the BSM answer sheet.

As in previous studies, accuracy of usage was determined by the ratio of the correctly formed and used functors to the obligatory occasions for them. Following Dulay and Burt (1973) a correctly used functor was scored as one point, a misformed functor as .5 and a missing functor as zero, e.g.

They   birds   (missing functor = 0)
They is   birds   (misformed functor = .5)
They are birds   (correct functor = 1)

RESULTS

Pearson product-moment correlations were performed on the relative accuracy of use of the eight grammatical morphemes between Spanish and non-Spanish speakers and among the eight instruction levels.

There was a significant correlation between relative accuracies of function words for Spanish and non-Spanish speakers ($r = .926$, $p < .005$, one-tailed test). The scores are portrayed in Figure 23-1. Correlations among the eight instruction groups are given in Table 23-2. There was a high degree of agreement as to the relative difficulty of the functors among all groups, with the exception of Level 3 in the English Language Institute program, which may be due to a ceiling effect caused by a high level of English language proficiency in this group. Percentages of accuracy are given in Table 23-3.

To test Hypothesis 2 adult relative accuracies were compared to Dulay and Burt's (1973) data for 5-8 year old children learning English as a second language. Relative accuracies for their "Sacramento" group (consisting of 96 children with

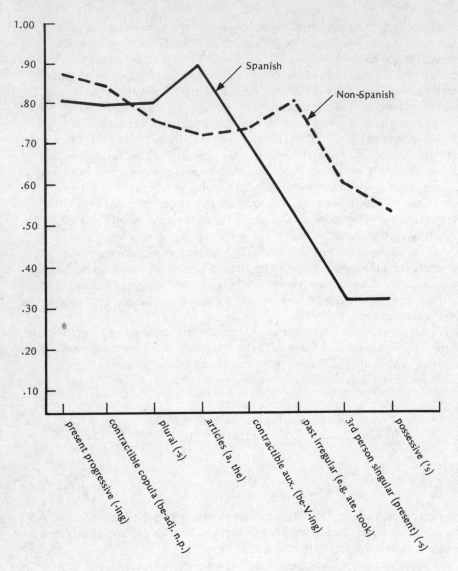

Figure 23-1. Comparison of Spanish and non-Spanish adults; relative accuracies for 8 functors

a relatively large amount of exposure to English) correlated significantly for both parametric and non-parametric measures ($r = .893$, $p < .005$, one tailed test, rho = .91, $p < .01$). Also, correlation between our subjects and Dulay and Burt's "San Ysidro" group (26 Mexican children exposed to English only in school) was significant ($r = .97$, $p < .005$, one tail, rho = .94, $p < .01$). The correlation between the adults and Dulay and Burt's "East Harlem" group (30 Puerto Rican

Table 23-2 Correlations between groups of ESL students for function word accuracy

	ELI 1[1]	ELI 2	ELI 3	ELI 4	CON ED 1[2]	CON ED 2A	CON ED 2B
ELI 2	.85[b]						
ELI 3	.53	.79[b]					
ELI 4	.93[b]	.82[b]	.51				
CON ED 1	.78[a]	.83[b]	.43	.69[a]			
CON ED 2A	.93[b]	.86[b]	.49	.88[b]	.90[b]		
CON ED 2B	.84[b]	.68[a]	.16	.78[a]	.84[b]	.93[b]	
CON ED 3	.71[a]	.80[b]	.52	.69[a]	.84[b]	.63[a]	.94[b]

[1]English Language Institute
[2]Continuing Education Program

a: p < .05 (one-tailed)
b: p < .01 (one-tailed)

Table 23-3 Percentage of accuracy for adult ESL learners in eight functors

	ing	cont cop	plural	art	cont aux	past irr	third per	poss
ELI 1	.84	.85	.72	.80	.77	.61	.34	.31
ELI 2	.87	.77	.71	.59	.55	.48	.38	.38
ELI 3	.90	.90	.88	.70	.66	.82	.65	.72
ELI 4	.90	.88	.81	.82	.81	.77	.54	.47
CON ED 1	.82	.80	.69	.81	.50	.25	.47	.21
CON ED 2A	.63	.64	.66	.83	.76	.13	.21	.13
CON ED 2B	.90	.88	.94	.93	.75	.40	.28	.19
CON ED 3	.89	.82	.88	.79	.33	.45	.32	.36

children in a "balanced bilingual program") did not quite reach statistical significance with the Pearson r but did with the Spearman rho (r = .60, p < .10, rho = .88, p < .01). Figure 23-2 exhibits the relative accuracies of the four groups. The lower correlation with the East Harlem group may reflect the fact that Black English is often the target language for these children since their main divergence from the order of the other two groups is due to lower accuracy in the use of the copula and contractible auxiliary, commonly deleted in Black English.

As predicted, the adult order did not correlate significantly with relative accuracies for functors reported by de Villiers and de Villiers (1973) for children (rho = .57, n.s.).

DISCUSSION

Despite the differences in adult learners in amount of instruction, exposure to English, and mother tongue, there is a high degree of agreement as to the relative

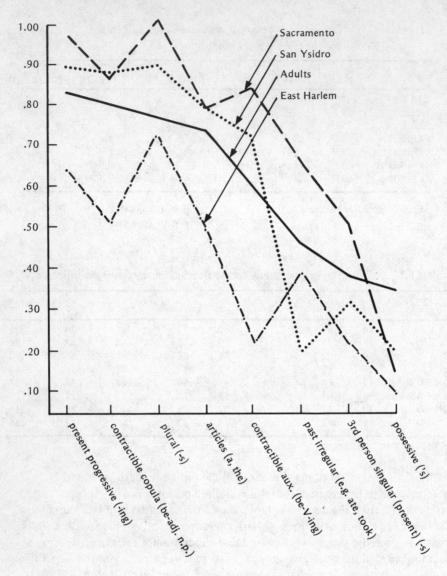

Figure 23-2. Comparison of child and adult relative accuracies for 8 functors.

difficulty of the set of grammatical morphemes examined here, supporting Hypothesis 1. This result in conjunction with error analysis research, indicates that adults use common strategies for second language learning. In addition, if relative difficulty corresponds to order of acquisition as implied by de Villiers and de Villiers' (1973) results with children, this result also suggests a common order of acquisition for functors in adults.

Comparison with Dulay and Burt's data reveals that relative accuracy in adults is quite similar to the relative accuracies shown by children learning English as a second language for the same functors, supporting Hypothesis 2. Thus, while adults may in general not achieve the level of performance achieved by first language learners or children learning English as a second language, and may need the isolation of linguistic structures and feedback provided by the classroom, these results indicate that they process linguistic data in ways similar to younger learners.

Since subjects with different first languages performed similarly, the results are also consistent with findings that errors in second language learning are not all the result of interference from the first language. Along with studies of errors in second language learning cited above, this argues against any strong version of the contrastive analysis hypothesis. While casual observation affirms that errors due to mother tongue interference do occur in second language learning in adults, our data imply that a major source of errors is intra- rather than inter-lingual, and are due to the use of universal language processing strategies.

Further evidence may be found for the use of universal language processing strategies in the study of aphasia, a non-interference situation. A very recent cross-sectional study of non-fluent aphasia (de Villiers 1974) reports a relative order of difficulty in functors nearly identical to that found here for adults learning English as a second language (for those six functors covered in both studies, rho = .94, p < .05). There thus seem to be two invariant orderings for functors: one for children learning English as a first language, and the other shared by children learning English as a second language, adults learning English as a second language, and adult non-fluent aphasics. It remains to be determined what combinations of factors account for this apparent uniformity in adult processing and why the adult order differs from the child's.

Finally, we need to consider the role of the classroom. Dulay and Burt (1973) conclude that their findings of an invariant order of acquisition in children learning English as a second language and its implications for a developmental theory imply that "we should leave the learning to the children" (p. 257); teaching syntax is not necessary. It may be the case that second language learning in children can effectively take place in the absence of a formal linguistic environment. The conclusion, however, while possibly correct, does not follow from their results on relative accuracy of function words. Adults, as demonstrated here, show nearly the same rankings and a similar degree of invariance, and as empirical studies (Krashen and Seliger, 1976, Krashen, Seliger and Hartnett, 1974, Krashen, Jones, Zelinski, and Usprich, in press) and years of experience in language learning and teaching show, instruction is directly related to English language proficiency in adults, while exposure to English in informal environments is not.

We are thus faced with an interesting conclusion: adults seem to profit from instruction, an instruction that often presents the grammatical morphemes in an order different from that implied here. An interesting and testable hypothesis is that the most effective instruction is that which follows the observed order of difficulty, one with a "natural syllabus." We will be prepared for such an experiment when we confirm the implied sequence longitudinally, and discover which aspects of language follow a universal sequence, and understand what factors determine such a sequence.

Note

We thank Helen Cairns, Miriam Eisenstein and the students from Linguistics 19, Queens College, Spring 1973 for their help.

An Explanation

24

for the Morpheme Accuracy Order[1]

of Learners of English as a Second Language

Diane E. Larsen-Freeman, *University of California, Los Angeles*

INTRODUCTION

Perhaps the most detailed 'baby diary' of all time is that written by Wilhelm Preyer in the 1870s. The Child Study Movement of the late 19th century culminated 25 years later in the next most influential book in child language by Stern & Stern in 1907. The period between these two great studies has often been called the Golden Age of child language. And during all that time, the arguments about the importance of frequency, the arguments about external and internal cause raged constantly. Stern & Stern's paper on the language of children finally defined what they felt was the proper position:

> We believe that the proper position is a synthesis. . . . In his form of speech a child learning to speak is neither a phonograph reproducing external sounds nor a sovereign creator of language. In terms of contents of his speech, he is neither a pure associative machine nor a sovereign constructor of concepts. Rather his speech is based on the continuing interaction of external impressions with internal systems which usually function unconsciously; it is thus the result of a constant 'convergence.' The detailed investigations pertaining to the development of speech and thought should determine the relative participation of both forces and also show how they accommodate each other. (Stern & Stern, *Die Kindersprache*. Trans. Lyon & Blumenthal, p. 87.)

Our notion now of the importance of frequency in second language acquisition incorporates this view. Yet we have had little notion of how important frequency might be as an explanation of the order in which various structures are learned. Few have tried to measure and compare frequencies in input and output data. Larsen-Freeman, in the following paper, has done just that in an attempt, as Stern & Stern suggest, to determine the relative participation of such forces in the acquisition process.

Second language acquisition researchers Dulay and Burt (1974a) found "virtually the same order of acquisition" of eleven English morphemes by young Chinese and Spanish-speaking ESL students as measured by the children's production of these morphemes in obligatory contexts in elicited speech.

Shortly thereafter, Bailey, Madden and Krashen (1974), utilizing the same procedure, corroborated this order of grammatical morphemes (using eight morphemes from a 1973 Dulay and Burt study) for adult ESL learners from disparate language backgrounds.

Speculations were made to account for the common morpheme order, but an acceptable explanation was not found.

Since these morpheme studies employed the Bilingual Syntax Measure (Burt, Dulay and Hernández, 1973) to elicit speech data, Larsen-Freeman was prompted to carry out her own investigation to discover if:

1. the same morpheme order would be found to exist if different data collection procedures were utilized; and,

2. the data from other collection procedures would be useful in helping to explain the morpheme order the Bilingual Syntax Measure (hereafter the BSM) consistently elicits.

A battery of five tasks—reading, writing, listening, imitating and speaking (the BSM) was administered to twenty-four adult learners of ESL. There were six subjects from each of four native-language backgrounds—Arabic, Japanese, Persian and Spanish. The data elicited by these tasks were scored for morpheme suppliance in obligatory contexts (Brown, 1973). The Group Score Method (Dulay and Burt, 1974a) was used to order the morphemes. To test for the effect of time and language instruction on morpheme ordering, this entire procedure was repeated after an interval of two months.

The results of this study showed individual variability and native language background to exert some influence on the way morphemes were ordered by language groups within a task. Despite these influences, significantly high Kendall's coefficients of concordance were found among the morpheme sequences produced by the various language groups for each task, thus confirming what previous researchers had reported, i.e., language background did not have a significant effect on the way ESL learners order English morphemes.

This same high degree of association determined for the morpheme orders produced by language groups within a task was not found when the morpheme sequences for the different tasks were compared. The morpheme sequences from the oral production tasks (speaking and imitating) did, however, correlate with that of Dulay and Burt (1974a) and with each other at both phases.

Table 24-1   Spearman rank correlation coefficients for ten morphemes

	Phase I	Phase II
Speaking Task/Imitating Task	.59[b]	.75[a]
Dulay and Burt 1974a/Speaking Task	.87[a]	.72[b]
Dulay and Burt 1974a/Imitating Task	.60[b]	.70[b]

[a] $p < .01$ [b] $p < .05$

     Since some of the findings of this study have already been dealt with elsewhere,[2] the remainder of this paper will focus on an attempt to explain why ESL learners consistently exhibit the oral production morpheme order that they do.

     In pursuit of an explanation (or explanations, as it is certainly feasible that more than one factor contributes to the morpheme sequence) for this common order, the data from the study just described were considered in light of conceivable determinants.

     One possible explanation for the similar oral production morpheme sequence is that the morphemes are ordered by the learners according to increasing grammatical complexity. It seems reasonable to expect that the more complex the morpheme, the less often a learner is likely to supply it accurately. Thus, for this explanation to be substantiated, the morpheme ranked first would have to be the simplest grammatically.

     In order to measure the syntactic complexity of morphemes, Brown (1973) adopted Transformational Grammar's "derivational theory of complexity." This theory would predict that given any two morphemes, the morpheme requiring fewer transformations in its derivation from the deep structure to the surface structure is the simpler syntactically. Brown modified this theory somewhat by employing a construct he termed "cumulative complexity." Cumulative complexity helps avoid the assumption that each transformation contributes a uniform increment of complexity.

     Brown used this modified measure of syntactic complexity to successfully explain the morpheme order he found for his three subjects—children learning English as their first language.

     Unfortunately, syntactic complexity is not a satisfactory explanation for the oral production morpheme order of ESL learners. Although the morphemes examined in the first and second language studies are comparable, the morpheme orders first and second language learners produce do not correlate. Thus, an explanation of the morpheme order produced by first language learners is not the answer to why ESL learners produce the morpheme order that they do.

     That learners order morphemes according to increasing semantic complexity seems also to be an implausible explanation for the morpheme order of second language learners, since Brown acknowledges that the evidence that enabled him to claim syntactic complexity as the cause for his subjects' morpheme acquisition order can be "alternatively interpreted as demonstrating that semantic complexity is a determinant of an order of acquisition" (1973:379).

A developing cognition in children which is manifest in their speech by their suppliance of certain morphemes more accurately than others seems a reasonable explanation for the morpheme sequence first language learners exhibit. Replication of such a sequence is hardly an enticing explanation for any order the adult second language learners produce since the orders of first and second language learners are so radically different.

Could it be, then, that the order found in second language acquisition is based on phonological complexity? This might help to account for why the different tasks in my study, some not phonic, produced different orders. But, this explanation, too, is not credible since morphemes with the same allomorphs are not clustered together, but possess diverse ranks in the morpheme sequence. Table 24-2 shows, for example, the short plural morpheme in the speaking task at Phase I is ranked fifth whereas the possessive morpheme (NP's), with identical phonological forms, occupies the tenth rank.

Perhaps the use of similar texts by second language learners is instrumental in giving rise to the common morpheme order. However, Bailey, Madden and Krashen found a high degree of agreement with regard to morpheme sequencing

Table 24-2   Rank order of morphemes on speaking and imitating tasks at both Phases

Phase	Morpheme	Speaking	Imitating
I.	cop	2	3
	prog	1	1
	aux	4	9
	art	3	2
	s. plu	5	8
	poss	10	10
	i. past	8	4
	3rd sing	7	7
	1. plu	9	5
	r. past	6	6
II.	cop	1	1
	prog	2	2
	aux	3	4
	art	4	3
	s. plu	5	8
	poss	6	10
	i. past	7	5
	3rd sing	8	7
	1. plu	9	6
	r. past	10	9

among the eight different classes from which the population sample for their study was drawn even though each had different teachers, different textbooks, different syllabi and were at different proficiency levels. Learner experience with particular language instruction does not seem to be a satisfactory explanation, then, either.

Even though the subjects learning ESL from the various morpheme studies represent different age groups, possibly they have similar attitudes or type of motivation. It is conceivable that shared effective factors might influence learner performance in similar ways. But a recent study by de Villiers (1974) provides challenging evidence to this explanation, too. She examined the speech of adult non-fluent (Broca) aphasics for the occurrence of fourteen morphemes. Of the eight morphemes which appeared regularly in the speech of the aphasics, six were identical to those Bailey, Madden and Krashen had studied in adult ESL learner speech. A highly significant correlation ($r = .94$, $< .01$) exists between the orders of these six morphemes by these two groups of adults.

While it is not impossible that aphasic adults and adult second language learners undergo a similar affective experience in speaking English, it is difficult to imagine that there is sufficient commonality between the two groups to account for almost identical morpheme orders.

Slobin (1971) has proposed "operating principles" to account for the order of acquisition of structures in children's language. He inferred these operating principles after a perusal of a vast amount of linguistic output. He alleged the operating principles existed as strategies in the minds of language learners. A typical operating principle might be: "Pay attention to the ends of words" (335). Although no one has as yet developed a hierarchy of operating principles (Dulay and Burt 1974b) from which successive ones could be applied when the conditions were appropriate, if an order of application of these principles were to be developed, this might help explain an acquisition sequence. At this point, however, it is premature to rely on operating principles as a solution to our investigation since the list is inadequate to explain any entire sequence, and since without an established hierarchy, a random application of the strategies would result in contradictory actions.

If underlying complexity, cognitive maturity, learner type and experience, and processing strategies all seem ineffectual by themselves to explain second language morpheme sequences, maybe an examination of the surface forms of the morphemes would be enlightening.

The progressive morpheme, for instance, was ranked among the highest morphemes. One reason for this might be its [+ syllable] feature which would give it a heightened saliency. Features of [± perceptual saliency] might influence the rank of a morpheme in the oral production tasks.

Perceptual saliency features of morphemes would include whether or not a morpheme were bound, stressed or a syllable. Other factors might be the length of a morpheme, its contractibility or whether or not any vowels it contains undergo vowel reduction in fast speech.

Finally, its position in a word if it is a bound morpheme and its position in a sequence, might affect its perceptibility. Although admittedly the amount and type of English input to the learner might vary according to the situation, there are probably stable characteristics of morphemes which would be cogent for all learners.

By now, however, the pattern should be patently clear: Perceptual saliency does not account for all the morpheme ranks. The copula, for instance, which presumably has low perceptual saliency, is ranked near the top of both the speaking and imitating task orders. There are examples from the other tasks, too, which defy an explanation based on perceptual saliency.

Another conceivable explanation based on the input to the learner is the frequency of occurrence of the various morphemes in native-speaker speech. Hatch (1975), for example, examined the English input a young ESL learner was receiving and noticed with a few exceptions, that the questions the learner was asked most frequently, he acquired first. While Hatch's observation should not be startling, it deserves attention because in the recent trend to disavow any connection between a developmental view of language acquisition and the old habit formation theory, we may have forfeited some valuable insights.

To test the frequency hypothesis, an examination was made of the number of obligatory contexts for the various morphemes in the transcripts of the subjects on the speaking task. (See Table 24-3.)

Indeed, the morphemes with the highest ranks, the article, auxiliary, progressive and copula, all seem to occur far more frequently than the other morphemes with the exception of the short plural morpheme which on the speaking task, at least, occupies a medial rank.

The reason the morpheme ranks obtained from the speaking task correlated with the number of times the morpheme was supplied in that task could be that when a subject has more opportunities to attempt a morpheme on a given task, incremental learning can take place. As a result, a score for a certain morpheme would increase in proportion to the number of times the morpheme is attempted.

However, another explanation is also plausible. Perhaps the frequency counts of morphemes on the speaking task reflect their actual occurrence in real communication. Thus, if a subject encountered certain morphemes more than others, he was likely to score higher on those morphemes, all other things being equal.

Since the frequency of occurrence of the morphemes was controlled in all but the speaking task, an independent measure of morpheme frequencies was needed. As there was no general morpheme frequency count available, the morpheme frequencies Brown (1973) determined for the three sets of native English-speaking parents of the subjects in his study were used. (See Table 24-4.) Brown's counts were made from transcripts of recordings taped during the periodic visits by researchers to the subjects' homes.

Since the plural morpheme in Brown's study was not divided into long and short forms as it was in the present study, nine morpheme frequencies in the parents' speech were summed. (See Table 24-5.) The two auxiliary and two copula

Table 24-3   Number of obligatory contexts for all subjects for ten morphemes at both Phases on speaking task

Morpheme	Phase I	Phase II
cop	108	116
prog	158	168
aux	129	147
art	397	428
s. plu	158	149
poss	59	67
i. past	91	97
3rd sing	81	82
1. plu	63	70
r. past	10	18

Table 24-4   Frequency of certain morphemes as listed in Brown's (1973) Table 52

Morpheme	Adam's Parents	Sarah's Parents	Eve's Parents
Uncon. cop	57	65	53
Con. cop	164	100	126
prog	65	28	67
Uncon. aux	35	5	16
con. aux	30	13	52
art	233	157	162
plu	57	57	33
poss	25	16	30
i. past	71	45	25
3rd sing	25	19	7
r. past	28	9	7

categories were combined as they were not scored separately in this study. The morphemes were ranked in descending order of frequency and Spearman rank correlation coefficients were computed between this order and second language acquisition researchers' order.

When the frequency order of morphemes based on the speech of the parents of Brown's subjects was compared with the morpheme order of second language acquisition researchers, significant correlations were found to exist. (See Table 24-6.)

Thus, the tentative conclusion is that morpheme frequency of occurrence in native-speaker speech is the principle determinant for the oral production

Table 24-5 Frequency order of morphemes based on parents of Brown's subjects

1. cop	(con. and uncon.)
2. art	
3. prog	
4. aux	(con. and uncon.)
5. plural	(long and short)
6. i. past	
7. poss	
8. 3rd .sing	
9. r. past	

Table 24-6 Spearman rank correlation coefficients

Second language acquisition morpheme difficulty order	Frequency order of morphemes in native-speaker speech (Brown, 1973)
Larsen-Freeman Phase I speaking task	.80[a]
Larsen-Freeman Phase II speaking task	.93[a]
Larsen-Freeman Phase I imitating task	.53
Larsen-Freeman Phase II imitating task	.87[a]
Dulay and Burt (1974)[c]	.87[a]
Bailey, Madden and Krashen[d]	.79[b]

[a]p < .01   [b]p < .05

[c]Dulay and Burt (1974a)

1. art
2. cop
3. prog.
4. s. plu
5. aux
6. r. past
7. i. past
8. 1. plu
9. poss
10. 3rd sing

[d]Bailey, Madden and Krashen (1974)

1. prog
2. cont. cop
3. plural
4. art
5. cont. aux
6. i. past
7. 3rd sing
8. poss

morpheme accuracy order of ESL learners. This conclusion must remain tentative until second language acquisition orders are compared with morpheme frequency counts from the speech of a larger sample of native speakers using different registers in conversing about a variety of topics. The conclusion is believed defensible, however, because:

1. The morpheme frequencies Brown reports are probably fairly representative of their actual occurrence in native-speaker speech. Brown states that there were significantly high correlations for the morpheme frequency orders among the three sets of parents and each set had its speech recorded independently at several different times.

2. The morphemes have disparate frequency ranks. The article, for example, occurred 552 times among the three sets of parents while the regular past tense morpheme occurred only 44 times. It is difficult to imagine these morpheme ranks being reversed, or even significantly altered, in a more general morpheme frequency count.

3. Morpheme frequencies, unlike lexical item frequencies, are probably less context-bound and would therefore be fairly stable in relation to one another so the morpheme frequencies in the parents' speech are probably indicative of overall frequencies.

If the frequency of occurrence of morphemes in native-speaker speech is confirmed as the main reason why ESL learners supply certain morpehemes more accurately than others, the implications are intriguing.

It would appear that second language researchers should pay more attention to the input to which the learner is exposed than has previously been afforded. It would also appear that at least with regard to morpheme form, an S-R explanation is not untenable—the more frequently a stimulus is encountered, the more often it is supplied accurately. Since grammatical morphemes have limited semantic weight, perhaps it is not in morpheme acquisition where the learner's cognitive involvement is evident in the second language learning task. Perhaps the creative talent of the second language learner is reserved for more complicated structures, while the learner concentrates on simply matching native-speaker input for structures at the morpheme level.

Resolution of these speculations will have to be postponed until more evidence is accumulated. Meanwhile, the tentative explanation for the ESL oral production morpheme order provided in this paper will hopefully free us to move on and address these new issues.

Notes

1. I have chosen to use the term "accuracy order" as I feel this is a more precise description of what morpheme studies reveal than the terms previously employed, i.e., "acquisition order" (Dulay and Burt) and "difficulty order" (Bailey, Madden and Krashen). What we are measuring in a cross-sectional study is the percentage of times a subject accurately supplies a morpheme form in an obligatory context.

2. See Larsen-Freeman 1975b.

Part III
Discourse
Analysis

Child-Child Discourse

25

in Second Language Acquisition

Sabrina Peck, *University of California, Los Angeles*

INTRODUCTION

In order to talk about process in second language learning, Peck has turned to a different research framework, the analysis of conversational discourse. The hope of this methodology is that the analysis of transcriptions of child-child or child-adult discourse might show us strategies of learning in progress.

The earliest motivation for child language learning, as other studies in this volume have shown, is the wish to talk with another child (cf., Kenyeres) or an adult (cf., Itoh). Fantini documents that children want to learn the language of their conversation partners:

Sitting by the side of the pool, Mario was speaking to his father in Spanish. A four-year-old child overhearing them, turned to her mother and asked:
Child: Mommie, why does Mario speak that way?
Mother: He's speaking another language.
Child: I want to speak a language too.
Mother: But you do speak a language. Everybody speaks a language!
Child: No, I want to speak like Mario!
(Fantini, 1974, p. 60)

Not only does the child want to speak the same language, but he wants to speak *with* someone even when he knows little of the language:

> ... while shopping, Mario met a small girl of about the same age. He tried to attract her attention by amusing her with facial expressions and motions as well as by speaking to her. Since his English was so limited he was able to say only: "Hey! Look! Watch! Here! Come!" and "Water!" (pointing to a nearby fountain). He judiciously avoided Spanish. . . . This is significant in that . . . he limited himself to only those linguistic items which were appropriate for use with the little girl. (Fantini, p. 66)

The following study looks at the language of the child second language learner as he and his partners strive to be 'cooperative conversationalists'—that is, try to use language appropriate for their conversational interaction. Peck describes cooperative conversation in Child L_2—Child L_1 discourse and in Child L_2—Adult discourse. By contrasting them, she is able to hypothesize what the child might be learning from each.

This paper will describe discourse patterns between an eight-year old acquirer of English and a child native speaker of English and will explore two questions relating to discourse analysis in second language acquisition. First, is the child-child discourse similar to another sample of adult-child discourse? Second, what is the child acquirer learning about English syntax, phonology and semantics in his discourse with the other child and with the adult? Before focusing on these two questions it will be necessary to define what I mean by "discourse," then to discuss briefly the issue of what Piaget has called children's "unsocial speech," and last to review work by researchers who have discussed first and second language acquisition through discourse. Following this background information, I will compare the discourse patterns and the kind of language learning which may result from them, in a child-child and a child-adult discourse sample.

By discourse I mean the flow and the structure of a conversation or topics within it. It is especially interesting to examine who nominates new topics and how, what are appropriate ways to respond to a topic, and what happens when one speaker ignores the other's remarks. One can analyze discourse patterns to see which speaker is dominant or to contrast the patterns through which a conversation develops. The first type of analysis (which can include the second) is relevant to developmental psychology (Corsaro). The second type of analysis is a little like a New Criticism literary analysis which seeks to define the patterns and devices in two poems that make them effective. The relevance of conversational analysis to language acquisition studies has been pointed out by Daden (1975). In a review of the literature, she showed that rules which govern discourse are as systematic as phonological and syntactic rules.

Since conversational or discourse analysis is such a new field, researchers have only defined a few patterns in adult discourse. Even so, another question that has been asked is whether children use the same discourse patterns that adults do (Keenan 1975). Piaget (1926) argued that much of what young children say to each other consists of *unsocial speech,* in other words, that children do not obey such discourse rules as the necessity of responding to the other's topic or nominating a relevant topic to which the other child is capable of responding. In contrast to Piaget, Elinor Keenan (1974) has argued that the 2-3 year-old children that she studied consistently adhered to Grice's maxim, "Be relevant." While they were sometimes relevant by addressing the topic at hand, another way to be relevant was to repeat or modify a phonological or syntactic form of the previous utterance. *Functions* are what Keenan calls the child's way of repeating, modifying, and recombining elements of the other child's utterance. She argued that to these children, repetition and sound play were relevant responses in conversation, and that when one child did not attend to the conversation, the other child would often force him to attend, for instance, by speaking more loudly and repeating until he paid attention.

Given that children do obey some form of adult discourse rules, one direction for research would be to look at the stages in which children learn discourse rules. Another direction would be to study the discourse of children who are still acquiring a first or second language to see in what ways they might be learning syntax, phonology and semantics through discourse. Scollon (1974) argues that first language learners develop syntactic structures through interaction with an adult. These interactions result in what he calls *vertical constructions,* for instance:

Brenda: hiding
Adult: Hiding? What's hiding?
Brenda: balloon

In monologues, the child also produces vertical constructions:

Brenda: bathtub
        scrub it
        scrub it
        paper napkin

Hatch (1976a) has given similar examples of vertical constructions in second language acquisition from Itoh's data, and of the child's repetition and recombination of parts of the conversation.

Takahiro: This
          broken
Adult: Broken.
Takahiro: broken
          This /əz/ broken.
          broken
Adult: Upside down.
Takahiro: upside down
          this broken
          upside down
          broken.

Hatch cites data from other sources in which native Spanish-speaking children use the same ways of gradually extending and building up their utterances. In this example, the child does the buildup as a monologue:

(Mazeika's data)

Carlito: in the boat
go in the boat
Mommy, him go in the boat
Mommy, go in the boat in a con esa
Mommy, go in the boat
Mommy, go in the boat con esa Daddy ride in the boat.

Another term for the child's repetition and recombination of previous utterances is what Wagner-Gough and Hatch (1975) call incorporation. They discuss the importance of studying the input data as well as the acquirer's production in second language acquisition studies. In other words, they urge that we study discourse.

While the above researchers have started to make a case for children's learning of the syntax of a first or second language through discourse, one wonders whether a child second language learner might go through the same process with another child. Anecdotal evidence from bilingual first grade teachers in Boston suggests that some Puerto Rican six year olds enter school with a working knowledge of English solely because their older siblings have spoken English with them. One wonders what sorts of conversations these were, and what was "learned" through them by the younger child. In comparing the child-child and child-adult data in this study, then, I will be asking two major questions. The first is whether child-child discourse is different from child-adult discourse, especially in how it is built on *functions* (Keenan), *incorporation* (Gough and Hatch), and *vertical constructions* (Scollon). The second question concerns what the child is probably learning through the two kinds of discourse which I will be reporting here.

DATA

The subject of this study is Angel, a native speaker of Spanish who came to Los Angeles from Mexico City at 7:4 with his parents and two younger brothers. The parents, who are fluent in English, are upper middle class Mexicans who used to own an English language school in Mexico City, and came to Los Angeles to attend graduate school. Both parents were interested in their sons' progress in English, and believed, as their friends did, that the boys would learn English quickly and with little effort. Angel had had no previous English instruction, except for a year at a nursery school in Mexico City. He had learned some English songs and games. In Los Angeles he was placed in a monolingual combined second and third grade where he received some supplementary help in reading. The positive attitudes toward Americans and the large amount of contact that Angel's family had with Americans suggest that they had, in Schumann's terms (1975), low social distance. The ease with which Angel made friends at school suggests that he experienced low psychological distance as well.

Weekly 38-minute tape recordings of Angel in free play sessions with an adult were begun when Angel was 7:4 and had been in Los Angeles for 45 days. The adult was in graduate school with Angel's mother, and Angel thought of her as his teacher. At 7:11, weekly tape recordings were begun of his free play sessions with Joe, a native English speaker and classmate in the second grade. The two sessions that are compared in this paper took place when Angel was 7:10 (with the adult) and 7:11 (with Joe). Both sessions involved the same two activities: putting together a jigsaw puzzle, and playing war with two toy airplanes, bombs, and two armies of toy soldiers.

CHILD-CHILD DISCOURSE

In looking at the child-child data, it is striking to see how closely Angel and Joe's discourse resembles that of Toby and David, the children in Elinor Keenan's study. In "Conversational Competence in Children," Keenan showed that one way for the 2-3 year old children in her study to respond relevantly to an utterance was to repeat or modify a phonological or syntactic form of the previous utterance. *Functions* are what Keenan calls the child's ways of modifying a previous utterance. The types of functions include *focus functions* and *substitution functions,* and all of them occurred in the tape of Joe and Angel.

Focus functions "take an initial conversational turn, focus on a constituent of it, and repeat it in a subsequent turn" (Keenan 1974). The following is a *basic focus function* because in it the constituent of an antecedent turn is repeated exactly as it appeared originally, including intonation.

> (Keenan)
> S_1 —Mommy to do /Daddy to do/
> S_2 —Daddy to do/
>
> Angel— /nə/ (=no)
> Joe — /nə/

A *focus + prosodic shift* repeats the constituent of an antecedent turn exactly as it appeared but changes the constituent voice quality or intonation.

> (Keenan)
> S_1 —↘flower broked/↘flower broken/
> S_2 —↗flower/
>
> Joe— I—will—*do* it.
> Angel— I *will* do it.

A *focus + constituent expansion* "focuses on a constituent within an antecedent turn and expands it syntactically. The expansion does not alter the grammatical status of the focused constituent."

> (Keenan)
> S_1 —flower broken/flower/its flower broken/eh/oh/end/
> S_2 —many many flowers broken

> Joe— One piece at least you do—at least one piece. (sing-song:) Where-where-where-where.
> Angel— Where are you?

A *focus + constituent embedding* "focuses on a constituent within an antecedent turn and embeds it in a larger construction."

> (Keenan)
> S_1 —big one/yes/big one/
> S_2 —I got/I got big one.

> Angel— Camera
> Joe— (Circus barker voice) Announcing the mighty camera! (laugh)

Substitution functions, along with the focus functions mentioned above, include, Keenan notes, Bloom's *expansions,* Braine's *replacement sequences,* and Weir's *build-ups* and *break-downs.* A substitution function "take(s) an utterance within a conversational turn and replace(s) a constituent within it with a constituent of the same grammatical category. (An entire utterance may not be replaced.)"

> (Keenan)
> S_1 —two moths
> S_2 —many moths

> Joe— You know what?
> Angel— You know why?

The following selections from the transcript of Joe and Angel illustrate how the children's discourse can be analyzed in terms of Keenan's functions:

Example	*Function type*
J— I can't do it. I just can't do it	focus + constituent expansion
Do what? Do this.	substitution
Do this—	basic focus
Do //what.//	substitution
A— //Do that.//	substitution
J— You know what?	
A— You know why?	substitution
J— You know why? (frustrated with puzzle) Oh!	basic focus
A— (starting to laugh) You know why—you /not/ why?	focus + prosodic shift substitution (sound play)

Keenan also found that the children in her study repeated and modified nonsense sounds as part of their discourse. Sound play was also a part of Joe and Angel's discourse:

A— (sing-song) Na (11x)

J— (sings, in a similar tune) Na (11x)

In the following example, Joe's repetitions of /d/ and /da/ remind Angel of the word "Daddy" so Angel starts to make up a song:

J— Do that, do what, /d/ (6x)—Umm /da/ (4x)

A— (making up a tune) My Daddy's in Mexico

Another interesting parallel to Keenan's study is the boys' use of songs and nursery rhymes. In this example, the rhythm of "Very, very funny" reminds Joe of the nursery rhyme, "Mary, Mary quite contrary."

A— Very, very funny.

J— Mary, Mary quite //contrary//—How does your garden grow

A— //(scream:) Get off!//

Or both boys may make an association to a song, and sing it together:

J— (sing-song) Where-where-where-where

A— Where are you?

J— Where are you?

A— /Id/ (sings:) "Scooby-dooby-doo, //Where are you?//

J— (sings)   //Where are you?//

Here, Angel begins by making grunting sounds (Oh. He!) and works into a recitation of the vowels, pronounced as in Spanish. He sounds as though he is remembering the kind of drill he probably did in Mexico when he learned to read through a syllabary method. Then Joe is reminded of the song, "The Witch Doctor," and Angel screams with frustration after three repetitions of the chorus:

Joe— (singing) doo-doo-dee (etc.)

A— Where is that piece? That more like it. Oh. He! /i/ /u/ /a/ /e/ /i/ /o/—/u/.

J— "Ooh, ee, ooh, ah-ah, ting tang, walla-walla bing bang, oo ee, oo ah ah ting tang walla-walla bing-bang, I calls it" (repeats above verse 2x)

A— (scream:) Oooh!

While the following example could probably be analyzed in terms of substitution functions and focus functions, the accelerated pace and high pitch suggest that it may be a "ritual" as defined by Garvey (1974). She studied young children in free play situations and described a type of interaction which she called a ritual. These play sequences were characterized by a changing, sing-song intonation, "a precise temporal integration of the participants' behaviors," a faster rate of utterances, and a high pitch.

A— I like *you*—like a silly boy.

J— Who?

A— You.

J— Who?

A— You!

J— You?

A— No.
J— You? You?
A— *No*!
J— You-you-who-who. You-who.
A— You-who.
J— (like a trumpet flourish announcing a king:) You-who-who-who who-who! Oooo!

CHILD-CHILD AND CHILD-ADULT DISCOURSE

Thus, in this study the child second language learner and his classmate use discourse patterns that are similar to those of the 2-3 year old children that Keenan studied. In contrast, there are only a few examples of language play by the adult involving functions. In this example, Angel and the adult were working on a puzzle. Angel had almost finished it, and was looking for a few more pieces. Then the adult tried to play, briefly, by singing, "Look here."

A— (sing-song) Looking—I looking, I look . . . I look . . . Hmm (laugh, claps hands) Puff. (makes clicks)
Ad— (singing:) Look here—
A— I look, I look, I look. Looking I look . . . (speaking:) Look. (singing:) Look. (speaking:) Look. Here.
Ad— Yes!

In this example the adult played along with Angel in naming the soldiers:

A— Your name this is—
Ad— Jim
A— (Pointing to a "dead soldier" in the pile under the bed) No. Jim's here.
Ad— (laugh) Oh, Albert.
A— No. This is— . . . Kalayra.
Ad— Kalayra?
A— Kalayrá!
Ad— Kalay—rá
A— No this is Mississippi.
Ad— Mississippi? //Mississippi Jim?//
A—   //(chuckle)//

There are few instances of "functions" in the child-adult discourse, perhaps partly because the adult does not know how to play this particular game with language or does not feel comfortable about playing.

The adult-child discourse differs from the child-child discourse in several ways: the number and types of questions, the number of requests for clarification, the ease of topic nomination; and the boundaries and prevalence of unsocial speech.

The adult relied heavily on questions to keep the discourse going with Angel. She asked 95 questions during the session, while Angel asked only 17. The adult's most frequent type of question (35 examples) asked for information.

Ad— What country are your soldiers from?

Angel tried to check the adult's meaning with his most common question type:

Ad— And these?

A— These?

In the child-child discourse, Joe asked only 58 questions, and Angel asked 27. For both children, the most common question types were rhetorical questions. Joe asked 43 rhetorical questions, for instance:

J— You know—what he did? Yesterday . . .

A— (laugh)

J— Yesterday I was playing—um—he just—*hit* me.

and Angel asked 10 rhetorical questions. Thus, the two boys use questions less frequently than the adult does with Angel. The boys often use rhetorical questions, while the adult asks many information questions and is met by a fair number of checking questions by Angel. These patterns suggest that the adult is more concerned with referential meaning than Joe is, and this suggestion will later be borne out.

An analysis of the requests for clarification yields further evidence of the essentially informational, semantic character of the discourse between the adult and Angel, in contrast to the playful character of the discourse between Joe and Angel. The adult asked for clarification the most often (7 times) and Joe the least (never). The adult needed clarification because a whole sentence, an unstated element, or one word of a sentence was not clear:

A— Have—este—/puzəl/ have a—a hundred piece. Is big.

Ad— What?

A— He . . . went here. A one day.

Ad— Who was here one day?

Angel asked the adult for clarification five times, and this process of checking may have been a response to the many information questions which were posed to him.

Ad— It's a machine gun.

A— Machine gun?

Ad— How old are you? (While looking at a baby picture, and meaning, "How old were you in this picture?")

A— Hmm?

Ad— What country are your soldiers from?

A— Mmmm?

Joe never asked for clarification, while Angel asked four times.

J— (previous part of utterance omitted) You know what you just did? Give me a clue. Thank you ve'—very *not* much.

A— Not much? Why //not much?//

J— //not much.//

(It is 5:30 in the afternoon)

J— I *know,* we're not gonna have war yet. War's—it's gonna start at ten o'clock. We're pretend it—it's gonna start.

A— Ten o'clock? Of night?

Often, Joe would not clarify when Angel asked him to, as in the first example. It seems that the adult and Angel needed to check for clarification because of the high number of information questions. Discourse never really broke down between Angel and Joe because it was one of their rules that it was all right for a sentence to be ignored in the sense that the other child responded to it by sound play.

In topic nomination, Angel had more success with the adult than with Joe. The adult tended to meet him more than halfway when Angel nominated a topic.

A— I want a—I go for—mm—another play.

Ad— Another play? Another toy? All right.

So the adult made an effort to understand Angel's use of "play" for "toy." The adult also tended to do what Angel asked:

A— Go—

Ad— Okay.

A— Go fast.

Joe, on the other hand, often would use Angel's non-standard word choice or pronunciation as a take off point for his free association and sound play. He sometimes would interrupt Angel with a different topic, as when Angel was making up a narrative about the toy soldiers and Joe tried at the same time to establish the rules of the game. When asked a question, Joe often ignored it. For example, he did not explain what "clown school" and "jackpot" meant when Angel asked for definitions. While Joe was often successful in nominating topics, Angel was often unsuccessful. Angel was most likely to receive a topic-relevant response from Joe when he sang, started sound play or a narrative, or did some action.

Even though Joe often ignored the topics that Angel tried to nominate, there is less unsocial speech between the two children than there is between Angel and the adult. Unsocial speech, as defined here, is a long section of monologue or of several turns by both speakers in which they are not attending to or responding to each other's utterances. The range of relevant response to an utterance is much wider for the two children than for the adult and Angel. The adult used language literally and referentially, and did not respond when Angel played with language. For instance, when Angel and the adult had almost finished the puzzle, Angel wanted to find the last pieces as soon as he could, and said to himself:

A— Mm Ay! (whiney:) where's a piece for that? (Laugh) (tries a piece but it doesn't fit) No, this not . . . (looks through pieces) /tiyu/

And he got even more excited about his progress with the puzzle:

A— (sing-song) I looking, I looking, I looking. I looking . . . I looking. /a/ more. (fits another piece) Ha-ha-ha-ha-ha-ha-ha.

The adult then said, "You're so good! Boy!" and in this way showed that she thought that the topic of Angel's play was something like "look what a good puzzle maker I am." But Angel did not respond to her compliment; he kept playing:

A—   xxx Ha (7x) (claps hands)

Thus, each was addressing a different topic. A few minutes later the adult felt more uneasy and made another effort to tell Angel what a good puzzle maker he was:

Ad— You sure are looking!

A—   I shirt! (amused)

Again, Angel did not attend to the topic that the adult was on. He recognized that "sure" sounded like "shirt." He responded to the form, not the meaning of her utterance, and made a pun, "I shirt!" So, this was a long stretch of unsocial speech because the adult never responded to Angel's topic of "language play" and Angel never responded to the adult's topics of "puzzle piece shapes" and "how Angel is working on the puzzle."

When we look at the discourse between the two children, most of their topics, including singing and sound play, are social because the children respond to each other's topics. There are some examples, however, of both boys talking at the same time about different topics. Sometimes one boy forcibly gets the other's attention and draws him back into a conversation by loud commands which may be repeated.

J—   //(singing:) doo-dee (etc.)//

A—   //Is gone! One piece (to himself) This piece—goes. (singing, own tune) Is gone! Is gone! Oh, is gone. Ah, is gone, la-la-la (etc.) (tune gets louder)//

J—   (mockingly) la-la-la-la

A—   (still singing) la la (etc.)

J—   *Hold* it! *Hold* it! *Hold* it! *Hold* it!

Joe broke up the two monologues by shouting "*Hold* it!" And in the next example, the native speaker, Joe, was involved in his own monologue, until Angel drew Joe back into the dialogue.

J—   (crackling, cartoon voice) I'm original redcoat and I'll get that fighting English! (own voice:) I don't get it.
       //I just// don't get it. Hey! //Who's a//—where's //xxx//

A—   //xxx //

J—   The other ending? I think we're missing a piece.

A—   Is missing—like //you!//

J—   //piece.//

By mentioning "missing," Angel was able to get Joe to continue with the topic of "pieces of the puzzle."

Thus, there is generally less unsocial speech on the tape of Joe and Angel, but this is probably due to the wider definition in child-child discourse of what is social. Angel and Joe responded to each other by word and sound play, or according to the meaning. Any utterance was potentially social, i.e., material for the free associatory play of the other child. In adult-child discourse, any utterances which express an appropriate meaning are social speech. Another area which is more narrowly defined in the adult-child than the child-child discourse is that of a relevant topic response. Because with the adult a relevant response is a meaningful response, there are more questions and requests for clarification in the child-adult discourse than the child-child discourse. Because the adult encourages Angel to express his ideas, Angel has more successful topic nominations with her than with Joe.

LANGUAGE LEARNING THROUGH DISCOURSE

Having described some of the main differences in the discourse patterns, we can now turn to look at what Angel may be learning about syntax, phonology and semantics through the discourse. It seems that the child-child situation gives him many chances to practice syntax and phonology, and the child-adult situation offers him many chances to practice syntax and semantics.

The kinds of modifications which Angel makes on Joe's speech (described in the section on "functions") mean that he only has to fill in one or two words to come up with an acceptable utterance.

A— (previous part of utterance omitted)
//Please—excuse me//
J— //I need it.//
Oh good! A teamwork who counts! Oh! *Good*! Now there's *one* piece.
A— (starting to laugh) There one piece!
//(laugh)//
J— //Oh//
A There different piece

Or another method is to slightly change the word order:

J— Nope. But it goes here. //xxx//
A— //Here!// Goes!

Sometimes Joe's teasing of Angel seems to go on until Angel produces a grammatical, standard utterance:

J— That's like on—Ernie and Bert—(roar)
A— No, like a crazy boy! (laugh)
J— (laugh) That's more like it. (high pitch:) What?
A— (chuckling) Like a crazy boy!
J— (even higher) What?
A— (softer) Like a crazy boy.
J— Like a mazy—like a—a—
A— *Crazy*!
J— I—I mean—li' li' (pretending to stutter) I mean—I—I—I mean—I mean—I mean—I mean—(normal voice:) I mean a crazy?

A— A crazy.
J— A crazy what, a crazy daisy?
A— No, a crazy you.
J— Oh! Oh! Oh!
A— //You are//
J— //Oh!//
A— Crazy.
J— Oh! (10x)

So Angel's original phrasing, "No, like a crazy boy!" becomes "You are/ crazy" and then the teasing ends.

Through sound play in which Joe mocks Angel, and sound play in which both boys enjoy themselves, Angel is practicing and probably learning something about phonology. In this example, through Joe's teasing about his pronunciation, Angel moved from pronouncing the initial /k/ of "camera" partially voiced, to a standard voiceless pronunciation and then, in frustration perhaps that the teasing continued, back to a nonstandard one again:

A— //That is//
J— //And—a//
A— Camera—/l/—is camera
J— (mocking his accent:) /gæməra/!
A— Camera.
J— /gæməra/.
A— Like—tha'—you have camera? //I like—//
J (to the tune of "Camelot") Ca//mera!// Camera! Camera!
A— *Ca*mera
J— (circus barker voice:) Announcing the mighty gamera! (laugh)
A— (louder) /kæ/—/mə/—/ra/
J— (sing-song) *Ga*mera.
A— (irritated, shouting:) *Camerá*
J— (laughing, loud) *Ga*mera. (softer:) /gamərə/
A— (soft, laughing) /gamərə/

In the following example, Joe mocked Angel's pronunciation of "pieces" and "simple," which were more standard than the mocking echoes of them that Joe produced. Angel became frustrated at one point, and screamed, "Ooooh!" but later he deflected the mockery by associating to "pizzas" and then, when Joe asked "/pɛpsiš/?" Angel sang the Pepsi Cola commercial.

A— That is mine—pieces
J— (laugh)
A— Oooh. That very simple
J— Got //it//.
A— //That// very simple
J— (mockingly, slowly) That—is—very—/sɪmpəl/
What /šɪmpəl/ mean?
/š/

A— /simpəl/!
J— /impəl/!
A— //Silly! (laugh)//
J— //You're//
silly!
A— Your are.
J— Your *are*.
A— (frustrated) Oooh!
J— Oooh!
A— Only one piece.
J— Only one /piš/ (4x) //I can't stop.//
A—   //This a old// piece. Piece
J— /piš/ /piš/. You like /pišəš/?
A— No. I like pieces.
J— What. Whatta you mean—you like /pišəž/?
//I like//
A— //Pizza//
J— //pišəs/
A— I like pieces, pizzas.
J— /pɛpsiš/?
A— (sing-song) Pepsi Coli—yeah.

There are also some examples of times where both boys enjoyed the sound play (somewhat as Toby and David did, in Keenan's study) and did not mock each other:

J— Oooh, I got! no—Dong!
A— Doyng!
M— Doyng, I said darn! //Doyng//
A—   //No, I said doyng,// doyng, boom.
J— Doyng, doyng, doyng.
A— Doyng.
J— /Id/ Dong. Ding-dong! That was—remember Dong?

A more precise analysis needs to be done to see which features Joe tended to imitate and exaggerate, and how Angel changed his pronunciation as a result of Joe's mockery.

In the area of semantics, Angel learned new words by listening and repeating to himself, but much of the time, as noted above, Joe responded to the form of Angel's utterances, and not the meaning. Here is an example of Angel's repeating a new bit of vocabulary to himself, and soon afterwards, using it:

J— I see it, I see it, I see it! And that's one more like it.
A— (laugh, then whispers to himself:) 's more like it!
J— *Really* more like it.

(a few minutes later)
J— (singing) doodle-doo-doo-doo (etc.)
A— Where is that piece? That *more* like it.

Here is an untypical situation in which the meaning of what Angel said was so important that Joe did not mock Angel's pronunciation:

J— Where's the other ending? I think we're missing a piece.
A— Is missing—like //you!//
J—   //Piece//
A— //You sitting in—//
J— //I still s'—//
A— The piece? Maybe.
J— See.

Joe was more concerned with finding an edge piece of the puzzle than with making fun of Angel.

While Joe's method of dealing with Angel's beginner's knowledge of English often seems to be to ignore Angel's meaning and respond to the form of his utterance, Angel often responds to the meaning of Joe's utterances. In the following two examples, he took "ten o'clock" and "bowl of soup" literally, and tried to question Joe about them:

J— I know we're not gonna have war yet. War's—it's gonna start at ten o'clock. We're pretend it—it's gonna start.
A— Ten o'clock? Of night?
J— No—/bə/—for pre*tend*! Yeah-uh—no, in the day—time. Ten o'clock in the daytime.

J— (telling soldiers to march) *Hup*! *Hup*! Hup-hup-hup-hup! Hup! Hup! Bowl of soup! Hup! Hup!
   Tomato soup! And/ //hike//
A—   //I don't// //have soup!//
J—   //Hup-hup// (laugh)

And in this example, both boys responded to meaning. They had just finished the soldier game, and were imagining what the next war would be like for the soldiers. It is a nice example of collective narrative play:

J— And they are gonna /čurǰ/ a //charge xxx//
A—   //And one day// the
   Tiaj'—Gua'—Guatemala.
J— Next time, we'll see a war! In the *South* America—and East America. It's over—cheap. Ha!

Although Angel has a difficult time expressing what he means to Joe, the adult helps him to express himself by asking questions and rephrasing what he says. In the following example Angel was looking at the puzzle box and talking about the puzzle.

A— Is big . . .
Ad— (doesn't understand) Oh, I see.
A— Have—este—/puzəl/ have a—a hundred piece. Is big.
Ad— What?
A— The /puzəl/ have a—a hundred.
Ad— (echoing his pronunciation) the /puzəl/?

A— /puzəl/. This. (touches the puzzle.)
Ad— Oh the puzzle!
A— Puzzle. (Standard pronunciation) //Has a hu—//
Ad—   //Oh it has a//
A— -ndred—piece. /xx//
Ad—   //A hundred pieces, right.//
A— Big. (points to the boxtop)
Ad— Whatta you see in the picture here?
A— Is like this the /puzəl/
Ad— Yuh,
A— Puzzle!!
Ad— Puzzle. What's happening there?

So the adult helped him to express the idea that it was a big puzzle with a hundred pieces, and at the same time, he learned to pronounce "puzzle" enough to monitor his error in the last utterance quoted above. The difference between what he learns with the adult and with Joe is not clearcut, then, but some tentative conclusions can be drawn.

CONCLUSIONS

It may be that Angel is learning more about the forms of words (phonology and syntax) with Joe, and he is learning more about the meanings of utterances, and how to express himself (semantics) with the adult. To explore this suggestion, it will be useful to contrast the input, output, and affective environment for Angel in each situation.

As far as input goes, from Joe Angel is receiving a wider variety of input than from the adult. From Joe he hears talk, sing-song, singing, exaggerated whispers, sound effects, imitations of T.V. program and advertisement figures, songs off the radio, parodies of "Camelot" and "Allouette" set to "Camera" and "My Dad, Your Dad, My Dad." He hears a fair number of grammatical errors or mistakes. From the adult he hears mostly talk about things in the room such as the puzzle, or things outside the room, such as his school. There's some singing, and, in the soldier game, a good deal of narrative fantasy. So the input that Angel receives from Joe is enormously more varied. The adult tends to listen to his *meaning* and respond to it only. She asks some questions about words or sentences she does not understand. Joe, however, interacts on various levels—form, meaning, his own free association, or a sudden impulse to tease Angel.

In terms of output, Angel probably responds in a greater variety of ways, and makes more short answers with Joe, but it is harder for Angel to nominate a topic or make a response with Joe than it is with the adult. With Joe, Angel is forced to respond to his corrections and mocking play. The number of utterances per unit of time seems much larger on the tape of Angel and Joe than on the tape of the adult and Angel. Angel sings, whispers, sing-songs and generally, responds in a greater variety of ways. He needs to challenge Joe or ask him questions more often than he needs to do so with the adult. He makes fewer, and shorter responses, filling in blanks, sometimes. With the adult Angel is often the instigator of the conversation and it is easier for him to nominate topics. He usually talks, although there is some singing and sing-song. He rarely needs to ask the adult questions, but he is asked a larger number of information questions, as well as to explain words and sentences which she does not understand. It is interesting to note that Angel says, "I don't know" six times as opposed to never with Joe because he can not always understand or field the questions. In a sense he plays more of a passive role with the adult, since she asks him questions to be sure that she understands, while with Joe Angel has to struggle more to figure out what Joe means to keep up with the conversation, let alone nominate a topic of his own.

One overly blunt way to characterize the difference between the child-child and child-adult discourse would be to say that Angel struggles to learn, or understand the other child's language, but that the adult works at trying to learn and understand Angel's language. With the adult, Angel is asked to respond to the meaning of her words, and if he does not understand, he has to say "I don't know" or in some other way ask for help. With the other child, Angel has freedom to respond on many levels, especially, to play with the sounds and forms of words, or to sing, or chant. The challenge of this type of discourse, however, is that the other child does not attend to the meaning that Angel is trying to express, and makes it very hard for Angel to nominate a topic. It looks as though the freedom in the types of responses that the child can give may be what allows the child (forces the child) to perfect his pronunciation and helps him to speak in a more standard form. The adult's concern with the child's meaning, and willingness to overlook the child's mistakes, is perhaps instrumental in allowing him to learn how to use language to express his ideas. It also seems clear, however, that not all child-child discourse is like that reported in this paper, but that the kind of teasing and play that happened to occur on the tape does occur between children, and not in adult-adult or child-adult dyads to such an extent.

The preceding analysis of what the child "learns" through discourse with Joe and with the adult is incomplete, and there are also many other questions which need to be answered:

1) What difference does the input of the other child make? In other words, how different are the kinds of functions that a child uses when he is alone from the ones he uses in his speech with another child? Probably many of them are the same. I suspect that the input of the other child makes a difference, and perhaps prolongs the play sequences, and gives them more variety of topics and sounds.

2) What kind of situation brings out this type of language play? Semi-isolation? The two boys engage in more sound play while doing the puzzle than while playing with the soldiers. Perhaps doing a puzzle induces the same feeling of isolation as does a semi-dark room. Perhaps when children do not have quite enough to play with (Toby and David had nothing to play with) they start to play with words.

3) What difference does the affective climate have on sound play? Toby and David both seemed to enjoy sound play, but much of the time, Angel is being teased by Joe, and Angel gets annoyed. There are also some play sequences that seem parallel to Garvey's "rituals."

4) How can we tell that a child has "learned" a given unit of language *because* of discourse? A working definition could be, as in this paper, that the child "learns" a word or structure enough to use it in following utterances. But is this definition enough?

5) And most important, how can we best study what a second language learner is "learning" through discourse? In analyzing transcripts of spontaneous speech, how can we define patterns which are relevant to language learning? What kinds of experimental elicitation techniques need to be developed to supplement the analysis of transcripts?

We will learn much about second language acquisition through a thorough analysis of patterns in child-child discourse, particularly language play. Since conversational analysis as applied to adult discourse is still developing, the work will be initially an attempt to establish categories and definitions. Difficulties will be the time-consuming process of transcribing data for discourse analysis, and, once transcribed, searching the data for patterns in which the process of "learning" seems to be going on. Researchers in first and second language acquisition have pointed out some kinds of language learning in child-adult discourse. Elinor Keenan has described some patterns in child-child discourse for first language learners. As far as second language learners are concerned, many people agree that children of immigrants to the United States often learn English from their older brothers and sisters, but no one has systematically studied what sorts of conversations these children have, and what the process of their language learning is like. Elinor Keenan states that children's language play contains the same discourse processes as adult discourse, but more clearly delineated and easier to see. If this is so, then a description of the process of second language learning through child-child discourse will have implications for second language acquisition research. There is a great deal of fascinating and fruitful work to be done.

Discourse Analysis

26 *and Second Language Acquisition*

Evelyn Hatch, *University of California, Los Angeles*

INTRODUCTION

Sabrina Peck's study has given us a first look at the possibilities of conversational analysis as an alternative methodology for second language acquisition research. The following paper is an attempt to draw together some of the work that has been done in discourse analysis for first language learners, and an attempt to apply the methodology to second language learning. The work in this area is, obviously, only in an embryonic stage. We don't have a good description of what the rules of conversation might be for native speakers, whether adult or child; naturally we have little idea of what the conversational analysis method might give us (or what kind of morass it might lead us into) for second language learning.

In view of the present state of development, perhaps it is best to be cautious and make no strong claims for discourse as the 'teacher of syntax.' Just as we have always been cautioned in the area of statistical research that we cannot claim *cause* when we find two variables highly *related* (that is, when we get a high correlation index between years of study and language proficiency or between frequency and order of acquisition of morphemes, we cannot say we have established a causal relationship), in the same sense, we cannot say that because we see a relationship between, e.g., early vertical patterns in discourse followed by horizontal patterns in discourse, that discourse is the causal factor. Nevertheless, in both kinds of research, we feel justified in making such claims in the weak sense. Whatever cautionary remarks might seem in order, I believe the search for explanations via discourse analysis is one of the more promising areas of research. That research is now underway in the work of Keller-Cohen, at the University of Michigan, and that of Peck, Schwartz, Gaskill, and Brunak & Fain at UCLA.

The purpose of this paper is to build a case for discourse analysis as a methodology for the study of second language acquisition. To do this I will first give a short historical sketch of the research methodology presently used in second language research and then look at examples from data which may justify a new approach. Hopefully, the data will show how discourse analysis gives us more revealing, if less formal and elegant, insights into the second language learning *process*.

Research of the '70s in second language acquisition has investigated the *form* of syntactic structures used by the learner. Since Berko (1958), Brown (1971) and others had shown that it is possible to solicit morphemes in a test situation as well as count them in observational data, it's not surprising that second language researchers also did morpheme counts as a way of looking at the acquisition of *form* in a second language. Morpheme counts, then, comprise the bulk of the studies since they are the easiest (though for the researcher surely the most tedious) to do, and because they are easily quantified.

The counts have been discussed in a number of ways. Swain, 1972, and Adams, 1974, looked at the occurrence of morphemes in the child's two languages and compared them not just in production but also imitation and translation tasks (Swain for French-English; Adams for Spanish-English). Another group, interested in whether children learning English acquired the morphemes in a similar order to that claimed for first-language learners, searched for an 'invariant' order of acquisition (Dulay & Burt, 1972, 1973, 1974, Hatch, 1972, Hakuta, 1974). Morpheme counts establishing a similar order for adults have also been reported (Bailey, Madden & Krashen, 1974; Larsen-Freeman, 1975). Explanations for the order of acquisition seen in the literature have been given in terms of Slobin's universal operating principles (Hatch, 1972, 1974; Dulay & Burt, 1974, Hatch & Gough, 1976) or in terms of frequency in the input to the learner (Hatch, 1974, Gough & Hatch, 1975, Larsen-Freeman, 1976).

Another area of investigation which again looked at the learner's production of *form* is the study of the development of the AUX system, particularly in negative and question formation (Huang, 1970; Adams, 1974; Young, 1974; Milon, 1972; Schumann, Rosansky & Cancino, 1974). A developmental sequence again has been recognized for second language learners in the above research and a number of explanations have been given in terms of similarities to first-language acquisition and universal operating principles. Further, the speed and success with which learners go through the developmental sequence has been explained in terms of social and psychological distance factors by Schumann (1975).

In reaction to these studies of *form* and in particular to the literature on morpheme acquisition, Gough (1975) pointed out that it is meaningless to talk about acquisition of any morpheme until the child also acquires the function of that morpheme. That is, *form* cannot be studied apart from *function.* Since ING is a morpheme that was claimed to be acquired early by both first and second language learners, she looked at the acquisition of the function of ING in the speech of a Persian child learning English as a second language. In adult speech, the ING form is used for a variety of functions; e.g., to mark immediate intent ("I'm just leaving for the movie right now."), to mark future intent ("I'm going to France next summer."), to mark repeated actions ("Oh, I'm singing in the chorus like always."), to contrast times ("I'm taking sign language at 7:00 now."), etc. Her question was which, *if indeed any,* of these *functions* does the child give evidence of knowing when he first begins to use ING forms. Her data show that the child produced ING early but that it appeared in variation with the unmarked form of the verb for all tense/aspect possibilities. That is, the form appeared long before its syntactic function was acquired.

Gough's criticism of *form*-counts as evidence of acquisition of language function echo those of Mikeš and Savič (1969). Under their methodological constraints one does *not* claim acquisition of any syntactic form until it appears in clear contrast to other forms in its class. We would not, using this method, claim acquisition of any of the tense/aspect system until the contrasts in function are clear. Any such study, then, would look at the *process* by which the child separates out the function of the various parts of the system. A description of that process would, hopefully, give us insights into language *acquisition.*

In an effort to link the learning of functions and forms, we have suggested that the researcher must transcribe and examine not just the child's production of speech but also the speech of those with whom he talks. We assume that input (some portion of which must be intake) is an extremely important factor in the order of acquisition of various syntactic forms and functions.

In all the research, however, an important link has been missing. In talking about the importance of input and the frequency of forms in that input, we have overlooked the most important factor of all, the link that explains *how* the child learns. I truly believe that to talk about child language learning as an automatic process is simply to say that we have nothing interesting to say about *how* that child learns a language. A turn to a new methodology might give us a way of looking at the *how.* One possibility for a new method is discourse analysis and, in particular, conversational analysis. It is not enough to look at input and to look at frequency; the important thing is to look at the corpus as a whole and examine the interactions that take place within conversations to see how that interaction, itself, determines frequency of forms and how it shows language functions evolving.

Our basic premise has long been that the child learns some basic set of syntactic structures, moving from a one-word phase to a two-word phase, to more complex structures, and that eventually the child is able to put these structures together in order to carry on conversations with others. The premise, if we use discourse analysis, is the converse. That is, language learning evolves *out of* learning how to carry on conversations.

In second language learning the basic assumption has been, if anything, stronger than it is in first-language acquisition literature. It is assumed that one first learns how to manipulate structures, that one gradually builds up a repertoire of structures and then, somehow, learns how to put the structures to use in discourse. We would like to consider the possibility that just the reverse happens. One learns how to do conversation, one learns how to interact verbally, and out of this interaction syntactic structures are developed. (This is not the same as a Newmark model as I hope the following section will make clear. Nor does it necessarily lead to the same pedagogical implications.)

In order to build a case for the study of discourse in second language acquisition, let me review first the evidence from studies of children acquiring first and/or second languages.

What does the child have to do to talk with others? Keenan (1976) has pointed out that the first step the child must make in conversation is to get the attention of the person with whom he wishes to talk. This can be accomplished in non-verbal ways (banging a spoon, pulling at mother's hand, etc.) or through verbal gestures. If immediate response is not forthcoming, the child usually becomes insistent in his repetitions ("mama, mama, mama") until he does get a response, and he may use additional non-verbal gestures to add to the attention-drawing verbalization. He does not continue until contact with a listener is established. This first step is also clear in data of second-language learning children. (For the convenience of the reader, I will use an indentation for the speech of the native-speaker of English throughout this paper. Reference on the data source will be given for the first citation; thereafter, the learner will simply be identified by name.)

Huang, 1970, Taiwanese, 5 yrs., Paul

Paul: (To Kenny) You-you-you-you.

K: Huh?

P: I-see-you
    Kenny.

Yoshida, 1976, Japanese, 3 yrs., Miki

Miki: Ryan, Ryan, Ryan

Paul: Oh-oh!

J: What?

P: This. (Points to ant)

J: It's an ant.

This does not mean that every time the second language learner wanted to nominate a discourse topic he called the listener's name, said 'oh-oh' or 'hey,' or any of the usual attention-drawing markers (though Keller-Cohen reports a large number of *lookit*'s in beginning conversations of second language learning children, 1976). When a child is being studied, the investigator is almost always attending to the child (unlike a more natural situation). We would expect to find more of this behavior in child-child interactions, and we would further expect that the second-language learning child would have a far wider range of non-verbal signals to check for listener-attention than have first language learners.

Once the learner has secured the attention of his conversation partner, the second task is to get the partner to attend to the topic of discourse. He can do this by pointing to what he wants to have noticed (Paul, pointing: Cat.) or he may use other deitics. Many children (c.f. Young, 1974) seem to favor 'that' /dæt/. Paul's favorite was the demonstrative 'this.'

Paul: (pointing toward drum) This, this, this!

In a frame, then, the first task is to get attention, the second is to identify the topic reference:

Paul: lookit.   Paul: oh-oh
J: What?   J: What?
P: ball.   P: that. (points at box)

One might claim that it is from these conversational exchanges that connected utterances of more than one word develop:

Paul: this
J: A pencil.
P: (echo) pencil.
Paul: this+++pencil. (falling intonation on each
          word)

It is possible that such 'two-word' utterances (or two, one-word utterances which follow each other) are propositions (There exists a pencil). It is more sensible, however, simply to gloss them as establishing the topic 'notice the pencil.' (In the same sense that Atkinson's 'There goes a mouse!' hardly seems to be other than 'notice mouseness' since *'There doesn't go a mouse' is quite impossible.) In turn (unless the task is one of looking at picture books and naming the objects seen), the adult does not interpret such utterances as 'this+++NOUN' as a piece of information. Rather, he accepts it as a topic for conversation. He does not seem to react as if the child were telling him names of things.

If one can accept that a call for attention ('oh-oh,' etc.), a pointing out of a topic ('this,' etc.) and the learner's and partner's identifying remarks serve to nominate a topic for conversation, then we have accounted for the presence of such utterances as 'This+++NOUN' in the early data. That is, we are saying that this particular structure evolves out of discourse. It evolves not because of some magic acquisition device which operates automatically on input but because of the conscious desire of the child to say something, to talk about something.

Once the child has secured the listener's attention and has nominated a topic, what happens in the discourse? Scollon, in his dissertation on a child learning English as a first language, shows how the learner and the partner together build a conversation once the topic is understood. In first language acquisition, of course, there is a good deal of difficulty in getting the topic understood:

Scollon, 1974, English, Brenda

Brenda: (a car passes in the street. R does not hear it at the time)
/kʰa/ (repeated 4 times)

R: What?

B: /gɔo/
/go/

S: XXX

B: /bəiš/ (nine repetitions)

R: What? Oh, bicycle? Is that what you said?

B: /na?/

R: No?

B: /na?/

R: No—I got it wrong. (laugh)

I have not found that second-language learning children have the same trouble in getting their topic nominations recognized (perhaps because I have only been looking at sequential data; there may be examples of this in Leopold); their problems in control of the vocal apparatus are much less severe. They do, however, have problems in getting close to the adult model for specific words (c.f., Itoh, 1973, where the child Takahiro makes repeated attempts at 'square' yielding /skueəl, skuəl, škuwee, fukueer, šukuwel, skweyl, skweə, šuwel, kuweəl/).

When the adult does recognize the topic, he responds to it appropriately:

Brenda: Kimby

R: What about Kimby?

B: close

R: Closed; What did she close, hmmm?

Brenda: (looking in picture book which shows an old woman at a stove)
cook
say

R: What'd the cook say?

B: something

Out of these interactions (which Scollon calls vertical structures) develop syntactic structures (which Scollon calls horizontal structures). That is, the words that the child produces one at a time *are* semantically linked. *When the adult asks for more information with questions, he asks for a constituent to fill out the construction.* It appears quite clear that the adult takes the child's first utterance as a topic nomination and then asks her to clarify it or comment on it.

Brenda: hiding

R: Hiding? What's hiding?

B: balloon.

The clarification or comment is semantically related by such questions and the relationship is later made more explicit through syntax. Scollon believes, therefore, that "this interaction with other speakers may well be the means by which Brenda has learned how to construct" syntactic relationships.

The child also produces vertical structures without adult prompting:

Brenda	my turn	this way	bathtub
see that.	do it.	hold it (3X)	scrub it (2X)
		holding (2X)	paper napkin

but obviously adult questions help her to get all the relationships out:

Brenda: tape corder
       use it (2X)
R: Use it for what?
B: talk
       corder talk
       Brenda talk.

From many such examples, Scollon has built a convincing argument that those vertical structures form the prototypes for longer horizontal constructions at a later period. *"This suggests that . . . discourse structure is at the heart of sentence structure from the beginning of its development."*

Is there evidence for this same sort of progression in the data of second language learners? If we look back at one of the first examples given for Paul:

Paul: Oh-oh!
J: What?
P: this (points to ant)
J: It's an ant.
P: ant

it seems that we do. If you glance through the following examples, it should look like there are direct parallels; and I believe that to be the case. However, there is a difference that must be taken into account. The learner in this case has already learned to make syntactic constructions (Scollon's horizontal structures) in his first language. Why doesn't he immediately do so in the second? He has little difficulty physiologically in getting out long streams of speech; therefore, we can't say that the problem is completely in controlling his vocal apparatus. Two explanations seem possible: 1) he needs more time for his automatic acquisition device to work on the input in building up syntax; or 2) conversation is what he is learning and the syntax grows out of it. I would like us to opt for the second explanation.

Let's look at the first example.

Paul: This boat.
J: Mmhmm boat.
P: this
       my boat.

Why doesn't Paul start immediately with "my boat" or "this my boat"? It would not be beyond his ability to do so. But if we look at conversation function, we know that he must first make sure that the adult has identified the referent for the following discourse (much in the same way that an adult might say, "You see that boat?" "Mmhmm." "Well, it's mine."). Following is another example of establishment of the discourse topic:

Paul: This
J: Yes?
P: this you?
J: It's Kenny's.

Again, Paul identifies the topic of discourse first before he asks who the ball belongs to.

In the following example, Paul tries to establish a topic but the adult, in turn, nominates another which Paul then must respond to:

Paul: fish
        see?
J: Where's the turtle?
P: turtle
J: Mmhmm. Is he in there?
P: no turtle
        fish

The next example from Huang's data shows the child establishing a topic and defending his vocabulary choice for that topic:

Paul: this
J: What?
P: window (looking at fish tank)
J: Where's the window? (challenge?)
P: window
        this
J: Another window. Show me.
P: another window (echo)
J: Hmmm. Is this a *window* here?
P: yah
        window fish
        not window car.

He even responds to requests for imitations as though they were topic nominations on which he should elaborate:

J: Paul, can you say 'teacher'?
Paul: teacher
J: Right, teacher.
P: teacher
        Elsie (Name of his teacher)
J: Very good.

The data from Paul, then, show a wealth of examples similar to Scollon's and the conclusions I draw from the examples is the same. The child wishes to interact, to say something with language, and in learning how to do conversations he learns first vertical and then syntactic constructions.

A number of people who work in the field of conversational analysis have said that the first rule of conversation must be to "say something relevant." The data that we have looked at so far shows that the child is doing just that. However, what happens when the child knows this rule for conversation from his first language but knows absolutely none of the second language? How does he 'say something relevant' when he wants very much to carry on a conversation with a speaker of a language he does not understand? What can he say that will be relevant?

Itoh's data (Itoh, 1973) shows the very first interactions between her subject, Takahiro, and his aunt. The child wanted very much to interact verbally with his aunt but he did not know any English. His strategy was to 'say something' even though he did not understand what he said. The only possible way for him to interact verbally was to repeat her utterances after her. However, the intonation of the repetitions made the repetition 'relevant.' He echoes her statements with rising intonation and her questions with falling intonation:

Itoh, 1973, Japanese, 2:6, Takahiro

A: (Parking cars and airplanes)
    Make it one at a time.
Takahiro: one at a time?
A: Park everything.
T: /ɛvrišin/?
A: Park them.
T: Park them?
A: Does it fly?
T: Fly.

As the data collection sessions continued, repetitions became less echolalic:

H: Do you want to race also?
Takahiro: Also racing car.
H: That's all. That's all.
T: Okay, that's all.

He then began nominating topics:

Takahiro: /gra:ž/
H: Garage. OK. I'll make a garage.
T: OK.

Takahiro: /flɔ/
H: Flower. Green flower.
T: Green flower.
H: Oh, what color is this?
T: Green.
    Green flower.

He repeated, used and recombined parts of the conversation:

Takahiro: this
    broken
H: Broken.
T: broken
    This /əz/ broken.
    broken

H: Upside down.
T: upside down
            this broken
            upside down
            broken

As in Scollon's data, vertical constructions take place even without adult interaction:

H: House.
Takahiro: This house?
H: House.
T: House.
            To make the house.
            To make the house.
            To make the house.
            This?
            House.
            Garage.
            Garage house
            house
            big house
            Oh-no!
            broken.
H: Too bad.
T: Too bad.
H: Try again.
T: I get try.
            I get try.
H: Good.

While repetitions always played an important role in Takahiro's learning, immediate repetitions began to die out:

H: It's a garage. Come in garage.
T: /kəmən/ garage.
            /nay/ your. (= not yours)
H: This is yours.
T: /nay/ yours. (note morphology correction)
T: (continuing) come back.
            You do garage /tə/ here.
H: No. The garage is too small.
T: Small garage?
H: Mmmm. I can't come in. Right?
T: Okay. You'll can.

Again, I think that the Itoh data is supporting evidence that syntactic constructions grow out of conversation. It is quite possible that other studies, if input data were only available, would show the same thing. Even without the complete data, there are examples from learner-production data that seem to suggest that this is true. Here, for example, are a few examples from production data reported by Mazeika:

Mazeika, 1973, Spanish, 2½, Carlito

Carlito: La daddy
un pato
pato a Daddy ('Daddy's foot')

Chicle
chicle a Baby
otro chicle a Baby ('another chewing gum for baby')

sí banana
sí una banana
Baby quiere una banana, Mommy. (Baby wants a banana, Mommy)

The longest utterance in the data given in the report is twelve words, resulting from a gradual extension build-up:

Carlito: in the boat
go in the boat
Mommy, him go in the boat
Mommy, go in the boat in a con esa
Mommy, go in the boat
Mommy, go in the boat con esa Daddy ride in the boat.

Similar examples appear in Young's data:

Young, 1974, Spanish, Juan and Enrique

Juan: hey
dat green
green.

Enrique: Close la eyes
no mine. (= you close your eyes, I'll keep mine open.)

Her study, like Itoh's, shows the children using a great deal of repetition not just of the experimenter's speech, but of self-repetition. In her study, this can be at least partially attributed to the child's need to compete with other children for her attention. But another issue which must be discussed here (but probably better elsewhere) is the issue of language play.[1]

It might well be claimed that the long segment from Itoh's data on *garage/ house* (p. 410) has no conversational function, that it is not social speech at all but language play. In an earlier resume of Huang's work, I pointed out the large number of 'language play' routines. Some of them, no doubt, were just that, but all of them did occur within conversations (not when the child was alone or talking to toys). They do serve a conversational function of keeping talk going, which may or may not be important. Secondly, I don't think that language play is necessarily an argument against structure growing out of discourse. Once the child begins nominating topics and enlarging on them, commenting on them, and showing semantic relationships within the conversation, there is no reason that he should not then practice those relationships and/or use language play as a way of further practicing or playing with new forms for his own amusement or for the pleasure of those around him.

Obviously there is not space here to trace through all the kinds of conversational interactions between adults and child second-language learners to look at the emergence of each syntactic structure. I would like, however, to review what we have said about input frequency to the child and the appearance of those particular structures in the child's speech. We have said that the emergence of questions in one child's speech, Paul, directly reflects the frequency of questions asked him. We thought this a very important finding for it showed that input was an important factor in the order of emergence of structures—an issue which has been raised by morphology studies which talk about a developmental *order* of acquisition in child second language acquisition.

We would now like to say that the order of acquisition is really a reflection of conversation growth. The child learns to call the adult's attention to very concrete objects and on-going actions. If the first rule of conversation is to make a relevant reply, there are few directly relevant replies to be made to the kinds of topics the child nominates. For example, if the child nominates 'this' pointing to a fish in a fish tank, the child and adult seem to talk about 'this' as a topic in a very few, very limited ways: What? Fish. What's this? It's a fish. Where's the fish? Who's fish is that? Is that yours? How many fish are there? What color is the fish? What's the fish do*ing*? He's swimm*ing*. Can he swim? *No,* it's *not* a fish. There are not many 'etc.'s' possible. And precisely these questions and responses to the topic can account for the order of acquisition in morphology and AUX development that we have talked about elsewhere.

The conversation puts the adult under two constraints as to what is a relevant response: 1) what information about 'this' is shared by adult and child; and 2) what are the attributes of 'this' that one can talk about? That is, there is nothing immediately obvious about 'this' that allows one to ask *result/cause* questions (unless the fish is floating on top of the water). There is nothing about 'this' to allow one to make a *relevant* remark about much of anything beyond what, where, whose, what color, how many, what doing, can X Verb, is X Verb-ING. And the first constraint prevents the adult from saying such things as "You know the price of tuna just went up again," or "What's an angel fish doing in a fresh-water tank?"

My conclusion, then, is that it's really not so much that the adult knows the child cannot answer questions with complex syntactic forms and therefore consciously *simplifies* the input to the child. Rather, the frequency of what/where/whose/is X VerbING, etc. is controlled by the child's conversation topics. The constraints that conversation puts on questions explain their frequency in the input. That the child then uses (acquires) these same questions first should not be surprising.

This may be a very labored working out of why the input frequency looks like it does, but I hope it is a revealing one. I think it would be worthwhile for those researchers who are interested in the order of acquisition of morphemes to look back through their observational data to see, for example, if this might account for the frequency with which ING forms appear in the input (and therefore the early *appearance* of the ING form in child speech). If so, then we might want to reconsider why plurals appear early (what kinds of conversations lead to questions about *how many*); what kinds of conversations ask for possessives, third-person singular, etc. I feel it would be worth doing.

Another worthwhile task would be to look at the acquisition of almost all speech acts for the child second language learner. The above examples (and they are plentiful in the data) of language play may show us how the child learns to argue in English, for example. In the very earliest exchanges in Yoshida's data, Miki tries to get the attention of one of the other children prior to nominating a topic for conversation. He calls the child's name several times. The child, instead of responding, in turn calls the name of another child three times. That child immediately picks up the 'game' and adds the traditional sing-song 'ynneh' tone (used for such taunting phrases as 'Billy's got a girl-friend'), and this continues among several of the children in the nursery school. Miki, if anything, is given a quick lesson in the speech act of 'how to tease/fight/argue.' Hopefully, Sabrina Peck's data on L_1 Child and L_2 Child interactions will have much to say on such topics (as well as conversational differences between child-child and adult-child interactions).

There is a large jump now to be made in the attempt to justify discourse analysis at another level, to the issue of adults learning second languages. Surely conversations between adults are very different; conversational ambitions are at a much more complex level. Nevertheless, I think discourse analysis can reveal much that speaks to the issue of adult vs. child success in second language learning.

The problem in gathering evidence for discourse analysis in adult second language learning is, again, the paucity of substantial data (data which includes both the learner's speech and the speech of his conversation partner) on which to check our intuitions. The majority of the examples that follow are taken from data collected by Guy Butterworth (1972) on a teenage Spanish speaker learning English by immersion. His subject, Ricardo, attended school where he was enrolled in regular classes; there was no ESL program and only two people in the school spoke Spanish. He is the closest to a true beginner in the data of older second language learners that I have looked at so far.

Other data, collected by Brunak, Fain and Villoria (1976), consists of their conversations with Rafaela, an adult Spanish-speaker enrolled in a community adult school for night classes in beginning English. Fragmentary data from other sources will be identified in the text as they are cited.

In the early sessions the experimenters (hereafter labelled as NS for native speaker), in order to cope with the learner as a conversation partner, took control of conversation primarily by asking questions. This is common in adult-child interactions as well (see Corsaro, 197--; Keenan, 1976). The NS, then, would nominate a topic for discussion by asking a WH-question. Some sort of preliminary signal was given to the learner to pay attention, that he was about to be asked to take a conversation turn. The signal might be a slight cough, a clearing of the throat, an introducer such as *ehhh* or *emmm,* or a repetition of the initial part of the question as sort of a stutter start:

NS: Who is, who is your math teacher?
Where is, where is the haunted house?
Where in, where in Dana Point?

These signals (probably accompanied by non-verbal gestures) secured the learner's attention much in the same way that *lookit, oh-oh* and name calls did in the child examples given earlier. Another device used occasionally by adults addressing Ricardo was *Okay* or *Okay, now, Ricardo.* This was particularly true of male school personnel.

During the first two months, *immediate* relevant replies to the questions asked were almost nil in the Butterworth data. Topic identification, obviously, was not clear to the learner. Since the NS, in nominating the topics, did not point to any concrete reference, did not always have a picture handy to establish the reference, the learner's first problem in conversation was to try to elicit the reference for the topic in some way.

The easiest way to ask for the topic referent to be clarified, when one does not have much language to use, is to say *huh?* And the transcripts are full of *huh's:*

NS: Do you wear them everyday?
Ricardo: Huh?
NS: Do you put them on everyday?

NS: Did you have a nice weekend?
Ricardo: Huh?
NS: Friday, Saturday . . . did you have fun?

NS: What do you wear there?
Rafaela: Hmmm?
NS: What do you wear in Panama? The clothes?
Rafaela: Oh.
The . . .
maybe six dollars.

The *huh* forces topic clarification in many ways. It may get the speaker to move the topic either to the beginning or the end of his utterance where the learner can more easily attend to it. It may also get him to 'shift down' his lexical choice in nominating the topic from general to more specific or higher frequency vocabulary.

Another way to solicit a repair on the topic is to echo part of the question:

NS: Did you ride the mules?

```
Ricardo:     Mules?
NS:                  The horses around. The pack mules.
R:           Pack mules?
NS:                  (Gives up; goes to new topic)

NS:                  Did you live by yourself in Panama?
Rafaela:     Self?
NS:                  Did you live alone?
R:           Alone?
             Oh!
             in Panama . . .
             I have . . .
             yes
             all the time.
```

Repeated use of echoes and huh's as repair-solicits also forced the native speaker to add gestures:

```
NS:                  Do you wear them every day?
Ricardo:     Huh?
NS:                  Do you put them on every day?
Ricardo:     Wear?
NS:                  Yeah, do you (+gesture) put them on every day?
R:           Ah! No. Muy XXX
```

Second and third repairs were most likely to be accompanied by a gesture or to involve a direct translation into Spanish to make the topic clear.

There is some evidence in Rafaela's data (the more advanced beginner) that *huh* repair requests also served as time-holding devices for the learner. That is, in some instances Rafaela really understood the topic immediately but, because of her problems with fluency, needed more time before she could get out her response. There is an example where her repair requests seem to serve this function, and the native speaker 'shifts up' rather than down in reselecting vocabulary:

```
NS:                  What do people do in Panama for fun?
Rafaela:     Oh!
             for fun?
NS:                  For good time.
R:           Fun?
NS:                  For entertainment.
R:           Fun? (Followed by a long and careful build up of shared
             information, see page 428.)
```

Requests for topic clarification usually made the topic evident to the learner, but there were a few bad repairs which only added to the confusion:

```
NS:                  What does he make in Colombia?
Ricardo:     Hnnn?
NS:                  In Colombia, what does your father make? In Buena
             Ventura?
```

R:	In Buena Ventura?
NS:	Yeh, your father.
R:	No.
NS:	Oh well . . . (gives up)

The native speaker did use a left shift to repair the topic but he made a mistake and moved the wrong constituent. The second repair emphasized the earlier definition of *he* as *father,* but the notion of 'father makes something' and 'what' are not clarified for the learner. It's not surprising that he responds as if the question had been 'Is your father in Buena Ventura?'

It is interesting that the native speakers in the Butterworth data seldom simplified the grammar of the sentences to the point of what has been called 'foreigner talk.' There are many more examples of such simplifications in Brunak, Fain and Villoria data. We need to find out whether 'foreigner talk' is a common reaction of native speakers when they have to carry on conversations with new learners. In the above example, it seems that an 'easier' repair would be to drop most of the syntactic markers and instead build up a common pool of information, using semantically related words, to nominate the topic.

As I have noted elsewhere, on the basis of visiting adult schools, simplification to the point of 'foreigner talk' is a much more prevalent phenomenon than I initially suspected.

(Teacher explaining 'bath' and 'to bathe')
In your house. You . . . house. A tub. You (+gesture) wash.

(Teacher explaining how to take telephone messages)
I want speak other person. He not here. What good thing for say now?

(Teacher talking about individual interviews)
Not other student listen. I no want. Necessary *you* speak. Maybe I say,
    'What is your name?' The writing not important.

Teachers also carefully build up to topics. For example, where students were being reminded to bring their books to class, a teacher said, "The book. We have . . . (holds up copy of the book) book. Is necessary for class. Right? Necessary for class. You have book?" etc.

This careful establishment of topic occurs in conversations between native speakers as well as in discourse of native speakers and language learners. That is, we do not immediately plunge into a topic of conversation without first asking the listener to attend to the topic, and establishing the shared information we have about a topic, before making a new assertion. Atkinson calls such examples as "Do you know Jack?" "Do you remember the man you met at the theatre on Friday" topic priming, a way of establishing topic reference before giving new information, such as "Well, he's in the kitchen." The *do you remember/do you know* forms are not yes/no questions about information or memory (the phonological form is considerably reduced which separates them unambiguously from information questions). Their function rather is to prime the listener and establish the topic before new information is given or asked for.

The native speakers in Rafaela's corpus seem to use this strategy at least to some degree. In the following example, the NS does not immediately ask "Do you like your English classes," but rather first establishes the topic:

NS: You're taking some English classes, no?

Rafaela: Aha?

NS: Where? Is it at—

R: Where? In Samoa High, Santa Monica.

NS: I think I know . . .

R: In Pico and Lincoln.

NS: . . . where that is.
                Do you like them?

However, in most cases learner were faced with topics for which s/he needed either clarification or additional information. The huh/echo strategy was the most effective way for them to tune in to what was happening.

The huh/echo strategy worked well in another way. It forced the native speaker to change the syntactic form of the question in the ways we had previously found in transcripts of telephone conversations between second language learners and various service personnel. The learner in the following examples is a French speaker, wife of a graduate student, approximately 25 to 30 years old. Like Rafaela, she is enrolled in a community adult school class, this time in intermediate English.

Pauline's task, in these examples, was to find out how much it would cost to get a thesis typed and when the typist could do it. Although the task required that she ask for information, the native speaker quickly took over much of the burden of conversation by asking questions.

Pauline & typist	Discourse pattern
NS: WHICH UNIVERSITY IS IT FOR?	WH-Q
P: Yes. I have a more 100.	t-rel (topic related response)
NS: PARDON ME?	repair request
P: I have a more 100 page.	repair
NS: YES, BUT IS IT FOR UCLA? OR USC?	Repair WH-Q→ YES/NO+ CHOICE
P: Ucla.	TRR (topic relevant response)

The typist used a WH-Q to which Pauline gave a response which, while topic-related, is not an appropriate answer to the question. The native speaker then repaired the question by putting it into an 'easier' form, the YES/No question. In fact, USC and UCLA are familiar vocabulary items for Pauline, giving her some cue as to the question being asked, and she chose UCLA (the school which her husband attends) as her answer. The change from a WH-Q on 'university' to a choice of answers between USC and UCLA made it possible for Pauline to respond, but it does not necessarily mean she understood the question being asked.

The second example shows that even the technique of offering possible answers in a Yes/No format will not always allow the learner to respond appropriately. You will also notice that Pauline's speech consists almost entirely of repair solicits in the following exchange.

Pauline & typist	Discourse pattern
NS: I SEE. WELL, IS IT TYPED?	Q_1
P: Type? Yes uh for the I don't I don't type.	t-related
NS: IS IT HANDWRITTEN?	Repair, 2nd CHOICE offered
P: Uh. Pardon me. Excuse me?	repair request
NS: IS YOUR THESIS NOW HAND-WRITTEN?	Repair, it = thesis definition
P: I don't understand you. Because excuse me I I speak a little bit English. I speak French. Do you speak French?	repair request request for lang. change
NS: NO UNFORTUNATELY NOT ENOUGH. NO, I KNOW A VERY LITTLE BUT I REALLY COULDN'T SPEAK IT.	TRR
MMM (searching for words) IS Y— IS YOUR THESIS NOW TYPEWRITTEN OR DID YOU WRITE IT BY HAND?	Repair, + OR CHOICE
P: Ah yes, by hand.	TRR + echo
NS: BY HAND.	Check
P: Now I I me I write my copy by hand but uh uh I like you type for me. You understand?	TRR Check
NS: OH YES	TRR
UH BUT IF IT— IS IT GOING TO BE A DRAFT OR THE FINAL?	Repairs, IF-Q repaired to YES/NO + OR CHOICE
P: Uh no uh excuse me.	repair request
NS: OHHHH (sympathetic sound)	
P: Do you repeat, please?	repair request
NS: YES	
IS, ARE YOU GOING TO NEED UH THE FINAL COPY?	Repair (No. 6) Typed = final, handwritten = draft

Perhaps one more example will show how difficult repair construction can be (particularly in phone conversations where non-verbal cues cannot be seen). Pauline, however, is able to respond when enough repairs with suggested answers are provided:

Pauline & typist
NS: WHEN DO YOU HAVE TO TURN IT IN TO UCLA?
P: Oh. Excuse me. I don't understand.
NS: OH. YOU DON'T UNDERSTAND. MMMM (sympathetic sound)
P: I uh what the paper, no?

NS:	PARDON ME?
P:	No, I don't know you say.
NS:	WHEN . . . WHEN DO YOU NEED THE THE-SIS? WHEN DO YOU WANT TO HAVE IT TYPED?
P:	Yes. When? (= Did you say 'when')
NS:	WHEN. (= Yes, I said 'when')
P:	When . . . ah . . . maybe ah two weeks?
NS:	TWO WEEKS?
P:	Yes.
NS:	TWO WEEKS FROM NOW? (checking) OR IS IT READY NOW? DO YOU HAVE IT READY? (= Is '2 weeks' when you need it or when you want it typed)
P:	Uh no I don't. I do not I don't have finished now. Maybe on July.
NS:	IN JULY. (checking)
P:	Yes. July.
NS:	I SEE. (= Answer was for 'when you want it typed' question) AND WHEN DO YOU HAVE TO FINISH IT FOR THE UNIVERSITY?
P:	Yes.
NS:	WHEN.
P:	'When' uh uh . . .
NS:	IN AUGUST? (possible answer suggested)
P:	No I finish uh uh uh uh July 30?
NS:	JULY 30TH. I SEE.

From the above examples it is clear that Pauline does not solicit repairs with *huh* in the same way as Ricardo and Rafaela. Rather she uses *Pardon me/ Excuse me/I don't understand* along with echoes. Her topic-related and topic-irrelevant responses also solicit repairs. The repairs solicited, however, do not 'shift down' the syntax difficulty. Rather they 'shift down' what is required of the learner in order to respond. He need only agree or disagree with the YES/NO questions, take one of the choices offered him by OR CHOICE questions, or take one of the answers suggested by the NS.

Using this evidence of question sequencing as one device for 'making it easier'[2] for the learner to participate in conversations, we turned to the Butterworth tapes and found many similar examples:

1. WH-Q repaired as YES/NO Q
   How is your team? Is your team very good?
   What did you do? Did you, didn't you ride your bicycle?
   Where in, where in Capistrano Beach? Did you throw it in the dump?
   Who is Kathi R? Is she the girl that's going to the Chili Pepper?
   Why not? Oh, is it too far?

2. WH-Q repaired as an OR CHOICE Q

No, how does it go, do they play like this or like this?

If you win today, then what do you get? You know, a prize, a trophy?

How do they—are they playing like this? Or are they playing like this?

3. Q + Answer

No, what not? She'd be scared?

It has a . . . in the dock does it have a big wheel?

What else is good over there? The Haunted House?

In a sense, these repairs go beyond helping the learner to identify the topic. The NS models for the learner what his response ought to be to the topic.

The strategies the NS uses to simplify questions seem to be reliable on the basis of a questionnaire test[3] but these repairs do not always allow the learner to make a relevant response. NSs also find it difficult to repair some of their utterances in ways that will allow the learner to respond appropriately. The following example shows the NS trying ten different repairs before finally giving up:

Butterworth & Ricardo	Discourse pattern
WHO IS THE BEST PLAYER IN COLOMBIA?	Q_1
Colombia.	Echo (or t-rel response?)
DOES UH . . . WHO IS *THE* COLOMBIAN PLAYER?	WH-Q → YES/NO repair fails
Me?	TRR (incorrect)
NO, IN COLOMBIA, WHO IS *THE* PLAYER?	Left shift, best = *the* repair
In Colombia plays. Yah.	T-related
NO, ON YOUR TEAM. ON THE MILLONARIOS.	Repair, Colombian team specified
Ah yah, Millonarios.	T-rel, recognizes team name.
WHO IS THE BEST PLAYER?	Q_1 exact repetition
Me?	TRR attempt repeated (incorrect)
NO. ON THE MILLIONARIOS TEAM.	Team specified again.
Millonarios play in Colombia. In Sud America. In Europa.	T-related comment
NS: DO, DO THEY HAVE SOMEONE LIKE PELE IN COLOMBIA?	Repair best = Pele, WH-Q YES/NO
R: Pele? In Colombia? Pele?	Echo, name recognized
NS: IN COLOMBIA? WHO IS, WHO IS 'PELE' IN COLOMBIA? DO YOU HAVE SOMEONE?	Repair left shift. Repair WH-Q YES/NO

R:	In Bogotá?	Repair request
NS:	YEH. WHO IS THE BEST PLAYER?	Q_1 exact repetition
R:	In Santo de Brazil?	Repair request
NS:	OKAY. (Gives up)	Give up
	AND YOU ARE CENTER FORWARD?	Q_2

Topic related and topic irrelevant responses such as those given in this exchange result in less than lucid conversational exchanges but they, perhaps, show us more about what strategies the learner is using in conversational discourse than do the topic relevant responses. For example, if one examines inappropriate responses, it is often possible to see what the learner thought the topic and subsequent questions on it were:

Butterworth & Ricardo

NS:	WHY, WHY ARE YOU GOING THERE?
R:	Why?
NS:	WHY ARE YOU GOING TO THE CHILI PEPPER?
R:	Today Mr. L., Mrs. T., ten boys and girls.

Ricardo's answer is to the question 'who is going.' There are many, many examples of close guesses in the data:

WHO ELSE DO YOU PLAY CHESS WITH? He play me. (Who does he play with?)

HOW LONG TO GO HOME? In bus. (How do you go home?)

WHEN YOU GET HOME, WHAT WILL YOU DO? I'm at home XXX thrée. (What time do you get home?)

WHAT SUBJECTS DO YOU HAVE HOMEWORK IN? House. (Where do you do your homework? / possible word association response.)

WHEN DO YOU WATCH CARTOONS? Aquaman. (What program do you watch?)

WHAT DO YOU DO WITH LOBSTERS? In morning. (When do you catch lobsters?)

5:00 IN THE MORNING! CAN YOU SEE AT 5:00 IN THE MORNING? Hmmm, me come by 4:00 . . . 3:00 afternoon. (What time do you come back?)

TIRED. ARE YOU SLEEPY? In mi house? (Where do you sleep?)

HOW BIG WAS THE BOAT? In Disneyland. (Where was the boat?)

Given such examples, it is possible to go back to the WHO IS THE BEST PLAYER sequence (p. 420) and then see that the first response Ricardo gives is his recognition of the topic 'Colombia' or, possibly, his response might be to answer 'Who is best, Colombia?' His 'In Colombia plays' may mean that he agrees that soccer is played in Colombia. The next response is a recognition of the team name. He later volunteers information about where the team plays. His next response might mean he wonders if Pele is actually in Bogotá. His next response might be to question just where Pele might be playing in Colombia. From his responses, it might be possible to hypothesize a discourse context and a set of concerns that Ricardo believes the conversation to be about; obviously it is not the same as Butterworth's.

In the following exchange it is not clear that the topic and/or the topic shift is recognized clearly by *either* party. Is Ricardo talking about what he did or about what he got? For some unknown reason, the NS (in this case, not Butterworth) assumes after 'bicycle' that Ricardo received a bicycle for Christmas. The final exchanges suggest that Ricardo had been talking about activities rather than gifts all along:

NS: DID YOU HAVE A NICE HOLIDAY?
R: Huh?
NS: (Slower) NICE CHRISTMAS . . . WAS YOUR CHRISTMAS NICE?
R: Yah.
NS: WHAT DID YOU DO?
R: Ehh baseball.
NS: PLAY BASEBALL. WHAT ELSE DID YOU DO?
R: Football
NS: FOOTBALL. WHAT ELSE DID YOU DO?
R: Bicycle.
NS: YOU GOT A BICYCLE.
R: Mmmm.
NS: WHAT KIND OF BICYCLE?
R: 10-speed.
NS: TEN-SPEED. WHAT ELSE?
R: Chess.
NS: CHESS SET.
R: Chess.
NS: DO YOU KNOW HOW TO PLAY CHESS?
R: Yah. I understand chess.
NS: VERY GOOD. WHO DO YOU PLAY WITH?
R: Huh?
NS: WHO DO YOU PLAY WITH? YOUR MAMA OR YOUR DAD?
R: Friends.
NS: FRIENDS. VERY GOOD. WHAT ELSE?
R: Huh?
NS: DID YOU GET ANY CLOTHES?
R: Huh?
NS: DID YOU GET ANY CLOTHES?
R: Clothes?
NS: YAH, CLOTHES. SHIRT (+ gesture)
R: Huh?
NS: YAH. DID YOU GET FOR CHRISTMAS?
R: Yah.
NS: WHAT DID YOU GET?
R: Huh?

From all these exchanges, it should be evident that the adult learner has a great deal of difficulty, in the beginning stages of second-language acquisition, in identifying topics accurately. It should also be evident that the learner has strategies to help clarify topics. He can ask for repetitions and clarifications in a number of ways: for Pauline, it was excuse me/pardon me and echoes; for Ricardo it was echo/huh. This allows the learner to get content words restated so that he can recognize the topic being nominated in the original question. Once the topic is recognized, he can further use his knowledge of the world and of discourse in his own language to predict the possible questions, the concerns which might be expressed in questions about that topic. Based on that prediction, he will respond in a less than random fashion. If his predictions on the probable questions (e.g. Christmas vacation and what he received as gifts) are correct and his order of the probable questions as to which might be asked first, second and third is correct (or his recognition of WH-Q words is correct), his chances of giving a topic-relevant response are high. Many topic-relevant responses may then be good guesses and not evidence of comprehension of specific questions at all. If his ordering of possible questions is faulty, he may give a topic-related response. If his predictions are completely wrong because he did not even get the topic of discourse correct, his responses would be topic-irrelevant responses. Our evidence suggests that this, indeed, is what is happening in the data that we have looked at thus far.

If this description is correct, we might want to reconsider our notions of the requirements of 'listening comprehension' at least so far as non-native speakers of a language are concerned. A number of models of listening comprehension have been suggested. One model (the one apparent in ESL textbooks) assumes the listener must discriminate all the small details of what he hears and simultaneously make phonetic decisions, phonemic decisions, syntactic decisions, and semantic decisions in order to understand each utterance. A second model suggests that we interpret utterances by trying to generate them ourselves, cross-checking to see whether our generated utterances match those being said. Obviously this must be a very rapid generation of guesses in order for the match(es) to take place while the auditory signal is still present in short term memory. A third model might be a discourse model in which the learner may, at the beginning of a discourse block, use a fine discrimination model, then through the priming questions, predict the discourse topic. Once the topic of discourse is set, the learner could shift to predicting possible questions and comments based on his knowledge of past discourse and shared information. The checking and matching would be in large units, then, rather than small, with repairs and new hypotheses being generated at discourse break-down points. Similar models for beginning rapid reading have also been proposed.

It seems quite possible that the adult learner transfers these strategies to second language learning, using a discourse model for as much as he possibly can. Once a topic is clear, he can form a grid for listening, based on his knowledge of discourse possibilities within that topic, which markedly improves his comprehension performance. Without the grid, he can become lost in phonetic and syntactic detail and understand nothing. In a sense, he is doing what the child does when he looks at his environment at the nursery school, watches the other children's actions, and thereby gives evidence (e.g., hangs up his jacket when the teacher tells him to do so) of comprehension of the second language when, in fact, he does not understand the syntactic form nor the vocabulary of the utterance when that context does not exist.

The problem, then, for the adult learner is that the discourse of Adult-Adult conversation relies much less on immediate environment than Adult-Child or Child-Child interactions. Topic identification is much more difficult. The adult learner must, *at the very least,* recognize the content vocabulary of a topic nomination in order to participate in conversation at all. Without vocabulary cues, he cannot make any of the predictions necessary for topic-relevant responses. We will get back to the pedagogical implications of this statement later.

While we have discussed how the adult language learner solicits repairs to make topics clear, this discussion has all been in terms of topics which the native speaker has initiated. I'd like to turn now to the learner's attempts to nominate topics.

One might expect that topic nominations would be quite different from those of the child learner. There are, however, a couple of examples in Butterworth's data that look somewhat similar to the child's attempts to establish topics:

Ricardo:	Lookit that. (Shows map, apparently wants to talk about skyscrapers.)
	This.
	Empire State.
NS:	Yeh, but it uh—
R:	This is New York.
Ricardo:	In Chicago.
	One more maybe.
	New.
	New one, new.
NS:	Yeh, there's a new round one there.

Such examples, however, are few and far between. Ricardo does prepare for topic nominations, however, either by using Butterworth's technique of stutter starts and repetitions, thereby building up vertical structures like those in our child language data:

Ricardo:	Who is	You go
	who is	you go
	who is more good freeway?	for bicycle racing
	San Diego Freeway?	Los Angeles?

or by getting vocabulary agreement before asking a question:

Ricardo:	Thruway and freeway
	similar?
NS:	Yeh, similar.
R:	Thruway was in city?
NS:	Uh city or country.
R:	You go de thruway?

These examples of topic nomination and of establishing the context for the question by priming of vocabulary, seem very similar to our examples from child data. However, establishing the topic and making observations on it seems to take the adult learner much longer since the topic is not tied to objects present or necessarily related to present activities:

Ricardo:	Saturday, Sunday (Trying to elicit 'last weekend'?)
	me
	how do you say . . .
	Saturday, Sunday.
	me in . . .
	in car of my father.
NS:	Where? In your father's car? Where did you drive?
R:	Capistrano
	me
	my mother me go for my mother watch.
	She watch house.
	Me (+ gesture of driving)
NS:	Oh, are you looking at a house in Capistrano?
R:	Yeh.
	Mama say me
	Mama say me
	Mama no understand car.
	You know?
NS:	Yes, she doesn't know how to drive.
R:	Mama say me . . .
	"Ricardo. You me go de Capistrano."
	Me . . .
	"Fred.
	Fred, please, keys for car.
	Me a this for police (+ gesture)"

The data on topic nominations is somewhat sparse in the Butterworth data. Most topic nominations came from the NSs. Rafaela, on the other hand, is quite willing to suggest topics in her conversations with NSs. The form of her nominations and comments on her topic are, in some ways, very similar to the child learner's:

| NS: | You're not working right now? |
| Rafaela: | No. |

NS: No?
R: Ahhh
for one week . . .
I . . .
the . . .
comp-any?
the company . . .
is inventory
inventory
aha
for one week.
NS: Oh.
R: Monday I work
I work . . .
Monday.
NS: You're going to start working Monday again.

Perhaps because the nominations and comments are so lengthy, the native speaker seems driven to paraphrase everything that has been said in one sentence. This occurs in all the data we've looked at for adults.

Raefaela: I like men American but I no no . . .
I no . . .
have nothing . . .
NS: Oh, I see. You don't have a boyfriend here.
R: No boyfriend American.

Rafaela: Before here 3, 2 months
I live my mother.
NS: For two months you lived with your mother.

The learner, then, tries to solicit vocabulary from the native speaker and drives the native speaker to restate his topics and his comments in a summary way. However, the native speaker does not always understand clearly and in many cases cannot restate what was said and instead changes the topic:

NS: There are some problems between the Americans and
Panamanians, no?
Rafaela: Yeah.
NS: Really?
R: For the students
for flag?
flag?
NS: Flag?
R: For the canal zone
the flag
is the Panama and students go to the Canal Zone
the students
the Canal Zone work

	the Canal Zone
	fight
NS:	With who? With who?
R:	The student Panamanian and the students the Canal Zone.
	Canal Zone is American.
NS:	Oh yeah?
R:	Yeah, is American
	in Panama.
NS:	They have . . . American schools and everything.
	Are there private schools?

It is not clear that the native speaker understood Rafaela to say that Panamanian students went to the American-controlled Canal Zone to fight with American students over the American flag flying there.

Restatement of learner speech by the NS could be viewed as a repair-by-another-speaker. However, its function seems to be one of reassuring the learner that he is understood. As Schegloff has pointed out, it is polite to allow the speaker to repair his own speech. The restatements do not appear to function as repairs. The learners, themselves, do solicit repairs (particularly of vocabulary items; c.f., rising intonation on vocabulary items in many of the examples above as both discourse and vocabulary checks). But, even more frequently, they repair their own utterances:[4]

NS:	You don't like shorts?
Rafaela:	No . . .
	my sister . . .
	my sister . . .
	oh . . .
	the lady . . .
	lady no, no, no use many short.
	For me is muy . . . (laughs)
NS:	(laughs) Latin American men . . . yeh!
Rafaela:	Sí.

In all of Rafaela's topic nominations, she uses a fantastic amount of topic preparation, a great deal of priming. Karen Schlue (1976) has also noted this in her data on adult second-language learners. The following example is given as a comparison of the amount of priming done by the NSs and the amount Rafaela seems to feel is necessary to make her comment clear.

NS:	Oh, that's a beautiful plant!
	I like that.
	Did you buy that?
Rafaela:	Excuse me . . .
	this is the . . .
	October 24.
	The how you say . . .
	the . . . (writes '1974')
	year, ah?

NS: 1974. Last year.

R: Ah! Last years.

NS: One. (note plural correction)

R: Last year.
Last year a friend gave me it.

NS: Oh, gave it to you! That's a nice gift!
Do you like plants?

R: Yes I like.
This is my . . .
Miss Fain give me.
In October 24.

This example and the following one gives us an idea of how much effort it takes to get out material which might take a native speaker two utterances at most.

Rafaela: (In response to 'What do people in Panama do for fun?')
Oh . . .
the people work, no?
ah . . . estudian? . . . study?

NS: Study.

R: Study.
Friday is Viernes Cultural.
This is in Panama Friday . . .
Viernes Cultural
Friday cultural.

NS: Cultural.

R: When finish the work . . .
many compañero? . . .

NS: Compañero?

R: I don't know is this is correct.

NS: Oh I see . . . companions, friends.

R: Friend and friend and—

NS: Friends from work? Co-workers?

R: Compañeros.
go to the . . . ah . . .
in Panama have a salon—
(Telephone rings and she leaves the room)

NS: So tell me what you were telling me about what people
do on Friday, in Panama.

R: Oh! Friday?
In Panama every Friday the companions, the work, talk for
going to, for to dinner.
Ever
for drink
dance every Friday.

NS:	Aha. And on Saturday?
R:	Saturday, Saturday is party!
NS:	Oh!
R:	Yeah
	every Saturday
	people party the Saturday.

Using the last two examples as evidence, we might say that the learner is trying to obey the conventions of discourse. She knows that one must first present some shared background information as a primer ('You know the fights about the flag,' before elaborating on the topic ('well, the Panamanian students come over to the Canal Zone to capture the flag').

A second possibility is that instead of obeying discourse constraints, she first is checking the content vocabulary necessary to establish the background information for what she wishes to say.

I believe the last example shows that she tried to do both. It is clear she could as easily have said, "Friday, Friday is party!" as she did for Saturday. However, she seems to be aware that conversations among adults call for much more elaboration than that. It is also clear that it is difficult for her to get all of her information (semantically related though it is) into a proper syntactic order. She has real fluency problems; this is clear from the ease with which she answers the question after leaving the room to talk on the phone. She has managed to get everything together by the time she gets back.

This does not mean that vocabulary elicitation is not the primary reason for the lengthy build-ups that occur in Rafaela and Ricardo's topic nominations. In the Butterworth tapes, vocabulary elicitation seems to be essential if Ricardo is to participate in conversations at all. This technique made it possible for him to nominate more and more topics himself rather than always acting as a passive, question-answerer:

1. Ricardo & NS
   Patinas. How do you say (+G)
   Skating.
   Yeh. They're skating.

2. This is pañuelo . . . ?
   Oh yeh, that's a scarf.
   Scarf.
   Scarf-pañuelo.

3. I don't know 'bull'?
   You know, 'toro.'
   No, no like.

4. Brother of my, how do you say,
   my my uncle woman, you know?
   Your uncle's wife.
   Yah . . . woman is my uncle.
   Oh, your aunt. Aunt.
   My aunt husband.

5. My uncle and esposa . . . ?
   And wife.
   And wife and niños . . . ?
   Oh, and children.
   Yeh.

Me go here and here.
And childrens put they in car.
And every city Cali.
 Oh, and you drove around Cali.

Ricardo also asked for judgments on vocabulary items:

Ricardo: In, in California 'super freeway'?
NS: They um call them . . . no, they don't. We don't call them 'super freeway.' We say 'super highway' or 'freeway.'
R: No 'super freeway.'

Even when definitions were not asked for, they were provided if the topic was not clear to the native speaker.

Ricardo: Ticket.
NS: You got a ticket?
R: Yah. A little bit.
 Is for one month.
NS: You have . . . ?
R: Ticket for one month.
NS: To do what?
R: Ticket for one month. No more.
NS: So you can drive?
R: Mmmm.
NS: You have a permit to drive.
 A driver's permit.

It is tempting, on the basis of these data, to hypothesize that the adult focus in second language learning is on vocabulary while for the child the focus is on something else. But, instead, it appears that the learner is only asking for enough vocabulary to allow him to nominate topics and participate in conversational discourse. Perhaps once the pressure of needing a particular word in order to take his turn in the conversation is gone, the vocabulary is also 'forgotten.' That is, eliciting vocabulary may only be a strategy to allow one to continue the discourse. I believe this to be the case, but I would like very much to find that a great deal of vocabulary acquisition is taking place at the same time.[5] The child does, of course, have many opportunities to work on vocabulary but it is a much more limited set of items. The practice for the child is more often in the form of word play or word-naming games which are played over and over again with pictures, objects, rhymes and songs.

Yet, with these qualifications in mind, it seems quite clear that vocabulary is an important concern of second language learners. Adult second language learners have been telling us that for years (and perhaps it's time we listened to their intuitions of what would help them in language classes). Stafford and Covitt (1976) and Schlue (1976) also point out that learners perceive 'errors' in their speech and in their writing as much, if not more, in terms of vocabulary choice as in terms of grammar. Krashen too has commented that such a finding is not surprising for, after all, adults carry around dictionaries, not grammar books.

Our research into child-learner and adult-learner discourse strategies shows that there are many marked similarities. The learner has the same difficulty in perceiving topics in discourse whether child or adult; they also have the same difficulty in nominating topics for conversation and developing their ideas in syntactic form. The differences in success seem to be a function of topic appropriateness for child and adult. Topics are limited by the amount of information that is shared by adult and child. The adult does not suggest topics for which the child has no background information. The child, in turns, nominates topics that are seldom displaced in time or space. Such topics severely limit the syntax and vocabulary used in child-adult discourse.

Conversational ambitions of adults are much more abstract; they cover an incredibly wide range of topics. This does not mean there are no predictable topics for the adult learner. He quickly learns to answer 'where are you from, how long have you been here, how do you like LOC, where do you work, what did you do last week-end'; and when conversation comes to a standstill, native speakers frequently revert back to these topics just to make conversation easier.[6]

Since the topics in adult discourse are much more varied and more abstract, it is much more difficult for the adult to identify conversation topics unless he knows the necessary vocabulary for that topic. One way he clarifies topics is with continued vocabulary solicitation. In nominating topics, he also solicits vocabulary. In a sense, this is no different than the procedure the child uses when he first gets the NS's attention by saying 'oh-oh,' then points to an object saying 'this.' While 'this' is a topic nomination it, in effect, also solicits the vocabulary item for that object.

Once the topic is recognized by the adult, he has strategies (that the child does not seem to possess to the same degree) for predicting what the entire discourse on that topic might be like. He can transfer discourse chunks from his first language, predicting questions on the basis of what he knows of the real world. The child can do this too, but the range of possibilities is much smaller for him.

There is strong evidence, I believe, that children develop syntactic form out of vertical constructions in conversation. The move from semantically related vertical constructions to horizontal ones shows how syntactic construction develops. The evidence is less strong for adults. The adults, in the data we have to look at, seem also to form vertical constructions of semantically related words and phrases. However, the function of their vertical constructions is not clear. It may be that their vertical constructions serve two other functions: first, to check out the vocabulary necessary in order to get important parts of the proposition together; or second, to observe the convention of polite conversation where it is necessary to first establish background information as a primer before elaborating on the topic with new information.

To make a case for discourse analysis as strong as possible, we must be able to show how syntax grows out of discourse for each learner. I think it is quite possible to do this with the child data that we have looked at thus far. But more data is needed. It will be more difficult, unfortunately, to establish as strong a case for the adult learner. Obviously, the adult transfers much more than just the discourse predictability from the first language. In nominating topics and commenting on them, the adult can try to order agent-action, agent-action-object, entity-attribute or any other semantic relationship he wishes to establish by mentioning them in an order which makes the relationship clear to him. That relationship has already been clearly arranged syntactically in his first language for many years. It would be strange to find the relationships evolving in ways radically different from those of his first language. Nevertheless, there are examples in the data that seem to violate the word order constraints of *both* the learner's first language *and* the second language. Perhaps word order violations are evidence of conversational forces at work.

To make our case a strong one, we also need to look for evidence within conversations that would predict the acquisition of English morphology as well. The literature shows a general order of acquisition that is similar for child and adult learners. We have tried to show how that order is a direct result of learning from discourse in child second-language learning. If that is so, why do we have the same order of acquisition of morphology in adult learners? The topics seem to control the input of structures to the child in a way that explains morphological ordering. Topics for the adult do not seem to be structured in the same way. We will need to look at adult data very thoughtfully for an explanation.

It is *possible* that topic nomination for the beginning adult learner requires establishment of semantic relationships using precisely the morphemes that are acquired early. The vertical constructions may consist of a set of such relationships as object identification, time reference, action, object identification, attribute description, etc. These would require such morphemes as the plural, the possessive, copula, etc. Secondly, it is *possible* that when the NS does not understand the learner, he asks for clarifications with questions like 'how many?' 'one?' (see Rafaela's data, p. 428), 'whose car?' Mistakes in the marking of verbs, however, would not be caught by 'when?' questions. Such question-corrections would more likely elicit a time adverb rather than a verb correction for morphology. This might explain late acquisition of certain verb functions in morphology. It is also likely that one would not question third-person singular present tense if the subject were clear. So it is possible that conversations could also determine the order of acquisition of morphology for the adult.

I do not want to go back to the 'frequency' argument without some under-standing of what determines that frequency in the input to adult learners. We need to know what kinds of conversations prompt use of such a large number of ING morphemes, why there are few -s endings for third person singular (do we always talk about ourselves rather than he/she?). This kind of evidence is crucial for the case. And I hope to find reliable data soon on which to base our claim.

This brings up a final problem for the establishment of discourse as an alternative methodology, the problem of reliable data. Transcription of taped data is an extremely time-consuming task; if you have tried to transcribe tapes carefully, you know *how* time-consuming. Even so, the tape transcriptions that I have looked at for data for this paper leave much to be desired. Pause length and intonation curves become crucial when you are looking for vertical structures. Contrastive stress is crucial in understanding semantic relationships which are not always clear from word order arrangements. For example, if a learner says, "He for long hair ties it," and we do not have the complete conversation, do not have the pauses marked, do not have intonation and stress information, we can only tally the utterance as aberrant word order based neither on the first nor the second language. We cannot say that the learner has first pointed to someone with long hair, then motions with rubber-band gestures, and tells us that the 'he' uses the rubber band for the long hair, making a pony-tail. If the data were transcribed in vertical constructions, if there were detailed notes on his gestures, if we were sure of stress and pauses, we could feel confident in making such statements. Our data, for the most part, are inadequate to serve our purpose. Videotaped data may be the only answer.

In spite of all these problems, I feel very strongly that only through discourse analysis can we answer the many questions that we have about second language acquisition. The fact that "chaos is the alternative to orderly systems of grammatical rules should not dismay workers in the field" (Atkinson, 1974, p. 24). I happen to think that chaos is the most productive possible position to be in. It lets us look at all the alternative methodologies for explanations rather than getting us locked into one way of doing research. While I believe that discourse analysis is the best alternative at the moment, I don't want to stop looking for evidence of Slobin's universal strategies; I just want to see how conversational analysis might explain them. Though I don't believe there is a real difference between acquisition and learning, I would like to look at behaviors that are operationally defined as learning or as acquisition to see what discourse analysis tells us about such behaviors. I don't want people to stop looking at the emergence of forms in the speech of second language learners, I just want to know how discourse analysis might explain that order of acquisition. I don't want to stop looking at function of verb forms but I'd like to know how the functions are acquired and why. For all these reasons, I would like to see researchers look through their findings once again from another viewpoint, a viewpoint that I believe will be extremely fruitful for the future.

Finally a word or two about pedagogical conclusions. I know that it is presumptuous and dangerous to make any recommendations on the small amount of evidence that I have presented in this paper. But I will anyway, just to let you know where I stand.

I think the study of discourse analysis might have tremendous implications for teaching, particularly for teaching *adults* a second language. While I have not thought out what these implications might be, I have a few ideas that do not necessarily draw on these data, but from my own observations in trying to learn second languages.

First, the learner needs to be able to talk about a small number of topics that s/he knows s/he will be asked (where are you from; how long have you been here; how do you like America, UCLA, etc.; if in school, what classes are you taking; if at work, where do you work; if at work, what do you do there, etc.). They should also learn to talk about their own major or occupation at a number of different levels. They should practice nominating topics about which they are prepared to speak. They should do lots of listening comprehension for topic nominations of lots of native speakers. They should practice predicting questions for a large number of topics. In their predictions they should be taught to listen for particular WH-words (when, where, who, etc.) which would clue the question being asked more accurately. They should be taught all the elicitation devices we have mentioned to get topic clarification. That is, they should practice saying *huh,* echoing parts of the sentences they do understand in order to get the rest of it recycled again, *pardon me, excuse me, I don't understand,* etc. They should be told to use uh-uh-ah-ah or whatever fillers they can to show the Native Speaker that they really are trying. Nothing stops the opportunity to carry on a conversation quicker than silence or the use of 'yes' and head-nodding when the learner does not understand. They should get lots of work on clarifying semantic relationships in 'second tries' using the proper morphological markers. That is, if the learner cannot identify the topic and does not know the vocabulary, he cannot also attend to the morphological markers. If the learner gets to recycle the same topic several times with the same or different native speakers, he will then have the vocabulary and know the possible questions that will be asked. When he's got that much, he can recycle the topic again with another person and pay attention to his syntax and morphology. We do this, in some sense, when we give students dialogues and/or role playing situations to do. The emphasis would be changed to fit these techniques into a discourse analysis framework. Finally, and most important, the learner should be taught not to give up. He should be encouraged to find a friend (in the Larson & Smalley sense) but he should also be taught not to give up in any contact he has with a native speaker. Pauline, for example, made tremendous progress because she didn't give up. She uses uh's and ah's and 'excuse me's' for all they were worth. No one ever hung up on her. The same could not be said for other learners who just said 'What?' or 'Yes,' showing little work in their attempts to keep conversations going. The most important thing of all has to be 'don't give up.' But it's hard not to when we know the learning task is going to demand that the adult learn thousands of vocabulary items, learn to use those items to predict topics, and work out ways to make his comments on that topic relevant not just in terms of semantically related notions, not just in terms of syntactic relations, but also in terms of the conventions of conversation for the English language.

Notes

1. For a discussion of language play as social speech, see Keenan, 1974. For a discussion of language play in second language acquisition, see Peck, 1976.

2. There are, of course, many ways that native speakers 'make it easier' for the learner to participate in conversations. They slow down, articulate more clearly, use contrastive stress, check for comprehension in a variety of ways, 'fill in linguistic gaps' for the learner by predicting what he meant to say, etc. For a more complete discussion of these discourse strategies, see my 'Foreigner Talk' paper, 1975.

3. To test whether other native speakers would use similar question repairs, a questionnaire containing 14 examples of WH-Q's asked by the NS and the learner's response were distributed to 38 adult speakers of English. They were asked to read the question and the learner's response, and then write down what they thought *they* would say next. The repairs used were similar to those used by the NS's in Butterworth's data, and in some instances they agreed exactly. For example, given: *(After Christmas) Did you have a nice holiday?/Huh?*, 24 native speakers changed *holiday* to *Christmas*; 4 topicalized *Christmas,* placing it first; 9 changed *Did you have* to a 'simpler' *Was your* question; 3 changed *have* to *like*; and 5 defined *nice* as either *good* or *fun*. In fact, the actual repair was: *(Slower) Nice Christmas . . . was your Christmas nice?*

Given: *Do you like bull fights?/I don't know 'bull.'*, 15 native speakers wrote, *You know, 'toro'*; 2 drew pictures, 11 said they would use gestures for horns, and others talked about cows, male cows and animals. The actual repair was, *You know, 'toro.'* Given: *(Talking about soccer) Will you win today?/Win?* 21 defined *win* in the repair (will you beat, have more points, be champion, get the prize, etc.); 6 changed *will* to *are you gonna*, and a few resorted to ungrammatical 'foreigner talk' (e.g., You win today? You champion? You número uno?).

Given: *(R has said he's going to the Chili Pepper for lunch) Why, why are you going there?/Why?*, 22 native speakers changed the WHY-Q to a Yes/No Q which suggested an answer (e.g., Is the food good?) while 18 also clarified *there* by changing it to the name of the restaurant. Three persons decided to translate *why* to *por qué* (e.g., Why, por qué, you go there?).

We concluded that native speakers do use the same strategies in repairing questions. The only clear difference between the data on the questionnaire and Butterworth's data was in the much higher incidence of 'foreigner talk' elicited in the questionnaire.

4. Self-correction by second language learners is an important issue in itself. For a discussion of this issue, see Schlue, 1976 and Dennis Godfrey, 1976 (paper given at TESOL conference).

5. Note that in Rafaela's data, after she returns from speaking on the telephone, p. 428, she uses 'companions'—the word suggested to her by the NS as an equivalent for compañeros.

Gayle Johnson, in her research on vocabulary (in progress, UCLA), taped a number of learners' comments on their acquisition of vocabulary. Here is one learner who feels that she definitely learns vocabulary from conversations: "For me it's easier to remember the word if somebody say it. If I can hear it. (Uh-huh) Even for one time. (Uh-huh) It's, it's easier for me to remember it. I can read the word for ten, twenty time, and I can, I still don't remember it. But, it's, it's, eh, okay if somebody only say me, say to me this word, I can remember it."

6. Schlue reports that adult learners who met with her once a week for conversation and subsequent analysis of their errors became extremely frustrated when they could not converse fluently on a variety of topics. One of her learners became so frustrated over his poor performance that he came to their next meeting with a prepared topic—customs in his country. Instead of allowing her to interact with him in a conversation on this topic, he gave his prepared lecture. After he had given the lecture, he was willing to try conversation practice again. That is, once she was forced to recognize him as a fluent speaker of English in this way, he was willing to be a non-fluent conversationalist again.

Part IV
Abstracts

Papers were selected for inclusion in the abstract section on the same basis as for the chapters: the reports must be based on empirical data, they must deal with second language acquisition, they must not be evaluation of formal instruction only, nor should they be reports of theoretical arguments unless they have substantial data analysis. This, of course, has limited us from including many excellent papers of relevance to second language acquisition. While an attempt has been made to make the abstracts as complete as possible, it is inevitable that some reports have been overlooked; any omissions are unintentional.

The abstracts are author abstracts, dissertation abstracts, journal abstracts, and conference abstracts with as little editing as possible. When such abstracts were not available or when they did not appear to include important issues discussed in the report itself, the editor has supplied an abstract.

Allwright, R.L., Bailey, K.M., Fullantes, L., Gasser, M. & Lim, C. Topics, turns, and tasks: a pilot investigation for a case-study approach to classroom language learning. Paper presented at the Second Language Acquisition Forum, UCLA, 1976.

Two UCLA English language classes were regularly audio-recorded to provide the basic data for a study of individual learners' classroom experience and behavior. Three types of analysis are involved. One, turn-taking behavior in terms of the manner in which a turn is obtained (e.g., simply 'accepted' after a nomination, or 'stolen' from another learner, etc.). Two, the topic or content-focus of a learner's turn in relation to that of the teacher's response (e.g., if a learner 'steals' a turn to ask a question, does the teacher answer the question or 'punish' the turn-stealer by focussing instead on the linguistic form of the question?). Using the above two types of analysis suggested the need for a third; in terms of the tasks classroom partici-pants set each other. Turns can be accepted, for example, but used to avoid tasks rather than to complete them. An analytical model is being developed of the decision-making processes potentially involved as classroom participants, including the teacher, negotiate the complexi-ties of turns, topics, and tasks.

Several specific research questions are being addressed. One, how do some learners get far more, and others far less, than their mathematical average share of turns? Two, how is it that some 'below-average' participators appear to make more progress than some 'above-average' participators? Is what they do with their turns the relevant variable? At present, however, the investigation is aimed primarily at throwing light on the methodological problems involved in this relatively novel way of studying language learning.

d'Anglejan, Alison & Tucker, Richard G., The acquisition of complex English structures by adult learners. *Language Learning*, 1975, *25*, 2, 281-96.

This study was designed to investigate the acquisition of a set of complex English structures by adult learners of English at two different levels of proficiency. We focused on the five constructions described by C. Chomsky (1965) in her study of child native speakers. The results showed a similar developmental pattern to that found for child native speakers. This suggested that the degree of linguistic complexity inherent in the sentence is indeed a critical factor in determining the order of acquisition of certain grammatical features and that this factor operates in both native language and second language learning.

Some interesting language learning strategies came to light. Contrary to expectation, second language learners did not process the target sentences by relating them to similar structures in their native language. Beginners tended to rely on semantic information more than on syntactic information to provide clues to the likely interpretation of certain ambiguous sentences. The advanced subjects tended to use a combination of syntactic and semantic information. We did not find evidence of language learning strategies different from those reported in the literature for child native language learners. Our data do not permit us to extrapolate these findings to any prediction about the acquisition of productive skills in the second language.

Bailey, Nathalie, Madden, Carolyn, & Eisenstein, Miriam. Developing question formation ability in adult language learners. Paper presented at the TESOL Conference, New York, 1976.

The purpose of this study was to (a) test the hypothesis that adult second language learners exhibit systematic stages of development in the formation of questions and (b) to show these stages are similar to those of children learning English as a first language and as a second language. This was a cross-linguistic study of full-time adult English Language Institute Students at Queens College, N.Y. Pictures were used to elicit spontaneous questions. A repetition task and an intuition task were also presented to each student. An analysis was done on Yes/No questions, WH-questions (progressive and do-support). A comparison was made between this study and studies concerning question formation of children, first and second language learners.

Results indicate that there are systematic stages of development for adults. Among these are the tendency for beginning language learners not to use the full form of a discontinuous verb construction, e.g., Wh- NP — V + ing, and a surprising tendency of advanced learners to omit or use incorrect forms of 'do' more than beginners. This was analyzed as the result of beginners' avoidance of do-support questions. Given these results, teachers should not insist upon early inclusion of the auxiliary in discontinuous verb forms or expect accuracy of do-support.

The data further suggest that learners are using perceptual strategies to determine the grammatical form of questions as evidenced by the early learning of the more salient end position items in discontinuous verb forms, e.g., -ing, and the slower learning of the minimally distinct inflections of middle position 'do.'

Bassan, Henrietta F. Spelling difficulties of Hebrew speakers of English: an error analysis of third graders in three bilingual schools. MA-TESL, UCLA, 1973.

The hypothesis of the study was that bilingual children would experience phonological interference from their first language, Hebrew, and that this phonological interference would lead to specific spelling errors in their written work. Data was collected from both Anglo and Israeli children at three bilingual (Hebrew-English) schools in Los Angeles over a three-month period. Errors in the written assignments and spelling tests of the children were then analyzed for the following factors: classification of errors as shared with Anglo children (using Schwab's analysis of Anglo children's spelling error patterns); errors classified according to principles of possible Hebrew interference; and relative frequency of errors. Additional data was also gathered on 8 adult foreign students from Israel for comparison purposes. While samples of individual students did show what appeared to be strong interference patterns based on Hebrew-English phonological contrasts and difference in spelling systems, the errors made by the children could be easily classified according to the list of common Anglo errors. Only one-third of the errors could be accounted for as Hebrew interference. The adult data showed that errors related to Hebrew interference were distinctly uncommon in the writing of the 8 Israeli adults tested.

Bebout, Linda. An error analysis: comparing the ability of learners of English as a first and as a second language to extract information from written material. Paper presented at the TESOL Conference, Los Angeles, 1975.

In discussions of language learning, the nearly-inevitable acquisition of a first language is often contrasted with the variability of second language learning. However, it is possible that research into the strategies used by the learner may show that these two tasks are not so distinct as is commonly thought. In connection with this question, a study was done concerning the English language ability of two groups of subjects, native and non-native English speakers. The major purposes of this study were as follows: (a) to compare the errors made by advanced learners of English as a native language (American monolingual 9 to 11-year olds); (b) to investigate the usefulness of a modified cloze test in obtaining errors for profitable analysis; and (c) to aid teachers and researchers in evaluating the potential of error analysis as a tool by providing a demonstration of what it can reveal about language learning.

A test was devised consisting of one or two-sentence items, each containing a blank. The items were constructed in such a way that the item sentence exerted a considerable amount of contextual constraint over the blank and thus over the material which could fill it. The subjects were asked to supply a word for the blank which would complete the sentence. A group of native English speakers rated the responses according to their accept-ability. Error responses were classified into six categories: (1) context alteration, (2) non sequiturs, (3) grammatical errors, (4) lexical confusions, (5) uninterpretable, and (6) other. Errors in each category by native and non-native groups showed an overall similarity in terms of quantity and quality.

The results were taken as evidence in support of the hypothesis that there are many parallels between the language learning strategies of first and second language learners.

Ben-Zeev, Sandra. The influence of bilingualism on cognitive development and cognitive strategy. Paper presented at the Stanford Child Language Research Conference, Stanford, California, 1976.

This paper presents findings from two massive studies involving bilingual children, aged from 5½ to 8½ years. In the first study, 98 Hebrew-English bilingual children and English monolin-guals from similar social and religious backgrounds were tested; the second study involved 188 Spanish-English bilinguals and English monolinguals from similar social groups. The children in each study were given a battery of tests investigating cognitive strategies: 1. Peabody Vocabulary Test—English. Monolingual children scored higher than bilinguals on English vocabulary. 2. Verbal Transformation Test. Warren & Warren found that when Ss listen to an unchanging verbal stimulus, they report hearing changes in what the voice says. Projecting auditory change where none exists is thought to result from processing efforts to make sense of the stimulus. Bilinguals heard a greater number of auditory changes than monolinguals. 3. Symbol substitution test. For this test, the S must substitute one meaning-ful word for another within a sentence frame. For example, "You know that in English this is named 'airplane,' right? (shows airplane) In this game its name is 'turtle.' Can the 'turtle' fly?" Or "For this game the way we say 'I' is to say 'macaroni.' So how do we say 'I am warm'?" To succeed in this task the child must treat the substitute word as merely a unit in an abstract system, ignoring its reference function. In the Hebrew-English study, the bilinguals performed better than the monolinguals; there was no difference between bilinguals and monolinguals in the second study. 4. Grammar Tests. In the first study, children were given an adapted Berko test; no differences were found between the groups. In the second study, grammar was studied in a story-telling task. English monolinguals scored higher on all subscales in English than the bilinguals except on percentage of clausal sentences and clausal sentences using illogical conjunctions. Ben Zeiv believes this shows the bilingual child's willingness to chance complex structures before simpler grammatical structures have been completely learned. 5. Paradigmatic Association Test. No statistical differences were found. 6. System Analysis Strategy Tests. A number of nonverbal tests were given with the hope that a comparison of monolingual and bilingual subjects might show differences in attainment of operational thought. A number of interesting differences were obtained but these did not clearly establish that bilinguals were precocious operational thinkers. A number of possible variables are discussed which might account for the differences obtained for the subject groups.

Bertkau, Jana. Comprehension and production of English relative clauses in adult second language and child first language acquisition. Ph.D. dissertation, University of Michigan, 1974. (Also see *Language Learning,* 1974, *24,* 2, 279-86 for a supplementary article on Bertkau's research.)

The study investigated comprehension and production of relative clauses by adult Japanese and Spanish learners of English as a second language and five-year-old native English speakers.

A picture-cued, 18 item test incorporated four relative clause structures: right, center or 'ambiguous' embeddedness; subject vs. object focus; absence or presence of the relative pronoun; and singular or plural number of the object complement of the clauses.

In the comprehension test, Japanese *S*s scored lower than Spanish. Focus had a significant effect for both Spanish and child *S*s. A significant effect for Japanese *S*s was limited to center-embedded clauses. The comprehension results indicated that native language structure interfered significantly for Japanese *S*s but not for Spanish, while object focus was inherently more difficult for all groups to understand than subject focus when both were center embedded.

The production data distribution showed that the adults did not possess a common 'learner language' but that individual learner idiolects existed. The study shows that any theory of second language acquisition must recognize that learners employ a simplification process. The notion of a simplification process is further substantiated in Bertkau's *Language Learning* article.

Boyd, Patricia A. Second Language Learning: the grammatical development of Anglo children learning through Spanish. MA-TESL thesis, UCLA, 1974. (Also see *TESOL Quarterly,* 1975, *9,* 2, 125-36 for a supplementary article on Boyd's research.)

Subjects for this study were 12 children in the third year (second grade) of the Spanish Immersion program in Culver City. Six tests were used to elicit spontaneous speech data from the children: Spanish morphology I, Spanish morphology II, Spanish Bilingual Syntax Measure, an oral storytelling measure, a repetition task, and a test of reflexives. Spontaneous speech was also recorded, and five hours of teacher language in the classroom was taped.

The children are very fluent in Spanish—they use it in conversing with each other, with their teacher, and with the Spanish-speaking children who joined the class during the third year. A detailed error analysis of the natural speech data indicated problems in the following areas: subject-verb agreement for number and person, adjective-noun gender agreement, and article-noun gender agreement. The same areas were identified as problems in the morphology tests. The low frequency of object pronouns and the use of other than present tense in the teacher input data correlated with the children's problems in these areas.

Similarities and differences between first and second language development of Spanish are discussed. The differences tend to argue against a strong version of the $L_1 = L_2$ hypothesis. Raw data is included in the appendix.

Bruck, M., Rabinovitch, M.S., Oates, M. The effects of French immersion programs on children with language disabilities—a preliminary report. *Working Papers in Bilingualism, 5,* 1974.

This study is particularly interesting because it reports on children with language learning difficulties. The progress of these children has been followed from kindergarten to grade 3. Preliminary results indicate that the children fare well. They have learned to read in both English and French; their school achievement is adequate. They can understand as well as communicate in their second language with some facility. Furthermore, their first language acquisition does not appear to have been slowed by this educational experience. (Ed. note: language learning disabilities should not be confused here with language disorders. The children studied appear to be those who were slow in learning to read, write and speak the first language or who were diagnosed as having language difficulties.)

Brunak, J., Fain, E. & Villoria, N. Conversations with Rafaela. Second Language Acquisition Project, UCLA, 1976.

The aim of this study was to discover how a Spanish-speaking adult acquired the negation system of English. The subject, Rafaela, is a 28-year-old Panamanian who had been living in this country for approximately nine months at the start of the study. While she attended an ESL class in a community adult school, her goals were more social than academic. Data was collected in taped conversations in a variety of social interactions (e.g., dinner at a restaurant); supplementary data were also collected using a variety of elicitation tasks. In both types of data her major negative pattern was *no* or *not* + VP (e.g., I no see.). Occasionally she would use *don't* as an allomorph of *no* (e.g., I don't know). In copula sentences, however, the negative was consistently placed following *be* (e.g., Is not red. This is not the family.). BE + neg should probably be considered as a separate category since there is the possibility that Rafaela has a good notion of how it is to be used in most contexts. It is possible that copula negation is acquired quite separately from other verb negation rules. Modals, where they do appear, are either exact repetitions as in the imitation tasks, or are unanalyzed units used in expressions learned in class. In instances where the negative is correctly supplied, it appears to be the result of immediate input, recitation of memorized forms, and/or learning which resulted from school instruction.

Buteau, M.F. Students errors in the learning of French as a second language. *IRAL,* 1970, *7,* 2, 133-46. (Reprinted in Schumann & Stenson (Eds.), *New frontiers in second language learning.*)

This article describes a qualitative and quantitative analysis of errors made by 124 students in an intermediate level class in French. In an analysis of errors made on a French grammar test and also on free writing compositions, the author concludes that many errors could not be explained as interference from the first language. The author concludes that error-based analyses are not only useful but necessary in order to test out hypotheses concerning the level of difficulty of various structures. The study supports the opinion that linguistically, difficulty is related to the number of choices involved, and psychologically, from the point of view of the student, difficulty is a function of awareness of contextual cues.

Cathcart, Ruth L. Report on a group of Anglo children after one year of immersion in instruction in Spanish. MA-TESL thesis, UCLA, 1972.

The nineteen children described in this report constituted the first year of the Spanish Immersion Program at Culver City. The children in the program are given no formal Spanish language lessons; instead, the regular curriculum is presented to them in Spanish. The teacher speaks no English in the classroom. At the end of the kindergarten year, the children studied could communicate with their teacher using a variety of different language strategies.

In the earliest stages, some children used one-word utterances, others used Noun Phrase sentences, and still others seemed to be practicing a form of extended listening where almost no Spanish data was available. The *S's* two-word sentences usually contained no verb: *Nina . . . chica.* When verbs were supplied, they seemed to function to hold the verb slot in the sentences rather than show specific semantic meaning. *Querer, ser* and *tener* were the most commonly-used verbs although they were used to cover a wide variety of verb meanings. The verb form was usually first person no matter what form would have been appropriate. Several children used only one form for all pronouns, usually first person *mi* or *mío* to express subject and/or object and/or possessive pronouns. Two of the children used a large number of *Este* + NP or *Este es* + NP sentences. Children imitated complete sentences or units which were said frequently by the teacher. There was evidence of substitutions in memorized Spanish utterances such as in *¿De quién es este?* to *¿De quién es día?,* etc. They also constructed original utterances which did not reflect the teacher's speech data.

All of the children used some mixing of Spanish and English, usually with English sentence structure and a Spanish noun, adjective, or noun plus adjective in final sentence position. Occasionally they began utterances in one language, then switched to the other.

One child showed strong evidence of English patterns in Spanish (e.g., *negro papel* rather than *papel negro*). One child also did a great deal of language play, picking up and repeating (or frequently singing) parts of the teacher's utterances: Así, así, así, así, así . . . a mí, a mí . . . (after the teacher had said, "Así me gusta a mí."). When reprimanded, the same child mumbled incomprehensible streams of sounds which were apparently Spanish to him interspersed with Spanish words. Partial data on each of the children is included and discussed. The report also covers the children's English Berko scores, English reading readiness, cross-cultural attitude, and Spanish repetition data scores.

Cazden, C., Cancino, H., Rosansky, E. & Schumann, J. Second language acquisition sequences in children, adolescents, and adults. Final Report, United States Department of Health, Education & Welfare, August, 1975.

The purpose of this project was to make a preliminary investigation of the processes of second language acquisition by children, adolescents and adults, and to develop a methodology appropriate to the study of second language learning. In the development of the methodology, applicable techniques from first language acquisition research were incorporated and new techniques appropriate specifically to second language acquisition were devised.

The research examined the acquisition of English by 6 Spanish-speaking subjects over a ten-month period—two subjects at each of three target ages: 4-6, 11-14 and over 18. Each subject was visited approximately every two weeks and speech samples were recorded in three situations: spontaneous speech recordings, elicitations and pre-planned socio-linguistic interactions. The subjects were 'free' second language learners with very little or no prior or current instruction in English. Thus they acquired their second language mainly by exposure to the English-speaking environment.

The analysis focused on the acquisition of the English auxiliary and its related structures, the negative and interrogative. A clear developmental pattern was found for both the negative and interrogative. A highly variable order of acquisition was found for the appearance of auxiliaries.

Cohen, Andrew D. The Culver City Spanish Immersion Program: how does summer recess affect Spanish speaking ability? *Language Learning*, 1974, *24*, 1, 55-68.

This study looks at one aspect of second-language mastery in depth: patterns of foreign language retention among young children after being removed from a language contact situation for a period of time. The *S*s were 14 Anglo children from the Culver City Spanish Immersion Program, a pioneering project in American public school education. These children were immersed exclusively in Spanish during their kindergarten year. English was gradually introduced in first grade. This report deals with the effects of summer recess between first and second grade upon the spoken Spanish of the students. They were given an Oral Language Achievement Measure individually on a test-retest basis. The results showed that a summer recess of three months took its toll on Anglo children's performance in Spanish. Utterances became shorter; at least one grammatical class (prepositions) was used slightly less while another (verbs) became more prominent; the children made more errors proportionate to what they said; problems with article-adjective agreement not only persisted, but in the case of the definite article, shifted in nature; the *ser* verb began to be used more than *estar* when children were in doubt; and inflection for person in present tense indicative verbs continued to cause minor problems.

Cohen, Andrew D. Forgetting a second language. *Language Learning,* 1975, *25,* 1, 127-38.

A previous study by this author investigated group patterns of foreign language retention among young children after being removed from a language contact situation for a period of time. The present study was undertaken to provide an in-depth look at three students in an effort to determine whether the first things forgotten are, in fact, the last things learned, and whether forgetting entails unlearning in reverse order from the original learning process. Three subjects were administered an Oral Language Achievement Measure individually on a test-retest basis at the beginning of June 1973, the 20th month of language contact, and again in September 1973, after the children had started second grade. Two subjects provided examples to support the notion that some of the things that are learned last are also the first to be forgotten when the learners are removed from second language contact for a period of time. The third subject provided an example of reversion to an earlier pattern in the use of the definite article, perhaps skipping stages in between. Some data suggest that forgetting may produce forms that were never tried out during the process of language acquisition prior to the respite. Other data suggest that a pause in the learning process may actually cause a reduction in certain problem areas. Although the findings from this study are merely suggestive, since they are based on insufficient data to make them definitive, they are a first step in investigating the ways in which children forget a language in which they have been immersed.

Cook, Vivian J. The comparison of language development in native children and foreign adults. *IRAL,* 1973, *11,* 1, 13-28.

The study compares the performance of native children and foreign adults on 1) imitation and comprehension of various relative clause types and 2) on the difference between active and passive focus in such sentence pairs as "The duck is happy to bite/the duck is hard to bite." In testing relative clauses, 20 adults enrolled in an elementary ESL class were shown a picture and then asked to repeat a sentence which the picture illustrated. Focus and position of the relative clause were varied, as was the presence or absence of the relative pronoun *that*. Errors in repetition were similar to those made by children whose native language is English.

The second experiment required the learner to identify the actor in such sentences as "The wolf is happy to bite" vs. "The wolf is hard to bite." The data could be described in stages similar to those reported by Cromer for children.

Correa-Zoli, Y. Lexical and morphological aspects of American Italian in San Francisco. Ph.D. dissertation, Stanford, 1970.

The author tape recorded the speech of 23 Italian-born adults living in San Francisco. The data was then analyzed for 1) adapted loan words, 2) loanshifts, and 3) switches. The glossary lists 203 items in phrase context. In the discussion section, syntactic interference is discussed as having a good deal of importance. The author also notes a trend toward the use of masculine gender as the preferred assignment for new American-Italian noun forms.

Dato, D.P. American children's acquisition of Spanish syntax in the Madrid environment. ERIC ED -53-508. Spanish verb phrase in children's second-language learning. In P. Pimsleur and T. Quinn (Eds.), *The psychology of second language learning*. Cambridge: Cambridge University Press, 1971, 19-34.

Data was first collected on Michael, an American child (4:11) for a nine-month period in a variety of situations in order to develop a workable model for data collection on the child's learning of Spanish as a second language in Madrid. During the second year, observation of Michael was continued and six children (age range: 5½-6½) were studied in detail. The children were exposed to Spanish communication situations for approximately fifty to sixty hours each week. Twenty to twenty-four recordings (approximately ten hours of data per child) were collected for each *S* over a ten-month period. The data was then analyzed within the transformational framework to allow for comparisons among the children and also to discover the rule stages which might be used to describe language acquisition. The order of occurrence of 'underlying structure and functions' was similar for all *S*s, suggesting a systematic pattern in learning Spanish as a second language. From the comparison data, Dato also suggests that differences in age may be of little or no consequence in second language learning.

Dickerson, Lonna J. The learner's interlanguage as a system of variable rules, *TESOL Quarterly*, 1975, 9, 4.

Reported in this paper is a longitudinal study of the acquisition and use of the English sound system by Japanese learners of English. The central point is that the learner's second-language system must be a system of variable rules if it is to account for the variability (wide assortment of pronunciations) in his production, the fluctuations beween his in-class and out-of-class performance, and the regularities in his process of acquisition. The model used in this research is the variability model of sociolinguistics.

The study has both theoretical and practical value. First, it captures the regular patterning of diversity in the learner's speech, giving the developing theory of interlanguage a firmer grounding. Second, the study provides insights to help the classroom teacher better understand and evaluate student performance in pronunciation.

Dickerson, Wayne B. Hesitation phenomena in the spontaneous speech of nonnative speakers of English. Ph.D. dissertation, University of Illinois, 1971.

Seventeen-minute recordings were made of the speech of six foreign students from 6 different language backgrounds. After the tapes were transcribed, the transcripts were then examined for an analysis of the hesitation phenomena. Four pause devices were found: silence, [a]-type fillers, non-phonemic lengthening, and filler words. Pause units consisted of a sequence of one or more pause devices. Two kinds of disfluencies occurred frequently in the data: repetitions and self-corrections. The study shows that non-native learners of English use identical hesitation phenomena as native speakers and that their speech exhibits rhythmic patterns of extensive pausing alternating with fluent speech. However, non-native speakers take more time to plan their utterances and are not able to store as much of their planned speech before uttering it. Therefore, their speech is not as free of repetitions and self-corrections as that of native speakers.

Hesitation phenomena are focused on delivering a message in the most linguistically and temporally unified manner possible. The message is served by pause devices, repetitions and self-correction. Repetition also serves continuity by preserving the grammatical integrity of units at all levels that are broken by prolonged pausing or self-correction. Self-correction serves the message by improving the match between form and content.

Dulay, Heidi C. Aspects of child second language acquisition. Ph.D. dissertation, Harvard, 1974.

This paper traces an attempt to discover underlying cognitive strategies children use in learning to produce second language syntax. It begins with a theoretical question—is second language syntax acquisition a process of habit formation or is it the creative construction of a syntactic system by the child? The dissertation contains a report of a series of empirical research studies (presented in numerous articles in *Language Learning, TESOL Quarterly,* and *Working Papers in Bilingualism*) which showed that the major portion of error types can be explained by the creative construction hypothesis.

Duškova, Libuse. On sources of errors in foreign language learning, *IRAL,* 1969, 7, 1.

This article presents results of a study of grammatical and lexical errors in the writing of 50 Czech students of English. The corpus for the study were the 50 essays written by students in a free writing assignment. The 1,007 errors collected were then classified and analyzed.

The influence of the first language was most evident in word order errors, errors in construction and government, preposition and article errors. In contrast, almost all morphology errors could be accounted for as interference of other English forms and functions. Lexical errors seemed to be due to similarity of forms in English and difference between Czech and English use of expressions. There were a few minor instances of interference from German on lexical items for those students who had also learned German before acquiring English. In conclusion, the author notes that the greatest problems exist in learning grammatical categories which do not exist in the first language. For example, Czech students continue, even when their command of English is near native, to make errors on English articles.

Fantini, A.E. Language acquisition of a bilingual child: a sociolinguistic perspective. Ph.D. dissertation, University of Texas at Austin, 1974.

The materials for this study of Mario, a Spanish-English bilingual, were collected from the child with considerable regularity from the age of 11 days until 5:8. The data was obtained either through direct observation or from occasional tape recordings of his speech. The purpose of these efforts was to produce a sizeable corpus of data as the basis for later analysis. Throughout the collection, the writer's attention focused on the prominent aspects of development at each stage. After the pre-speech period, phonology and lexical development were the main concern. By 2:3, the child began to produce two and three-word utterances and attention shifted to syntax. From 2:6 on, morphological detail began to form part of the child's speech patterns. From 3:0 on, the reporter's interest focused increasingly on contextual aspects of the child's speech. Notes concerning the setting, participants, and interaction among speakers provide the basis for possible discourse analysis. Notes were made on both verbal and non-verbal aspects of communication. It is this information—not simply the linguistic notations—which permits examination into infant bilingualism, language differentiation, switching, interference, and the effect of social factors on the child's developing styles and language use.

Fathman, Ann. The relationship between age and second language productive ability, *Language Learning,* 1975, *25,* 2, 245-54.

This study examines the relationship between certain aspects of the second language acquisition process and age. An oral production test was developed to assess the ability of non-native English-speaking children to produce standard English morphology and syntax. The test was administered to approximately 200 children (ages 6-15) who were learning ESL in American public schools. The results of this testing were used to examine the relationship between age and 1) the rate of acquisition of certain English grammatical structures and 2) the order of acquisition of these grammatical structures.

    The results indicated that there were some relationships between age and rate of learning. Among children exposed to English the same amounts of time, the older children scored higher on the morphology and syntax subtests, whereas the younger children received higher ratings in phonology. There were, however, no major differences observed in the order in which children of different ages learned to produce the structures included in the test. These results suggest that there is a difference in the rate of learning of English morphology, syntax and phonology based upon differences in age, but that the order of acquisition in second language learning does not change with age.

Fathman, Ann. Language background, age and the order of acquisition of English structures. Paper presented at the TESOL Conference, Los Angeles, 1975.

This study examines the order of acquisition of certain English morphemes and syntactic structures by children learning English as a second language. An oral production test was designed to test specific morpheme categories (e.g., present participle, plural, past) or syntactic patterns (e.g., negative, WH-question, yes/no question). This paper reports the results of testing 60 Korean and 60 Spanish children, between the ages of 6 and 14, who were learning English as a second language in Washington, D.C. schools. All Ss had been in the United States one year and came from families who spoke only their native language at home.

    Few differences were found in the order in which the Korean and Spanish children learned to produce the items included on the test. In addition, the order in which structures were learned was similar for children from various schools. These results suggest that neither language background, age, nor learning situation in this study seems to have a great effect on the order of acquisition in second language learning.

Felix, S.W. Interference, interlanguage, and related issues. Paper presented at the conference on German in Contact with Other Languages, Essen, Dec., 1975.

In this paper, Felix asks for more sophisticated and careful analysis of second language data in answering questions as to whether or not interference/transfer is an important factor in second language learning. To illustrate this point, he displays data which might be interpreted as interference if it appeared in the speech of speakers of one language background and as a developmental, or interlanguage, stage if it occurred in the data of speakers of other first languages.

Felix uses data from the Kiel project collected from English-speaking children learning German from German playmates in a natural setting to illustrate this contention. The age range of the children is from four to eight years. Data were collected two to three times a week; two or three hours of recorded data were obtained at each visit.

In the syntactic data from these observations Felix found that examples of transfer were rare and unsystematic. The examples could as easily be attributed to other factors. He concludes that "neither the stages themselves nor the sequence of stages are in any significant way determined, influenced, or affected by language transfer."

One of the subjects, a seven-year-old, used *warum* (why) both appropriately as the why-question marker and inappropriately in place of a 'because' element. If this subject had been a Spanish speaker, it is likely that interference from Spanish would be claimed since Spanish uses *porque* both as a question-word and as a because-marker. Obviously, since the child is a native speaker of English, interference cannot be claimed. The subjects in the project also deleted copula, as has been noted in studies of first language acquisition. They also deleted *it* (e.g., *Ist nicht meine*), a phenomenon which for native speakers of Spanish has frequently been attributed to Spanish interference since such sentences are acceptable in Spanish.

Further examples (word order errors, interrogatives, etc.) are given to show that we must be much more careful in attributing the source of such 'errors' to interference/transfer. Felix is careful to point out that interference was found in the data in the area of phonology. The important question, he suggests, is why transfer/interference does occur in some areas of second language acquisition and why it is not an important source of 'error' in syntax.

Flores, M.A. An early stage in the acquisition of Spanish morphology by a group of English-speaking children. MA-TESL, UCLA, 1973.

The acquisition of Spanish as a second language by fifteen children enrolled for the second year in the Culver City Spanish Immersion Program is discussed in this paper. Observational data was collected from each of the children. Two morphology tests and a story-telling task provided additional data on their acquisition of various syntactic structures. By the end of the second year, the children were quite fluent; utterances up to 11 words in length were recorded; they seemed to be able to express whatever they wanted to say in Spanish. Yet the data showed a variety of non-acceptable linguistic forms particularly in the agreement rules of Spanish. Subject-verb, article-noun, noun-adjective agreement rules showed constant fluctuation in form. While there was no formal language instruction built into the academic curriculum, the teacher in the second year began to offer corrections on the children's language output. The author sees this as one reason for the fluctuation between forms in many of their utterances. A partial analysis of each child's progress along with raw data is included in the thesis.

Gaskill, William. Correction in adult native speaker—non-native speaker conversation. MA-TESL Thesis, UCLA, 1977.

This thesis focuses on correction in native speaker—non-native speaker conversation. Included in the study are a summary and discussion of Schegloff, Jefferson and Sacks' "The Preference for Self-Correction in the Organization of Repair in Conversation" (1977) and an analysis of corrections in conversations involving one adult, Iranian, non-native speaker of English and six adult, native speakers of English. The transcripts of the conversations are included in the study.

Analysis of the other-corrections, i.e. corrections of one speaker's utterance by another speaker, in these data suggest that other-corrections parallel those described by Schegloff, Jefferson and Sacks in native speaker conversation. Other-corrections were frequently done after a slight pause. They were often modulated to display uncertainty; that is, they were done as questions such that the correction was proffered for acceptance or rejection rather than asserted. Some evidence suggested that other-corrections of substandard forms of English may be done as restatements which may be modulated in the form of affirmations suggesting agreement with what was said rather than made as an overt correction. When unmodulated other-corrections were found, i.e. in the format "No + correction," they occurred in special environments, relative to a previous utterance, which tended to elicit the correction. Instances of "No + correction" also were found where disagreement was a major issue.

The author suggests these findings are relevant to current research in classroom interaction. Additionally, the study illustrates the relevance of conversational analysis to the study of second language acquisition.

Gasser, Michael. A stage in the acquisition of Amharic by an adult. Psycholinguistics-TESL Project, UCLA, 1975.

Wimmi, the 30-year-old subject of this study, worked in Ethiopia as a nurse for three years. During that time she received no formal instruction in the language. Her native language is Panjabi; she also speaks Hindi and English. In her work, even during the first few days, she was required to use Amharic in order to ask her patients for biographical data. After three years in Ethiopia, Wimmi came to the United States. She had had little chance to speak Amharic for the four years prior to this study. Tape recorded conversations were collected of her speaking Amharic with a native-speaker of that language and with the investigator.

An error analysis of the transcripts revealed an interesting problem with word order. She made no errors in basic word order which is SOV (the same as it is in her first language but different from English). However, in embedded clauses, she used SVO order which is incorrect. Wimmi also showed her awareness of verb suffixing as an important part of the language. She always attached some suffix to the verb, but her choice of suffixes was seemingly random. She also produced forms she could never have heard by combining several suffixes. Other forms produced, however, were certainly due to forms she had heard very frequently. In contrast to what a pidginization process might predict, she did not omit the copula in equational utterances. Perhaps this is due to its sentence-final position in Amharic. Wimmi also overgeneralized vocabulary. For example, the word *t'äyyäk'ä* is used to mean 'to visit.' Some English speakers frequently use 'see' for 'visit.' Wimmi, then, extended *t'äyyäk'ä* not only to visit but also to all meanings of the act of seeing. She also extended *antä*, the second-person masculine form to third person masculine. The evidence shows that, like Zoila and Alberto in the Shapira and Schumann studies, Wimmi is quite fluent; the author expressed surprise at how unsystematic the *S*'s choice of verb forms is in Amharic and compares this to the data on Gough's subject, Homer.

Gillis, Mary & Weber, Rose-Marie. The emergence of sentence modalities in the English of Japanese-speaking children, mimeo paper, McGill University.

To investigate the validity of the hypothesis that second language learning in school age children follows the same development as first language acquisition, specifically with respect to negatives, interrogatives, and imperatives, the English of two Japanese boys acquiring English in a natural setting was observed over a five-month period. The children were Akio, 6:11 and Haruo 7:6. The analysis and comparison to first language acquisition (especially to

Klima & Bellugi, 1966) showed a striking basic similarity between the second language learners and the young children, even though the older children differed from one another in some details. There was no clear evidence of transfer from the children's mother tongue.

Hamayan, Else. French oral production and awareness of errors by English children educated bilingually. Paper presented at the TESOL Conference, New York, 1976.

Two studies were carried out investigating the acquisition of specific structures in French. The performance of third and fifth grade English-speaking children, who were learning French as an L2 in the St. Lambert immersion program, was compared to that of children whose native language was French.

In the first study, children were read a story in French, and asked to repeat the story as they heard it. Native-speakers rephrased the story but produced grammatically acceptable sentences most of the time. The bilingual children, however, showed consistent patterns of error.

In the second study, children's awareness of grammatical errors was investigated. It was of interest to see whether children would recognize as 'ungrammatical' some of the errors that they themselves produced which presumably formed part of their interim grammar system. The same children who participated in the first study were given a series of sentences, some of which contained errors which were typically made by them, and others which were grammatically correct. The experimenter, after showing each sentence on a card and reading it aloud to the child, asked him to say whether he thought the sentence was correct (i.e., was said by somebody who spoke French well), or whether it was incorrect (i.e., was said by somebody who couldn't speak French very well). Group analysis indicated that older children in general made more correct grammaticality judgments than young children. Furthermore, there seemed to be a similarity between the two language groups in the relative order of difficulty of different structures, although the native-speakers performed better than the bilinguals.

Hamayan, E., Markman, B.R., Pelletier, S. & Tucker, G.R. Differences in performance in elicited imitation between French monolingual and English-speaking bilingual children. *Working Papers in Bilingualism, 8,* Feb., 1976.

This study represents an attempt to describe the second-language competence of English-speaking children who are learning French as a second language. The performance of 4th and 6th grade children, taking part in a French immersion program, was compared to that of French-speaking children of the same age using an elicited imitation task. The Ss' performance on 8 syntactic features was measured. French-speaking children, in general, performed better than the English children. A consistent pattern of errors by the English children indicated that they possessed a rule system for several of the features which was different from that of the child native speakers. By giving a digit span task in both languages, it was possible to rule out a confounding memory factor which may have offered an advantage to French speakers in a sentence-repetition task.

Hamayan, E., Saegert, J. & Larudee, P. Elicited imitation in second language learners. *Working Papers in Bilingualism, 6,* 1975.

Three groups of subjects were tested in an elicited imitation study. They were 8-year-old, 11-year-old, and adult native speakers of Arabic who were learning English as a second language. The Ss were asked to repeat sentences of seven different grammatical structure types.

Previous research with 4-year-old native speakers of English (Smith, 1973) has found that three of the structures were easy to repeat (Type A structures) while four were difficult to repeat (Type B structures). In the present study, a similar difference in the repeatability of A and B structures were found for the youngest Ss but there was no such difference for the adults, and only a moderate difference for the intermediate group. The pattern of results suggested that this was not a function of differences in the Ss' English-language backgrounds, but represents a developmental difference in the ability of second-language learners to repeat certain grammatical structures. The theoretical reasons for the variability in repetition difficulty for the different structure types were considered.

Hanania, Edith. Acquisition of English structure: a case study of an adult native speaker of Arabic in an English-speaking environment. Ph.D. dissertation, Indiana University, 1974.

This work is a longitudinal case study of the early stages of natural second language acquisition by an adult native speaker of Arabic in an English speaking environment. The subject, a 19-year-old Saudi wife of a Saudi graduate student knew no English on her arrival in the United States and received very little formal instruction thereafter.

Data were collected at one-month intervals over 18 months. Additional elicited speech was collected as well. An informal framework of semantically based generative grammar was used to describe the data.

The subject's earliest constructions were constrained to two-word utterances held by one relation. Development took place in three directions: new relations emerged between elements; two-element sentences were expanded to include three elements; and the main constituents of each sentence were extended through the acquisition of inflections and of modifiers, prepositions and determiners. Substantive elements preceded functors. Correct English word order was preserved throughout. There was no evidence of surface structure interference from the learner's first language.

The development of the subject's acquisition of English was similar to that of a child first language learner, although the rate was much slower and there were differences in the order of acquisition of modulators. The differences may be accounted for in terms of social and psychological variables. The subject had limited meaningful exposure to the language, little pressing need for it, and she was inhibited by her fear of making errors. Another factor may be the higher sensitivity of the child to phonological detail and a greater reliance of the adult on semantic salience. The overall similarity, however, suggests that many of the same kinds of cognitive processes underlie adult and child language acquisition.

Hansen-Bede, Lynne. A child's creation of a second language. *Working Papers in Bilingualism, 7,* 1975.

Three stages of the developing second language of a 3:9-3:11-year-old English-speaking child in an Urdu speech milieu were examined and compared with findings that have been accumulated about the order and process of first language acquisition. The study showed that in the development of many syntactic and morphological features the child used strategies characteristic of mother-tongue learners; an exception, the development of the negative, was interpreted as evidence that knowledge already available to a second language learner from learning a first may contribute to an acceleration of progress in some details of acquisition.

Hartford, Beverly. The English of Mexican-American adolescents in Gary, Indiana: a sociolinguistic description. Ph.D. dissertation, University of Texas at Austin, 1975.

This study isolates 14 phonological features of English of 30 Mexican-American adolescents in grades 9 to 11 in Gary, Indiana. Certain of these phonological features co-occur and therefore define linguistic sets which may be used to define subgroups within this population.

Overall, this study shows that the regular linguistic variability of a socio-economically homogeneous group may be described either by its linguistic patterns or by certain psychosociological descriptors as sex, occupational choice, and linguistic and culture attitude. Thus, once the set of linguistic and psychosocial parameters has been defined, the occurrence of the variables of one set may be used to make predictions about the other.

Hébrard, P. & Mougeon, R. La langue parlée le plus souvent entre les parents et les enfants: un facteur crucial dans l'acquisition linguistique de l'enfant dans un milieu bilingue, *Working Papers in Bilingualism, 7,* 1975.

This study attempts to show that in a bilingual environment, the language most often spoken between parents and children plays a major role in the language acquisition of the children. For the study we have analyzed the spoken English of a sample of 15 grade 2 children selected in the French language schools of Welland and Sudbury. This sample has been divided in two groups. Group I included children who spoke mostly French with their parents at home and Group II children who spoke mostly English. The result of an error analysis showed: 1) that Group II children commit fewer errors than Group I children in spoken English; 2) that Group II children commit a lower proportion of interference errors (errors attributable to the influence of French) than Group I children.

On the basis of these results we can say that the language most often spoken between children and parents seems to have a significant influence on the language acquisition of Grade 2 children in a bilingual environment.

Heckler, Edward E. The acquisition of English verb morphology by non-native speakers. Ph.D. dissertation, Michigan State University, 1975.

Using a modified and expanded Berko test which included 70 items (oral production, written production, and written receptive), 36 students were tested on acquisition of verb morphology. *Ss* were from Spanish, Arabic, and Japanese language backgrounds; 4 beginners, 4 intermediate and 4 advanced students from each language group. Student proficiency level was accurately reflected in the *S*s responses to the test. Native language showed an ascending effect from Spanish to Arabic to Japanese in number of correct responses. The infinitive (to MV) was acquired earlier than progressive (-ing V); past tense before present -s; the -en of passive before be in *be + -en*; the *-en* of perfect before *have*; and *be* of progressive before *-ing*. Of structures that can follow a modal, MV and *be* were acquired before *have.* For present *s,* /s/ and /z/ were acquired before /ɪz/. For past and for *-en* perfect, /t/ and /d/ were acquired before /ɪd/.

Isman, Jakub. The acquisition of English syntax by Indonesian children. Ph.D. dissertation, University of Indiana, 1973.

Three, newly-arrived Indonesian subjects, seven to ten years of age, were enrolled in schools where no special language instruction was available to them. Their 'untutored' acquisition of English was studied using Chomsky's Aspects model. The study was conducted over 52 weeks with data collected each week. The data were broken into two stages. Stage 1 consisted of weeks 1 through 18 and fell into three periods. In Period 1, the children acquired affirmative interrogatives with copula *be.* In Period 3, they acquired negation and interrogatives with do-support. The second stage consisted of weeks 19 through 52, and was divided into two periods. In Period 4, the children acquired complex sentences with embedded Noun Phrase and Verb Phrase complements. In Period 5, relative clauses and conjoined simple and complex sentences were used. Isman notes that there was a good deal of overlap between the various periods in the two stages.

Johnson, Nancy A. A psycholinguistic study of bilingual language acquisition. Ph.D. dissertation, University of Texas, 1973.

The Berko test was used to test the control of English plurals by Spanish-English bilinguals over a wide age range. The test was given to 115 Spanish-English bilinguals and monolingual English speakers. Approximately 36 Ss from each of four grade levels were tested: Grades 3, 6, 8, and 10. Johnson found a gradual and constant rate of improvement in control of the plural inflection over the age range. However, there was a slight drop in scores at the tenth grade level. Phonological interference was an important factor at all grade levels.

Johnston, Mary Virginia. Observations on learning French by immersion. Paper for UCLA Psycholinguistics-TESL Project, 1973.

This paper reports on the acquisition of French by an adult learner, the author. Following a short period of formal French instruction, the author spent seven weeks working at a summer camp in the South of France. During her stay she spoke no English, determined to learn French by immersion through extended listening and a willingness to use one, two or three-word sentences, whatever was needed to communicate, rather than trying to speak French filtered through instruction. She describes her control of various language structures as follows: in the beginning stages she was unaware of errors; in a second stage she would make a mistake and then realize that she had made an error. In the third stage, she would 'hear' an error coming up but would be unable to stop herself in time; in the fourth stage, she would be able to stop an impending error. Finally, she was no longer aware of any problem with the structure and felt she had 'acquired' it. This model has been tested by Schlue and by Robbins in studies with second language learners. Johnston also comments on her inability to use other than very direct speech when incidental 'by-the-way' comments would have been more appropriate, her inability to use the language effectively for self-justification, and the differences between the French she used when speaking to French people and the French she used when speaking with those who also understood English.

Self observations by trained researchers can give us much information on the acquisition process. A number of researchers are presently using the diary-journal method to follow their acquisition of new languages.

Keller-Cohen, Deborah. Repetition in the non-native acquisition of discourse. Paper presented at the Stanford Child Language Research Forum, April, 1976.

The paper presents some of the initial findings of this study of second language learners acquisition of discourse skills in the new language. The on-going project is investigating two broad areas: the structures and processes that create cohesive discourse and the difference between adult-child and child-child discourse. The children, age range 4½ to 8 years, are videotaped in play situations on a regular basis. The discourse processes being investigated include repetition, expansion, substitution, anaphora, ellipses and conjunction. Keller-Cohen has examined the interaction between the processes creating cohesive discourse and the functions of utterances. Her current research considers the process of repetition. The second area of investigation is the difference between adult-child and child-child discourse. Longitudinal data from the four non-native children interacting with a native-English speaking adult and a native English speaking peer are being analyzed.

Kempf, Margart K. A study of English proficiency levels of the composition errors of incoming foreign students at the University of Cincinnati during 1969-74. Ph.D. dissertation, Ohio State University, 1975.

The data from the entrance exams (Michigan Test of English Language Proficiency) of 423 foreign students were analyzed in this study. Fifty-five error types were identified and 31 were cross tabulated by native language and proficiency level of the students. Significant differences among native languages were found for 9 error types while 15 error types were significantly different with respect to proficiency level of students. Thirty-five of the 55 error types were among the list which H.V. George has attributed to 'redundancy.' Because of the importance of redundancy in this study, it was suggested that Contrastive Analysis procedures be adapted to indicate points of relative redundancy as accounting for more errors than native language transfer alone.

Kenyeres, Adele. Comment une petite Hongroise apprend le français. *Archives de psychologie,* 1938, *26,* 321-366.

The language development of Eva, the author's six-year-old daughter, was observed in this classic study of adding a second language by immersion. Eva was enrolled in a French school in Geneva. French, Hungarian and German were used at home though Hungarian was the true home language. In answering the questions of that era, Kenyeres attested to the fact that Eva's intellectual development did not suffer because of her bilingualism, that she maintained her national identity despite periods of homesickness which were painful, and that by six months her French was, in many respects, comparable to that of her schoolmates.

Kenyeres believed that early errors could be attributed to reliance on the first language. These areas included gender agreement for nouns and their articles and adjectives, and the object pronouns. In the first stage, object pronouns were correctly used in phrases learned via imitation (e.g., *Je ne l'aime beaucoup*), then they were omitted as is possible in Hungarian (*Je dis pour rire*), then appeared for feminine but not for masculine or ellided forms, then appeared but were incorrectly placed (*C'est moi qui a l'invente*), and finally occurred in proper word order (*Je l'ai vu*) but with many relapses. (Note the similarities to the Ervin-Tripp data.) Verb tense, person and number also caused her some lasting difficulties. Verbs requiring reflexive pronouns also posed a problem for Eva.

Kenyeres concludes that Eva's language development differed from first language acquisition since much of her learning was on a conscious level, because much of her early French was based on Hungarian, and because she did not go through the same developmental stages as an infant. It differed from adult second language learning in that her articulatory and grammatical habits were not set, she used global understanding rather than analysis in her early learning, and she invented games which helped motivate her learning. At the end of six months the second language began to take over the functions of the first language. Since the manuscript is extensive, the reader is referred to it for further information on order of acquisition of various structures and for the interesting psychological discussion included. Of note is Eva's reaction to language change on her return to Budapest. Laughed at by her friends because of her imperfect Hungarian (which she quickly corrected within a few weeks), she rejected French and withdrew to play with her dolls. There are many parallels in the reactions of Eva and Leopold's Hildegard when faced with the change of language environments.

Kessler, C. *The acquisition of syntax in bilingual children.* Washington, D.C.: Georgetown University Press, 1971.

Twelve Italian-English bilingual children participated in this study which asked if structures common to Italian and English develop in the same order and rate in the bilingual child. The children, aged 6:1 to 8:3, performed several tasks which checked their comprehension of 16 language structures. Listening to a taped sentence, they chose the one picture from three choices which best depicted what they had heard on the tape. These sentences tested comprehension of various inflections and syntactic structures in each language. The children also listened to sets of three tape-recorded sentences, two of which formed a synonymous pair. The child matched the first sentence given with one of the two following choices. The sentences were either within language (all English or all Italian) or between languages. The data thus gathered from the children were subjected to statistical and linguistic analyses.

Findings show that the children were balanced bilinguals; they did as well in one language as in the other. Structures common to both languages had been acquired at the same rate and in the same order. Linguistically complex (within case grammar framework) structures were learned last; and in the synonymous pairs of sentences, synonymy was less easily recognized when additional transformations were involved or when one of the pair involved a language-specific realization rule. The reader may wish to compare these conclusions with those of Mikes̆ and Imedadze.

Krashen, S.D. & Pon, Pauline. An error analysis of an advanced learner of ESL: the importance of the monitor, *Working Papers in Bilingualism*, 7, 1975.

The spontaneous speech of a woman, a native speaker of Chinese in her forties, was tape recorded. The subject had immigrated to the United States in her late twenties. She was enrolled in college when this study was undertaken and graduated with an A average. Data were gathered over a three-week period during which 80 errors were tabulated. Immediately after an utterance containing an error was recorded, it was presented to the subject. In nearly every instance (about 95% of the time), the subject was able to correct the error. Another finding was that the rules violated by the subject were rules presented in most beginning classes in ESL (e.g., third person singular present tense, irregular past, etc.). In addition, the subject is able to write error free English. In writing, and in careful speech, she is able to use her knowledge of English rules, while in casual speech she does not have time or perhaps is too preoccupied with the message to monitor her output. It is hypothesized that the conscious knowledge of linguistic rules may act as a monitor, altering the output of the acquired language system. For a more complete notion of the Monitor Model, see the reports of the Second Language Acquisition Forum, 1975, 1976, for Krashen's papers.

Lagarreta-Marcaida, Dorothy. An investigation of the use or non-use of formal ESL training on the acquisition of English by Spanish-speaking children in traditional and bilingual classrooms. Ph.D. dissertation, University of California, Berkeley, 1975.

This dissertation contains a comparison of gains made by Spanish-speaking children in English proficiency in five different kinds of programs: 1) traditional, no ESL, 2) tradition, with ESL, 3) bilingual, unbalanced input of languages, no ESL, 4) bilingual, balanced language input, no ESL, 5) bilingual, unbalanced input with ESL. Balanced input means the use of each language on alternate days. Traditional means a regular English-language classroom.

The measures used to test gains were 1) an oral comprehension test, 2) vocabulary (home, school, and street subscales), 3) oral production, and 4) the author's communicative competence test. All tests, except for the communicative competence test, were peer administered.

Group 4 (bilingual, alternate days, no ESL) showed the greatest gains in the communicative competence test in both languages, but especially in Spanish. They also showed greater gains in oral comprehension although the difference was not statistically significant.

The bilingual classes scored higher on the vocabulary for the home section than the traditional groups. There was no significant difference in the production test among the five class types.

LaMarche, Maurice M. The topic comment pattern in the development of English among some Chinese children living in the United States. Ph.D. dissertation, Georgetown University, 1972.

Sixty-six recordings were made of six children, ranging in age from 2½ to 8 years, during a six-month period. It was expected that during their earliest acquisition of the second language, the children would use a large number of topic-comment language patterns because of interferences from their first language. This pattern was then expected to become less important since the child would not receive reinforcement of such patterns from those with whom they used their second language. Topic and comment are defined as follows: "The person or the things about which something is said is called the topic; and the statement made about that person or thing is called the comment." The tapes yielded 162 instances of topic-comment patterns. Instances were then analyzed to show the gradual differentiation of language patterns by the children.

Lebach, Susan M. A report on the Culver City Spanish Immersion Program in its third year: Implications for language and subject matter acquisition, language, and attitudes. MA-TESL thesis, UCLA, 1974.

While this study looks at a wide variety of questions, perhaps the most interesting is its documentation of the child's attitude toward learning a second language and his notion of how competent he is in his two languages, English and Spanish. One child, for example, admitted to being puzzled the first day of kindergarten when he thought the teacher called him 'stupid.' She had called him Esteban, the Spanish version of his name. All students interviewed were proud of their bilingualism and felt that they 'talked both good.' Some claimed to be 'better' in Spanish, their second language. The study includes evaluation of subject matter courses (all of which are taught in Spanish) and a section on teacher attitudes toward the project as well.

Linde, Richard. A diagnosis of grammar errors made by Japanese persons speaking English as a second language. Ph.D. dissertation, American University, 1971.

The data consist of conversations with five adult learners of English as a second language. The tabulation of errors in the data showed: 1) each subject made the same error many times in his speech sample; 2) error ranks across subjects did not always agree—that is, not all students made the same errors despite their common first language background; 3) the assumption that prepositions and a/the article usage would show the highest number of errors was true when simple frequencies were counted, but they were no more common than simple present tense, past tense and plural errors when correction for frequency was computed, or simple percentage figures were used.

LoCoco, Veronica. An analysis of Spanish and German learners' errors. *Working Papers in Bilingualism, 7,* 1975.

This study analyzes Spanish and German errors committed by adult native speakers of English enrolled in elementary and intermediate French and German classes. Four written samples were collected for each target language over a period of 5 months. Errors were categorized according to their possible source. Types of errors were ordered according to their frequency. The hierarchies of relative difficulty thus obtained varied for the target languages. The production of some errors seemed to be based on proposed universals of language acquisition; other errors appeared to be directly related to the languages involved.

LoCoco, Veronica. A comparison of three methods for the collection of L2 data: free composition, translation, and picture description. *Working Papers in Bilingualism, 8,* 1976.

Three methods for L2 data collection are compared: free composition, picture description and translation. The comparison is based on percentage of errors in a grammatical category, and in a source category. Most results obtained from the free composition and picture description tended to be similar. Greater variation was found for some error categories between these two tasks and the translation task. Analysis of the errors suggests that differences in results could be reduced through slight adjustments in the method of data analysis, and a variation of the translation task. Results obtained from the three methods should then be very similar.

Markman, Barbara R., Spilka, Irene, & Tucker, G. Richard. The use of elicited imitation in search of an interim French grammar. *Language Learning,* 1975, *25,* 1, 31-41.

The study was an initial attempt to tap the French language competence of two groups of English speaking pupils who are being educated via French. Third and fifth grade English-speaking pupils were compared with French-speaking children of the same age using a sentence repetition task constructed to test control of selected French linguistic features. It was hypothesized that the English speakers would have a different internalized grammar of French than would French speakers; furthermore, that the different internal grammars would be reflected by differences in task performance. The results of the study can best be explained with reference to two factors: an 'internalized grammar' factor as was hypothesized; and a memory factor attributable to familiarity with, and exposure to, French.

Martínez-Bernal, Janet. Children's acquisition of Spanish and English morphological systems and noun phrases. Ph.D. dissertation, Georgetown University, 1972.

The purpose of this thesis was to develop a measure that would give reliable information on the bilingual child's language development. A series of pictures was devised, similar in some ways to the Berko test of English morphology, with a procedure similar in some ways to the Berko test to elicit grammatical forms. The measure was then used to collect data on both English and Spanish morphology of 5 to 8 year old bilingual children in Arizona. The results were then compared with monolingual children and it was found that the two groups did not differ substantially.

Mazeika, E.J. A description of the language of a bilingual child. Ph.D. dissertation, University of Rochester, 1971. See also: A comparison of the grammar of a monolingual and bilingual child. Paper presented at SRCD Conference, Philadelphia, April, 1973.

2100 utterances of the child Carlito were collected from 26 to 30 months of age. The data consisted of both Spanish and English utterances. The data were recorded during play time monologues in order to compare the data with that presented by Weir for her first language learner, Anthony. The data were first examined for phonological development. Among the findings were: 1) late development of /v, ǰ, Ө, ð/ (accounted for in terms of non-occurrence of these forms in Spanish); 2) that the child could use words from his other language that are easier to articulate (similar to Celce-Murcia's findings); and 3) relatively, the phonological development chronology was the same as for L1 children. The data were also analyzed for various morphological inflections of both Spanish and English. Similarities, again, were found to the chronological development of L1 children. Some of the strategies used by the child were then compared to the monologues of Weir's subject, Anthony. Build-ups similar to those reported by Huang, Young and others in this volume, occur in the data. Carlito says, for example: "Bathroom. Mommy, truck in bathroom" or "Sí, banana. Sí una banana. Baby quiere una banana, Mommy." Breakdowns also occurred: "That's a tractor man. Tractor man." Some interesting explanations of this phenomenon are given in Clark (1974), Scollon (1975), and Peck (1976). Finally, the utterances were analyzed for sentence type using the Stockwell, Bowen & Martin system.

Mikeš, Melanija. Acquisition des categories grammaticales dans le langage de l'enfant. *Enfance,* 1967, *20,* 289-98.

Mikeš presents data from infant girls who acquired Hungarian and Serbo-Croatian simultaneously. The study gives a careful annotation of when the grammatical form of the elaborate case, gender, person, number, tense, and mode system is acquired in each language. She then contrasts the acquisition of these forms by her bilingual subjects with a child learning Serbo-Croatian as a first language. The basic findings of the study were that interference between the two systems was not lasting for either of the two children so that by age four the systems were perfectly balanced. Also of interest is the discussion of how one decides that a particular form is acquired. Mikeš believes that only when a form appears in proper contrast to other forms in its category can one truly claim acquisition. This has served as a basis for Gough's insistence that one not claim acquisition of a form until the function of the form has also been acquired. Since certain forms in one language are acquired before parallel forms in the other, this study has also served as a source for supporting data for various operating principles proposed as universals in language acquisition.

Milon, J.P. The development of negation in English by a second language learner. *TESOL Quarterly,* 1974, *8,* 2, 137-143.

The speech of a seven year old Japanese boy recently arrived in Hawaii was examined in light of the hypothesis that non-native speakers, if they are well below the age of puberty, will acquire the grammatical structures of negation in English in the same developmental sequence which has been described for the acquisition of those structures by native speakers. Video tape recordings were made over a period of more than six months at regular intervals. It was found that there was a striking similarity between the developmental substages of negation in the acquisition of English as a first language as described by Klima and Bellugi (1966) and the development of negation in the speech of the subject.

    The reader will want to compare the findings of this study with that of Cancino, Rosansky and Schumann in this volume. Their analysis of negation for their learners does not conform to that of first language learners, a position opposite that of Milon. With so many studies of negation available (cf., Huang, Young, Adams, Shapira), a summary project now seems both possible and desirable.

Murrell, M. Language acquisition in a trilingual environment: notes from a case-study. *Studia Linguistica*, 1966, *20*, 9-35.

Murrell's daughter, Sandra, learned English in a trilingual environment: Finnish, Swedish and English. The study covers her language development from age 2 to 2:8 at which time her environment had become bilingual, primarily English with some Swedish.

The study is of special interest in light of perceptual strategies that have been discussed in the literature since the appearance of this article. A number of the operating principles discussed by Slobin and others appear in this paper in a somewhat different form. One of Slobin's principles is that the learner will pay attention to word order. The Murrell study shows that Sandra used relatively free word order. This is also characteristic of the data collected by Bowerman for acquisition of Finnish as a first language; Finnish is one of the three languages with which Sandra had contact. Certainly free word order is atypical of most children learning first and second languages, and it is unclear why Murrell and Bowerman's data show children not attending to basic word order (whether SVO, SOV, or verb initial. Their data presents problems for the basic claims of conversational analysis (Hatch) and for Greenfield's analysis of the early stages of language acquisition.

A second operating principle which has since appeared in the literature is that the learner will pay attention to the ends of words. Sandra did not acquire suffixed morphology. However, certain suffixes did *appear* before unstressed prefixed morphemes. For example, she produced 'bord*et*' and 'tables' before she produced 'the table.' Paying attention to the ends of words may really not be the underlying strategy as much as paying attention to stress for Sandra produced stressed forms like '*the* table' before 'the table' with no stress on the article. Stressed *can* and *can't* also appeared in her speech long before the unstressed forms.

A third strategy that has been discussed at length since this study appeared is that the child will learn simple forms before complex forms. This might, for example, account for the child's learning of simple morphological endings which have only one form (e.g., *-ing*) before those which have several forms (e.g., the three forms for possessives).

Murrell also presents data on many of the same questions asked in other studies of infant bilingualism: when does the phonology of the two languages become separated? when does the child realize he has more than one language to cope with?, etc. The reader must be impressed with the careful analysis that Murrell is able to do because he transcribes the child's output using phonetic script. This is a paper well worth many careful re-readings.

Naiman, Neil. The use of elicited imitation in second language acquisition research. *Working Papers in Bilingualism, 2*, 1974. (Based on a Ph.D. dissertation, University of Toronto.)

This paper reports on a study undertaken to investigate the relationship between elicited imitation data and comprehension data (as measured by a picture-identification task, and an L2 to L1 translation task), and between elicited imitation data and production data (as measured by a spontaneous speech task, and an L1 to L2 translation task). The *S*s were native English-speaking children attending a French immersion program at the grade 1 and 2 levels. Generally speaking, the results suggest that elicited imitation data present a conservative estimate of second-language comprehension skills and a non-conservative estimate of second language production skills.

Differences in performance between 'good' learners and 'poor' learners on the tasks are unaccounted for on the basis of sex, age, or exposure to the second language.

The errors made by the children are categorized and discussed within Selinker's (1972) interlanguage framework.

A model which allows for the interpretation of elicited imitation data is presented, and it is noted that accurate interpretation of these data are dependent upon the location in the model sentence of the syntactic structure being investigated, and the number of test items employed as well as the length of the model sentence.

Nam, Eileen. "Child and adult perceptual strategies in second language acquisition." Paper presented at the TESOL Conference, Los Angeles, 1975.

Bever and Denton have shown that Spanish-speaking children learning English as a second language go through the same stages in use of the NVN = SVO strategy (take the first noun as the agent and the second as object) as do native children. Adults learning a second language, however, appear to rely on strategies different from those available to the child. Bever, Nam and Shallo showed that Spanish speaking adults learning English as a second language do not go through the stages used by children with respect to the NVN = SVO strategy. To further test these findings, Nam is collecting data on adult and child speakers of Spanish and Korean who are learning English to determine whether children and adults (irrespective of their first languages) perform in a way similar to those reported in the research to date on child vs. adult use of the NVN = SVO strategy.

Natalicio, Diana S. & Natalicio, Luiz F.S. A comparative study of English pluralization by native and non-native English speakers. *Child Development,* 1971, *42,* 1302-06.

144 males, four groups of 36 in the first, second, third, and tenth grades, respectively, equally divided at each grade level according to native language, were presented a randomized list of nonsense syllables designed to elicit the plural forms of these pseudonouns. Results indicate that the pattern of acquisition of noun plurals in English is comparable for both children having English as their first language and those acquiring English as a second language.

Nielsen, Thelma H. Early stages in the non-native acquisition of English syntax: a study of three children from Zaire, Venezuela, and Saudi Arabia. Ph.D. dissertation, Indiana University, 1974.

The study investigated the developmental trends in the acquisition of English syntax by three children of diverse language backgrounds in an attempt to find out whether processes undergone by each child, during a six-month period, were similar to those of each other child. Four basic sentence types were analyzed: imperatives, declaratives, negatives, and interrogatives. The data were divided into four developmental stages. While the findings indicated that children learning a second language go through similar stages regardless of their mother tongue, some individual differences were present in the data that Nielsen attributes to phenomena such as overgeneralization, individual learning strategies, and other factors. In addition, each child showed certain consistent idiosyncracies in his speech. Comparison with first language learners suggests that second language learners acquire certain features at a much greater speed than native speakers do. The second language learners were found to use two-word utterances for an extremely short time and used adult-like forms as early as the third month of exposure. This was attributed to the cognitive ability of the child and his knowledge of language *per se.*

Oksaar, Els. Implications of language contact for bilingual language acquisition. Paper presented at the IXth International Congress of Anthropological and Ethnological Sciences, Chicago, 1973.

The author provides a model of emerging Swedish-Estonian bilingualism based on data from her son, Sven, collected from age two. During this early period her analysis was focused on the rules of code-switching. Data were collected when the child was playing alone or before falling asleep (monologue situation), or together with other children and adults (dialog situation). To account for the child's language use, Oksaar has created a model which posits an L3 as the child's language when he is constantly exposed to L1 and L2.

L3 contains elements and rules from L1 and L2 as well as elements and rules typical only for L3. The rules are activated according to the requirements of the language situation. In certain speech events, L1 parts dominate, in others those from L2, in others again the autonomous parts of L3. The contact with languages gives the child an opportunity of choosing the linguistic medium of expression. Characterizing the early stages of infant bilingualism as a 'mixed system' allows one to overlook this point. The emerging grammars of unilingual children include rules and elements that do not exist in the adult's code. The repertoire of children simultaneously acquiring two or more languages also contains rules and elements that cannot be found in either of them. Code-switching reveals that language contact operates at least on two levels: it creates awareness of two languages, which make it possible to use the 'right' sequences in 'right' situations. However, it also seems to develop awareness for rationality in performance; interference can occur on one occasion and not on another, where each language could be 'possible.' The L3 model shows how sociolinguistic factors create an overall code.

Oller, John W. & Ziahosseiny, Seid M. The contrastive analysis hypothesis and spelling errors, *Language Learning*, 1970, *20*, 2, 183-97.

The implications of three versions of the contrastive analysis hypothesis (CAH) are explored. The strong and weak forms are rejected in favor of a more moderate version which predicts the results of a spelling error analysis on the dictation section of the UCLA placement examination in English as a second language. Spelling errors of foreign students whose native language employed a Roman alphabet (Group R) were compared with spelling errors of foreign students whose native language used some non-Roman system (Group NR). An analysis of covariance with non-spelling errors as the covariate, and spelling errors as the dependent variable showed NR superior to R ($p < .025$) with a significantly smaller percentage of spelling errors. These results support a more moderate CAH which predicts that spelling errors are based on "interference" of similar patterns due to false generalizations.

Olmstead-Gary, Judith. The effects on children of delayed oral practice in initial stages of second language learning. Ph.D. dissertation, UCLA, 1974.

The purpose of this five-month study was to determine the effects on children's listening comprehension *and* speaking skills of delayed oral practice in initial stages of second language learning. Fifty English speakers, aged 5 to 8 years, were randomly assigned to experimental and control treatments consisting of 85 twenty-five-minute lessons in Spanish. The control group received oral practice (mimicry and drill); the experimental group did not. Their mode of response was gross motor movements such as jumping or running. The experimental group received totally delayed oral practice for 14 weeks followed by 7 weeks in which oral practice was introduced during the second half of each daily lesson. Tests were given each day and at two intermediate points during the project. Results showed that the experimental group surpassed the control group on question formation scores and their general rate of learning was quicker than the control group. It was speculated that with additional lesson time, the experimental group would also have exceeded the control group in oral performance.

It would be interesting to investigate the differences among the children in this study as well as the differences between the two groups in an attempt to understand why some children (see the diary studies presented in this volume) use an extended listening period before trying to use the new language while others immediately plunge into verbal communication in the new language. Looking at individual children who did well in the experimental group and those who did poorly in the oral language control group might give us some clues to this problem.

Oyama, Susan. A sensitive period for the acquisition of non-native phonological system. *Journal of Psycholinguistic Research,* 1976, *5,* 3, 261-284.

Sixty Italian-born immigrants who had learned English at various ages and who had been in the United States for various amounts of time were judged for degree of accent in English. Pronunciation was scored from two speech samples: 1) *S* read a short paragraph specially constructed to elicit typical pronunciation problems for Italians learning English and other phonological variables linked to sociolinguistic stratification and stylistic shift (Labov). 2) *S* was asked to recount an experience where he thought he was in danger of losing his life (Labov's 'danger-of-death technique'). a 45-second sample from each passage was then judged by two native-speakers of English on a 5-point scale (no accent to heavy accent). The casual story samples showed less accent than paragraph reading. While native-speakers appear to monitor their speech in reading tasks towards more prestige-valued pronunciation, for the non-native speaker, increased attention seemed to have a deteriorative effect on pronunciation.

Age of arrival in the United States was the best predictor of accent, better than years in the United States. The author concludes with a discussion of the 'sensitive period' for acquisition of native-like pronunciation including claims made in pedagogical and neurolinguistic literature.

Pavlovitch, Milivoie. *Le langage enfantin: acquisition du serbe et du français par un enfant serbe.* Paris: Champion, 1920.

"M. Pavlovitch traces the speech development of his son Douchan acquiring simultaneously Serbian and French. His study would have been more interesting for our present purposes if he had not stopped when the child was two years of age; it would have been interesting, for instance, to compare the learning of declensions in the synthetic Serbian with that of the analytic French. In their results Pavlovitch and Ronjat are largely in agreement; Pavlovitch does not believe in heredity and says that if there is any, it is a predisposition of a more general than of a national character. His study contains many generalizations on bilingualism, although his child does not seem to have been really bilingual, and an extensive bibliography, in the opinion of Leopold drawn largely from Stern supplemented by French titles." Vildomec, V., *Multilingualism.* A.W. Sythoff-Leyden, 1963, 25-26.

Perkins, Kyle & Larsen-Freeman, Diane. The effect of formal language instruction on the order of morpheme acquisition. *Language Learning,* 1975, *25,* 2, 237-43.

We conducted a study to determine if informal learners of ESL had the same acquisition order of morphemes as formal learners have been found to possess. Secondly, we wanted to find out what would happen to the established order if only certain of the grammatical morphemes were to be explained and drilled. We found that we had overestimated the ability of our informal subject pool to produce English sentences; that we had to structure our tasks which caused the loss of some 'naturalness'; that language instruction might result in improved performance in morpheme usage but not a change in the order of acquisition of morphemes; that a rank ordering type of statistical analysis is inadequate for morpheme acquisition studies.

Plann, Sandra. The Spanish Immersion Program: towards native-like proficiency or a classroom dialect? MA-TESL, UCLA, 1976.

A cross-sectional test was carried out on English-speaking children in grades one through four in the Culver City Spanish Immersion Program to investigate acquisition of two areas of agreement rules in Spanish: verb subject and number, and article and adjective gender and number.

While a definite acquisition order could not be determined for all verb forms, all groups seemed to master the third person singular first; they overgeneralized this form, using it for other forms as well. Although there was a slight improvement of children across grade levels, this feature of Spanish grammar cannot be considered mastered even by the fourth grade. Adjective and article agreement were not mastered by any of the groups either. The large majority of these errors, however, involved only gender, not number errors. The children overgeneralize in their use of the masculine forms.

The main cause of these persistent errors was believed to be the large amount of incorrect peer-input, which far exceeds correct teacher-input. The children have their own immersion-classroom dialect. The emphasis has always been on communication, not on grammatical correctness, and this dialect is adequate for classroom needs. These problems by the fourth grade level seem to be fossilized forms which may prove difficult if not impossible to eradicate unless the immersion program can be supplemented with increased contact with native-Spanish-speaking peers.

Raffler, W. von. Studies in Italian-English bilingualism. Ph.D. dissertation, Indiana University, 1953.

Taped data of second-generation, Italian-English bilingual informants provided a corpus for investigating whether bilinguals make use of one, two, or one and a half phonemic systems. The author concludes that mispronunciations show the learner bases his second language phonological system on that of the first language. That is, they "try to superimpose additions or alterations." Yet, she concludes that, "The comparison of the American-English and the Italian-American speech of the same bilingual informant leads to the conclusion that bilinguals on the phonological level operate with two separate systems."

Ramírez, A.G. The spoken English of Spanish-speaking pupils in a bilingual and monolingual school setting: an analysis of syntactic development. Ph.D dissertation, 1974, ERIC 904-569.

The purposes of this study were 1) to describe the developmental trends in the control of spoken English grammatical constructions produced by Spanish-speaking Mexican-American schoolchildren learning English in the elementary grades, and 2) on the basis of this description to assess the comprehension development of English structures in pupils schooled bilingually in English and Spanish and those instructed in only English. The Ss were 115 Mexican-American school children in grades Kg through 3rd. The data were assessed using Hunt's T-unit count. Bilingually-schooled pupils produced more language overall and more structurally complex units.

Ramírez, A.G. The acquisition of Spanish grammar by native English-speaking pupils in a Spanish Immersion Program, grades K-4. Mimeo report, UCLA, 1976.

The Spanish Grammar Production Subtest of the Spanish/English Balance Test, developed at the Stanford Center for Research & Development in Teaching, was administered to 40 pupils randomly selected across grades K-4 (8 Ss, 4 males and 4 females, at each grade level) in the Culver City Spanish Immersion Program. The grammar production subtest consists of 10 grammatical categories (2 items per category) which require the subject to make changes from 1) singular to plural, 2) plural to singular, 3) present to past tense, 4) affirmative past tense to negative present tense, 5) prepositions of location, 6) interrogatives—indirect to direct, 7) imperatives—indirect to direct, 8) interrogatives—direct to indirect, 9) imperatives—direct to indirect, and 10) comparatives. Responses were analyzed by grade, sex, and grammatical category in order to establish developmental trends across grade level. The utterances produced were further categorized by "errors" (e.g. the type/frequency of intralingual vs. interlingual errors) and strategies of communication. A Spanish writing sample was obtained from pupils in the third and fourth grades, and additional comparisons were made between the oral and written proficiencies in Spanish at the two grade levels.

Rizsk, Nazli. A comparative study of the learning of English morphemes by an Arabic-speaking child. M.A. thesis in progress, UCLA, 1976.

Spontaneous and test data were gathered on the speech production of a six-year-old subject, Lydia. The child, an Arabic speaker from Egypt, was enrolled in a regular California school where no formal language instruction was given her. The elicited data consist of imitation, translation data and responses to the Bilingual Syntax Measure. The data collected are being analyzed for morpheme development, using the Brown procedure of 80% correctly supplied in obligatory instances over two samples. For a final report on findings, please consult the thesis.

Robbins, Margaret. The effects of feedback on the eradication of errors in verb forms by ESL students. MA-TESL, UCLA, 1976.

The focus of this study on verb errors in compositions was on the learner and the information he can furnish the researcher about his errors. The purpose of the study was to investigate the effectiveness of eliciting student explanations about verb errors on the eradication of those errors. Secondary areas of investigation were whether any patterns developed in the types of errors made and whether any patterns developed in the explanations given. Eight intermediate-level adult ESL learners, 2 from each of 4 native-language backgrounds (Arabic, Japanese, Persian and Spanish) were randomly placed into either a control group or an experimental group. Both groups were administered a pre- and post-test on verb usage and verb forms. Weekly errors explanations were conducted with each experimental subject during which the learner examined his uncorrected compositions. He attempted to locate his errors, correct them, and then he was asked to give an explanation for each error. This study shows that error explanations from the learner provide useful insights concerning the production of errors and the second language learning process. It is suggested that the effectiveness of this technique appears to be dependent on the personality of the learner and the learner's past language learning history.

Ronjat, J. *Le développement du langage observé chez un enfant bilingue.* Paris: Champion, 1913.

This volume reports on the simultaneous acquisition of French and German by the author's child Louie. Ronjat attributes much of the child's balance development in both languages to the "one language-one person" principle. The father always spoke French and the mother German. Fortunately, unlike the Leopold study, there were other speakers of each language present in the child's environment on a regular basis so that, at least after the first year, he had adequate contact with each language. Ronjat noted only a few isolated instances of language interference in the development of phonology. If Louie used a French word in a German utterance, he would pronounce it with a German accent, and vice versa. He was clearly aware of the phonological system of each language. His acquisition of phonology showed the same processes of consonant cluster simplification, assimilation and dissimilation, etc., in each language. The child could translate easily from either language. From the 36th month on, he constantly asked for lexical equivalents. The child showed precocious metalinguistic awareness. Louie could also skillfully change dialects to his own standard in singing songs, and attempted to teach German to a French-speaking servant. Ronjat discusses earlier studies where children were not as successful in attaining fluency in both languages. Most of these problems he attributed to violation of the one person-one language principle.

Rosansky, Ellen J. The critical period for the acquisition of language: some cognitive developmental considerations. *Working Papers on Bilingualism, 6,* 1975.

This paper reviews the biological origins of the critical period hypothesis and the neurophysiological evidence which was initially supplied in support of a critical period for the acquisition of language. Noting the inconclusive nature of neurophysiological evidence, the author suggests that we look at the interplay of affective and cognitive factors in discussing the acquisition of a second language. The main focus in the paper is the consideration of Piagetian cognitive developmental theory in general, and the development of the symbolic function in particular as it relates to the problem of second language acquisition. The suggestion is offered that the onset of Formal Operations may well mark the beginning of the end of a critical period for the acquisition of language.

Rouchdy, Aleya A. A case of bilingualism: an investigation of lexical and syntactic interference in the performance of a bilingual child. Ph.D. dissertation, University of Texas at Austin, 1970.

This study examined interference in the speech of a 12-year-old child, the writer's son, whose languages are Arabic and English. The *S* spoke only Arabic on his arrival in the United States at age 8. The analysis demonstrates that interference has occurred on the syntactic level as well as at the lexical level from English to Arabic as English became the child's major language. The data for the study were collected over a six-month period when the *S* was twelve. It consists of systematic tests as well as spontaneous speech. Both measures showed the impact of one language system on the other in the quality and quantity of production in the *S*'s now-weaker language, Arabic. The author concludes, from the tests given, that the child's production of Arabic does not reflect his competence in that language. That is, his passive knowledge of his language is superior to his active knowledge. This is related to the notions of competence and performance in transformation grammar theory.

Savignon, Sandra J. Talking with my son: an example of communicative competence. In Grittner, F.M. (Ed.), *Careers, communications and culture in foreign language teaching.* Skokie, Illinois, National Textbook Co., 1974.

Savignon's primary concern in this article is the development of communicative competence rather than simply linguistic competence. She collected data on conversations with her son, Daniel, age 9, who began speaking French when the family spent the summer in France. The transcribed conversations provide examples of communicative competence which the author contrasts to models used in formal language classes. She also categorized the "errors" in the child's speech in terms of: 1) interference-like errors, 2) developmental errors, 3) ambiguous errors, and 4) unique errors. The data showed the child's wide range of comprehension as compared with production, and the semantic richness of his speech as contrasted with structural simplicity. Savignon states that linguistic competence "is not the same thing as an ability to engage in spontaneous interpersonal transaction, and that the development of communicative competence is greatly enhanced by the opportunity for creative, spontaneous expression." The article includes many sensible comments for language teachers.

Schachter, Jacquelyn. An error in error analysis. *Language Learning*, 1974, *24*, 2, 205-14.

Presently, a number of proponents of an error analysis approach to the investigation of second language learning argue that contrastive analysis (CA) apriori is inadequate as an account of target language learning problems. They claim that the only tenable version of CA is an aposteriori approach, i.e., CA is just those areas that have been proven by error analysis to be difficulties in production. This claim is disputed in a study involving the acquisition of English relative clauses by speakers of Persian, Arabic, Chinese and Japanese. The aposteriori approach obscured the fact that the Chinese and Japanese learners have more difficulty with relative clauses and therefore avoid them, a fact predicted by the apriori approach.

Schlue, Karen. An inside view of interlanguage, MA-TESL thesis, UCLA, 1976.

Three university ESL students, one Persian, one Korean, and one Spanish-speaking, were tape-recorded while conversing with a native English speaker. The subjects then listened to their speech and attempted to recall their awareness of grammar during the encoding/speaking experience, using the following categories: 1) no problems with this sentence, 2) recognized error and corrected it before speaking, 3) recognized error before speaking, but no time to correct, 4) recognized error after speaking, 5) recognized error after hearing the tape, 6) not sure if this is correct or not. Individual sessions were held once a week for ten weeks. It was hypothesized that each subject would gain some control over at least one area of grammar during the ten weeks, and that his analysis of utterances containing that structure would move upward on the scale, e.g., from insecurity toward total mastery. Preliminary results, however, show that categories 2, 3, and 4 were infrequently chosen (they perhaps represent experiences which are not common to these subjects or are not easily recalled); category 6 was rarely chosen (reflecting, perhaps, a reluctance to admit uncertainty); category 1 was frequently chosen for error-ridden as well as error-free utterances. In areas of grammar where the subjects made progress, the pattern was a shift from category 1 (sentence contained unrecognized error) to category 5 (belated awareness of error) to category 1 (no error, no problem). The few examples of categories, 2, 3, and 4 being chosen do not constitute intermediate 'stages' of control.

Schmidt-Mackey, I. Language strategies of the bilingual family. ERIC ED 060-740. Paper presented at Conference on Child Language, Chicago, 1971.

This paper contains a literature review of several important second language acquisition studies along with a discussion of the importance of language separation for ease of learning, including one-language, one-person, separate languages for home and school, etc. It also includes a discussion of the language strategies of the author's own multilingual family.

Schwartz, Joan L. Repair in conversations between adult second language learners of English. MA-TESL Thesis, UCLA, 1977.

The study was conducted to investigate how adult second language learners deal with errors and other trouble sources in their conversations with one another. The specific aims were to describe the repair work done by the learners during conversations, to describe the extralinguistic features which accompany repair, to describe the differences between repairs made by speakers at different proficiency levels, and to compare the description of repair for these learners with native speakers of English.

Three videotaped conversations of pairs of friends from varying language backgrounds and proficiency levels were collected. The tapes were then transcribed according to conversational analysis transcription techniques. Extralinguistic features were transcribed using a system of detailed glosses.

The data indicate that adult second language learners were successful in dealing with errors and other trouble sources in their conversations with one another. While the verbal repair work done by the learners was similar in many aspects to repair of native speakers, their corrections were the outcome of incompetence in phonology, syntax and lexicon. Extralinguistic features were significant in the repair process, in terms of facilitating the process of negotiation for understanding. The data show that these students were able to learn specifics (such as vocabulary) as well as conversational strategies (such as negotiation) from conversing with one another.

Selinker, L., Swain, M. & Dumas, G. The Interlanguage hypothesis extended to children. *Language Learning*, 1975, *25*, 1, 139-53.

The purpose of this paper is to demonstrate that the Interlanguage hypothesis should be extended from 1) adult second language acquisition settings to 2) those non-simultaneous child language acquisition settings where the major sociolinguistic variable is the absence of peers who are native speakers of the target language. The paper first established the need to postulate the existence of an interlanguage. Data from the Toronto French immersion program are then described in terms of language transfer, simplification, and overgeneralization. The possibility that interlanguages may develop as dialects in their own right is also discussed.

Smith, Madonah E. A study of five bilingual children in the same family. *Child Development*, 1931, *2*, 184-187.

Five English-speaking children (Ruth, Jane, John, Lois and Mary) lived with their family in China. During their stay in that country, they learned Chinese from the family servants. The study does not specify which Chinese language. The study consists of a discussion of the then current issue of whether or not bilingualism may or may not have retarded their vocabulary acquisition and/or I.Q. The study contains vocabulary lists (English) and I.Q. measures.

Sodhi, S.S. Uznadze's set and second language learning. *International Journal of Psychology*, 1969, *4*, 4, 317-19.

Studies of simultaneous acquisition of two languages have shown a first stage of mixed speech where both languages are used interchangeably in the same context. Uznadze's theory of set has been suggested as a model for the evolution of two separate systems. In this study, Sodhi tested set fixation and extinction among 160 Ss who had studied French for three years in high school. The Ss were divided into good vs. poor learners on the basis of MLA tests in French normalized against their scores on SCAT. The results showed that poor second language learners were not capable of extinguishing one set readily and beginning another. This difficulty in shifting from one set to another is suggested as a significant source of variance in second language learners. For a similar study, see Cummins & Gulutson, 1975.

Stafford, Cynthia & Covitt, Regina. An investigation of the Monitor Theory, Psycholinguistics-TESL Project, UCLA, 1976.

This study attempts to ascertain the reality of the Monitor Theory of adult second language acquisition as proposed by Krashen (1976). In particular the study focuses on trying to determine the extent to which rules are consciously used in adult second language production. A questionnaire was administered to 38 advanced level ESL students at UCLA. On the basis of the questionnaire, 4 individual students, 2 seemingly rule oriented and 2 seemingly non-rule oriented, were chosen for in-depth interviews. Transcripts of student interviews reveal four different kinds of rule usage behavior: 1) correct application and conscious reliance on rules, 2) incorrect application and conscious reliance on rules, 3) successful reliance on intuition or 'feel' with no conscious rule reference, 4) unsuccessful reliance on intuition or 'feel' with no conscious rule reference. The transcripts also reveal a definite psychological need for rules on the part of all students interviewed. The study concludes by posing several questions concerning the Monitor Theory which warrant further investigation.

Swain, Merrill & Wesche, Mari. Linguistic interaction: case study of a bilingual child. *Working Papers in Bilingualism, 1,* 1973.

The phenomenon of 'linguistic interaction' in bilinguals is examined through a case study of a child growing up in a French-English home in Quebec City, Canada. Approximately 25 hours of his speech were recorded during regular play sessions over a period of nine months with two adult unilinguals, one an English speaker and the other a French speaker. From this corpus all instances of within-sentence lexical mixing as well as examples of syntactic and semantic interaction are examined.

Developmental changes in the kinds and frequencies of language mixing occurring during the nine-month period (age 3:1 to 3:10) are described. The linguistic junctures at which switches occur are discussed, and several are examined in detail to seek evidence of the psychological reality of grammatical constituents.

Swain, Merrill. Writing skills of grade three French immersion pupils. *Working Papers in Bilingualism, 7,* 1975.

This paper analyzes short stories written in English and French by French immersion pupils at the Grade 3 level. Their English writing skills are compared to those of Grade 3 pupils in a regular English program. Aspects of their writing skills which are examined include vocabulary skills, technical skills (punctuation, capitalization, and spelling), grammatical skills and creativity. The errors made by the pupils are discussed in detail and data are provided. For a similar study, see Bassan, 1975.

Syngle, Bishan. Second language (English) acquisition strategies of children and adults: a cross-sectional study. Ph.D. dissertation, Louisiana State University, 1973.

The purpose of this study was to empirically test whether children and adults learning English as a second language use similar strategies. One hundred ninety-eight foreign adults and 16 foreign children (from different language and culture backgrounds) who had been in this country from a few weeks to two years were administered tests to evaluate their comprehension of structures involving 1) the Easy-Eager distinction, 2) the non-identity condition to pronominalization, and 3) the Ask-Tell distinction. In addition, negatives, WH-questions and some inflections were elicited from the children. No relationship was found between Ss' native languages and strategies in decoding the structures. In the Easy-Eager test, native child, foreign child, and foreign adult groups appeared to perform similarly. All expect and seek the marked form of the adjective. The results on pronominalization and Ask-Tell support this finding of 'essential similarity' in the processing strategies of the three groups.

Tanka, Judith. An error analysis of the speech of Russian ESL students. Psycho-linguistics-TESL Project, UCLA, 1975.

Twenty-four Russian students of ESL participated in this study. All were enrolled in adult school ESL classes; their age range was from 25 to 55 years. Each S was asked individually to describe two pictures from the Peabody Language Development Kit. Their responses were recorded and transcribed, and a frequency count of the most salient errors was made. The largest number of errors were made in the English article system followed by copula errors in the present tense and omission of *be* in continuous *be + ing*. Subject-verb agreement, preposition errors in possessive phrases also were important sources of errors. Word order errors also occurred in the data. The findings of this paper are similar to those found for Czech students (Duškova) in an error analysis of written, rather than oral, language production.

Tarone, Elaine E. Some influences on Interlanguage phonology. Paper presented at the TESOL Conference, Los Angeles, 1975. See also *Working Papers in Bilingualism, 8,* 1976.

There has been a great deal of speculation about the nature of the processes which shape the phonology of second language learners. Oller (1974) has suggested that the phonology of the second language learner is shaped not by processes active in first language acquisition but rather by those of language transfer. Oller has pointed to such phenomena as reported epenthesis as evidence of different processes for first and second language learners. Tarone (1972) has shown that the simple open syllable, as a possible universal articulatory unit, may be influential in shaping second language phonologies, affecting the production of consonant clusters and 'blending' of speech sounds across linguistic boundaries, and thereby affecting speech rhythm.

In this study the interlingual phonological systems of six speakers are described in detail. Two of the Ss were Cantonese speakers, two were Portuguese speakers from Brazil, and two were Korean. Each speaker was asked to describe a sequence of pictures, narrating a story in the process. Each S's narration was transcribed using standard IPA with diacritics where needed to note deviations from standard transcription (transcriptions are included in the study). The data thus obtained were subjected to a detailed analysis in order to shed light on the relative importance of the syllabic articulatory unit, language transfer processes, and first language acquisition processes in shaping the interlingual phonologies of these learners.

Taylor, B.P. Overgeneralization and transfer as learning strategies in second language acquisition. Ph.D. dissertation, University of Michigan, 1974.

A test requiring translation of 80 Spanish sentences was administered to 20 Spanish-speaking students of ESL, ten each at the elementary and intermediate level of instruction. The test required the use of 8 English sentence types. These sentences were given orally in Spanish and the Ss attempted to write correct English translations for them.

The Ss' choices of AUX and Verb Phrase were then analyzed using a taxonomy of 20 error types. Errors were classified as due to 1) overgeneralization, 2) transfer, 3) translation, or 4) errors of independent origin. While common errors occurred and could be characterized as 'systematic,' Ss more frequently used a correct response than an incorrect one. The notion of Interlanguage as an internally consistent linguistic system might, therefore, be invalid. Since no syntactic theory seems capable of accommodating language behavior which involves random vacillation between conflicting rules, the concept of Interlanguage as a "system" seems highly suspect. The Ss' decision to use a particular rule in a given situation may be completely arbitrary or it may arise from confusion as to which rule is appropriate.

Tits, D. Le mécanisme de l'acquisition d'une langue se substituant à la langue maternelle chez une enfant espangnole agée de six ans. Bruxelles, 1948.

"The case studied by D. Tits is somewhat different from that of Kenyeres and the treatment less careful. The little Spanish refugee girl who found a new home in a Belgian family was in poor health when she got there and she heard only L^e (Ed. note: = the second language) in her new home. The L^e was, however, related to her L^m (Ed. note = mother tongue), which led to her using Spanish as a starting point. At the age of 6:4, she started attending a French school, where she learned also Flemish. In the author's opinion, the process of adaptation to the new milieu did not have any retarding effect on the child's mental development or on her articulation of French sounds, but, on the contrary, was a linguistic, physical, moral and mental stimulant. Whereas for an adult such a change of milieu means embarrassment, for her it was a sort of play. Very soon, i.e. on the 93rd day, she declared she did not know Spanish any more although her foster-parents had tried to preserve her L^m. She started learning Spanish again two years later. At the chronological ages of 8:6 and 10:3, her speech was tested with the results of 10:3 and 12:7 respectively, which means that her French was considerably above average, although in other spheres she was not so advanced. On the whole, Tits traces in her linguistic development the same phases as are those of a baby learning his L^m. Her acquisition, of course, was faster than is the acquisition of L^m by a baby as it lasted ten months only; the various stages were not as pure and clear-cut as they are in a baby's speech." Vildomec, *Multilingualism,* 27-28.

Tran, Thi Chan. Concepts of development in second language learning and teaching. Ph.D. dissertation, University of Toronto, 1972. See also *IRAL,* 1975, *13,* 119-43.

The questions asked in this dissertation deal with whether contrastive analysis (using the Stockwell, Bowen & Martin model), error analysis, or the student's statements of his perception of difficulty would best account for the errors actually made by students learning a new language. 149 high school students studying Spanish participated in the study. The author found that 51% of the errors were due to interference and that 27% of the errors could be accounted for by subsystems of the target language interfering with each other. The conclusions were that 1) contrastive analysis is valid but the student perception of difficulty provides a more accurate device to diagnose problem areas; 2) that to predict difficulty accurately, contrastive analysis, error analysis and student perception of difficulty combined would be useful for the teacher.

Van Mettre, Patricia D. Syntactic characteristics of selected bilingual children. Ph.D. dissertation, University of Arizona, 1972.

The study is an analysis of selected syntactic structures of bilingual children who scored either high or low on a state mandated reading test. The structures tested were: 1) interpretation of Ask/Tell, and of Ask questions which violate the minimal distance principle for determining the implicit subject of a complement verb; 2) interpretation of Promise sentences which violate the minimal distance principle; 3) interpretation of syntactically complex sentences in which the underlying relationships are not expressed in the surface structure; and 4) interpretation of restricted pronominal reference.

Thirty-two subjects were interviewed individually and their responses to the test items were tape recorded and transcribed for analysis. The findings show that 1) children who scored high on measured reading achievement knew the syntactic structures significantly better than those who scored low; 2) there were no differences between bilingual subjects tested in the study and monolingual children (Chomsky). The study substantiates earlier research findings of both an orderly sequence of acquisition of structures and the advent of acquisition of some structures based more on individual rate of development than on age.

Warshawksy, Diane R. The acquisition of four English morphemes by Spanish-speaking children. Ph.D. dissertation, University of Michigan, 1975.

This paper is concerned with the acquisition of four English morphemes by five Puerto Rican children learning English in a natural setting. The age range of the children was from 8 to 15 years. Four morphemes studied were plurals, possessives, third person singular present tense, and the negative of present tense. The hypothesis tested was: If, at a given time it is crucial for a child to differentiate between two possible meanings and if a certain expressive device to which he has access enables him to do so, then the acquisition of this expressive device will be favored.

The research was divided into two phases: a training phase and a test phase. The training served the function of increasing the frequency of the forms in the learner's input and of making syntax and semantic conditions governing their use apparent to the learner. The test consisted of a series of comprehension and production tasks which required the learner either to process or produce a minimal difference in meaning.

Observational data, the results of tests and samples of both spontaneous and elicited speech from the five subjects showed that, in every case, a form was acquired and used productively only when it assumed a critical role in transmitting essential information. Grammatical structure appears to develop in the learner's speech in response to communicational need.

Wong-Fillmore, L. The second time around: cognitive and social strategies in second language acquisition. Ph.D. dissertation, Stanford, 1976.

This study concerns five Spanish-speaking children and their second language acquisition in social context. The five children were studied in play situations with friends at school. The study presents not only what the children learned (the language product) but also investigates the social strategies and cognitive aspects of second language learning.

In examining the data from the children, Wong-Fillmore sketches three operational stages (while recognizing overlap) as follows: Stage 1: the aim is to establish a social relationship with speakers of the language. Children use nonverbal gestures. They learn names of objects and learn formula expressions. Stage 2: The children need to express new ideas so they begin to create novel sentences by combining formulas, substituting within formulas in sort of a slot-filler manner. They also seem to use more lexical items from their first language as they try to say more. Stage 3: While all children used the 'speak now, learn later' strategy, two of the children reached stage three which is a 'concern for correctness' stage. They began to sort out morphological signals for tense, etc.

In terms of social strategies, the good learner: 1. Joins a group and acts like he understands even if he doesn't. 2. Gives the impression with a few well-chosen words that he can speak the language. 3. Counts on his friends. The native-speaker peers were highly supportive of the learners, convinced that they could and did speak English. They also simplified their speech to the learners in a number of interesting ways which included repetition, limited lexical choice, use of vocatives and attention callers, using narratives to describe what they were doing in play situations, etc.

The learners follow the maxims listed below: 1. Guess. Assume that when people are speaking they are saying something relevant to the situation at hand. 2. Get some expressions you understand and start to talk. 3. Start analyzing the formulas you have learned as chunks into their parts. 4. Make the most of what you've got (string the formulas together, add new lexical items as you can). 5. Work on big things first; save details til later (morphology can wait).

Wong-Fillmore discusses a wide range of personality variables, the special needs and motivation of the children, their temperament, interests and skills in accounting for the wide variation in second language acquisition among the five learners.

Young, Denise I. The acquisition of English syntax by three Spanish-speaking children. MA-TESL, UCLA, 1974.

Three Spanish-speaking children (Enrique, Juan and Alma) were observed in their kindergarten class over a 9-month period. The data were tape recorded, in some instances using wireless microphones, twice each week. The massive amount of data collected in this way was then analyzed in three main sections: acquisition of negation, question-formation, and the acquisition of definite and indefinite articles. The methodology used for the analysis was an error analysis in the Chamot model. The data for Enrique and Juan identify a number of persistent problem areas which in some cases could be attributed to first-language interference. The data for Alma showed little or no learning of the second language. When she did begin to speak in the last days of the data-collection period, her speech did not represent a 'sudden flowering' after an extended listening period. There seemed to be a number of explanations possible for her delay in attending to and producing English. This is discussed in detail. The use of intentional repetition in speech patterns, and of build-ups, breakdowns, and completions (using the Weir terminology) in the data of Juan and Enrique is also presented. Raw data are included in the appendix.

References

Adams, M.A. The acquisition of academic skills and a second language through a program of total immersion. MA-TESL Thesis, UCLA, 1974.

d'Anglejan, A. & Tucker, R.G. The acquisition of complex English structures by adult learners. *Language Learning,* 1975, *25,* 2, 281-296.

Asher, J.J. & Garcia, R. The optimal age to learn a foreign language. *Modern Language Journal,* 1969, *8,* 334-341.

Atkinson, M. Prerequisites for reference. Paper presented at B.A.A.L. Seminar, University of Newcastle-upon-Tyne, April, 1974.

Bailey, N., Madden, C. & Eisenstein, M. Developing question formation ability in adult language learners. Paper presented at the TESOL Conference, New York, 1976.

Barik, H.C., Swain, M. & McTavish, K. Immersion classes in an English setting: one way for les Anglais to learn French. *Working Papers in Bilingualism, 2,* 1974.

Barik, H.C. & Swain, M. Third year evaluation of a large scale early grade French immersion program: the Ottawa Study. *Language Learning,* 1975, *25,* 1, 1-30.

Bassan, H.F. Spelling difficulties of Hebrew speakers of English: an error analysis of third graders in three bilingual schools. MA-TESL Thesis, UCLA, 1973.

Bebout, L. An error analysis: Comparing the ability of learners of English as a first and as a second language to extract information from written material. Ph.D. dissertation, Cornell University, 1974.

Belen Balagtas de Jesus, M. The development of English grammatical structures of elementary school children learning English as a second language: a linguistic analysis. Ph.D. dissertation, Stanford, 1975.

Bellugi, U. & Brown, R. (Eds.), *The acquisition of language.* Lafayette, Indiana: Purdue University Press, 1964.

Ben-Zeev, S. Influence of bilingualism on cognitive development and cognitive strategy. Paper presented at the Child Language Research Forum, Stanford, 1976.

Berko, J. The child's learning of English morphology. *Word,* 1958, *14,* 150-177.

Bertkau, J. Comprehension and production of English relative clauses in adult second language and child first language acquisition. Ph.D. dissertation, University of Michigan, 1974.

Bever, T.G. The cognitive basis for linguistic structures. In J.R. Hayes (Ed.), *Cognition and the development of language.* New York: J. Wiley & Sons, 1970, 279-362.

Bever, T.G. The nature of cerebral dominance in speech behavior of child and adult. In R. Huxley & E. Ingram (Eds.), *Language acquisition: models and methods.* New York: Academic Press, 1971, 231-254.

Bloom, L. *Language development: Form and function in emerging grammars.* Cambridge, Mass.: The M.I.T. Press, 1970.

Boyd, P.A. Second language learning: the grammatical development of Anglo children learning through Spanish. MA-TESL Thesis, UCLA, 1974. See also *TESOL Quarterly,* 1975, *9,* 2, 125-36.

Braine, M.D.S. The ontogeny of English phrase structure. *Language,* 1963, *39,* 1-13.

Braine, M.D.S. On two types of modes of the internalization of grammars. In Slobin, D.I. (Ed.), *The ontogenesis of grammar.* New York: Academic Press, 1971.

Brown, R. *A first language.* Cambridge, Mass.: Harvard University Press, 1973.

Brown, R. & Bellugi, U. Three processes in the child's acquisition of syntax. In Lenneberg, E.H. (Ed.), *New directions in the study of language*. Cambridge, Mass.: The M.I.T. Press, 1964.

Brown, R., Cazden, C. & Bellugi, U. The child's grammar from I to III. In A. Bar-Adon & Leopold, W.F. (Eds.), *Child language, a book of readings*. Englewood-Cliffs, N.J.: Prentice-Hall, 1971, 382-424.

Bruck, M., Rabinovitch, M.S., & Oates, M. The effects of French immersion programs on children with language disabilities—a preliminary report. *Working Papers in Bilingualism*, 5, 1974.

Brunak, J., Fain, E. & Villoria, N. Conversations with Rafaela. Second Language Acquisition Project, UCLA, 1976.

Burt, M.K., Dulay, H.C. & Hernández, E. *Bilingual Syntax Measure* (Restricted Edition). New York: Harcourt Brace Jovanovich, 1973.

Buteau, M.F. Students' errors in the learning of French as a second language. *IRAL*, 1970, 7, 2, 133-146. (Reprinted in Schumann & Stenson (Eds.), *New frontiers in second language learning*. Rowley, Mass.: Newbury House, 1975.)

Cathcart, R. Report on a group of Anglo children after one year of immersion in Spanish. MA-TESL Thesis, UCLA, 1972.

Cazden, C.B. Environmental assistance to the child's acquisition of grammar. Ph.D. dissertation, Harvard, 1972.

Cazden, C., Cancino, H., Rosansky, E. & Schumann, J. Second language acquisition sequences in children, adolescents, and adults. Final Report, United States Department of Health, Education & Welfare, 1975.

Chamot, A.U. Phonological problems in learning English as a third language. *IRAL*, 1973, 11, 3, 243-250.

Chomsky, C. The acquisition of syntax in children from 5 to 10. Ph.D. dissertation, Harvard, 1968.

Clark, E. What's in a word? On the child's acquisition of semantics in his first language. In Moore, T.E. (Ed.), *Cognitive development and the acquisition of language*. New York: Academic Press, 1973, 65-109.

Cohen, A.D. The Culver City Spanish Immersion Program: how does summer recess affect Spanish speaking ability? *Language Learning*, 1974, 24, 1, 55-68.

Cohen, A.D. Forgetting a second language. *Language Learning*, 1975, 25, 1, 127-138.

Cohen, M. (Ed.) *Etudes sur le langage de l'enfant*. Paris: Scarabee, 1962.

Cook, V.J. The comparison of language development in native children and foreign adults. *International Journal of Applied Linguistics*, 1973, 11, 13-28.

Corder, S.P. The significance of learners' errors. *IRAL*, 1967, 5, 161-169.

Corder, S.P. Idiosyncratic dialects and error analysis. *IRAL*, 1971, 9, 2, 147-159.

Corder, S.P. 'Simple codes' and the source of the second language learner's initial heuristic hypothesis. Paper presented at the Colloque 'Theoretical Models in Applied Linguistics' IV. Université de Neuchâtel, 1975.

Dato, D.P. American children's acquisition of Spanish syntax in the Madrid environment. Preliminary edition, HEW Fund Rep/ 3036, 1970, ERIC ED 053-631.

Delacroix, H. *Le langage et la pensée*. Paris: Champion, 1924.

de Villiers, J. & de Villiers, P. A cross-sectional study of the acquisition of grammatical morphemes in child speech. *Journal of Psycholinguistic Research*, 1973, 2, 267-278.

Dickerson, L.J. The learner's interlanguage as a system of variable rules, *TESOL Quarterly*, 1975, 9, 4, 401-408.

Dickerson, W.B. Hesitation phenomena in the spontaneous speech of non-native speakers of English. Ph.D. dissertation, University of Illinois, 1971.

Dulay, H.C. Aspects of child second language acquisition. Ph.D. dissertation, Harvard, 1974.

Dulay, H.C. & Burt, M.K. Goofing: an indicator of children's second language learning strategies. *Language Learning*, 1972, 22, 235-252.

Dulay, H.C. & Burt, M.K. Should we teach children syntax? *Language Learning,* 1973, *23,* 245-258.

Dulay, H.C. & Burt, M.K. Errors and strategies in child second language acquisition. *TESOL Quarterly,* 1974, *8,* 129-136.

Dulay, H.C. & Burt, M.K. Creative construction in second language learning and teaching. In Brown, H.D. (Ed.), *Papers in second language acquisition,* proceedings of the 6th Annual Conference on Applied Linguistics, Ann Arbor, Michigan, 1975, 65-80.

Dumas, G. & Swain, M. L'apprentissage du français langue seconde en classe d'immersion dans un milieu torontois. In Carey, S. (Ed.), *Bilingualism, education, and Canadian West,* in press.

Duškova, L. On sources of errors in foreign language learning. *IRAL,* 1969, *7,* 1, 11-33.

Ervin-Tripp, S.M. Some strategies of the first and second years. In Dil, A. (Ed.), *Language acquisition and communication choice.* Stanford, Calif.: Stanford University Press, 1973, 204-238.

Fantini, A.E. Language acquisition of a bilingual child: a sociolinguistic perspective. Ph.D. dissertation, University of Texas, 1974.

Fathman, A. The relationship between age and second language productive ability. *Language Learning,* 1975, *25,* 2, 245-254.

Fathman, A. Language background, age and the order of acquisition of English structures. Paper presented at the TESOL Conference, Los Angeles, 1975.

Flores, M. Early stages in the acquisition of Spanish syntax structures by a group of English-speaking children. MA-TESL, UCLA, 1973.

Fraser, C., Bellugi, U., Brown, R. Control of grammar in imitation, comprehension and production. *Journal of Verbal Learning and Verbal Behavior,* 1963, *2,* 121-135.

Gasser, M. A stage in the acquisition of Amharic by an adult. Psycholinguistics-TESL Project, UCLA, 1975.

Gatbonton-Segalowitz, E. Systematic variation in second language speech. Ph.D. dissertation, McGill, 1975.

Genessee, F., Tucker, G.R. & Lambert, W.E. Communication skills of bilingual children. *Child Development,* 1975, *46,* 1010-1014.

Gillis, M. & Weber, R. The emergence of sentence modalities in the English of Japanese-speaking children. Mimeo paper, McGill University, 1975.

Greenfield, P.M. Informativeness, presupposition, and semantic choice in single-word utterances. Paper presented at the Third International Child Language Symposium, London, 1975.

Hakuta, K. Learning to speak a second language: what exactly does the child learn? Paper presented at the 26th Annual Georgetown Roundtable, Washington, 1975.

Hamayan, E. French oral production and awareness of errors by English children educated bilingually. Paper presented at the TESOL Conference, New York, 1976.

Hamayan, E., Markman, B.R., Pelletier, S. & Tucker, G.R. Differences in performance in elicited imitation between French monolingual and English speaking bilingual children. *Working Papers in Bilingualism, 8,* 1976.

Hamayan, E., Saegert, J. & Larudee, P. Elicited imitation in second language learners. *Working Papers in Bilingualism, 6,* 1975.

Hanania, E. Acquisition of English structure: a case study of an adult native speaker of Arabic in an English-speaking environment. Ph.D. dissertation, Indiana University, 1974.

Hansen-Bede, L. A child's creation of a second language. *Working Papers in Bilingualism, 7,* 1975.

Hartford, B. The English of Mexican-American adolescents in Gary, Indiana: a sociolinguistic description. Ph.D. dissertation, University of Texas, 1975.

Hatch, E. Studies in second language acquisition. Paper presented at the Third International Congress of Applied Linguistics, Copenhagen, 1972.

Hatch, E. Studies in language mixing and switching. Paper presented at the IX International Congress of Anthropological and Ethnological Sciences, Chicago, August, 1973.

Hatch, E. Second language learning—universals? *Working Papers on Bilingualism,* 1974, *3,* 1-18.

Hatch, E. & Wagner-Gough, J. Second language acquisition. In Celce-Murcia, M. (Ed.), *Methods in teaching English as a second language.* Rowley, Mass.: Newbury House, in press.

Hatch, E. Language teaching and language learning. In Carterette, E. & Friedman, M. *Handbook of Psychology, Vol. 7, Language and Speech.* New York: Academic Press, 1976.

Hatch, E. & Wagner-Gough, J. Explaining sequence and variation in second language acquisition. In Brown, H.D. (Ed.), *Papers in second language acquisition.* Proceedings of the 6th Annual Conference on Applied Linguistics, Ann Arbor, Michigan, 1975, 39-58.

Hatch, E., Shapira, R., & Gough, J. Foreigner Talk. Paper for USC-UCLA Second Language Acquisition Forum, 1976.

Hatch E. The metalinguistic awareness of child second language learners. Paper for the USC-UCLA Second Language Acquisition Forum, 1976.

Hébrard, P. & Mougeon, R. La langue parlée le plus souvent entre les parents et les enfants: un facteur crucial dans l'acquisition linguistique de l'enfant dans un milieu bilingue, *Working Papers in Bilingualism, 7,* 1975.

Heckler, E.E. The acquisition of English verb morphology by non-native speakers. Ph.D. dissertation, Michigan State University, 1975.

Henzl, V. Cultivation and maintenance of literary Czech by Americans. Ph.D. dissertation, Stanford University, 1975.

Hill, J.H. Foreign accents, language acquisition and cerebral dominance revisited. *Language Learning,* 1970, *20,* 2, 237-248.

Hymes, D.H. *Pidginization and creolization of languages.* Cambridge: Cambridge University Press, 1971.

Imedadze, N.V. K psikhologicheskoy prirode rannego dvuyazychiya. *Vopr. Psikhol.,* 1960, *6,* 1, 60-68.

Ingram, D. The inversion of subject NP and Aux in children's questions. Paper presented at the meeting of the Linguistic Society of America, December 30, 1973.

Isman, J. The acquisition of English syntax by Indonesian children. Ph.D. dissertation, University of Indiana, 1973.

Jashni, V.M. The effects of the Spanish Immersion Program on the kindergarten and primary students in affective and cognitive domains. Ph.D. dissertation, Brigham Young University, 1976.

Johnson, N.A. A psycholinguistic study of bilingual language acquisition. Ph.D. dissertation, University of Texas, 1973.

Katz, J.J. & Postal, P.M. *An integrated theory of linguistic descriptions.* Cambridge, Mass.: The M.I.T. Press, 1964.

Keenan, E.O. Conversational competence in children. *Journal of Child Language,* 1974, *1,* 2, 163-184.

Keenan, E.O., Schieffelin, B. & Platt, M. Propositions across utterances and speakers. Paper presented at Child Language Research Forum, Stanford, California, 1976.

Keller-Cohen, D. Repetition in the non-native acquisition of discourse. Paper presented at Child Language Research Forum, Stanford, California, 1976.

Kempf, M.K. A study of English proficiency levels of the composition errors of incoming foreign students at the University of Cincinnati during 1969-1974. Ph.D. dissertation, Ohio State University, 1975.

Kennedy, G. & Holmes, J. Discussion of creative construction in second language learning and teaching. In Brown, H.D. (Ed.), *Papers in second language acquisition.* Proceedings of the 6th Annual Conference on Applied Linguistics, Ann Arbor, Michigan, 1975, 81-92.

Kenyeres, A. & Kenyeres, E. Comment un petite Hongroise de sept ans apprend le français. *Archives de Psychologie,* 1938, *26,* 104, 322-366.

Kessler, C. *Acquisition of syntax in bilingual children.* Washington, D.C.: Georgetown University Press, 1971.

Klima, E.S. & Bellugi, U. Syntactic regularities in the speech of children. In Lyons, J. & Wales, R. (Eds.), *Psycholinguistic Papers.* Edinburgh: Edinburgh University Press, 1966, 183-208.

Krashen, S. Language and the left hemisphere. Ph.D. dissertation, UCLA, 1972.

Krashen, S. Lateralization, language learning and the critical period: Some new evidence. *Language Learning,* 1973, *23,* 63-74.

Krashen, S. The critical period for language acquisition and its possible bases. *Annals of the New York Academy of Sciences,* 1975, in press.

Krashen, S. & Seliger, H. The essential characteristics of formal instruction in adult second language learning. *TESOL Quarterly,* 1975, *9,* 173-183.

Krashen, S. & Pon, P. An error analysis of an advanced learner of ESL: the importance of the monitor. *Working Papers in Bilingualism, 7,* 1975.

Krashen, S. Monitor theory: a model of adult second language performance. Paper presented at the USC-UCLA Second Language Acquisition Forum, 1976.

LaMarche, M.M. The topic comment pattern in the development of English among some Chinese children living in the U.S. Ph.D. dissertation, Georgetown University, 1972.

Lambert, W.E. & Tucker, G.R. *The bilingual education of children.* Rowley, Mass.: Newbury House, 1972.

Lambert, W.E. & Gardner, R.C. *Attitudes and motivation in second language learning.* Rowley, Mass.: Newbury House, 1971.

Larsen, D.A. & Smalley, W.A. *Becoming bilingual.* New Canaan, Conn.: Practical Anthropology, 1972.

Lebach, S.M. A report on the Culver City Spanish Immersion Program in its third year: Implications for language and subject matter acquisition, language and attitudes. MATESL thesis, UCLA, 1974.

Lenneberg, E. *The biological foundations of language.* New York: John Wiley & Sons, 1967.

Leopold, W.F. *Speech development of a bilingual child: a linguist's record.* Vol. 1, Vocabulary growth in the first two years. Vol. 2, Sound learning in the first two years. Vol. 3, Grammar and general problems in the first two years. Vol. 4, Diary from age 2. Evanston, Ill.: Northwestern University Press, 1939, 1947, 1949a, 1949b.

Leopold, W.F. The study of child language and bilingualism. In Bar-Adon, A. & Leopold, W.F. *Child language: a book of readings.* Englewood Cliffs, N.J.: Prentice-Hall, Inc., 1971.

Leopold, W.F. The study of child language and infant bilingualism. *Word,* 1948, *4,* 1, 1-15.

Leopold, W.F. *Bibliography of child language.* Evanston, Ill.: Northwestern University Press, 1952.

Levelt, W.J.M. Grammar inference and theories of language acquisition. Report 73 FU 17, Psychology Dept., Nijmegen University, Netherlands.

Linde, Richard. A diagnosis of grammar errors made by Japanese persons speaking English as a second language. Ph.D. dissertation, American University, 1971.

LoCoco, V. An analysis of Spanish and German learners' errors. *Working Papers in Bilingualism, 7,* 1975.

LoCoco, V. A comparison of three methods for the collection of L2 data: free composition, translation, and picture description. *Working Papers in Bilingualism, 8,* 1976.

LoCoco, V. A cross-sectional study on L3 acquisition. *Working Papers in Bilingualism, 9,* 1976.

Malmberg, B. Ett barn byter sprak. *Nordisk tidskrift,* 1945, *21.*

Malmberg, B. *Spraket och människan.* Stockholm: Aldus, 1964.

Markman, B.R., Spila, I. & Tucker, G.R. The use of elicited imitation in search of an interim French grammar. *Language Learning,* 1975, *25,* 31-41.

Martínez-Bernal, J. Children's acquisition of Spanish and English morphological systems and noun phrases. Ph.D. dissertation, Georgetown University, 1972.

Mazeika, E.J. A description of the language of a bilingual child. Ph.D. dissertation, University of Rochester, 1971.

Mazeika, E.J. A comparison of the grammar of a monolingual and bilingual child. Paper presented at SRCD Conference, Philadelphia, April, 1973.

McNeill, D. The capacity for the ontogenesis of grammar. In Slobin, D.I. (Ed.), *The ontogen- -esis of grammar.* New York: Academic Press, 1971, 17-40.

McNeill, D. & McNeill, N.B. What does a child mean when he says 'no'? Paper presented at Inaugural Conference of the Center for Research in Language and Language Behavior, University of Michigan, 1966.

Menyuk, P. *Sentences children use.* Cambridge, Mass.: The M.I.T. Press, 1969.

Mikeš, M. Acquisition des categories grammaticales dans le langage de l'enfant. *Enfance,* 1967, *20,* 289-297.

Miller, W. & Ervin, S. The development of grammar in child language. In U. Bellugi & R. Brown (Eds.), *The acquisition of language,* Monographs of the Society for Research in Child Development, 1964, Ser. No. 92, *29,* 35-39.

Moskowitz, A.I. The two-year-old stage in the acquisition of English phonology, *Language,* 1970, *46,* 2, 426-441.

Murrell, M. Language acquisition in a trilingual environment: Notes from a case study. *Studia Linguistica,* 1966, *20,* 9-35.

Naiman, N. Comprehension, imitation, and production of certain syntactic structures by children acquiring a second language. Ph.D. dissertation, University of Toronto, 1975.

Natalicio, D.C. & Natalicio, L.F.S. A comparative study of English pluralization by native and non native English speakers. *Child Development,* 1971, *42,* 1302-1306.

Nelson, C. *Structure and strategy in learning to talk.* Monographs of Society for Research in Child Development, *38,* 1-2, 1973.

Nemser, W. Approximative systems of foreign language learners. *IRAL,* 1971, *9,* 2, 115-123.

Nielsen, T.H. Early stages in the non-native acquisition of English syntax: a study of three children from Zaire, Venezuela, and Saudi Arabia. Ph.D. dissertation, Indiana Univeri- ty, 1974.

Oksaar, E. Implications of language contact for bilingual language acquisition. Paper presented at IXth International Congress of Anthropological and Ethnological Sciences, Chicago, Illinois, 1973.

Oller, J.W. & Ziahosseiny, S.M. The contrastive analysis hypothesis and spelling errors. *Language Learning,* 1970, *20,* 2, 183-197.

Olmstead-Gary, J. The effects on children of delayed oral practice in initial stages of second language learning. Ph.D. dissertation, UCLA, 1974.

Pavlovitch, M. *Le langage enfantin: Acquisition du serbe et du français par un enfant serbe.* Paris: Champion, 1920.

Penfield, W. & Roberts, L. *Speech and brain mechanisms.* Princeton: Princeton University Press, 1959.

Perkins, K. & Larsen-Freeman, D. The effect of formal language instruction on the order of morpheme acquisition. *Language Learning,* 1975, *25,* 2, 237-243.

Pfuderer, C., Drach, K. & Dobashigawa, B. The structure of linguistic input to children. Berkeley Language Behavior Research Laboratory, University of California, Working Paper No. 14, 1969.

Plann, S. The Spanish Immersion Program: towards native-like proficiency or a classroom dialect? MA-TESL, UCLA, 1976.

Politzer, R.L. Developmental sentence scoring as a method of measuring second language acquisition in bilingual and monolingual schooling, *Modern Language Journal,* 1974, *58,* 5-6, 245-250.

Politzer, R.L. & Ramírez, A.G. An error analysis of the spoken English of Mexican-American pupils in bilingual and monolingual schooling. *Language Learning,* 1973, *23,* 1, 39- 62.

Preyer, W. *The mind of the child*. Trans. by H.W. Brown. New York: Appleton-Century-Crofts, 1889.

Raffler, W. von. Studies in Italian-English bilingualism. Ph.D. dissertation. Indiana University, 1953.

Ramírez, A.G. The spoken English of Spanish-speaking pupils in a bilingual and monolingual school setting: an analysis of syntactic development. Ph.D. dissertation, Stanford, 1974, ERIC 094-569.

Ramírez, A.G. The acquisition of Spanish grammar by native English-speaking pupils in a Spanish Immersion Program, grades K-4, Mimeo report, UCLA, 1976.

Ravem, R. Second language acquisition; A study of two Norwegian children's acquisition of English syntax in a naturalistic setting. Ph.D. dissertation, University of Essex, 1974.

Ravem, R. Language acquisition in a second language environment. *IRAL*, 1968, *6*, 2, 175-185. (Also in J.W. Oller, Jr. & J.C. Richards (Eds.), Focus on the learner. Rowley, Mass.: Newbury House, 1973.)

Ravem, R. The development of WH-questions in first and second language learners. In Schumann, J. & Stenson, N. (Eds.), *New frontiers in second language learning.* Rowley, Mass.: Newbury House, 1975, 153-175.

Reich, P.A. The early acquisition of word meaning. *Journal of Child Language*, 1976, *3*, 1, 117-124.

Richards, J.C. A non-contrastive approach to error analysis. *English Language Teaching*, 1971, *25*, 204-219.

Richards, J.C. Error analysis and second language strategies. *Language Science*, 1971, *17*, 12-22.

Riebel, D.A. Language learning strategies of the adult. In P. Pimsleur & Quinn, T. (Eds.), *The psychology of second language learning.* Cambridge: Cambridge University Press, 1971.

Rivers, W.M. *The psychologist and the foreign-language teacher.* Chicago: University of Chicago Press, 1964.

Rivers, W.M. *Teaching foreign-language skills.* Chicago, Ill.: University of Chicago Press, 1968.

Rivers, W.M. The natural and normal in language learning. In Brown, H.D. (Ed.), *Papers in second language acquisition.* Proceedings of the 6th Annual Conference on Applied Linguistics, University of Michigan, 1975, 1-8.

Robbins, M. The effects of feedback on the eradication of errors in verb forms by ESL students. MA-TESL, UCLA, 1976.

Ronjat, J. *Le développement du langage observé chez un enfant bilingue.* Paris: Champion, 1913.

Rosansky, E.J. Methods and morphemes in second language acquisition. Paper presented at Child Language Research Forum, Stanford, 1976.

Rosansky, E.J. The critical period for the acquisition of language: some cognitive developmental considerations. *Working Papers on Bilingualism*, 1975, *6*, 93-102.

Rouchdy, A.A. A case of bilingualism: an investigation of lexical and syntactic interference in the performance of a bilingual child. Ph.D. dissertation, University of Texas, 1970.

Sachs, J. Effect of age on the ability to imitate speech sounds. Language Acquisition Laboratory, University of Connecticut, Report No. 4, 1972.

Savignon, S.J. Talking with my son: an example of communicative competence. In Grittner, F.M. (Ed.), *Careers, communication and culture in foreign language teaching.* Skokie, Ill.: National Textbook Co., 1974.

Schachter, J. An error in error analysis. *Language Learning*, 1974, *24*, 2, 205-214.

Schlue, K. An inside view of Interlanguage. MA-TESL thesis, UCLA, 1976.

Schmidt, Mackey, I. Language strategies of the bilingual family. Paper presented at Conference on Child Language, Chicago, 1971. ERIC 060-740.

Schumann, J. The implication of pidginization and creolization for the study of second language acquisition. In Schumann, J. & Stenson, N. (Eds.), *New frontiers in second language learning.* Rowley, Mass.: Newbury House, 1975, 137-152.

Schumann, J. Second language acquisition: the pidginization hypothesis. Ph.D. dissertation, Harvard, 1975.

Scollon, R.T. One child's language from one to two: the origins of construction. Ph.D. dissertation, University of Hawaii, 1974.

Scovel, T. Foreign accents, language acquisition and cerebral dominance. *Language Learning,* 1969, *19,* 3-4, 245-254.

Selinker, L. Interlanguage. *IRAL,* 1972, *10,* 201-231.

Selinker, L., Swain, M. & Dumas, G. The Interlanguage hypothesis extended to children. *Language Learning,* 1975, *25,* 1, 139-153.

Shapira, R. A study of the acquisition of ten syntactic structures and grammatical morphemes by an adult second language learner. MA-TESL, UCLA, 1976.

Sinclair, H. & Bronckart, J.P. SVO: a linguistic universal? *Journal of Experimental Child Psychology,* 1972, *14,* 329-348.

Sinclair-de Zwart, H. Language acquisition and cognitive development. In Moore, T. (Ed.), *Cognitive development and the acquisition of language.* New York: Academic Press, 1973, 9-26.

Slobin, D.I. Cognitive prerequisites for the development of grammar. In Ferguson, C. & Slobin, D.I. (Eds.), *Studies in child language development.* New York: Holt, Rinehart & Winston, 1973.

Slobin, D.I. Universals of grammar development in children. In Flores, G.E., d'Arcais & Levelt, W.J.M. (Eds.), *Advances in psycholinguistics.* Amsterdam: North Holland, 1970, 174-186.

Slobin, D.I. Abstracts of Soviet studies of child language. In Smith, F. & Miller, G.A., *Genesis of Language.* Cambridge, Mass.: The M.I.T. Press, 1966, 361-386.

Slobin, D.I. & Welsh, C.A. Elicited imitation as a research tool in developmental psycholinguistics. In C. Ferguson & D.I. Slobin (Eds.), *Studies in child language development.* New York: Holt, Rinehart & Winston, 1973, 485-496.

Smalley, W.A. Culture shock, language shock, and the shock of self discovery. *Practical Anthropology,* 1963, *10,* 49-56.

Sodhi, S.S. Uznadze's set and second language learning. *International Journal of Psychology,* 1969, *4,* 4, 317-319.

Stern, C. & Stern, W. *Die kindersprache: Eine psychologische und sprachtheoretische Untersuchung.* Leipzig: Barth, 1907.

Stockwell, R., Bowen, J.D. & Martin, J.W. *The grammatical structures of English and Spanish.* Chicago: University of Chicago Press, 1965.

Swain, M. French immersion programs across Canada. *The Canadian Modern Language Review,* 1974, *31,* 117-129.

Swain, M. & Wesche, M. Linguistic interaction: case study of a bilingual child. *Working Papers on Bilingualism, 1,* 1973.

Swain, M. Writing skills of grade three French immersion pupils. *Working Papers on Bilingualism, 7,* 1975.

Syngle, B. Second language (English) acquisition strategies of children and adults: a cross-sectional study. Ph.D. dissertation, Louisiana State University, 1973.

Tanka, J. An error analysis of the speech of Russian ESL students. Psycholinguistics-TESL Project, UCLA, 1975.

Tarone, E. Some influences on Interlanguage phonology. Paper presented at the TESOL Conference, Los Angeles, 1975. See also *Working Papers on Bilingualism, 8,* 1976.

Tarone, E., Frauenfelder, U. & Selinker, L. Systematicity/Variability and Stability/Instability in Interlanguage systems. In Brown, H.D. (Ed.), *Papers in second language acquisition.* Proceedings of the 6th Annual Conference on Applied Linguistics, University of Michigan, 1975, 93-134.

Tarone, E., Swain, M. & Fathman, A. Some limitations to the classroom application of current second language acquisition research. *TESOL Quarterly,* 1976, *10,* 1, 19-32.

Taylor, B.P. Overgeneralization and transfer as learning strategies in second language learning. Ph.D. dissertation, University of Michigan, 1974.

Tits, D. *Le mécanisme de l'acquisition d'une langue se substituant à la langue maternelle chez une enfant espagnole ageé de six ans.* Bruxelles, 1948.

Tran, Thi Chan. Concepts of development in second language learning and teaching. *IRAL,* 1975, *13,* 119-143.

Van Mettre, P.D. Syntactic characteristics of selected bilingual children. Ph.D. dissertation, University of Arizona, 1972.

Vildomec, V. *Multilingualism.* Netherlands: A.W. Sythoff-Leyden, 1963.

Wagner-Gough, Judy. *Comparative studies in second language learning.* CAL-ERIC/CLL Series on Languages and Linguistics, *26,* 1975.

Wagner-Gough, J. & Hatch, E. The importance of input data in second language acquisition studies. *Language Learning,* 1975, *25,* 2, 297-308.

Waldman, E.L. Cross-ethnic attitudes of Anglo students in Spanish Immersion, bilingual, and English schooling. MA-TESL Thesis, UCLA, 1975.

Wardhaugh, R. The contrastive analysis hypothesis. *TESOL Quarterly,* 1970, *4,* 2, 123-130.

Warshawsky, D.R. The acquisition of four English morphemes by Spanish-speaking children. Ph.D. dissertation, University of Michigan, 1975.

Waterhouse, V.A. Learning a second language first. *International Journal of American Linguistics,* 1965, *15,* 106-109.

Weinreich, U. *Languages in contact.* New York: Linguistics Circle of New York, 1953.

Young, D. The acquisition of English syntax by three Spanish-speaking children. MA-TESL Thesis, UCLA, 1974.